FEMINIST ART ACTIVISMS AND ARTIVISMS

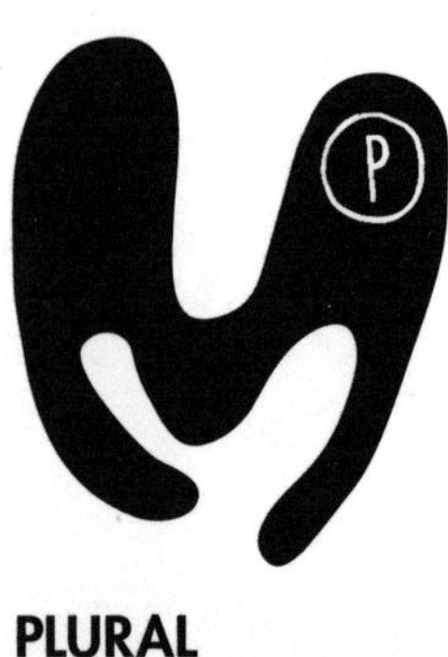

PLURAL
Valiz, Amsterdam

FEMINIST ART ACTIVISMS AND ARTIVISMS

Katy Deepwell (ed.)

With contributions by:

Linda Aloysius
Marissa Begonia
Sreyashi Tinni Bhattacharyya
Marisa Carnesky
Paula Chambers
Amy Charlesworth
Emma Curd
Katy Deepwell
Tal Dekel
Emma Dick
Lior Elefant
Christine Eyene
Abbe Leigh Fletcher
GraceGraceGrace
Alana Jelinek
Sonja van Kerkhoff
Alexandra Kokoli
Elke Krasny
Loraine Leeson

Laura Malacart
Rosy Martin
Alice Maude-Roxby
Kathleen Mullaniff
Louise O'Hare
Tanja Ostojić
Martina Pachmanová
Gill Park
Pune Parsafar
Roxane Permar
Anne Robinson
Stefanie Seibold
Pam Skelton
Mare Tralla
Christina Vasileiou
Camille Waring
Michelle Williams Gamaker
Virginia Yiqing Yang

CONTENTS

ARTIVISMS AS ART ACTIVISMS

ART ACTIVISMS AND ARTIVISMS

FEMINIST ART ACTIVISMS AND ARTIVISMS
Introduction

Katy Deepwell

1. Carol Hanisch, 'The Personal is Political' (1969, 2006); Martha Rosler 'Well, *is* the Personal Political?' (1980), in *Feminism–Art–Theory: An Anthology 1968–2014*, ed. Hilary Robinson (Malden, MA, and Oxford: Wiley Blackwell, 2015), p. 68.

An anthology is always a "plural" entity: different voices participate in its construction. Anthologies by design are ensembles of ideas, projects and approaches. How does this "plural", composed of singular chapters (describing events and actions, individual authors/artists/artworks and collective projects), represent feminisms (in the plural) on the question of art activisms and/or artivisms? This book seeks to demonstrate how art engages with feminist politics and, at the same time, how thinking about feminist politics reinvents art, changing and transforming existing categories, concepts, and distinctions.

Feminist Contentions on Art and Activisms

Feminist art activisms are not just an extension into art of the political agenda of the women's liberation movements since the 1960s, when women have repeatedly taken to the streets as activists to protest in their own name and for other women about rights, equal pay, sexual politics (liberation) and social justice amongst many other causes affecting women. Feminist art, as feminist politics in general, has redefined traditional political agendas and party lines, challenging the divisions between private/public spheres and the separation of Politics with a capital P—of political groups and Unions—from a micro-politics of the everyday in their questioning of the personal as political.[1] Alongside this, feminist thought has challenged the binary thinking in knowledge production between nature/culture, mind/matter, and analysed how the world is organized socially, economically and politically between two sexes/spheres as a "gender order", a hierarchy of power and privilege. Feminist art, as a result, responded to and transformed these concerns, introducing new approaches, subjectivities, sensibilities, ways of seeing as well as new forms of art into the art world, capitulating neither to agit-prop, nor to art's irrelevance as bourgeois elitism and continuing to question the routes of art's canonical logic.[2]

Is feminist art activism only a visual response in art to existing "hot" topics in contemporary politics mimicking, copying or reproducing existing media representations of that struggle?[3] Art made with a view towards social and political change aims to transform our understanding of how social and political issues are experienced, felt and understood, but art made in this way is not just about producing sympathy or empathy for "good causes" or pre-existing issues. The promise of art activisms is that they can redefine both how art and politics can be understood by bringing together unexpected elements and new configurations, encouraging us to see the world and how it operates differently and presenting different models of art production and social organization. Martha Rosler's project, *If You Lived Here...* (1989) did just this dual work in both art and social politics on homelessness; as did Sanja Iveković's *Women's House/Frauenhaus* (1998–2003) on violence against women.

Discussion of art, at the service of activism, has moved away from its early focus only on the visual symbolism used in campaigns: in logos, slogans/placards, banner designs, zines, murals and posters, not only because of conceptual art or "critical art" or institutional critique, but because of the development of more participatory art projects (on different scales) and an art for social change that involved different communities or audiences in new ways, manifest in New Genre Public Art and different forms of artivisms in collective projects.[4] Separating "art" from "propaganda" has been the typical mechanism for divisions between art and politics and this was often made because artworks in the first group served the purpose of Art (in indirect, opaque, or autonomous ways, as a critique or negation), while the latter delivered a singular message

2. On this encounter, see Griselda Pollock, 'Action, Activism, and Art and/as Thought: A Dialogue with the Artworking of Sonia Khurana and Sutapa Biswas and the Political Theory of Hannah Arendt', *e-flux journal* #92 (June 2018).

3. See special issue on Visual Activism, *Journal of Visual Culture* 15, no. 1 (April 2016) with contributions from T.J. Demos and Trinh T. Minh.

4. See Lucy Lippard, *Get the Message: A Decade of Art for Social Change* (New York: Dutton, 1983); Arlene Raven, *Crossing Over: Feminism and the Art of Social Concern* (Ann Arbor, MI: UMI Research Press, 1988); Suzanne Lacy (ed.), *Mapping the Terrain: New Genre Public Art* (Seattle: Bay Press, 1995); Nina Felshin, *But is It Art?: The Spirit of Art as Activism* (Seattle: Bay Press, 1995); Suzanne Lacy, *Leaving Art: Writings on Performance, Politics and Publics, 1974–2007* (Durham, NC: Duke University Press, 2010). Mónica Mayer et al., *Si tiene dudas... Pregunte: una exposición retrocolectiva/When in Doubt... Ask: A Retrocollective Exhibit* (Rio Pánuco: Editoriual RM, MUAC-UNAM, 2016) or the artivism/ activism of Tania Bruguera: www. taniabruguera.com. Alana Jelinek, *This is Not Art: Activism and Other 'Not Art'* (London: I.B. Tauris, 2013).

5. See Lucy Lippard, 'Hot Potatoes: Art and Politics in 1980', *BLOCK* 4 (1981), pp. 2–9.

6. See Grant H. Kester (ed), *Art, Activism, and Oppositionality: Essays from Afterimage* (Durham, NC: Duke University Press, 1998).

aligned to the stated objectives of party, State, government, trade union, company or campaigning charity. If art with a social purpose is no longer seen as "propaganda" in this sense, to what extent is it offering us a different kind of argument, or is it just a different type of engagement with a visual politics and visible political histories? Can we really separate (except perhaps theoretically) art, its imagery and its conscious adoption of thought from Politics in general, from its support systems, when governments continue to fund art institutions and cultural activities as part of their strategy for governance and building civil society, as much in authoritarian regimes as modern democratic ones?

Art is frequently presented (in art history and art criticism) as "taking a position", manifesting a political viewpoint held by the artist in terms of sympathies or identifications, even when there are many ambiguities, complexity, or multi-layered meanings in how the artwork is written about and understood. The intentions of the artist do not fully explain the impact of different works on communities: as many unexpected effects are often present in which works are valued or recognized. Similarly, can the question of all cultural patronage—inside as much as outside the art world—as "interference", be defended only in the "intention" of the artist as "free" or "undirected", or by attention to the philosophical problem internal to the work itself? When certain artworks start to acquire a reputation as a "political intervention" and circulate in the art-world distribution systems of galleries and museums, does this reveal more about art's context, or histories, or "favouritism" for certain kinds of art and certain kinds of politics? Are we then judging the artivism of the artwork based on its political "effect" or simply on how it gains currency (in the artworld) as an example of the "political" in art and as a dissenting voice?

"Art" and "Politics" also used to be regarded as distinct where a very specific limited, rarefied conception of art as "apolitical" was deemed central to a late modernist studio-based practice, an "Ivory-Tower" practice (and it was this form that was critiqued by Lucy Lippard[5] among many other writers[6]). This notion of the privileged place of the studio, as a space apart from the world, collapses when it is widely recognized today that an artwork's distribution is always wholly political/ideological and that how an exhibition is "marketed" is also a form of propaganda, generating the art world's "star system" and maintaining particular associated values for "good art". Is it only in the selection processes in which some artworks are chosen, selected, rewarded, honoured and discussed, that a cultural feminist politics which seeks to intervene "on behalf of women" can emerge, and would this intervention or protest (for more representation, better prices, or programming of women artists' work) register as an artivism or art activism?[7]

Any discussion of art and politics in art activism today has to begin with the idea that there is no Art which is "non-political", no art without ideology (even as systems of beliefs and values are challenged or questioned by art, as this is where art's autonomy lies). Chantal Mouffe goes further and argues 'there is an aesthetic dimension in the political and there is a political dimension in art'.[8] Feminism has demonstrated this complex dialectical relation between art and politics many times from the Suffragists to Femen. Not all street protests are recognized as art, nor is all performance—human action—enacted on the street, nor are all placards used in protests valued highly as art forms. Is this definition of activism as a politics on the street too narrow? The distribution of art outside a gallery space or in "non-art" spaces can no longer be in itself a definition of art activism, or even artivism,[9] nor is it a signal of art with a political intent (as murals or banners can be decorative, they are not always "political" in content). Should the politics of the museum be scrutinized more carefully, including its separation between curatorial and educational programmes? Is the distinction about artivism vs activism really a question about the non-utility/utility of art, its relative elitism vs. popularity? How do interventions in art's language prioritize different kinds of politics pursued or built outside of a politics built around conventional parties, unions or national, ethnic, race-based, or gender-identified loyalties? If defining activism is only a question of the effects and effectiveness of acts, interventions or artworks in serving an ideological function, then can this be measured in terms of how art invents, projects or presents a present/future society in utopian or dystopian visions of the world as it is and could be?

Art is widely accepted as offering a projection of

7. The Guerrilla Girls' posters are now displayed in Tate Modern; has this protest now become "art" or was it always so?

8. Chantal Mouffe, 'Artistic Activism and Agonistic Spaces', *Art and Research* (Studio 55, Glasgow School of Art, online) 1, no. 2 (Summer 2007) www.artandresearch.org.uk/v1n2/mouffe.html.

9. Kirsten Dufour, 'Art as Activism, Activism as Art', *The Review of Education, Pedagogy, and Cultural Studies* 24, nos. 1-2 (2002), pp. 157–167.

10. Boris Groys, 'On Art Activism',
e-flux journal 56 (June 2014).

11. Ibid.

future worlds (its utopian gesture), manifesting a desire for projecting change, presenting a harsh critique of existing realities or institutions, being an allegorical form, symbolizing ideas, or being known for political irony or satire. Some of these functions help us identify those important icons of "political art" (as an art historical category), but these are seemingly the boundaries or limits to its work as artivism, however inspiring they may be. If the subjects art tackles, represents or addresses are "about" campaigns for better health care, housing rights, human rights, anti-nuclear campaigns, arrangements for childcare, equal pay, environmental issues, campaigns for social justice, against exploitation at work, violence against women, does this make the artwork, "art with a social purpose" or just an "individual" perspective in which the subject alone signals a "politics" and a social conscience about the contemporary moment? If it is admitted that art addresses, references or responds to political issues, it is generally suggested that art cannot change them because it rarely has any direct impact upon them. The recognition process of art as "Art" is never instant—even when art becomes the object of an immediate news story or scandal—and the effect of art can rarely be measured in any precise concrete terms as "instituting" change. The situation appears polarized by either the critique of "aestheticization" of politics in the production of anti-spectacular art (as a form of anti-Fascism) or a critique of the status quo as "dead" (thus upholding avant-garde's nihilism in a critical negation of the status quo).[10] Feminism's negotiation of this situation is rarely considered by these discussions of art activisms, largely because its politics are not discussed, especially its continuous critique of the status quo in limiting women's roles/positions/lives/potential. Much as we each value particular and specific images and traditions that we have familiarized and accustomed ourselves towards, do we really see art itself as capable of producing a policy change or bringing about a revolution, or can it only acquire value as a symbol of a particular mind-set, a manifestation of a political position? Mouffe's argument about an agonistic approach which contests the dominant liberalism in democracy, is that 'critical art is art that foments dissensus, that makes visible what the dominant consensus tends to obscure and obliterate'.[11] Feminism has been doing this for more than fifty years in and with art.

In 1995, in another anthology, I argued that feminism was moving from practical strategies to strategic practices.[12] This was my attempt to present and characterize how a multiplicity of ideas, practices and interventions across the women's art movement and in relation to many feminism(s) was institutionalizing itself and developing new pathways for action. It was a means to signal how the debate had changed since the 1970s and it keeps on changing, both as we look back (to twenty years ago) and today move forward.

The 1990s (now two decades in the past) is frequently characterized in terms of a split between academic forms of feminism (as women's studies became gender studies) and activisms which remained outside the University, where the emergence of feminist theory risked becoming separated from the activities of the women's movement's institutions and methods for organizing.[13] Is it useful to describe feminism in these terms today, except where it reminds us to think of feminism as combining a politics in practice, in knowledge, in daily life, which rethinks how to represent women's experiences of the world? Feminist debate is marked by differences for and on behalf of different constituencies of women and as alliances between women seeking change in the position of women in society, locally, nationally and transnationally.[14] This type of coalition or alliance between different women's groups, interests, and areas of work (on both a global and local level) is the workable definition of a "strategic feminism" which exists to counter sexism, sexual harassment, all forms of discrimination, and the oppression of women (or even in Gayatri Spivak's infamous "risk of essentialism" where one still needs to act for and on behalf of and in the name of women).[15] It is around the use of feminist politics as a term for organizing, that any "solidarity" is produced in alliances between women,[16] and a vision of feminism "beyond borders" is actually created.[17]

Dividing the strategies or tactics of feminisms beneath the umbrella term feminism is never easy, given the extent of feminism's reach into all areas of everyday life, thought and knowledge. The common strategy of adding another kind of politics: "black", "socialist", "neo-liberal", "anarchist", "third-wave", "culturalist", "queer" quickly

12. Katy Deepwell, 'Introduction', in *New Feminist Art Criticism: Critical Strategies* (Manchester and New York: Manchester University Press, 1995).

13. Diana Coole, 'Feminism without Nostalgia', *Radical Philosophy* 83 (May/June 1997), pp. 17–24.

14. 'Cheryl Hercus offers a fractal model of the process of becoming a fem-inist, which involves four intertwined components of subjectivity: knowing (consciousness), feeling (emotions), belonging (identity), and doing (action).' Cheryl Hercus, *Stepping Out of Line: Becoming and Being Feminist* (New York: Routledge, 2005), quoted in Yin-Zu Chen, 'How to Become a Feminist Activist after the Institutionalization of the Women's Movements: The Generational Development of Feminist Identity and Politics in Mexico City', *Frontiers* 35, no. 3 (2014), pp. 183–207.

15. Gayatri Spivak affirms strategic essentialism in these terms, 'No representation can take place, no *Vertretung*, representation, can take place without essentialism'. Sarah Harasym, 'Practical Politics of the Open End: Interview with Gayatri Spivak', *C Theory*, 21C017 (2 June 2016), http://ctheory.net/ctheory_wp/spivak-cjpst-test/.

16. Donna Haraway, 'A Manifesto for Cyborgs: Science, Technology and Socialist Feminism in the 1980s', Socialist Review 15, no. 2 (1985), pp. 65–107; Linda Nicholson, *Feminism/Postmodernism* (London: Routledge, 1990) pp. 190–233.

17. Chandra Mohanty, *Feminism Without Borders: Decolonizing Theory, Practicing Solidarity* (Durham, NC: Duke University Press, 2004) and Nancy Fraser, *Fortunes of Feminism: From State-Managed Capitalism to Neoliberal Crisis* (London: Verso, 2013).

underlines its plural character, allegiances, and alliances with other political movements. When we qualify feminism, are we "doubling/expanding" or "dividing/reducing" the meaning of its politics in distinguishing between kinds of feminisms? Is a certain "fuzzy thinking" about women's lives, allegiances, experiences productive for thinking about feminisms? Does declaring oneself or one's actions, artworks or protests as feminist signal just "a political identification" or does it mean that one is really "doing feminism", enacting social and political change or engaging in the struggle to do so, in and through words, acts, actions or projects, in which other people participate or are asked to participate? Feminist critique has regularly highlighted how there is always a part of political experience that the mainstream of most political movements and groups continues to overlook, erase or exclude in its conception; is it this element which concerns women that gains the name "feminist"? Will homogenizing feminism, even with a qualifying marker, into one position really assist us with understanding important differences between "black feminisms" around the world: Afro-Caribbean feminisms, Brazil's black feminisms, feminisms in diverse African countries, varying Afro-American feminisms and womanisms, feminisms of diasporic Africans living and working in Europe, and their particularities in relation to distinct issues in women's civil and human rights across the world? If "white feminisms" has become a term of abuse, who is contained in this term by an identification of a "white feminism" as an unmarked, unlocated term, or an inherently racist and negative one, and does this label really condemn the thought of all European, American, Australian, Canadian forms of feminisms by a skin colour, or only some of those in the Northern hemisphere, where those politics are genuinely exclusionary and those using this term don't agree with an "us"? Similarly does the label queer feminism assist or confuse any understanding of distinct lesbian feminisms in different decades or countries, does it make sufficiently apparent the work of lesbian or bi-sexual artists/writers in relation to either gay liberation, gay rights or other LGBTQI activisms of different kinds and on different social and political issues or, in art terms, to reclaim different histories of women and modernism or the global contemporary?

Feminisms (as a plural) is widely used today to

draw attention to gender differences but it has always been
clear that feminist conceptions of sex/gender, race and class
produce multiple variations within and across locations,
ethnicities, sexualities, dis(abilities), or concepts of the
nation and nationalisms. In these complex configurations, we
need to identify the lines of thought, genealogies, separate
traditions manifest in different kinds of continuities over
certain forms of political actions or protests identified with
women, political histories and different forms of local/
global politics. The changing, and always charged, value of
thinking about feminist identities in terms of race/sex/class/
sexualities/(dis)abilities/ethnicities has often positioned feminism as just another form of "identity politics" for women,
an identity situated within or rather amongst a list of visible
protest groups from queer politics, indigenous politics, black
politics or anti-racist politics, disability rights activisms and
anti-nationalist, anti-authoritarian, anti-fascist politics:
which are ambivalently but always eventually recognized as
having a "gendered dimension" to them. This link between
identitarian politics and new social movements post-1960,
especially on the question of representation, and how individuals are made representative of such unitary identities,
requires much further consideration than it is often given.
Attaching "identity politics" to the women's movement's
social and political activities and campaigns for civil and
political rights across 170 years, indigenous rights activists,
disability activisms, civil rights movements, third world
politics for independence, struggles and campaigns against
racism, against slavery and for ethnic minority and migrants'
rights, alongside gay liberation protests, is well-known as a
feature of political representation after the 1960s. However,
as a combined list, this ignores the interactions between
these multiple struggles and overlooks their own internal
differences. These forms of identity politics are regarded
as sharing their critique of the dominance of (white, but
not always) heterosexual male privilege from one ethnic/
racial group in a country and the pursuit of their interests
in mainstream politics, governance and business over
that of the "Others" in their discourses, but is this binary
critique of power enough? When it comes to considering
the impact of political definitions of feminism in the visual
arts, it cannot be reduced to "identity politics", to labels,

18. 'Women artists have been undoing the autonomy and the universality of the aesthetic image, by developing their art, not only for the production of effects in signification or communication, but as a form of agency.' Elisabeth Lebovici, 'This is not my body', *Radical Philosophy* 156 (July/August 2009), www. radicalphilosophy.com/article/this-is-not-my-body.

19. Mouffe 2007; Chantal Mouffe, *The Return of the Political* (London: Verso, 1993).

to "representativeness" of a few more women artists in the mainstream, although it unfortunately often is, especially in debates around the representation or use and abuse of women's bodies and labour.[18]

If we want a radical vision of democracy which is inclusive and diverse and attends to the needs of the many, not just a few, how can we work with a vision of agonism and its accompanying antagonisms as a necessary part of civil society while we question its hegemonies,[19] and how should we address questions about the situation, co-operation and alliances between people in shifting the power relations, and privileges, within these hegemonic configurations. Feminism has frequently declared that its aim is social transformation—a change in society and its attitudes towards women. Is art just a tactic in this general movement, a part of the "how"? Feminisms' insistence on the personal as political has regularly cut across the distinction between a macro-politics of governance, economies, wars and administrations and emphasized the importance of a micro-politics of everyday life. In the list of social, economic and political problems today, there are feminist perspectives developing on austerity, social struggle, war, the situation of refugees, mass migrations across continents because of war, economic and social hardship, climate change (floods, tsunamis, volcanic activity) and famines. Feminism has insisted that the "private" sphere—the home, the family, social organization of relationships, the maintenance and reproduction of life itself—is not distinguishable from the "public", and in its impact on political agendas has brought whole areas of social, sexual, psychological, emotional concern into Politics with a capital P. The same feminist challenge critiques any neat separation between the realms of production and reproduction in "productivist" logics about capitalism—arguing for the importance of a more fundamental reassessment of production in relation to social reproduction of life, love and care in families, the organization of labour, our institutions, health and education systems. The exclusion of socially reproductive activities from sources of value is doubly marked in works where women's labour and protests about women's labour—as carers, mothers, housewives, teachers—is present because this has been a major focus in art produced by women artists.

This focus on social reproduction is against the orthodox Marxist view that only waged industrial workers qualify as makers of the (next) revolution.[20] The question of the division between waged and unwaged labour has shifted into another dimension when we look at how the forms and modes of labour are costed or monetized in capitalism, and this prompts the question of where we want future feminist visions of a different world.[21] Dimitris Papadopoulos contests the idea, still so prevalent on the Left, that social change is principally about a unified social (human) subject taking over political institutions in order to direct and distribute nature (resources) towards better ends. Against this, Papadopoulos proposes 'alter-ontological organizing' in his call for a decolonizing politics of matter that is not about taking charge of matter, but 'instituting direct changes on the material level of existence'.[22] This is at the heart of what Papadopoulos calls 'more-than-social movements' that 'do not attempt to contest power by organizing protest; rather, they attempt to create the conditions for the articulation of alternative imaginaries and alternative practices that bypass instituted power and generate alternative modes of existence'.[23] Feminist art production has created many kinds of social campaigns organized with and through art which focus on "art/life" boundaries to raise awareness for political action,[24] in this imaginary way, and they join a long tradition of avant-garde practices in this regard. The tactics of small-scale meetings, group discussions, deployment of national/ international social networks, production of campaign literature, imagery, logos, slogans also form part of this alter-ontological organizing. Some of these mesh with early feminist use of consciousness-raising activities in women's groups, but others do not, especially when there is a focus on only producing product or "leaders".

About this Book

These are some of the many contentions in this book. The structure of this book is conceived as a dialogue between two categories: Art Activisms and Artivisms. The two halves of the book, like that of the same coin, present where art approaches, develops or transforms into activism and its

20. Alessandra Mezzadri, 'On the value of social reproduction: Informal labour, the majority world and the need for inclusive theories and politics', *Radical Philosophy* 2, no. 4 (Spring 2019) www.radicalphilosophy.com/ article/on-the-value-of-social-reproduction.

21. Silvia Federici — on the work of Mariarosa Dalla Costa, Selma James and Leopolda Fortunati — emphasizes how their attention to 'redefining the capitalist function of the wage as a creator of labour hierarchies, and an instrument serving to naturalise exploitative social relations and to delegate to wage-workers power over the unwaged….unmask[ed] the socio-economic function of the creation of a fictional private sphere, and thereby re-politicising family life, sexuality, procreation.' Silvia Federici, 'Social reproduction theory: History, issues and present challenges', *Radical Philosophy* 2, no. 4 (Spring 2019) www. radicalphilosophy.com/article/ social-reproduction-theory-2.

22. Dimitris Papadopoulos, *Experimental Practice: Technoscience, Alterontologies and More than Social Movements* (Durham: Duke University Press, 2018), p. 17. He defines alter-ontological organizing as 'the capacity to set up alternative forms of everyday existence and mundane practices that later come to force power and control in a specific field to reorganize itself and subsequently to reengage the actors involved in the field in new and often unexpected ways', p. 198.

23. Ibid., p. 198.

24. Bojana Kunst, *Artist at Work: Proximity of Art and Capitalism* (Winchester and Washington: Zero Books, 2015) argues that 'doing less' is also a refusal and offers a space for resistance to the neo-liberal logic of the art market's productivist ethic, renegotiating art/life boundaries.

converse, where activisms become artivisms. In both, art emerges in differing forms of political intervention, at both an individual, shared or collective level, apparent in actions, events, identifications and practices. Different types of art activism are named and explored: monument activism; fictional activism; memory activism; activisms in art's histories; actions in performance as well as the activism of participatory and socially engaged art projects. The works discussed include poster campaigns; photo-therapy; curating queer historiographies; performance art in the gallery, the theatre, and on the street; as well as documentaries recording the activisms of others; and even writing about art as one's own contribution to activism. Many different political issues are discussed: from anti-nuclear protests to placing menstruation at the heart of environmental protest; from protesting against sexism to public art made for the streets; from the labour of social reproduction and differing ideas about motherhood to the exploitation of workers in the domestic labour market or education; from activisms about older women to campaigns for better health care or childcare; from considering representations of historical experiences of trauma and memory in art to representing women activists' work as the subject of art. While the contributors came together at a one-day conference in London and most live and work across the UK, women also travelled from Austria, Italy, Germany, the Czech Republic, Israel and the Netherlands for this event. However, the countries and contexts discussed in the contributions extend beyond these countries and contexts to the former Yugoslavia, China, India, Russia, Iran, Estonia, USA, Lithuania, Poland, South Africa and New Zealand.

This book presents examples of activism in political life—in the authors' thoughts, reflections, ideas—and how they inform their practices as artists, activists, curators, and writers. Their first-hand accounts do not form a ready-made toolkit for change, however inspirational, they are reflections upon these art activisms and their difficulties. The accounts are written in art historical as well as first-person and diaristic modes and offer different ways of speaking to and thinking about art practices as interventions, challenges, and possibilities for seeing the world differently, while drawing attention to the limited realities of the status quo for women in the present. Only when understood as a whole, in their challenges to existing modes of patriarchal and sexist thinking, do these different projects reinforce the point that there are always a multiplicity of ways to think about or conceive what are feminist strategies today in art and activisms. This plural is not a defence of pluralism, which is often regarded as a defence for the maintenance of the status quo in a liberal democracy. Instead, these chapters contain many tactics for how to change art, how to pursue particular lines of enquiry into feminist thought, many differing techniques, practices, sites or contexts pursued at different moments in time (as history is far from absent in this presentation of contemporary artworks) and across different media.

The feminist plural in this book does not offer any special pleading for the collapse of distinctions. We need greater recognition of how these distinctions limit consideration of the full relationship between activisms and artivisms in contemporary art and where feminism occurs in these debates. The promise of changing the terms of this dichotomy into new and surprising coalitions or new kinds of politics beckons, especially when mediated by the internet/social media, or experimental and discursive approaches to understanding art. However, be it a new radical democratic, a socialist or an anarchist revolution we seek, someone will still have to wash the socks after the revolution, even if this is no longer seen as a maintenance act of privatized labour (as women's work), but done by a machine in a shared, participative, communal or collective fashion in the future. And we all still want time to dance![25]

25. Emma Goldmann's now infamous allusion to dancing has been taken up by many feminists including the feminist arts festival in the Netherlands, If I Can't Dance. The closest phrasing from her autobiography: 'I want freedom, the right to self-expression, everybody's right to beautiful, radiant things. Anarchism meant that to me, and I would live it in spite of the whole world—prisons, persecution, everything. Yes, even in spite of the condemnation of my own comrades I would live my beautiful ideal.' *Living My Life* (New York: Knopf, 1934), p. 56 (see Alix Kates Shulman, 'Dances with Feminists', *Women's Review of Books* IX, no. 3 [December 1991]). The problem of 'who will wash the socks' is taken from Mirijana Stojčić, 'Proleteri svih zemalja—ko vam pere čarape? Feministički pokret u jugoslaviji 1978–1989' (Proleterians of the World—Who's *Washing* Your Socks?), *Društvo u pokretu*, eds. Đorđe Tomić and Petar Atanacković (Novi Sad: Cenzura, 2009), pp. 108–121, but also appears as a topic in Mierle Ukeles' 'Manifesto for Maintenance Art, 1969!'.

ARTIVISMS AS ART ACTIVISMS

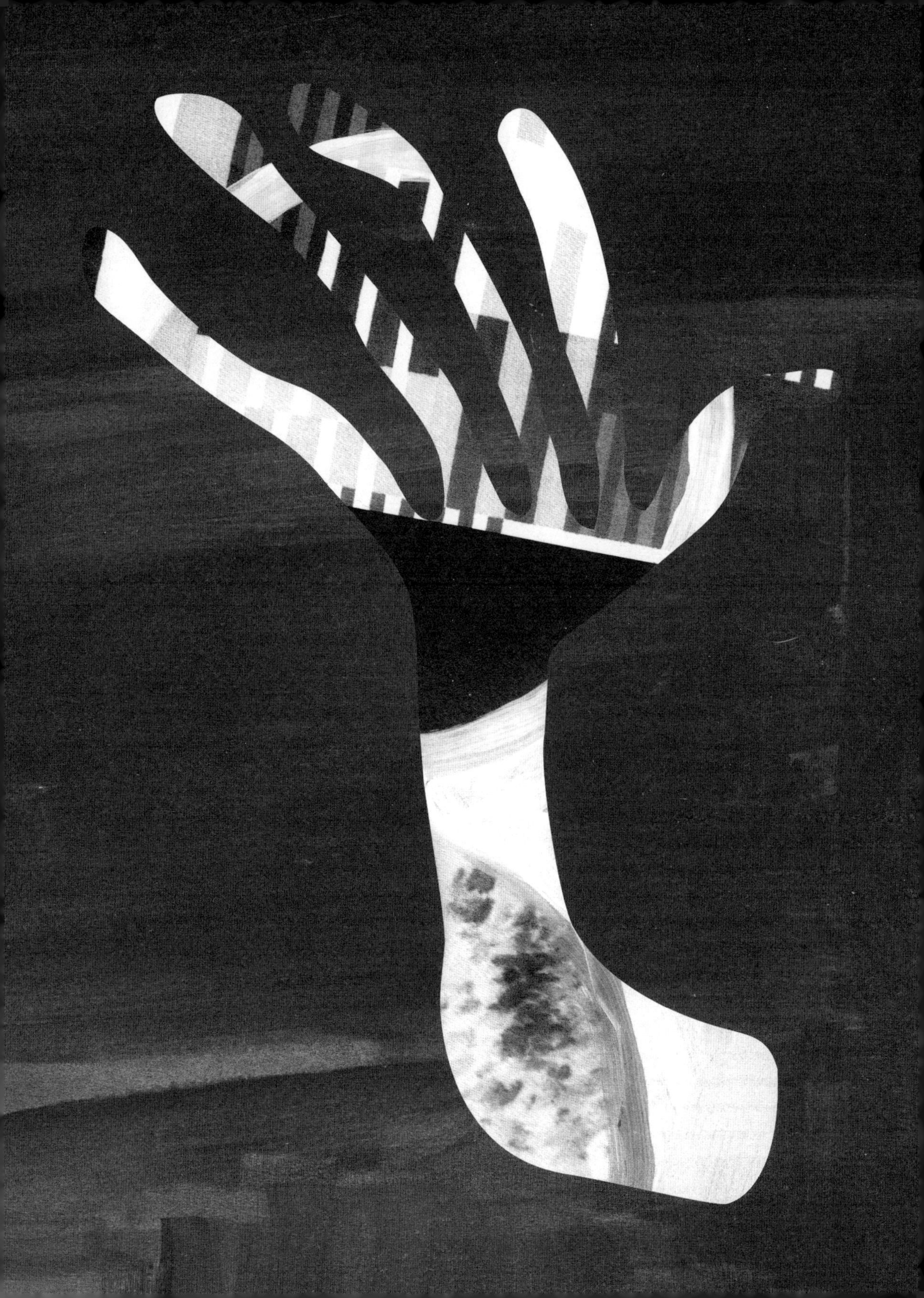

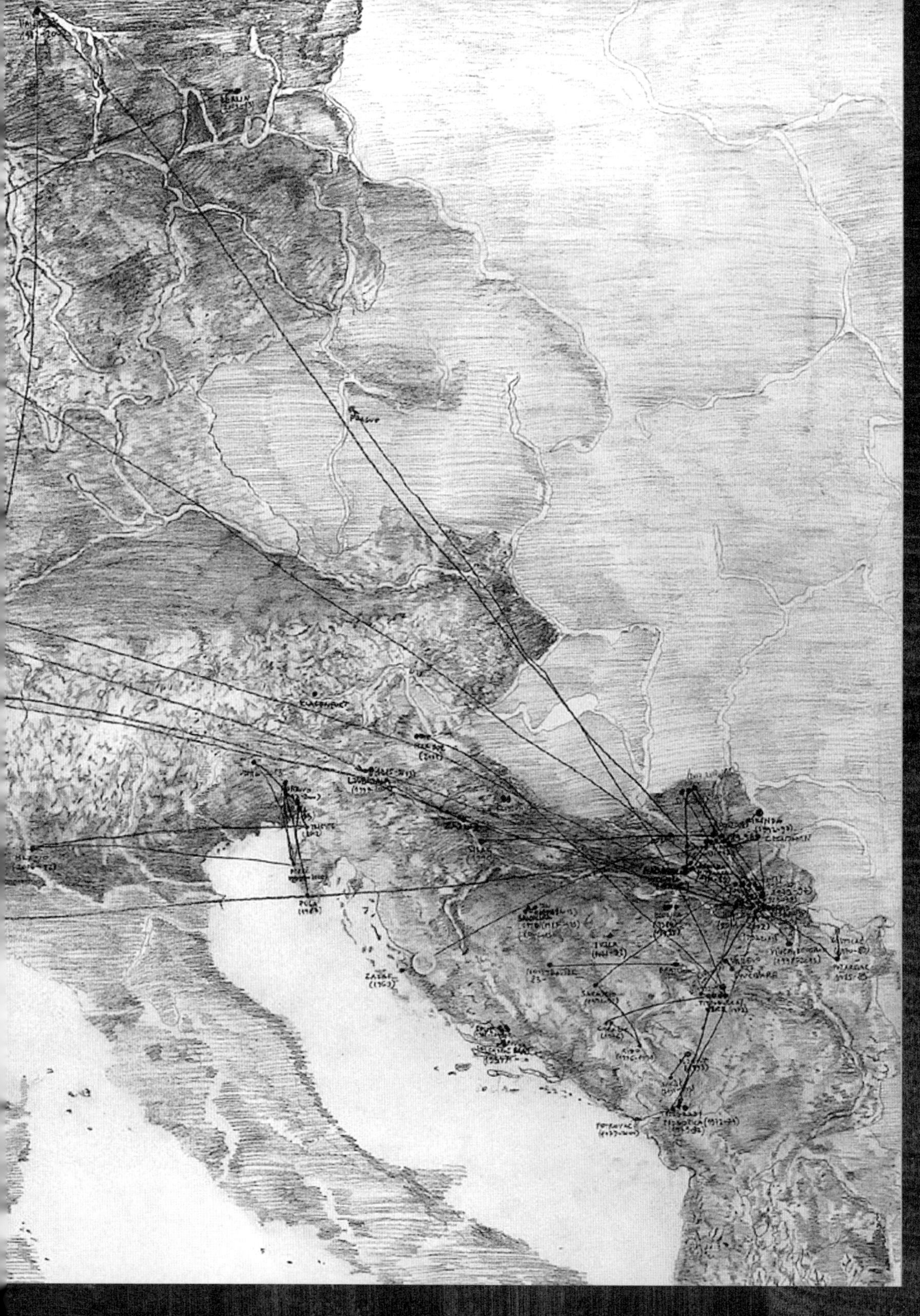

Tanja Ostojić, *Lexicon of Tanjas Ostojić: Migration Map of 30 Tanjas Ostojić*, 2013, drawing in pencil on aquarelle paper, detail.
© Tanja Ostojić

ON THE DEVELOPMENT OF INTERDISCIPLINARY FEMINIST METHODOLOGIES AND PERSPECTIVES WITHIN MY OWN ARTISTIC PRACTICE
I'll Be Your Angel (2001) and *Lexicon of Tanjas Ostojić* (2011–2017)

Tanja Ostojić

It's Saturday, 15 June 2019. Yesterday I had a very inspiring studio visit by researcher Lena von Geyso and we had an in-depth discussion of the politics of my *I'll Be Your Angel* (2001) project, the facts surrounding my participation at the 49th Venice Biennale and its consequences. We both agreed that it is about time for a new reading of this work in the light of changed discourses in the past eighteen years, especially after the #MeToo movement.

 Strategies of Success/Curator Series (2001–2003) was a conceptual art project that focused on the relationships of power and gender within the art system, analyzing how gender operates within power structures and how economies of professional, and professional & private merge and interrelate. The work offered a pioneering institutional critique of artist-curator-art critic-institution relationships in the context of "East and West", across the division of the

Global South and Global North. It included the following performances, conceptual body artworks, photos, collages, videos, etc.: *Black Square on White* (1995/2001), *I'll Be Your Angel* and *Be My Guest* (2001), and in 2003, the following four works: *Sofa for Curator, Politics of Queer Curatorial Positions: After Rosa von Praunheim, Fassbinder and Bridge Markland* (with Marina Gržinić), *Strategies of Success* installation and *Vacation with Curator.* The last one was produced for but ultimately censored in large portion by the Tirana Biennale in Albania.[1] In 2017, I tried to extend this project by exploring the artist-collector's gender & power relationships, attempting two times to produce *Vacation with Collector*, with one of the most influential art collectors in Southeast Europe—once on my own, and the second time with an informal collective of my name-sisters—but, on both occasions, the project remained unrealized or was censored. After Lena's visit, I wonder if it would be somehow possible to revisit the project now after eighteen years, especially given the extremely hierarchical setting of academic work-shops in which I've been invited to speak recently, where I found the relation to certain international theoretical male stars has produced new power and gender dynamics between academic institutions, theoreticians and artists. The constant recuperation of the same models, the inappropriate language and attitudes they tend to use, seem to actually belong to the same matrix of power they attempt to criticize. How can one act in these contexts to change things?

 I had been invited by Harald Szeemann to take part in his 'Plateau of Mankind' exhibition at the 49th Venice Biennale (2001) via e-mail and he asked me what I would like to propose to him for this exhibition. Well, first of all, I proposed renaming the exhibition 'Plateau of Humankind' as a step towards gender equality, but I did not ask to be credited for this. Powerful men simply gather and use knowl-edge of anonymous women, and this can be found multiple times throughout art's history and in humankind. The use of terms and the changes in language that feminism has tried hard to bring about is an important part of our struggle. Szeemann changed the title of the show as I advised, and this was a term by which I would prefer to be represented, but I got the impression that he accepted my proposals for an artistic intervention without giving it too much thought.

1. The first phase of the *Vacation with Curator* project in May 2003 included the successful production of a series of quasi-paparazzi photographs with the Biennale's curator Edi Muka and me captured at various locations on the Albanian coast. I produced two photo collages from this and they were supposed to have been shown at the Biennale exhibition when it opened a few months later. In the framework of my project, the organizers also produced a small quasi-paparazzi webpage with some of those images, which was linked to the official Biennale website. The webpage was not visible either in the exhibition or on the Biennale homepage. The important part of this project was, however, banned, as I was told, because it could have directly ruined the re-election campaign of Edi Rama who was, at the time, city Mayor of Tirana and the director of the Tirana Biennale (Mayor of Tirana 2000–2011, then Prime Minister of Albania 2013–present). There were already some rumours present in Albanian press at the time that accused Rama, who had served earlier as Minister of Culture, Youth and Sport, of laundering money through art. As the success of the Tirana Biennale was supposed to work in support of his re-election campaign, I was told all of a sudden that it was not suitable or acceptable to have topless and beach photos of Edi Muka and myself in the Albanian press at the time. An integral part of my initial artistic concept was to provide Albanian press with photos of this work and to see what happens. The resultant press clippings would then become an integral part of the work. However, as a result of the ban, not one of the photos was ever allowed to be part of the press images of the Biennale or given to the press. Additionally, as a participating artist I was not invited to attend the Biennale opening, but Harald Szeemann apparently was there.

2. *Jugoslovenka* = Yugoslav woman (in Serbo-Croatian language).

We should not forget the stakes here: on the one side, we have a male "genius" curator who was working on his third and last Venice Biennale… and on the other side, myself, as Jasmina Tumbas brilliantly termed a *Jugoslovenka*[2]! — *uninvited guest*, in her 2019 article in *Art Monthly*:

> Ostojić provocatively made visible what so many women already know—and since [the] #MeToo movement has become poignantly evident—that a career in arts often lies in the hands of men whose gatekeeping powers are habitually sexually charged.

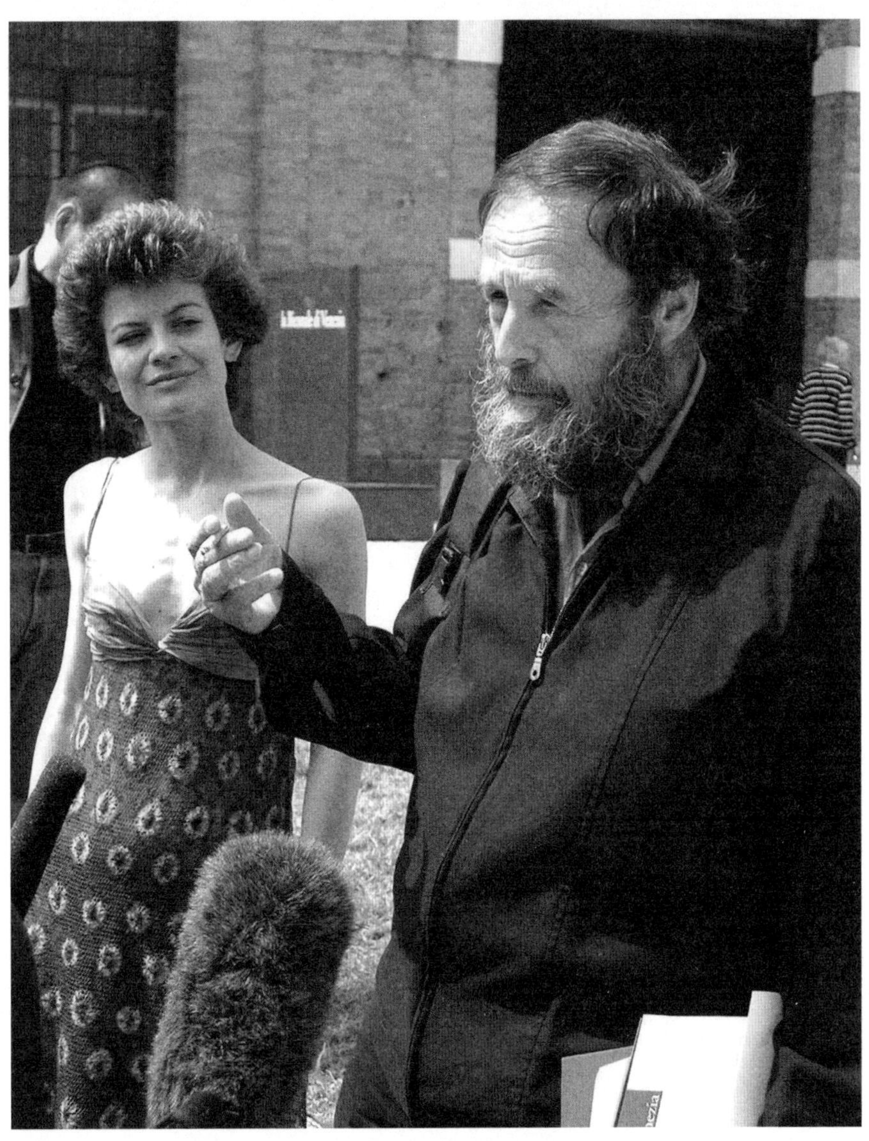

Tanja Ostojić, *I'll Be Your Angel*, 2001, four days performance with Harald Szeemann, *Plateau of Humankind*, 49th Venice Biennale. Photo: Borut Krajnc. Courtesy of Tanja Ostojić. © Krajnc/Ostojić

Choosing to act as the obnoxious, over-friendly and uninvited guest who Szeemann could not easily get rid of, Ostojić also brilliantly exhibited the powers of immigrant *Jugoslovenka's* survival in Europe: smiling and persisting while enduring the humiliating position of constantly being "lesser than".[3]

"Lesser than" resonates strongly with me and that has been part of the production and treatment of my artworks and my career in many international exhibitions and conferences. With this text I want to highlight not only the specific artworks, but rather to include circumstances of production and presentation, representation, reception and consequences as they all create a unity that needs to be considered. Hopefully, this will open the door for more complex and profound analyses of this practice in the future. In that light I include here my text from 2001 for the official 49th Venice Biennale catalogue, so we could see what this young artist Tanja Ostojić was intending to do and what she wrote back then:

> Provocation is a speciality of mine. My experience tells me that while art cannot quickly change social or political reality, it is important art not be apolitical.
>
> My need for direct communication led me into using my body and personality as a medium for art works. Sometimes I radically "sacrifice" my intimacy to confront certain existential, social or political subjects. *Looking for a Husband with EU Passport*, an interactive web project addressing gender and capital, criticizes the 1990s politics of Yugoslavia, and describes the collision of isolation, poverty and the elitism of European Union politics.
>
> The personal contemporary space of individuals and human relationships, in and out of art circles is in crisis. How can one revitalise essential human values through art? The Venice Biennale attracts the world press, art lovers and professionals; it seemed a natural opportunity to pose these questions here.

3. Jasmina Tumbas, 'Yugonostalgia', *Art Monthly* 425 (April 2019), pp. 6–10.

4. *Black Square* (1915) is an iconic painting by Kazimir Malevich.

5. Tanja Ostojić, 'I'll be Your Angel', in *La Biennale di Venezia: 49. Esposizione Internazionale d'Arte*, eds. Harald Szeemann and Cecilia Liveriero Lavelli, exh. cat. Venice 2001, pp. 274–275.

Black Square on White,[4] made of pubic hair on my Venus Mound, allows me to reconstruct a previous artwork (*Personal Space* Photo Series 1995–96) in a very different context. Only the Biennale director, Mr. Harald Szeemann, will have the right to see this "hidden Malevich" in order to declare it an official part of the 49th Venice Biennale. Walking around Venice during opening days, elegantly dressed, my work of art will be hidden. This intervention can provoke a reinterpretation of Eastern European spirituality, and non-material ideas; it is essentially about trust and power.

I'll Be Your Angel consists of my accompanying Mr. Szeemann during the opening days around Venice (including cocktails, dinners, press conferences). I will be naturally performing as his escort—his *Angel*. This piece, integrated in everyday life, poses potential ambiguous narratives concerning the scandalous artist (and the curator). It provokes an invitation/invasion, and questions the power structure in the art world. Speculations of morality, and art world strategy will spin out; while the press will possibly construct a media support for this, it is not necessary. The structure of the piece is the process of mystery, both personal and public, encased in the glossy gossip of art world whispers.[5]

In the English version of the catalogue my signature (unlike signatures of all other text authors) was not published, but more significantly the following part of the text was also completely missing both in the English and Italian versions of the catalogue as well (without any authorization from or agreement with me).

Why such a radical strategy? The Venice Biennale is a global phenomenon: A tourist attraction, a financial party of the art world, an intellectual soup; yet, it happens that many art works in Venice are either missed or misconstrued. So, I asked Harald Szeemann for his collaboration. His openness and trust of the potential nature of me 'being his escort and his angel', owes a critical debt to him. He is a respected and powerful personality with a "loaded name"; he becomes the material for my work and a "guarantee" for a platform for fragile questions.

> The opportunity to make an active/interactive artwork out of Mr. Szeemann proves infinitely rich and complex. It allows me to blend the immaterial and intellectual in a process-oriented work, a work that is not only "officially" sanctioned, but also "unofficially" snakes in and out of the language of the art system.

Szeemann, who was the main person responsible for editing the catalogue, claimed one year later that he still hadn't had time to double-check why one third of my text was missing, when I, Tanja Ostojić, "lesser than" *Jugoslovenska*, explicitly asked him in writing about it.

In two earlier projects, staged unofficially at the Venice Biennale during its opening days, I, as an uninvited guest, tried to address some very serious concepts in art's reception, namely the dissolution of the self in contemporary life, and the destruction of life in neighbourhoods—and visibly (almost forcibly, but with a "smile") opened my ideas for communication, interaction and contact with the art world public of the Biennale. And I wrote about my earlier project for the Venice Biennale *Unofficial Chronologies* as well in the second part of my text for the catalogue[6] that had been shortened for unknown reason and by an unknown editor.

> *Would You Digitalize Your Soul/Death Is In My Sight Today* was realized as a set of posters and flyers, and unofficially exhibited on the streets on the occasion of the 47th Venice Biennale (1997), together with Saša Gajin. This work attempts to stage the conflict of real-time communication and contemporary digital systems of understanding, which are focused largely on speed and little else.
>
> Two years later, following the NATO bombing campaigns of Yugoslavia and (by chance) the elections in Italy, I conceived my own campaign for the international crowd at the 48th Venice Biennale (1999): *I Want You to Ask Your*

6. Ibid.

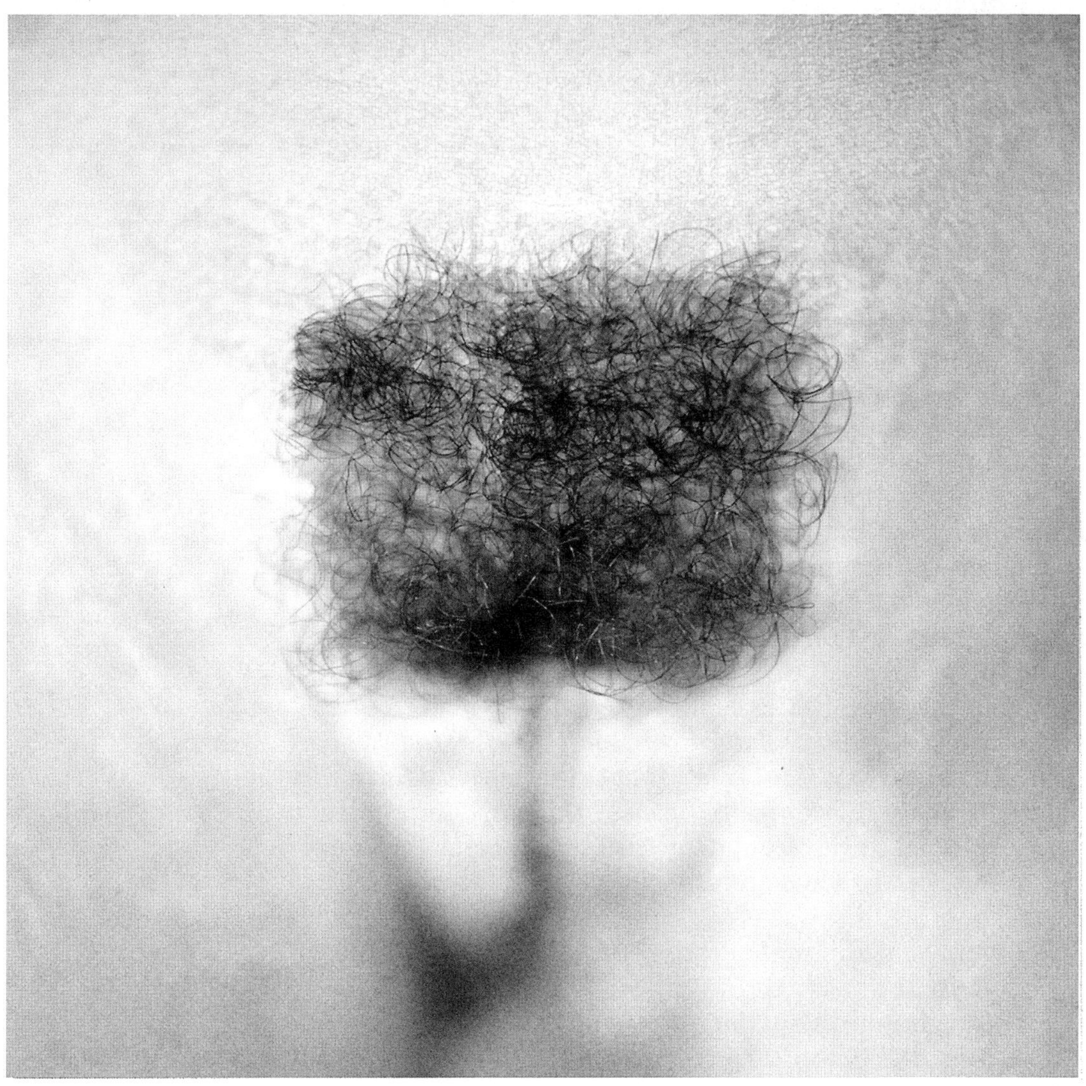

"Black Square on White," Pubic hair on my Venus Hill, reconstructed from Personal Space Photo Series 1995-96, for the 49th Venice Biennale. Only Mr. Harald Szeemann, director of the 49th Venice Biennale, will have the right to see this "hidden Malevich" in order to declare it an official part of the exhibition. I will be his elegantly dressed Angel/Escort, during the opening days of the exhibit, and my work of art will be hidden.

Tanja Ostojić, *Black Square on White*, 2001, postcards, 49th Venice Biennale.
Photo: Saša Gajin. ©/Courtesy of Tanja Ostojić

Government's Responsibility for the Consequences of Bombing Yugoslavia. I again personally distributed posters and postcards (in four languages) during the opening days of the Biennale.

In my written correspondence with Szeemann preceding the exhibition I referred to Alexander Brener's dollar sign[7] intervention over a painting by Malevich in the Stedelijk Museum in Amsterdam as a strategy of critique towards the Western dominated art market and Western art history's recuperation of Eastern European art, and in particular to my feminist perspective, both as my references for the *Black Square on White* body artwork that would not be visible in the exhibition, only on my naked body. And he (kind of) promised to write about it in the catalogue but that did not happen. As I attempted to announce in my Biennale catalogue text (in the missing section though), my performance, which spanned four days, was not only "officially" sanctioned, but also "unofficially" sneaked in and out of the language of the art system, as rumours started to circulate about this in the press. After I published the postcards documenting my action (*Black Square on White*, 2001), the *Venice Diary*[8] (2002) and the *I'll be Your Angel* video, Mrs Szeemann formulated a written attempt to "close" the work and halt its further development or circulation and so I received a long private letter from Szeemann himself:

> I want that Biennale piece remains limited in time and use, no more quotes about it in your upcoming works, no more cuts in video and text. The Biennale is over and belongs to the past.
> (Date, 6 June 2002, First day of Documenta in Kassel).

Furthermore, he wished me "good luck" with my "immigrant projects" and I consequently appear to have been blacklisted by this family's influence, particularly in Switzerland, where my work has never been shown to date, or in "Balkan Shows" held across Europe. This project functioned as a litmus test to a form of applied performative sociological research that I then pursued, even though it did contribute to a decisive downward turn in my career.

---

7. Александр Бренер (Alexander Brener), one of the main figures of Moscow Actionism was jailed in 1997 for spraying a green dollar sign on Kazimir Malevich's painting *White Suprematist Cross* (1920–1921).

8. Tanja Ostojić, 'I'll be Your Angel' and 'Venice Diary', in *Venice Diary*, ed. Tihomir Milovac, exh. cat. Zagreb (Museum of Contemporary Art) 2002.

9. Tanja Ostojić, *Strategies of Success: Curators Series 2001–2003*, exh. cat. Bourges (La Box); Belgrade (SKC) 2004.

10. Suzana Milevska, 'Spectacle of the Invisible', *NU: The Nordic Art Review* 3, no. 5 (2001); Suzana Milevska, 'A Gaze at the Naked Truth', *Venice Diary*; Suzana Milevska, 'The Portrait of an Artist as a Young "Strategic Essentialist"', in *Strategies of Success*.

11. Marina Gržinić, 'Between Ostojić's Legs', in *Situated Contemporary Art Practices: Art, Theory and Activism from (the East of) Europe* (Frankfurt a.M.: Revolver; Ljubljana: ZRC Publishing, 2004); Marina Gržinić, 'Tanja Ostojić: "Yes, it's Fucking Political – Skunk Anansie"', in *Strategies of Success*, pp. 11–31.

12. Angela Dimitrakaki, 'Labour, Ethics, Sex and Capital: On Biopolitical Production in Contemporary Art: Andrea Fraser and Tanja Ostojić', *n.paradoxa: international feminist art journal* 28 (July 2011), pp. 5–15; Angela Dimitrakaki, in *Gender, artWork and Global Imperative: A Materialist Feminist Critique* (Manchester: Manchester University Press, 2013).

13. Please visit *Misplaced Women?* project blog with over one hundred contributions: https://misplacedwomen.wordpress.com.

My feminist strategy was, despite everything that happened, to go on with the *Curator Series* project, exploring the topic further with other curatorial perspectives hoping it might serve as empowerment to other women as well. To shed more light on these issues I published the *Strategies of Success: Curator Series 2001–2003*[9] book in 2004, and this included some of a number of brilliant essays and articles analyzing the work, among others by Suzana Milevska[10] and Marina Gržinić.[11] Angela Dimitrakaki also later wrote about the work.[12] In other major projects of 2000–2004, *Waiting for a Visa* and *Illegal Border Crossing* in 2000, *Looking for a Husband with EU Passport*, 2000–2005, *After Courbet* in 2004, the *Crossing Borders Series* (2000–2005) and *Integration Project* I started to develop my methods further. All these works were profoundly involved with issues of migration, examining bio-politics, the concept of "integration", different forms of racism and social/cultural economies in which people work across borders.

The *Strategies of Success* (2001–2003) project had involved clear strategies of over-identification and confrontation, and, after these experiences, I turned towards more constructive strategies, trying to avoid and to go around and beyond addressing the position of power directly by working on several large, long-term and low/no-budget projects. The twelve-year research-based performance project *Naked Life* (2004–2016) focused in the first place on claiming historical and contemporary racism against the Roma minority throughout Europe and expressing solidarity with them. Another project, the complex *Misplaced Women?*[13] platform, ongoing since 2009, is an ever-growing example of constantly working on a small scale with inclusive creative and performative activities, and is resulting in the creation of a global community of women of all genders and beyond, by exploring the diverse aspects of misplacement and variety of public spaces.

Transformative Encounters

My recent project, *Lexicon of Tanjas Ostojić* (2011–2017) develops further the strategies of a conscious ethical politics in artistic production, the creation of a community with shared authorship and ownership, and the emancipatory potentials of collective autobiographical methodologies as the basis for art-making. *Lexicon of Tanjas Ostojić* is a complex, long-term, interdisciplinary, participatory research art project, in which I used online social media networks, as well as collaborations with women, to trace and contact people sharing my first name and family name. These name-sisters are of diverse nationalities, ages, and levels of education and have different professions, social backgrounds, and life experience, but all of them are able to communicate in Serbo-Croatian, and they, or their parents, are from the Socialist Federal Republic of Yugoslavia.

In this project, I felt somehow liberated from the political struggle of the art world and from the academic market's use of the terms praxis-based research and artistic research, as I did not have an obligation to deliver something according to any particular academic standards and it was not a doctorate, but a project developed in the first part in the frame of my interdisciplinary fellowship at the Graduate School, University of Arts Berlin, and beyond. That was liberating, as I could orient myself particularly towards the ethics of research and of artistic production, and the methodology of chance, enabling me to embrace the diversities that I met on my way.

Through a form of inter-personal sociological research, I devised a standardized list of questions to interview these women and in order to direct social and creative exchange, I created a map that documents the ways in which over 33 name-sisters—the project participants (including myself)—migrated (as refugees for reasons of war and post-war resettlement, for education, marriage, or economic reasons). Specifically, I tried to look at various identity and gender issues with which their lives were concerned. One of the important threads of the project is the labour conditions of the name-sisters, including women who are proud of their work, even when they have experienced being unemployed, underpaid, and/or exploited. The coming together of these different experiences is reflected in a 20 metre long multi-lingual "Women Talk" freeze made for the first exhibition of this project, a separate patchwork of joint embroidery, and some works in pottery inspired by women's coffee circle culture (that we practised together). This and our

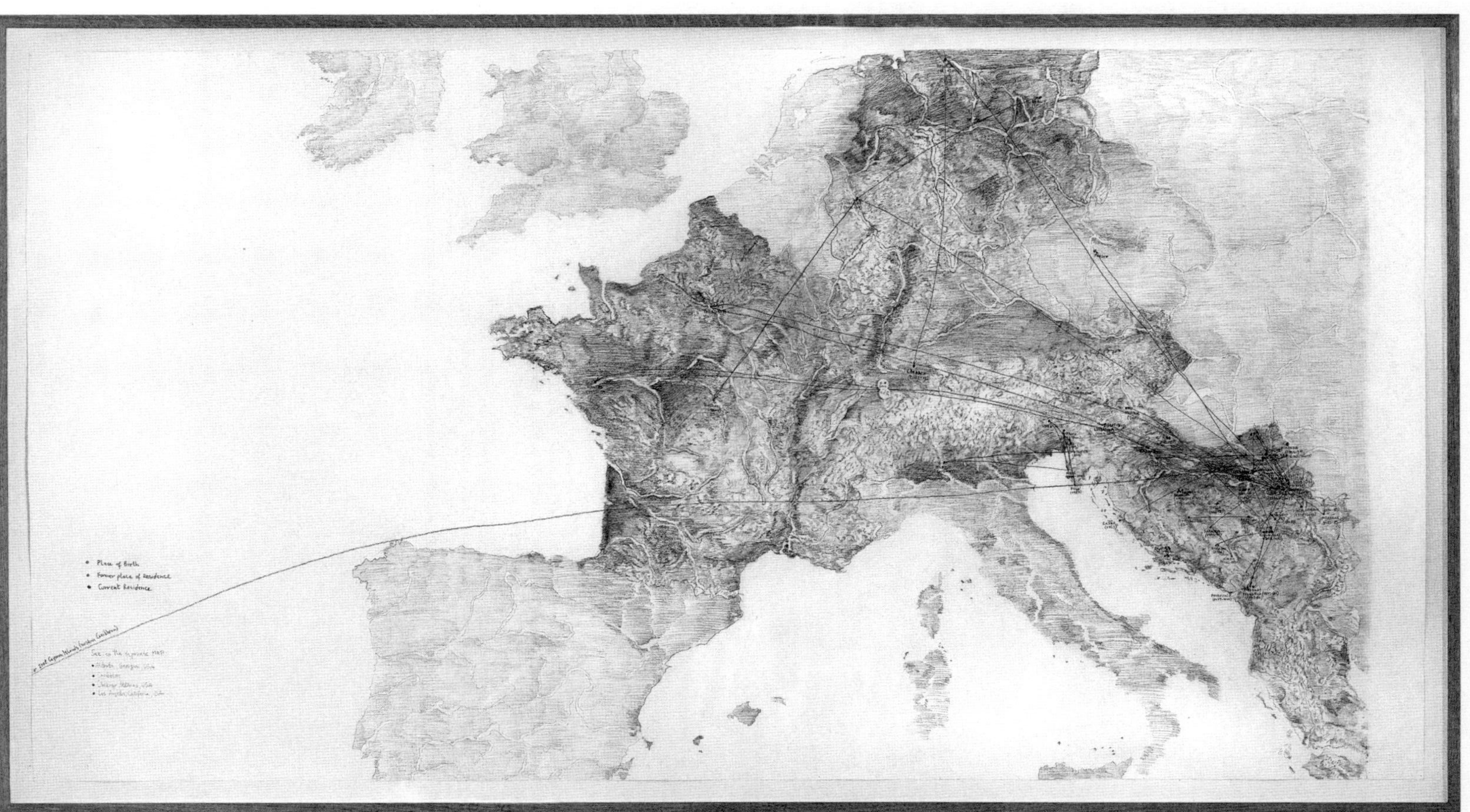

Tanja Ostojić, *Lexicon of Tanjas Ostojić: Migration Map of 30 Tanjas Ostojić*, 2013, drawing in pencil on aquarelle paper, 254 × 138 cm, installation view of the Salon of the Museum of Contemporary Art Belgrade. Photo: Nikola Radić Lucati. © Tanja Ostojić

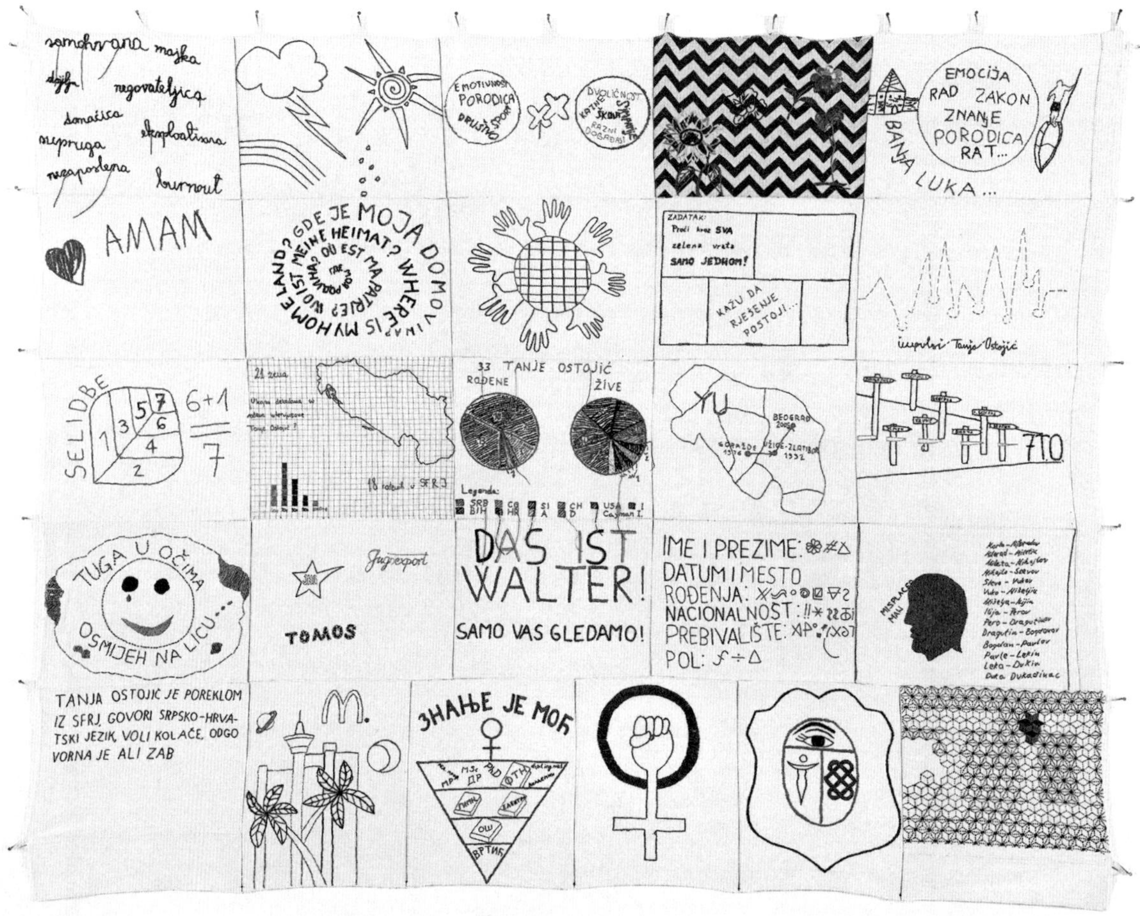

Tanja Ostojić, *Embroidered Lexicon of Tanjas Ostojić*, 2017, embroidery on cotton, 200 × 160 cm. Coauthors: Jelena Dinić, Tanja Ostojić (Banja Luka), Tanja Ostojić (Berlin), Tanja Ostojić (Trn), Tanja Ostojić (Udine), Tanja Ostojić-Guteša, Tanja Ostojić-Petrović, Tanja Petar Ostojić, Tatjana Ostojić (Beograd), Tatjana Ostojić Alabama, Sunčica Šido and Vahida Ramujkić. Workshops facilitators: Tanja Ostojić (Berlin) and Vahida Ramujkić. Photo: Nikola Radić-Lucati. ©/Courtesy of Tanja Ostojić

The work has been created over the course of three documentary embroidery workshops, hosted by the Goethe-Institut Belgrade, the Museum of Contemporary Art Republic of Srpska, Banja Luka, and the Museum of Contemporary Art, Zagreb. Together with a group of women (the name sisters) gathered around the interdisciplinary project *Lexicon of Tanjas Ostojić*, large-scale tapestry has been completed. This work reflects diverse aspects of female identity vis-à-vis work, knowledge, community and other issues in various ways. The work is the common property of the twelve coauthors.

14. Bojana Videkanić, 'Lexicon of Tanjas Ostojić and Feminism in Transition', *Sociologija* 60, no. 1 (2018), pp. 142–162, www.sociologija.org/admin/published/2018_60/1/578.pdf.

15. The Ethical Code is as follows:
• Participants have the right to step out of the project at any time.
• Nothing will be published without their knowledge or consent.
• Participants have the right to take back certain information or censor parts that they do not wish to be accessible to the public. Participants can/will get all material produced in the project frame for their own use. In the case of public events participants could additionally decide, for example, whether they are willing to take part in it or not; which questions they might be ready to answer and which not; what facts can be disclosed about them and which should stay secret; if they want to be filmed, photographed, or not, etc.

domestic work (as well as experiences of domestic violence) is discussed in the "Women Talk" chapter of the resulting book and the *Embroidered Lexicon of Tanjas Ostojić*. The anecdotes of individual women and changes of identity due to marriage are also featured as far as the women decided to authorize them with the distance of time.

Bojana Videkanić described the process very well in her writing about this work in the journal *Sociologija*:

> The methodology of chance was further employed through the interviews conducted with all Tanjas. Each interview became a moment in which women found out about each other, but also entered a dialog through which the stories that they heard about others' lives prompted them to share their own, sometimes forgotten or repressed, memories and experiences. Creative workshops served a similar role; as women discovered new information about each other they could then immediately share and embroider into the work that was collectively made. In short, *Lexicon*'s methodology was to include all aspects of women's subjective experience, of their perceptions, feelings, natural, cultural, and political opinions as part of its overall structure, and as a valid methodology of assessing and critiquing socio-political context.[14]

For me, the ethical line of the project development at all stages remained a crucial one. I tried to avoid some of the exploitative traps associated with participatory art, and particularly regarding the position of power of sociological/anthropological researchers that can be problematic. In order to be able to deal with ethical dilemmas of research conducted on living participants, at the earliest stage I defined an Ethical Code,[15] which related to the entire project. The guiding strategies during the project's development, involved investing a lot of time and trying to balance fairly what I asked of the participants, and what I had to offer, while staying uncompromising in those terms for the sake of the final outcome and what was discovered through this process.

In conversation with my cousins, neighbours, and
friends, and following what was going on in society,
I had the impression that the new national states,
new religious identity, wars, transition, and poverty
in the region were a huge step back for what were, in
large part, emancipated Yugoslav women, and I was
very curious to find out more about this through this
research project. I wanted to find out, among other
things, whether access to education and employment, and working conditions had changed after the
workers' self-governance and Yugoslav Socialism
vanished, and especially with migration, if and
how this has influenced the position of women in
families and in societies that have been transformed.
Additionally, in the past several decades there seems
to have been a strong trend for erasing all traces
of Yugoslavian tradition and history, including a
proper interpretation of the anti-fascist struggle, the
turn to the Non-Aligned Movement, and the tradition of workers' self-governance. This project has the
modest intention of going against such mainstream
discourse, and to engage with oral histories of some
of the women from post-Yugoslav geographies.[16]

16. Tanja Ostojić, 'Transformative
Encounters: From the Author's
Perspective', *Lexicon of Tanjas
Ostojić*, ed. Tanja Ostojić (London:
Live Arts Development Agency;
Rijeka: Museum of Modern and
Contemporary Art, 2018).

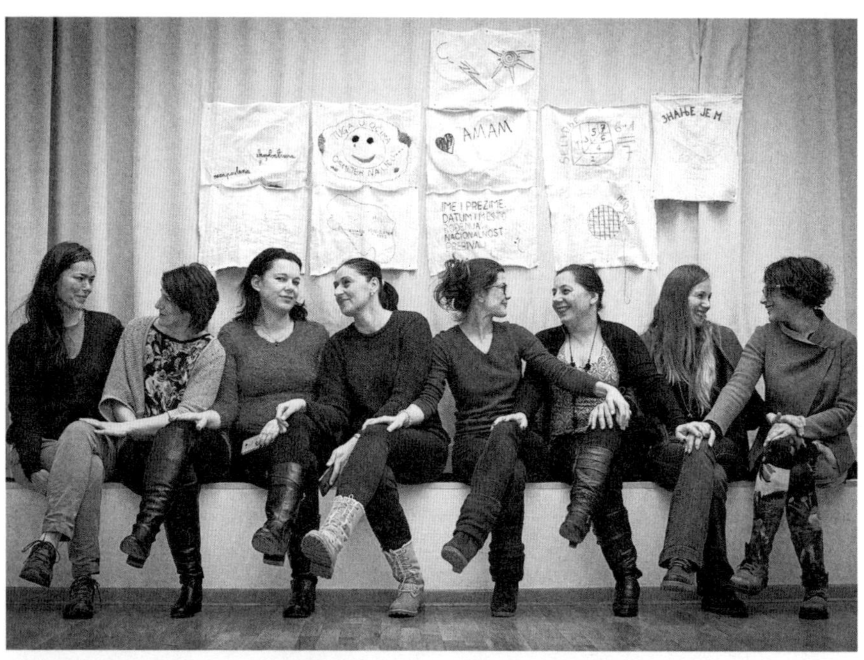

Embroidered Lexicon of Tanjas Ostojić, Workshop, Goethe-Institut Belgrad, January, 2017.
Photo: Marija Piroški, ©/Courtesy of Tanja Ostojić

As a consequence, this project created long-lasting friendships and has significantly enhanced the quality of the lives
of the participating women via creative work, social interactions and transformative encounters. More precisely, the
project offered an opportunity to discuss personal ideas and
life situations with a diverse group of women with different
life experiences, who were able to exchange ideas with people
of a different social status and from different backgrounds.
Self-analysis via interviews based on emancipatory collective
autobiographical methodologies and the recognition that
perhaps it's time to change something in one's life were
also very important. The project provided an introduction
for some of these women to participate in artistic life via
pedagogical work, including joint museum and exhibition
visits, guided tours, the production of tapestry, pottery,
joint performances in public spaces, project presentations,
a talk show, and many new experiences in their lives. The
co-authorship and co-ownership of a joint artwork, and the
importance of this collaboration, could be discussed both in
ethical and economical terms. Further work on the project
could include analyses of certain topics and statistics that
become apparent in the interviews and through art production. The crises and transition to a new economic system,
and the pride that these women take in their work, their
access to education, as well as the history of Yugoslavia, and
related identities, should all be noted. In particular though,
the wishes, plans, hopes, and perspectives of the participants
could all be observed via diverse inputs in the exhibition
and project book including artefacts, visual documentation,
recipes, interviews, and texts.

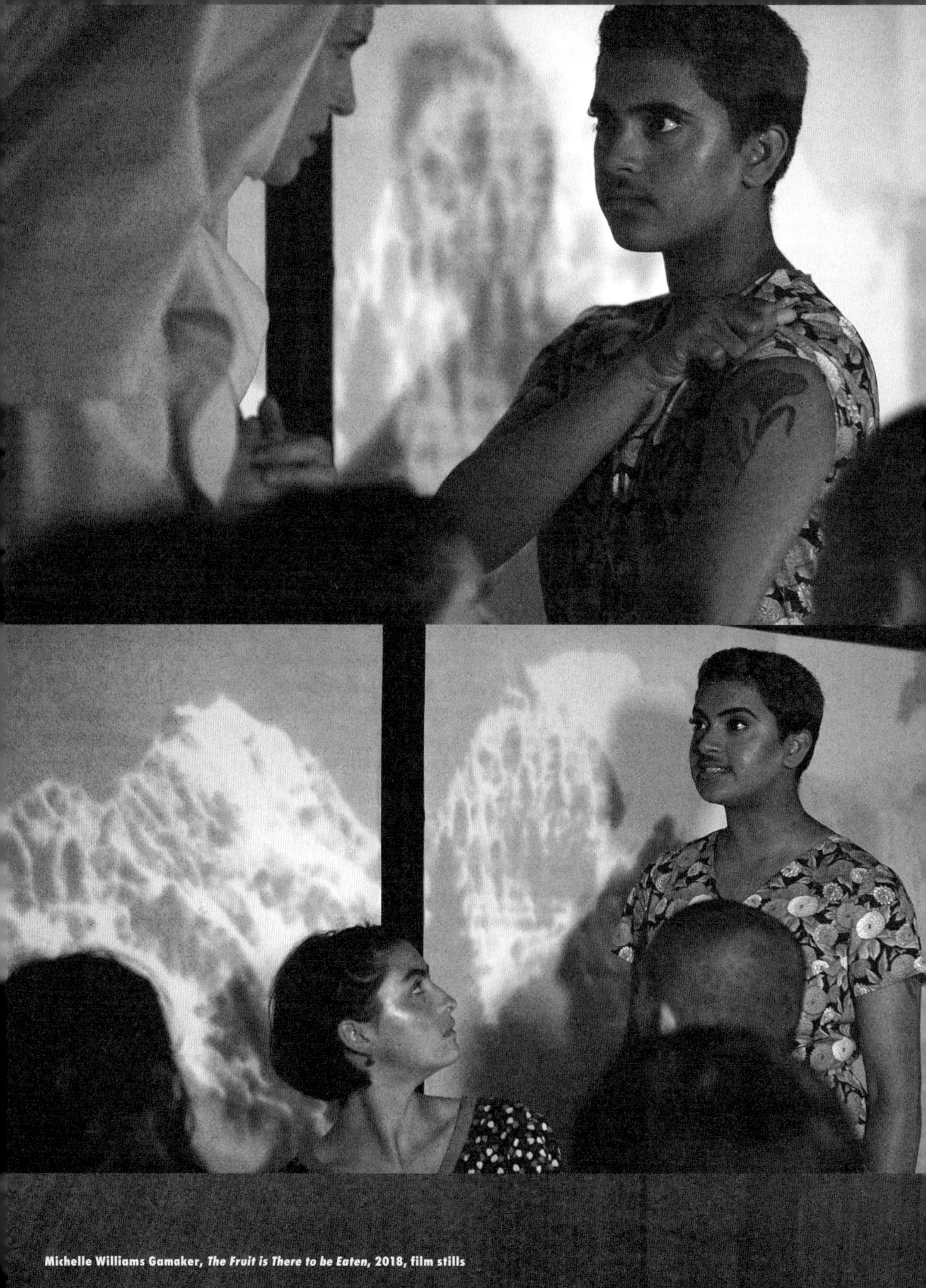

Michelle Williams Gamaker, *The Fruit is There to be Eaten*, 2018, film stills

ON FICTIONAL ACTIVISM
Exploring the Film Trilogy
Dissolution (2019)

Michelle Williams Gamaker

1. The trilogy *Dissolution* comprises *House of Women* (2017), *The Fruit is There to be Eaten* (2018) and *The Eternal Return* (2019).

2. Sarita Malik, *Representing Black Britain: Black and Asian Images on Television* (Thousand Oakes, CA: Sage, 2001), p. 112.

As an artist filmmaker who is also a woman of colour and self-confessed cinephile, I spent my childhood and teenage years watching television and film rather indiscriminately. I would like to draw upon these early encounters with screen culture—and my attendant preoccupations therewith— to highlight how they inform my recent body of work, *Dissolution* (2017–2019).[1] In those early years, I ravenously consumed images with little or no parental interference about quality or content to learn about the world not quite mine to explore. In spite of more positive moves in the film and television industry, the visibility of people of colour continues to be subject to problematic structural mediations in how their images are disseminated in mainstream culture, often in limited or stereotyping ways perpetuating social inequality and reinstating spectres of Imperialism.

I cannot say if I registered the paucity of characters that looked like me as actively as I do now, but from my memory the mainstream British media of the 1980s did not image brown female bodies, nor did they represent the stories of first generation British South Asians with any alacrity or attention to detail. More often than not, I was subjected to weak comedic representations, a rather embarrassing legacy of 1960s and 1970s TV, which included white stars in blackface who latterly resurfaced—without editorial apology—in re-runs. As cultural critic Sarita Malik has emphasized in her analysis of the BBC's *Black and White Minstrel Show* (1958–1978), in which white actors similarly donned blackface, the policy appeared to reject Black-British acting talent.[2]

There is a violence hard to comprehend in such images of imperialism and inequality, despite the Technicolor schmaltz the films of the 1940s exude. As a child, this dearth of "brownness" amongst actors affected me in strange but meaningful ways; firstly, an over-identification with Fijian-Indian-German pop/folk singer–songwriter Tanita Tikaram's renditions of *A Good Tradition* and *Twist in My Sobriety* on *Top of the Pops*, and secondly thanks to BBC2's afternoon programming *Saturday Matinee* in the 1990s, I accessed a great deal of lush Technicolor film, in particular ambitious and lavish set productions that inadvertently contributed to an ongoing obsession with two figures from British film directors Michael Powell and Emeric Pressburger's 1947 film classic, *Black Narcissus*.[3]

My films, and the fictional characters within them, reflect on the long-term effects of this exposure to such depictions of inequality and loss of agency, and my own response became a rewriting of their fictional injustices. My "fictional activism" is a claim for subtle, but potent acts of fictional treachery. Fiction offers huge freedom in representation, but all too often produces lazy, non-reflexive repetitions. I am deeply interested in repeating and revisiting older content, in particular British and American Studio films of the 1930s, 1940s and 1950s, by utilizing contemporary critical awareness to challenge the structural sloppiness of their representations. While I aim my critique specifically at the twentieth-century film industry, I would argue this is a condition symptomatic of many industries today. So, I proceed with caution to suggest that "fictional activism" rests with the filmmaker, her text and its activation through the tools of fiction to touch the inequalities she finds in the source material. It does so by actively producing images and texts that interrogate and trouble the viewer on an emotional and political level.

In 2014, I began making *Casting Kanchi*, a four-channel video installation that was later edited into the short film *House of Women* (2017). In this work, I reinstated what I termed a "brown protagonist" as a lead character in my moving image work.[4] The film is part of a larger project to explore individuals structurally marginalized due to their race, class and gender in studio films produced during the British Empire.

3. Michael Powell and Emeric Pressburger, *Black Narcissus* (London: Pinewood, 1947). Originally published in 1939, Rumer Godden, *Black Narcissus* (London: Virago Modern Classics, 2006).

4. Michelle Williams Gamaker, *House of Women* (2017) screened at Channels Festival, Melbourne, Dokfest Kassel, Internationale Kurzfilmtage Winterthur, Switzerland, L'Alternativa, Barcelona in 2017; Transmediale, Berlin, International Women's Film Festival, Cologne, Visite Film Festival, Antwerp, 62nd BFI London Film Festival Experimenta, *Living Beyond Limits*, MIMA in 2018, 'Women, Power, Protest', Birmingham Museum Art Gallery, and 'As Seen on Screen: Art and Cinema' at Walker Art Museum, Liverpool in 2019). The film is now part of the Arts Council of England's national collection.

5. The name Kanchi is a Nepali word for a 'young girl' who is 'sweet.'

6. The Indian extras for *Black Narcissus* were cast from local dockyard workers at Rotherhithe, it is likely the children in the film were family members. In the follow-up to *House of Women, The Fruit is There to be Eaten*, I locate the entire film at Rotherhithe at Sands Pictures Film Studio and The Brunel Museum's rooftop garden, making reference to Rotherhithe's working class history. It is likely many of these extras would have been allocated to the garden sequences, the convent's Lace Room and the adjacent classroom. Rather than presenting the source texts' image of the 'docile native' I presented somewhat lacklustre, disinterested schoolgirls, who would rather paint their nails and begrudgingly repeat the alphabet of British flora in their botany lesson.

7. Utilizing a similar strategy in *Elephant Boy*, in his silent documentary *Nanook of The North* (1922) Flaherty employed elements of docudrama, 'casting' locals for fictitious roles and incorporating staged sequences, such as the anachronistic hunting narrative. See Erik Barnouw, *Documentary: A History of the Non-Fiction Film* (Oxford: Oxford University Press, 1993), pp. 33–36.

In the original film, the character of Kanchi was played by white British actor Jean Simmons, made famous by her earlier role as Estella in David Lean's *Great Expectations* (1946).[5] Simmons willingly participated, as did so many actors of the time, in the age-old studio tradition of blackface. Her skin covered in brown Panstick make-up and her body adorned with jewels and coloured silks, Simmons was transformed into the South Asian dancing girl, a lascivious, mute troublemaker whose burgeoning sexuality threatens the chaste values of the convent, shaking the colonial benevolence of the sister's mission to its foundations by tempting the Young General to run away with her. This subplot follows the story of the Prince and the Beggar Maid. The irony that my identification with a white woman playing a South Asian woman does not escape me, but cements my earlier assertion that "brownness" as I desired it had no home in Western screen culture. I was also preoccupied with the character of The Young General, played by Indian-born American actor, Sabu, because I imagined that my maternal grandfather might have looked like him as a young man. Here was an "authentic" brown body, *sans* make-up, and an individual who appeared to have some parity to his white co-stars in the film's billing, despite his "sidekick" role. Sabu was assigned lines that held narrative weight, a far cry from the silent, passive character of Kanchi who barely passes as authentic anything. Simmons' performance can only draw from a poor copy based on imitation veering into parody. While these two "brown protagonists" now occupy a leading role in the trilogy, I then became interested in the idea of agitation and finding power from the margins, and in my second, *The Fruit is There to be Eaten*, I looked at how the film's extras, dock workers from Rotherhithe, were cast and mobilized.[6]

How Sabu was cast for the film also strikes a chord. In 1936, while gathering footage in a Maharajah's palace in India, documentary filmmaker Robert J. Flaherty came across twelve-year-old Sabu Dastagir (born Selar Sheik Sabu), the son of a *mahout* (elephant rider) from Mysore.[7] Mirroring the realities of Sabu's young life, Flaherty cast Sabu in Alexander Korda's film *Elephant Boy* (1937), based on the short story *Toomai of the Elephants* from Kipling's *The Jungle Book* (1894), an adaptation that earned Korda's brother Zoltan the Best Director award at the 1937 Venice Film Festival. Sabu went on to major roles such as Abu in *The Thief of Bagdad* (Michael Powell & Ludwig Berger, 1940) and Mowgli in *The Jungle Book* (Zoltan Korda, 1942). His apparent willingness and "charm" led to a meteoric rise in fame that meant the studios took full advantage of their new child star. Sabu became a household name, appearing on stamps, endorsing cereals, opening the 1939 San Francisco World's Fair and featuring in lifestyle magazines in the UK and US. Sabu in effect became the go-to actor for such films: the studios now had someone who did not need to be "blacked up" and, crucially, like all collections built on colonial premises, they had found their authentic specimen to parade for general consumption.

The British studio system, like its American counterpart, looked to the colonies to provide the exotic backdrops audiences demanded, but paradoxically they commonly did so by constructing sets. These offered a controlled colonial vision of the British Raj and its people, including the casting of white British actors in the roles of Indians. *Black Narcissus* was shot almost entirely at London's Pinewood Studios; utilizing matte painting to create the illusion of the glinting peaks of Kanchenjunga.[8] According to film critic David Thompson, '*Black Narcissus* is that rare thing, an erotic English film about the fantasies of nuns'[9] and indeed the Technicolor melodrama, based on the 1939 novel of the same name by Rumer Godden,[10] unleashes the emotional tensions of Anglican nuns, sent to the Himalayas with the colonial mission to civilize and educate the local natives of Darjeeling. The film was actually released only a few months before the declaration of Indian Independence in August 1947. Film critic David Kehr suggests that the nuns' hasty retreat from the mountain in the film's closing sequence could be read as 'a last farewell to their fading empire'.[11]

For *House of Women*, the first in the *Dissolution* trilogy, I decided to recast the character of Kanchi by asking only ex-pat or first-generation British Asian women and non-binary individuals living in the UK to apply.[12] Shot on 16mm film, the four candidates, Krishna Istha, Jasdeep Kandola, Tina Mander and Arunima Rajkumar, introduce themselves to an anonymous reader, voiced by actor Kelly Hunter. They each recite a personalized alphabet including

8. The film's exterior location at Leonardslee Gardens in West Sussex, was home to an Indian army retiree, who had cultivated the appropriate plants to mimic the foothills of the Himalayas. See David Kehr, *Black Narcissus* (The Criterion Collection, 2001), www.criterion.com/current/ posts/94-black-narcissus (accessed 1 June 2019).

9. David Thompson, *The New Biographical Dictionary of Film* (London: Little Brown, 2002), p. 694.

10. Rumer Godden, *Black Narcissus* (London: Virago, 2013 [1939]).

11. David Kehr, *Black Narcissus* (The Criterion Collection, 2001).

12. In 2014, I placed a Facebook call out asking for individuals interested in auditioning for the role. The subsequent scripts reflect a conversation between the prospective Kanchis and myself about their personal politics to incorporate this into the structure of the script.

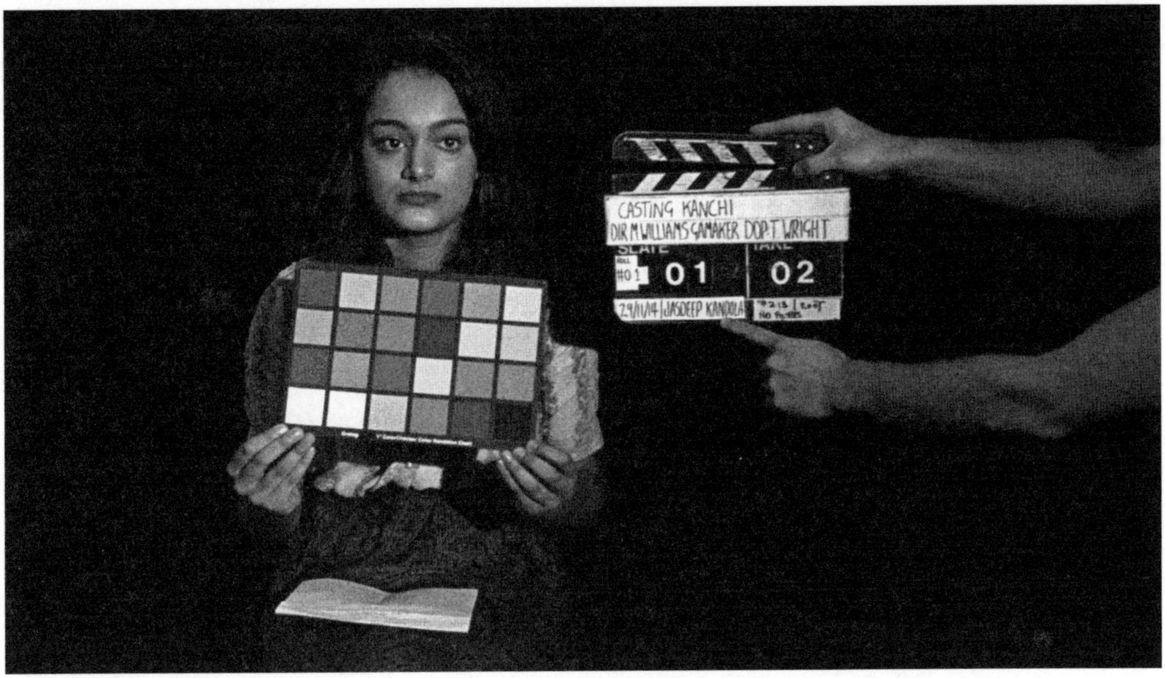

Jasdeep Kandola, screen still from: Michelle Williams Gamaker, *House of Women*, 2017, 16mm film transferred to HDV, colour, sound, 14'05, Arts Council of England Collection

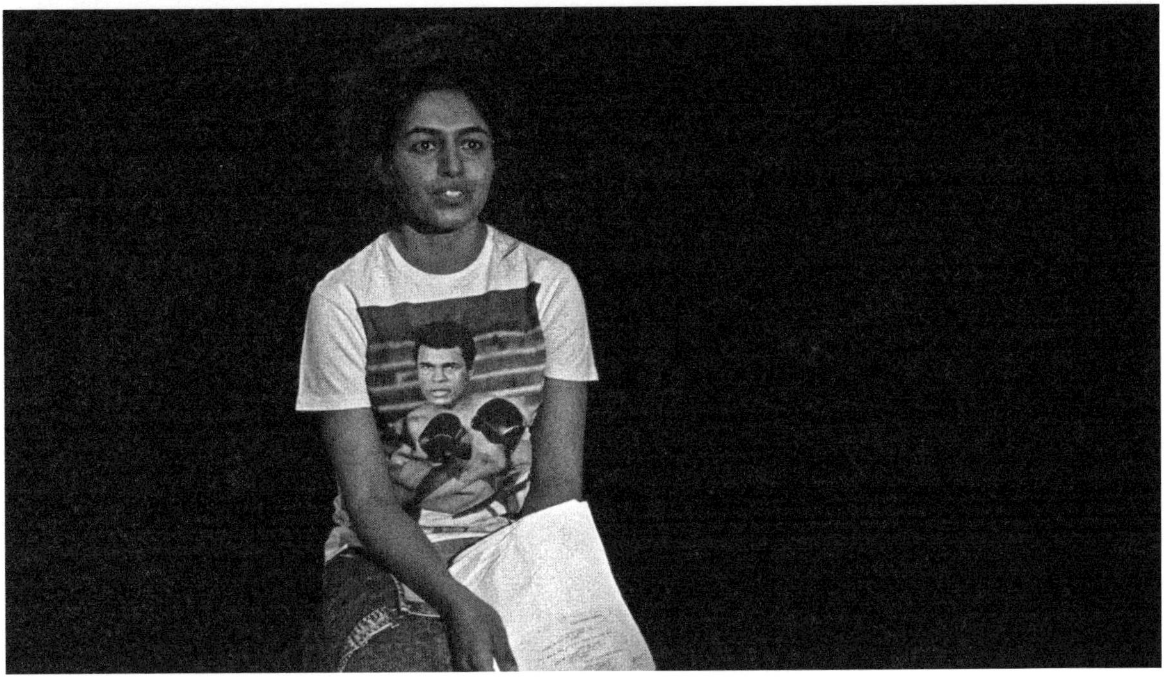

Tina Mander, screen still from: Michelle Williams Gamaker, *House of Women*, 2017, 16mm film transferred to HDV, colour, sound, 14'05, Arts Council of England Collection

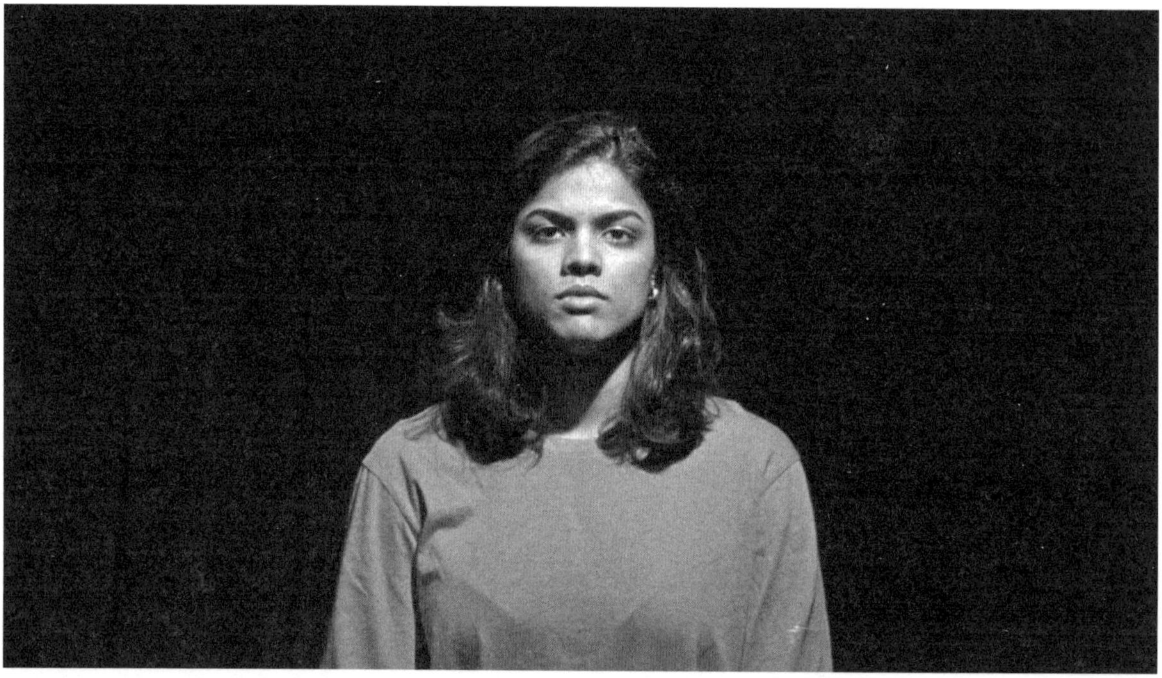

Arunima Rajkumar, screen still from: Michelle Williams Gamaker, *House of Women*, 2017, 16mm film transferred to HDV, colour, sound, 14'05, Arts Council of England Collection

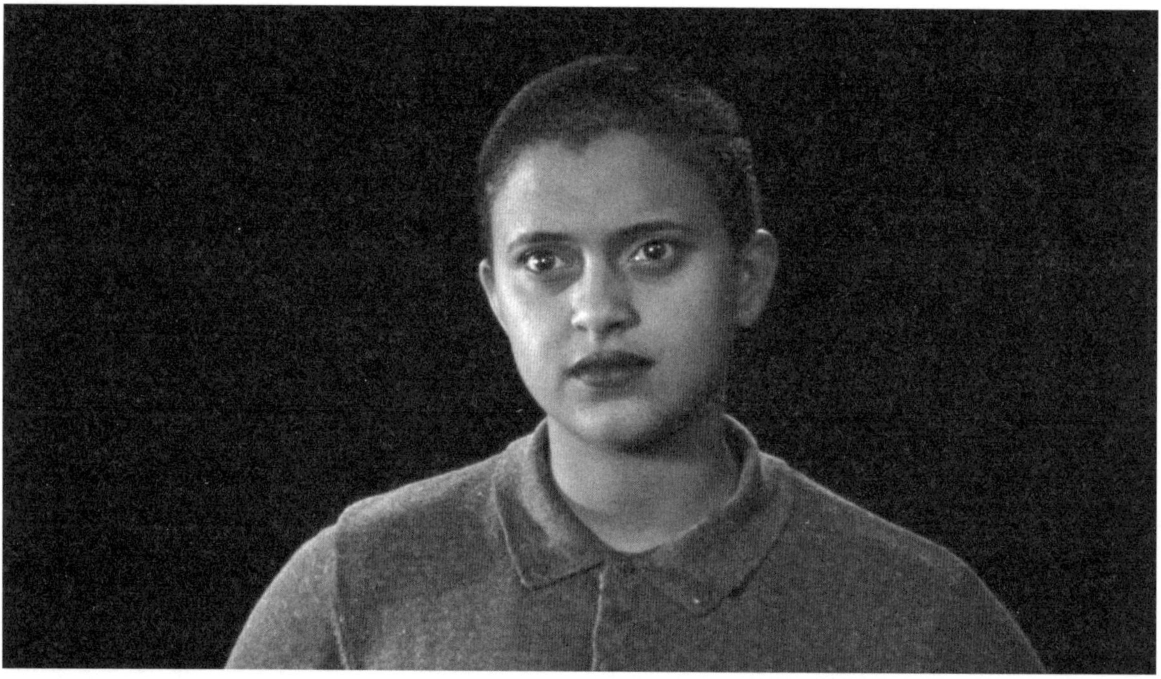

Krishna Istha, screen still from: Michelle Williams Gamaker, *House of Women*, 2017, 16mm film transferred to HDV, colour, sound, 14'05, Arts Council of England Collection

13. This extreme scrutiny is part of the framework of whiteness that I have alluded to.

references to the history of photography, colonialism, and gender politics. They also read lines sourced from Godden's *Black Narcissus*. Their presence marks a return as prospective vocal protagonists with their own agency to challenge the strange conditions of the casting studio they find themselves in. It was important to engender some of the structural violence as a direct provocation to encourage the viewer to see the artificiality of all fictional constructions. Perhaps this is part of what *Fictional Activism* might seek to enact, to puncture our polite collusion in suspension of disbelief, an object that draws from the realities of the subjects and the fantasies of the source material. Creating an intentionally ambiguous object that introduces doubt in the viewer, I shaped a space that applies to any hopeful seeking a role: a somewhat functional, sparse environment to record the auditions. But crucial here was to make visible the conditions for the brown protagonists of my film, who not only enter a casting room, but also a purposefully reconstructed framework of whiteness. This framework could also be understood as a space of vulnerability not only in the inherent nature of a competitive casting scenario, but also one that in its aesthetic minimalism aimed to push their brownness to the fore, rather like the clinical conditions of a laboratory, where subjectivity slips into specimen. Pushed to its furthest point, such practices of pseudo-science and their subsequent documentation have seen individuals tracked, classified and archived. The film certainly does not forget the lineage of photographic history and the precipice on which it sits.[13] Therefore I incorporated visible filmmaking mechanisms, including the seemingly infinite space of the black box studio, which simultaneously frames and isolates its subject, the snap of the clapperboard, the racially problematic colour chart and the sound of the crew working in the background to show the somewhat alienating quality of the film set. It was also important that the voice of Kelly Hunter, who plays the anonymous interlocutor, delivered her lines in crisp "Received Pronunciation" to echo the voices of the film's nuns, in particular Deborah Kerr, who plays Sister Clodagh.

Part of the process of *Fictional Activism* is to resist drawing from one source, but to take multiple sources to encourage a plurality of sources as a strategy to make the film that we encounter harder to digest as a fictional object.

An example here is how the script was developed for *House of Women*, which became a methodology for the subsequent scripts in the trilogy. As the excerpt below from the script written for Krishna Istha shows, we can see that I draw from Krishna's history and what was going on in their life during the time of filming, alongside elements from the source material—a fictional object in need of a revisionist reappraisal for the twenty-first century. It was important to listen to the individual story of my film subjects, and to ask them to meet me halfway. So, the resulting script borrows from both spaces resulting in a docu-fictional text:

KANCHI 4
I was born on April 1st in
St Petersburg, Florida. A lot warmer
than its namesake. No-one is ever
shocked that I was born on April
Fool's Day... My parents are from
Kerala, although I know nothing
about my Dad's side of the family.
At the age of three we moved to
Bangalore. School dragged on for an
eternity... It was a convent where
the nuns ruled the roost...
Needless to say I had to find my way out.

READER (O.S.)
Why are you here today?

KANCHI 4
Well I'm here in London on
a three-year study visa.
I live with my Mum and Uncle,
I'm very close to both of them.
I'm here today because I love to perform.
I'm currently working on a Queer version
of Midsummer Night's Dream,
I'll be playing Hermia.

14. Joseph Campbell, *The Hero with a Thousand Faces* (Princeton, NJ: Princeton University Press, 2004 [1949]). p. 45.

15. Virginia Woolf, *Orlando: A Biography* (London: Vintage, 2016 [1928]).

16. Masc-presenting is a term used to denote a person who chooses to present masculinely without identifying as a cis man. Cisgendered individuals relate to a people whose personal identity and gender corresponds with their birth sex.

READER (O.S.)

Did you know that Hermia has to make a choice: marry Demetrius, enter a nunnery or die?

KANCHI 4

Ha ha, I'm not going back to a convent...

Excerpt from the original script for the four-channel installation *Casting Kanchi: Krishna Istha* (2015). Michelle Williams Gamaker (16mm film transferred to HDV, colour, sound, 06'20)

Within this introduction to Krishna Istha, we learn something about their family circumstances, that they attended a convent in India (a serendipitous echo with the fictional character of Kanchi) and that their work as an actor led them to play Hermia, in a Queer version of Shakespeare's *A Midsummer Night's Dream*, which also opens a correspondence as to whether or not the character will enter a nunnery.

Through repeated viewings of Powell and Pressburger, I began to find herald-like figures, arguably the gender queer character of the muse in disguise, Nicklaus, played by Pamela Brown in *Tales of Hoffmann* (1951) and Marius Goring as Conductor 51 in *A Matter of Life and Death* (1946). The Herald narratively speaking is often one who brings about the call to adventure to the hero/protagonist;[14] they are also agents of change whose influence sets things in motion. I began to imagine that someone could embody this, moving from film to film with new information. Working with Krishna also enabled me to resist narrative norms by embracing mutability: Krishna's transformation as a non-binary individual complemented a flexible, ever-changing protagonist. We have seen this in Virginia Woolf's *Orlando: A Biography* (1928),[15] adapted by Sally Potter into a film *Orlando* (1992). Here, Tilda Swinton plays a poet who changes sex from man to woman and defies time by living for centuries, meeting key figures from English literary history. As my trilogy progresses, Krishna becomes increasingly Masc-presenting,[16] noticeably through a deeper voice and more facial and body hair. My fluid protagonist allowed both Kanchi and Sabu to be played: an *Orlando* in reverse. This mutability is also applied to the form of the material of the moving image, which meant a necessary transformation of format. Thus, *House of Women* was shot on 16mm film, and the aim was that the chosen Kanchi would step out of the source material (film) into a future digital 16:9 format (4K HD video) in *The Fruit is There to be Eaten*. In the final instalment, *The Eternal Return*, the format changes again, this time to a 4:3 screen ratio. The work also moves from colour to black-and-white to match the British Pathé stock that shows sequences of the treatment of elephants in British circuses during the 1950s and 1960s.

    The Fruit is There to be Eaten (2018), second in the trilogy, shows the "winner" of the audition (Krishna Istha) entering the set of *Black Narcissus* to re-engage with the re-cast nuns of the convent, carving out a decolonized, more politically relevant narrative. Here I imagined that Kanchi and the nuns find themselves on the film set of *Black Narcissus*, a space of limbo, but it is only Kanchi who can see that Empire is over and that they should no longer be there, as it is set in 2017. It was essential that Kanchi did not simply regurgitate lines from the original script but found a way to dislodge the notion that the character had arrived at the convent to receive charity from the nuns. The opening up of the constructed nature of the film set is made ever more visible in the sequel, by incorporating the film crew and myself as director within the film. The aim here is to highlight our/my complicity in the inherent construction of fiction and to also highlight the voyeurism that exists through filmmaking as a process. I tried to encapsulate some of the more melodramatic elements of *Black Narcissus* by revisiting the famous lipstick sequence, in which Kathleen Byron applies a fire engine red coat to her lips to mark her decision to leave the convent for civilian life. In *The Fruit* the decision for Sister Clodagh is also one of choosing one path for another. Here, Clodagh decides to meet Kanchi halfway by listening and heeding their message. To end this film, Kanchi and Clodagh meet on the set's floor and unite in a kiss, dissolving in part the idea of hierarchy and allowing a space for desire to replace notions of colonial benevolence.

In the third film, *The Eternal Return* (2019), Krishna transforms again into Indian-born actor Sabu to tackle more concretely Sabu's typecasting as sidekick. The film explores the experience of how a performer of colour might be treated and thought of in a way analogous to the animals he appeared with during his professional life. In Sabu's case, this was the conflation of his background as mahout's son with his career as actor that imposed a seemingly inescapable relationship with elephants: the animals recur throughout his filmography, from his debut role of *Elephant Boy* (1937) to his life as entertainer in Harringay Circus near the end of his career in the early 1950s. Indeed, the word "elephant" follows his first name in almost every press release or editorial about the actor. It also highlights how, in spite of his extraordinary fame Sabu was always the sidekick and never the leading man or love interest, an early example of being shackled or typecast to the classification the studio assigned and desired for their contracted talent.

What recurs throughout all the films is the deployment of alphabets or the listing of names to mimic the mechanical or habitual repetition of something to be learned. The idea of learning by rote in childhood struck me as part of the regurgitation of culture that my "fictional activism" has sought to disrupt. I wanted to upend the formulaic nature of such repetitions, and reverse the logic of our expectations. All the alphabets in *House of Women* pertain to the individual interests of each auditionee, thus Jasdeep Kandola's alphabet explores law and social justice, Tina Mander's explores play and Arunima's references photography. Krishna Istha's alphabet is one that in its structure reveals an interest in LGBTQ+ issues and makes reference to a de-centred, non-western geography to challenge or shake the inherently western-centric and classist nature of the knowledge distributed in the English alphabet:

A beat. The reader shuffles through paper.

READER (O.S.)
OK, let's warm up. First of all,
could you go through the alphabet text?

Kanchi 4 settles herself, focuses and begins to read.

KANCHI 4

Ann is African.
Bill is bisexual.
Caroline is a cartographer.
David is from Darjeeling.
Edward is in Egypt.
Freddy is female.
Grace is a guy.
Henry speaks Hindi.
Ian is Intersex.
John is jaded.
Kitty loves kwaito.
Lucy loves Lucy.
Mary is a masochist.
Nancy knows Nehru.
Oliver is open.
Peter is Pan.
Queenie is questioning.
Robert has rabies.
Simon is Sinhalese.
Tommy is Tamil.
Ursula is undecided.
Vera visits Venus.
William is worldly.
Xena dabbles in xenomancy.
Yolanda says yes.
Zachary is a zealot.

Excerpt from the original script for the four-channel installation *Casting Kanchi: Krishna Istha*, 2015. Michelle Williams Gamaker (16mm film transferred to HDV, colour, sound, 06'20)

17. Catherine Lord with Michelle Williams Gamaker 'House of Preposterous Women: Michelle Williams Gamaker re-auditions Kanchi', *OAR: The Oxford Artistic and Practice Based Research Platform* 3 (2018), www.oarplatform.com/house-of-preposterous-women-michelle-williams-gamaker-re-auditions-kanchi/.

Writer, actor and theatre-maker Catherine Lord, suggests that

> By bringing together British names from now and from Empire, and by interlacing them with transgender and post-colonial subversions, the four Kanchis bring to life a subaltern who can find their words, ventriloquizing then releasing the silent source through a past made future.[17]

To respond to Lord's insight of a past made future, my *Fictional Activism* consistently tries to work with this dialectic, which involves a return to one's own history to seek out images that trouble and persist in one's memory. Other than obsession, what might this "image haunting" signify? Perhaps *Fictional Activism* cannot leave things alone, nor let historical objects get a pass for their lack of knowledge. Can *Fictional Activism* enable these obsessions to resurface in a new form? This could be seen in my examples of critical affection for Powell and Pressburger's classic, but I return to their work with a pointed desire to construct an alternative outcome, one beyond the usual doomed narrative. *Fictional Activism* produces an object to reconcile the fictional injustices absorbed over time. By returning, I follow my own journey and that of my lead actors to see how we mirror the fictional realm.

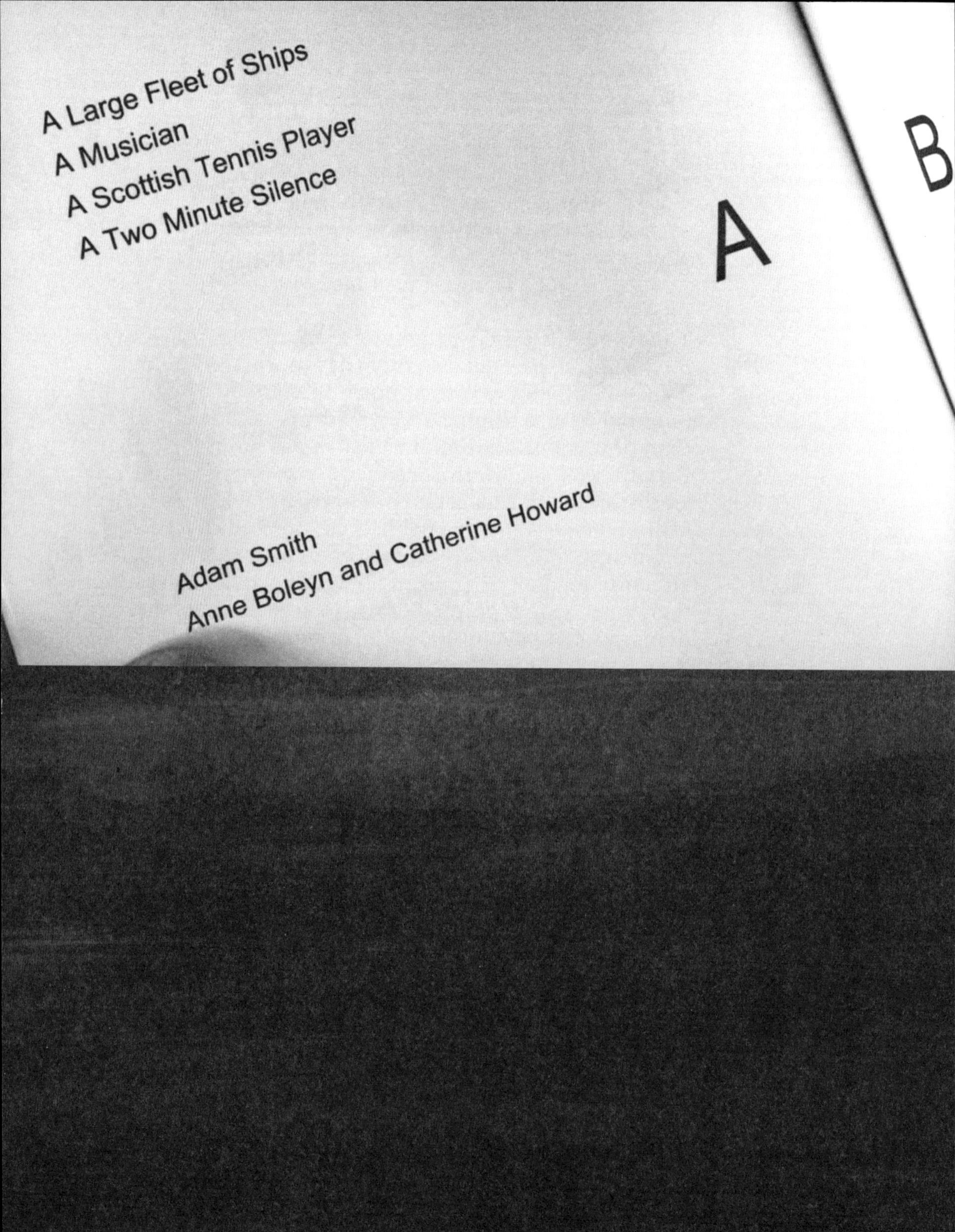

A Large Fleet of Ships
A Musician
A Scottish Tennis Player
A Two Minute Silence

A

B

Adam Smith
Anne Boleyn and Catherine Howard

THE LITTLE BOOK OF ANSWERS
Voice, Embodiment and Autopoiesis as a Methodology for Resistance

Laura Malacart

1. My relationship to this subject comes from my experience of naturalisation having lived in the country 27 years and then being required to take the *Life in the UK* test. If this requirement seems redundant in my circumstances, as sociologist and collaborator Bridget Byrne points out, the test itself is questionable for anyone who qualifies to take it because they must already have lived in the country at least six continuous years to be eligible to apply for citizenship: https://citizenshipceremonies.files.wordpress.com/.

2. Passing this test fulfils the mandatory requirement of "sufficient knowledge of life in the United Kingdom" introduced by the UK Government as a precondition of naturalisation on 1 November 2005 and of settlement on 2 April 2007.

3. Selected iterations of the work: 2015 Tate Modern, Turbine Hall, Three activities and Info Point; Laura Malacart, 'Artist's Pages: THE LITTLE BOOK OF ANSWERS VOL. 1 Polemics/Contestations', *n.paradoxa: international feminist art journal* 38 (July 2016), pp. 33–38; symposium and artists respond to the Book, Manchester, Manchester Central Library, 2016 ; 'Dancing the Answers to Hip Hop Music', Brixton Market, 2016 (ArtLicks, Workweek Prize winner); four scholarly responses are written after a discussion at Accademia di Brera, Italy, 2017; *A (Very British) Pictionary Game* is played by teams in the gallery (Margate, Turner Contemporary, 2017); a night-long soundtrack composed live with readings of the *Answers*, Oval Cricket Ground, 2018.

The Little Book of Answers is a work challenging the political praxis of citizenship as it investigates the content and role of the citizenship test (*Life in the UK*) as an essential requirement for naturalization in the UK.[1] The artwork utilizes the correct answers of the UK citizenship test but offers these to the audience separated from the questions in order to draw attention to the ideology that underpins it.[2] This artivist project was launched in 2015 as a participatory performance in the Turbine Hall at Tate Modern but then evolved into distinct iterations, in other exhibitions and publications,[3] while developing a methodology for resistance designed to enable the audience to interact with the content of the test and, as a result, short circuit its premises.

In 2017 I framed *The Little Book of Answers* as an artwork conceived as a methodology that challenges current citizenship praxis.[4] In Bianca Frasso's reading, this work 'avoids an analysis of the observed system in terms of representational forms, but instead it sets it within an experiential dimension which is ecological and multidisciplinary'.[5] In my own conception of the artwork, this method concerns the formulation of the work *a priori* as a script with a set of instructions but also *a posteriori* as the piece evolves into distinct iterations "applicable" to diverse cohorts and locations.

For its launch in the Turbine Hall, I devised a participatory performance with a set of three main activities through which the public embodies the content of the test:

A *Memorising the Answers* (kinetic memorisation): the public enrols to a class to learn to memorise the answers by associating them with specific movements.
B *Pronouncing the Answers:* the public enrols to a class to learn to pronounce the most common answers "True" and "False" in received English pronunciation.
C *Expressing the Answers:* the public is invited to sing, read, and declaim their own chosen selection from The Compendium of Answers.

The installation contained an Info Point, with samples of *The Little Book*, a class enrolment desk and the possibility to interact with the project via social media: for example, by guessing the questions to a selection of displayed answers. *The Little Book of Answers* compiled the correct answers of the text in alphabetical order without the questions. As printed pages, *The Book* becomes a score or script activated by a set of instructions during the series of participatory events.

As the audience engage through movement, pronunciation and vocal expression with the content of the test, they are also affected by the evocative nature of the textual clues. It becomes apparent that this is no conventional learning since the learning focus is shifted onto the

4. The presentations in Brera, Italy became the document "four-texts". https://citizenshipceremonies.files.wordpress.com/2019/06/four-texts.pdf.

5. Bianca Frasso, William Shakespeare West Africa True, trans. Laura Malacart (Milan 2017), https://citizenshipceremonies.files.wordpress.com/2019/06/four-texts.pdf.

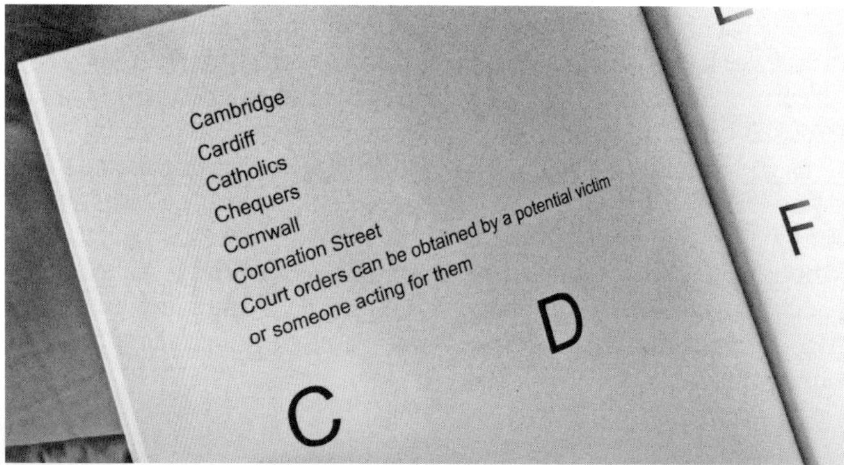

Laura Malacart, *The Little Book of Answers*, limited edition artist book, 2015

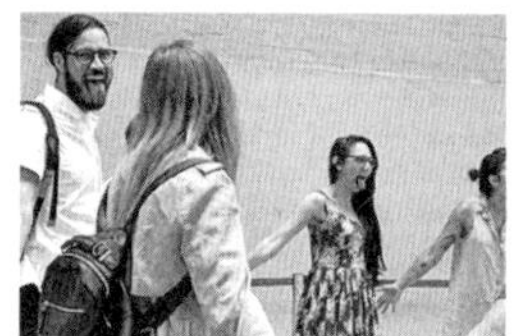

Laura Malacart, *The Little Book of Answers*, participatory installation view (Pronouncing the Answers) at Turbine Hall, Tate Modern, London, 2015

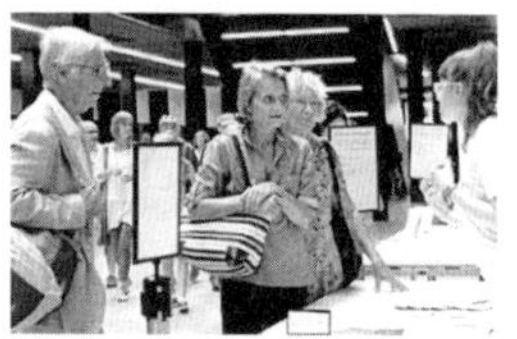

Laura Malacart, *The Little Book of Answers*, participatory installation view (The Info Desk) at Turbine Hall, Tate Modern, London, 2015

body and the original learning content is decontextualized. Simultaneously, the absurdist nature of the actions signals a critique of the presumed emancipatory nature of the test and of the fact that this knowledge requirement is necessary for citizenship acquisition and the indefinite right to stay in the UK.

The Info Point on the other hand operates in a different way. It offers the audience an opportunity to consider their own perspective, regain any sense of agency after the spurious dance actions or the phonetic breakdown of the word "False", pause for reflection, and share conversations and experiences.

In this area the public is also encouraged to contribute by suggesting what the original questions to the selected answers displayed on the counter might be. Here the audience can implicitly contribute in two ways: either to guess the government's perspective with the actual question to the answer, or to use this opportunity to formulate a critique via questions that are deliberately incorrect but reveal something about the subject using sarcasm, exaggeration or humour. A third option is also possible when the public sets out to fulfil the first goal and inadvertently carries out the latter.

This can be exemplified by the Answer "India". What is the question in the test for which "India" is the answer? The association with British colonial history is immediate and people might consider formulating a type of question related to the history of empire, migration, the question of Indian independence, its partition from Pakistan, or even cuisine.

The question for which "India" is the actual answer is 'What is the birthplace of Rudyard Kipling?'.

A lingering puzzlement over the relevance of this information to naturalization or knowledge of life in the UK is replaced with the questionable ideological message conveyed by this reference to a very "English" writer born abroad in today's post-colonial multicultural Britain.

In the following section I explore whether *The Little Book of Answers'* role as an activist/artivist work operates via the format of the multiple choice test and you, as reader, are invited to answer.

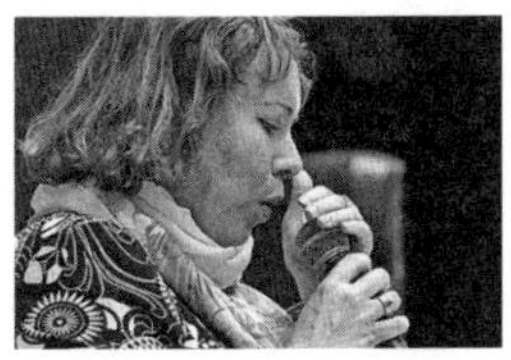

Laura Malacart, *The Little Book of Answers*, participatory installation view (Expressing the Answers open mic, Iris Erderer jazz improvisation of the Answers) at Turbine Hall, Tate Modern, London, 2015

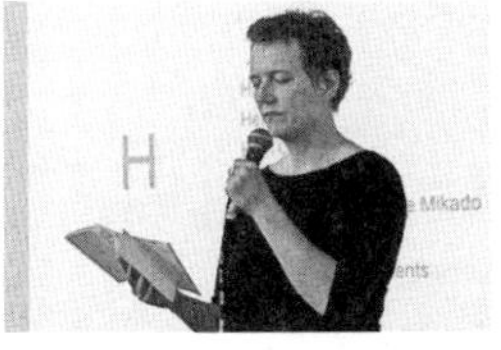

Laura Malacart, *The Little Book of Answers*, participatory installation view. Musician Naomi Graham performing a song inspired by *The Little Book of Answers*, at Manchester Central Library, June 2016.

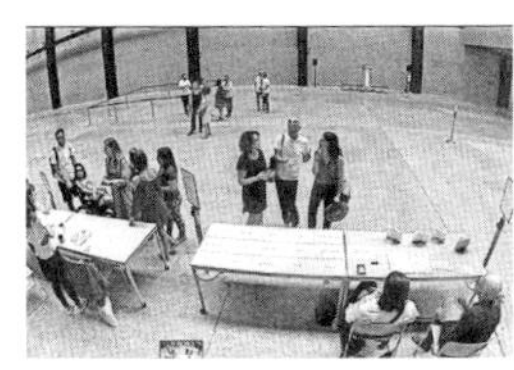

Laura Malacart, *The Little Book of Answers*, participatory installation view (The Info Desk) at Turbine Hall, Tate Modern, London, 2015

Laura Malacart

THE LITTLE BOOK OF ANSWERS IN THE UK

1. Does the piece de-territorialise the official narrative of the UK represented by the citizenship test form within?
◊ True
◊ False

2. Does the work re-configure the content and approach of the test?
◊ True
◊ False

3. Is *The Little Book of Answers* political in that it addresses the social sphere?
◊ True
◊ False

4. Does it work as a collective enunciation at the expense of an authorial voice?
◊ True
◊ False

5. Does *The Little Book of Answers* re-configure the content of citizenship praxis?
◊ True
◊ False

6. Is the knowing subject affected?
◊ True
◊ False

7. Is the knowing subject a collective or singular body?
◊ Singular
◊ Collective
◊ Both
◊ Neither

8. Does a collective body emerge via the participants engaged in kinetic memorisation?
◊ True
◊ False

9. Does a collective body emerge via the stuttering of the pronunciation class learning to say 'True' and 'False' in received pronunciation?
◊ True
◊ False

10. Does a collective body emerge via the hip hop dance of the *Answers* in Brixton market?
◊ True
◊ False

11. Does *The Little Book of Answers* help foreground the ideological motivation of the test?
◊ True
◊ False

12. Which of its iterations was able to apply a feminist critique to the test?
(You may select more than one option)
◊ *n.paradoxa*
◊ The Oval Cricket Ground
◊ Brixton Market
◊ Manchester Library

12. Which iteration was able to re-address the multi-lingual, transnational, post-colonial make up of British society?
(You may select more than one option)
◊ *n.paradoxa*
◊ The Oval Cricket Ground
◊ Brixton Market
◊ Manchester Library
◊ Mostyn Open Turner Contemporary
◊ Turbine Hall, Tate Modern
◊ Woodland in Basilicata

The playful layout of the above section hints at the seriousness of the format of the multiple choice test when it comes to naturalization, just as dancing the *Answers* of *The Little Book* hints at a different kind of dance when it comes to the praxis of citizenship. The multiple choice test is typical of a neoliberal administrative mode in that that it performs a speedy, mechanized, efficient and apparently fair and objective evaluation task.

Yet this user-friendly format conceals a number of problematic aspects such as the notion of citizen or subject that it creates and the finite and closed nature of learning where the boundaries of expression are pre-defined and potential dissent pre-empted.

In the humanities, a second generation of "studies" areas are evolving in a trans-disciplinary post-anthropo-centric manner re-organizing dualisms of mind-body and human-nature-technology relations as well as previous disciplinary boundaries. In the face of this, the notion of the posthuman, in a nomadic or critical posthumanities, is often an attempt to react, debunk or de-territorialize dominant features of this logic (often by introducing the problem of "dis-identification" with Man/Anthropos). Rosi Braidotti notes that while posthuman critique often presents its own emergent subjects and subjectivities, these seem to occur at the same accelerationist speed as the advanced capitalism they are trying to contain or resist; what actually distinguishes their politics is evident only in their affirmative ethics and 'a collective counter-affirmation of the virtual'. Instead, she suggests, it is necessary that:

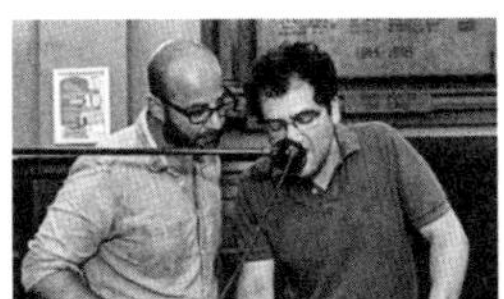

Laura Malacart and Andrej Bako, *The Little Book of Answers (Drone Britannia)*, participatory installation view at Art Night, Kia Oval Cricket Ground, London, 2018

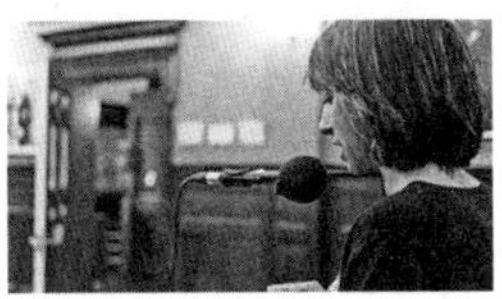

Laura Malacart and Andrej Bako, *The Little Book of Answers (Drone Britannia)*, participatory installation view at Art Night, Kia Oval Cricket Ground, London, 2018

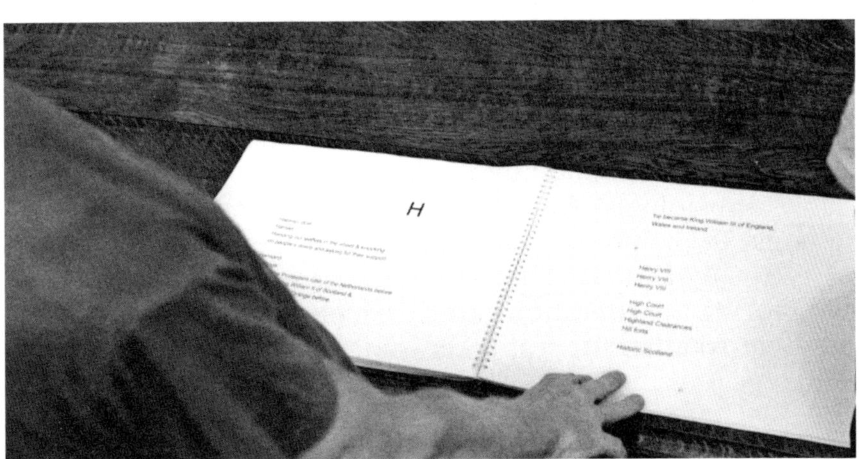

Laura Malacart and Andrej Bako, *The Little Book of Answers (Drone Britannia)*, participatory installation view at Art Night, Kia Oval Cricket Ground, London, 2018

The political starts with de-acceleration through the composition of transversal subject assemblages that actualize the unrealized potential of what Deleuze calls "a missing people". In the old language: de-accelerate and contribute to the collective construction of social horizons of hope.[6]

The strategy and architecture of *The Little Book of Answers* aspires to be this kind of de-accelerated method for resistance in a neoliberal society governed by the logic of cognitive capitalism and in which the process of naturalization, with its characteristic machinic and accelerationist style embodied in the multiple choice questionnaire, is nevertheless geared toward questioning its quantitative processes and economic logic.

This project has also been discussed using a number of different frameworks in the context of multidisciplinary, systemic and ecological thinking, as demonstrated by four texts written in response to this piece across sociology, art theory, cultural analysis (as discussed below).[7]

But first, since *The Little Book of Answers* is geared to disturb structural relationships and foreground the subaltern state of the non-citizen, citizand, or pre-citizen, I would like to explore its potential using the notion of the "minor" to focus again on how exclusion is framed in producing a subject/citizen. Like that of the posthuman, this enables us to ask 'what kind of knowing subjects are we in the process of becoming and what discourses underscore the process'.[8] The framework regarding the revolutionary potential of the "minor" was devised by Deleuze and Guattari originally in reference to Kafka's fiction. We can ask whether the term "revolutionary" now sits comfortably in the context of advanced capitalism or whether it belongs to the "old language" and needs transposing to meet today's notions of activism, artivism and resistance. The "negative gaze" of *The Little Book of Answers* offers a creative method that is embodied, prolific and adaptable.

Sociologist Anne Marie Fortier in her textual response to the project[9] emphasizes that the apparent objectivity and equality of the test reinforces societal inequalities by ignoring the conditions under which the test is taken. For example, whether the test taker is an English speaker or not,

6. Rosi Braidotti, 'A Theoretical Framework for the Critical Posthumanities', *Theory Culture & Society*, Special Issue: Transversal Posthumanities (2018), p. 11.

7. https://citizenshipceremonies.files.wordpress.com/2019/06/four-texts.pdf.

8. Braidotti 2018, p. 2.

9. Anne Marie Fortier, *The Little Book of Answers and the Artifice of Citizenship* (2017). https://citizenshipceremonies.files.wordpress.com/2019/06/four-texts.pdf

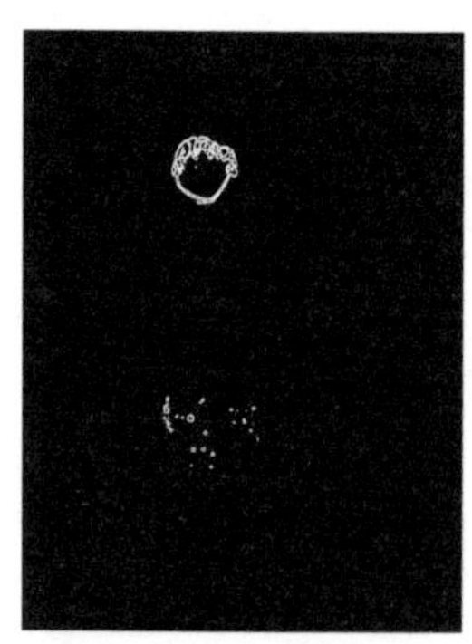

Laura Malacart, *The Little Book of Answers (A Very British Pictionary Game)*, 'Margaret Thatcher', drawing from participatory installation at Turner Contemporary, Margate, 2017

 Feminist Art Activisms and Artivisms

10. Karin Anzivino, *DO IT YOURSELF INBURGEREN Or How the Netherlands Decided to Abandon its (New) Citizens* (Amsterdam 2016), https://citizenshipceremonies.files.wordpress.com/2019/06/four-texts.pdf.

11. Bridget Byrne, *The Little Book of Answers and National Stories* (Manchester 2017). https://citizenshipceremonies.files.wordpress.com/2019/06/four-texts.pdf.

whether they are affluent or not, whether they need to work extensively in order to pay for the test (study, study materials and exam), or if they are an asylum seeker or a permanent resident.

Karin Anzivino, a cultural theorist based in Amsterdam,[10] complemented this point by providing a case study of citizenship praxis in the Netherlands. Anzivino had volunteered with Boost to assist refugees with *inburgeren* or with their naturalization process. They receive government instructions in Dutch and are officially advised to 'seek help with their naturalisation with friends and families'. Anzivino confirms how the automatization of the citizenship process as a top-down process creates a paradoxical situation where the more the state disappears from the process the more it is present. Here *The Little Book of Answers* harnesses a trans-national conversation when it comes to peoples' movements and the structural inequalities of global economies.

Sociologist and project collaborator Bridget Byrne emphasizes how *The Little Book of Answers* challenges us to ask what story is being told about Britain to those who are applying for citizenship or permanent residency.[11] This is because nations and national identities are created via stories and it is through a range of technologies beyond the legal dimension that all nations create a sense of "us". While the nation is addressed as "a cohesive people" via the use of these technologies, like the weather forecast, for example, or the newspapers, Byrne emphasizes how such cohesive "us" is

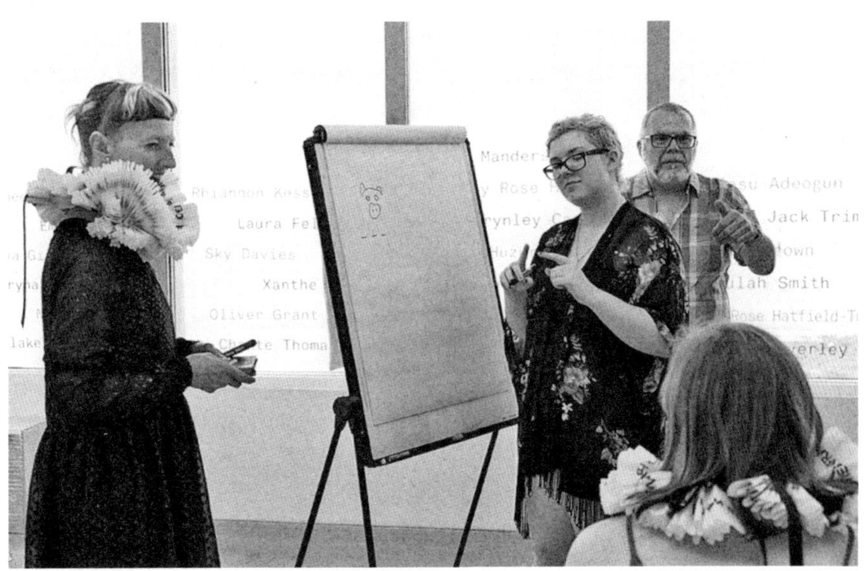

Laura Malacart, *The Little Book of Answers (A Very British Pictionary Game)*, participatory installation view at Turner Contemporary, Margate, 2017

at odds with the range of "othering" that has emerged out of the radicalized, classed and gendered history of colonialism and postcolonialism.

The "negative gaze" created by the *Answers*, as Bianca Frasso describes it, enables the viewer or the knowing subject, to dismantle the coherence of the "us" implied by the test. A feminist gaze cast onto the *Little Book of Answers*, as per the project's partial reproduction in *n.paradoxa's* volume 38, reveals extra results over and above the expected. The assumptions that the British narrative "naturally" contains a disproportionate majority of white males *vis-à-vis* any women and/or ethnic minorities is very obvious but something else was noted about the way women were represented in the test. When it came to the Royal Family, Queens were described differently to Kings: the latter were assertively named, while the former referred to via vague or circumstantial details about their lives: 'She spent much of her childhood in France' 'She was suspected in the involvement in the murder' 'She was only two when she became Queen'.

Bianca Frasso's contribution expanded her reading of *The Little Book of Answers* using ideas from thinking about complexity in science and cybernetics with Gregory Bateson. In his approach the organizational forms of human-nature-technology exist on a continuum in a self-generative manner through autopoiesis:

> To introduce a test that reflects a unidirectional pedagogical model, inside the autopoietic circle that structures every globalised context, means to stop the natural progress of that contest. Laura Malacart elaborates here the short-circuit capable of reactivating the recursive mechanism.[12]

In other words, the project is seen to re-enable the autopoiesis that was halted by the format of the multiple choice test: a creative self-determining process that re-instates the original proposition through the strategic mode of the work. This reading aligns it to multidisciplinary ecological approaches, because the project is conceived as a critical intervention in the contemporary domain of advanced capitalism as a moment of resistance and de-acceleration.

12. Bianca Frasso, *William Shakespeare West Africa True*, trans. Laura Malacart (Milan 2017) https://citizenshipceremonies.files.wordpress.com/2019/06/four-texts.pdf.

   Feminist Art Activisms and Artivisms

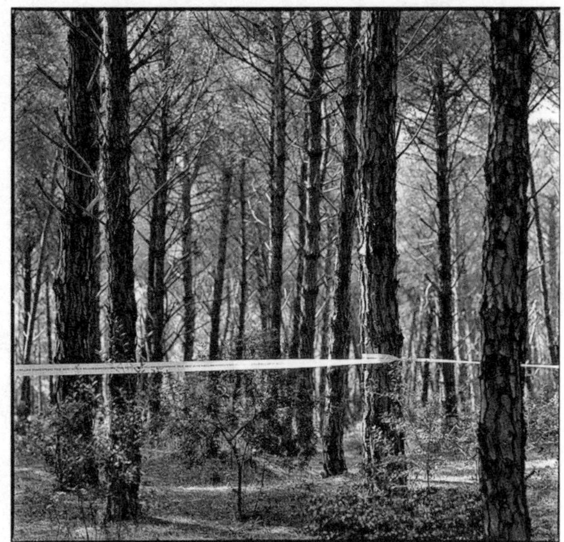

Laura Malacart, *The Little Book of Answers (William Shakespeare West Africa True)*, installation view, Basilicata, Italy, 2017

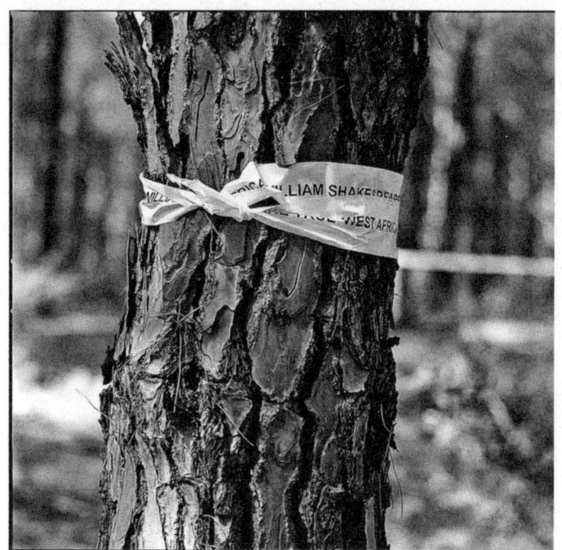

Laura Malacart, *The Little Book of Answers (William Shakespeare West Africa True)*, installation view, Basilicata, Italy, 2017

13. Braidotti 2018, pp. 4, 16.

This is both a moment that conceives time as cyclical rather than linear but also one that can therefore return in ever more diverse iterations. In Frasso's terms, the intervention is an attempt to resist the quantitative mode of the computational and machinic mode of global capitalism and offer instead the antidote of a qualitative embodied experience.

Rosi Braidotti emphasizes how important it is to find new critical cartographies which bring forth alternative figurations or *conceptual personae* that can expose not only the 'repressive structures of dominant subject-formations (*potestas*) but also the affirmative and transformative visions of the subject as nomadic process (*potentia*)'.[13] Paraphrasing her words, *The Little Book of Answers* attempted this 'cartographic accuracy, with the corollary of ethical accountability, and the combination of critique with creativity, including a flair for paradoxes and the recognition of the specificity of art practices.'

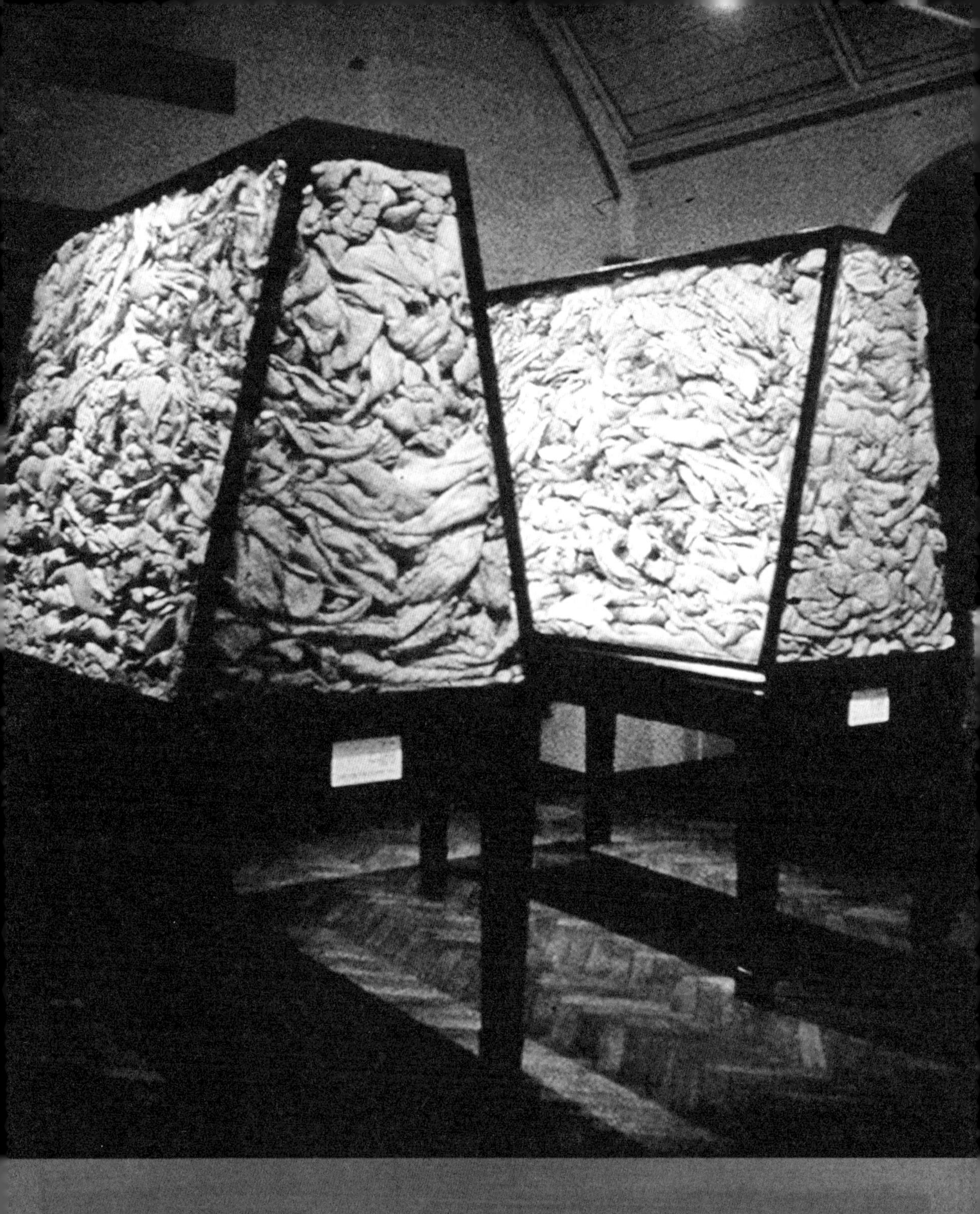

Roxane Permar, *Human Remains, The Nuclear Family 172.289,* **1989, temporary sculptures in museum vitrines, exhibited in 'Women Sculptors' at The Maidstone Museum, Kent**

FROM *THE NUCLEAR FAMILY TO COLD WAR PROJECTS*

Roxane Permar

1. Neil Postman and Charles Weingartner, *Teaching as a Subversive Activity* (New York: Doubleday, 1969), pp. 4–16.

2. Mary Kaldor, *The Imaginary War: Understanding the East-West Conflict* (Oxford: Blackwell, 1990), pp. 4–6.

3. Thérèse Delpech, *Nuclear Deterrence in the 21st Century: Lessons from the Cold War for a New Era of Strategic Piracy* (Santa Monica, CA: RAND, 2012), p. 5.

4. Chloe Chaplain, 'From Poll Tax to the People's Vote March: The Biggest Protests in Recent British History—and the Impact They Have Had', *Inews.co.uk*, 22 October 2018, https://inews.co.uk/news/brexit/peoples-vote-march-poll-tax-political-protest-impact-list/ (accessed 30 May 2019).

5. Suzanne Moore et al., 'How the Greenham Common Protest Changed Lives: "We Danced on Top of the Nuclear Silos"', *The Guardian*, 20 March 2017, www.theguardian.com/uk-news/2017/mar/20/greenham-common-nuclear-silos-women-protest-peace-camp.

In the early stages of my career I believed that art could change the world. The turbulent social and political climate into which I was born instilled in me and, indeed, many of my generation, a strong sense of social justice and a desire to make a difference in the world. The book, *Teaching As A Subversive Activity*,[1] published not long before I went to university, opened my eyes, both as a student and an educator in the making. It galvanized me to question everything I had been taught including the prevailing ideologies of the Cold War. The threat of nuclear war bedevilled my generation from childhood. It was presented as an imaginary war animated by images of nuclear attack, underpinned by the conflicting ideologies of two super powers.[2] Unfortunately the nuclear threat continues, for no sooner did the Soviet regime topple, than the second nuclear age crept almost unnoticed into our world as more countries around the world acquire nuclear capability. The French strategic thinker, Thérèse Delpech, asserts that in addition to these factors, the term 'second nuclear age' signifies a period in which there are still nuclear weapons but that the old rules have changed.[3]

In the late 1970s and 1980s, feminism awakened me to many other political campaigns such as those against racism and nuclear disarmament.[4] I went to Greenham Common twice in the early 1980s, both times with my long-time friend Susan Timmins, once to participate in 'Embrace the Base' and on another occasion to be part of a human chain linking Burghfield, Aldermaston and Greenham, organized by CND.[5] In the late 1980s I joined the Shetland

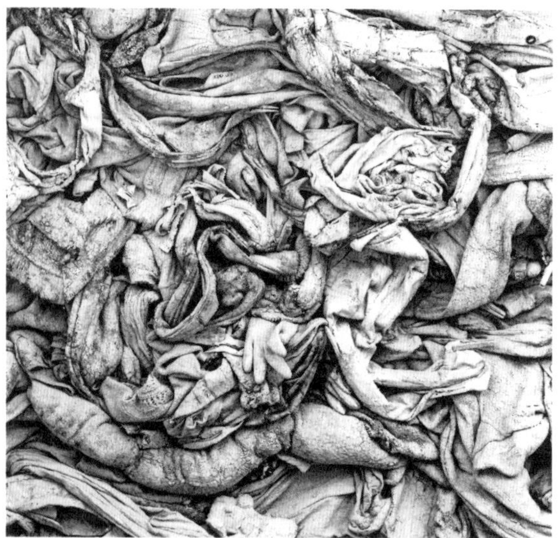

Roxane Permar, *The Nuclear Family 19832688*, 1988, detail of wall installation, 370 x 370 cm, in the exhibition 'From Inside Out: Françoise Dupré, Roxane Permar and Ann Tappenden', The Bedford Hill Gallery, London. Photo: Peter Whyte, 1988

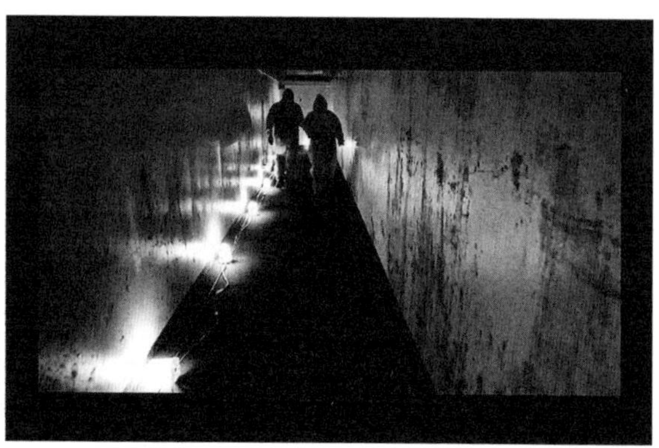

Roxane Permar and Susan Timmins, *Countdown*, 2012, film still, 4'31

branch of C.A.D.E. (Campaign Against Dounreay Expansion) as a protest against the importation of nuclear waste from Europe.

Diverse strategies adopted by feminist artists also shaped my art practice during the formative early years of my career. Many events, including a major series of feminist art events at the ICA, London in 1980 were hugely influential, particularly the conference, Questions on Women's Art.[6] I joined The Brixton Artists Collective, specifically the group Women's Work, as it provided significant collective agency to organize projects, events, workshops, exhibitions and conferences. This ability to take action, initiate and lead has driven my practice ever since.[7]

In addition to feminism, my art practice is equally defined by places, London, Moscow and Shetland, all of which hold a particular resonance in relation to the nuclear issue and Cold War politics. In late 2000 I moved permanently to Shetland. My practice, and especially my politicized voice, manifests very differently in the context of this geographically remote, small island community. New technologies, increased mobility and collaborative working practices have utterly transformed my working and personal

6. Lucy R. Lippard, *Issue: Social Strategies by Women Artists: An Exhibition* (London: Institute of Contemporary Arts, 1980).

7. Roxane Permar, 'Why Join the Collective?', in *Women's Work: Two Years in the Life of a Women Artists Group* (London: Women's Work, 1986), pp. 5–9.

life. Today my art practice is embedded in the Shetland context and is probably not perceived as overtly political. However, it is social, and it is responsive to my local culture, community and society while sharing concerns about what are global issues.

The Nuclear Family (1983–1991), my first body of work around the nuclear theme, served to untangle some of the horror and fear embedded in my subconscious by the nuclear propaganda that permeated my generation's early years. The Brixton Art Gallery provided the first public space for *The Nuclear Family* in the exhibition 'Textiles: Making and Meaning', curated by Teri Bullen. In this essay I will look at this work and how it led to my current on-going collaboration with artist Susan Timmins for *Cold War Projects*, starting in 2011.

The Nuclear Family used and presented objects, largely clothes treated with plaster and powder pigments, in temporary installations to address both the aftermath of the nuclear bomb and the ideology of the nuclear family. By contrast *Cold War Projects* offers more explicit and varied ideas about cultural memory and employs a variety of media, including film, photography, textiles and sound. The working processes in *Cold War Projects* are also distinct from those of *The Nuclear Family* in that we actively employ methods drawn from socially engaged art practices, including the potential for co-authorship among collaborative participants.

My continuing interest in this theme is ironically triggered by and responds to the dismantling of the first-generation of Cold War installations in the UK as a visual archeology of memories and sites. What I had imagined would be a short-term exercise, has seamlessly snowballed into an on-going project. Several years into our work, world tensions began to increase again and suggestions of a second Cold War emerged. Fuelled by this new situation, we continue to unearth the largely invisible memories and ordinary stories from this era to explore our past in relation to the nuclear present and future.

NUCLEAR FREE ZONE

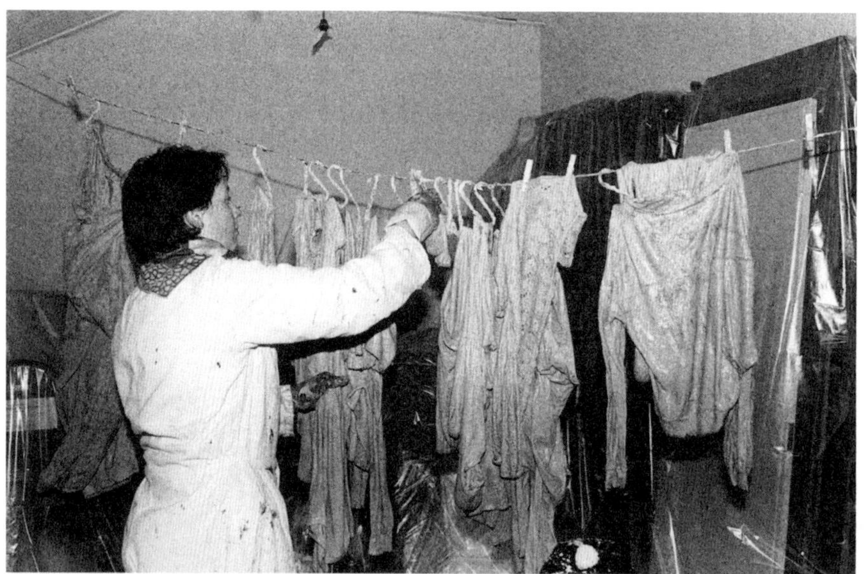

Roxane Permar and Susan Timmins, *The Nuclear Roadshow*, 1990, participatory public art work located across six sites in Shetland. Krystyna Goudie helps to make plastered sculptures, Lerwick, a Projects UK Live Art commission. Photo: Susan Timmins

The Nuclear Family

The Nuclear Family comprised objects made largely from clothing soaked in plaster and grew from just four individual pieces to a large body of work, many hundreds of 'individual' crumbling objects and dust, symbolic of human remains. The work referred to the nuclear family unit and the horror of nuclear holocaust. It was not meant to be permanent, nor did it always appear in the same form. New pieces were created, added and presented differently each time, depending on location and whether it appeared in group or solo exhibitions. By using clothes, it was possible to work with materials and processes familiar since childhood—soaking, sewing, stuffing, shaping, suspending, laundering, painting and colouring. These treated clothes could be suspended from a clothesline, stuffed in crates, architectural spaces or windows, laid out on the floor or suspended using meat hooks. The materials and processes of making reflected qualities linked to women's work. The making process was a little haphazard and unpredictable, which echoed the random and indiscriminate ravages of war.

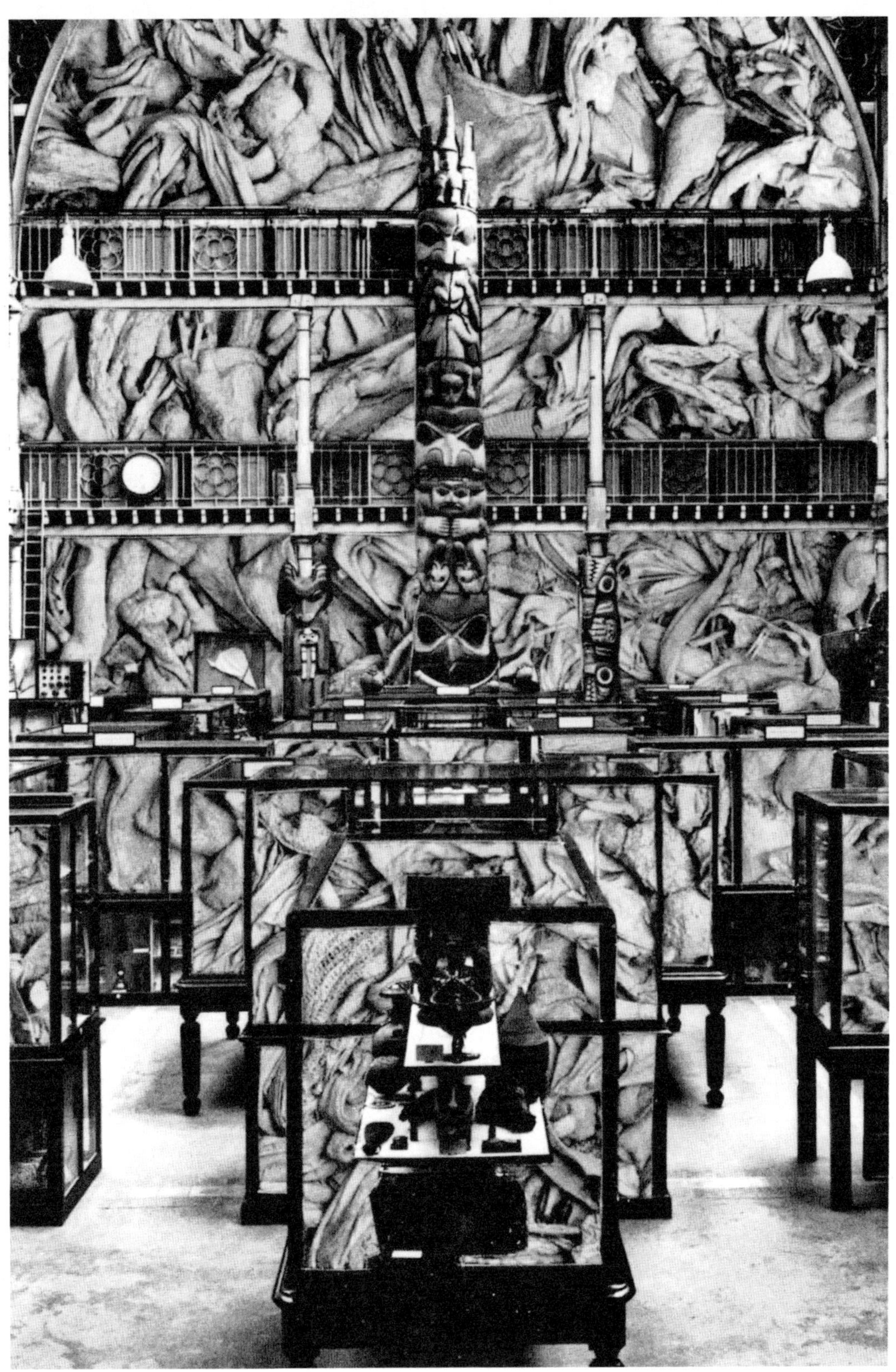

Roxane Permar, *The Nuclear Family*, artist montage produced as an original postcard for the exhibition 'Gathering Rites', Pitt Rivers Museum, Oxford, 1988

Some of the individual pieces resembled bones or fossils and the textures emerged from burnishing and manipulating the clothing as the plaster dried.

The building plaster, rather than artist's casting plaster, was fundamental for its colour and physical qualities. It was very unstable when applied to textiles and would begin to fall away as soon as a piece was moved, a metaphor for ruination and decay. Powder pigments were applied by hand, burnishing the surfaces to bring out the textures in the fabric as well as to suggest flesh, bruising, blood. The clothes were chosen very carefully, for their meaning, texture and personal histories. I used my own clothes, my family's clothes, and clothes that friends donated. They emphasized the personal reality of the nuclear threat, the horror of which was brought home vividly to me when I learned that Clapham Common, very near to my home on Battersea Rise, was designated as a site for mass burial in the event of nuclear attack.

By spending time with the work in public, it was possible to learn a lot from people's reactions and thus gain understanding and insight into the work's ability to generate meaning and evoke response. Media reviews also helped to confirm whether ideas were clear. In one review, for example, about the exhibition 'State of the Nation' in which *The Nuclear Family* was exhibited as thirteen individual items of clothing suspended from a washing line stretched across a ten-foot span, the critic Andrew Graham-Dixon wrote, 'It is a rare exception in a show that prefers to make its political statements rather more obviously: Roxane Permar's *The Nuclear Family* is a washing line strung with lurid rags dyed the colour of flesh—no explanation required.'[8]

The clothes and occasional soft toys made the work feel familiar and lent an air of domesticity. Visual signs of impermanence and ephemerality, such as the dust and powder, or display methods such as hanging, laying and layering, hinted at cyclical processes, destruction and perpetual renewal. The work operated on different levels, visually seductive, demanding; deeply emotional; fragile and durable, beautiful yet horrific; haunting, obsessive, and, as the work physically grew in size over the years, monumental. It carried symbols of past, present and future, albeit a horrible, unimaginable one.

8. Andrew Graham-Dixon, 'The Journey of the Maggie: Andrew Graham-Dixon', 28 August 1987, www.andrewgrahamdixon. com/archive/the-journey-of-the-maggie.html (accessed 30 May 2019).

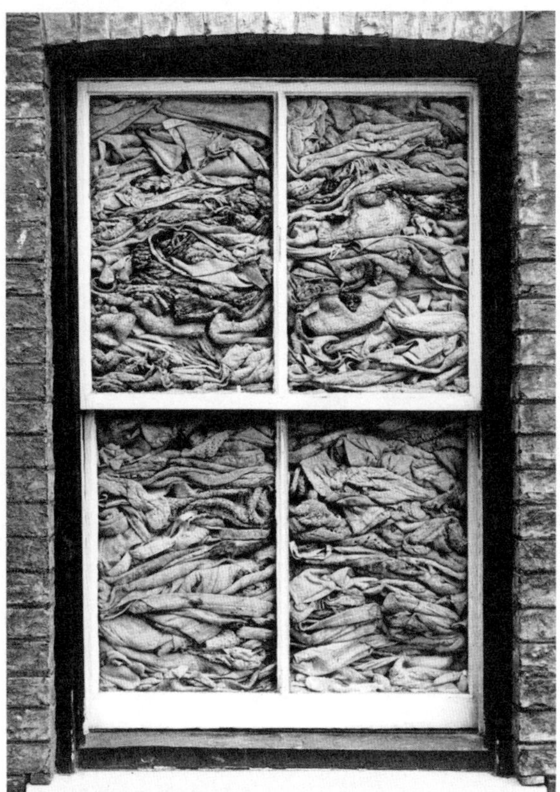

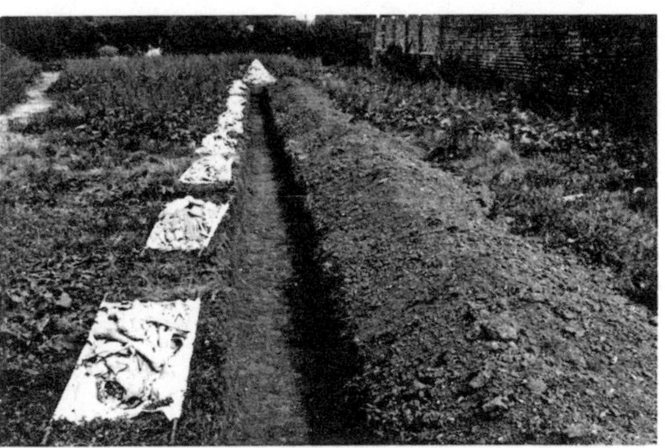

Roxane Permar, *Burial and Preservation*, site-specific participatory work, 61 × 61 × 4267 cm, Gunnersbury Park, London, July to September 1990. Photo: Roxane Permar

Roxane Permar, *The Nuclear Family 2415588*, detail of interior wall installation, 335 × 290 × 335 cm, seen from the street for the exhibition 'Death', Cambridge Darkroom and Kettle's Yard, 1988. Photo: Roxane Permar

For the group exhibition 'Death' (Cambridge Darkroom and Kettle's Yard, 1988) I installed this body of work in a vacant terrace house on a fairly busy residential street. People walked by the window and became curious. There was no electricity, and thus no light after the window was completely filled. An invigilator gave visitors a single hurricane lamp to carry inside thus giving them control over the way they would see the work in the interior.

Looking back, it is apparent that two projects realized in 1990, *Burial and Preservation* (London) and *The Nuclear Roadshow* (Shetland), realized in collaboration with Susan Timmins, form a connection between *The Nuclear Family* and my future collaboration, *Cold War Projects* which they anticipate in terms of relationship to site and place, ways of working and critical positioning.

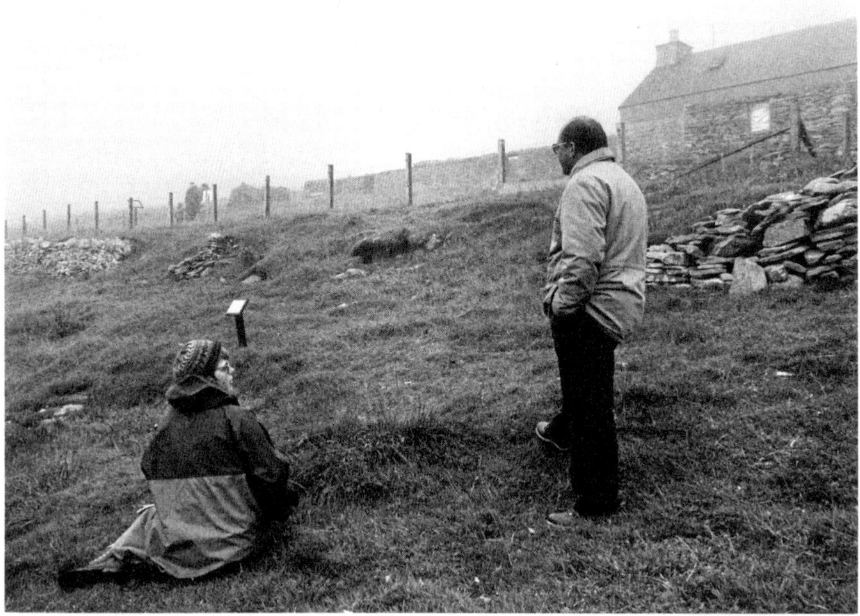

Roxane Permar and Susan Timmins, *The Nuclear Roadshow*, 1990, public engagement at Bressay, Shetland, one of six locations in Shetland, a Projects UK Live Art commission. Photo: Susan Timmins

These projects brought closure to *The Nuclear Family*. I publicly buried all of *The Nuclear Family* in a trench, 150 feet long, on the anniversary of the Hiroshima bombing, in *Burial and Preservation*.[9] This attempt to both purge and commemorate nuclear atrocity was intended to give my practice a fresh start. In spite of having done that, there is no escape from the shadow cast by the nuclear era. Unlike *The Nuclear Family*, which posed a general view in response to the nuclear theme, both *Burial and Preservation* and *The Nuclear Roadshow* offered a critical position in direct reference to nuclear incidents, the first to the bombing of Hiroshima by staging the burial on its anniversary; and the second to the nuclear accident at Chernobyl in 1986 and the plan to expand the importation of nuclear waste for burial at Dounreay.

These projects marked a turning point, too, in terms of public engagement and participation. Because *Burial and Preservation* was realized in a public park, the work invited participation among the park's regular users, enabling them to take part as they liked, e.g. through digging, talking or

9. Roxane Permar, 'Burial and Preservation', *AND: Journal of Art and Art Education* 21 (1990), p. 24.

 Feminist Art Activisms and Artivisms

10. Roxane Permar and Susan Timmins, 'The Nuclear Roadshow: Shetland 1990', *Shetland Life* 120 (1990), p. 24.

leaving offerings and watching it slowly change. Ultimately many did in fact feel it belonged to them. This project ran parallel to *The Nuclear Roadshow*, in Shetland, for which public participation was equally important. Our engagement with the local Shetland community, however, followed a very different process in which we worked to identify six empty buildings sited throughout the islands, using local radio interviews, telephone conversations, personal visits, newspaper articles and word of mouth alongside two thousand miles driving around the islands.[10]

Happily people responded to the work in their own way. The crofter, Robbie Johnson, who lived by the site in Eshaness, would flag down tourist coaches so passengers could look at the house and he could tell them about the project. The fact that he had his own thoughts about the work was important as well as his assertion that he didn't quite know what was intended. He is one of a number of crofters who shared stories about those who had lived in the houses in the past or lambs being born deformed following the accident at Chernobyl.

A number of unexpected attitudes were revealed, too, during the project. Somewhat alarmingly, *The Shetland Times* published an article suggesting a nuclear bomb had hit Shetland houses, which might have worried the property owners who had been assured no damage would be done. Most interestingly, some members of the community showed mild surprise or even astonishment on hearing which Shetlanders had given permission to use their properties.

Cold War Projects

Cold War Projects began by investigating the legacy of the Cold War in Shetland as it exists both physically in the landscape, and in memory. This work is grounded in Shetland but expands across different cultural and political borders, exchanging memories, knowledge and perceptions of the nuclear era by connecting communities in the northern and Arctic region. During the Cold War period Shetland, Norway, Faroe, Iceland, Greenland, Canada and Alaska played an important strategic role by hosting NATO's early warning defence system. There is much evidence remaining,

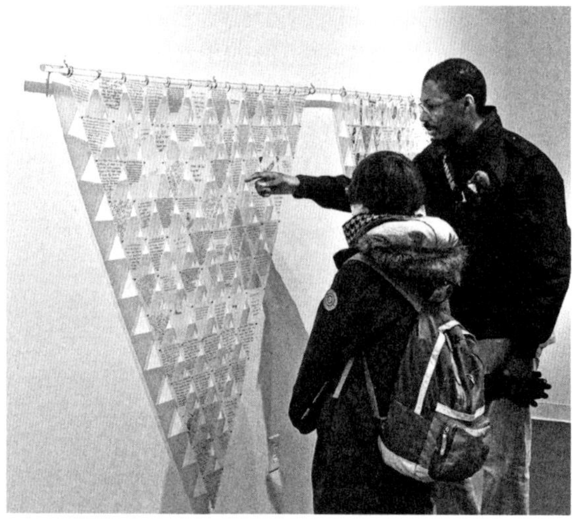
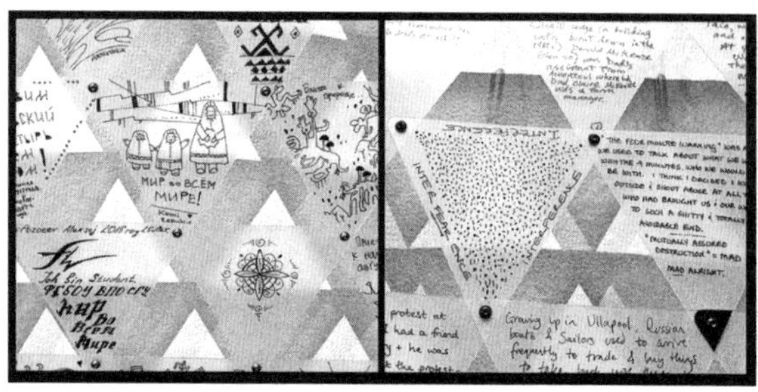

(left)
Roxane Permar and Susan Timmins, *Northern Exchange*, installation view of 'Relate North 2015: Culture, Community and Communication', Kimora Gallery, University of Alaska Anchorage, 2015. Photo: Cold War Projects

Roxane Permar and Susan Timmins, *Northern Exchange*, 2015, details of triangles created by participants in Scotland, Canada, Philadelphia and students from the Piritim Sorokin Syktyvkar State University and Shetland College University of the Highlands and Islands.
Photo: Cold War Projects

particularly in Shetland, of listening stations, bunkers and radar installations.[11] It is quite shocking to encounter this Cold War landscape in Shetland in comparison to London where I lived in the 1980s and 1990s. The visual landscape of Shetland is very different; big skies and almost no trees create open vistas where the presence of the Cold War is highly visible. Conversely, in London the presence of the Cold War was very hidden, secret, and couched in terms of reference defined by paranoia and fear. Today NATO, including US and British military forces, are returning to some of these sites signalling an escalation in defensive measures against the threat of self-destruction.

Bringing together work across sculpture, photography, film, the Internet and sound, *Cold War Projects* aims to encourage a different understanding of the remote North through consideration of its historic significance as a new Front Line for defence against the perceived Soviet threat in the Cold War era. Ways of working play on methods used during the Cold War to acquire information through listening and in turn relaying, or sharing. Thus the project encourages listening, learning and gaining knowledge and experience; to share and exchange in order to stimulate debate, trigger collective memory and promote engagement with issues that are not only unique to the Cold War but have continuing relevance to today's global society.

11. Roxane Permar and Susan Timmins, 'Art and Engagement with the Cold War in Shetland', in *Relate North: Art, Engagement and Representation* (Rovaniemi: Lapland University Press, 2014), pp. 35–36 and p. 42, https://lauda.ulapland.fi/bitstream/handle/10024/62240/RN_2014_LUP_PDFA.pdf?sequence=2.

Cold War Projects presents firsthand accounts of ordinary people's experiences of the Cold War so that they can be collected, preserved and shared with younger generations in an effort to consider our nuclear futures. To date three separate art projects are complete, *Countdown* (2012); *Recount* (2013); *Northern Exchange: Cold War Histories and Nuclear Futures* (2016, Iceland). One work, *Northern Exchange*, is on-going, in progress since 2015, elements of which have been exhibited in Scotland and Alaska. A new project is in the planning stages to take place in Unst, Shetland's most northerly island, which hosted the Royal Air Force for more than fifty years. It benefits from a slow development that enables relationship building and trust to grow among the collaborative partners.

Each project uses a different approach to address the nuclear threat. Each was designed to work within the Shetland context and drew extensively on previous projects and connections in the community. *Recount* was a socially engaged project based on activities undertaken by civilian volunteers for Shetland's Royal Observer Corps (ROC) in underground Posts from 1961 to 1991. The content of the project is informed by personal recollections of ROC Observers, creating a poignant and powerful narrative. The Observers displayed huge commitment and revealed a strong sense of public duty to the people of Shetland, as did the civil volunteers at all 1500 Posts operating throughout the

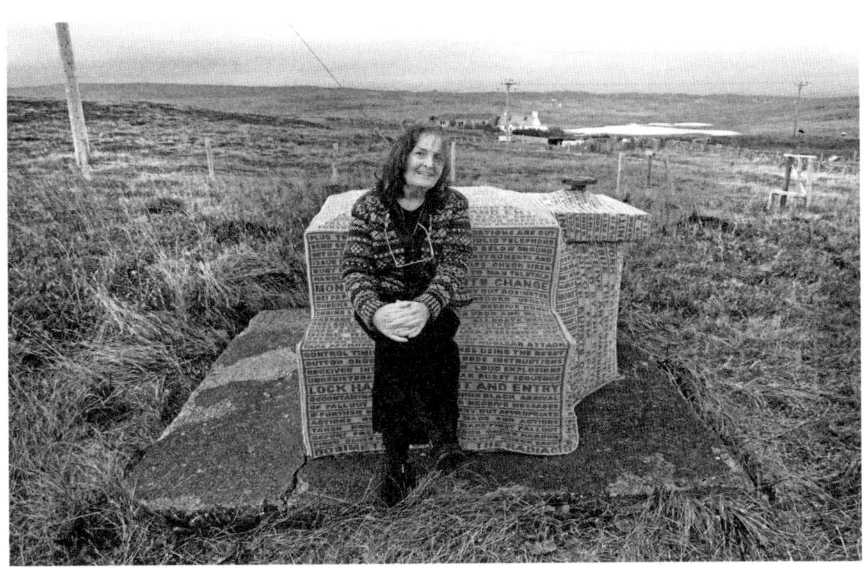

Roxane Permar and Susan Timmins, *Recount*, 2013, project participant Gwen Jamieson, the last Chief Observer at the Walls ROC Post, Shetland, seated on entrance to bunker, covered by glow-in-the-dark knitted artwork.
Photo: Cold War Projects

United Kingdom. The volunteers were well aware of the dangers and risks involved in their work yet firmly believed that serving in the ROC was a way to help their community.[12] *Recount* comprised four elements that offered very different forms of engagement and thus broadened access to the work. These included artworks sited at three extant ROC underground bunkers, comprising glow-in-the-dark knitted covers for above-ground structures; public events in each of the communities where there had been ROC Posts; a Focus Display in the Shetland Museum and Archives; and a web page containing edited sound recordings and photographs.

In *Countdown* a very different approach was used to address the question of the nuclear threat. The work was made in the studio, without direct social engagement, then subsequently used in public situations to stimulate discussion and debate about nuclear issues past and present. The work comprises two elements, eighteen photographs and a film. The photographs show the exterior buildings and landscape surrounding the military base, RAF Saxa Vord in Unst, the largest and most complex Cold War site in Shetland. The film was shot inside the operations block and bunker. The title *Countdown* alludes to the British Government's much derided public alert system, the Four Minute Warning, which would warn the public that in the event of a nuclear attack it would have four minutes to count down to zero, the moment of annihilation.[13] The photographs are displayed inside cellophane bags normally used to package disposable, protective masks. The flimsiness of the bags recalls the absurdity of the civil defence measures put in place not only in Britain but on both sides of the Iron Curtain.[14] The imagery in *Countdown* evokes shared associations for people across northern

12. Roxane Permar and Susan Timmins, *Recount: Bunker Stories*, exh. cat. Shetland, Cold War Projects, 2014, pp. 2–7, https://issuu.com/home/published/recount-permar_timmins.

13. N.J. McCamley, *Cold War Secret Nuclear Bunkers: The Passive Defence of the Western World during the Cold War* (Barnsley: Pen & Sword Military, 2013), p. 58.

14. E. Geist, 'Was There a Real "Mineshaft Gap"?', *Journal of Cold War Studies* 14, no. 2 (2012), pp. 3–28.

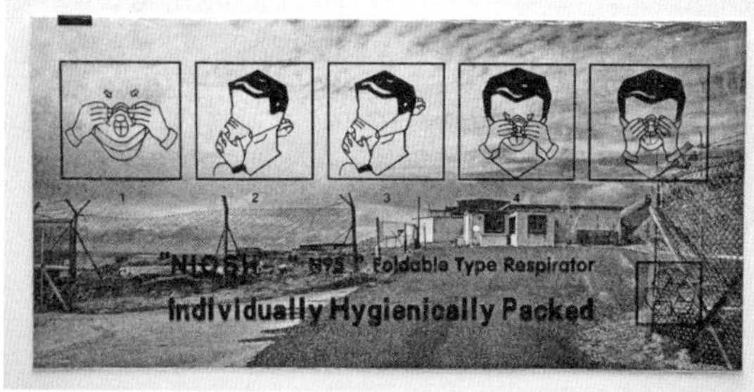

Roxane Permar and Susan Timmins, *Countdown*, 2012, one of 18 photographs comprising the installation. Courtesy of Cold War Projects

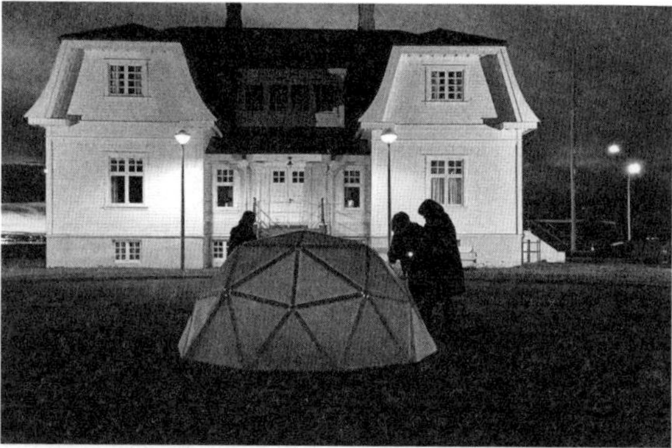

Cold War Projects, *Our Dome, Northern Exchange: Cold War Histories and Nuclear Futures*, 2016, sited at Höfði House, Reykjavik, the location of the 1986 summit between Mikhail Gorbachev and Ronald Reagan, regarded by some as the beginning of the end of the Cold War. Photo: Cold War Projects

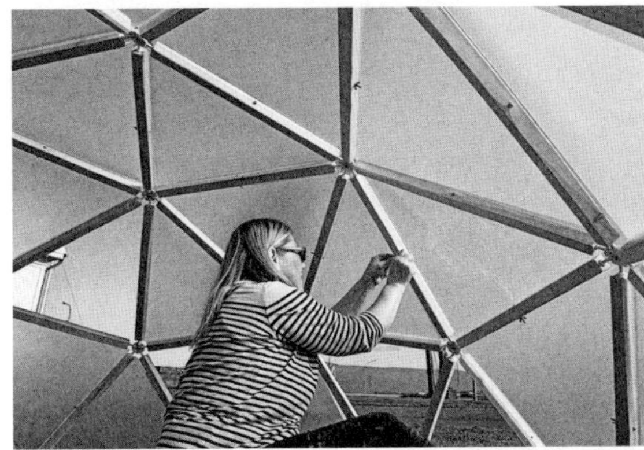

Cold War Projects, *Our Dome, Northern Exchange: Cold War Histories and Nuclear Futures*, 2016, one of the participants, Dagrún Magnúsdóttir, is setting up our mobile dome outside Höfði House, Reykjavik. Photo: Cold War Projects

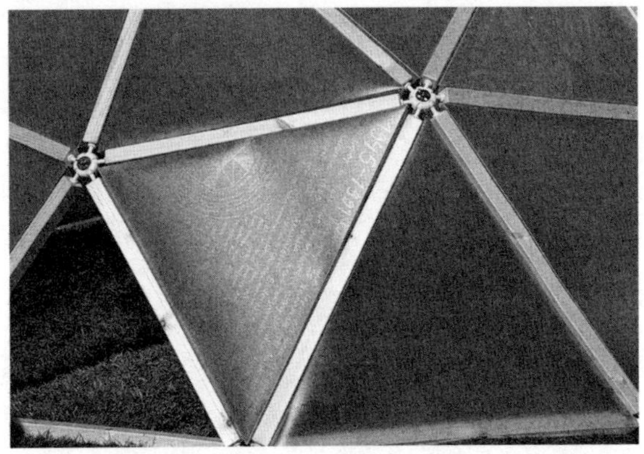

Cold War Projects, *Our Dome, Northern Exchange, Cold War Histories and Nuclear Futures*, 2016, detail of one of the triangles with invisible message illuminated at night by uv light. Photo: Cold War Projects

15. Roxane Permar and Susan Timmins, 'Cold War Projects|Fairbanks' (images of Murphy Dome and H-3 Radar Station at Stokksnessi), 2016, www.coldwarprojects.com/fairbanks-alaska.

16. Roxane Permar, 'Night Photos|Cold-war-projects', 26 August 2016, www.coldwarprojects.com/iceland.

regions, whose landscapes are similarly occupied by Cold War structures.[15]

Northern Exchange: Cold War Histories and Nuclear Futures explored the nuclear issue by using a combination of approaches to re-imagine the period and ask how the presence of Cold War military installations impact on local populations in Iceland, both past and present. The project revolved around four communities, Höfn, Keflavík, Bolungarvik and Þórshöfn, linked to bases operated by the American military during the Cold War. The operations have subsequently been updated, re-situated and are now operated by the Icelandic Coastguard for NATO.

The project brought together artists and students with volunteer participants who together represented different generations of people who live and work in the remote communities that hold historic significance in NATO's early defence warning system. Collaborative inter-action and dialogical exchange were central to the project. A mobile geodesic dome served as a tool for engagement, attracting attention and sparking curiosity as well as providing the framework to display participants' contribu-tions written or drawn in invisible ink on triangles.[16]

Icelandic artist, Ásthildur Jónsdóttir, and Finnish artists Elina Härkönen and Timo Jokela, brought their students while Susan Timmins and I worked with Elizabeth Crichton and Rebecca Boyd from the University of the

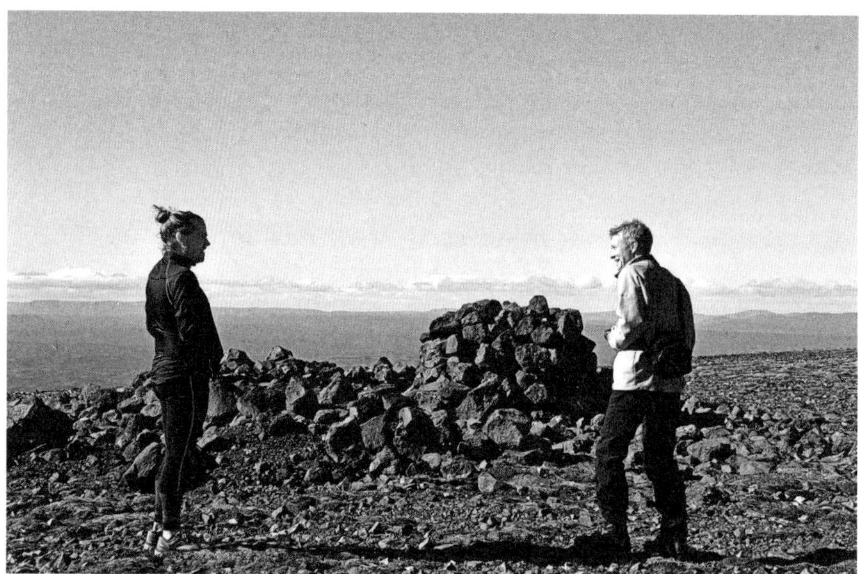

Rebecca Boyd and Rúnar Jónsson during site visit to the former American base at Langanes near Þórshöfn, Iceland, 2016. Photo: Cold War Projects

Highlands and Islands. Participants and collaborative partners, or the specific ensemble of social actors, as Grant Kester has described them, are fundamental to a project like this one, and without them it would have been impossible, in fact inconceivable, to go ahead.[17] Ásthildur Jónsdóttir was a key collaborative partner, who served as gatekeeper and helped choreograph the invitations to work within each community as well as steering our historical and contextual learning from the Icelandic perspective.

Attitudes to the nuclear issue and the Cold War varied across the different communities, from no interest at all to highly politicized or strident positions. It is not, however, the differences in views or the passion with which they are held, but the fact that the project brought people together to engage with each other, to talk, to learn and become more aware of the histories embedded in the Cold War period that are relevant to the nuclear issue now and in the future. One of the collaborative participants in the project, Rebecca Boyd, clearly articulates the value of this experience and identifies the importance for military leaders as well as ordinary people to take note of this process.

17. Grant Kester, 'Art and Answerability in Jay Koh's Work', *Art-Led Participative Processes: Dialogue and Subjectivity within Performances in the Everyday* (Helsinki: Academy of Fine Arts, University of the Arts Helsinki, 2015), pp. 1–6.

18. Rebecca Boyd, *Collaborative Art in Iceland: Northern Exchange: Cold War Histories and Nuclear Futures: A Student's Perspective*, University of the Highlands and Islands (Shetland: Cold War Projects, 2016).

It is the rich yet intangible network of relationships woven with people and places, knowledge gleaned and awareness raised, that is the real and powerful outcome of this journey of creative engagement.
… And perhaps it would be no bad thing if today's global military leaders took more notice of that all-important human element, not only in their awareness of 'Cold War Histories' but in their strategizing for 'Nuclear Futures'.[18]

The nature of engagement shifted over time, evolving as more people became involved and the project moved across different virtual and geographical spaces. Each person and community of people brought new ways of working, different expectations and background experience. Speaking and talking, conversation and discussion, formed the heart of the project, giving it meaning, purpose and momentum, whether face-to-face, by email, Facebook or through Skype, all processes and tools that were used.

Through both bodies of work, *The Nuclear Family* and *Cold War Projects*, knowledge is extended, awareness raised and discussion about the nuclear threat encouraged, not only as it was experienced in different periods, whether the Cold War era or the second nuclear age, but as it relates to life as we live it and aspire to live in the future. The processes by which these aims are achieved are different, shaped by the changing contexts of world politics, personal circumstances and the contemporary art world. Regardless of these shifts in situation, the drive to use art as a means to address the nuclear issue, whether overtly or with subtlety, endures. The need regrettably remains urgent. We can use our skills and knowledge of art practice to keep the issue in the public eye, emphasizing that this threat has not disappeared or lost relevance.

NUCLEAR FAMILIES

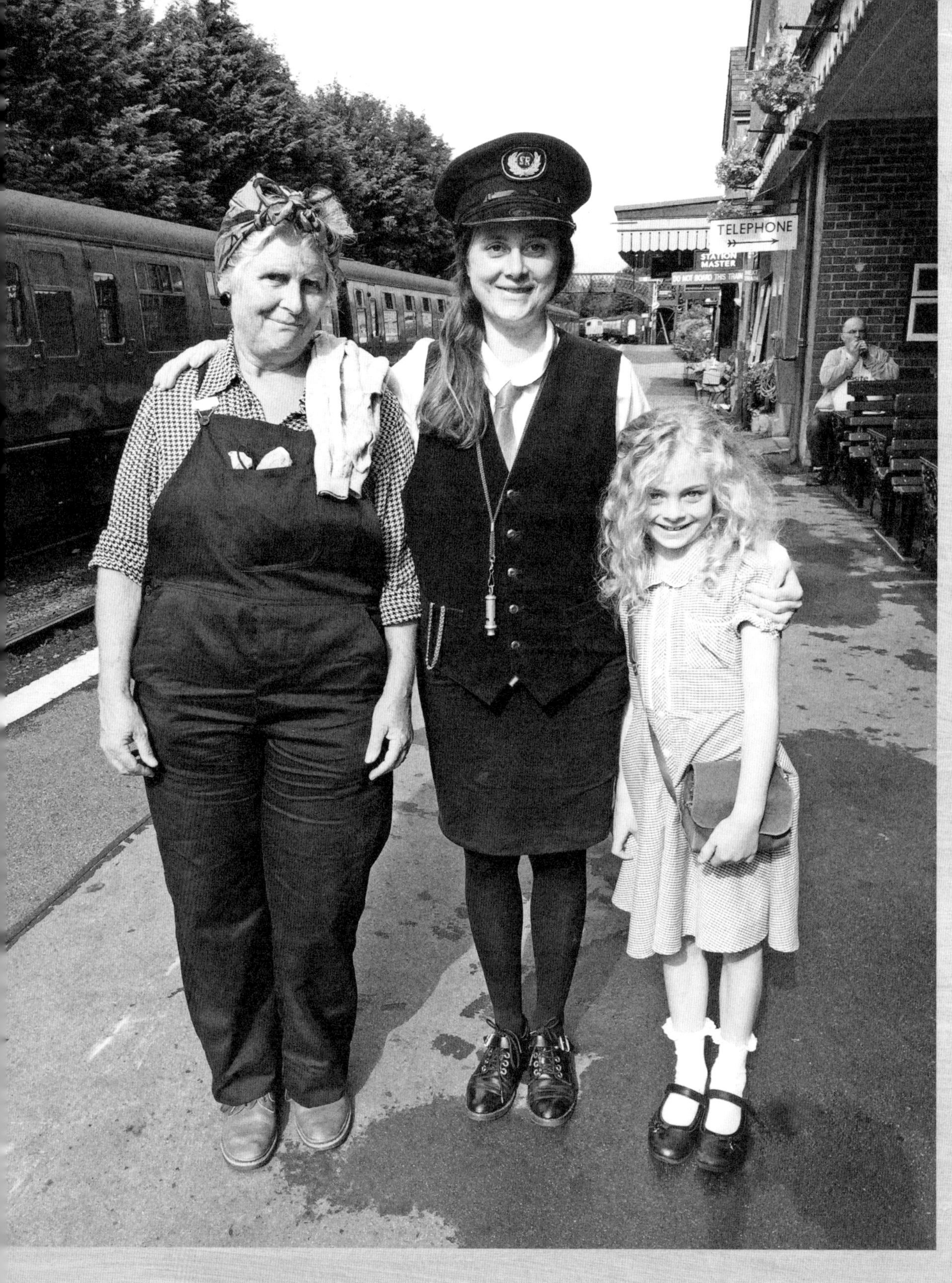

The cast of *Railwaywomen*, Shielagh Finlay, Jessica Akerman and Lois Leonard

FILM MAKER IN THE FAMILY
The Impact of Family Life on Creativity

Abbe Leigh Fletcher

1. Cyril Connolly, *Enemies of Promise* (London: Routledge, 1938).

2. www.enemiesofgoodart.org.

3. 'The idea that the artist must sacrifice himself to his art. (I use the pronoun advisedly). His responsibility is to his work alone. It is a motivating idea of the Romantics... This heroic stance, the Gauguin Pose, has been taken as the norm—as natural to the artist—and artists, both men and women, who do not assume it have tended to feel a little shabby and second-rate.' Ursula K. Le Guin, 'The Fisherwoman's Daughter' (1988), in *The Mother Reader: Essential Writings on Motherhood*, ed. Moyra Davey (New York: Penguin Random House, 2001), p. 171.

4. Mary Shelley's Introduction to *Frankenstein* (London, 1831).

'There is no more sombre enemy of good art than the pram in the hall', according to Cyril Connolly.[1] This writer may have had the luxury of partitioning off childrearing by sealing himself within his study but what of the parent/ mother artist who doesn't have that opportunity. The Enemies of Good Art Collective (started 2009)[2] openly acknowledged the hypocrisy of Connolly's quote in their choice of name, while campaigning to increase participation by parents, but especially mothers, and their children in public discussions and art events. The implication in this quote remains that openly combining artwork with family responsibility is somehow impossible if working as an artist is defined, in the Romantic tradition, as shutting oneself away to work alone, rather than working amidst the chaos of family life. The compartmentalization of family life from "working life" is always seen as necessary for artists and work in general and refusing to do so regarded as 'a little shabby and second-rate', according to Ursula Le Guin.[3]

Creative work does not happen in a vacuum but is inspired, spawned by, reacted to, rebelled against, embraced, nurtured alongside life itself. As Mary Shelley reminds us, 'Invention does not consist in creating out of a void but out of chaos'.[4] Creative work is a way of interacting with our surroundings, a form of physical and mental play. Whilst we raise and socialize the next generation of workers (and artists), some spark of inspiration comes from the drudgery of the domestic and the quotidian. Children are excellent at this as they have not yet had it drummed out of them in favour of productivity and politeness.

The barriers between work and leisure are widely recognized today as being eroded with the rise of the casualization of work. This could perhaps offer intervals for cross-pollination, or at least a visibility and acknowledgment of the importance of the filmmaker as both parent and artist, and a re-evaluation of the mother/artist. As Le Guin suggests:

> The advantage of motherhood for a woman artist is that it puts her in immediate and inescapable contact with the sources of life, death, beauty, growth, corruption… If the woman artist has been trained to believe that the activities of motherhood are trivial, tangential to the main issues of life, irrelevant to the great themes of literature, she should untrain herself. The training is misogynist: it protects and perpetuates systems of thought and feeling which prefer violence and death to love and birth, and it is a lie.[5]

The project, *Film maker in the Family* (2011–2018), constitutes an investigation into the relationship between family life and creative work and is an example of documentary-based filmmaking practice that addresses and develops the impact of having children within the work. Adopting a rhizomatic approach to filming, in the sense of using Deleuze and Guattari's rhizome, as an organically developing system of connections that form out of necessity and creativity to produce networks of becoming, where the process of making is equally significant to the final outcome.[6] This rhizomatic way of working, through informal networks, and playful collaborations is lateral rather than hierarchical.

Before having children, I was exploring how to work collaboratively as a filmmaker, with a specific aim of challenging hierarchical and dominant approaches to film-making in teams with highly specialized skill sets and demarcated roles. The *Four Shores* project (2004–2005) documented artworks inspired by the environment of the Isle of Sheppey with a visual artist, architect and poet. We each operated from within our established disciplines,

RHIZOMATIC

5. Le Guin, whom I stole the quote from says: '… have you ever heard anyone say that before? The *advantage* of motherhood for an artist?' Le Guin 1988, p. 176.

6. 'The rhizome is reducible neither to the One nor the multiple. … It has neither beginning nor end, but always a middle (*milieu*) from which it grows and which it overspills…. In contrast to centred (even polycentric) systems, … the rhizome is an acentred, nonhierarchical, nonsignifying system without a General and without an organizing memory or central automaton, defined solely by a circulation of states.' Gilles Deleuze and Félix Guattari, *A Thousand Plateaus*, in *Capitalism and Schizophrenia*, vol. 2, trans. by Brian Massumi (London: Continuum, 1987), p. 23.

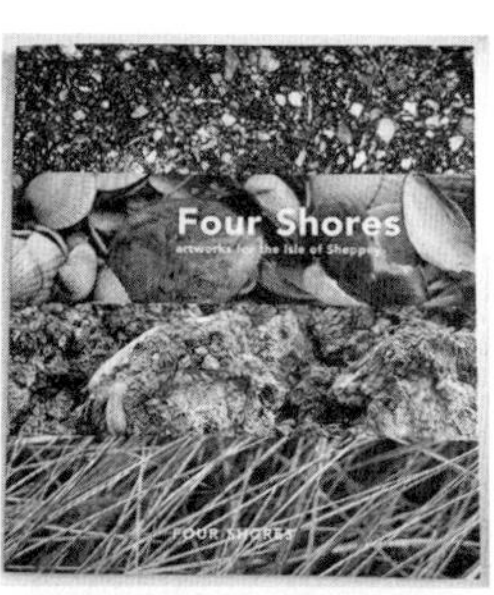

Catalogue *Four Shores: Artworks for the Isle of Sheppey*, 2005

7. www.raisingfilms.com/portfolio-items/making-it-possible/.

8. Tillie Olsen, *Silences* (New York: The Feminist Press, 2003 [1965]), p. 33.

9. Mihaly Csikszentmihalyi, *Beyond Boredom and Anxiety: Experiencing Flow in Work and Play* (New York: John Wiley, 1975).

10. This particular essay very much chimes with the writing of this paper, rupture and interruption has been the process of thinking and writing this, from submitting the proposal to the performing of it at the 'Feminist Art Activisms and Artivisms Conference' (Middlesex University, 2 July 2018) to the writing up for it for this publication a year later, through constant interruption, writing around my academic job, during the short school day, around domestic chores, using pockets of time to reflect on it and add to it, thankfully with a constructive editor to give deadlines and feedback.

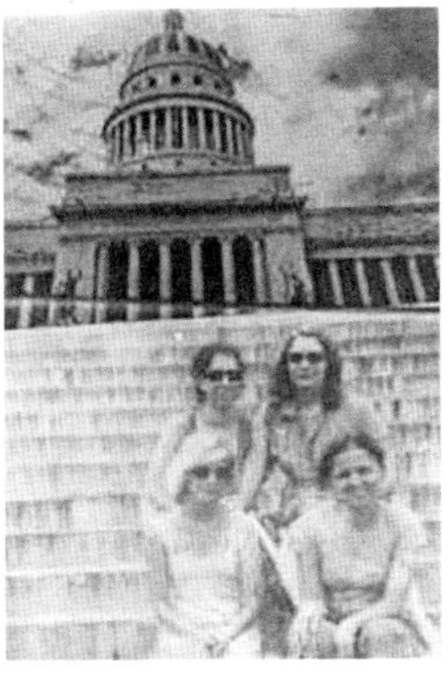

w.in.c films: Sabela Pernas Soto, Abbe Leigh Fletcher, Petra Niskanen and Claudia Vasquez Ramírez in Havana, 2009

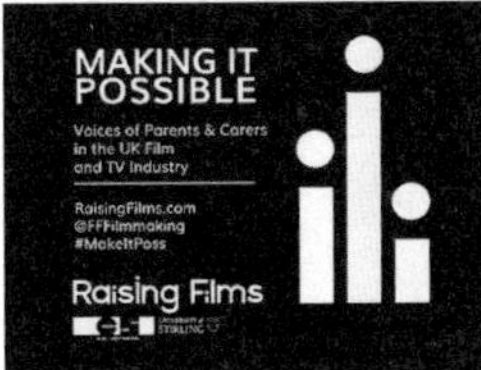

Raising Films logo

collaborating but contributing in our specific modes and I was the documentary filmmaker of these meetings and working processes. To make *The Road to Gibara* (22 min., 2010), our collective, w.inc. films, was formed to travel to the Cine Pobre No-Budget Film Festival in Cuba founded by Humerto Solás in 2003. When filming in Gibara, we regularly rotated the production roles so that we each took turns to direct, shoot and record sound, refuting the industrial model of specializing in a specific production role.

Since its foundation by filmmaker Hope Dickson Leach in 2016, Raising Films has been campaigning for the rights of parents working in the film and television industries—an industry notoriously brittle and male dominated—to encompass flexible working and include parents rather than exclude them or make them feel they have to choose between parenthood and career.[7] As Tillie Olsen confirms, motherhood is characterized by interruption: 'More than any other human relationship, overwhelmingly more, motherhood means being instantly interruptible, responsive, responsible. Children need one *now*… It is distraction, not meditation, that becomes habitual; interruption, not continuity.'[8]

Pockets of time are precious to all, they are guarded, savoured, and can sometimes be used with wizard efficiency to produce something that was not there a moment ago. After having my daughter in 2010, I found every moment was accounted for, I was booked in, on duty bodily all day and night. In the creative process, rather than wading into Csikszentmihalyi's flow,[9] we get to put a toe in puddles, a wetted finger, a drop of rain here and there, rather than a drenching.

Playwright Sarah Ruhl's *100 Essays I Don't Have Time to Write*, documents the flurry of ideas that spark, more ideas than time available to write them (as) fully (as she might like). Titles of her unwritten essays: 'On interruptions',[10] 'On the loss of sword fights', 'On lice', 'On motherhood and stools (the furniture kind)', 'Children as dramaturgs' to name a few, indicate the cross-fertilization of the imagination, the reluctance/impossibility of separation, the juxtaposition of contexts enriches rather than diminishes. They provide insight into the parental juggle but also the capacity for creativity and the concise nature of communicating these ideas when time is fragmented and fitted around the needs of others.

> I found that life intruding on writing was, in fact, life. And that, tempting as it may be for a writer who is also a parent, one must not think of life as an intrusion. At the end of the day, writing has very little to do with writing, and much to do with life. And life, by definition, is not an intrusion.[11]

Stan and Jane Brakhage documented the coming into the world of their child in the film *Window Water Baby Moving* (1959). The final shot of the film, when Jane takes the camera, captures Brakhage's awe at the event of birth, after Brakhage's camerawork had been intimately examining Jane's body. Can you imagine agreeing to be filmed in extreme close-up during labour? Jane's final shot as the camerawoman is the denouement of her labour and a reminder of separation within this event… that the woman bodily produces the baby and the man witnesses it. Where does this awe at production disappear to…?

In the reflective materialist and feminist approach of Mary Kelly's *Post-Partum Document* (1973–1979) her work representing the mother's view of her child, documenting the traces of different foodstuffs as evidenced in nappies, casts of hands with notes on fabric, deciphering mark-making, embraces her child's productions with curiosity and structured presentation. While based on a critique of Lacan, this work foregrounds for me, D.W. Winnicott's notion that there is not a baby and mother separately, but a mother-baby symbiosis, her work is a co-production.

Ever the inspiration, Agnès Varda came up with a tactical solution to merging motherhood with filmmaking when she was commissioned by German television in 1974 and given a year to make a film after the birth of her second child.

> She knew from experience how difficult it was to care for a small child while on a film set so she resolved to make her next film without leaving home. [writing in 1975] 'I told myself that I was a good example of women's creativity—always a bit stuck

    Feminist Art Activisms and Artivisms

11. Sarah Ruhl, *100 Essays I Don't Have Time to Write: On Umbrellas and Sword Fights, Parades and Dogs, Fire Alarms, Children and Theater* (New York: Faber, 2015), pp. 4–5.

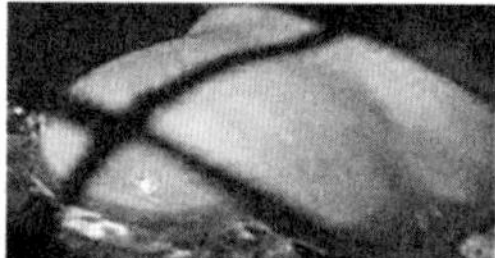

Still from *Window Water Baby Moving*, 1959

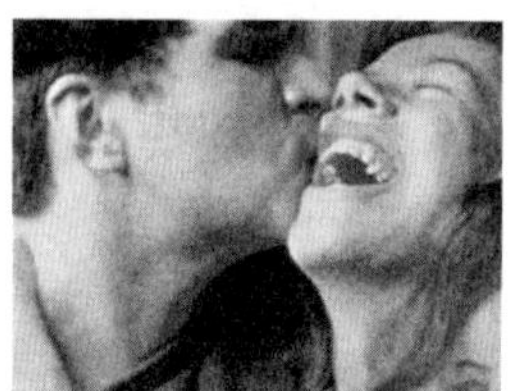

Stan and Jane Brakhage in *Window Water Baby Moving*, 1959

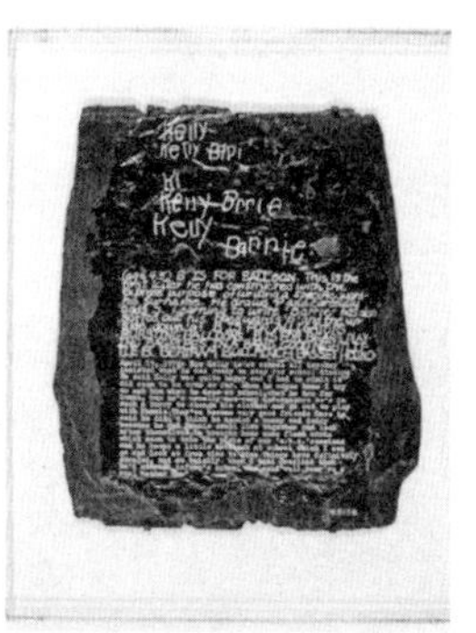

Mary Kelly, *Post-Partum Document*, 1973–1979

12. Mason Currey, citing Agnès Varda in *Daily Rituals: Women at Work* (New York: Knopf , 2019), pp. 262–263.

and suffocated by home and motherhood... Could I manage to restart my creativity from within these limitations? ... So I set out from this idea, from this fact that most women are stuck at home and I attached myself to my hearth. I imagined a new umbilical cord, I had a special eighty-meter electric cable attached to the electric box in my house. I decided I would allow myself that much space to shoot [her next film].'[12]

In this way, Varda made *Daguerréotypes* (1975) a portrait of the street where she lived, documenting the shopkeepers and community.

Eleven months after my first child's birth, I was getting restless, wanting to make something, feeling rusty and so I started a new film project. In collaboration with artist Jessica Akerman, we began a film about her mother-in-law who grew up in Dalston (London) in the 1950s, treading the same streets on walks with our children. Dalston was changing rapidly and this was a way of mapping the changes in the area as well as seeking stories (and tactics) of child-rearing from the generation before us for tips, strategies and reassurance from other women's embodied experience.

My Mild-Mannered Mother-in-Law from Mildmay (completed, 2013, 20 min.) was filmed over three time periods: when both of our first babies were eleven months old (my daughter strapped to my back to film, twittering into the mic, cable-bashing), then when they were 22 months

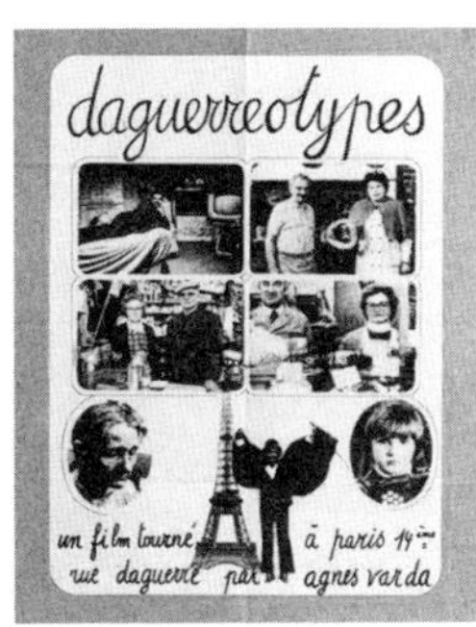

Agnès Varda, *Daguerréotypes*, 1975

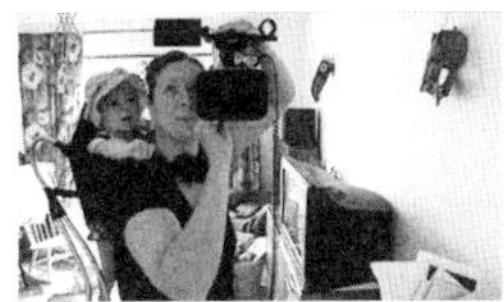

Filming *My mild-mannered Mother-in-Law from Mildmay* together

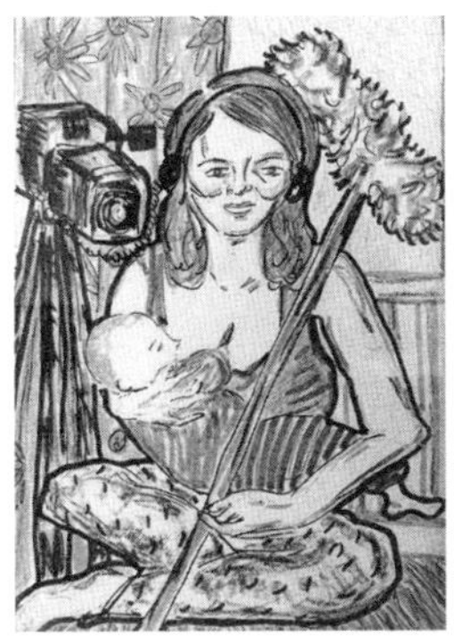

Behind the camera, drawing by Jessica Akerman

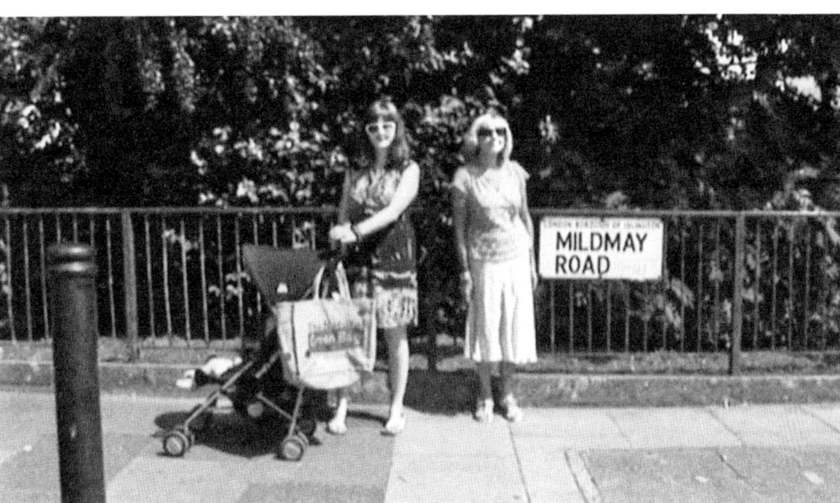

Jessica Akerman and Stella Robinson in *My Mild-Mannered Mother-in-Law from Mildmay*, 2013

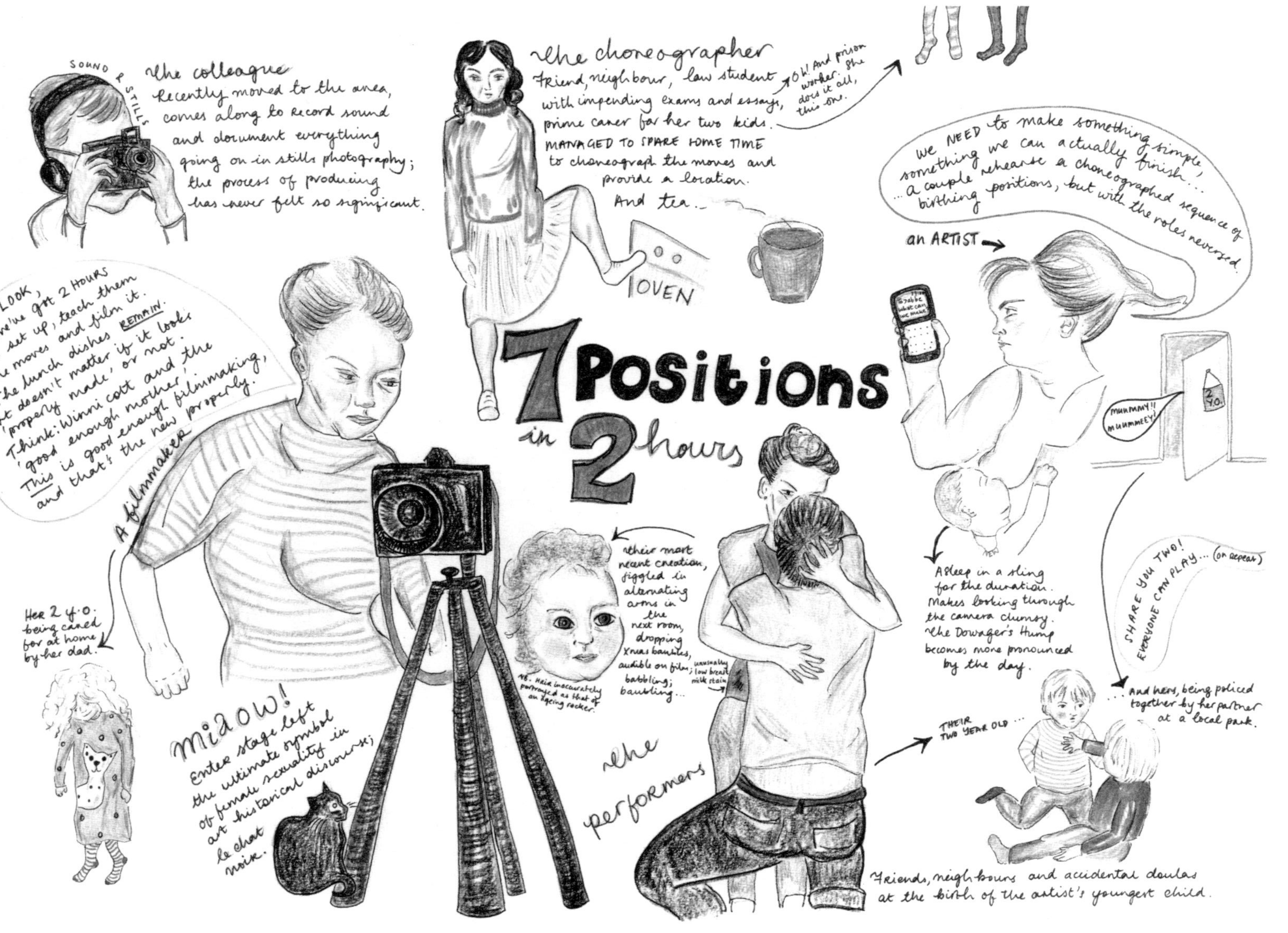

7 positions in 2 hours, 2013, drawing by Jessica Akerman

13. Rhizome, a botanical term for a subterranean plant stem borrowed by Deleuze and Guattari as a practical refutation of hierarchical arborescent power structures in favour of the subterranean possibilities of the rhizome to make connections, 'it is composed not of units but of dimensions, or rather directions in motion. It has neither beginning nor end, but always middle (milieu) from which it grows and which it overspills'. Deleuze and Guattari, *A Thousand Plateaus*, p. 23.

14. Ibid., p. 13.

15. Ibid., p. 8: 'A rhizome ceaselessly establishes connections between semiotic chains, organizations of power, and circumstances relative to the arts, sciences and social struggles. A semiotic chain is like a tuber agglomerating very diverse acts, not only linguistic but also perceptive, mimetic, gestural and cognitive …'

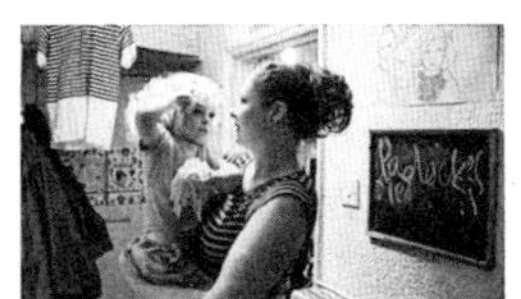

Abbe Leigh Fletcher, *First Trip Away*, 2013, film still

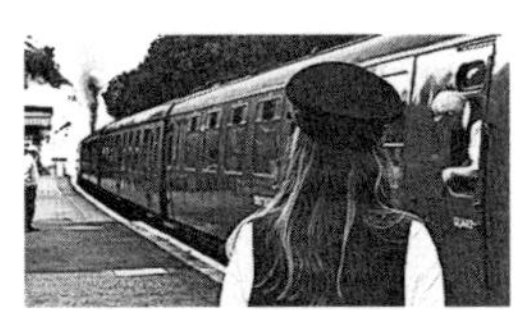

Railwaywomen, 2018, film still

old and Jess was pregnant with her second child; and after the arrival of that baby, with the two-year-old toddlers. The narrative structure skips between these different time periods, cutting associatively back and forth, reflecting the non-linear processes of memory. While making the film, we were multitasking: filming, recording sound and breast-feeding. The film communicates the chaos of child-rearing, but also those moments of reflection, or collaboration, of interaction between the children and what we were trying to do.

Later, when the kids were three, we planned a film for the Birth Rites Trust Collection, researched and choreographed the action in the film, roped in cast and crew, arranged childcare, and brought our children along. The day of the shoot was set. The filming happened in a flurry and when we looked back at the footage, we realized that everything that was interesting was happening behind the camera, off-screen. All the arrangements, the positions of the crew, the babies strapped to Jess and Colette when she wasn't performing in front of the camera, the Christmas tree lights, the ad hoc nappy changes, feeding of babies, sound effects suggestions brought in by the choreographer's slightly older children with hushed reverence, the rapt attention. We had edited all of this out of the finished film and it was all the duller for it. Jessica captured the arrangements in her drawing *7 Positions in 2 hours* (2013), mapping the detail of the rhizome—as dimensions and actions in motion, growing from the middle and overspilling[13]—that we created behind the scenes.

Deleuze and Guattari call to 'make a map not a tracing' differentiating 'what distinguishes the map from the tracing is that it is entirely oriented toward an experimentation in contact with the real'.[14] Akerman's drawing maps the diverse perceptive, mimetic, gestural and cognitive acts[15] that made up the experience of making the film, practical, creatively tactical actions that were not captured by the camera, thus rendering them visible and mapping the interplay in contact with the real conundrum of how to make a film with offspring present and to document a collaboration that is inclusive and multiple.

Later that year I made a film about visiting another w.inc. films member in Galicia. This became the film *First*

Trip Away (2013, 15 min.). It was a documentation of the visit, the humbling inspiration of Santiago de Compostela to a place of pilgrimage. The reconnection with my fellow filmmaker is bracketed with a scene of me saying goodbye to my daughter and partner and at the end of the film returning home, key in the door, luggage in the hallway and straight into the plot of Cinderella. My daughter doesn't greet me, she presents me with a shoe, and I slip into the prince's role, 'it fits' I exclaim and she retorts, 'I'm married with you!' and hugs me—a warmer and more imaginative homecoming I could not have anticipated. Every child is an artist.

      The final film in the series, *Railwaywomen* (2018, 4 min., 42 sec.), came later, once I had had my second child, a son. I emerged from the heavy fog of postpartum depression, moved out of London but kept my job in the outer boroughs, and hence kept my commute. The station where I commuted from was the starting point for the heritage Mid Hants Railway. I became obsessed with steam, and with the history of women's roles on the railway throughout its history. This film would not be a documentary but rather an experiment in micro short form drama. I would portray the fascination of a little girl with a brownie camera (my daughter) when she sees the elder female train driver (my mother). With Jessica Akerman appearing as the guard on the platform. Three generations of women, intersecting at three different points in their lives. The fascination and inspiration of childhood, juxtaposed with the professionalism (or the slog) of middle age (sorry Jess) and the reflection of

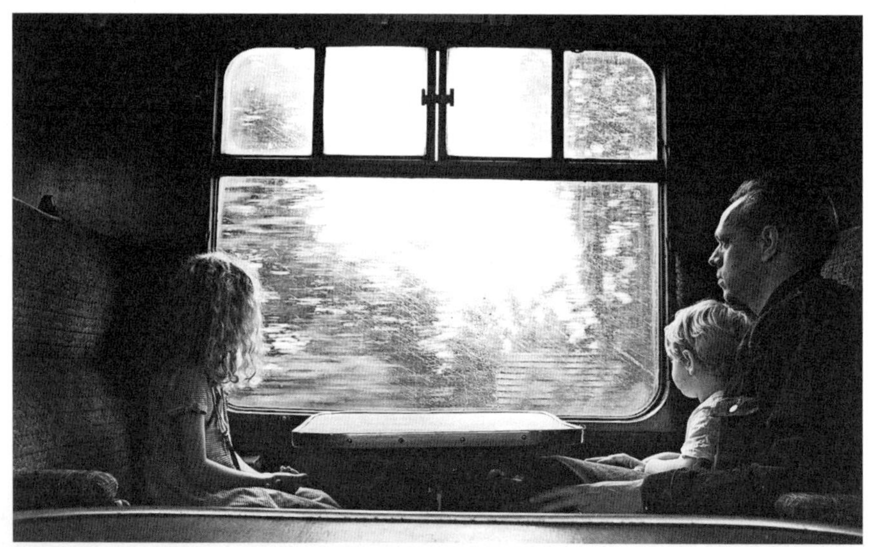

Lois, Frank and Dan Leonard in *Railwaywomen*, 2018, film still

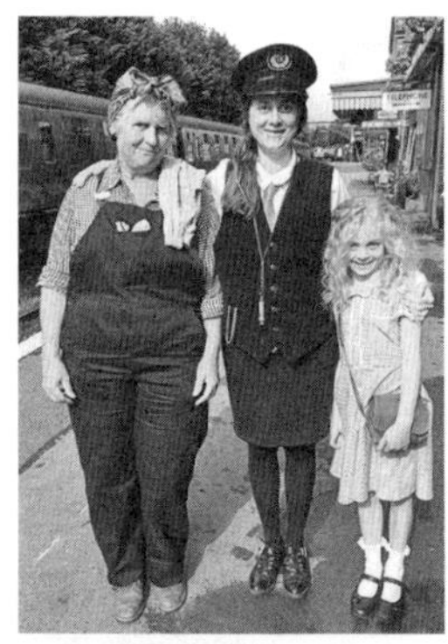

The cast of *Railwaywomen*, three generations

16. The Mid Hants Railway has adopted the film, and to my delight, show it with their talks on women working on the railway.

17. 'One can distinguish "ways of operating"—ways of walking, reading, producing, speaking, etc. These styles of action intervene in a field which regulates them at a first level… but they introduce into it a way of turning it to their advantage.' Michel de Certeau, *The Practice of Everyday Life* (Berkeley, CA: University of California Press, 1988), p. 300 and 'A tactic is a calculated action determined by the absence of a proper locus. No delimitation of an exteriority, then, provides it with the condition necessary for autonomy. The space of a tactic is the space of the other. This it must play on and with a terrain imposed on it and organized by a foreign power…. It takes advantages of "opportunities" and depends on them…. It can be where it is least expected. It is a guileful ruse. In short, a tactic is an art of the weak.' p. 37.

older age coming full circle as it inspires youth. This evolving way of working collectively with other women underpins the feminist artivism aspect of this practice. *Railwaywomen* sought an alternative to documentary aesthetics to produce something more polished, but in order to sustain the project the scale of it is micro, it is a very short film (4 min., 42 sec.), and thereby difficult to get shown. It remains a document of a specific moment, a collaboration between people to create something that didn't exist the day before.[16]

Michel de Certeau's concept of tactics,[17] is my operational guide to circumnavigating restrictions in my everyday environment through actions designed to resist established power structures. The tactics of working around possibilities, pragmatism, and scale, combined with the new experience of time not being your own that comes with raising children and the parental/carer role. Time in film, as in life, is fragmented, broken into smaller, jewel-like moments, and less able to disappear into a flow of time. Meanwhile, less time makes for less procrastination, more decisiveness, and action. The chaos of *in media res* & the multifaceted juggle although tiring and confusing most of the time does offer opportunity for cross-pollination, association, daydreaming, play, refuting linear, arborescent structures in favour of multiplicities, becoming, developing, a changing landscape in flux: and this is a rich grounding for the artist. Varda's umbilical cord of electricity to simultaneously limit and power her physical distance from home (and thereby her infant son) is an example of imaginative and practical

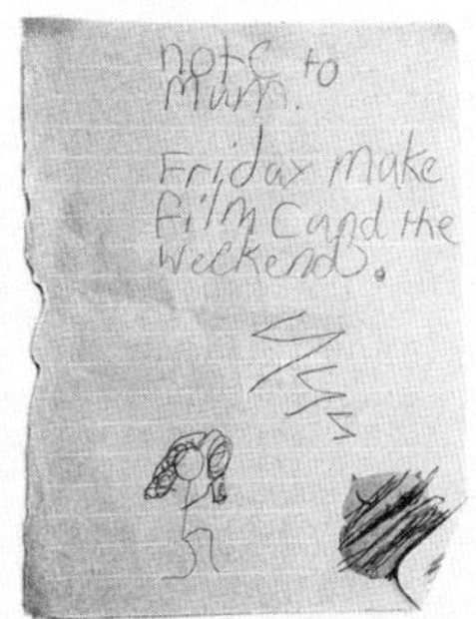

An invitation to make a film

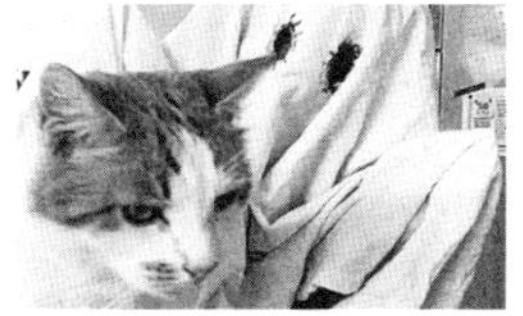

Abbe Leigh Fletcher, Lois Leonard and Frank Leonard, *A ghostly visit*, 2018, film still

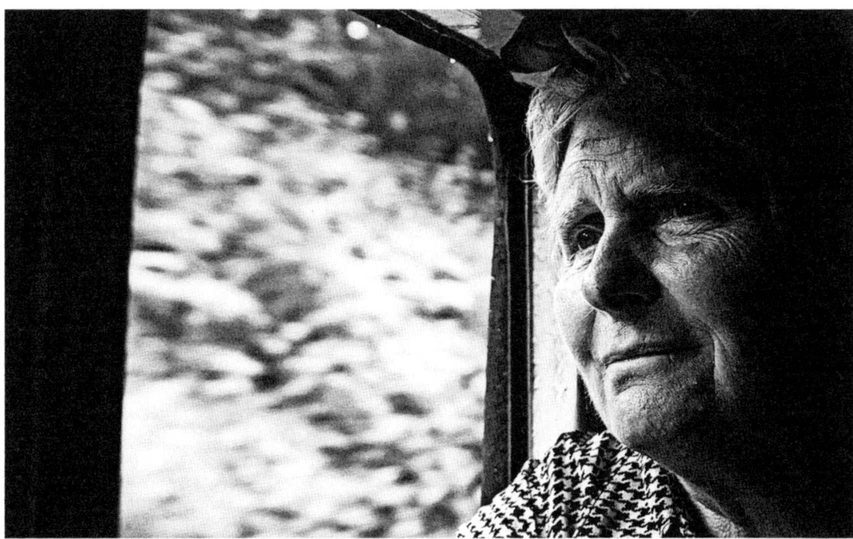

Shielagh Finlay in *Railwaywomen*, 2018, film still

De Certeau style tactics—her identifying the power cable as distinctly maternal positively claims this necessity as part of her artivism.

The *Film maker in the Family* project provides a modest documentation of a body of work across an eight-year period. Looking back at the project films, they are imperfect, awkward, roughly put together in places, polished in others but they constitute an output over a specific eight-year period. They show children growing, parents adapting creatively, they show an attempt to communicate, to make ideas visible. As an artist with an interest in aesthetics that do not aspire to the industry standard with its emphasis on production value, but that are related to social economic conditions and as an academic, in a position to ask questions, to champion other routes, and other aesthetics less mainstream. It has its limitations and restrictions. It is a no-budget way of working and thereby remains on a small scale, with quite particular aesthetics.

There is also the significant issue of putting your child on screen. I became increasingly uncomfortable about this, about the impact on the children, what they think of being on screen, where the film goes and how it will affect them. *Railwaywomen* was filmed in one day, but unlike with *7 Positions in 2 hours*, the web of arrangements behind the scenes to make this possible (as with any production) were kept hidden, the connections on screen between archetypes are what resonate.

After this film, my daughter asked if we could make a film together. We made *A Ghostly Visit* (2 min., 26 sec., 2018). I became her cinematographer and editor with her directing and taking turns with her brother to star in the film under a sheet with eye holes as the disappointed ghost who fails to scare anyone and ends up on the washing line. This is a good place for the project to finish, in that she has taken control of the process of filmmaking and that it has become a form of play, more about process than product: a documentation of an idea, a spark, of us playing together one afternoon. That this is a valid process and a good use of filmmaking in a family context, despite it being small scale, seemingly trivial, not counting for much, is nevertheless a creative application of storytelling and filmmaking as expression, and collaboration with family, for fun.

18. Deleuze and Guattari, *A Thousand Plateaus*, p. 28.

19. Jean-Cristophe Bailly's description of movement in German Romanticism in Deleuze and Guattari, *A Thousand Plateaus*, p. 28, note 25.

20. Jonas Mekas, 'A Call for a New Generation of Film-Makers', *Film Culture Reader*, ed. Adams P. Sitney (New York: Cooper Square Press, 2000), p. 75.

While Virginia Woolf was right about needing a space of one's own to create, rather than retreating from the world and shutting oneself away, where this is not possible, work thought through in the hubbub of family life, planned in snatched moments of quiet and produced in any way possible, shows versatility as an adaptable tactic of creativity and collaboration and community as lateral facilitators in a collective rhizomatic approach that is both in constant flux and becoming.

'The rhizome is alliance, uniquely alliance. The tree imposes the verb "to be", but the fabric of the rhizome is the conjunction "and…and...and."'[18] Rather than starting at the beginning, seeking a beginning, which implies a false conception of voyage and movement, a rhizomatic approach precedes 'from the middle, through the middle, coming and going rather than starting and finishing'[19] which captures the *in media res* of making with children in tow, inclusively, collectively, pragmatically and creatively.

This is a small contribution towards a cinema that could be a combination of Winnicott's statement that a mother (or parent) has only to be *good enough*, combined with the logistically collective possibilities of the rhizome building on work-in-progress and spurred on by Jonas Mekas' call for 'less perfect, more free films'.[20]

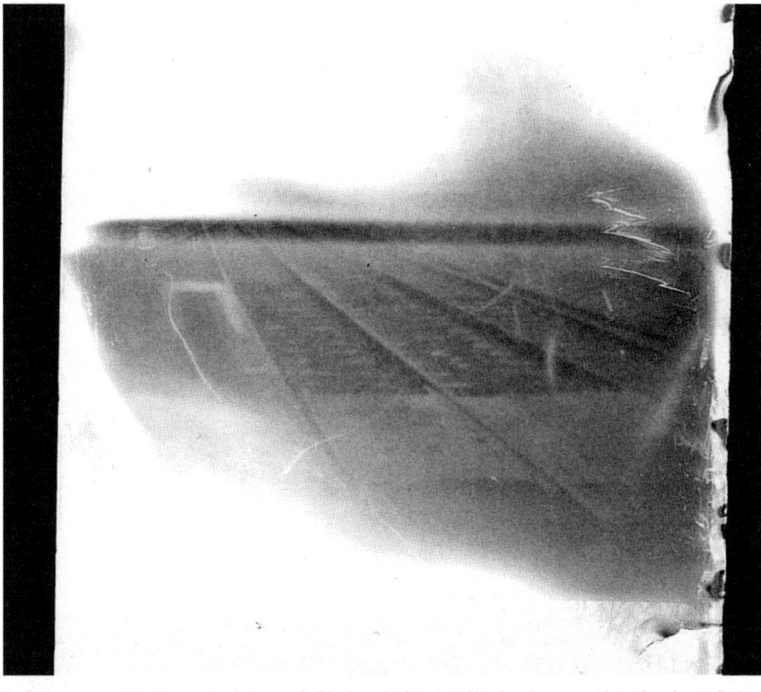

Railwaywomen, 2018, Brownie photograph, black and white 120 film, hand processed (cut [track copy])

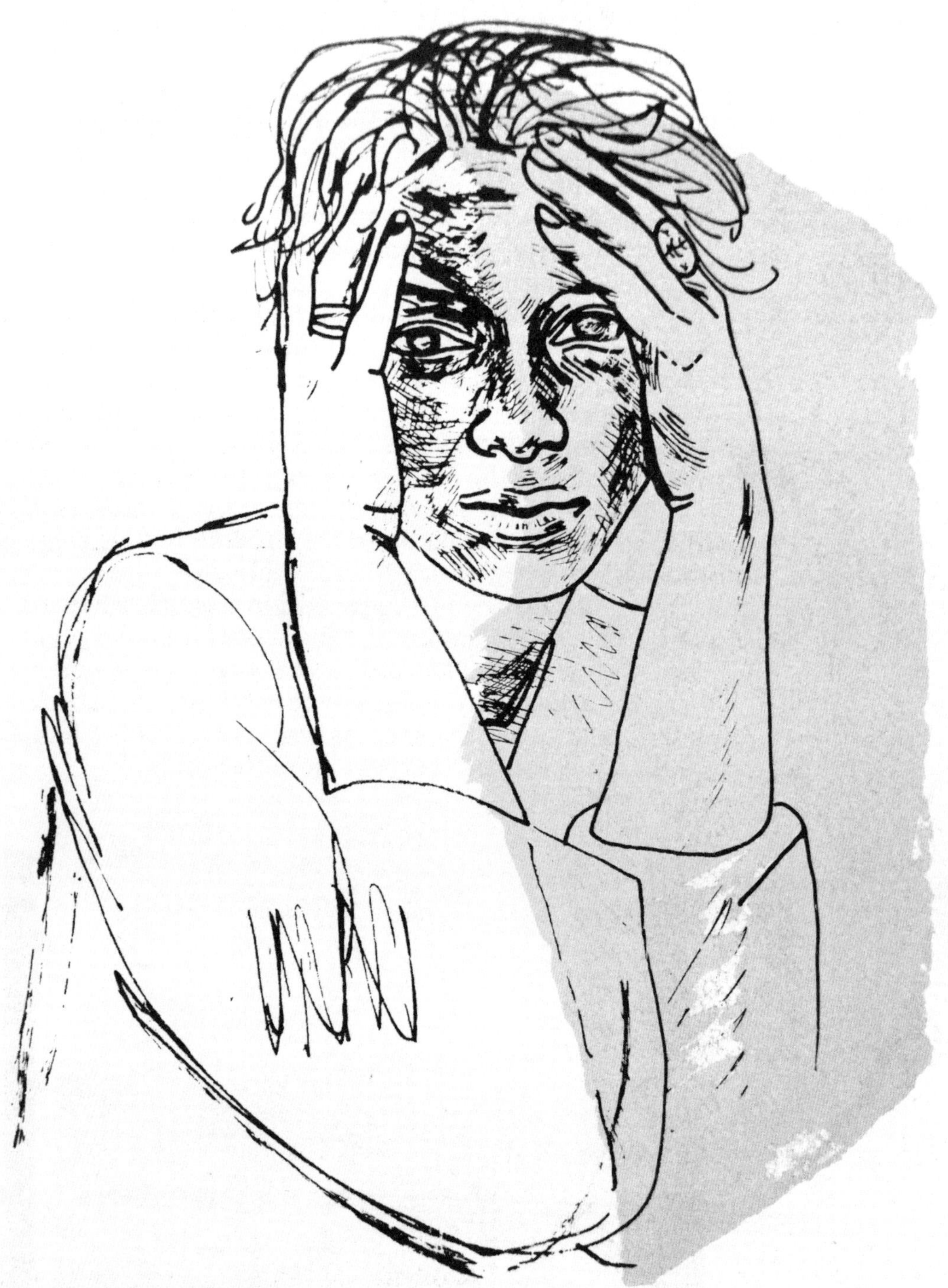

Fig. 1
Sonja van Kerkhoff, *Fran*, 1985, silkscreen on paper, 35 × 20 cm, edition of 30

FUZZY-EDGED FEMINISM
When the Artist is a She

Sonja van Kerkhoff

I was aware that being female was problematic growing up in conservative rural Aotearoa/New Zealand. My first fight was to stay at school past age fifteen when my father wanted me to leave to work on the farm. Then it was to get the courage and the means to go to art school. I was nineteen when I quit my job and hitchhiked 1100 km to attend the Dunedin School of Visual Arts. But my biggest journey was moving into a world of reading.

Fig. 1 Sonja van Kerkhoff, *Fran*, 1985
A year or so later an older man asked me if I would call myself a feminist. I said I wouldn't. He said he was disappointed in me. For me at the time, any label was problematic. I was dealing with my working-class background in a world where few others had literacy issues.

Fig. 2 *In the Woods*, 1989

I was making art as a woman and women were often protagonists in my work. But that was not the same as being informed by feminism in a sociological or mindful sense. The man was possibly disappointed because he saw my independence as a feminist stance. In truth I was struggling and couldn't give myself any label. It infuriated me that the woodwork tutor refused to teach me basic woodworking skills because unlike the males I had had no basics in high school. I refused to give up and time after time wood would go flying across the room because I had used the clamps incorrectly. And I would pick up the pieces and start over. So I was certainly aware of the different gendered expectations at art school. It was expected that because I was a female I would stick to painting or drawing like the others. It was also assumed that I didn't question the tradition of the female form as an object rather than subject. But to call myself a feminist was too much for me.

Fig. 3 *Portrait of the artist as a bottled peach*, 1989

In 1989 I moved to the Netherlands to do a Masters in Fine Arts and everything changed. Now the sexism hit me in the face. I was even told that my brushes were too small. Initially in response I made a series of angry female ancestor forms with open vaginas. The tutors called them "monsters" and the sexism was so vile that one teacher saw nothing wrong with yelling at the top of his voice 'here comes the feminist', to which

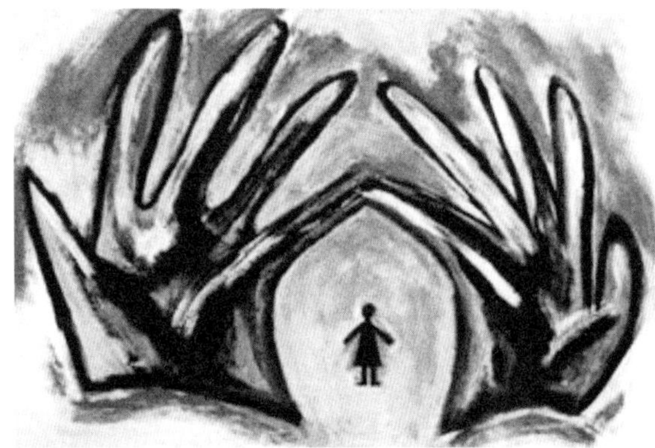

Fig. 2
Sonja van Kerkhoff, *In the Woods*, 1989, acrylic on paper, 40 x 70 cm

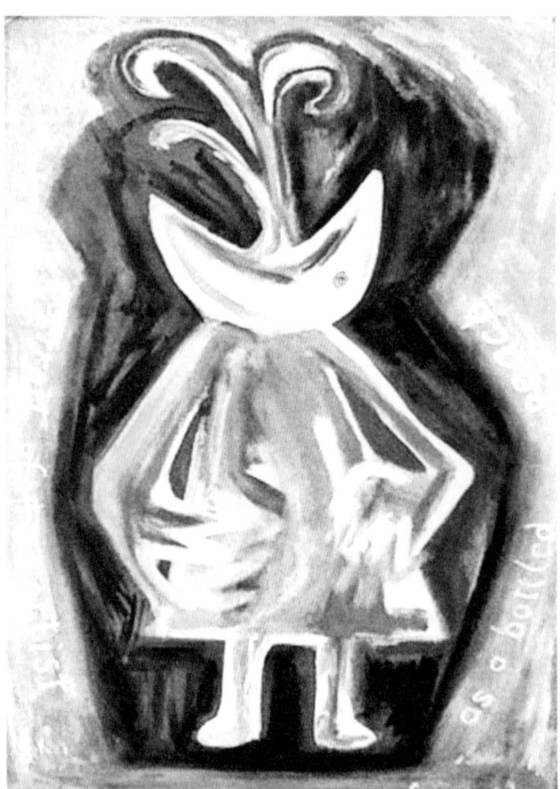

Fig. 3
Sonja van Kerkhoff, *Portrait of the artist as a bottled peach*, 1989, acrylic on canvas, 80 x 50 cm

Feminist Art Activisms and Artivisms

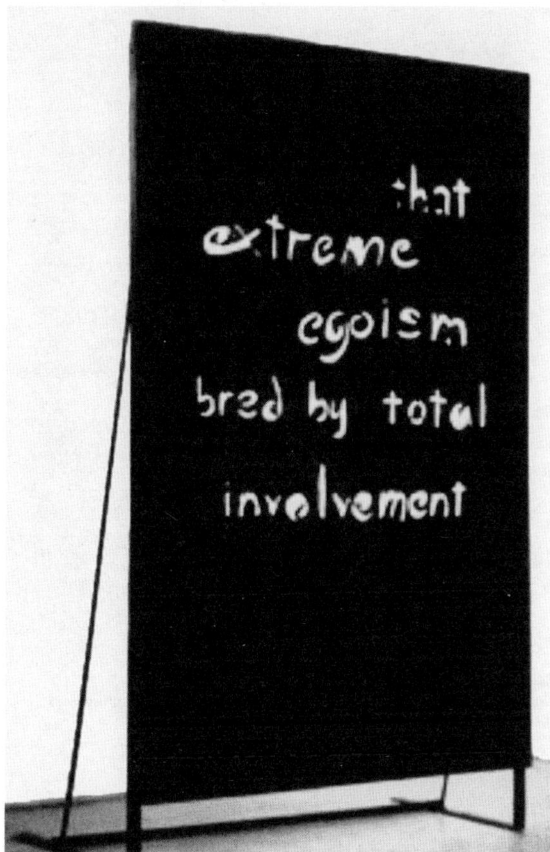

Fig. 4
Sonja van Kerkhoff, *That extreme egoism*, 1990, canvas, metal, tar, 200 x 100 cm

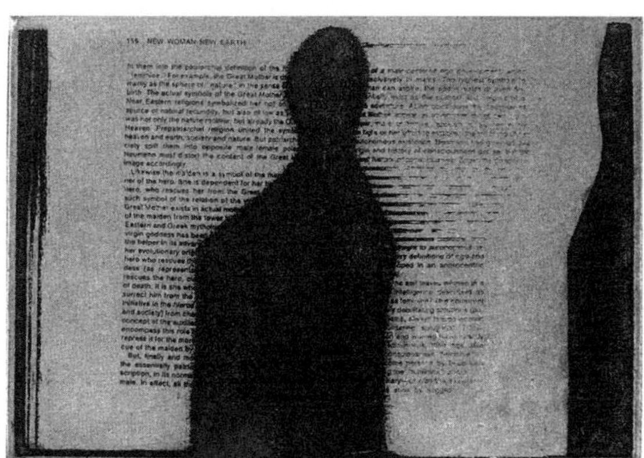

Fig. 5
Sonja van Kerkhoff, *Schaduw* (Shadow), 1990, etching on paper, 10 x 15 cm, edition of 40. The barely legible text is p. 155 from Rosemary Radford Ruether's New Woman New Earth.

I responded, 'it is not an insult'. I upped the ante, saying to my seven male tutors 'where are the female tutors?'

Fig. 4 *That extreme egoism*, 1990
I was told to make independent art, which meant making abstract expressionist art like the other students. In response I put a canvas on legs, cut out the text 'That extreme egoism bred by total involvement' and tarred it. There was no comment from any of the tutors but some students in the sculpture department saw this, which was a life saver because that led to contacts with other tutors.

Fig. 5 *Schaduw [Shadow]*, 1990
I realized I needed to find a language to fight with so my work could not be so easily dismissed. Finding feminist literature in the library helped, as well as discovering the Women Artists Slide Library in London. My subscription to their journal' became a valuable connection to what other artists were making and doing. This gave the reading I was doing a grounding. Here artists were also dealing with a world where the artist was a woman.

Note 1. *Women Artists Slide Library Newsletter* (1985–1990) became *Women's Art Magazine* (1990–1995), then *Make* (1996–2002), as the Women Artists Slide Library became the Women's Art Library (MAKE) in the UK and moved from an independent arts organization and charity to an archive in a University setting: www.gold.ac.uk/make.

Fig. 6 *Feminism as an active desire*, 1993

And now my work became more political. Feminism became a strategy for my Otherness in this Dutch male environment. Many of the feminist artists I was reading about brought the domestic into the frame. Although my day-to-day life too had nappies and babies, finding my feminist voice meant making my art more conceptually oriented.

Fig. 7 *Dress it up*, 1993/2004

I returned to art school three days after the birth of my first child to find that the tutors had taken my studio as a staff room for themselves. My stuff was lying in the corridor. I had no studio. I was told I should leave because I now had a baby. I rang the head of the department at his home and told him I needed a space. He barked back that it was not his responsibility. He was the one who had taken my studio away. None of my fellow students offered to help but I also didn't ask them. They were about five years younger and the school had not had a female student with a baby before. This was in 1990 in the Netherlands! I solved this by finding a room the caretaker used for storage and finding unused shelves and corners in other departments throughout the art school buildings. Some students in other departments also let me leave materials in their studios. In being forced to find my own working spaces, I met students and studio assistants outside of the painting department and some who didn't think it was odd to be a mother and an art student.

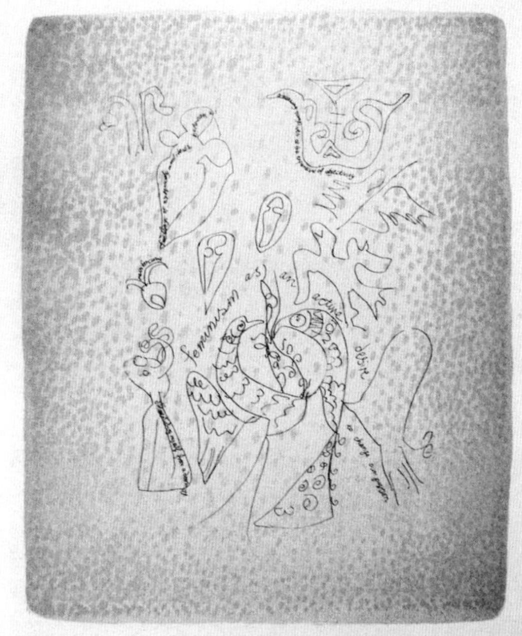

Fig. 6
Sonja van Kerkhoff, *Feminism as an active desire*, 1993, lithograph and silkscreen on paper, 35 × 20 cm, edition of 15

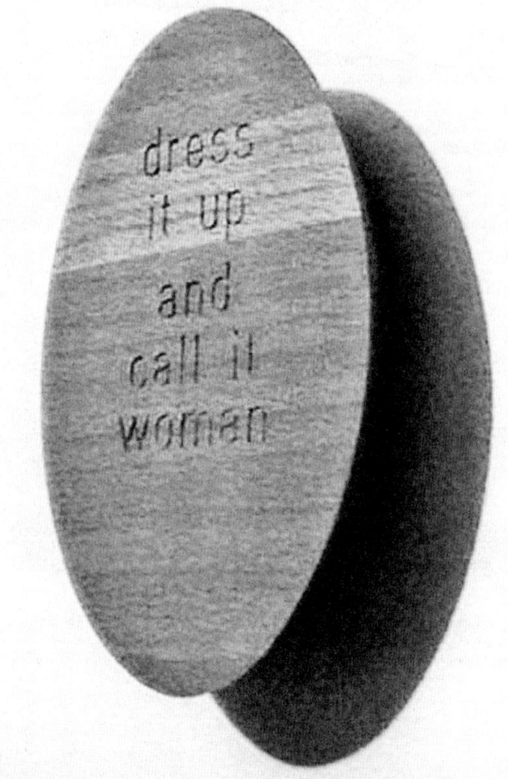

Fig. 7
Sonja van Kerkhoff, *Dress it up*, 1993/2004, engraved wood, gold paint, 12 x 8 x 5 cm

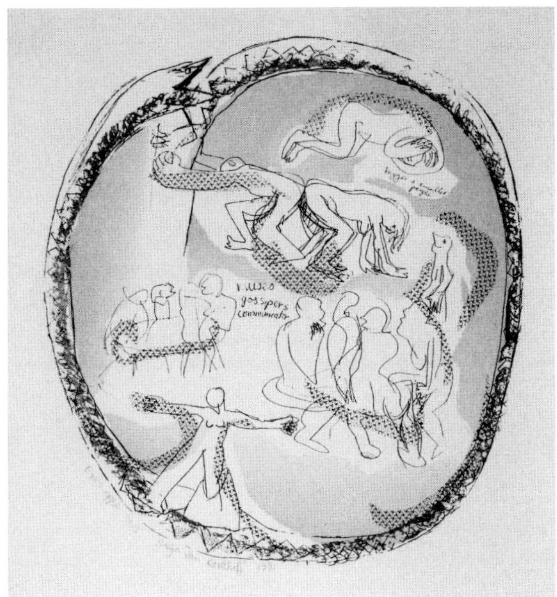

Fig. 8
Sonja van Kerkhoff, *Eve's Apple*, 1992, lithograph and silkscreen on paper,
25 x 25 cm, edition of 15

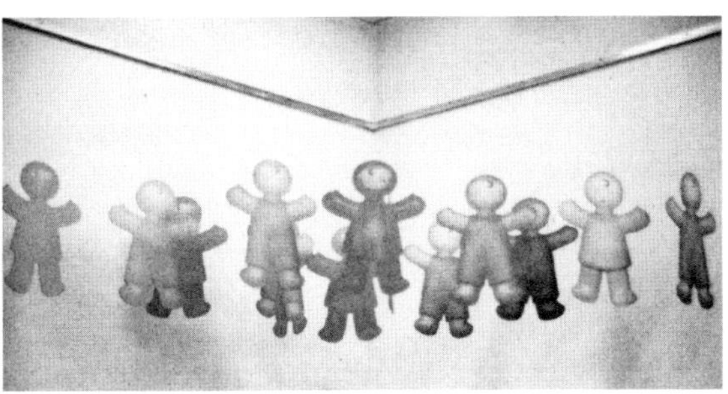

Fig. 9
Sonja van Kerkhoff, *First Lessons in Relativity*, 1992, suspended cardboard
silkscreened on both sides, 50 × 30 cm (each). The colours change in a range
from pink to blue.

Fig. 8 *Eve's Apple*, 1992

So having a room of my own was
not so vital because I had found
other spaces. One had video editing
equipment in it. Within a year I was
making videos, thanks to a tutor
in another department. So, I ended
up working in many areas of the
school. The rigidity of that painting
department still amazes me. Once, to
teach me a lesson, the caretaker locked
me inside the building with my baby
so I had to hand the baby out through
a top window to a friend standing
outside on a ladder.

Fig. 9 *First Lessons in Relativity*, 1992

The idea that a mother should stay
at home and babies were not allowed
in the public domain was a new
experience for me and a battle. On
the bus, on the train, I was berated by
strangers. Taking my baby, alone, on
public transport, became a political
act and I started to understand why
women would stay at home. It wasn't
all negative, at a theory conference in
Amsterdam ('The Point of Theory',
1993, coordinated by Mieke Bal and
Inge Boer), my breastfeeding presence
was welcomed but one of the male
presenters sat on the floor beside me
and hissed 'This is disgusting'. I hope
he ate his words later when, for a
group photo, they wanted the equally
bald baby next to him. Today he is
a Professor of Literary Studies in a
Dutch university.

Months later, it shocked me to
be thrown out of the World Wide
Video Festival in The Hague because
of my son's presence. But I didn't
leave without a discussion about

how unreasonable this was given that everyone was wearing headphones. I was told 'No one else does this'. In the Netherlands, female artists, it seems, have children extremely rarely. I forced myself to move past how upset I was and wrote the script for the video *Wrapping for a marginal citizen* on the train home.

Fig. 10 *Wrapping for a marginal citizen, 1994*

In my final year, the painting department said they had listened to me and were going to hire a female guest tutor. She seemed afraid of me, spent her time with the males and gave me a "C" which was used against me by the male tutors when they tried to get me to leave again. Decades later she apologized to me.

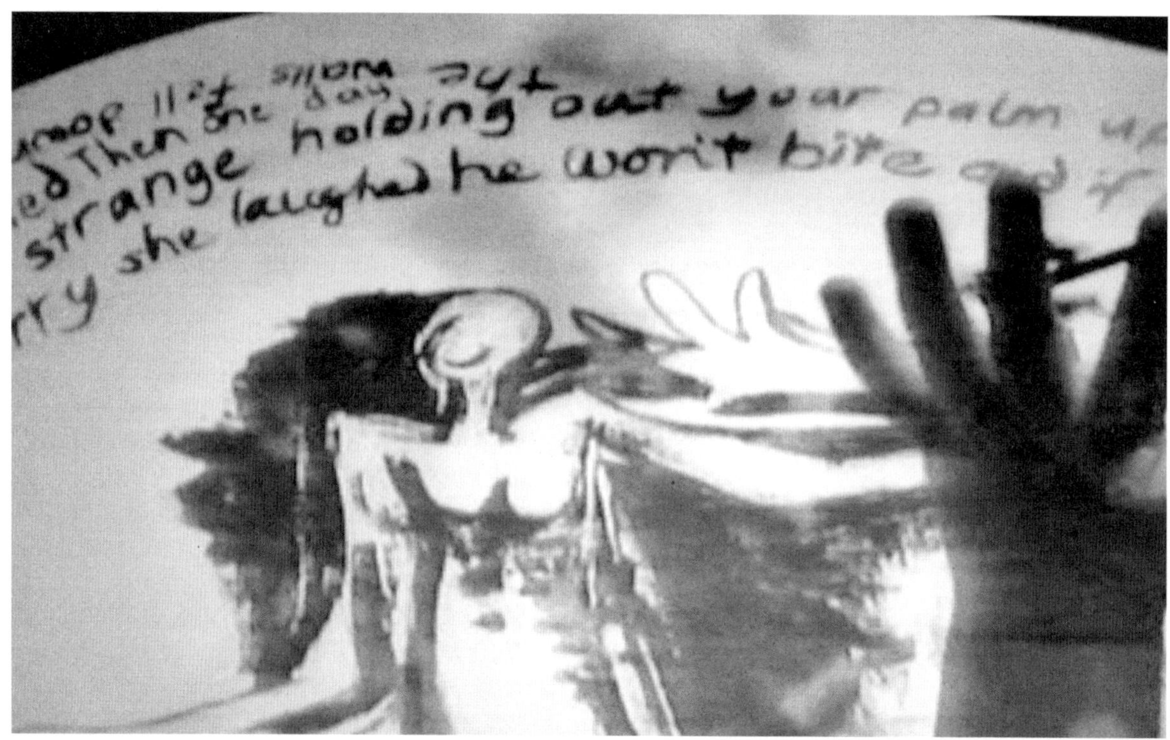

Fig. 10
Sonja van Kerkhoff, *Wrapping for a marginal citizen*, 1994, 13', video still.
Inspired by Rebecca Horn's use of her own sculpture in her films, the props in this film were my sculpture, such as the detail of 'Bijzettafel' (Side Table) in this still. Here, a handwritten text under the glass top of a custom-made table tells of two women joking about blind fools and walls falling down. It is a text you read as you walk around the table, and become dizzy.

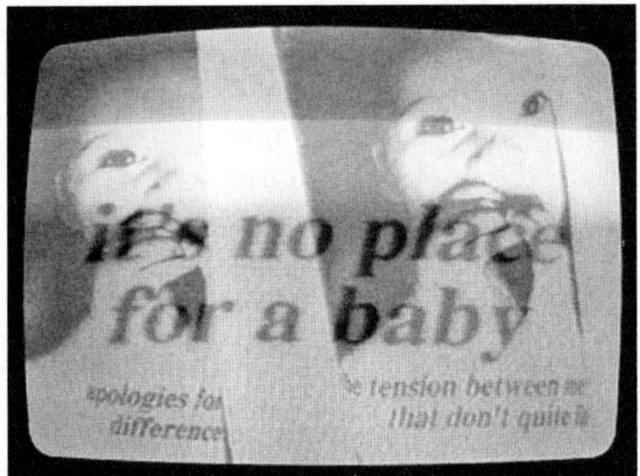

Fig. 11
Sonja van Kerkhoff, *Wrapping for a marginal citizen*, 1994, 13', video still

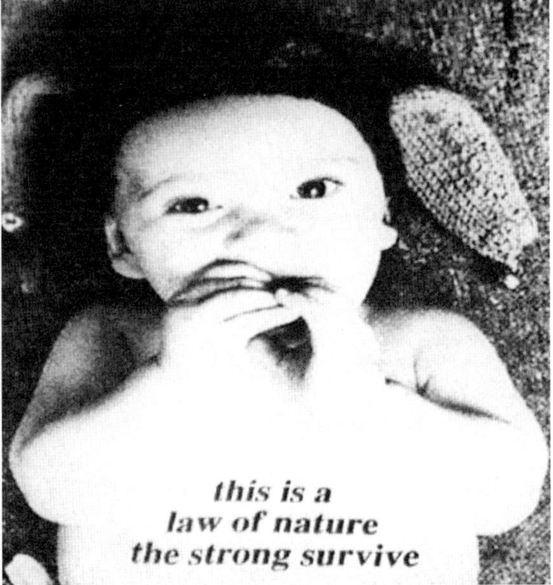

Fig. 12
Sonja van Kerkhoff, *Wrapping for a marginal citizen*, 1994, detail of a
1200 × 50 cm silkscreen print and the image used in the 2002 performance
Mother and Child

Fig. 11 *Wrapping for a marginal citizen, 1994*

These experiences were partly because in the Netherlands the word feminist is polarized more than it was or is in New Zealand. Breastfeeding in public spaces was not exceptional in New Zealand and in the 1980s it was not an issue for a woman to have a baby and be a full-time student. In the Netherlands even today, when I say 'I am a feminist' there is often the knee-jerk response or some sign of discomfort, which I generally ignore because there's little point in explaining that feminism is a way of looking at the world.

Fig. 12 *Wrapping for a marginal citizen, 1994*

I refer to my approach as fuzzy-edged feminism, not as a form of apologetic but as a strategic position. Feminism slides into all worlds and in general I choose a conceptual approach in my artworks as a means to address multiple issues blurring the edges of the binary artifice of the object/subject as well as the dichotomy between the marginalized Other and the unmarked Subject at the centre.

Fig. 13 *Your honour*, 1992

I found that using words with objects or imagery to muddy the waters was a way to give a twist—be it humour, a mismatch or poeticism—to statements with fuzzy edges. It was also a response to the pressure that an artist should present a consistent style. These days this is nothing new but then it was a battle and even Alexis Hunter told me that I should only present one type of work so the galleries would give it value. She divided her work into the photographic and the painterly[2] (and sometimes performance) and kept the presentation of these in distinct art worlds. Later she told me that she decided not to exhibit her paintings anymore, so her early photographic works from the 1970s and 1980s would not be negatively affected in the art market. Just before she died in 2014, her last work was an unfinished painterly landscape. It seems to me that a feminine or female tendency is to multi-task, whether out of necessity or from our training since babyhood, and that could be why many female artists work across media. For me it is both strategic and political, and seems natural.

Note 2. See Sonja van Kerkhoff, 'Alexis Hunter: The Feminist is in the Room', *EyeContactSite*, September 2015, http://eyecontactsite.com/2015/09/alexis-hunter-the-feminist-is-in-the-room. Alexis Hunter lived in London but was from and showed regularly in New Zealand.

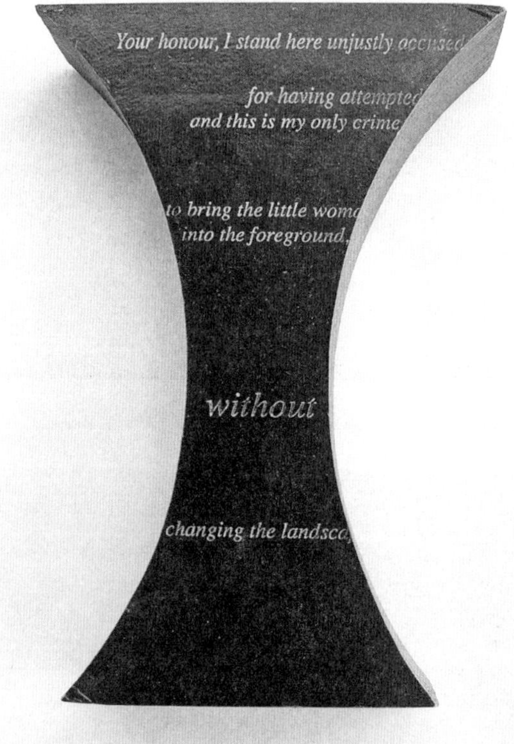

Fig. 13
Sonja van Kerkhoff, *Your honour*, 1992, etching on 19 layers of cardboard which can be stood or hang, 20 × 15 × 8 cm, edition of 19. The text reads: 'Your honour, I stand here unjustly accused for having attempted and this in my only crime to bring the little woman into the foreground, without changing the landscape.'

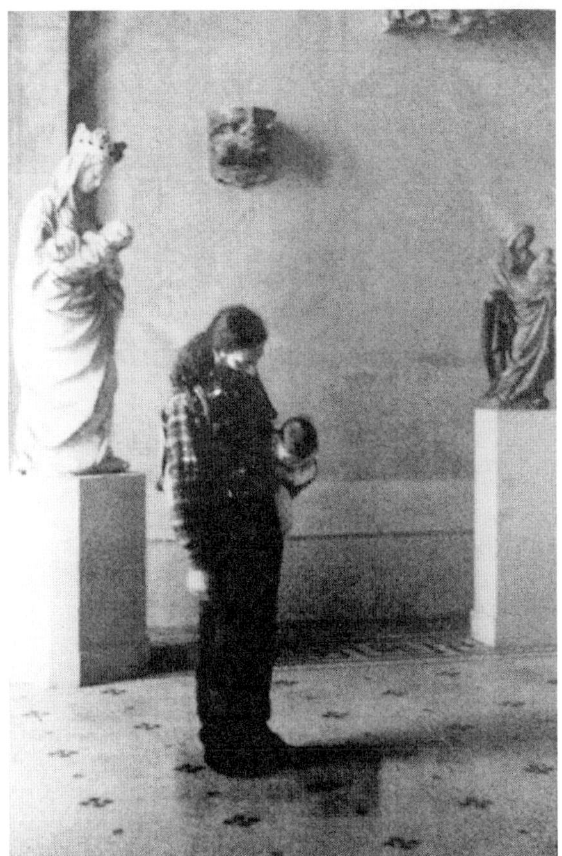

Fig. 14 *Mutability*, 1994

In 1994, *Mutability* was selected by the Amsterdam feminist gallery, Amazone, and as part of a public talk for the *Prima Donna* show, I was asked why my Madonna was a man. My response was that until men become mothers we won't have equality and until men can see or read feminism, the imbalance won't change.

This work relates to the idealization of motherhood, which distances and fossilizes the reality of mothering, so for me it wasn't just about the validation of subjectivity (the mutable pedestal), although this was not excluded, but about questioning norms that put motherhood into certain boxes. As a mother, I didn't have to limit my career as an artist. Things changed but I had a partner who did as much mothering as I did so I had a good night's sleep and was able to continue working in a career with little monetary reward. It meant also attending conferences and gallery events as a single woman (the self-employed husband had the kids) so I was taken more seriously as an artist.

Fig. 15 *Movement for Mother and Child, 2002*

This freedom also made it a choice, for me, to show my motherhood in my artworks. The performance *Movement for Mother and Child* addresses 'the gendered nature of knowledge claims'[3] while acknowledging that the domestic can be a prison if there are no escape routes. The piece ends with the two of us walking into the audience (and dissolving "the stage"), then out onto the street, while giving out cards with the text 'It is a law of nature the strong survive'.

Note 3. Julia Rothenberg, 'Form, Utopia, and Feminist Performance Art: Toward a Rehabilitation of Adorno's Aesthetic Theory', *telos* 137 (Winter 2006), pp. 36–66.

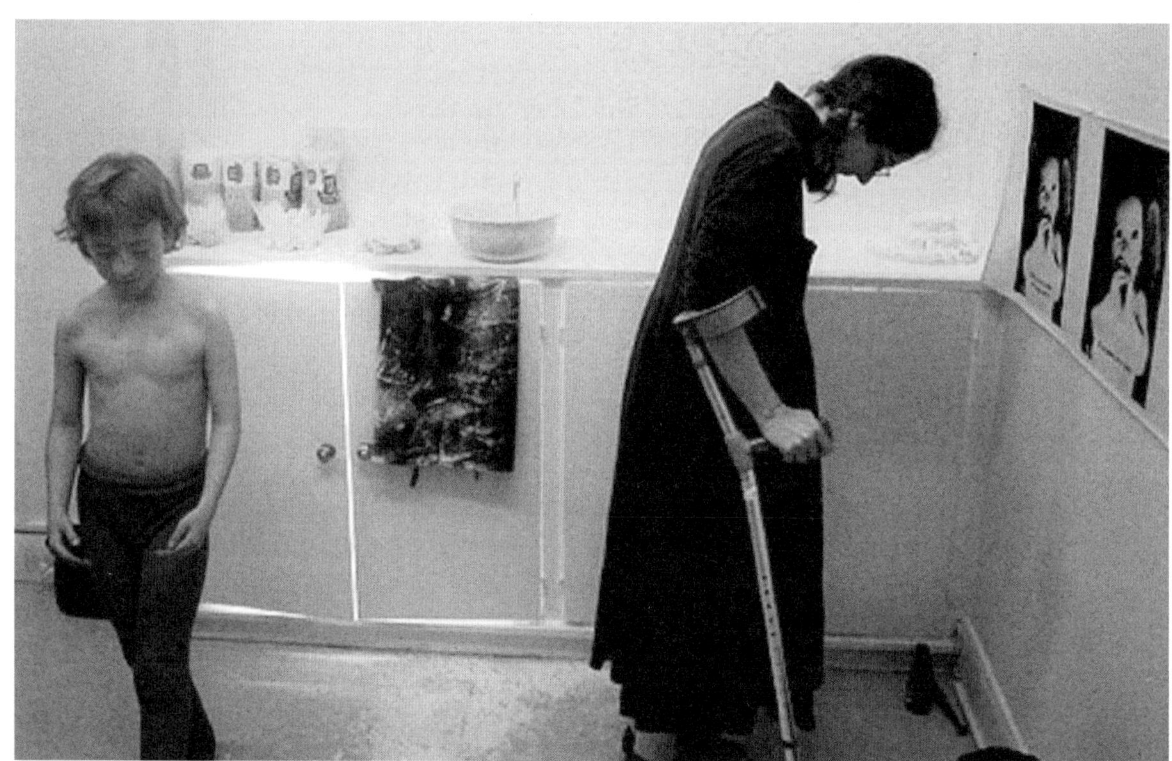

Fig. 15
Sonja van Kerkhoff, *Movement for Mother and Child*, 2002, 10' performance with my 9 year old son, in 'Domestically Spaced', Space Station Sixty-Five, London. Photo: Rob Weinberg

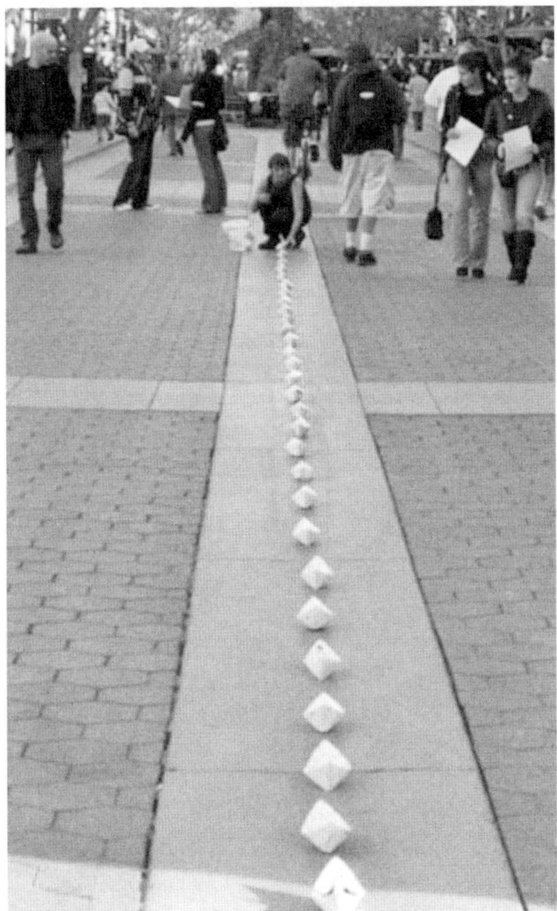

Fig. 16
Sonja van Kerkhoff, *Colonizing Santa Monica*, 2009, paperboats made out of pages from my son's school writing exercises. Performance in the Santa Monica Promenade, Los Angeles. Photo: Tony Lee

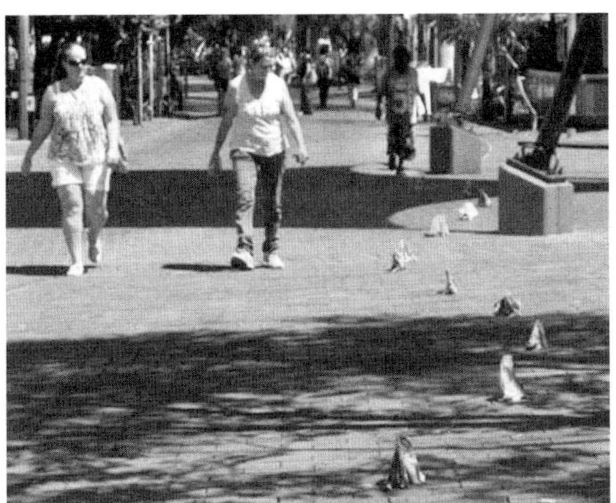

Fig. 17
Sonja van Kerkhoff, *Caravan From Istanbul, Mparntwe*, 2012, performance in Alice Springs, Australia. This caravan of origami elephants began in 2011 at Istanbul and were folded from newspapers collected enroute.

Fig. 16 *Colonizing Santa Monica, 2009*

My performances where I "colonialize" are equally strategic when it comes to expressing a feminist take on the world. I was well aware that as a small white woman I posed no threat to police, then security, then another branch of the police, each time they attempted to move me on from the Santa Monica pedestrian way. I was also aware that they would not take me as seriously as a man in a suit. The colonizers didn't ask for permission so neither did I, and with each argument they presented I came back with a counter argument until I had reached the end of the street.

Fig. 17 *Caravan From Istanbul, Mparntwe, 2012*

In 2012, in Alice Springs, a similar performance was stopped when I was ordered off the street by men with big cages on their truck. I was prepared for their arrival because, minutes before, all the Aboriginals watching and commenting had suddenly disappeared from the main street. I had expected that I would have been able to argue my way as I had in other places but these men were in no mood for a poetic intervention of folded paper elephants on their near empty pedestrian street. However, choosing to blur the edges between the art and public space means sometimes people will perceive this as a transgression.

Fig. 18 *19 Gay Men and The Throne of God*, 2017

Other works that transform spaces are my choreographed walks in which I direct people (attending an event) to walk slowly and film them. The men in the video, *19 Gay Men and The Throne of God* were part of a tour group. I blur the borders in my feminist activist works because as I read it, feminism is not one thing nor a particular level of attention or focus. I love art that moves me in diverse ways and so I think there are all manner of ways of being an activist as an artist. In *19 Gay Men and The Throne of God* an all-male cast took my directions, and the gaze is mine, a woman's. Some could argue that this is not a feminist work because the protagonists are male and the work is about giving them space, but the camera whose voice is heard is female because it is mine. More importantly the viewer is whatever the viewer wants to be with fuzzy edges—you see men walking and hear women singing. Some might ask, why I as a straight cis female have made a work featuring gays. I am a Bahai and it irks me that many of my co-religionists see something wrong with homosexuality, so in another of my worlds, I write a blog centred on gay rights. Essentialism has the danger of not only limiting one's subject matter but also one's responsibility.

Fig. 19 *Pop-up onna-bugeisha*, 2013

This is not to suggest that there isn't a place for works that foreground feminist concerns such as visibility. For a call on "Samurai Heroes" for a Leiden exhibition, I thought why

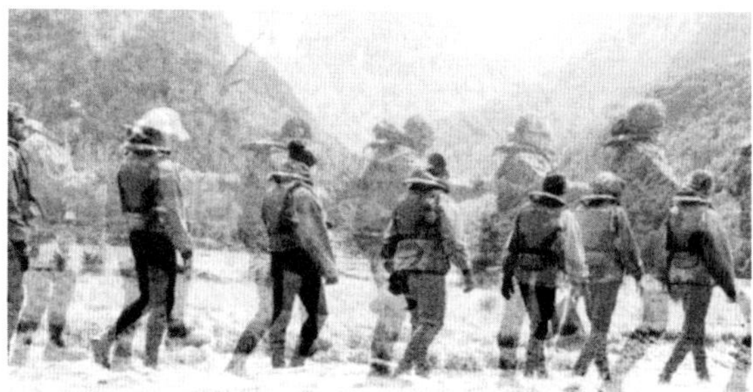

Fig. 18
Sonja van Kerkhoff, *19 Gay Men and The Throne of God*, 2017, still, 5'10. Filmed during the 2015 Toto Tours New Zealand excursion north of Glenorchy. Music by The Gazebo Girls (Penni Bousfield and Janet Muggeridge), a traditional Shaker hymn, arranged by Penni Bousfield, New Zealand.

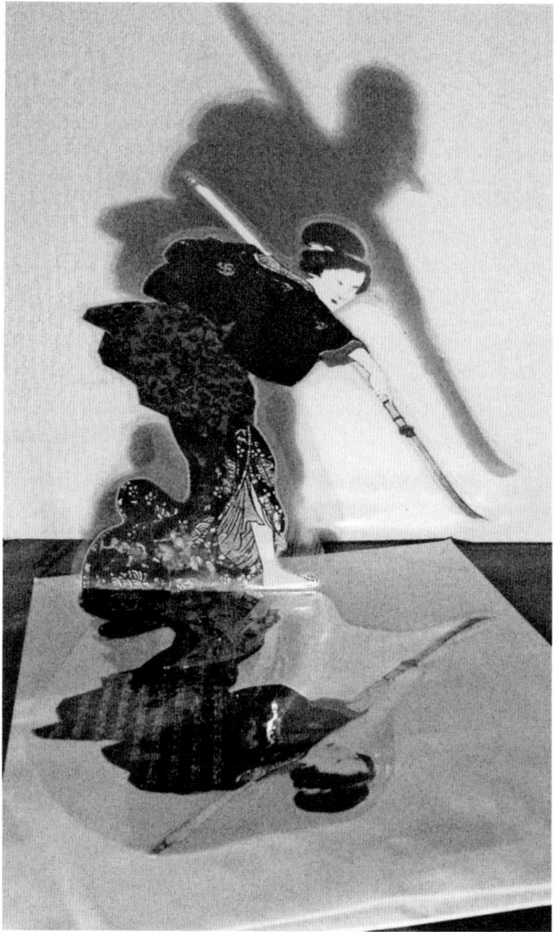

Fig. 19
Sonja van Kerkhoff, *Pop-up onna-bugeisha*, 2013, computer print on transparency, Dutch TNT (postal service logo in use between 1998 and 2011) envelope, 20 × 25 × 27 cm, edition of 19

Feminist Art Activisms and Artivisms

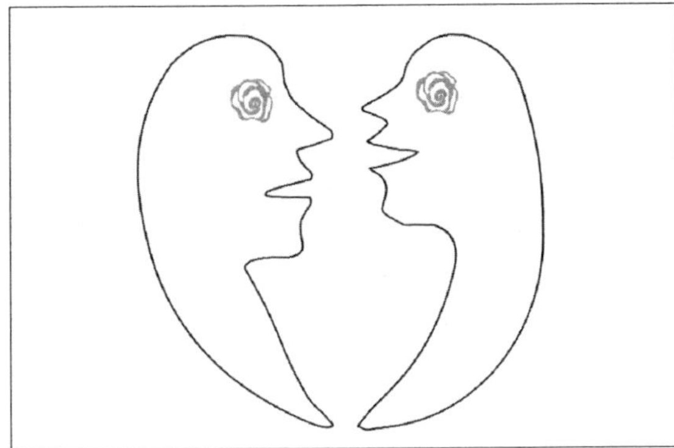

Fig. 20
Sonja van Kerkhoff, *Fading Roses*, 2004/2014, 4'20 animation,
music by Kath Tait

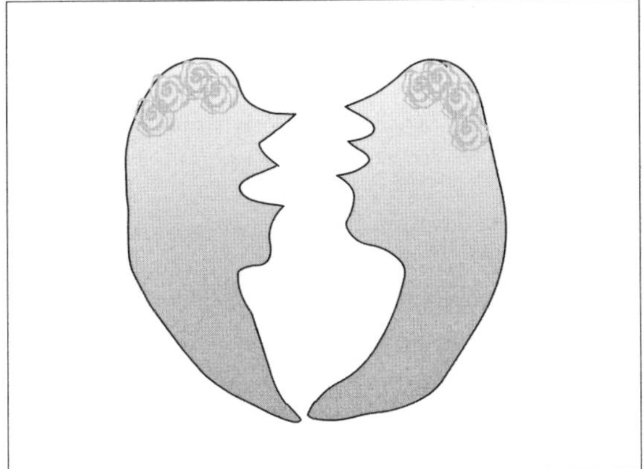

Fig. 21
Sonja van Kerkhoff, *Fading Roses*, 2004/2014, 4'20 animation,
music by Kath Tait

only men? My research found the *onna-bugeisha*, a female warrior in the Japanese upper class who predated the Samurai. The materials I chose, a fold-up illustration of a historical figure (a sixteenth-century illustration of Ishi-jo wielding a naginata) fixed on an envelope bearing a bygone Dutch postal logo, was not just a making visible of the female, but an example of an alternative to the mainstream. While the agency of gender visibility is an important aspect here, this work was also about transience—she stands up now and the shadow gives her a presence because of being put in the spotlight, but she or anything else can just as easily be folded down and slid into the envelope (and forgotten).

Fig. 20 and Fig. 21 *Fading Roses,* 2004/2014

Fading Roses is an animation on ageing. The use of white space and simple lines with sparse imagery was in part to deal with my awareness of data limitations for those on low incomes (in 2004) but also as a pointer towards using new media in 'non-traditional ways, and a use of reflexivity that exposes materiality and a sense of process'.[4] I chose cartoon-like animation as a front for references to materiality and immateriality as well as more specifically to fertility goddesses, so like a work of art, the recycled re-referenced imagery illustrates and questions the narrative.

Note 4. Miriam Harris, Lilly Husbands and Paul Taberham, eds., *Experimental Animation: From Analogue to Digital* (London: Routledge, 2019), p. 8.

Fig. 22 *Tomorrow will never be the same,* 2007

At the age of 45, frustrated with my limited programming skills, I embarked on a Masters in Computer Science, while my children were teenagers, and while working part-time for Dutch Educational Broadcasting as a multimedia designer. It was yet another world dominated by men and male ways of operating, but now my age and experience helped, I think, to have a stronger effect on the lecturers and other students. The title, *Tomorrow will be the same but not as this is* is the title of a famous painting by New Zealand artist Colin McCahon, an iconic artist in the New Zealand art world. In this work, the projected image of Mondrian's *Broadway Boogie Woogie* is infected with random repositionings of its own colours set in action by the visitor's mouse clicks. This chain reaction of pixel-by-pixel colour swapping starts to dissolve the original image, which continually mutates until the computer is turned off, the image is refreshed to start over, or the screen eventually mutates to black. The assignment for this work was to create a system that mimicked artificial intelligence (here each click swaps with another colour in the image, then that pixel creates 7 "children", which land randomly on the same image and in turn swap colours and so on). My fellow student, Jiang Yiwei, was happy to work with me on an assignment that also had aesthetic and cultural ramifications.

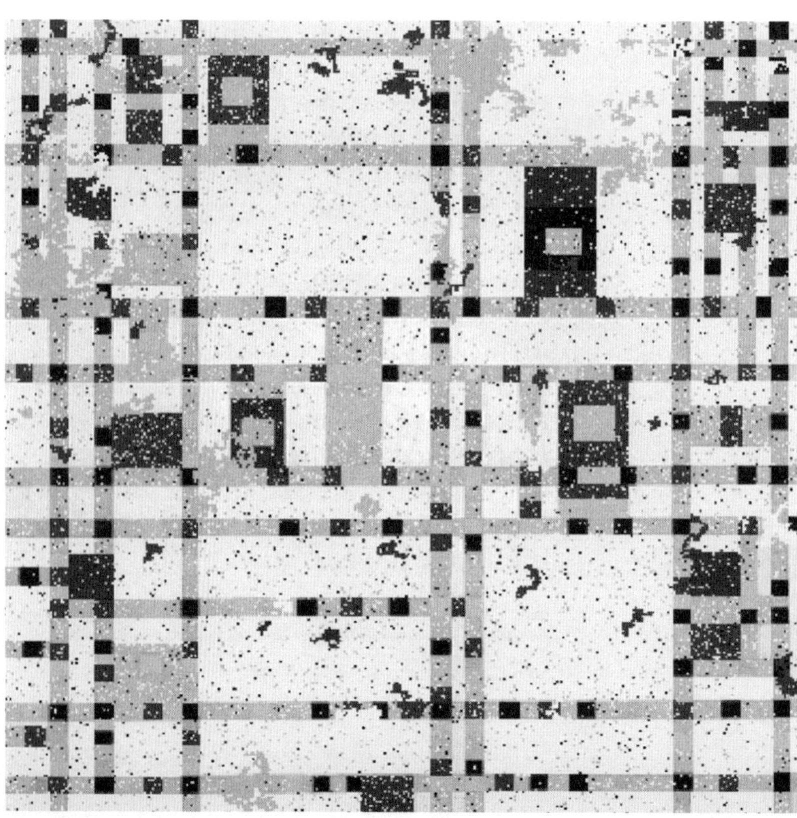

Fig. 22
Jiang Yiwei and Sonja van Kerkhoff, *Tomorrow will never be the same,* 2007, interactive projection, screenshot

Fig. 23 *Waka Huia* (Feather Vessel), 2009

While feminism has been and is important to me, the Maori world is and has been an equally important part of my ways of thinking and reading the world. The work *Waka Huia* foregrounds colonialization from a New Zealand Maori cultural background. I have access, as a *Pakeha* (of European descent), because I speak and sing in this language. Having the Maori culture as part of my baggage has helped me deal with sexism because of my dual experiences in New Zealand European and Maori worlds. I stopped painting *matua* (ancestor figures) in the early 1990s for the same reason I dropped painting my vagina paintings, because I was sick of them being dismissed as "monsters" or the exotic. I wanted to be an artist engaged with the Western contemporary art world, which meant using visual languages that couldn't easily be labelled outsider. However, it is not that I have stopped using figuration or non-Western imagery, but I have changed how to present this. In *Waka Huia*, each line of the feather is drawn with fine spiralling lines (a loose referencing of *kowhaiwhai*, a type of rafter pattern on Maori meeting houses symbolizing the ribs of the ancestor), while the colour and contour of the feather is from a scan of an actual feather of this extinct New Zealand bird, found in the collection of the Leiden Museum of Natural History. The title can mean feather vessel or boat, and treasure box. *Huia* is a common but not exclusively female name. *Waka Huia* was also made in response to the Leiden exhibition, 'Rijns Water' (Rhine Water).[5] The Rhine flows through Leiden past the door of this gallery. For this exhibition in the Netherlands, some of this water was poured into the feather-boat as if the vessel might transport some drops back to its New Zealand homeland.

Note 5. *Waka Huia* was shown in 'Rijns Water' (Rhine Water), Sidac Studio, Leiden, The Netherlands, July–August 2009. Sidac Studio (1995–2018) was a gallery and project space coordinated by Dutch artist, Piet Franzen.

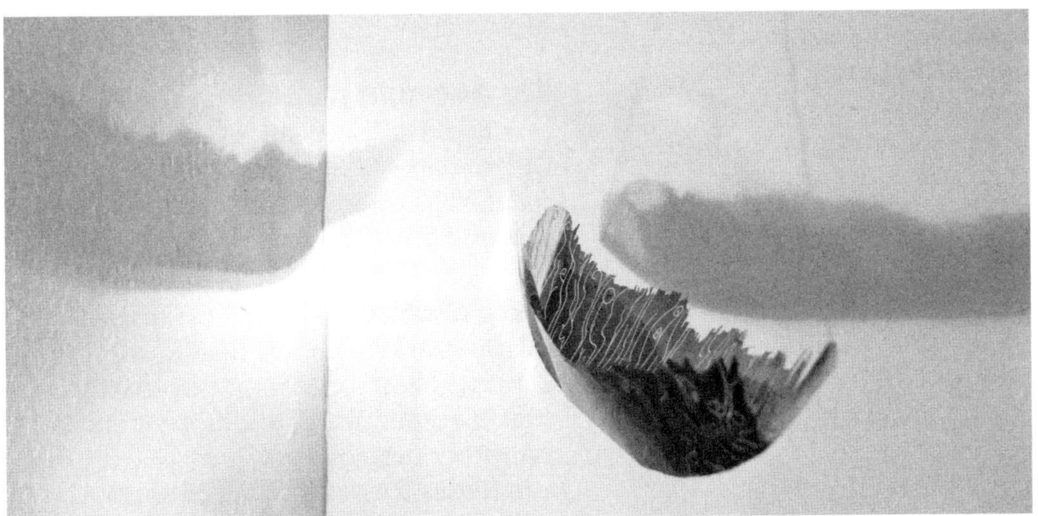

Fig. 23
Sonja van Kerkhoff, *Waka Huia* (Feather Vessel), 2009, computer print, nylon cord, edition of 35.
Shown at Blanc Compound, Quezon City, in the multi-venue international 'Nothing To Declare' exhibitions, performances and talks on migration in a contemporary art context in Manila, The Philippines, October 2011–January 2012. Curated by Flaudette May Datuin (College of Arts and Letters, University of the Philippines), Josephine Turalba (Dean, School of Fine Arts and Design, Philippine Women's University) and Precious Leano (Executive Director, Filipino Visual Arts and Design Rights Organization), https://nothing2declare2011.worldpress.

MANIFESTO

We demand recognition of our grace which has been hard won over many years on contested ground, not handed to us by approval.

We share and recognise our debt to each other.

We reject an art market capitalising on the myth of uniqueness and narratives of the singular heroic figure, with traction and trend dominated by the cult of youth and warped notions of beauty.

We intend to rupture the symbolic from within, and borrow from the saboteurs of the big daddy mainframe.

We demand the abjuration of male-controlled and imperialist systems of oppression which we understand as exploiting women for labour and demeaning our grace.

We hold violence in contempt.

We hold deliberate ignorance and narrow horizons in contempt.

We hold patriarchal geo-political justifications for greed and power in contempt.

We hold the laws of our forefathers and current tyrants which renders a person illegal or deserving of poverty, in contempt.

We demand vegetables, tenderness and trust.

We demand clean water and poetry.

We demand blankets, dappled light and a woman's right to choose.

We demand mechanisms to grace and protect feminist liberties.

We demand pluralism, promotion of ideas and innovative methods to break the monopoly enjoyed by patriarchs and messianic preachers of cultural orthodoxies.

We demand an understanding of life as a truly communitarian experience and expect a population that is respectful of older women as infinitely precious and possessed of capacities for reason, art and love.

GRACEGRACEGRACE

THEREFORE:

We demand the revocation of all contracts for military purposes, and a total ban on the use of fossil fuels. We demand sustainable agriculture, a comprehensive renationalisation of our public health and social care, education and transport systems and all other commonly held necessary structures.

We demand rigorously implemented, loophole free, fair and progressive taxation to pay for the well-being of all—according to need and awarded with grace.

AND WE DEMAND our rightful place in the aesthetic values of our culture, securing and ensuring the recognition that we are exquisite, beguiling and learned, for ourselves, for each other, and for all to see.

Signed:

Grace
Grace
Grace

PROTEST FEMINIST LIBERTIES

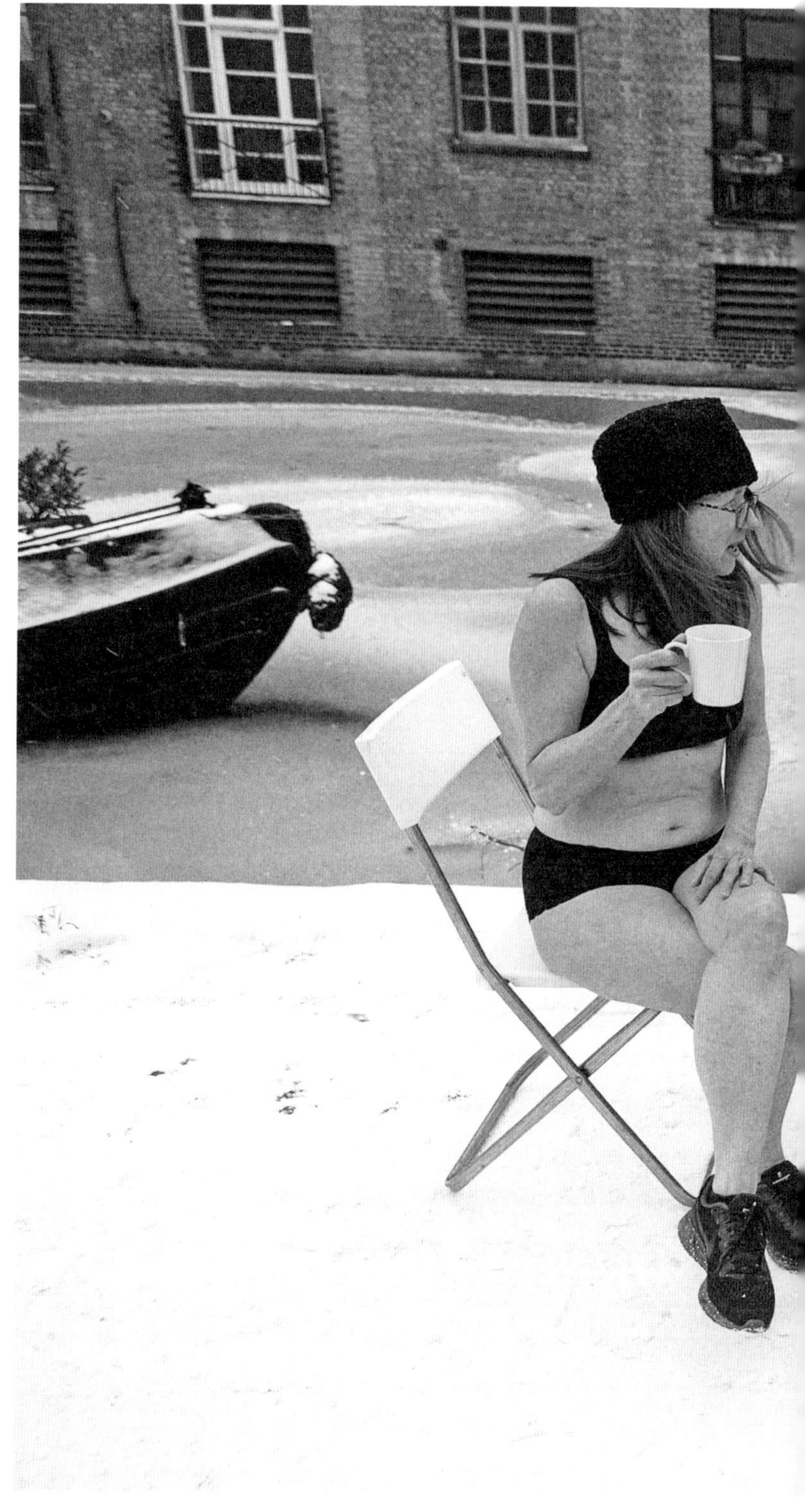

   Feminist Art Activisms and Artivisms

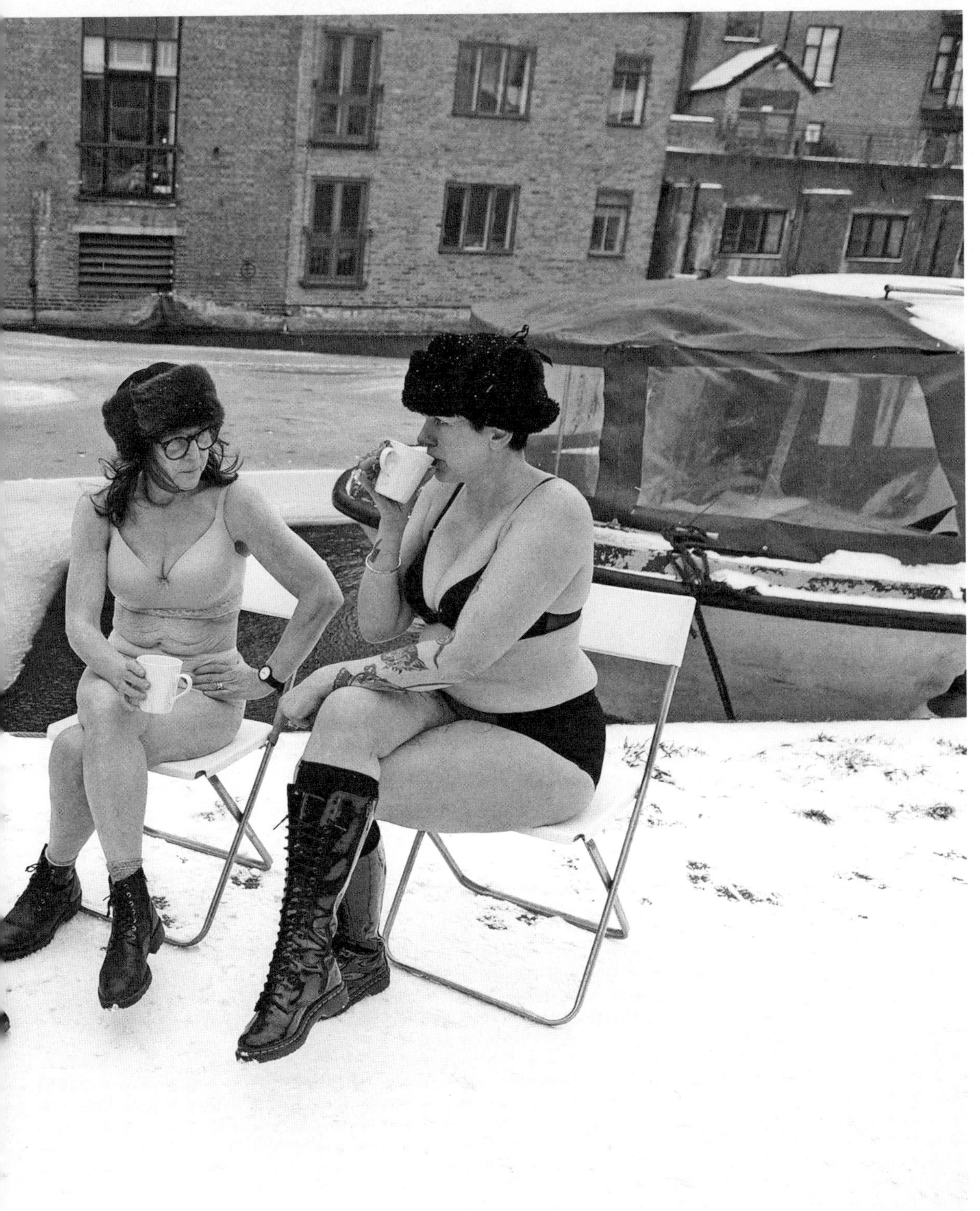

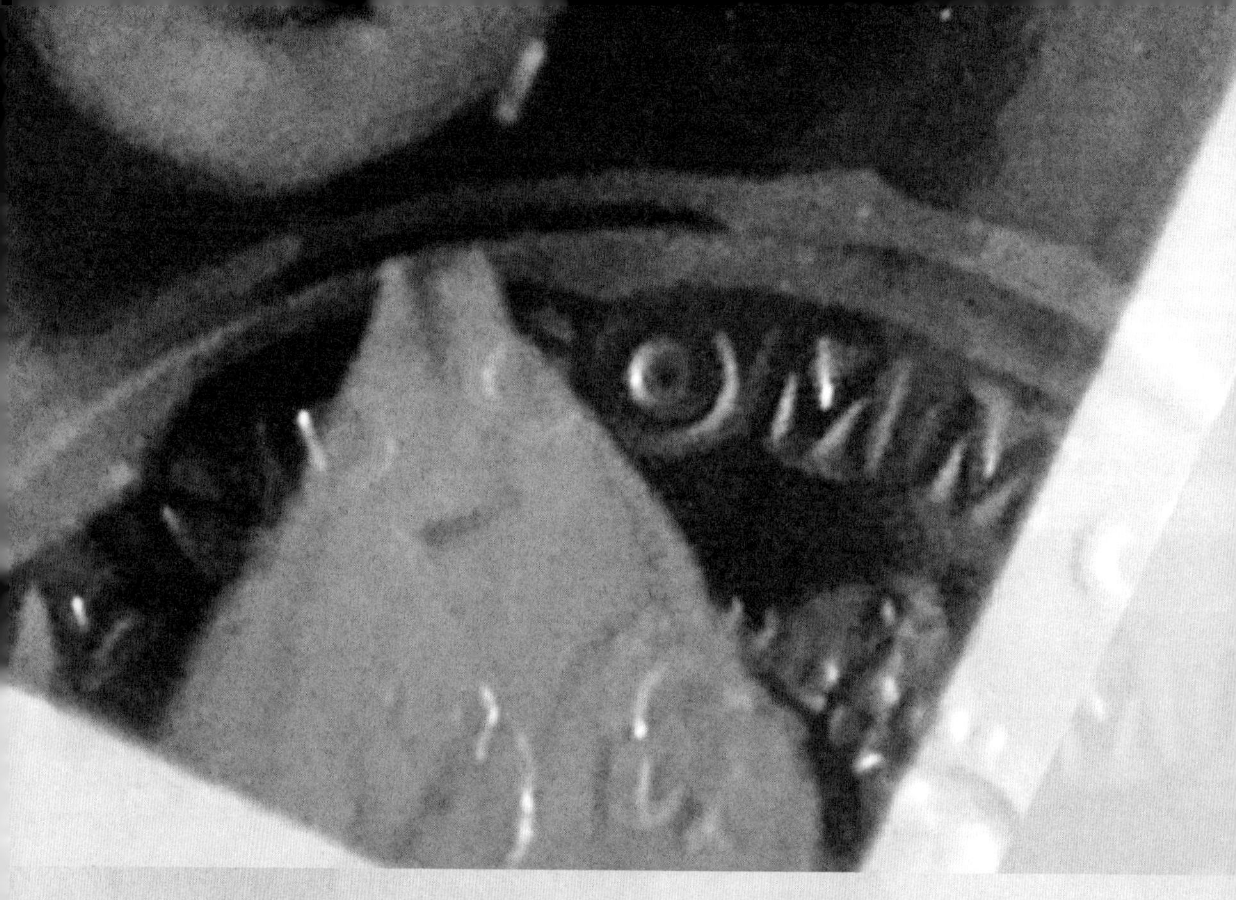

Anne Robinson, *Common Birds*, 2017, close up

REAL WOMEN/ COMMON BIRDS

Anne Robinson

1. Wildtrax, *Real Woman*, 1985, video still 1, video: U-Matic, 3 min., 40 sec. Available on Vimeo at: https://vimeo.com/329990965/311c37a600.

2. Anne Robinson, *Common Birds*, 2017, archival digital print, 840 x 170 mm, exhibited in 'Common and Garden', CGP London, 16 August–3 September, 2017, https://southwarkparkgalleries.org/common-garden (accessed 21 May 2019).

3. Artichoke, *Processions*, 2018, an Artichoke project commissioned by 14-18 NOW, various venues, 2018, www.processions.co.uk (accessed 19 May 2019).

4. Walter Benjamin, 'Theses on the Philosophy of History, in *Illuminations*, ed. Hannah Arendt (London: Pimlico, 1999), p. 247.

Interspersed across the following pages are images from three works: *Real Woman* (1984)[1], a music video collectively made with anarcho-punk band The Poison Girls showing a group of women on a seaside day out; *Common Birds* (2017)[2], an art work in the form of a printed booklet showing several generations of women, and *Processions* (2018), images of the colourful, creative women's street marches[3] throughout Britain to mark the centenary of the moment in 1918 when (some) women were given the right to vote.

I will focus on these three "gatherings" of women: collective, familial and "activist"… three flocks of "birds" across almost two hundred years: peeling back layers of time and stratigraphic image-making to ask what their collective voices can tell us about the "now" of art and activism. Perhaps it is hard to grasp, this "present" where the art world obsesses over radical signs, "class" is obfuscated and the poor get poorer. A different sense of time may be essential. As Walter Benjamin reminds us, 'The true picture of the past flits by… flashes up at the instant when it can be recognized'.[4]

In 1977, I left home for art school, the first of my family to do so, and in 1978 obtained a passport for the first time. In the early 1980s, inspired by feminism, "collective" practice and punk, I worked with See Red Women's Workshop and then made films as part of the Wildtrax collective, including *Real Woman*. In 1980s Britain, oppositional politics meant working against the ideology of the Thatcher government that set out to turn the clock back, putting women, queers, people of colour, the disabled, trade unionists, the entire working class, firmly back in their places. Thirty-odd years on, I am a working artist and it seems a new, conservative and neoliberal power-machine

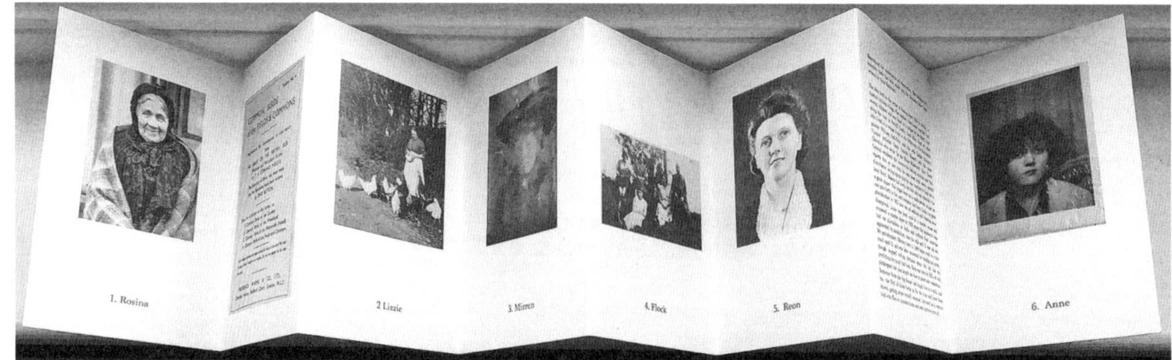

Anne Robinson, *Common Birds*, 2017, archival digital print, 840 x 170 mm

is trying to finish the job in a world where resistance is just a click away on social media and signs of resistance and protest from the past may be picked up and worn like a vintage frock. Recently, Amelia Jones said: 'we do not know what we mean any more when we say "woman", "lesbian", "queer", or "feminist" … this is a good thing'[5] and I agree. Our understanding of gender(s) has moved on and definitions like "nonbinary" offer new possibilities; yet the "personal" remains "political" for my queer, "othered" body at the heart of this matter, as I tentatively draw on images from my subjective past at this moment in flight. This paper is personal: 'here, now, alive, active, subjective'[6] and I remain "common"—a term used pejoratively with reference to the working classes and especially women—whilst I embrace the "commons" and the possibility of the solidarity in sharing common ground.

First of all, the music video, made in 1984–1985, by me, Caz Sheldon, Jenia Iljon and Clare Glasman, working as Wildtrax with the Poison Girls, who weren't all girls but were all anarchists, linked to the Crass collective, and whose lead singer Vi Subversa was some twenty years older than most punks. As Matthew Worley argues: 'punk opened up a space where feminist ideas were culturally played out'.[7] This was a turning point then for young women in terms of physical transgressions, refusing conventional expectations of womanhood or femininity. Some of us engaged in "culture jamming": spraying street graffiti on adverts combining both political message and physical exhilaration, reclaiming

5. Amelia Jones in *Imagining Queer Feminist Art Histories*, eds. Amelia Jones and Erin Silver (Manchester: Manchester University Press, 2016).

6. Raymond Williams, *Marxism and Literature* (Oxford: OUP, 1977), p. 128.

7. Matthew Worley, *No Future: Punk Politics and British Youth Culture, 1976–1984* (Cambridge, MA: Cambridge University Press, 2017), p. 193.

8. *Greenham Common protest, dancing on the silos at dawn New Year's Day, 1 January 1983, USAF air base, Berkshire, photo by Raissa Page of Format. Format's archives are held at Photofusion, London.*

9. *Vi Subversa, I'm Not A Real Woman,* Lyrics, 12" single, London: X-N-Trix Records/Rough Trade.

gender-forbidden space on the street. This rebellion of the physical body protesting was also visible at Greenham Common, in the incredible moment captured for the camera of a group of women dancing on top of the missile silos, behind the fence, their bodies a physical challenge to the most powerful military-industrial complex in the world.[8]

At this moment, as young feminists and queer activists, we worked collectively, questioning production methodologies and individualism making images for fast (as fast as the 1980s could muster) reproduction: what would later be called "DIY" culture. At this time, there were no rewards for doing politics or making collectives in art schools or galleries, especially for girls. *Real Woman's* lyrics concern resistance to feminine stereotypes or submissiveness, including the refrain:

> I'm generous I'm mean
> I'm a law onto myself
> And I just laugh at everything you say
> Don't be surprised
> If I don't look into your eyes
> My eyes are on a million miles away[9]

The video was filmed in London and Southend and shows a diverse group of women leaving their homes in a minibus and setting off to the quintessentially English and working-class seaside town of Southend for a day out. Joyous footage of dancing, sandcastles, roller coaster rides and dodgem cars is interspersed with footage of Vi and the band playing the song and cartoon scenarios where women refuse to behave. The women in the band and Vi's daughter Gemma

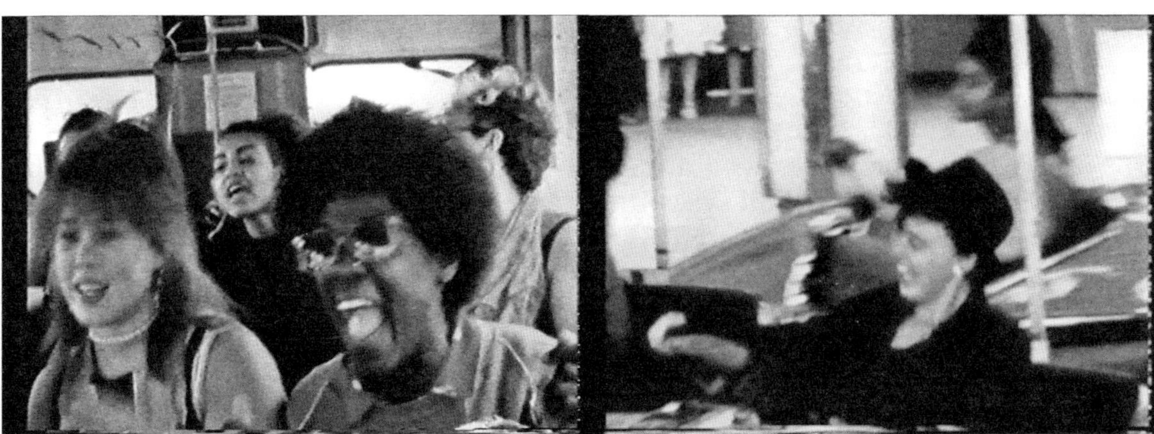

Wildtrax, *Real Woman*, 1985, video still 1, U-Matic, 3'40

are also part of the seaside trip. Hostility to these exuberant female day-trippers as they dance, laugh, sing, play, hug one another and reject any interruptions, is caught on Super-8 and partly filmed in Southend's Kursaal amusement park, by then looking seedy and run down, but reportedly the first ever theme park and once the home of female lion tamers.

As artists, our politics determined conscious choices not to be confined to small, art audiences, not to compromise. This is a hybrid work, experimental, but also inside pop culture, prefiguring debates in the later 1980s about "accessibility", "community", and the "burden of representation". Three points here about *Real Woman* as we move on to the next piece: firstly, a key element that audiences enjoyed on its release, was the sense of women misbehaving: the sheer joy of the final sequence of Vi burning her laundry on the washing line. Secondly, watching it recently, people comment on the diversity of this gathering of women and its "working class" settings: the amusement park, the day out and there was indeed behind this work, what would now be called an "intersectional" feminism that wanted to speak beyond the experience of white, straight, middle class women. Thirdly, I welcome contemporary enthusiasm for such imagery, and yet feel some ambivalence, even discomfort, in potential fetishization of the appearance of working class-ness, at this time when working class women are pushed into greater economic hardship, when as Bev Skeggs says: 'a great deal of energy goes into inscribing, depicting, categorizing and degrading the working classes as enemy'.[10] She goes on to suggest that while we value diversity as a resource, this is not the same as the neo-liberal agenda about empowerment and 'we need to understand the interests and investments made in the relationships that enable difference to be mis-recognized'. As bell hooks argues and I believe: 'broader perspectives can only emerge as we examine the personal that is political'.[11]

The second "flock" is a tale of my matrilineal family line… with asides.

It is a small artwork called *Common Birds* (2017). The title plays on two British colloquialisms: "common" meaning lower class and "bird" meaning woman. This work is a concertina style booklet, based on an illustrated nature pamphlet from the 1930s, entitled *Common Birds of the Fields and Commons*, and showing photographs of female members

10. Beverley Skeggs, *Class, Self, Culture* (Hove: Psychology Press, 2004), p. 180.

11. bell hooks, 'Feminism: A Movement to End Sexist Oppression', *Feminist Theory Reader*, ed. Sŭng-gyŏng Kim (Hove: Psychology Press, 2003), p. 52.

of my family: Rosina, Lizzie, Mirren, Reon, and myself
along with a speculative history. The piece was displayed on
a shelf at eye level so that spectators could read the text at
the centre of the work:

> Reproduced for convenience of observation. The
> selection of common birds has been made and
> the footnotes have been written by Anne Robinson.

> The first bird in the series is Rosina, born 1830 in
> Dailly, a Scottish mining village. Her mother, Ann
> never married, had several children and was listed
> as a pauper at her death. Just along the road in
> Penkill Castle lived Alice Boyd an artist who lived
> in a ménage à trois in the 1850s with Pre-Raphaelite
> painter William Bell-Scott and his wife Letitia
> Margery. Visitors included Dante Gabriel Rossetti
> and his sister Christina who wrote In the Bleak
> Midwinter there. Dante Gabriel wandered the coun-
> tryside feeling anxious and Bell reports that on one
> visit, he was beset with severe mental disturbance:
> seeing spirits and tempted to leap into a local
> "burn". Rosina had lovely red hair and was reported
> to be a great singer. She began work as a maidser-
> vant at age ten and gave birth to the next common
> bird here, Elizabeth, my great grandmother in 1857
> also out of wedlock and drawing some disapproval.
> Elizabeth was head cook in a country house
> and witnessed a murder there in 1918 when the
> landowner who owned tea plantations in India and
> suffered from sunstroke aggravated by alcoholism,
> shot his wife and 15-year-old son. My grandmother,
> Mirren, born in 1888 began work as a table maid
> aged 12 and was later renowned for reading tea
> leaves, though stopped telling fortunes when she felt
> she was predicting too much bad luck. Reon was
> born in 1920. An avid picture-goer, she also taught
> me how to paint with watercolour. Someone "from
> the big house" had taught her as a child. And me,
> the first of these birds to fly the coop and leave these
> shores, stamped "common" as a common bird who
> flies in common time and over common ground.

12. A quote from the title of Sonia Boyce, *Big Women's Talk* (1984), pastel and ink on paper, 148 x 155 cm.

Three recent "finds" came together prior to making the work: my first passport, a photograph of my great, great grandmother Rosina and the nature pamphlet. The passport is a blue one, from the time when bearer's photographs were stamped 'Britain and Commonwealth', except the stamp across my eighteen-year-old self had come out looking like "uppity and common", an identity I fully embrace. The photograph of Rosina, I had just recently been given, knowing something of her history and that of her mother Ann, but having no idea what they looked like. The photograph here is good quality because it has been taken by a professional photographer visiting the "big house" where her family worked. The booklet, I bought along with others for 50p from a market stall because I loved the beautiful illustrations… and the title! The other fragments of "history" within the text I knew already from local and art histories and from listening to 'big women's talk'[12] as a child: hearing second-hand, the narrative of servants' lives with little leisure and my mother's unfulfilled desire to paint, as she had to leave school for work at fourteen. These three elements were brought together to form *Common Birds*.

Moving on to the third "flock": a much larger one. *Processions* (2018) was arranged by public arts creators Artichoke and supported by 14-18 NOW. A hundred artists were commissioned to work with different communities of women to create 100 centenary banners for the parade

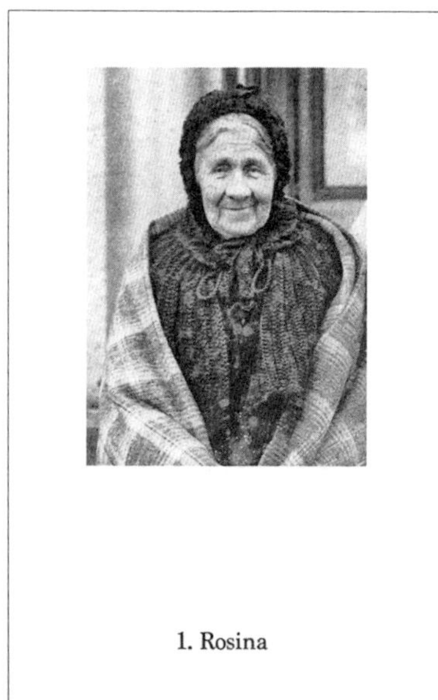

1. Rosina

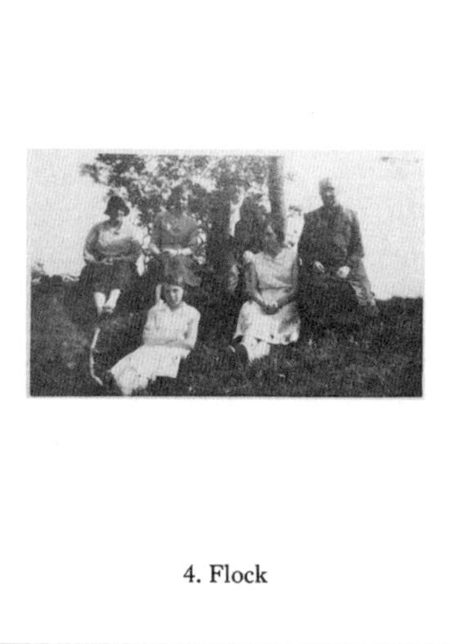

4. Flock

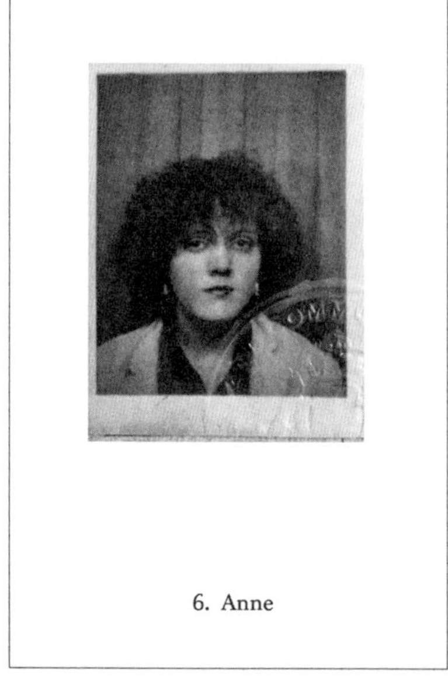

6. Anne

Anne Robinson, *Common Birds*, 2017, three details, archival digital print, 840 x 170 mm

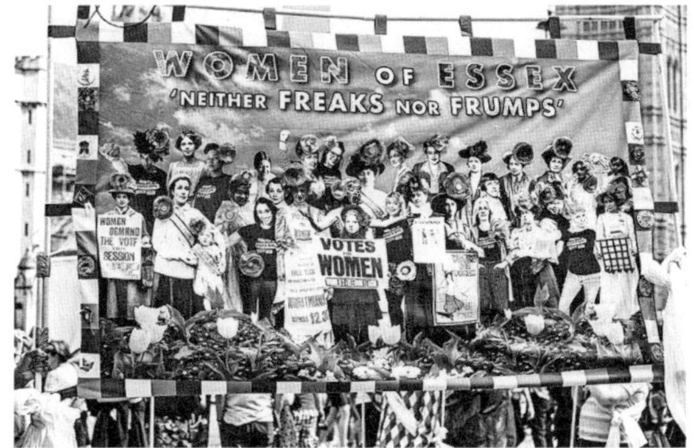

Artichoke, *Processions*, 2018, an Artichoke project commissioned by 14-18 NOW. Photo: Amelia Allen

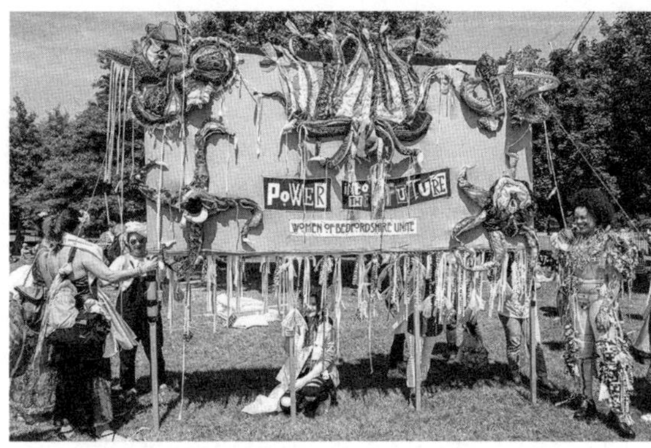

Artichoke, *Processions*, 2018, an Artichoke project commissioned by 14-18 NOW. Photo: Amelia Allen

13. Further details may be found at: www.parliament. uk/about/living-heritage/ transformingsociety/ electionsvoting/womenvote/ case-study-the-right-to-vote/ the-right-to-vote/birmingham-and-the-equal-franchise/1928-equal-franchise-act (accessed 19 May 2019). The voting age changed to 18 in 1969 with a further Representation of the People Act.

commemorating (some) women getting the vote in 1918, and re-enacting the suffragists' rallies and marches. Free scarves in the suffragist colours of white, green and violet were handed out: 400,000 were handmade in India for the event and choreographed for this procession to form, from above, one giant suffragette banner. *The Guardian* estimated that more than 100,000 women marched through London, Edinburgh, Belfast and Cardiff on Sunday 10 June 2018.

Those brackets, that word: "(some)" have disturbed me. I will expand here on the implications. The Representation of the People Act (1918) added 8.4 million women and 5.6 million men to the UK electoral register. This was the first enfranchisement of women in the UK, but only those over 30 and meeting the minimum property ownership qualification got the vote in 1918. Some men with a "university" vote retained two votes, while men over 19 who had seen active service and all working-class men over 21 were enfranchised. Working class women, including most women of colour, were not. They had to wait until 1928, when the whole adult population over 21 was enfranchised by the Representation of the People (Equal Franchise) Act.[13]

Rosina died in 1920 with no democratic rights as a citizen, a few weeks after Reon my mother was born with none. No-one knew in 1920 whether working class women would ever be allowed to vote.

During the suffragette celebrations of June 2018, I had no desire to rain on anyone's procession, but I found myself remaining silent as (some) friends went on marches.

Of course I admire the suffragettes. They were strong women, brilliant campaigners, truly and absolutely brave in the best sense of that word. Their struggle is deeply moving and they achieved a lot. However, the 1918 decision was, in part, a reward to the campaign's leaders in the NUWSS and WSPU (the two large suffrage societies)[14] for supporting Britain's war effort in what we now know was mass slaughter. The war was actively opposed by women in the labour movement, including Sylvia Pankhurst who, unlike her mother and sister, chose to take a stand against the war and worked tirelessly for a radical socialism, against capital and empire, campaigning with working women in East London and running *The Workers' Dreadnought* newspaper.

One persistent question for me was: what did it feel like to be a working class woman in 1918 who had campaigned for twelve or fifteen years for the vote, alongside wealthier suffragettes and suffragists, only to be told: these

14. Women's Social and Political Union (WSPU) (1903–1917) was founded by the Pankhursts and supported the militant suffragettes. In 1907, a split occurred because of the militant tactics and the Women's Freedom League was founded. National Union of Women's Suffrage Societies (*NUWSS*), founded 1897, are known as the suffragists, led by Dame Millicent Garrett Fawcett, and believed in peaceful campaigning for women's suffrage.

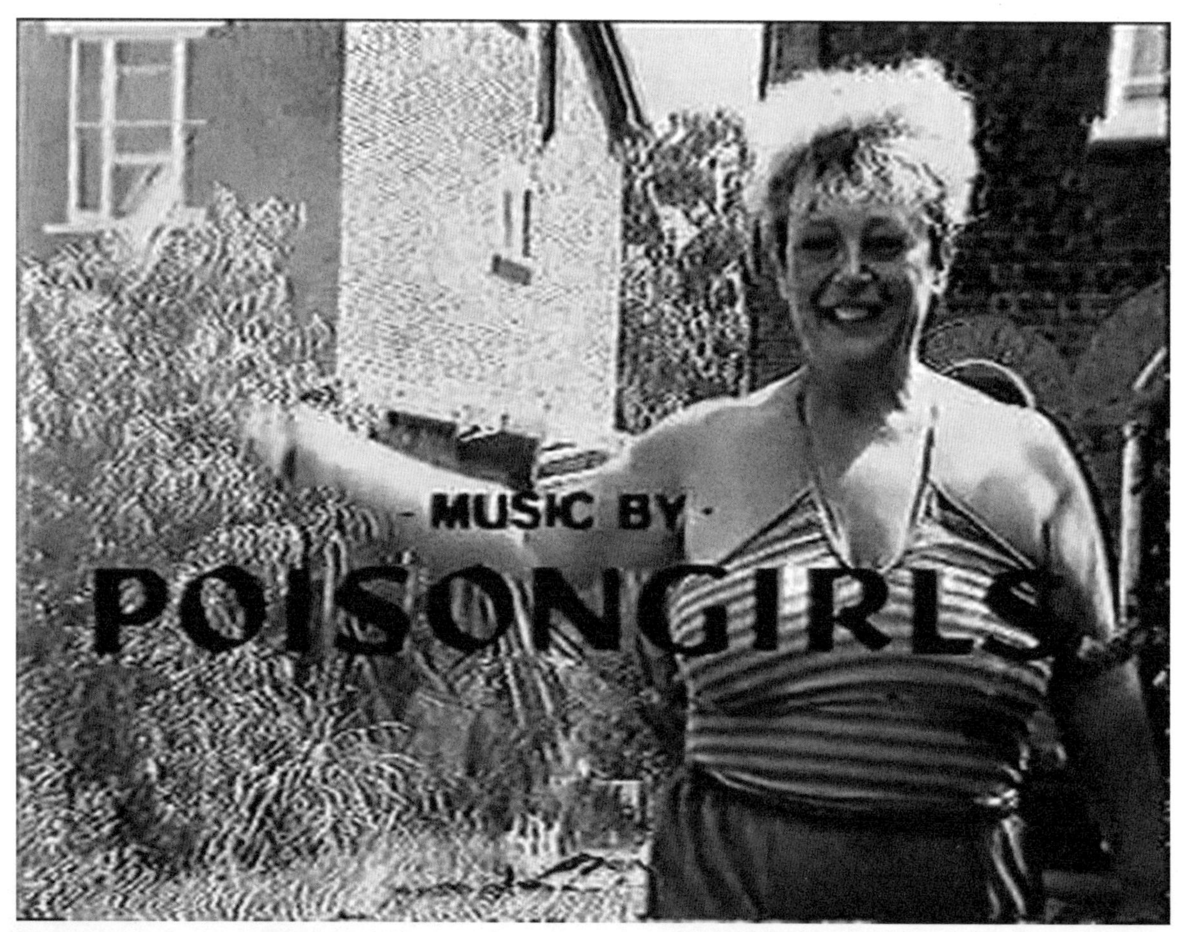

Wildtrax, *Real Woman*, 1985, video still 1, U-Matic, 3'40

15. Owen Jones, *Chavs: The Demonisation of the Working Class* (London: Verso, 2016).

women here can have the vote because they have property, wealth, stability, and easier lives. We trust them. You are poor, worth less, and so cannot vote. Nobody knew for sure that the law would change again in 1928 or ever. What did this celebration of achievement for (some) women conceal and what do such divisions mean for artivisms and activisms now? How might it have felt for activists who had worked so very hard together in struggle and even risked their lives, to be divided along those class lines? I believe we can learn from listening to these three flocks of birds...

The first was made collectively, at a time of resistance. We did not really expect the art world to look out for us, yet some of us "common birds" had flown over the walls of the art school on full student grants.

The second is made by drawing on personal family history, but stretching this to consider broader perspectives on class, history, and the creative desires of working class people, and using this material to reflect on this moment now: the need for education, economic resources, and time for art.

The third is a work with excellent intentions, to celebrate strong women, and yet I could not join in. I felt excluded. Even a hundred years on, the (brackets) were not enough. I was caught in parenthesis and struck down by sadness. I felt the day-to-day, invisible hurt of my ancestors: lighting fires, fetching, carrying, visible only to be chastized for their loose morals, their enjoyment of sex, their inappropriate desires...

In today's art world, the radical politics of the past and politicized art collectives are fetishized. However, in the West, we live in a culture which vilifies "working class-ness" characterizing "common" people as benefit scroungers or "chavs",[15] who lack taste and good judgement, who don't read, eat bad food: who are, in short, stupid. This stereotyping has got worse in the wake of Brexit with "working class" spat out like an insult. The most vicious generalizations are reserved for people who live in social housing, on estates and/or state benefits. The property division that meant that (some) women couldn't vote in 1918 persists. The wealth created from property ownership and inheritance still goes unquestioned. It is often the bodies and behaviours of the working classes, especially women, which are demonized, as documented by Owen Jones and Bev Skeggs and in controversies over reality TV shows like *Benefits Street*.[16] Recently, for the first time since records began, the gap in life expectancy between rich and poor women is widening.[17]

This retrograde shift has happened since the time of *Real Woman*. I have been asked in recent years, as a former member of DIY/art-making collectives, particularly See Red, to contribute to today's art/curatorial projects on feminism. Much of this has brought fantastic creative rewards, especially engaging with young, diverse, dynamic collectives like OOMK based in East London[18] but I observe that the art world remains overwhelmingly populated by the propertied classes.

Drawing on these three works, I offer some reflections. Property rights in terms of land wealth, inheritance and built property persist and entrench social divisions. Culture continues to establish relations of entitlement, but all too often may not be converted by working class individuals into the capital required to make progress, to gain recognition for their creative subjectivity or agency. Class struggle is alive and well. Returning here to Bev Skeggs:

> Whilst the middle-classes are busy propertizing their accumulative, exchange-value selves through the use of, attachment to, detachment from and experimentation with cultures not of their making… the working classes make culture that is defined as deficit, their selves as abject, and their value use-less… in the contemporary, the impossibility of a working class self is not articulated widely … instead a universalistic self is presented as if it is available for all, where in fact the access to the resources to make the self is not equally available.[19]

At worst, those who have nothing are demonized as their "cultures" are stolen from them to become the property of the wealthy. Members of these vilified classes will find it hard to be artists unless, ironically, they play at being the chav, by loudmouthing or shouldering the yoke of "representation" so that this engagement can be recognized by curators from more privileged backgrounds who sneer at and yet want to exhibit only this kind of creativity. The arts

16. *Benefits Street*, Channel 4 television programme, UK, production company: Love Productions, original broadcast: January 2014.

17. For further information, see: Damien Gayle, 'Women's life expectancy in poor areas falls by almost 100 days', *The Guardian*, 27 March 2019, www.theguardian.com/society/2019/mar/27/womens-life-expectancy-in-poor-areas-falls-by-almost-100-days (accessed 19 May 2019).

18. OOMK stands for 'one of my kind', http://oomk.net (accessed 21 May 2019).

19. Skeggs, *Class, Self, Culture*, p. 176.

CLASS MATTERS

are still a relentlessly middle class milieu. Tuition fees have risen, grants have gone and working class students pile up mountains of impossible debt. Children go hungry. The cycle persists. It is slippery: blink and you will miss the nuances.

Can contemporary artists avoid recuperation and acquisitive exploitation? How can the divisions created through property wealth and gentrification be resisted amongst groups of artists? What has to happen to make places for working class art making? And finally, for feminists engaged with intersectionality: are we really stuck with class?

Anne Robinson

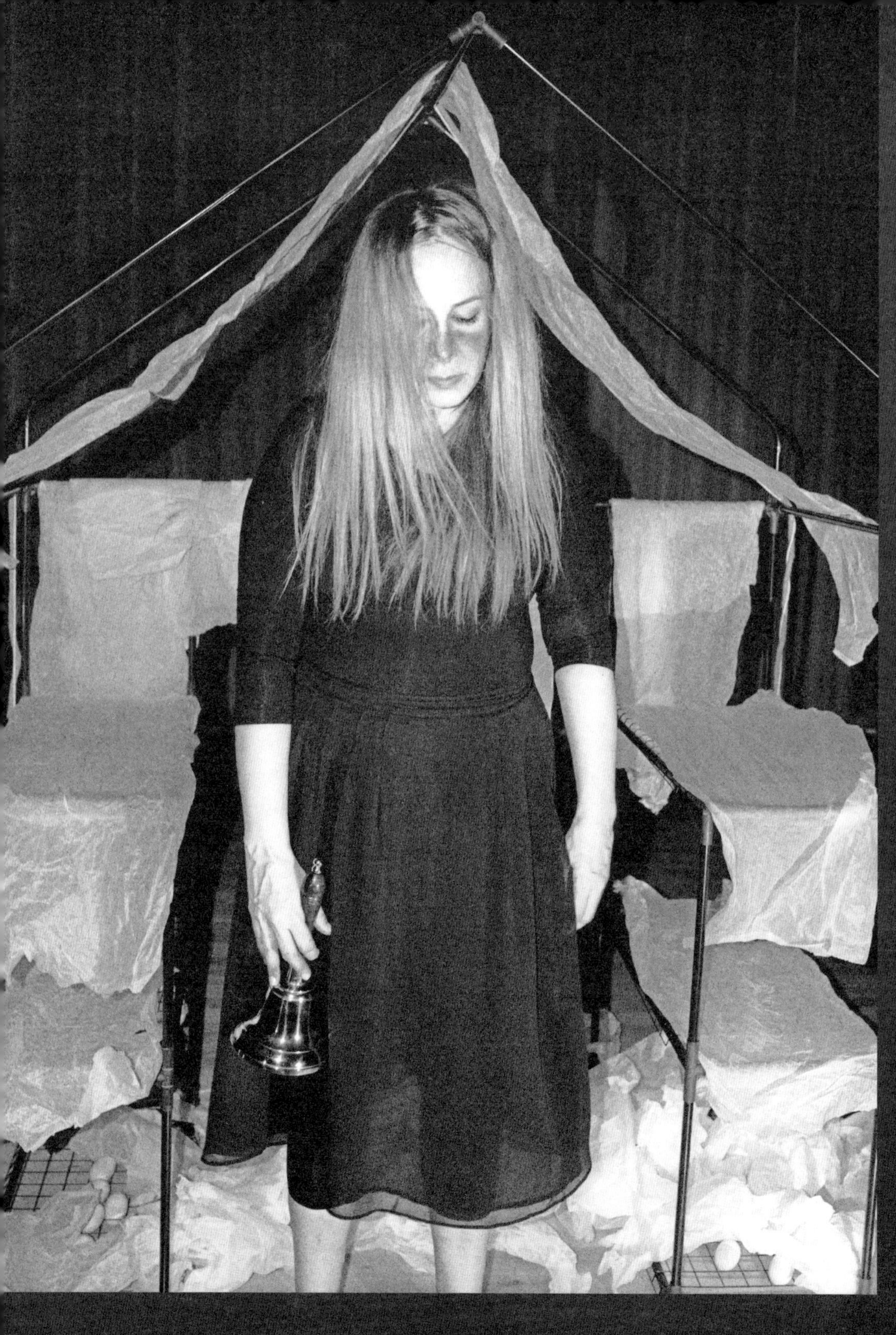

Christina Vasileiou, *PaperCare*, 2018, performance show.
Photo: Dimitra Dede. Courtesy of the artist

PAPERCARE
Performance Art Making as Voicing and Representation of the Feminine Caring Teaching Experience

Christina Vasileiou

1. Lisa Baraitser, *Maternal Encounters: The Ethics of Interruption* (East Sussex: Routledge, 2009), p. 67.

PaperCare was a one-woman performance art show, first staged at the Barbican OpenFest, London, in March 2018. The piece was strongly autobiographical, drawing on my experience of being a teacher and a mother, and was devised around themes that circle around the reality and practice of teaching: the repetitiveness, the mechanistic and suppressed, the interruptions, the messy and noisy, the care, love, satisfaction, and gratification, the psychic frameworks of self-sacrifice or self-alienation. These themes span the dynamics of both the teaching and the maternal, and suggest that women teachers' care extends beyond educational delivery and instruction. Mobilizing affective notions of intimacy and ambivalence, the piece reveals the woman teacher as "other—mother", and as someone who, like a mother, is 'subjected to relentless interruption'[1] by small children at any time.

This photo-essay describes the aesthetic devices I used in the performance. It also contains poetic sections. In these, I seek to offer a glimpse into the first-hand subjective experiences of a woman negotiating her identity as a teacher, artist, activist and mother.

In her significant essay 'Caring: A Labour of Love' (1983), Hillary Graham argued that 'caring defines both the identity and the activity of women in Western society.… It should be the place we begin, and not end our analysis of modern society.'[2]

With the introduction of universal primary education in the modern industrialized world at the end of the nineteenth century, primary school teaching became a female-dominated profession. In her examination of the historical development of teaching, Madeleine Grumet considers the links between the 'feminization of teaching and the [pedagogical] cult of maternal nurturance'.[3] According to her, women's association with the nurture of children is inscribed in the ways women teachers are considered, producing the strong correlation between the "good teacher" and the "good mother". While school and home are often contrasted as public and private spaces, the feminine teaching experience still contains intimacies of the private sphere in the form of a "maternal" pedagogy that 'seems personal [and yet] not quite defensible in [the] public space'.[4]

The framework of performance of care that *Paper Care* suggests, addresses the lack of these aspects of teaching in artistic representation. It presents a (re)-conceptualization of teaching as the performance of "doing care" in schools and disrupts dominant narratives that aim to rationalize and organize the feminine teaching experience. In the piece, I wanted to interrogate how such narratives tend to recognize only the rationality of duty or see docility and obedience as part of the teaching work, and question how these may suppress the human ambiguities inherent in any form of caring work. *Paper Care* positions the teacher and the practice of teaching in the foreground by looking into the classroom as 'an intimate place'.[5] The piece evokes a conceptualization of the classroom as another private environment as the domestic. In this, it echoes Mierle Laderman Ukeles' pioneering performance work and manifesto on domestic art[6] within institutions as a way of diagnosing the artistic in the laborious.

The show was one hour long and set around the structure of a metallic installation, which could be seen as an enclosure, a house or a school building.

2. Hillary Graham, 'Caring: A Labour of Love', in *A Labour of Love: Women, Work and Caring*, eds. Janet Finch and Dulcie Groves (London: Routledge and Kegan Paul, 1983), p. 30.

3. Madeleine R. Grumet, *Bitter Milk, Women and Teaching* (Amherst, MA: The University of Massachusetts Press, 1988), p. 56.

4. Ibid., p. 87.

5. Jill Dolan, *Geographies of Learning: Theory and Practice, Activism and Performance* (Middletown, CT: Wesleyan University Press, 2001), p. 147.

6. Mierle Ukeles, 'Manifesto for Maintenance Art, 1969!', Arnolfini, www.arnolfini.org.uk/blog/manifesto-for-maintenance-art-1969/Ukeles_MANIFESTO.pdf (accessed 1 May 2019).

 Feminist Art Activisms and Artivisms

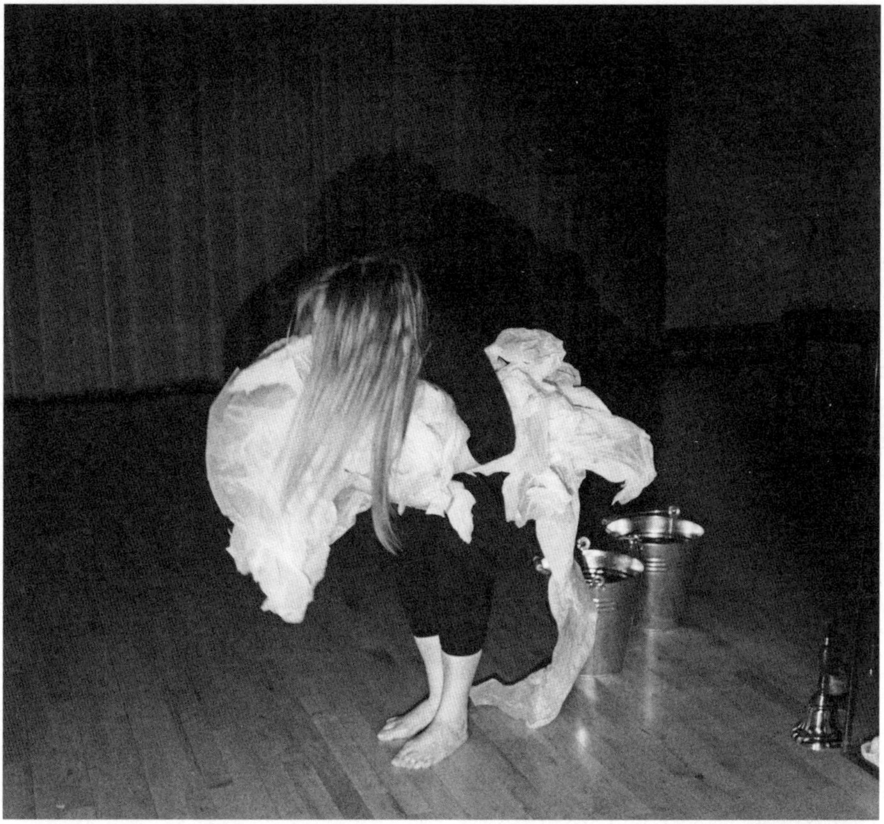

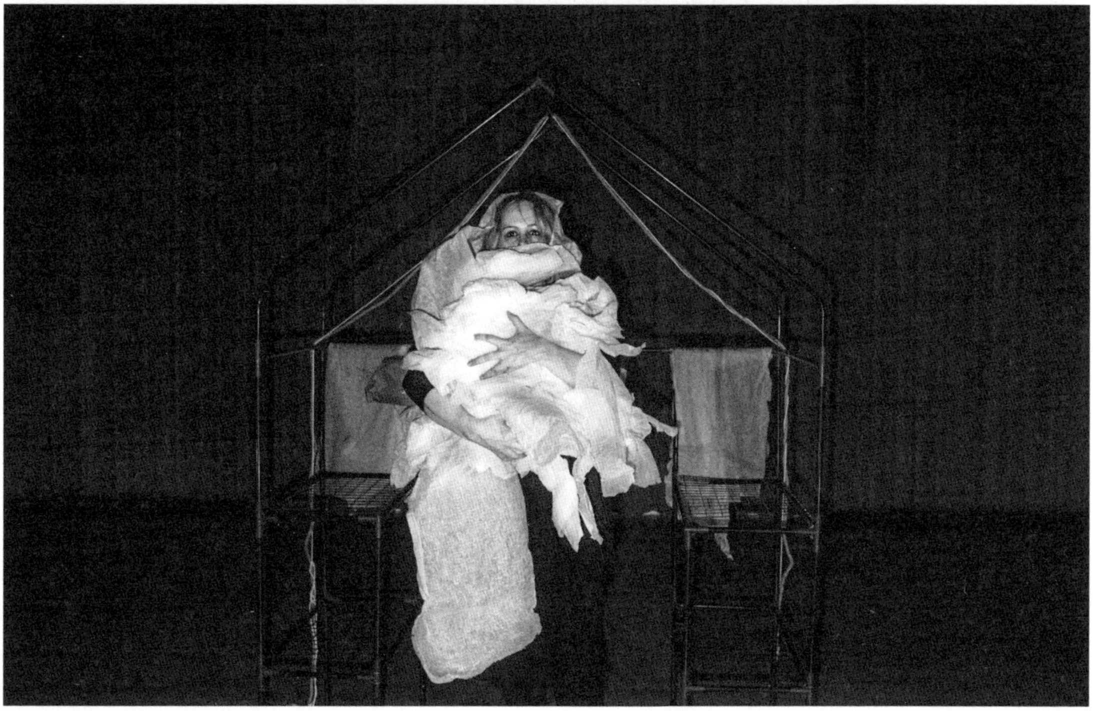

Christina Vasileiou, *PaperCare*, 2018, performance show. Photo: Dimitra Dede. Courtesy of the artist

I spend so many hours of the day at school.
I feel that
I live here.
I live with them.
This structure is my visual and material
representation
Of "walls".
A constrictive environment.
But I put this up
With my hands
I have trained myself to build these walls
Very fast
Fast as possible
And I gather my children in here
I teach them to stay within the frame.
We stand constricted
Stand corrected.
In control. Close, very close.
We don't fit, it's too much.
But I stay.

In a room filled with scattered, almost unruly papers and eggs, we see a woman performing rituals that seem caring: collecting, tidying, attending to, folding, managing or non-managing, washing and watering—papers, creating nests out of paper that she hands to the audience. My teaching care is presented as labour: emotional, physical, affective, maternal. My classroom caring practices seem repetitive, laborious, timed, and interrupted by the sound of a school bell that I am obsessively ringing. I seem gentle, care-full, humble, somewhat humiliated in the exaggeration and paradox of my "paper burden".

Papers and eggs demand to know their symbolization: How do I relate to them? What are they? Are they a visual representation of my students, "my children"? They are deliberately too many, too noisy and loud. They are unmanageable and disobedient. Equally, could they indicate the "layers" of my multiple identities of an artist/mother/teacher in constant shifts, frictions, and dysfunctions?

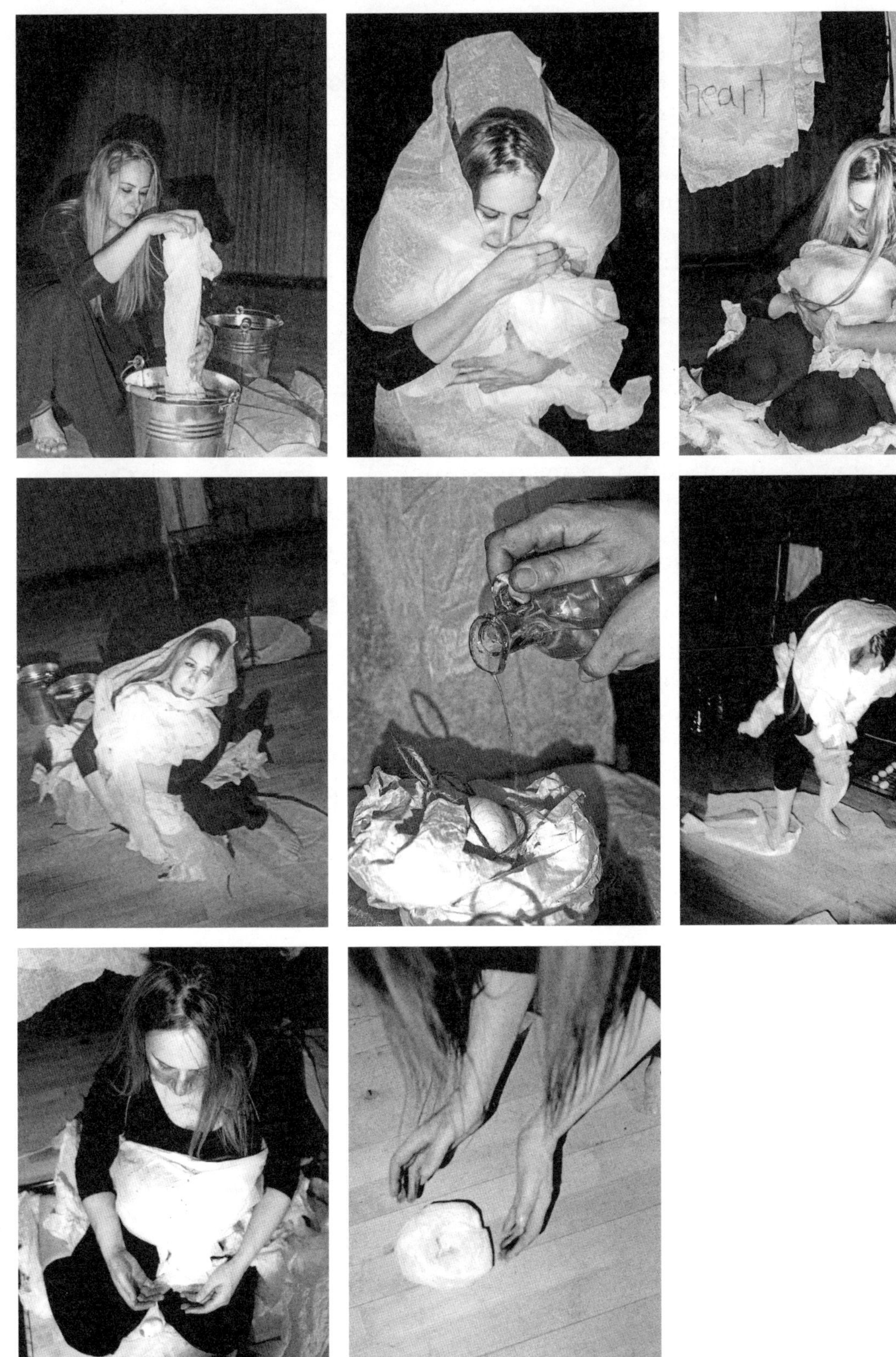

Paper
Is transparent and malleable.
Is lightweight, but fills up the space, can overflow.
Carries inscriptions of meaning and memory,
absorbing children's careful attempts to learn.
Is noisy like the teaching reality.
Scattered around in the room, it is messy,
like care also is.
Is difficult for me to manage.
Is unsettled, uncertain on my body.
Commands me to physical labour in order
to collect it.
Is fragile and ephemeral.
With paper, I:
Collect, tidy up, and wash; I wash papers (?)
Submit to the absurdity of my ritualistic,
mechanistic doings of care.
Submit to the mundane and the humble.
Uncover layers of oppression under the layers of
my paper.

Alluding to phenomenological notions of care,[7] in *PaperCare*
we see a human burdened, imprinted, and also constituted
by caring activities and the labour involved in caring for
others. This care is performed as a form of corporeal
morality, acquired through the body. Such embodiment
marks the body as a site of "caring events", imprinted by the
care that existed sometime, somewhere, on bodies, on objects.
We thus see the female body exposed in its enduring effort
of bearing the "load of care". Yet, the performativity of

7. Martin Heidegger, *Being and Time* (Albany, NY: State University of New York Press, 2010).

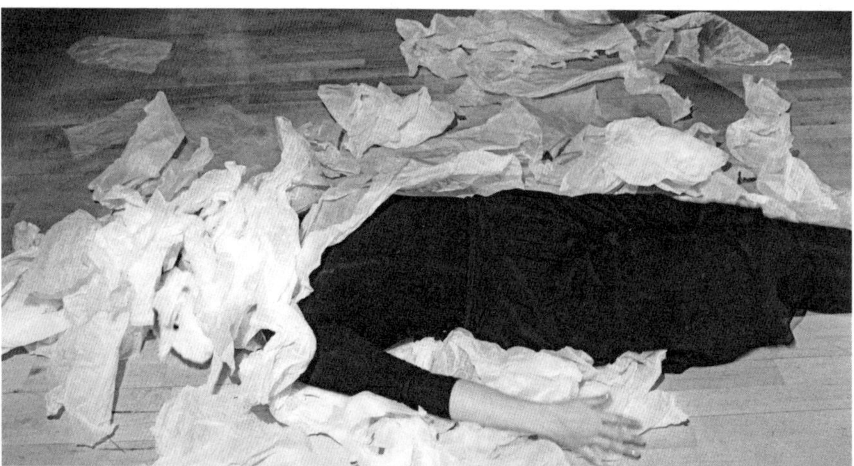

Christina Vasileiou, *PaperCare*, 2018, performance show. Photo: Dimitra Dede. Courtesy of the artist

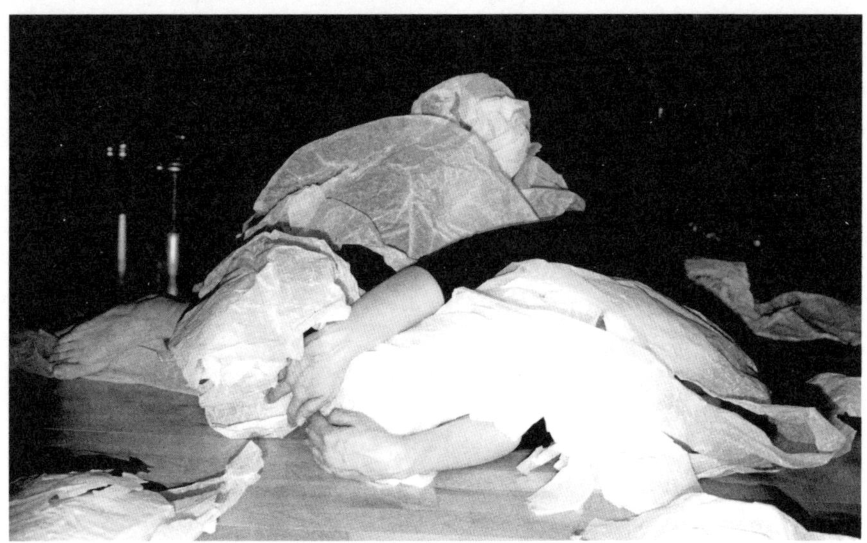

Christina Vasileiou, *PaperCare*, 2018, performance show. Photo: Dimitra Dede. Courtesy of the artist

8. Heather Piper and Ian Stronach, *Don't Touch! The Educational Story of a Panic* (London and New York: Routledge, 2008).

9. Maurice Hamington, *Embodied Care* (Urbana and Chicago: University of Illinois Press, 2004), p. 54.

institutionalized disciplines working on the teacher's body do not cease to propagate educational narratives of corporeal invisibility and somatophobia.[8]

> I am performing
> The Paradox of a
> "Teacher's—Body".
> I have a body—and I am exposing it to the audience.
> I need this body in order to practise my care.
> The embodiment of my care
> Radicalizes subtle or prominent systems of
> corporeal alienation
> that work on my body and
> Disrupts dominant narratives of
> How a teacher's body should do care.
> My body is my means of doing care
> A site of caring possibilities.

Care, therefore, emerges as a form of craft, an embodied artistry, perceived, controlled by the body, that appraises the quality of my care through 'an understanding in the flesh'.[9]

Through performance, the suppressed experience of teaching care claims a (re)connection with the body in its

caring, ethical doings and the actualization of the feminine
in teaching care.

> My care 'is making me'. I become care, I AM care,
> my performance IS care.
> I appear as an artisan of care.
> My performance extends into generating affective,
> Caring forces filling up the room.
> My body summons the strength and accuracy of my
> movements,
> The cultivation of patience for my care to be
> "complete", for the audience and me.
> I experience this effort as a form of maternal labour.
> I create, I procreate care,
> My care is generated through my body suggesting an
> embodied morality
> that extends to my audience.
> Wondering if they also feel cared for, by me,
> Stretching my caring performance into a form of
> ethical doing.

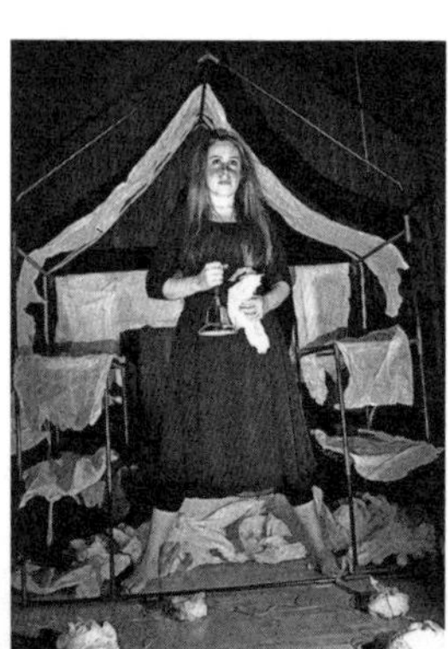 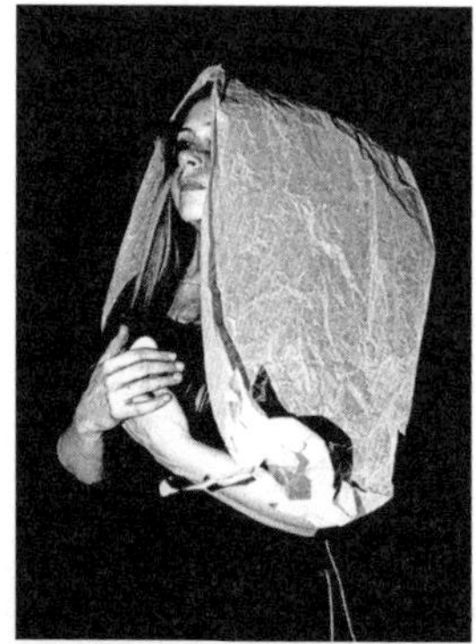 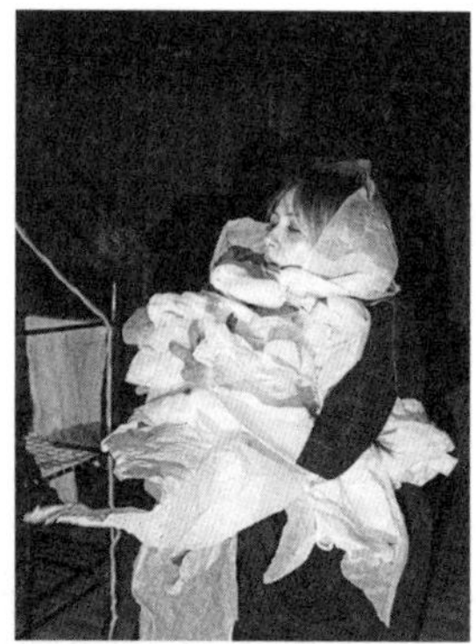

all images
Christina Vasileiou, *PaperCare*, 2018, performance show. Photo: Dimitra Dede. Courtesy of the artist

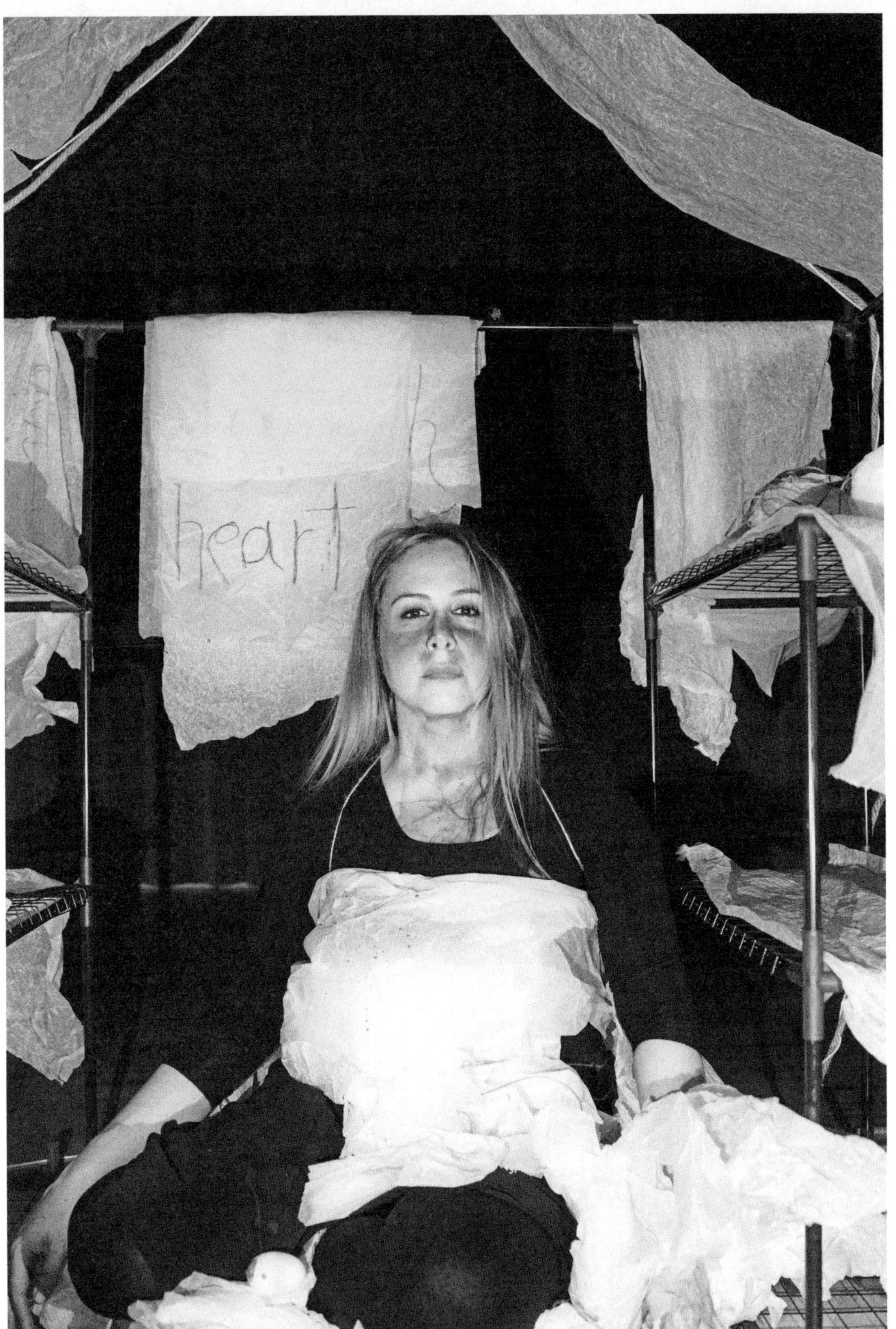

heart

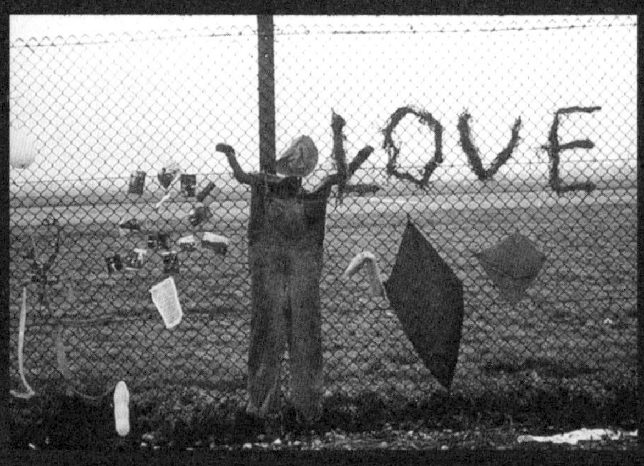

The fence at Greenham Common with additions by protesters from the peace camp, c. 1982.
Photograph by Sigrid Møller, the Women's International League for Peace and Freedom, slides scanned by
Holger Terp, June 2006, from *The Danish Peace Academy Greenham Common Women's Peace Camps Songbook*.

'DYING TO LIVE'[1] Bad Endings & the Afterlives of Greenham Common

Alexandra Kokoli

1. This is the title of a first-person narrative of a die-in demonstration in London by Greenham Common protester Gillian Booth: 'Dying to Live', in *Greenham Common: Women at the Wire*, eds. Barbara Harford and Sarah Hopkins (London: Women's Press, 1984), pp. 57–60.

2. Wendy, in Alice Cook and Gwyn Kirk, *Greenham Women Everywhere: Dreams, Ideas and Actions from the Women's Peace Movement* (London: South End Press, 1983), p. 21.

The end of the world as we know it through global war or man-made nuclear and environmental catastrophes elicits a wide range of collectively negotiated and socio-politically contingent responses. It is a philosophical and psycho-analytic truism that the living are burdened with a life-long preoccupation with death. Mortals are not only obsessed with but shaped by their mortality, against which they develop personal and cultural displacements and distractions serving to simultaneously deflect and signpost its inevitability. Yet if the death of oneself and one's loved ones is a defining given, the threat of death on a mass scale by nuclear war represents another turn of the screw, if not a qualitative transformation of a common issue: 'Knowing that everyone else is going to die makes the horror […] seem all-embracing, somehow bigger.'[2] This chapter examines some of the ways in which feminist anti-nuclear, anti-militarist movements have dealt with the paradox of simultaneously recognizing the unthinkability of the end of (nearly) all life on earth, and striving to lend form to it, in ways that are rhetorically striking, politically persuasive, and eminently shareable. The chapter is also haunted by the spectre of a far less important but personally vexing bad ending: the conclusion of a previous effort to get to grips with the poetics of feminist anti-nuclear art and visual activism, which did not live up to the radical aspiration of the practices under consideration but fizzled into apparent defeatism. I am adopting a quasi-auto-ethnographic perspective in the hope of conveying something of the vicissitudes of academic work on this topic, its broken temporalities, disappointments, and discoveries.

In an earlier article, 'Pre-Emptive Mourning Against the Bomb: Exploded Domesticities in Art Informed by Feminism and Anti-Nuclear Activism' (2017)[3], I began by exploring an anomaly from my perspective as a feminist art historian whose work focuses on the 1970s and early 1980s and tends to foreground maternal and filial ambivalence. This anomaly was that while social reproductive labour had largely been the target of protest and subversive revisions in feminist theorizations, activist interventions, and art practices, in the visual and material manifestations of feminist anti-nuclear activisms, motherhood and gendered care-giving were simultaneously challenged and mobilized. Rather than ambivalence, it was care and responsibility that were highlighted, as well as pre-Oedipal maternal authority. Mourning and motherhood were mobilized, often together, and their mobilizations were given concrete form: objects were repurposed and/or made and performatively deployed, such as a child-sized coffin with the inscription 'Human Race' delivered to one of the gates at USRAF Greenham Common and subsequently taken inside by the military police, providing opportunities for powerful photographic documentation. In an anti-nuclear poster made for distribution across community centres and eventually the Greenham Common peace camp, Shirley Cameron of Sister Seven,[4] a collaborative group including also artists Monica Ross and Evelyn Silver and poets Mary Michaels and Gillian Allnutt, wrote of the unexpected and unimaginable—and yet repeatedly represented—premature death of her prematurely born babies, exemplifying the strategy that I named "pre-emptive mourning" against the fallacy of Cold War nuclear deterrence.[5]

This designation of "pre-emptive mourning" as maternal, implicitly or explicitly, led me to research the broader ways in which mothering is evoked in feminist anti-nuclear activism. By the early 1980s, the maternalism of earlier women's pacifism and anti-nuclear movements,[6] was morphing into a non- (or perhaps less) essentialist re-confirmation of women's special role in contemporary pacifism, which in the context of the Cold War arms race

3. Alexandra M. Kokoli, 'Pre-Emptive Mourning Against the Bomb: Exploded Domesticities in Art Informed by Feminism and Anti-Nuclear Activism', *Oxford Art Journal* 40, no. 1 (March 2017), pp. 153–168.

4. Sister Seven, Posters and Actions (1981–1984), www.monicaross.org/artworks/SisterSeven.html.

5. Kokoli, 'Pre-Emptive Mourning Against the Bomb'.

6. See Jill Liddington, *The Long Road to Greenham: Feminism & Anti-Militarism in Britain since 1820* (London: Virago, 1989), especially the chapter 'War, Motherhood and The Hague', pp. 87–106. It is interesting that Women in Black (est. 1988), a women's anti-militarist anti-war group, mobilizes the iconography of the grieving mother while on the other hand explaining their women-only constituency in non-essentialist terms, making note of the disproportionate impact of war and displacement on women as well as the well-known links between militarism and toxic masculinity. Women in Black, 'Who are Women in Black?', http://womeninblack.org/about-women-in-black/.

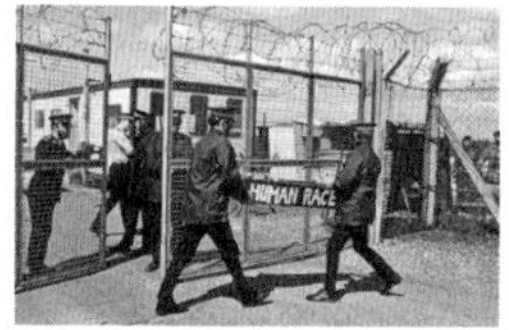
Coffin delivered at a gate of USRAF Greenham Common, n.d. In Beeban Kidron, Lindsay Poulton and Guardian Films, *Your Greenham.*

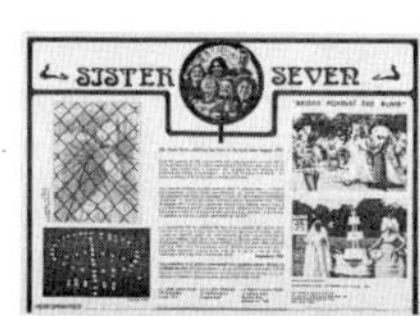
Sister Seven poster, c. 1981, Monica Ross Archive

Feminist Art Activisms and Artivisms

7. Liddington, *The Long Road to Greenham*, p. 226.

8. Olive Schreiner, *Woman and Labour* (1911), Project Gutenberg ebook, www.gutenberg.org/ebooks/1440, n.p.

9. Liddington *The Long Road to Greenham*, p. 227. For an overview of the nuances of maternalism in women's peace movements see Sasha Roseneil, *Disarming Patriarchy: Feminism and Political Action at Greenham* (Buckingham: Open University Press, 1995), pp. 4–7. Although I do not wholly agree with the distinctions that this overview draws, it falls outside the scope of this paper to critique them.

10. Cook and Kirk, *Greenham Women Everywhere*, p. 14.

11. Nick Higham, 'Margaret Thatcher Aides Used Prince William in Media War', BBC News, 21 July 2016, www.bbc.co.uk/news/uk-36847895.

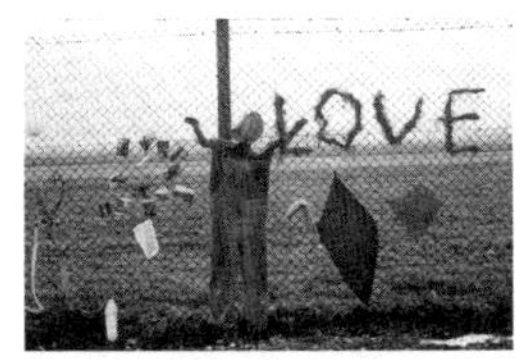

The fence at Greenham Common with additions by protesters from the peace camp, c. 1982. Photo: Sigrid Møller, the Women's International League for Peace and Freedom, slides scanned by Holger Terp, June 2006, from *The Danish Peace Academy Greenham Common Women's Peace Camps Songbook*.

was also specifically anti-nuclear. In Britain, the decline of the Campaign for Nuclear Disarmament through the 1970s (compared to the previous decade) presented a need and also opportunity for the revitalization of anti-nuclear campaigning on different terms. The formation of the group 'Women for Life on Earth' in Wales exhibited an "earthy pragmatism"[7] which was reminiscent of but not the same as, for example, Olive Schreiner's rhetorically romanticized description of "men's bodies" as "women's works of art".[8] Rather, an emergent womanist anti-nuclear politics foregrounded the recognition that the arms race affects women disproportionately by diverting funding from social care and putting pressure on unpaid carers; and claimed a more active role for women in the anti-nuclear movement, noting that they, already conditioned to unpaid labour, had long been squeezing activist work in their "spare" time.[9] Childbearing and childcare were approached both in terms of affect and the compromising, unpaid and undervalued labour of social reproduction. Although the gendered character of women's motivations to protest against nuclear deterrence exceeded their maternal labour and responsibility, including, for instance, the fear of 'being thought hysterical' in sharing one's fears with others, and the systematic denigration of women's peace camps and other initiatives as "'naïve", "sincere", "emotional'" in the press,[10] the centrality of the maternal dimension was well understood and exploited by both protestors and the establishment alike.

UK government documents released to the National Archives in Kew in 2016 revealed serious worries over the influence and impact of anti-nuclear activism in the early 1980s, threatening to escalate to mass civil disobedience that would require violent intervention. In addition to the chilling recommendation that, should it become necessary to shoot at protestors, the task must be performed by any of the British forces present (constabulary police, MoD police, or the British military) and not the US military, in order to avoid an international incident, Prime Minister Margaret Thatcher's press secretary Bernard Ingham published a list of suggestions for stealing the thunder from a large anti-nuclear demonstration in London on Easter Monday, 4 April 1983.[11] Ingham's suggestions included the promotion of what he considered to be traditional British bank holiday

Alexandra Kokoli

activities, such as 'pigeon or whippet or tortoise racing', and photographs of the then newly appointed Secretary of State for Defence Michael Heseltine's visit to the Berlin Wall, the one material manifestation of the Iron Curtain in Europe. Another suggestion, which is confirmed to have been acted on, was originally redacted from the documents: pictures of baby Prince William, then aged ten months and on his first visit to Australia and New Zealand, were released to the press and widely published. The royal baby was extensively photographed with his parents as well as his staff, including nannies and security detail. Such "soft" publicity offensives were targeted against small women's anti-nuclear groups, like Babies Against the Bomb, established in 1981, who eloquently articulated a new maternalist anti-nuclear paci-fism. The group understood childcare as both a challenge to and invigoration of activist commitment and made no distinction between the lives of one's own children and those of others across the globe.[12] Babies Against the Bomb were simultaneously ridiculed for the perceived frivolity of their chosen name and self-presentation, and accused of participating in seditious conspiracies orchestrated by Moscow.[13] Motivated at least partly by such bizarre and disproportionate attacks, the Greater London Council (GLC) supported Babies Against the Bomb in the context of its "Peace Year 1983", under the auspices of which a number of art projects, publications, exhibitions, and performances were funded. Hazel Atashroo describes such offensives and counter-offensives in terms of a heated publicity war,[14] even as both sides claimed to strive to avert war through directly opposed means: the covert accumulation of nuclear weapons versus the highly visual campaigning for their abolition. This really was baby to baby combat—in representation.

When I presented a paper on "pre-emptive mourning" at the conference 'Replacement', organized by BRAKC: Birkbeck Research in Aesthetics of Kinship and Community in December 2016,[15] I kept the same ending as my article for the *Oxford Art Journal*, which had not yet been published but had been accepted in its final form.[16] I closed with a quote from Jacqueline Rose paraphrasing Virginia Woolf's call to pacifism in *Three Guineas*, in an effort to express the continuity of feminism's contribution against militarism:

12. Tamar Swade, 'Babies Against the Bomb', in *Keeping the Peace*, ed. Lynne Jones (Women's Press: London, 1983), pp. 64–67.

13. For example, Conservative peer Max Beloff named Babies Against the Bomb alongside the women of Greenham Common as Soviet spies in a House of Lords speech in 1984, although such accusations appear not to have been uncommon. See Hazel Atashroo, 'Weaponising peace: the Greater London Council, cultural policy and 'GLC peace year 1983', *Contemporary British History* 33, no. 2 (2019), pp. 170–186.

14. Ibid.

15. BRAKC: Birkbeck Research in Aesthetics of Kinship and Community, *Replacement Conference Programme*, www.brakc.bbk.ac.uk/wp-content/uploads/2015/05/Replacement-recd-18-July-WEB.pdf.

16. Kokoli, 'Pre-Emptive Mourning Against the Bomb'.

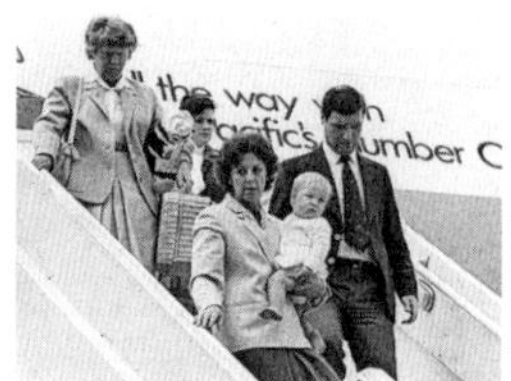

Prince William landing at Gatwick Airport, with nannies Barbara Barnes, Olga Powell, and unidentified staff, April 1983

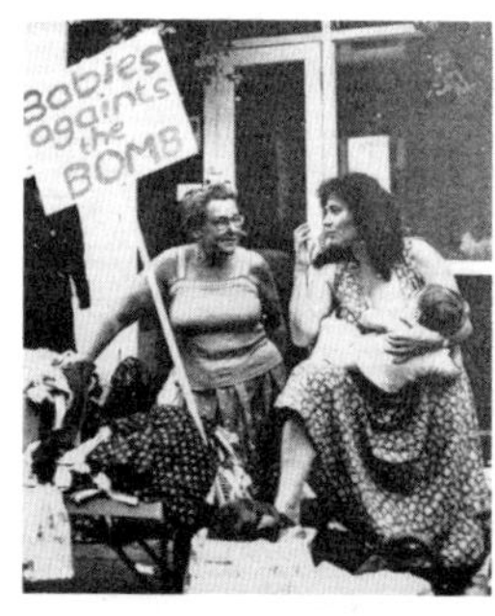

Uncaptioned and undated photograph with Tamar Swade on the right, from 'Babies Against the Bomb: A Statement by Tamar Swade', in Lynne Jones (ed.), *Keeping the Peace* (London: Women's Press, 1983), p. 66

17. Jacqueline Rose, *Why War: Psychoanalysis, Politics, and the Return to Melanie Klein* (Blackwell: Oxford, 1993), p. 37; Virginia Woolf, *Three Guineas* (Harmondsworth: Penguin, 1977), p. 90.

Virginia Woolf proposes ridicule, censure, and contempt as the great antidotes to vanity, egotism, and megalomania, and then poverty, chastity, derision, and freedom from unreal loyalties (all mostly imposed on the female sex) as the conditions for women's entry into a world of professionalism which, without them, will inevitably lead to war. Hang on to failure, hang on to derision—a failure and derision that would not invite a reactive triumphalism but pre-empt it—if you want to avoid going to war.[17]

I found this free indirect speech whereby Woolf's words are revisited and rewritten by Rose compelling, while the counter-intuitive emphasis on the minor mode conveyed something of the DIY craft aesthetics of the Greenham women's temporary interventions on the fence surrounding the base: my audience was embarrassingly small yet, to my delight, included Juliet Mitchell, who gave me very positive feedback but also urged me to change the ending. However much it was qualified, failure did not make for an adequate conclusion in the immediate aftermath of the election of Donald Trump to the US presidency and the recognition that such heretofore unthinkable events were symptomatic of a wider resurgence of anti-progressive and specifically anti-feminist forces. I felt remorseful and embarrassed that it was too late to change the conclusion to my article. I spent the following months looking for reasons to support my misguided emphasis on failure and hoping not to find them.

I had come across many anecdotal references to the role of Greenham in bringing the Cold War to an end thanks to the strong impression it made on Mikhail Gorbachev, who reportedly viewed the global peace movement favourably, perhaps because its most visible manifestations were conveniently in the West. Ann Pettitt gives the most sustained defence of this position in her memoir *Walking to Greenham*, which also relates her travels to the USSR to liaise with the Moscow Group for Trust, one of the few semi-covert Soviet anti-deterrence groups. Pettitt proposes that Gorbachev's personal experience of agricultural work as a teenage boy inculcated in him a different attitude to the planet, reminiscent of the "earthy pragmatism" of Women for Life of Earth:[18] 'whatever is dividing us, we live on the same planet and Europe is our common home—a home, not a theatre of military operations'.[19] The real reasons behind the end of the Cold War (or rather the cold war that ended in 1989), are complex and obviously fall outside the scope of this text as well as my research in general. I was, however, highly intrigued by Pettitt's ambition: she goes much further than anecdotally claiming that Greenham Common helped convince Gorbachev to end the Cold War, offering instead a pervasive interpretation of his beliefs, attitudes, and modus operandi, which foreground the influence of his wife Raisa and attribute to him some stereotypically feminine characteristics of emotional intelligence and a willingness to de-escalate inter-personal tensions and put a good face on difficult situations.[20] Rather than women's peace movements making an impression on him, Pettitt suggests that confluence and affinity might better describe the relationship between Gorbachev and the Greenham women.

David Fairhall, a sympathetic reporter on Greenham throughout the 1980s for *The Guardian*, concludes his 2006 book *Common Ground* with a "Straw poll" on the question: 'what did the Greenham women's protest achieve, and what difference, if any, did it make to the outcome of the Cold War?'[21] *Guardian* columnist Polly Toynbee is surprisingly ungenerous in claiming that Greenham may have galvanized the women's movement but had no effect on the Cold War whatsoever,[22] with other interviewees, including British and American military officers and Newbury residents, expressing much less favourable views. Instead, the cost of repairing the damage to the perimeter fence of the base and the nuisance of the encampment to the locals come up time and again. Even those most invested in asserting the value of Greenham concede that it is not simple to argue for the success of these years of women's protest. If not in its politics, Greenham did embrace failure in some form in its aesthetics. The inexperience of the majority of the protesters is a well-documented fact, and is often elevated to one of its distinct features, even a virtue:

> In my view, it is thanks to the millions of people in the western world for whom protest was a relatively easy option, and to a brave few in the East for whom

18. Liddington, *The Long Road to Greenham*, p. 226.

19. Mikhail Gorbachev cited in Ann Pettitt, *Walking to Greenham: How the Peace Camp Began and the Cold War Ended* (South Glamorgan: Honno, 2006), p. 295.

20. Pettitt undertakes a close reading of Gorbachev's memoirs particularly in regard to his representation to the press of the Reykjavik summit of October 1986. Mikhail Gorbachev, *Memoirs* (New York: Bantam, 1997), and Pettitt, *Walking to Greenham*, p. 300.

21. David Fairhall, *Common Ground: The Story of Greenham* (London: IB Tauris, 2006), pp. 191–202.

22. Ibid., p. 202.

23. Pettitt, *Walking to Greenham*, p. 309.

24. Ibid.

25. *Greenham Women Everywhere*, project and exhibition information, http://greenhamwomeneverywhere.co.uk/about/.

26. Carly Guest, *Becoming Feminist: Narratives and Memories* (London: Palgrave Macmillan, 2016), p. 145.

it wasn't, that the arms race ended with a whimper (the end of the USSR) and not with a bang (the end of the world as we know it. [...] We did this [...] not because we were good at campaigning, but because we were bad at it; not because we went about things in a professional way, but because we were amateurs; not because we were clever, but because we were naïve.[23]

Pettitt continues that although no formula can be gleaned and applied to other situations, the Greenham lesson is that any effective response to new threats 'too will appear amateurish, apparently naïve, and coming from the most unexpected of places, [and] will at first be beneath notice'.[24] Pettitt's future orientation and counterintuitive recommendations helped me realize that looking at the retrospective views of the participants would only reproduce the oppositions by which they were originally and continue to be divided. My reorientation was helped further by the announcement, in Autumn 2018, of a new oral history project organized by Kate Kerrow of the Heroine Collective and Rebecca Mordan of Cornish feminist theatre hub Scary Little Girls, with the aim of disseminating the legacies of Greenham through a free website, a nationwide exhibition, and by archiving the collected oral histories at the Women's Library at the London School of Economics.[25] The success or lack thereof of feminist anti-nuclear protest should not be judged by whether and how it may have contributed to an ending (of the Cold War) but in that it refuses to ever fully bring itself to an end. In her book *Becoming Feminist: Narratives and Memories*, Carly Guest considers the ways in which the development of feminist consciousness is transmitted through story-telling, images, and cultural artefacts, and how new feminists remember, narrativize, and share their own coming to feminism. Greenham Common features prominently in 'Ruby's Story', where a young woman describes herself as 'completely, completely, utterly obsessed' with Greenham Common, and mesmerized by the Greenham songbook.[26] Rather than fandom, this obsession initiates her into feminist politics, allowing her to imagine herself as a heroine and to eventually become an activist. In reference to another research participant, Beth, Guest

DEATH

explores visualizations (and materializations) of shared emotion in visual activism, and stumbles on a familiar if unsettling protest prop: the inscribed coffin. 'Part of the power of the image is its familiarity, not only as a social and cultural practice and a symbol of loss and grief, but also as a form of protest.'[27]

Coda: Towards a Virtual Feminist Museum[28]

To the question 'what makes a feminist masterpiece?', posed by the call for papers of the conference 'Mistress-Pieces: Iconic Artworks by Feminists and Gender Activists' (November 2018),[29] I responded with the performative activist strategies of women protestors at the Greenham Common Women's Peace Camp and their craft-based DIY interventions on the periphery fence of the Greenham Common USRAF airbase, in lieu of any single feminist or gender-critical "mistress-piece". Taking stock of feminist art historical critiques of the monographic approach as well as the post-medium materialist emphasis on "(art)work" as labour rather than completed output, I suggested that a virtual archive of diverse documentation (visual, material, textual, oral historical) is better suited to represent the aesthetic, political and ethical legacies of the feminist 1980s in Britain than any single artwork or project. Crucially, the protesters at Greenham Common showed a precocious aptitude for visual activism, knowingly mobilizing women's crafts, with all their ambiguous connotations, in the service of anti-militarist and anti-masculinist resistance. The peace camp brought together intersecting feminist issues, including pacifism, domestic politics, social reproduction, and the fight against poverty and global inequalities, and it remained profoundly intergenerational and international, while also bravely negotiating class and ethnic divides among women.

In the course of researching and writing my contribution to 'Mistress-Pieces', I came to the realization that although casting the expanded women's peace camp— its content, periphery and material commemorations, reflections, extensions—as a "mistress piece" initially seemed plausible, such a designation would not do justice to its significance. Rather than a feminist masterpiece, the

27. Ibid., p. 154.

28. Griselda Pollock, *Encounters in the Virtual Feminist Museum: Time, Space and the Archive* (London: Routledge, 2007).

29. SARChI, University of Johannesburg, Mistress Pieces Conference Announcement, www.uj.ac.za/faculties/fada/Pages/SARChI-Conferences.aspx.

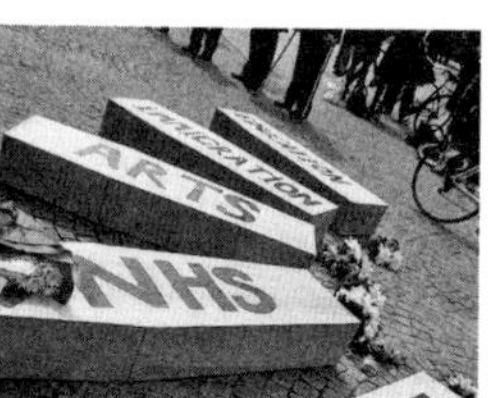

Coffins in anti-cuts demonstration, 2011. Photo: Beth, from Carly Guest, *Becoming Feminist: Narratives and Memories* (New York: Palgrave Macmillan, 2016), p. 153

peace camp and its Berkshire site are now beginning to be recognized as an important example of English (and Welsh) heritage with a transnational reach. Through my work, I now strive to consolidate, elaborate, and further promote this recognition, while also troubling the notion of "heritage" with the tool kit of feminist art history. Viewed through the lens of feminist intergenerational transmission, Greenham Common perfectly exemplifies Griselda Pollock's formulation of the virtual feminist museum.[30] Mobilizing Aby Warburg's *Nachleben* (afterlife/survival by metamorphosis), the virtual feminist museum untethers artefacts, images, and practices from their historical contexts and sets them in motion, tracing their travels, re-occurrences and transformations across time and space. For Pollock, virtuality is not opposed to actuality but vibrates with the possibility of imminent realization. I believe that the virtual museum of Greenham Common is fuelled by the intersection of ever-growing scholarship devoted to it and the enduring fascination that it exercises on young feminist activists in their continuing fight for change, be it against war, the arms trade, nuclear power, global inequalities, or austerity. Although the afterlife of Warburg's legacy is guaranteed thanks to Pollock and many more scholars, his notion of *Nachleben* is transformed when applied to a movement for which survival was not merely metaphorical.

Alexandra Kokoli

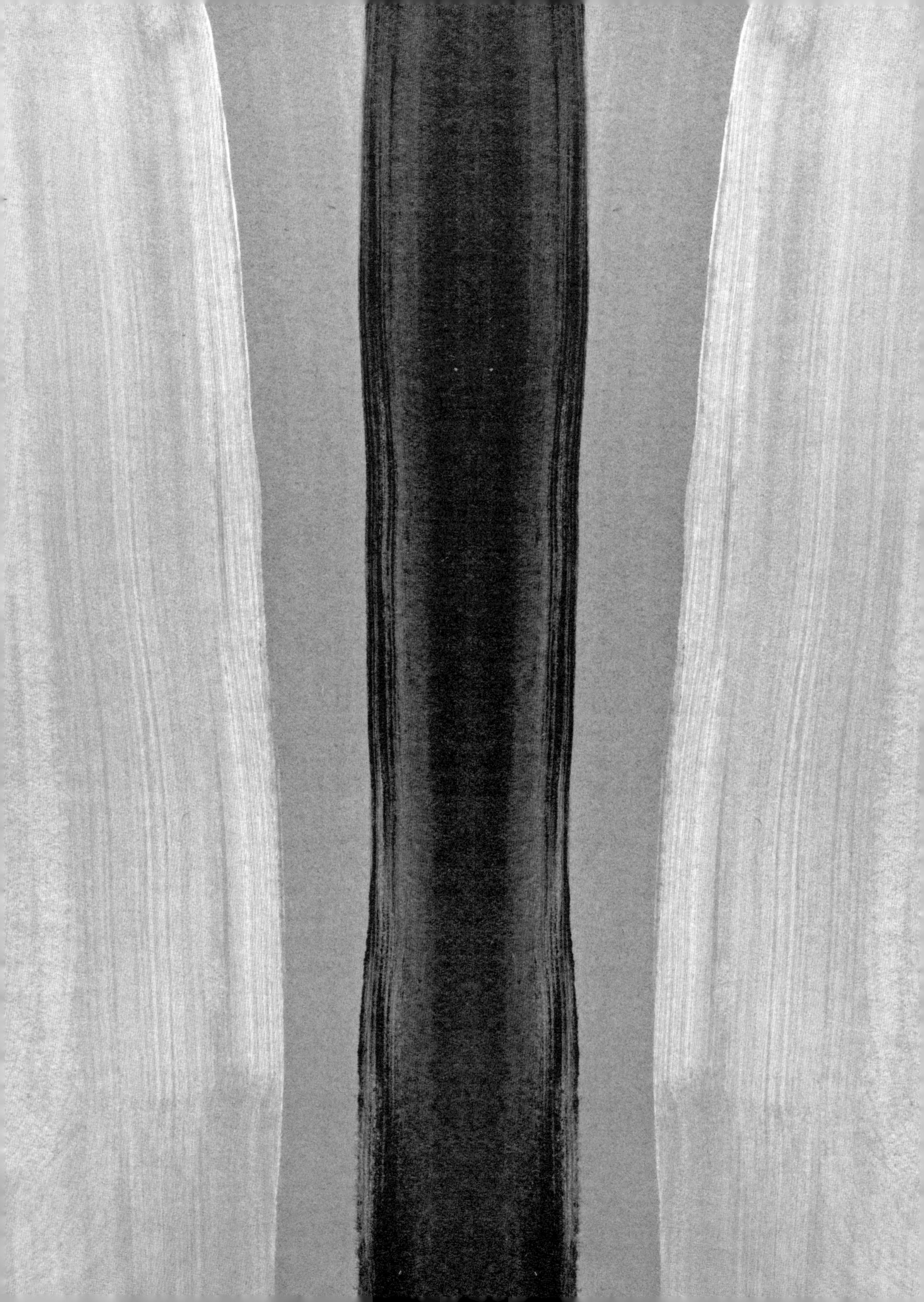

CENTREFOLD 1974: A MEMOIR
A Series of Excerpts

Louise O'Hare

1. References to comments by Lynda Benglis in 'Oral history interview with Lynda Benglis', Judith Tannenbaum, 20 November 2009, Archives of American Art, Smithsonian Institution, www.aaa.si.edu/collections/interviews/oral-history-interview-lynda-benglis-15741#transcript and Will Pavia, 'Lynda Benglis: The woman who refused to take her clothes off for Warhol', *The Times*, 3 February 2015.

My eyes are bleeding. I've been trying to read every single bit of press on Lynda Benglis from 2004–2017. I'm attempting to gather the various ways the story of Lynda Benglis' 1974 *Artforum* advert is dropped in, inserted, summarized. In this I have a couple of lovely assistants: the interns at Cheim & Read and Thomas Dane, my imaginary friends in New York and London, workers who I've already assumed are white, female, degree-educated, and slightly bored.

In 1966 when Lynda worked at Bykert in New York and then briefly for Paula Cooper, she says it was all about talking with artists and collectors, working out how everything works, so that she could see the shortcuts—the logical conclusions—tell Robert Ryman to paint directly on the wall, and Dan Flavin to just use the light itself—'he went blink, blink'.[1]

In 2004 when I was interning, I didn't have long black hair or long woollen skirts, or ever get mistaken for a starlet. It was all about photocopying to produce thick folders of press, then weighing them in, leaning in, and offering the collector a chance to find a critic-academic-art writer-journalist-curator (it didn't matter) to validate their taste. I wonder if my assistants still produce printed ones, alongside the pdfs they upload to the gallery website.

I guess the broad time span of my survey, 2004–2017, might seem arbitrary—especially when I tell you that this is when the "Selected Press" starts on Cheim & Read's website. But this moment, when Cheim & Read started representing Benglis (ten years after her final show at Paula Cooper Gallery), also, and not coincidentally, marks the beginning of her market and critical reappraisal, including as it does, the blockbuster "feminist" art shows, in Europe and the US: Venice 2005, 'WACK!', 2007.

*

I've been understanding *Centrefold* (1974) as its gossip, the performance expanded, circulating, ongoing, due to its continued appearance as quick two-line descriptions, tit bits dropped into conversation, inserted into interviews and articles.

I've been through 99 pieces of gallery press now, but I haven't quite finished—and I've slightly extended the constraint of only looking at what her galleries provide because I keep coming across articles they've missed, in the same types of publications they have previously archived. In my spreadsheet I note what paragraph the mention appears in, how many words it contains, and how many sentences. So far the average number of words is 66 and the number of sentences to describe "this act",

2. Michael Warner, 'Publics and Counterpublics', *Public Culture* 14, no. 1 (Winter 2002), pp. 49–90.

3. Pavia, 'Lynda Benglis'. See also William Poundstone, 'Dear Artforum: About That Lynda Benglis Ad...', *ArtInfo* [online], 1 August 2011.

4. Richard Meyer, 'Bone of Contention: Richard Meyer on Lynda Benglis' Controversial Advertisement', *Artforum*, November 2004, pp. 73–74 and 249–250. The idea that a way of understanding Benglis' practice is through what appears and is presented as peripheral, or diversionary is also suggested by James Boaden discussing her work *Parenthesis*, 1975. See James Boaden, 'Lives in Exchange: The Collaborative Video Tapes of Lynda Benglis and Robert Morris', *Tate Papers*, Spring 2016, www.tate.org.uk/research/publications/tate-papers/25/lives-inexchange.

this "single, notorious gesture", this "flagrant reminder", "this satire", this "explicit parody", "her mockery", "and the ensuing art-world rumpus", "seismic", "so outrageous", "a great scandal"; a "succès de scandale" … is most often one and at maximum four. These "passing mentions" seem to occur after the third paragraph, when we have been told other things about Benglis, when we know her and her work and so the story might seem interesting. Michael Warner in 2002, differentiating gossip from public address: 'gossip is never a relation among strangers'.[2]

The delayed timing of this dropping in, to conversation, to discourse, is formally similar to a gossipy aside—faux casual, you are aware the conversation has been leaning towards the opportunity to tell the story. Sometimes the rhythm of the delivery means the it reads like a joke: the punch-line is always the dildo, the "huge *double-ended* dildo", disrupting otherwise earnest criticism. An "unsolicited dick pic" arriving unexpectedly, again, and again.

*
I tried to make Conceptual poetry out
of the short descriptions. Sorting them
out into themes—the cat eye glasses,
the way her body is described, the size
of the dildo (rarely belittled, but only
once a "phallus"), the way she holds it:

**defiantly clutching, and
wielding, wielding, wielding,
wielding, wielding,
and holding, holding,
holding
and brandishing,
brandishing, brandishing,
a gigantic,
large,
gigantic,
giant,
massive
improbably long,
cartoonishly large,
formidable**

*
Searching through old issues of
Artforum is a heavy job—its thick
square format was as unwieldy then as
it is now, and Central Saint Martins
library has compounded this problem
by binding four issues together into
a dusty oversized hardback book.
October, November… I am pleased
to discover the page still there—not,
as apocryphal, ripped out. I consider
stealing it, just for a moment.

The body of Lynda Benglis seems
more explicit, more naked, in full-
colour glossy print than in the smaller
images I have seen online and in books
and magazines. It's only now that I
note the detail in the textures of the
skin, the wrinkles on her hands; the
way the fingers of her right hand splay,
her thumb and forefinger clenching
her waist; the way the light falls on her
protruding ribs. Looking at Benglis'
body here feels more like seeking out
pornography, perhaps because I am
confronted with these realities of the
body. Or is it that skulking between the
bookshelves, finding this page hidden
in an expected spot, reminds me of
stealing a look in the drawer by my
brother's bed?

But libraries cancelled their
subscriptions[3]—the context, furtive in
the library, is not the right one.
*
Richard Meyer says the key to
Centrefold is only for insiders, it is
left to be gathered not explicated,
and he both states and performs this
position—at the end of footnote
number nineteen, in small text, is the
note: 'A series of complex relations
between privacy and publicity, between
secrecy and exposure shaped this
episode in ways that remain fairly
(and perhaps necessarily) opaque to
outsiders.'[4]

His article was first published
in *Artforum* in November 2004, in
celebration of *Centrefold*'s thirtieth
anniversary, and so its publication
is self-historicizing—it presents the
Artforum (rather than the *October*)
version. It was later reproduced
in full colour, an object on the
page, in the 2009 monograph that
accompanied Benglis' international
touring exhibition, which sped up her

recent reappraisal, and its inclusion here makes me think it might also be Lynda's top recommendation for you to read—the Benglis approved version, as well as the *Artforum* version, or at least—"a" Benglis version.[5] Though I'm pretty sure she'd get visibly impatient—imply you should perhaps move on, get over it, introduce you to her dachshund Pi, and invite you to please pay attention to the large cascading polyurethane sculpture in her 2015 Hepworth Wakefield exhibition: translucent plastic, crystal-like and tinted coral pink, it looked a bit like an indoor water fountain from a try-hard restaurant, three teetering stacks, hard to take seriously, pushing again, almost to pastiche, her play with the decorative.[6]

*

'"Vulgarity is gendered, of course." — T.J.Clark' — Richard Meyer

Displaying your scholarship and starting with a quote, potentially completely out of context, is a classic trope of writing about art. This is how Meyer opens his article, neatly indicating a position: a very nice use of the Marxist art historian, to back up Lynda Benglis, who is normally positioned as anything but.

Of course! A confident bold assertion—we can trust him. Clark is writing about Greenberg, and De Kooning's misogynistic comment, 'the black battle stain on a soldier's face is not vulgar, but the dirty face of a housemaid is'.[7] Soldier and housemaid are of a similar class. But one is a hero, the other a slave. It's the domestic or female here that's vulgar, the muck is not transubstantiated through heroism. Still, as we are out of context, I want to add "…and classed" (which he should know)—because I keep noticing reference to her Southern accent, her Louisiana upbringing. But I suppose it goes without saying that ideas of taste are classed, ideas of who can be critical and decorative, who can perform an equivocality and who is enjoying themselves a bit too much.

*

I am, we are, at an event for The World Transformed (a politics, art and music festival running alongside the Labour Party national conference 2017). A small red plastic table and some chairs, coloured pens and paper have been set up for children in the corner. One of the stewards seems to be looking after another toddler, though I can't work out if it's his child, or someone else's. Selma James, one of the founders of the Wages For Housework campaign, is one of the panellists for a discussion titled 'Radical Childcare', and in my delegate's report to the local party I quip that this demand from the early 1970s 'sounds radical, but isn't if you take a few minutes to think about it'.

5. Franck Gautherot, Caroline Hancock and Seungduk Kim, eds., *Lynda Benglis* (Dijon: Les presses du réel, 2009).

6. Lynda Benglis, *The Graces*, 2003/2005, cast polyurethane, lead, stainless steel.

7. T.J. Clark, *Farewell to An Idea: Episodes from a History of Modernism* (New Haven, CT and London: Yale University Press, 1999), p. 393.

8. Silvia Federici, *Wages against Housework* (Bristol: Power of Women Collective/Falling Wall Press, April 1975).

9. Mariarosa Dalla Costa and Selma James, 'Women and the Subversion of the Community', 29 December 1971, first published in *The Power of Women and the Subversion of the Community* (Bristol: Falling Wall Press, 1973).

The Wages for Housework campaign was launched in 1972 in Padova by the International Feminist Collective, and in New York, Spring 1974, Silvia Federici wrote *Wages against Housework*. The lines opening her book: 'They say it is love. We say it is un-waged work', succinctly gathering and developing the arguments of the movement.[8]

I heard about the event from Vanessa Roberts, who told me that James had set up Crossroads Women's Centre, which, its website tells me, 'began as a squat in Drummond Street near Euston Station in 1975 opened by the Wages for Housework campaign', before being chased by developers from Euston, to Kings Cross and arriving at its current location in Kentish town where it is constituted as a charity which now owns the building, 'thanks to the generosity and commitment of volunteers, core users and supporters'.

I start to think of the London-based Selma James as the overlooked, grass-roots focused activist, compared to Federici, the better-known New York-based counterpart. But flicking through my tasteful pale green copy of Federici's collected writings I see that James' collected writings were published by the same press, the same year. Was missing James simply a personal oversight, or is Federici referenced more in the contemporary art discourse that I come across? Does James' writing have a stronger emphasis on class and race, that doesn't appeal to "the art world"? Is it because Silvia is a professor and Selma is not? Is it because there is more cash available for feminism in the US?

*

Selma James' mini-bio on the publicity states that she is one of the founders of Global Women's Strike, launched in 1999 by the Wages for Housework campaign with a demand for 'payment for all caring work'. The strike was inspired by the Women's "day off" in Iceland in 1975, but they've always been clear this is not about a holiday, a reward for work, but rather (as indeed with Wages for Housework) thinking about the power of collective action and unionization.

December 1971—Mariarosa Dalla Costa and Selma James declare 'we have worked enough'.[9] The Wages for Housework campaigns were "*against* housework"—they sought to refuse the myths of liberation through work, and they drew parallels and established solidarity between the housewife and the factory worker that she supported—promoting an awareness of the fact that care—reproductive "women's" work—was as much part of what enabled production as punching in and out at the factory. If the figure of *both* the unionized factory worker and the housewife now seem passé, the Global Women's Strike updates the argument, attempting to demonstrate that this out-modedness is not because the question of gendered labour is over, but rather due to the erosion of union power and the fact that the majority of women with children now not only undertake unpaid care but also low-paid exploitative part-time work. James calls this "the double day" in her speech, describing how mothers, in particular lone parents, get home from work to do more.

*

February 2016—I give birth to a girl in the Royal London Hospital on Whitechapel High Street—I become more local, circle my area. The park, the baby clinic for weighing, 'please take off all her clothes and put her in the metal dish on the scale', the best green grocers is the one with the orange signage on the corner, Superdrug for cheaper nappies, the park, the park again. I need the toilet and realize I can't leave her outside alone, and I can't take her in the cubicle. I learn to make use of disabled toilets, where there is room to park a pram inside. I learn that most of the Tube is *not* accessible for wheelchairs. I go to a baby "Sing and Sign" class in the church hall. I am no longer singular and placed only in an imaginary constellation of ideas of places and escape—but am breathing and shitting and delicate skinned dependent on help and support here in this overpopulated polluted city, in a borough with, I discover, 49% child poverty (it's now 53%).

I join Momentum and meet Jenny, Alena, Apsana, Leah, Gabi and Paula, and I find the skills needed to set up a small-scale not-for-profit arts organization or run an events programme can be easily re-applied to helping promote a political campaign. I find that more enthusiasm to work for free is now more forthcoming, from myself, from others. Perhaps it comes easy because I'm inured by a culture

of volunteerism in the arts, or because it is a relief to be *doing something*. I ask an artist friend, Daniel, to design some posters for signs. He makes badges too and it's exciting to produce something quickly, running them off the photocopier, clicking the parts together. The badges are just for fun, are perhaps a distraction, a guilty pleasure, but they perform an identification—*art magic*—they seem, somehow, to protect us.

*

I'm doing the endnotes and looking at a picture of Benglis' cartoonishly tall fountains—water cascading from tree-height into a leafy landscape[10]—and I share a text from Mierle Laderman Ukeles with Leslie, a note from 1970 'on being a woman maintenance artist':

> I want to use my freedom to move not only "up" and "away" but also "sideways", "backwards", "through", and "around and around" to weave and loop and loosen up existing structures: never forget the feelings of powerlessness [...] not cease to know the taste in the mouth of

10. Three identical fountains titled *Bounty, Amber Waves,* and *Fruited Plane* (2014, 25 feet tall, cast bronze) installed at 'Lynda Benglis: Water Sources', Storm King Art Center, Hudson Valley, New York, 16 May–8 November 2015.

11. Mierle Laderman Ukeles, 'A Note on Being a Woman Maintenance Artist', c. 1970, reprinted in *Mierle Laderman Ukeles: Maintenance Art*, ed. Patricia C. Phillips (Munich and London: Prestel and DelMonico Books; New York: Queens Museum, 2016), p. 212.

12. Leslie Kulesh, *Anthropo-scenester*, 2016, installed at 'is it rude or polite to leave the room?', Cell Project Space, London, 30 June–7 August 2016

the hatred of dependence that this society encourages."

When I first met Leslie at her opening she had made an odd hanging structure of various mass produced fabrics stitched together, printed with words "farmers market", "intellectual property" and "one size fits all" repeated over and over, and she had Avy strapped to her and later she told me that it needed to be a work she could make in pieces.[12] I wore Dora to the opening too, wanted to show that I could do two things at once, and it was a pleasant evening, but I guess it would have been more feminist to point out how difficult it can be.

*

In the car Jenny—credit her—Jenny Fisher—asks what the thesis is about and I describe *Centrefold* quickly and clumsily—revealing my embarrassment that this is my day job. Later she sends me an email, subject: "ambivalence". I imagine her deadpan tone, slightly amused at me, slightly amused at this her own history she describes:

> The fight for Liberation was a struggle against and a struggle for. We knew what we were against. Almost. We knew some of the things we were for. And we knew we knew less about what we were for and we knew we shared fewer common assumptions about what we were for than what we were against.
>
> Could an individual act of defiance be part of the struggle? Of course it could—because the

struggle was not defined, it was not finite, and anything which the individual perceived as a defiance of patriarchy or capital or both had to be part of the struggle against and part of the struggle for which was born out of the experience of struggle against. And of course it couldn't— because the struggle against had to be collective struggle—else it wasn't a struggle for women's liberation but just a struggle for individual liberation.
>
> …

Jenny reminds me that tabloid tales of scorned Generation Sex might hold secrets of threatening female working-class disorder—does this sound patronizing? Am I reading too much into these throwaway comments from a friend? Is quoting something out of context ever useful? Can the performance of any individual act threaten capital or patriarchy? *Trust I've got this ambivalence sorted.*

*

I'm a delegate, elected by delegates of the local branches of Tower Hamlets Labour party, to attend the conference, and elected largely because I was on the Momentum slate. I'm a hand-waver, a "foot soldier"—I consider myself mandated—not here as an individual. Much of my note-taking will focus on gathering quotes that damn privatization from Labour MPs that I can then gather into my report to be circulated to the local party on our return, and add fuel to our challenging of the Labour Mayor over his plans to privatize Tower Hamlets' three remaining public nurseries.

Tracy Brabin, a newly elected Labour MP and Shadow Minister for Early Years, speaking on the "Radical" panel starts me off well. She describes the details—the precise ways the underfunding of the Conservative's 30 hours childcare scheme is impacting nurseries, the growth of enormous nursery chains, and the problems caused by it being such a fragmented sector. Later, writing up, I include James' disgust that Labour abolished lone parent social security (in 1997) and her disappointment that the restoration of universal Child Benefit was missing from the 2017 Labour manifesto. Framed this way I start to see it represented a small step towards women's reproductive work being financially recompensed, and kick my knee jerk acceptance that means-testing Child Benefit was fair.

What does it mean to 'redefine what it means to do politics and debate new ideas'? I can't reconcile this panel, which is in the same format of every talk I have ever been to, with its marketing speak of "doing politics differently". "Radical Childcare"— apparent oxymoron—someone decided that "childcare" is boring, monotonous and needed some heroics. Still, it got me along, this promise of the new I'm struggling with, whilst trying to insist upon a revaluing of the repetitive, the done before, the needs doing, saying, again (and again). The marketing also niggles because "radical" reads like "Radical Feminism", which is conflated with conservative and

essentialist varieties (more than a niggle itself), and because "childcare" is already so often used in a derisory way that misses the chance to value the work nursery staff and childminders do—trained to provide structured early years education. If we value their work, it works two-fold—becomes much clearer how unjust the system is for children too, education denied to those most in need of it.

Over a thousand nurseries across the country have closed under funding pressure since the 30 hours "free" childcare scheme was introduced, and others have raised their fees.[13] In this funding environment every parent or carer is left to make consumer choices—find the most affordable option, pay extra for your child to be cared for by people with more training and experience.

Dora loves going to the local Montessori, it has a great ethos, an emphasis on the developmental importance of play, and is right next to the park, ten minutes' walk from our flat. I put her name down while she was still in my belly, punting a non-refundable fifty quid deposit to add her to the waiting list (they explained that it was very long, and still didn't guarantee a place).

13. Donna Ferguson, 'A thousand nurseries close as free childcare scheme falters', *Observer*, 18 November 2017.

14. Dalla Costa and James, 'Women and the Subversion of the Community'.

15. Hackney Flashers, *Who's holding the baby?* was first exhibited in 1978 at Centreprise, Dalston, London.

16. Hackney Flashers, *Women and Work* combined '250 photographs mounted on panels with text and statistics about women and work' as part of the exhibition '75 Years of Brotherhood: 1900–1975 Trades Union Exhibition', Hackney Town Hall, 20 September–2 October 1975. See https://hackneyflashers.com.

Someone on the panel starts talking about how pre-schools in Sweden have a really great model, and about the New Zealand playgroup movement, and I feel my eyes rolling in my head, before I imagine Selma giving me a stern look, along with Mariarosa, pulling me up: 'Women have always been forced by the working-class parties to put off their liberation to some hypothetical future.'[14]

I know, I know, but I don't think we've got time to re-imagine society right now, we've got to talk about how we preserve what we've got.

*

February 2018—Despite all our efforts, campaigning, petitions, speaking in council, and the motions passed almost unanimously by the local Labour party—the draft manifesto, written by the cabinet, and presented to the GC holds no promise to protect the nurseries from privatization. We attempt to interject with comments, but nothing of what we say is taken on—the consultation with party members is lip-service—meaningless. One section of the crappy manifesto talks about "new parent-led models" of childcare and exasperated I find my hand automatically raised (none of the earlier reticence to speak, or the earlier habit of blurting something out— now trained to behave as the meeting requires): For pities sake cut out "new". Women were self-organizing this kind of thing in the 1970s, and not for fun, only because the government wouldn't provide it.

'Who's (still) holding the baby?'[15] With a Labour Mayor closing public nurseries, the idea of celebrating parent-run cooperative nurseries becomes part of the problem. I know it's a form of DIY empowerment but am guarded when a curator friend suggests we self-organize our own (hot-desking) crèche. She suggests we follow the instructions in an old pamphlet she's found by Jo Spence, but I'm not sure this is really what the Hackney Flashers intended.

September 1975—they display the Hackney Trades Council's 'Working Women's Charter' on a panel next to a photograph of a cleaner. '6—Improved provision of local authority day nurseries, free of charge and with extended hours to suit working mothers. Provision of nursery classes in day nurseries. More nursery schools.'[16]

A woman is standing beside a chalkboard marked with a complex looking diagram, she wields a wide brushed broom and is laughing through thick spectacles.

This is an edited series of excerpts from Victoria Louise Everall O'Hare, *Centrefold 1974: A Memoir*, PhD thesis, University of Northumbria at Newcastle, April 2019.

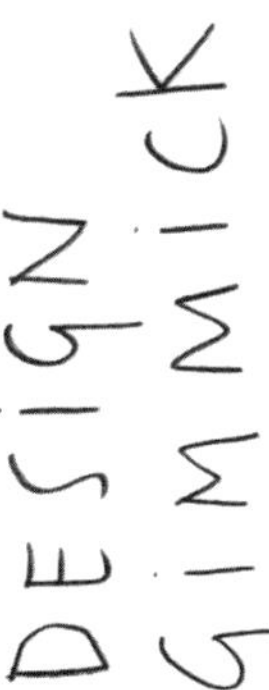

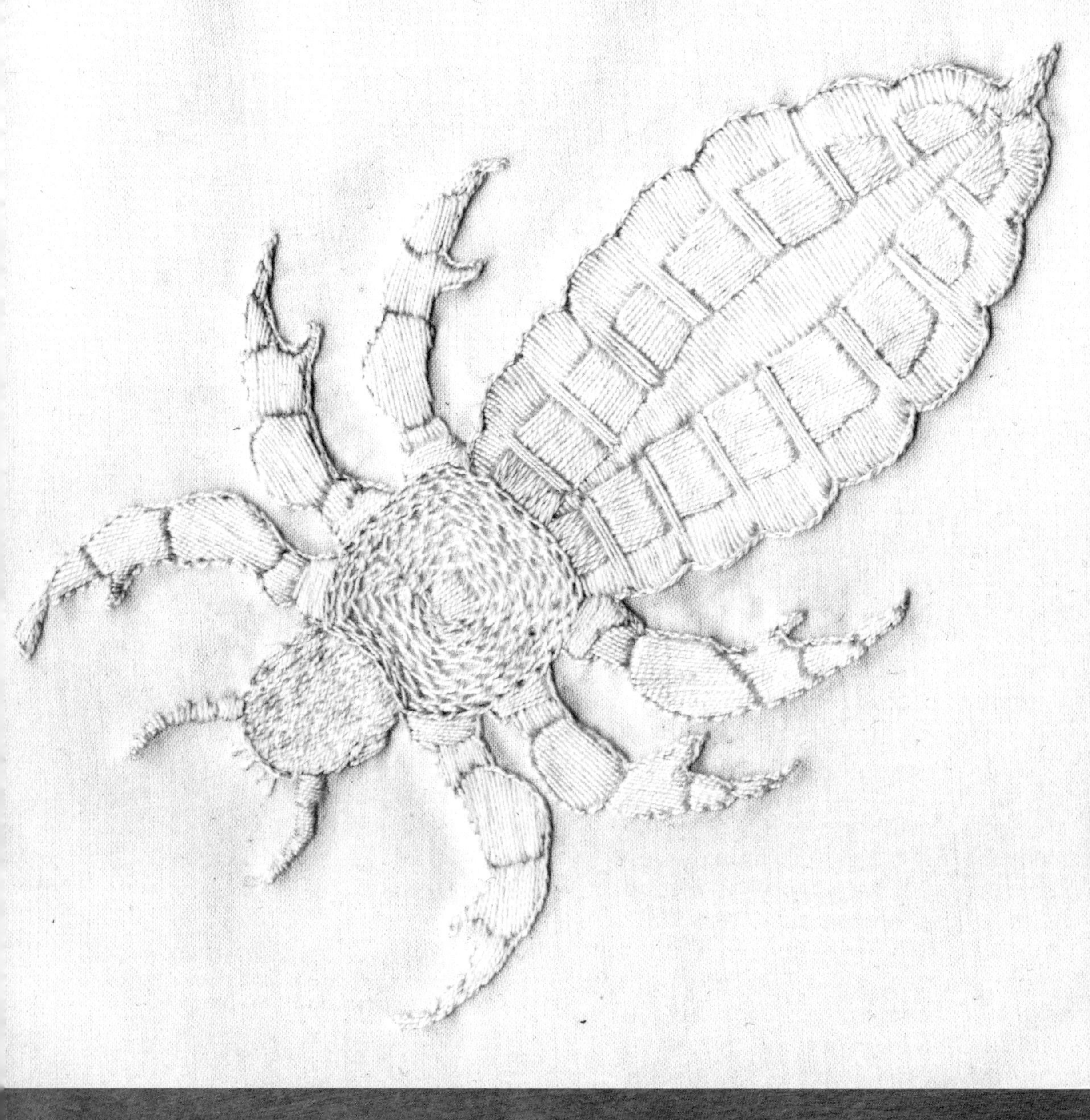

Louse (from Burns' poem *To a Louse*) made by Victoria Mount, Dean Castle Textile Team

REFLECTIONS ON TEXTILE AND MEMORY
The Invisible Hand and Women's Work: Dean Castle Textile Team at the Dick Institute, Kilmarnock

Emma Dick and Kathleen Mullaniff

1. Kathleen Mullaniff and Emma Dick, 'Garland at MYB Textiles (Newmilns)', London, 4 June–31 July 2015.

Our work with the Dean Castle Textile Team is the second socially engaged project since 2013, where we have linked textiles, women's history and Irish-Scottish diasporic cultures.

The Dean Castle Textile Team visited the result of our first collaboration, in a 2015 exhibition with MYB Textiles in Newmilns, Ayrshire, where we had investigated the relationships between lace-making, technology, painting and the feminine.[1] We established an immediate rapport with Linda Fairlie and the volunteers from the team because of our common interests and shared values. Our initial conversations developed in so many interesting directions, reminiscing about textiles we used to make at school and sharing a joy in the collection of christening gowns held in Dean Castle. Meeting Linda Fairlie and the women of the Dean Castle Textile Team in 2015 was a meeting of minds. We decided to visit Dean Castle in Kilmarnock and learn how the team of volunteers worked together, conserving the historic textile collections of Dean Castle; creating costumes for local youth theatre groups and providing a real focus for community engagement and the celebration of local textile and craft skills in Scotland.

Our collaboration brings together our different skills and interests in textiles, dressmaking and entrepreneurship. Over many years, Kathleen has developed a body of painting works influenced by the stories and experiences of her family who migrated from Longford in Ireland to London in the 1960s. Her mother apprenticed as a tailor and did piecework for a factory at home and as a child growing up Kathleen learned how to mend and stitch things such as dresses for dolls and make samples. As she developed as a painter, Kathleen transferred many of these stitching skills into her painting and drawing techniques, meditating on the layers of oil and brush strokes just like she believed her mother was entranced in stitches. Kathleen's sister Pauline, who also learnt dress-making from her mother, went on to become a fashion designer and she later became an integral part of this project as it evolved.

Emma's family on her father's side came from Cookstown in Northern Ireland and migrated to Glasgow in the early 1900s, whilst her mother's family came to Glasgow from Aberdeenshire. Her great aunts worked on clothing alterations and in a slipper factory in Glasgow and one of her aunts emigrated to America in the 1960s and still runs a successful clothing alteration business in Wyoming, Pennsylvania. One of Emma's earliest memories as a child is sewing through her own finger whilst playing with her grandmother's Singer sewing machine—all black metal and gold décor with a side turning wooden handle that you wound manually. It produced just a solid straight stitch but its early use marks the starting point of a lifelong passionate interest in sewing and textiles, gender and development.

On our first visit to Dean Castle, over a well-worn wooden table laden with homemade fruitcake, tea, coffee and biscuits, we met and learned about the life stories of an extraordinary group of women who have been meeting in the fifteenth-century kitchens of Dean Castle every Wednesday for thirteen years to work on the conservation of historic textiles in the museum collections, patch up community treasures such as the Provost's robes, and contribute their wealth of knowledge and expertise to making costumes for the local youth theatre group and other community clubs

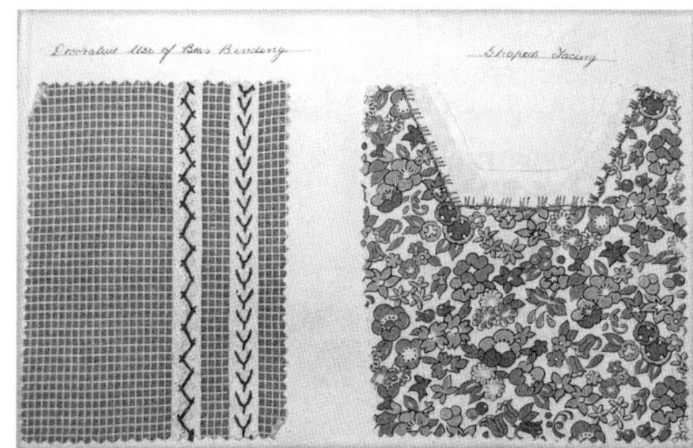

School sample book by Doreen Flett from Domestic Science class in 1940s/1950s. Photo: K. Mullaniff

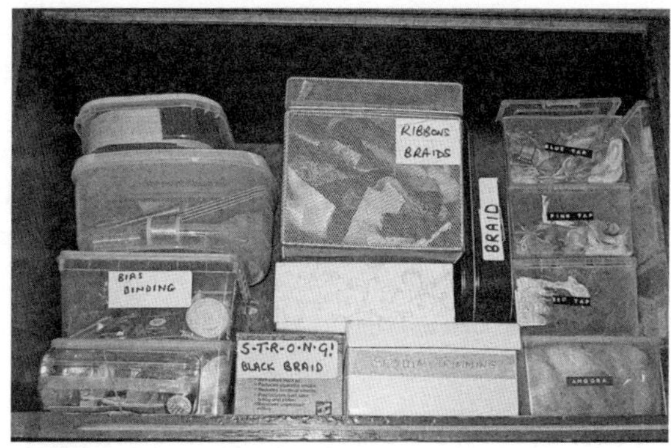

Ribbons and braids, Dean Castle textile studio. Photo: K. Mullaniff

2. Loraine Leeson, *Art : Process : Change: Inside a Socially Situated Practice* (Routledge Advances in Art and Visual Studies) (London: Routledge, 2017), p. 78.

and events. At the present time, the Dean Castle Textile Team comprises members ranging in age from 24 to 92, and the team acts together as a community of practice with different members bringing new skills into the group to share, co-develop artefacts and projects together, pick skills up from observing and talk through the practicalities of making with each other. The group generally acts as a crucible for the generation of new work as well as the transmission and preservation of textile craft skills through their continued enthusiasm for and engagement with their local community within East Ayrshire.

Over several visits between 2015–2019 we visited Dean Castle on a Wednesday morning. We got into a rhythm, always starting the day with tea and biscuits, and a gentle gradual welcome into the lives of these talented makers. Loraine Leeson (2017) writes with great insight on the interrelatedness and complexity between being "invited" to create an artistic response to a social context and how process and product evolve within community-based artistic settings. Leeson has learned though her considerable experience that, 'top-down forms of arts patronage, which attempt to control and limit outcomes, can fail to encourage the innovation they seek unless applied with a great deal of flexibility'.[2] This "warning" and "encouragement to do otherwise" mirrored exactly the fluid and gentle conversations which became the main touchpoints for developing the project together with Linda and the team, and gradually textile and memory began to flow.

As the women worked busily away in the kitchens or in the Dower House, we would sit and observe and learn and sometimes join in. Kathleen would draw from life in pencil sketches, capturing the quiet industriousness of the women absorbed in their work. Emma would offer to help with mechanical tasks that needed an extra pair of hands, and Kathleen also documented the groups and their emerging artefacts in photography. As we began to become a regular part of the group over several visits, we asked them to bring us some of the artefacts they had made over the years and to tell us their stories. With great modesty, they brought specimens of the most beautiful knitting, crochet, quilting, needlework, beading, weaving, dressmaking, bags, cushions, feltwork, dolls, christening gowns, wall-hangings, counted thread work, gold thread work, and blankets and they began to tell us the stories of how each item was made and why, and the memories each piece invoked for them.

Most of the pieces we were introduced to were closely intertwined with memories of their families and friends. Many of the pieces shown led to associations and stories of mothers and grandmothers, fathers and brothers, husbands, grandchildren, neighbours and friends. Some of the pieces had already been exhibited several times in group exhibitions or solo shows in Scotland and beyond. Some pieces had never left the maker's house but held a very special memory for them. We listened in awe as these stories unfolded, learning of the fantastic tapestry of people who had inspired and helped in the creation of these textile pieces. We initially wanted to capture these as oral histories, to make East Ayrshire come alive. But as we grew closer to the group and situated ourselves within it, it became more and more difficult to do this, and we felt it was an intrusion, on some very personal spaces and memories. So instead we captured their memories through poetry, written primarily by Emma, both in and out of time with our visits, which we eventually published in the catalogue to accompany the exhibition, *Textile and Memory* (Dick Institute, Kilmarnock, 2019–2020). The poetry suggests the feelings and narratives of the makers and captures the essence of the conversations in the kitchens.

3. Kathleen Mullaniff and Emma Dick, *Textile and Memory* (Kilmarnock: Dick Institute; London, 2019), p. 12.

When we initially asked these women to bring examples of their favourite thing that they had made over the years responses were slow, quiet, shy at first,

'och, this, it's not very good'
'it's just a bit of rubbish'
'it's nothing special.'
And slowly, gradually, we earned their trust,
'is this the kind of thing you were looking for…?'
And we kept coming back for more,
to drink more tea, eat more fruitcake and more biscuits, to sketch Irene and Patsy stitching up miracles for the stage, we watched the Lion from the 'Wizard of Oz' emerge from an old pair of pajamas
We learned how to do beautiful Ayrshire Whitework with Doreen, flower posies, scalloped edges and delicate lace infill, drawn with pure cotton yarn and short needles on a fine cotton lawn,
(probably imported from America,
'as we don't weave the fine stuff in Scotland anymore')[3]

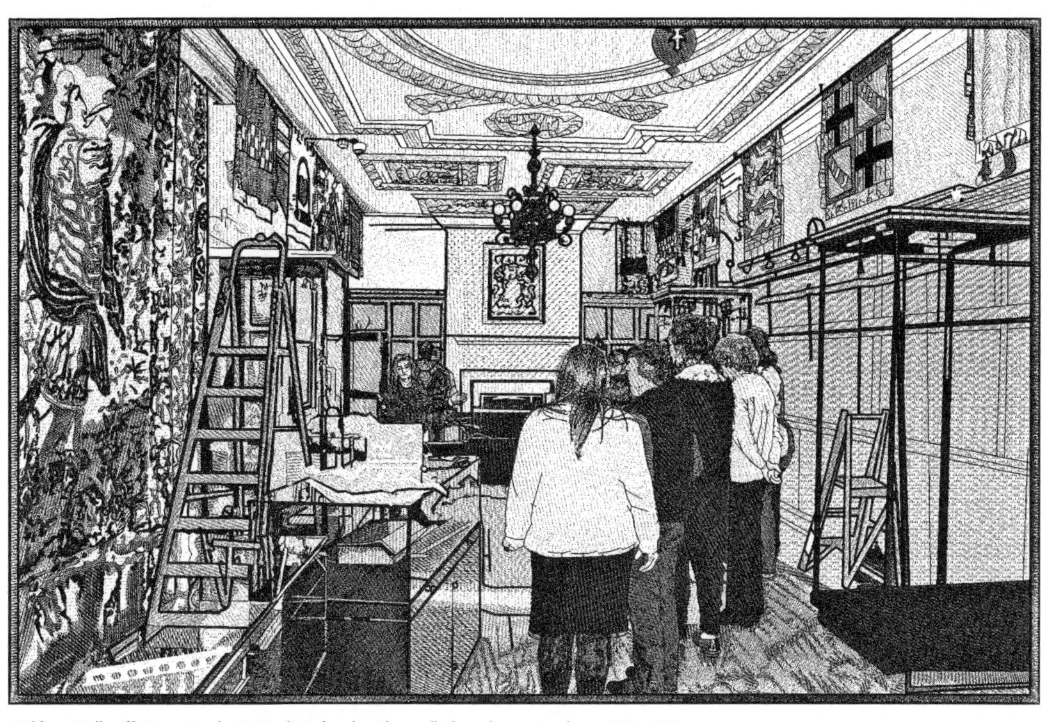

Kathleen Mullaniff, *Dean Castle*, 2018, digital embroidery, silk thread on cotton base, 16" × 24". Made by Netdigitizing embroidery digitizing: netdigitizing.co.uk

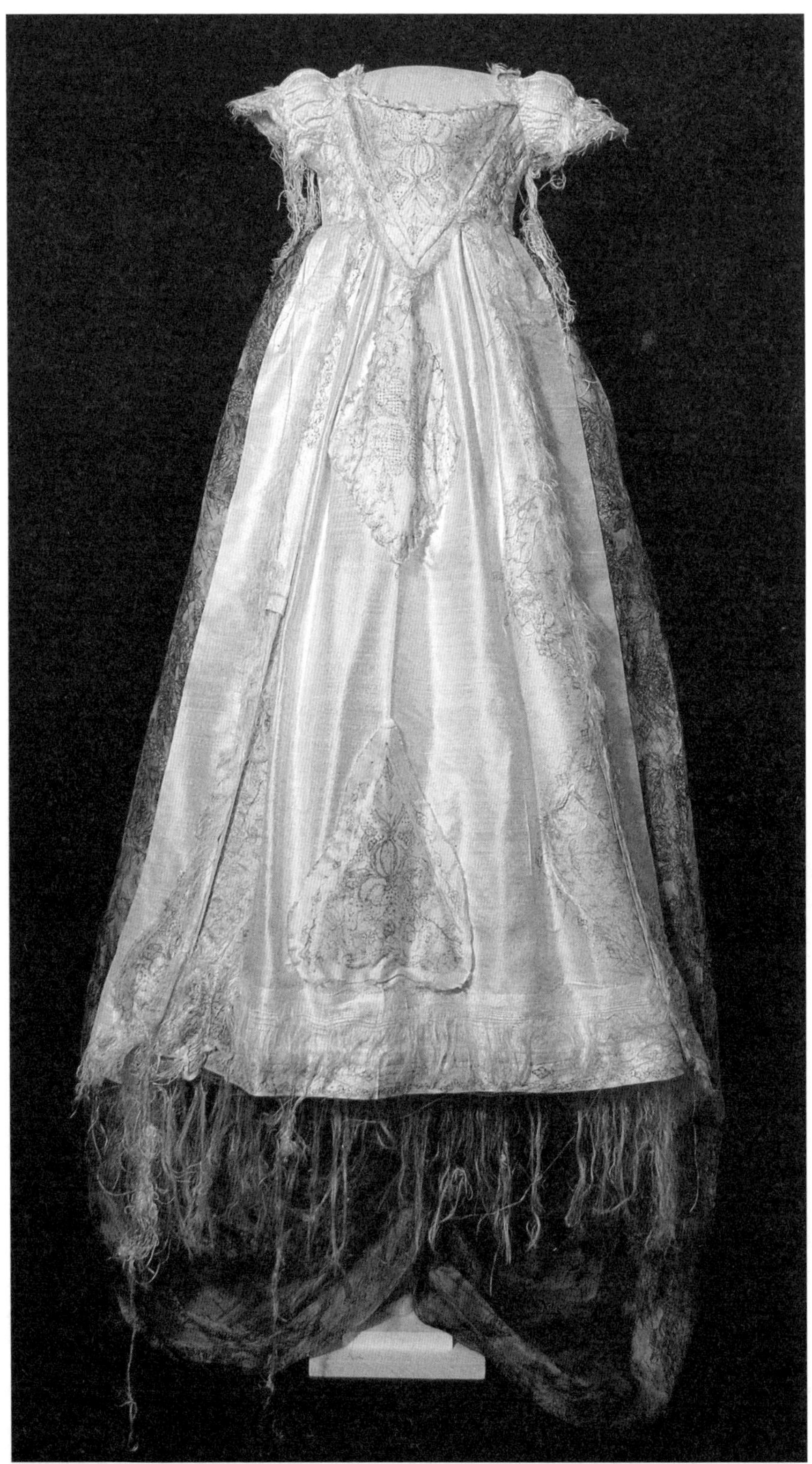

Textile and Memory, contemporary interpretation of Ayrshire whitework christening gown in silk and pencil drawings, designed and made by Pauline Mullaniff with digital print based repeat pattern based on original drawings by Kathleen Mullaniff. Photo: East Ayrshire Leisure

4. Margaret Swain, *Ayrshire and Other Whitework: (Shire Album)* (London: Shire, 1982); Agnes F. Bryson, *Ayrshire Needlework* (London: Batsford, 1989).

Kathleen's artistic responses to the group aimed to capture these narratives of making, celebrating the processes and people behind the artefacts themselves and not just the final outcomes. The quick life pencil sketches were translated and worked up later into more detailed oil paintings on circular bases, echoing the shape of embroidery frames. As Kathleen generated more and more work in response to the conversations about textile making, themes began to emerge, which very loosely became structuring principles for the rest of the work. The relationships between text, textiles and technology became embodied through experiments with digital embroidery, as Kathleen worked with digital embroidery specialists to translate her photography documenting behind the scenes at Dean Castle into brilliant full colour panels of digital embroidery, complementing the 500-year-old tapestry being re-hung in the gallery, depicted in the poem. Kathleen worked with her sister Pauline to create an interpretation of a full-scale christening gown from silk digitally printed with some of Kathleen's pencil drawings.

As we examined the textile collections of Dean Castle and Glasgow School of Art Archives we came across countless examples of what is known as 'Ayrshire Whitework', a form of embroidery made by thousands of unknown hands, and often catalogued as 'artist/ maker: unknown'.[4] Ayrshire Whitework is a good example of how many textile-making practices link the spheres of the domestic and the industrial together, and, occupied a transitional position between handwork and machine work as industrialization advanced.

Pauline began to work with the material we had been collecting throughout our visits and she began to focus on the white-on-white tracery of the Ayrshire whitework embroidery, as seen on the christening gowns. She asked Linda if we might get all the women to contribute one piece of whitework stitching to be incorporated into a dress. In actual fact only one of them, Doreen, felt proficient in the art of whitework. When asked by Linda, Doreen readily agreed to teach the other women how to achieve the best outcomes for whitework, using all the skills she had learned from Agnes "Bunty" Bryson, author of *Ayrshire Needlework* (1989) and former member of Dean Castle Textile Team, who passed away in 2006.

Each member of the Textile Team applied their own design ideas to the principles of whitework stitching that Doreen encouraged them in, and what emerged is a beautiful series of contemporary renderings of a revived eighteenth-century form, with a whole new range of novel subject matters, close to their hearts. The louse from Robert Burns' poem, a love heart in cross-stitch, wheat, barley and oats, a prayer branch, a simple cross and flowers, flowers, a depiction of a castle, flowers and mouse, a map where Ayrshire needlework was produced, Pauline was very clear that she wanted each of the pieces to be signed in pencil by the authors of the textiles, according the same value to textile narratives as text, assigning distinct indications of authorship for each piece of stitching, the pencil marks also emulate the fading of history and the passing of time. Pauline's original intention was to assemble the samples into a dress for the exhibition, but as the pieces progressed, she encouraged the team to think of these as individual 'texts' in their own right, in addition to the beautiful interpretation of a christening gown which emerged from Kathleen's drawings and Pauline's design intervention.

Very early on in our dialogue with Dean Castle Textile Team we realized through our collaboration with the women that we had an opportunity to make visible their own contribution to their preservation of cultural heritage to the community. *Textile and Memory*, the project that has emerged slowly and organically from this meeting, over a period of months and years, was driven by a will to celebrate the hidden work and commitment the members of the Dean Castle Textile Team have made both within and for their communities. These women have contributed throughout their very diverse, interesting and varied lives to the intangible cultural heritage of East Ayrshire. UNESCO underlines the significance of 'intangible cultural heritage' as being not merely about the cultural manifestation itself (i.e. the textile artefacts created) but rather, 'the wealth of knowledge and skills that is transmitted through it from one generation to the next'.[5]

Ayrshire Whitework was instigated initially as a cheaper alternative to lace in the late eighteenth century by an Italian embroiderer Luigi Ruffini (1760–1804) and produced in a semi-industrial system established through

5. UNESCO, 'What is Intangible Cultural Heritage?', 2003, https://ich.unesco.org/en/what-is-intangible-heritage-00003 (accessed 22 July 2019).

small networks of "putting out" the embroidery to rural farmers' daughters which was overseen by a woman called Mrs Jamieson from Ayr. Ruffini's innovation was to modify existing hand techniques by introducing cloth rollers at both ends of the standard rectangular hand embroidery frames. The scale of the operation made this the first mass-production of tambour work (embroidering using chain stitch and an embroidery hook) in Britain. The textile industry that was established gave many poorer women an entry into the labour market at early stages of industrialization and capitalist development, without leaving their homes. By the mid-nineteenth century there were estimated to be some 80,000 whitework embroiderers in Scotland and the business model had spread to Ireland where there were as many as 400,000 active stitchers. The designs were drawn by professional draughtsmen in Glasgow and the completed embroidery pieces were sent back there to be washed, bleached, boxed up and marketed. Ayrshire Whitework became extremely popular and was widely marketed to other countries, notably North America.

It is a fact that even today, most textiles and garment manufacturers worldwide have not been automated to the extent of other industries. In most factories, small businesses, shop floors and sweatshops, there is still a woman sitting at a sewing machine manipulating the cloth through the machine, as her manual dexterity and labour cost cannot yet be bettered by a robot. The social implications of this are huge and "ethical fashion campaigns" rarely focus on this aspect of the business model, except for highlighting poor working conditions in sweatshops. The invisible hand of the textile or garment worker is still ever-present, and closely connected to the artefact of mass-produced clothing and textiles. As globalization has increased, and towns like Kilmarnock have lost their manufacturing base, the production of mass-produced garments has been increasingly outsourced to developing countries, this discourse of industrialization and development travels around the globe and the social histories of nineteenth-century Britain are replayed by textile-workers in precarious environments around the world in the twenty-first century.

"The invisible hand" of the market is a term associated with the Scottish Enlightenment economist and philosopher Adam Smith (1723–1790) and the phrase has come to capture his notion that individuals' selfish efforts to pursue their own self-interest may frequently benefit society more than if their actions were initially directly intending to benefit society. This concept is often quoted as the foundation of contemporary economic "neoliberal" thought.

The community-spiritedness of the Dean Castle Textile Team is in stark contrast to Adam Smith's notion of free-market self-interestedness. These women do not function in a market and money-based system, but one where care, community, friendship, heritage, history and culture have considerably more value. *Textile and Memory* celebrates the contribution these women make to the material culture of their community.

Our project seeks to make visible the invisible, to celebrate these women and the collection they look after, including the unknown artists and makers who made these beautiful textiles historically and to link textiles with the memories they evoke. The exhibition took place in the wonderful setting of the Loom Room of the Dick Institute, Kilmarnock, and we placed the contemporary handwork of sixteen members of the Dean Castle Textile Team alongside fragments of industrial history in the museum, and artistic responses by Kathleen Mullaniff and Pauline Mullaniff and Emma Dick. Linda Fairlie gathered together the oral histories of the sixteen makers as they reflected on their own personal memories of textiles and how these are woven into the fabric of the histories of Kilmarnock and the surrounding area.

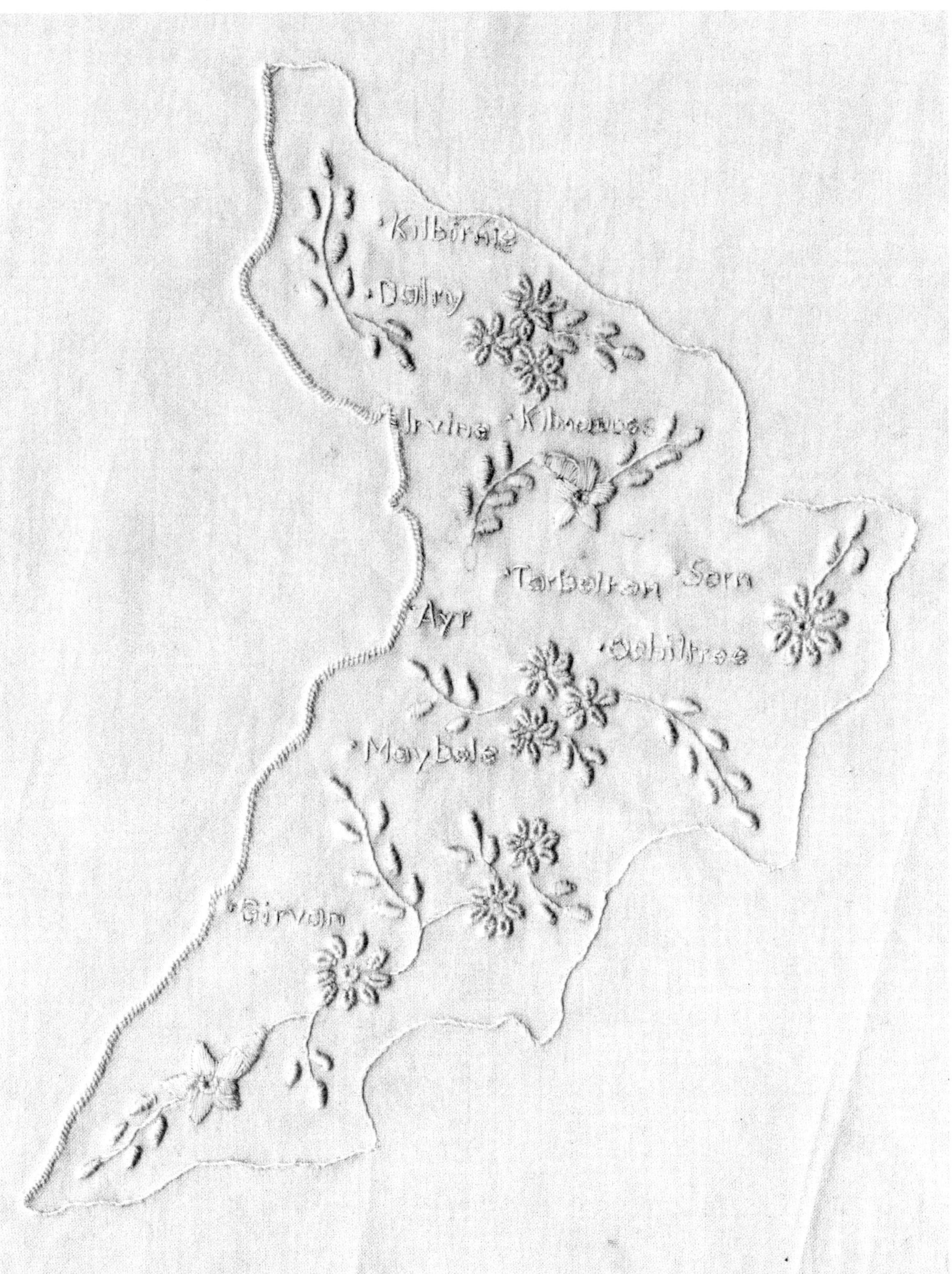

East Ayrshire map (local towns where Ayrshire needlework was produced), Ayrshire whitework sample made by Doreen Flett, Dean Castle Textile Team

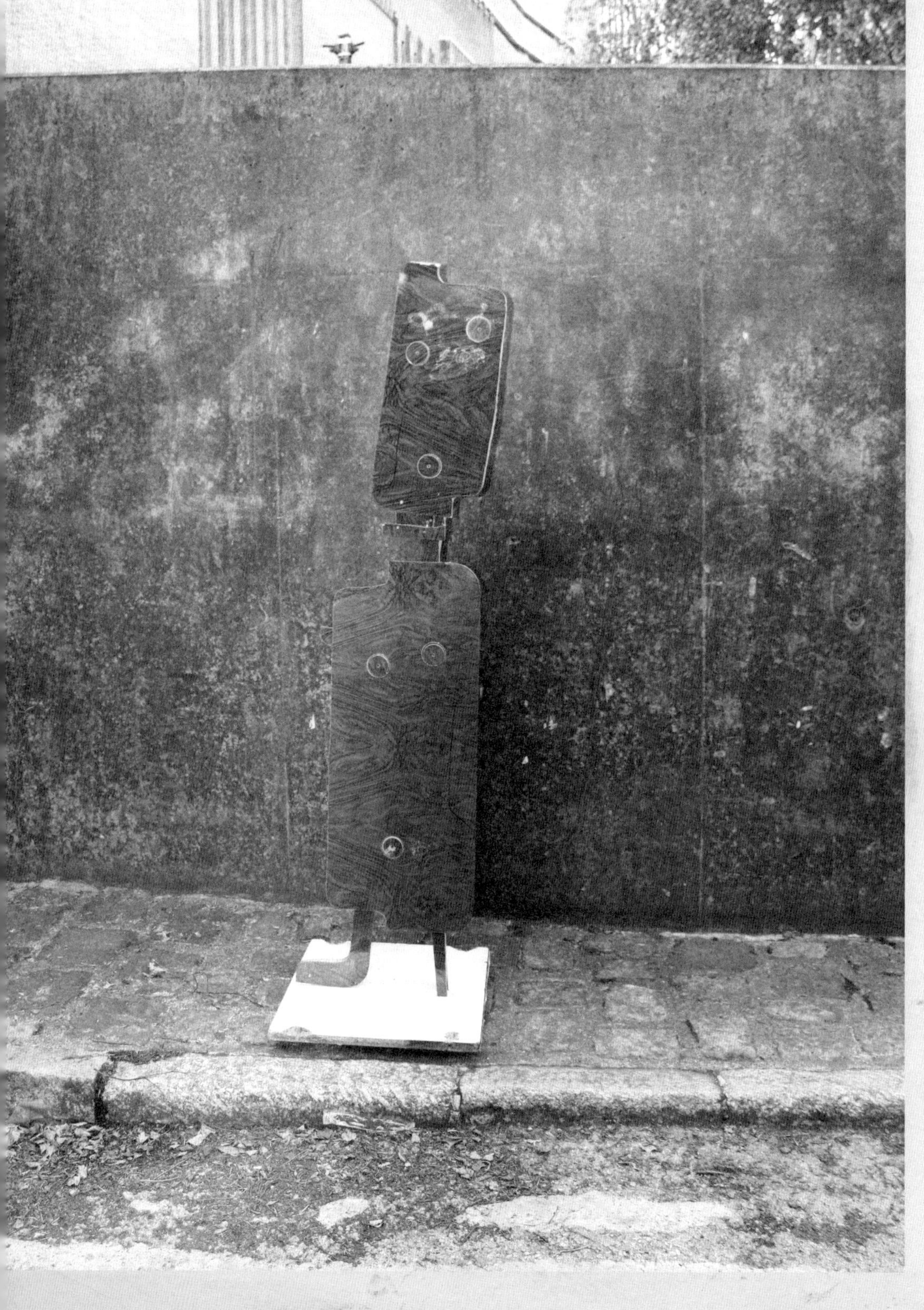

Linda Aloysius, *Groovy for New Model Army: Behind Tate Modern; Morphological Looking and Space-Making and Working Class Single Mothers* (2018–19), sculpt-photograph

NEW MODEL ARMY
Behind Tate Modern: Morphological Activism and Working-Class Single Mothers (2018–19)

Linda Aloysius

1. 'Single Parents: Facts and Figures', Gingerbread, www. gingerbread.org.uk/what-we-do/media-centre/single-parents-facts-figures/ (accessed 31 May 2019).

2. Linda Aloysius, 'New Model Army: Invisible Labour (2017–18)', *Feminist Review* 120, no. 1 (2018), pp. 122–129.

Given the fact that almost one quarter of UK mothers are single mothers,[1] I find it acutely painful that the negative effects of the historical pathologizing of working-class single mothers as artists and as subjects for art is widespread in art institutions, and especially in museums and art schools in this country. Art institutions have yet to acknowledge the complexity of the greater structures of inequality, social injustice and poverty underpinning the longevity and scope of the exclusion of working-class single mothers.

Through my Fieldworks—as trans-site and trans-disciplinary projects of sculpture, photography and writing[2]— I reflect on the representation of women's experiences of inequality. This has brought the realization that there are some things that I have to voice more publicly and more pointedly with regard to working-class single mothers and their creativity:

> One: the absence of diverse and inclusive representations, within the realms of artistic and cultural production, of the creativity and differently lived histories of (originally) working-class single mothers, who are, like myself, also artists.
> Two: the exclusion from history and history-making of a mode of looking and space-making that I call 'morphological looking and morphological space-making', which I suggest are particularly

generated by working-class single mothers, due to their political and structural positioning under patriarchal capitalism and, conversely, their strengths in resisting this.

As Joan Scott suggests when considering the evidence of the experiences of women under patriarchal capitalism, history making is not only a selective, exclusive process, in terms of content—that which is selected—but also an approach to the way(s) in which history is made and in terms of which persons—both groups and individuals—are formally acknowledged as history makers.[3]

In recent decades in the UK, and somewhat paradoxically, there has been a government-wide, strategic deflection of the public gaze away from the enormous amounts of invisible labour carried (out) by working-class women as the majority of carers, cooks, clerical and retail workers and cleaners in the workforce and in their families. Amongst the working-class, working-class single mothers are extremely burdened with different forms of invisible labour because they often lack the support of a partner, and sometimes extended family, especially if they attempt to defy their structural positioning under patriarchal capitalism and to insist on a futurity which may involve combining childcare duties, work, study and creative and artistic endeavour. As Lynn Abrams has stated, working-class women, particularly those who are mothers, have historically been actively undermined by their original families in their attempts towards self-autonomy.[4] Whilst the public gaze is turned onto and against them, the actual labour of working-class single mothers as sole carers and bread-winners for their families remains invisible and, as such, devalued. There has been a lack of progressive debate on their rights in all public institutions of education, health and culture when issues of equality and inclusion are discussed. Instead, they are widely regarded as a symptom of societal breakdown if not also its cause.

Jennifer Harding has asserted that a 'pathologized single mother' has been 'constructed in contemporary political and moral discourses' and that 'political discourse has identified single mothers as "responsible for social problems in the wider society"'.[5]

3. See for example: Joan Scott, 'The Evidence of Experience', *Critical Inquiry* 17, no. 4 (Summer 1991), pp. 773–797.

4. Lynn Abrams, 'Pursuing Autonomy: Self-Help and Self-Fashioning Amongst Women in Post-War Britain', podcast lecture, Royal Historical Society, 11 May 2018, https://royalhistsoc.org/category/rhs-video-archive/.

5. Jennifer Harding, *Sex Acts: Practices of Masculinity and Femininity* (London and Thousand Oaks, CA: Sage Publications, 1998), p. 116.

6. Peter Lilley, 'I've Got a Little List' cited *Your Favourite Conference Clips*, BBC News, 3 October 2007, http://news.bbc.co.uk/1/hi/programmes/the_daily_politics/6967366.stm (accessed 31 May 2019).

7. Alison Hadley, 'Young Mothers Face Stigma and Abuse Say Charities', BBC Newsbeat, 2014, www.bbc.co.uk/newsbeat/article/26326035/young-mothers-face-stigma-and-abuse-say-charities (accessed 31 May 2019).

Having experienced, first hand, the historical pathologizing[6] to which Harding refers, I suggest that the public gaze which has been forcefully turned onto and against working-class single mothers can only be challenged by works which place their experiences centre-stage and reverse the negative gaze and stigmatization of working-class single mothers. Such issues gain poignancy when we consider that, even today, scant art institutional recognition is given to the inequalities experienced by working-class single mothers who want to work as artists, and whether this inequality is considered historical, current, or both.

Alison Hadley, OBE, a key figure dealing with strategies aimed at supporting young parents, argues that many single parents 'often feel like they are being looked at in a judgmental way and that's why it's important professionals understand that and make them feel comfortable'.[7]

Hadley describes here how young parents are affected by the looks they receive from others. In so doing she touches upon what I know from my own and others' experiences to be a very extreme situation, in which the politics of looking are brought to bear on working-class single mothers. This is particularly acute for those perceived as biologically "young", as the judgemental looks they receive constitute the end points of longstanding oppressive structures designed to fix them into place, at a level of embodiment, and this gaze reproduces and engenders their social and economic marginalization and exclusion. In this situation, "equal opportunities" for young women's growth and movement—to socialize, to form supportive communities and relationships, to gain employment, to secure appropriate accommodation and to be given a fair chance in prospering—are effectively closed.

I want to suggest there is a need to place a productive doubt on the efficacy and authenticity of the current diversity and inclusion policies deployed by our art institutions. As a disadvantaged demographic, working-class single mother artists remain unrecognized by diversity and inclusion policies even when they may also be BaME and/or LGBTQI and/or disabled and, for these reasons, are not recognized in the same diversity agendas. Part of this is to do with the framing of government legislation which identifies structurally disadvantaged and discriminated groups as automatically part of diversity and inclusion criteria, while only "pregnant" women suffer discrimination in their employment, not mothers in general. This framing is problematic for many reasons. It means that those working-class single mothers who do not fall into categories currently recognized by these agendas receive no support at all, whereas those who do fall into those categories receive only partial support. Worryingly, this begins to illuminate the more complex problem of how to properly, rather than superficially, account for class difference in relation to the same currently supported categories. For example, should a middle-class BaME subject receive the same level of support as a working-class BaME subject? And should a working-class single mother receive the same level of support as both? The possible complexities generated by this thought are vast, but this vastness also illuminates the ethical fragility of current agendas and the need for progress.

Dr Kimberly Jamie of Durham University argues there is a need to change the expectations placed on those single mothers who identify as working-class:

> We need to stop accepting the middle-class life trajectory as the "right" way for young people, especially women, to live their lives.
> The school to university to career to house to marriage to children isn't possible or desirable for all young women, yet those who take a different route through life are positioned as irresponsible, or as having somehow failed.[8]

Policies aimed at including "mothers with young children" in education and/or museums are typically founded on a normalized presumption that all women want to, can and should behave only as middle-class subjects educating their children. Are these policies appropriate? What is the depth of their sensitivity to, and understanding and valuation of, working-class sensibilities particularly where working-class single mothers and their creativity are concerned?

In my experience of attempting to engage with art colleges and art galleries, in my various and overlapping capacities as single mother, student, artist and employee, I have been introduced to barely any art works made by

8. Kimberly Jamie, 'We Are Middlesborough: Pregnant Teenagers Tell Their Story', Philippa Goymer for BBC News, 22 May 2019, www.bbc.co.uk/news/uk-england-tees-48315469 (accessed 31 May 2019).

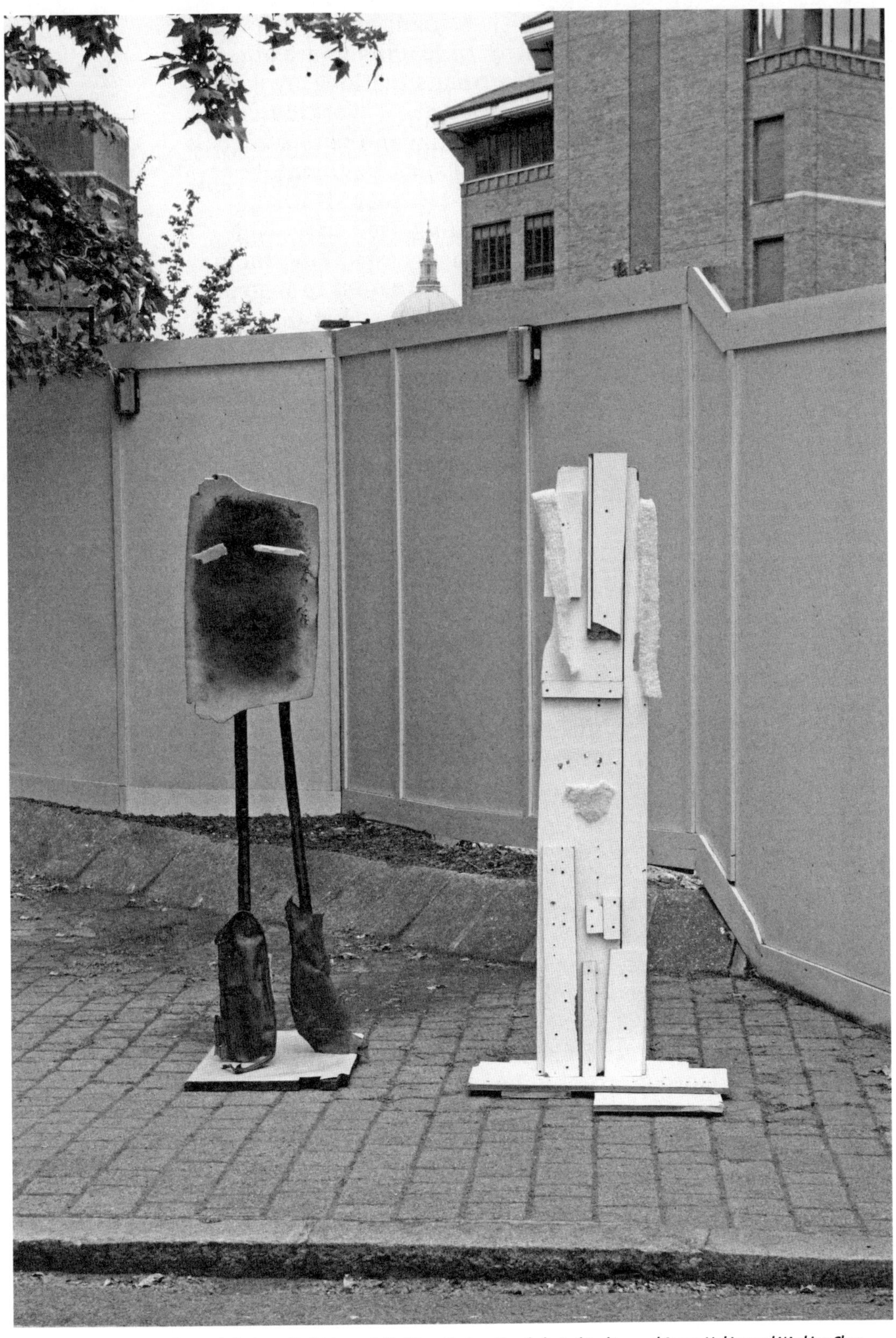

Linda Aloysius, *Strange with Straight* for *New Model Army: Behind Tate Modern: Morphological Looking and Space-Making and Working Class Single Mothers* (2018–19), sculpt-photograph working-class single mother artists recognized as such and promoted as emerging, prominent, or leading. Here, it is important to admit that, in the current situation, my own and other women's empirical knowledges of working-class single mother artists can only be "partial and perverse".[9] Nevertheless, this does not mean that such fragmental knowledges are and must remain fixed as such. Rather, I would contend that there is an ongoing need to actively refuse to work against these fragments by mistaking them for deficiencies to be corrected or added to, and to instead reflect through and across them, towards the idea that women's experience, in being drawn from as a form of knowledge, is not and cannot be presumed to be anything other than *positively* (from a feminist perspective) "instable" and, as such provides a potent, fluid basis from which to proceed with the intention to engender a "critical displacement"[10] of the central narratives of art history as framed by patriarchal capitalism.

To date, however, I have yet to come across lectures, conferences or critical debates specifically about working-class single mother artists, or about their absence from art's representations. As a lecturer, I have had the privilege of working with a few, often extremely talented working-class single mothers at undergraduate level, and who have also variously identified as white, black, mixed-race and disabled. But I have yet to meet many other university lecturers who are working-class single mothers, whether this is in a fine art department or any other department. As Jo Spence wrote, the presumption is that higher education makes you "middle-class", and lecturers can "only" be middle-class people on this count.[11] Also, in my experience, there is an unspoken presumption that to admit to being an originally working-class single mother who is now a lecturer must mean that I have never experienced employment in middle-class environments and perhaps chose lecturing because I wanted to become or be known as "middle-class". In fact, I have very extensive experience of combining art practice, motherhood and, through a combination of determination, necessity and utter naïvety, climbing the employment ladder to eventually work in profoundly upper middle-class environments.[12] In the latter I was treated with a certain kind of respect and encouraged in certain ways to prosper, receiving

9. Alison Wylie, 'Feminism in Philosophy of Science: Making Sense of Contingency and Constraint', *The Cambridge Companion to Feminism in Philosophy*, eds. Miranda Fricker and Jennifer Hornsby (Cambridge, Cambridge University Press, 2000), p. 157.

10. Clare Hemmings, *Why Stories Matter: The Political Grammar of Feminist Theory* (Durham and London: Duke University Press, 2011), p. 36.

11. Jo Spence, *Cultural Sniping* (London: Routledge, 1995), pp. 156–159.

12. Early experiences of interviews had established that, if I admitted my status as a single mother, I would not be employed. Although my single mother status was never given as a reason, it became obvious that this was why I was not offered roles and, as soon as I did not mention this at interview, I was offered a job. I therefore, through absolute necessity, did not tell my employers of my single mother status until after I had demonstrated that I was able to fulfil and, indeed, exceed my employment role which was sometimes after I had left a particular role. It hurts to remember that I effectively had no choice but to deny my child's existence for periods of time and to hide from my employers the difficulties I experienced in organizing childcare and the exhaustion I often experienced. No mother should have to do this.

promotions and increased responsibilities and authority within environments easily described as luxurious. It would have been all too easy to stay, and remain treated thus, but I only ever wanted to focus entirely on my art practice and to become a lecturer. Being the first and only member of my original family to attend university[13] and to study fine art, I was extremely naïve in regard to how I would subsequently be positioned and treated by art institutions. Other working-class single mothers' experiences may be different, but my experiences of working with fine art institutions resonate uneasily with the fact that I have rarely seen working-class single mother artists progress beyond undergraduate level education and I have not seen anyone—whether student, tutor, administrator, sociologist, artist, critic—question why.[14]

As it stands, middle class approaches ultimately entail seamlessly performing and reproducing a game of domination rife and normalized in the art world. This is a game predicated on extraction and, for it to continue, others, somewhere, somehow, anyhow, must be exploited, including by being rendered invisible. This is, to my intense boredom, and in the larger view of things, responsible for the mass dissemination of what I call *the middle class gaze*; a mode of looking normalized through an approach I would describe as that of continual project management, historically ingrained into the approaches of middle class subjects from birth and now extended, whole-scale, to art-making. This sanitizes visual languages to ensure their palatability for investors whilst serving the "star system"[15] that secures those investments.

There is a need for new, intelligent, trans-disciplinary and trans-class debate of how and why working-class girls and women become single mothers, particularly with regard to the parameters of motherhood: where these parameters lie, who sets them and how they become so fixed that they continue beyond one generation into the next.

Art institutions must overcome their fear of disrupting the subjectively and structurally embodied, middle-class frameworks and approaches they remain financially and habitually beholden to, and instead develop a sense of curiosity, a willingness to listen differently to and learn from working-class women students, some of whom are single mothers. Art schools, in particular, can choose, now, to intervene in this situation by seeking answers to the following questions:

- What needs to be discussed with regard to how working-class single mothers and their creativity is addressed in the curriculum?
- How should we listen and what can we learn from identifying and understanding traits in working-class mother artists' approaches?

More attention needs to be paid to the conditioning effects of languages used within art institutions, the values under-pinning their automatic conditioning towards this as "not important", how those values connect to larger political structures and how they can impact upon working-class single mothers already oppressed by them. Might some form of mediation between different classes and class attitudes be appropriate, here?

As a tutor, and speaking from my own experience, I have found that working-class single mothers may be conditioned into single motherhood, long before the biological act of giving birth. I have consistently found that my students who identify as or become working-class single mothers have experienced some form of early trauma, either their own or inherited from parents, in a family that is often toxic or struggling to function. Additionally, I have also found that, within their original family, they typically experience exposure to care duties that are either intense or prolonged and frequently involve prioritization of other people's needs combined with denial of their own. Significantly, this suggests that the parameters of single motherhood are not confined to the biological act of giving birth but instead pre-date it and, under patriarchal capitalism, can begin in childhood. In at least these ways the girls, even prior to becoming pregnant and giving birth, are pushed into a marginalized space.

Experiences such as these set them apart, psychically, from their peers, because they may not, as a consequence, have any opportunity to develop and convey the "nice personality"[16] which has been implied as being highly instrumental in gaining positive peer bonding and

16. Rebecca Coleman and Jessica Ringrose, *Deleuze and Research Methodologies* (Edinburgh: Edinburgh University Press, 2013), p. 131.

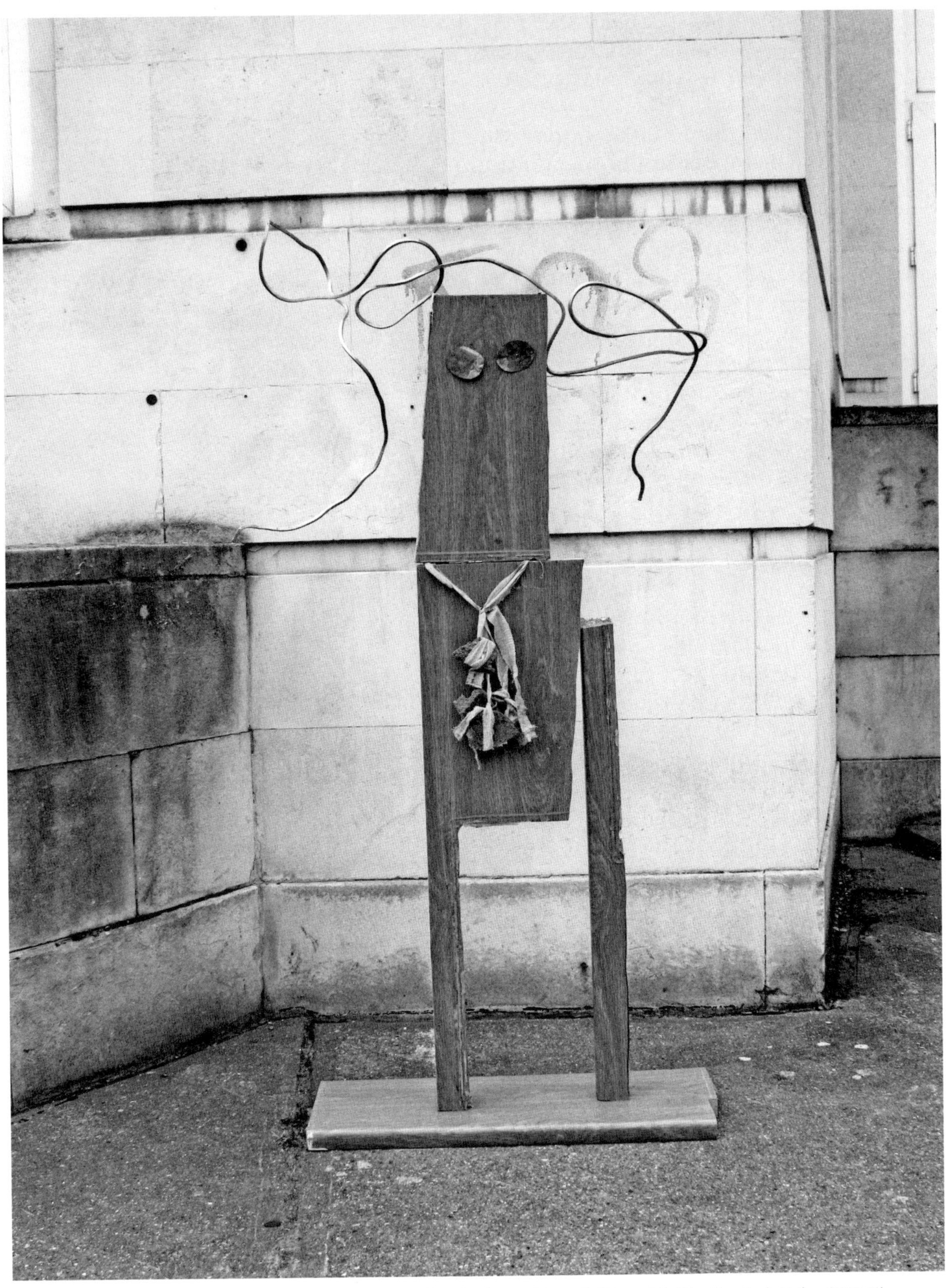

Linda Aloysius, *Teen* for *New Model Army: Behind Tate Modern: Morphological Looking and Space-Making and Working Class Single Mothers* (2018–19), sculpt-photograph

support. Although such experiences may prepare them to take on the responsibilities, hardships and struggles of single motherhood under patriarchal capitalism, when biological motherhood then takes place and they become categorized as working-class single mothers, they are subjected to the technologies of oppression in social attitudes which I have described above.

One consequence of their situation is that the subjectivities of working-class single mothers become differently structured by continually thinking and acting across and between at least two subjectivities: their own subjectivity and that of their child(ren). This continual "between-ing"[17] constitutes morphological looking and morphological space making as a mode which I understand as being particularly structurally connected to working-class single motherhood.

One might think that such a model of subjectivity and space making deserves to be supported and promoted in societies where #MeToo culture has become problematic, to the extent that the earth is now dying. Instead, this capacity for morphological looking and being, and the potential to extend this mode by example, through morphological activism, is obstructed and thoroughly exploited by patriarchal frameworks.

Hilary Robinson says: 'Irigaray insisted on the distinction between anatomy and morphology from an early point' and that: 'the term "morphology" … does not refer to deterministic analysis of forms in themselves, but to a method of discerning patterns of relationships between forms'.[18] Irigaray had argued that overly-simplistic, anatomical readings of the body deny the possibility of more complex relationships between, for example, the mind, the body and the symbolic world and instead engender a patriarchal 'economy of the sameness of the One'.[19] Irigaray was in favour of more complex, morphological readings between different elements, which she found to be capable of engendering women's "social signification"[20] as full, equal and different subjectivities. Notably, for Irigaray, morphology constitutes a highly serious mode of play, which draws from women's excess of patriarchal frameworks to re-structure patriarchies and allow for women's equality. So, morphological looking could become a mode of thinking and acting against the terms of the phallic and phallicising

17. In my doctoral thesis, I introduce and extensively discuss the morphological potential denoted by the phrase 'between-ing'. Linda Aloysius, 'Developing Productive Mimesis in the Age of Screened Oppression: Rhetorics of Flattening and Fragmentation in the Making of New Model Army', doctoral thesis, Goldsmiths, University of London, 2018.

18. Hilary Robinson, *Reading Art, Reading Irigaray: The Politics of Art by Women* (London and New York: I.B. Tauris, 2006), p. 97.

19. Luce Irigaray, *This Sex Which Is Not One*, trans. Catherine Porter and Carolyn Burke (Ithaca, New York: Cornell University Press, 1985), p. 132.

20. Ibid., p. 112.

 Feminist Art Activisms and Artivisms

21. Ibid., p. 132.

22. See my paper, 'When Girlhood is Motherhood: Towards New Looking and Being: The Desiring and Creative Gazes of Working-Class Single Mothers' at the conference 'Girling Feminism: Towards a Feminist Theory of Girlhood', organized by Girlhood Gang, Glasgow University, 14 May 2019.

23. Coleman and Ringrose, *Deleuze and Research Methodologies*, p. 130.

24. Ibid.

25. I discussed this aspect of my practice at greater length in conjunction with my paper presentation '(Im)Personification in the Making of New Model Army' for the conference 'Personification Across Disciplines' (Durham University, 17–19 September 2018).

"One" in order to challenge its 'economy of the sameness of the One'[21] and instead generate a particular "morphological" space of between-ness.

Drawing from Robinson's and Irigaray's ideas, I suggest that morphological looking is not restricted to the ocular—to the eye—and does not seek to establish hierarchical, linear relations of dominance. "Morphological looking" establishes pluralized connections between the ocular, the bodily, the psychic, the emotional, the behavioural; in brief, every aspect of whole subjectivities and their symbolic worlds, generating morphological spaces within and through which feminist values are produced.[22]

Art works can be structured in ways that help to form such relations between different elements, allowing their differences to speak to one another, engendering new morphological spaces which work to unfix the territories overlaid onto the symbolic by patriarchal capitalism. In so doing, morphological looking works through artworks to generate new relationships capable of constituting what Coleman and Ringrose might refer to as 'unknown spaces for movement',[23] and which I refer to as morphological spaces.

My *New Model Army* sculptures are built and deployed to do this work. The sculptures in my Fieldworks collectively constitute my *New Model Army*—an army of sculptures of working-class single mothers who would occupy spaces differently, with the specific aim of undoing the exclusion of working-class single mothers and their creativity, via the politics of looking which Hadley touches upon, and in ways that 'resist and fight back against the fixing of the body through looking'.[24]

The impetus to make *New Model Army: Behind Tate Modern: Morphological Activism and Working-Class Single Mothers (2018–19)* emerged through the sculptures and their anthropomorphic aspect.[25]

Leaving aside the many possible psychoanalytic interpretations of my motivations for anthropomorphizing my sculptures, it often seems to me that they do not or cannot easily accept my care for them or that I want an equal, working relationship with them. Instead, like the women whose experiences they momentarily represent, they are simultaneously tough and vulnerable due to their previous experiences of exploitation. They can be highly demanding, insisting on equality in their own terms, through their materiality and their gestures. This means they consistently assert their differences from me, refusing to allow me to fall into the trap of universalizing my experiences by veering between ignoring me entirely and/or educating me into what they need in order to activate their unique morphological potential and the solidarity this offers. This can be, for example, by exhausting and even injuring me during the making process, or by refusing to co-operate when I photograph them outside or, more recently, seeming to demand, in a variety of ways, improved working conditions. In these moments, I sense I am expected to learn from them, but I don't always know, immediately, what it is that I am expected to learn.

So, by building, transporting and photographing my sculptures behind the major art museum known as Tate Modern, and by writing about this, I sought to place the creativity of working-class single mothers in the sphere where it should be, but is not present: inside this major British art institution.

In these photographs, I choose to withhold any full view of the sculptures in the round, instead presenting them frontally as only photographic works, visual documentation of a moment in which my sculptures are situated outside of and *behind* the parameters of Tate Modern. The word *behind* is important. Positioning the sculptures in this way allows me to reflect back to Tate Modern, as a mother would to a child, its own behaviour, to highlight an awareness of that behaviour and, therefore, a choice of how it might be changed. Although Tate Modern could benefit from this new awareness of how it might choose to develop, it is not a child.

In the process of physically positioning and photographing the sculptures and writing this essay, this Fieldwork was challenging, logistically and psychically; the effects of marginalization and exclusion are embodied and cannot always easily be confronted or undone. Whilst I photograph the army to suggest a new form of feminist solidarity is possible between women, this is not a solidarity that can or should be presumed to already exist, for example, through the friendships and allegiances that working-class single

26. See 'Wages Against Housework' (pp. 15–22) and also 'Feminism and The Politics of the Common in an Era of Primitive Accumulation' (pp. 138–148), in Silvia Federici, *Revolution at Point Zero: Housework, Reproduction, and Feminist Struggle* (Oakland, CA: PM Press, 2010).

mother artists may have forged. Such a presumption of solidarity would be dangerous, alleviating governments and art institutions of a duty of care to working-class single mother artists, instead naturalizing any ability they may have to form supportive friendships, in ways that mimic the naturalization of women's ability to carry out domestic work, and which women like Silvia Federici have protested against.[26]

So, confronting the effects of embodied marginalization, as I did through the production of this Fieldwork, inevitably renders one vulnerable. Perhaps I should say, then, that I wanted to instil within Tate Modern and its ilk a feeling that even the most intelligent adults often have, that there is something at the back of the mind, on the periphery of consciousness. A nagging doubt that, when illuminated, can reveal something very difficult to face up to.

My decision to photograph the sculptures outside Tate Modern can, then, be understood generally as a material and political protest against the intricately interwoven and complex political violence of negation and non-representation of working-class single mother artists and as material testimony to their strength and vulnerability in insisting on an equal future for their creativity.

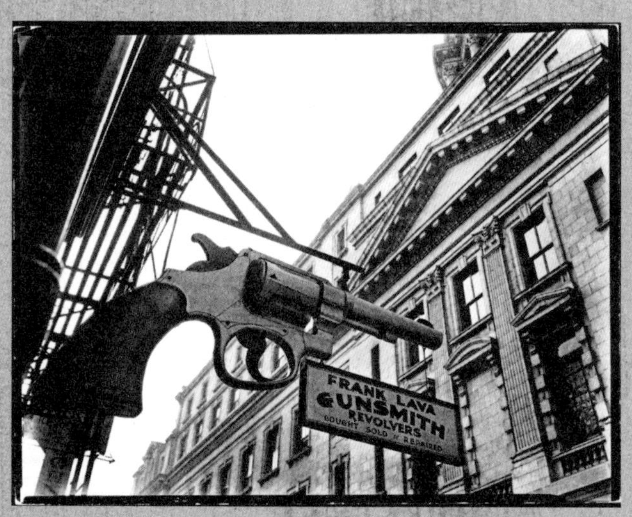
FRANK LAVA
GUNSMITH
REVOLVERS
BOUGHT SOLD & REPAIRED

A DIALOGUE WITH STEFANIE SEIBOLD AND ALICE MAUDE-ROXBY

Katy Deepwell

Katy Deepwell: *In your book* Censored Realities/Changing New York *(Camera Austria, 2018) you restage the intended relationship between text/image in Elizabeth McCausland and Berenice Abbott's plans for* Changing New York (1938), *how did your own collaboration on this project develop in relation to an equality between text/image and each other? Can you outline how previous projects led you to this work?*

Stefanie Seibold: We met through shared interests and through research we had each conducted separately in projects relating to 1970s avant-garde performance artist Gina Pane's work. It was immediately clear to us that both of us were bringing important aspects to light about Pane's complex practice, but approaching this from very different angles, fields of interest and specific knowledge relating to our respective backgrounds in artistic production and teaching. We were fascinated by how such different approaches could lead to such equally compelling readings without ever using the same tools or even questions.

Alice Maude-Roxby: What we shared, in relation to these separate approaches to Gina Pane, was that we were investigating her work via means which were considerably distanced from a traditional art historical approach. Our starting points were anchored in physical and live processes: explorations giving insight into the lived experience of these 1970s actions and the production of works. My intervention came through interviewing the photographer who had recorded all of Pane's actions and considering the Pane documentation in the wider context of Masson's day-job in commercial photography. Leafing through boxes of contact prints, light tests and dusting down photographic equipment, I was asking questions about Pane's direction of Masson and of Masson's experience taking the images, of being part of the action, and at times blocking the audience's view. Stefanie's re-staging of Pane's actions involved the re-making of Pane's props to explore the work in the contemporary, through a heightened understanding of the lived experience of the work in the present, now. It also highlighted important aspects of Pane's iconography and interest in poetic image-narratives, as well as her unique approach to performance from a female non-heterosexual position in the 1970s.

SS: Traditionally text is often seen to determine the meaning of an image, more than the other way around. We were very interested in questioning that hierarchy and also found this to be true in the proposed relationship between original texts and images for *Changing New York*, as envisioned by Abbott/McCausland in 1938, which is a rare thing actually: a collaboration of text and image on equal terms. In this regard we can maybe pinpoint the collaboration of Douglas Crimp with Louise Lawler in his book, *On the Museum's Ruins* [MIT, 1993], where the images contribute very precise statements of their own, and yet together a whole new dimension is achieved. That is of course what makes collaboration interesting, that things can be said that one medium or artist alone will not be able to say.

AM-R: Our collaborative work on Berenice Abbott and Elizabeth McCausland began with a hands-on engagement with materials: our unpacking of a box of 100 transcripts by Elizabeth McCausland that had lain pretty much undisturbed in the archive of the Museum of the City of New York since 1939. Our first job was to set up a numbering system via which we could start to re-unite each of these individual texts with the photographs that they had been intended for as captions. This sounds simple but was actually complex since the Dutton press editors had changed the titles, image selection and ordering from those intended by Abbott and McCausland. We found this process of physically transcribing from the 'hand written' typed pages, then mapping and moving between written notations, numbering systems and between published or online photo resources to be something that should be translated as an integral element of the book that we would go on to develop.

SS: One of the most important conceptual decisions for the project was our decision to publish the captions alone without Abbott's images, and develop a system of indexes as a key tool with which the reader can now do that herself. We wanted to show what had been missing from this history rather than trying to claim a "completeness" or even worse some kind of "original" state of the book, which is impossible to know. It was amazing to see how far their planning and collaboration had gone before it was more or less truncated to oblivion. It also asks the question again about the myth of modernism's unengaged "indexicality" in depicting scenes during the great depression.

AM-R: Since we were asked to give public lectures during the development of the book, we then realized how powerful McCausland's texts are when

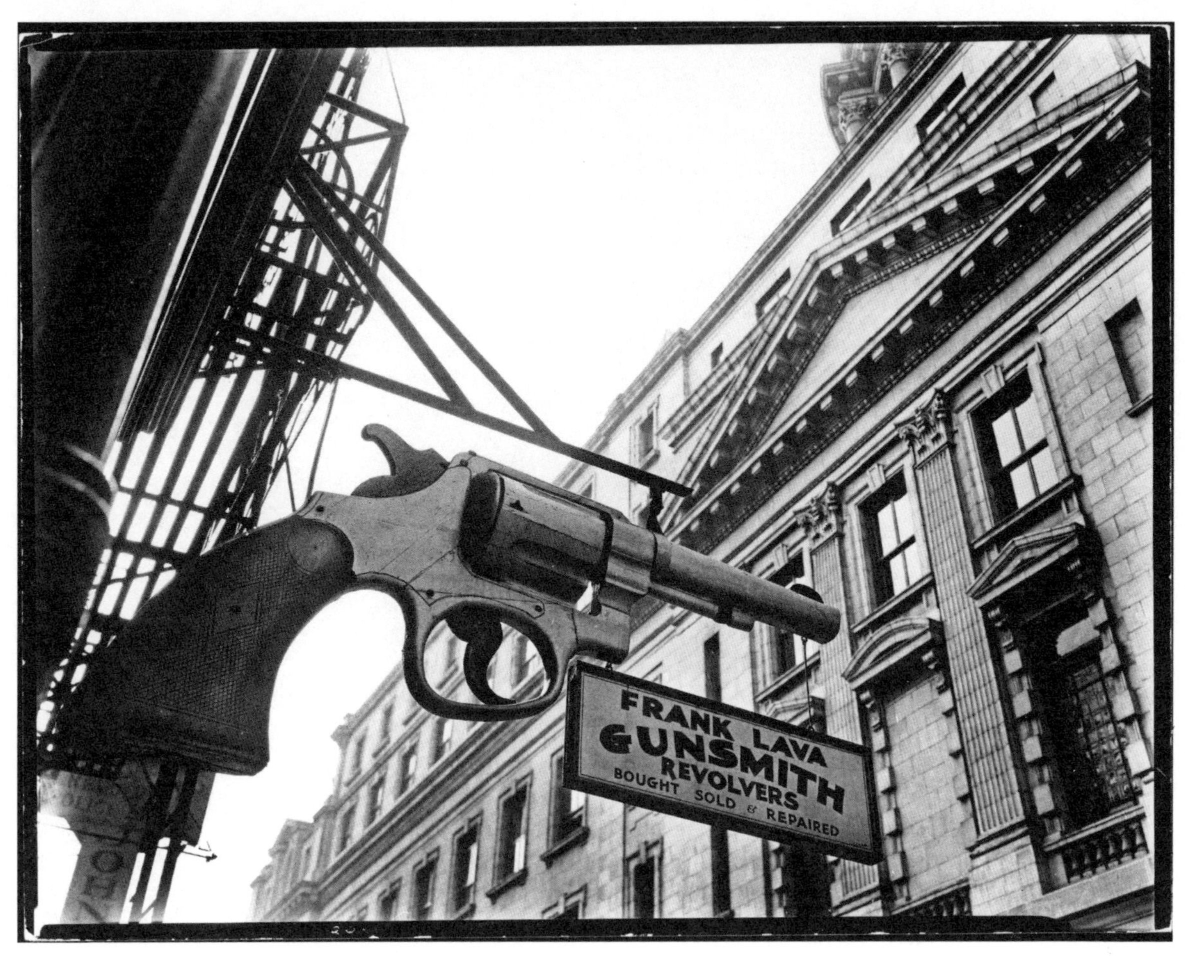

Berenice Abbott (1898-1991), *Gunsmith and Police Department Headquarters*
for Federal Art Project/Museum of the City of New York

pp. 184–186
Excerpt from: Alice Maude-Roxby and Stefanie Seibold, *Censored Realities/
Changing New York* (*Camera Austria*, 2018), including *Gunsmith* by Berenice
Abbott (1898–1991) for Federal Art Project/Museum of the City of New York

Gunsmith and Police Department

Full intended caption
by Elizabeth McCausland

Content is inseparable from form here. Of other photographs
in this series, it has been said that composition is dynamic,
form powerful, organization of parallel and diagonal lines rhythmic and moving, as if subject matter and style could be divided.
In this picture, subject matter is form. Later ages may look at
Gunsmith and Police Department with the same detachment
that we show in viewing African sculpture, unaware of ceremonial signification. But to the New Yorker of 1937 the photograph says one thing: Here is a gun, pointing at a police
department. It is an unavoidable comment. No doubt many
people have seen the gun over Frank Lava's shop. Some
have photographed it. This conception, however, is the artist's
unique contribution of significance. Again, the basic truth of
photography as a medium for art is demonstrated, that the act
of creation must be envisioned before the shutter is clicked.
The completed picture must be seen mentally before a finger
is lifted to expose the negative.

16

Gunsmith and Police Department

Published caption
as edited by Dutton

Frank Lava's gun shop was founded in 1850 by Eli Parker.
It closed up during the Civil War, but was re-opened in 1870
by ancestors of the present owner. The Lava shop used to do
repair work for the police, until the department retained its own
armorers. It still does work, however, for the sheriff's staff.

17

**Katy Deepwell, Stefanie Seibold and
Alice Maude-Roxby**

APRIL 2, 1939

MRS AUDREY McMAHON
ASSISTANT TO THE DIRECTOR
FEDERAL ART PROJECT
110 KING STREET
NEW YORK CITY

MY DEAR MRS. McMAHON:

WILL YOU KINDLY INFORM ME WHAT IS THE CORRECT PROCEDURE
FOR ME TO FOLLOW IN PROTESTING THE POLICY OF DUTTON IN
PLAYING DOWN OR COMPLETELY ELIMINATING MY NAME IN ALL
PUBLICITY IN CONNECTION WITH <u>CHANGING NEW YORK?</u>

SHALL I MAKE MY PROTEST DIRECTLY TO THEM? OR WILL YOU
FORWARD IT?

I CONSIDER THAT MY NAME SHOULD HAVE BEEN MENTIONED ON
THE FLAP OF THE BOOK JACKET.

IN THE ADVERTISEMENT APPEARING IN TODAY'S HERALD TRIBUNE
BOOK SECTION, THE WORKS "VALUABLE DESCRIPTIVE TEXT" SHOULD
HAVE BEEN FOLLOWED WITH "BY ELIZABETH McCAUSLAND."

IN VIEW OF THE YEAR'S WORK WHICH I DEVOTED TO MY PART
OF THIS COOPERATIVE PUBLICATION, I FEEL THAT MY SHARE OF
THE BOOK SHOULD BE PROPERLY PUBLICIZED.

I SHALL APPRECIATE YOUR ASSISTANCE IN THIS MATTER.

SINCERELY YOURS

ELIZABETH McCAUSLAND

spoken, especially when read while the audience view the Abbott photographs. The unpredictability, for the listener, of the collision of McCausland's content and its articulation of Abbott's images brings another dimension to considering text and image. In my case this then led to making an image/sound work where visitors hear recordings of McCausland's texts whilst seeing the Abbott photographs projected, this was shown as part of the exhibition, 'Resist: Be Modern (Again)' [John Hansard Gallery, 2019].

Whenever we did a talk about the book, we'd have several questions (notably from men in the audience) wanting to know why on earth we had not produced a book which included all of Abbott's photographs. If we had gone down that route, we would have ended up with a coffee table picture book neatly "closing off" an art historical chapter where our intention has been to bring these remarkable writings into a different conceptual and discursive framework.

KD: *In both the book and your next collaboration on the exhibition,* Resist: Be Modern (Again) *(2019), through working with archives, forgotten histories and artists/writers marginalized by mainstream canons, you draw attention again to "marginalized" and "censored" or "ignored" art practices by women. How did you arrive at this way of working together?*

AM-R: The practices we are drawn to are ones which have been ignored, we are not seeking them out for this reason but rather these are the ones that fascinate. In the process of finding out about these artists, the thing that is very obvious is that they were often extremely well known within the time of making their work. The most important aspect is finding forms that allow us to bring works back into view, or back into circulation whilst avoiding a "biographical" approach. In this way, it is much more interesting to us to find a form, like the *Censored Realities* book structure, that actively engages a reader in a process of re-finding the connections for themselves.

We live in different countries, our process of collaboration has been through occasional blocks of time where we work together in a studio but for the most part we're speaking via skype. For the John Hansard Gallery show we produced a huge wall chart on which we mapped the names and networks from the 1920s women to contemporary artists who we included in the exhibition—this network became an artwork but actually, similar to our development of the book, was also part of a process for communicating with each other since our different backgrounds/contexts meant that we were introducing trajectories/lineages that were new to each other.

KD: *What do you mean in one of your texts by bracketing the (iograph) in your work as a form of queer feminist history(iograph)y? How do you want to redraw these histories?*

Katy Deepwell, Stefanie Seibold and
Alice Maude-Roxby

SS: Making visible the gaps and also active marginalization within the canon, people who were well-known in their times and later sidelined or pushed into complete oblivion produced amazing work which we see as very, if not more, relevant for today than those currently well-known and canonized in the mainstream. Also, we want to re-claim important producers and artists for their meaningful and groundbreaking works outside of a heterosexual matrix, especially women.

KD: *Do you see announcing/re-presenting queer feminist positions in themselves as a form of activism? What is the value/ importance of intervening to remind people of particular historical events to any future-orientated activism?*

SS: It's just a way to move through the world, making sense of it for me. Things that I see and others don't. Things that I know and others don't. Things that I read, think are important, and others don't and that I see as having relevance in re-presentions today. Being sidelined and belittled hurts, has always hurt; making things and people invisible erases certain positions. And I also want to set the record straight: non-heterosexual women did make exciting, experimental, avantgarde art, before (and after) they were framed as "lesbians". But it is not activism, it is a critical reading of contemporary art and art history. And that might be as important and meaningful to others as any more direct form of activism might be.

AM-R/SS: We believe that those works, facts, stories and materials we find in history and re-introduce today in our projects have extremely relevant aspects for today. They lay a new base to start from and point to future ideas and concepts for today's generation. Looking back it becomes extremely clear how and why certain practices or individuals were cut out of view, perhaps this heightens an awareness in the present of how this process, which is less easy to see as it happens, is quite obviously still taking place today. Again, the questions raised when we did public talks related to the book and show are good indicators of this, for example, being asked how our research relates to the #MeToo movement.

SS: We had a complex research process, with multiple aspects and parallel directions to it over the course of five years. The final mapping and concrete display solutions speak about our employment of unconventional research methods and experimental visual approaches towards our topic(s). Our interest lies in making connections, rather than creating divisions, which seems to be the more classical approach to the concept of researching or curating. We also risked making some more speculative claims, knowing that by doing this we might end up being wrong in certain aspects or miss some important details. We did not want to make the usual divisions by fields of practices or productions, in generations or locality. Traditionally our stories are told separately:

the Harlem Renaissance and Art Nouveau, Textiles and Crafts, Fine Arts and Literature, Now and Then. These divisions are mostly ideological strategies and thus political, giving some people the power to define them and not others. As was to be expected, visitors to the exhibition have pointed out some blind spots in this web we have established, but we did get very positive responses to the many links that we did manage to make here.

AM-R: One thing we noticed, in giving gallery tours, was that it was a bad idea to speak about the Baroness Elsa von Freytag-Loringhoven's work, which spatially is encountered quite early on in the layout of our exhibition, before visitors had seen quite a lot of the other works on show. Notable, yet eclipsed, art historical research now indicates it is very likely that the urinal credited to Duchamp was actually a work by von Freytag-Loringhoven gifted to him. Whilst this story is also prominent in the media right now, via very recent press coverage of Siri Hustvedt's novel, *Memories of the Future* (2019), to groups of visitors unfamiliar with this concept, we'd find that if we talked about this piece too early on everything else in the show would be overcast by a sense that we were telling lies or creating fictional encounters.

KD: *Would you see your projects as "artivisms" or "activisms"—and how would you define these differences strategically?*

AM-R: I would make a distinction between these two terms in regards the different paths negotiated, one seems to specifically be framed within an "art" route, being worked through in making art, the other more broadly across all sorts of interventions and frameworks. Neither term actually feels right for us, perhaps our intervention is felt to be "activist" by those who don't want to question the traditional art history canon.

SS: My projects come out of my artistic practice and address interests and needs that I see within the field of contemporary art. To understand fine art and aesthetics as part of any society's biases, prejudices and dominant ideologies is for me the prerequisite of engaging with art in any meaningful or exciting way.

CENSORED REALITIES / RE-WRITING HISTORY

Katy Deepwell, Stefanie Seibold and Alice Maude-Roxby

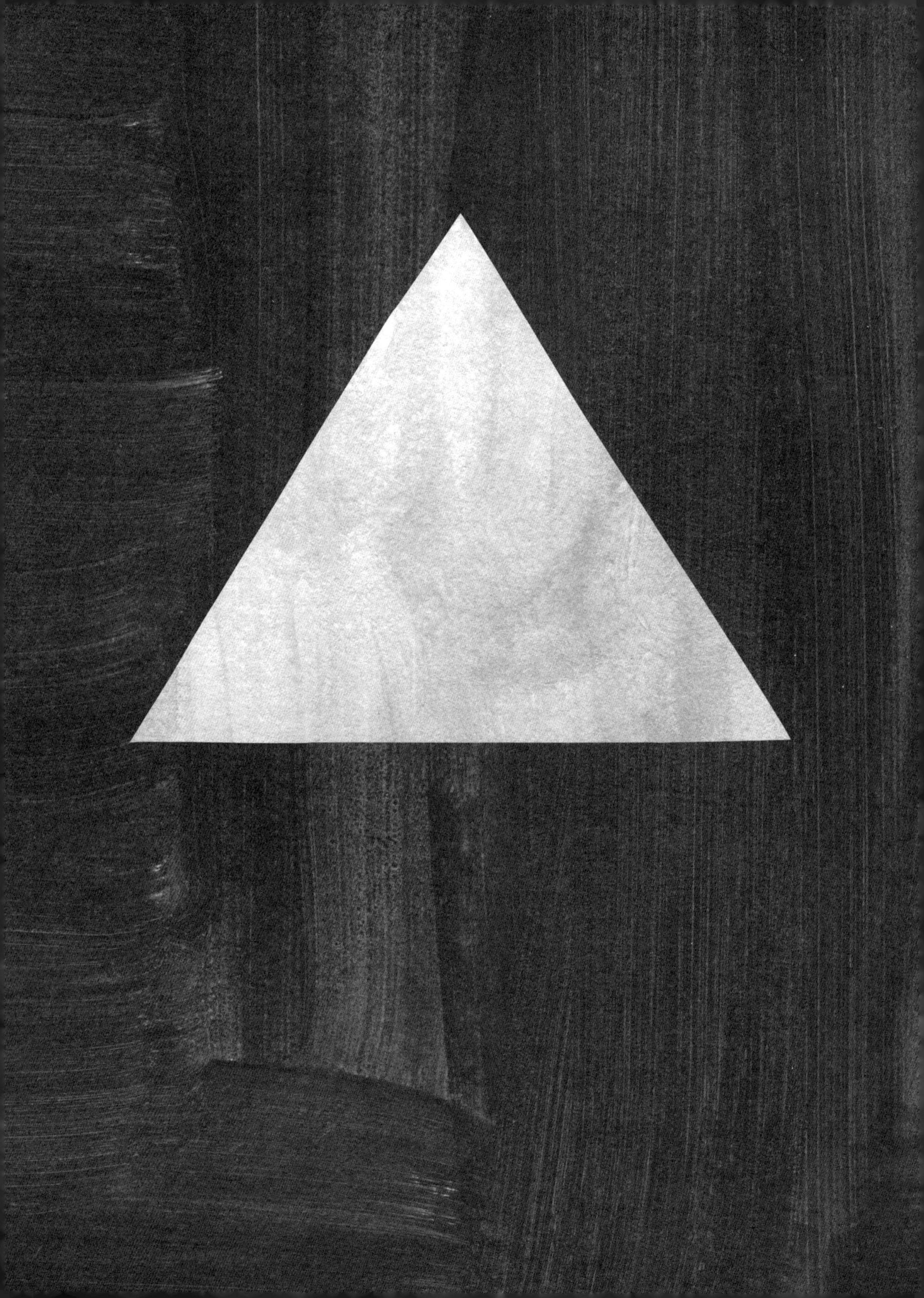

IDENTIFYING TOUCHPOINTS IN BRITISH AND CHINESE WOMEN'S ART IN THE TWENTY-FIRST CENTURY

Virginia Yiqing Yang

As a Chinese feminist living and undertaking a PhD in the UK, I suggest that there is a need in the twenty-first century to generate an in-depth study into contemporary women's art between these two countries.

The picture of gender imbalance in the contemporary art world is dispiriting in both the UK and China: according to a 2017 report in *The Guardian*, the majority of solo exhibitions in the UK were still by male artists.[1] The British Broadcasting Corporation also points out that male buyers at auctions are a driving force in the art market, and that they are more likely to think that women's art is inferior.[2] In China, now the third largest art market in the world, *The Art Newspaper* suggests that, among all the artists who were born after the 1980s and had successful careers, only ten percent are women. In group exhibitions, the proportion of women artists is even less because (mostly male) gatekeepers tend to choose male artists to participate in exhibitions, often promoting their friends first and then female partners.[3]

However, a shift may be occurring that is driven by women who have taken the helm of some of the major art institutions in both the UK and China. There is considerable momentum behind contemporary female artists in the twenty-first century, yet the signs of this imbalance changing are "painfully slow".[4]

Consequently, questions have been raised such as: what can we do for contemporary women artists to speed

1. Hannah Ellis-Petersen, 'How the Art World Airbrushed Female Artists from History', *The Guardian*, 6 February 2016, www.theguardian.com/lifeandstyle/2017/feb/06/how-the-art-world-airbrushed-female-artists-from-history (accessed 16 April 2019).

2. Anny Shaw, 'Female Artists Really Do Earn Less than Men, Survey Finds', *The Art Newspaper*, 14 December, 2017, www.theartnewspaper.com/news/female-artists-really-do-earn-less-than-men-survey-finds (accessed 6 May 2019). Original report cited is Renée B. Adams et al., 'Is Gender in the Eye of the Beholder? Identifying Cultural Attitudes with Art Auction Prices', 6 December 2017, SSRN: https://ssrn.com/abstract=3083500 or http://dx.doi.org/10.2139/ssrn.3083500.

3. 'Artists Come First, Then Female: "Women Artists" in Their Words' ('"艺术家在先，女性在后"：她们眼中的"女性艺术家"'), *The Art Newspaper*, 29 July 2016, www.tanchinese.com/feature/19802/ (accessed 2 November 2017).

4. Shaw, 'Female Artists Really Do Earn Less than Men, Survey Finds'.

up the process? Are there any touchpoints between women artists from different nations? How can these touchpoints help us understand their artwork? And in the future, can these touchpoints lead to meaningful exchanges and artistic creation?

I offer here one example from the eight British and Chinese women artists and their work which forms the basis of my PhD. My overall aim is to maximize the benefits of transnational and transcultural communications and to generate readings to understand and (re)evaluate women's art. Determining this method of reading women's art practice represents an artivism in knowledge production, in which feminist ideas find their form in women artists' works.

In an attempt to approach the phenomena in which women's art is produced, I started by examining women's artistic experiences as well as the readings of their artworks. Phenomenology[5] became my chosen approach to developing qualitative research that focuses on the commonality of a lived experience within a particular group (women artists) and within the everyday social contexts (the UK and China).

I wanted to consider if there is any commonality in taking women's issues into consideration in the subject-matter and imagery in their art.[6] My ambition became to identify touchpoints as a means to refer to the subtle and implicit overlaps (of technique, belief, or circumstance etc.) and harmony between different artists/ artworks, without reducing these to only that which is identical. The subject-matter of women-related issues—identity and body, domestic labour, and motherhood—is central to this idea of touchpoints as a means to connect different women's artistic experiences. However, to develop this observation, this project also draws on feminist standpoint theory, as a methodological set of debates interested in understanding knowledge from women's place in the world.

Feminist standpoint theory analyses 'causes of the gaps between the actual knowledge and power relations and those desired by women's movements'.[7] It takes gender as one of the defining characteristics of human experience. Standpoint theory is a way of investigating how women experience life differently from men as they live in specific social relationships and in situations where male power is exercised. Much contemporary feminist scholarship and

5. Dawn Hobson and Angie Titchen, 'Phenomenology', *Research Methods in the Social Sciences* (London and Thousand Oaks, CA: Sage, 2005), pp. 121–130; John W. Creswell, *Qualitative Inquiry and Research Design: Choosing among Five Approaches* (Thousand Oaks, CA: Sage, 2013); Cristian Hainic, 'A Few Uses of Phenomenology within Art History', *Journal for Communication and Culture* 1, no. 1 (June 2011), p. 71.

6. It can be traced from Aimin Tao's *Women's River* made from washboards used by rural Chinese women; Jingjing Lin's *Dress* with pictures attached of sexual dolls; Helen Gorrill's *Fushë Kosovë Sex Café Chair* assembled with reclaimed prosthetic limbs; Lana Locke's *Nappy* series; among other women's issues touched upon in their artwork.

7. Sandra Harding, 'Feminist Standpoints', *Handbook of Feminist Research: Theory and Praxis*, ed. Sharlene Nagy Hesse-Biber (Thousand Oaks, CA: Sage, 2012) 2nd ed., pp. 46–64.

8. Abigail Brooks, 'Feminist Standpoint Epistemology: Building Knowledge and Empowerment Through Women's Lived Experience', Feminist Research Practice: A Primer (Thousand Oaks, CA: Sage, 2007), pp. 53–82.

9. Judith Grant, 'I Feel Therefore I Am: A Critique of Female Experience as the Basis for a Feminist Epistemology', Women & Politics 7, no. 3 (1987), pp. 99–114.

10. Harding, 'Feminist Standpoints'.

11. Patricia Hill Collins, 'Learning from the Outsider Within: The Sociological Significance of Black Feminist Thought', Social Problems 33, no. 6 (October-December 1986), pp. S14–S32.

12. Patricia Hill Collins, Black Feminist Thought: Knowledge, Consciousness, and the Politics of Empowerment (New York: Routledge, 2000).

13. Anne Anlin Cheng, 'Ornamentalism: A Feminist Theory for the Yellow Woman', Critical Inquiry 44, no. 3 (Spring 2018), pp. 415–446.

14. For instance, scholar Monica Merlin, artist Xinmo Li, and critic Yujie Tong have conducted a series of research with Chinese women artists in the twenty-first century.

15. Harding, 'Feminist Standpoints'.

research strives to give voice to women's lives and to uncover knowledge, which has been ignored or hidden, within women's experience, in order to bring out women-centred solidarity and social change.[8] Standpoint methodologies have been considered problematic because they automatically privilege women's ways of knowing but they have also been central to feminist research methods.[9] Another criticism has focused on the practice of essentializing "women's lives", where a unified category of women is established that ignores the significant differences in the conditions of women in different ethnicity, race, class and other social and cultural contexts.[10]

The combination of phenomenology and feminist standpoint theory in my research aims not to sanction the notion of essentialism, nor to seek a universal "women's position"; rather, it attempts to gain an understanding of the diversity of women's artistic experiences. Patricia Hill Collins, for example, develops this into the "outsider within position" of disciplinary researchers from marginalized social groups.[11] She explores the specificity of African-American women's experience through the idea of black feminist thought which is grounded on the specificity of black women's experience of inequalities.[12] Yet Asian women, like black women, have 'suffered long histories of brutal denigration and relentless prurience',[13] with little work exploring or acknowledging Asian (Chinese) feminist standpoints in the contemporary art world.[14] Of course, one can never completely become an "outsider" of one's own cultural group, but finding even just a little critical distance from "the normal" (or the majority) can be sufficient to enable new perspectives to come to light.[15]

As a result of these considerations, I tried to develop a composite analysis of selected artists and their art-making to identify "what" they conveyed and "how" they presented in their work. The project investigates whether any touch-points could help with grasping the meaning of the artwork, and therefore enrich current research on comparisons between British and Chinese women's art.

For the larger project, I chose a small group of eight women artists from the UK and China as a starting point on the following basis [(Table 1)]:

Filters	Chinese Artists / British Artists
Gender	Cis Female
Generation	Born in the sixties, the seventies and the eighties
Occupation	Work as professional artists or art educators
Influence	Presence in major exhibitions locally and internationally; been studied and interviewed by scholars and researchers
Medium	Work across media, including object-based installations
Subject matter in their artwork	Involvement in many fields, including women-related issues

Table 1

I then interviewed Chinese artists Jingjing Lin, Jie Jiang, Aimin Tao, and Rong Gao during summer 2018 and British artists Rowena Harris, Helen Gorrill, Lana Locke, and Jemima Brown during spring 2018 and 2019. Two main areas were explored in all the semi-structured interviews: the form of their installations and how they saw female identity in their art-making. I wanted to understand the current situation of British and Chinese women artists and the difficulties they encounter; second, to establish the potential of installation art; and third, to point out any common aspect of their answers. The interview results provided necessary knowledge of selected women artists' experience and thoughts and a solid foundation to interpret their artwork.

Within the scope of this research, into post-2000 object-based installation work, I identified a number of ideas that appear relatively frequently in the selected artists' works:

> **a)** Female identity and body: the artists convey the idea of existence through the female body.
> **b)** Domesticity: the artists represent the everyday scene of domestic life.
> **c)** Motherhood and maternity: the artists describe the experience of becoming or being a mother.

16. Gillian Rose, *Visual Methodologies: An Introduction to Researching with Visual Materials* (London: Sage, 2016), 4th edn.

17. Victorino Tejera, *Semiotics: From Peirce to Barthes: A Conceptual Introduction to the Study of Communication, Interpretation, and Expression* (Leiden and New York: E.J. Brill, 1988).

Semiotic methods offered me the analytical tools for taking the image apart and tracing how a broader system of meaning could be established.[16] Peirce's semiosis process (Table 2) involves a triadic relationship between a Sign, a Semiotic Object and an Interpretant, which offers a rich potential for an analysis purpose.[17]

A Sign (or Representamen) indicates in the broadest possible sense of "represents". A Semiotic Object is a subject-matter of a Sign, while an Interpretant can be anything discussable or thinkable. An Interpretant is the effect of a sign on someone who reads or comprehends it.

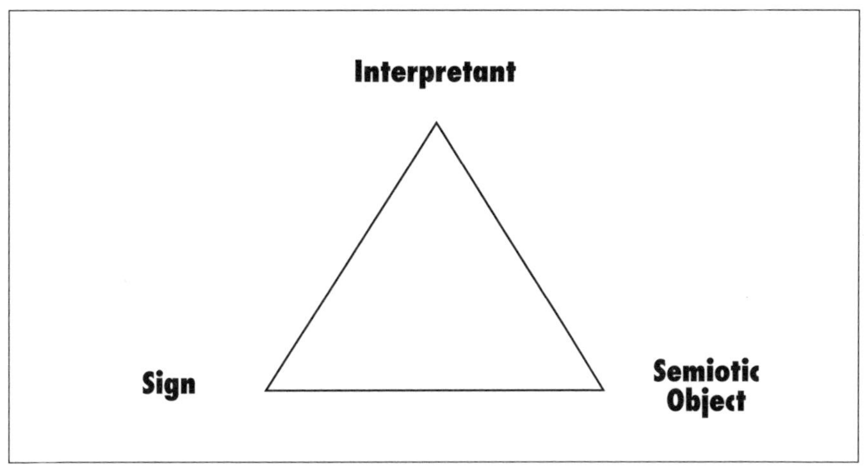

Table 2

Step \ Category	Description	Composition	Interpretation
Sign (or Representamen)	Qualisign (Tone): carrier of the sign	Sinsign (Token): carrier of the sign	Legisign (Convention): collection of identical signs
Semiotic Object	Icon	Icon Index	Icon Index Symbol
Interpretant	Rheme (a sign of qualitative possibility)	Rheme Dicisign (a sign of actual existence)	Rheme Dicisign Argument (a sign of law)

Table 3

Virginia Yiqing Yang

Based on Peirce's sign-theory [Table 3], in this study, the strategy of analysis was then developed in the following three steps:

1) Description: utilizing an innocent eye for observation without being concerned with its socially and culturally coded meanings, simply perceptions of the artwork.
2) Composition: looking at the work as a whole but then breaking it down into detailed components.
3) Interpretation: as the method that combines the artist's experience and interpreter's perspective for the purpose of opening up possibilities to read and make meaning of the artwork.

To further develop the interpretation of the work, the following sub-steps are considered:[18]

- Architext: the cluster to which the artwork belongs, for example, genre, discipline, or movement. (In this study, the artworks are in the form of installation.)
- Paratext: the material supplied by artist, for example, the title of the artwork.
- Pretext: historical and original background of the artwork.
- Antetext (Not necessarily included): the influence of previous work.
- Metatext: discussions and reviews of the artwork.
- Hypertext: the artwork in relation to other artwork (lead to touchpoints).

Let's take the idea of "female identity" from the initial categories as an example to show how this grid of steps helped to create a comparison between Helen Gorrill's *Fushë Kosovë Sex Café Chair* (2010) and Jingjing Lin's *Dress* (2006–2009) as examples.

Step 1: Description

Gorrill's *Fushë Kosovë Sex Café Chair* shows a sculpture made in a chair form that we might sit in every day but presents a complex of qualisigns—reclaimed prosthetic limbs, sex toys, steel, leather, fishnet, nylon, and resin.

18. Zhao, Yiheng, *Semiotics: Principle and Problems* (符号学：原理与推演) (Nanjing, 2016).

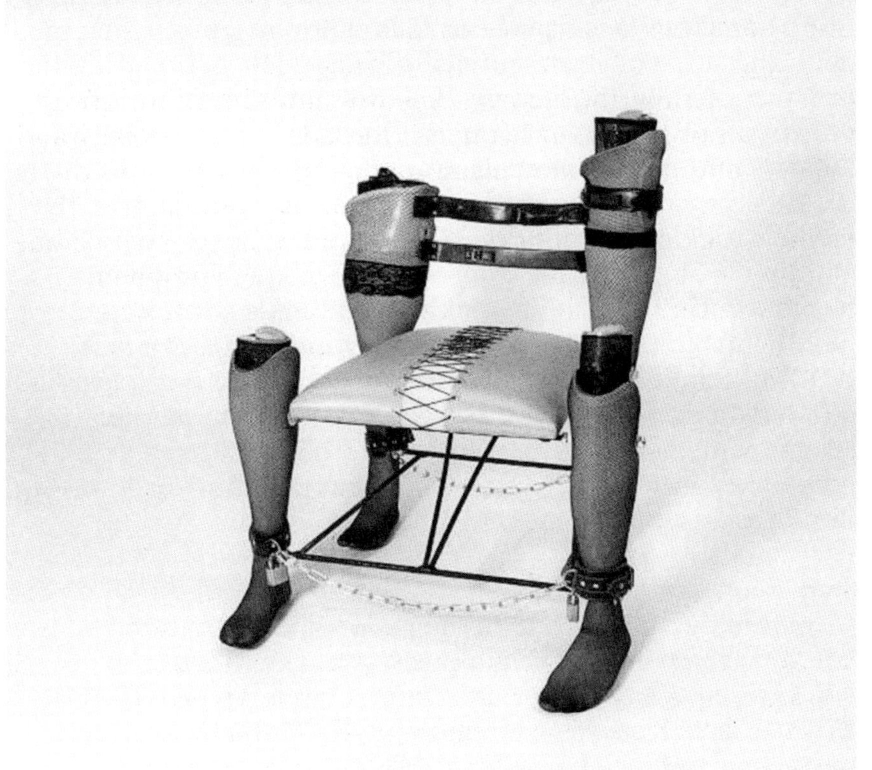

Helen Gorrill, *Fushë Kosovë Sex Café Chair*, 2010, installation view, 83 × 93 × 74 cm

The latter are signs that consist in qualities of feelings and possibilities before we try to understand the work in-depth. The support of Gorrill's chair is composed of four broken legs of varying lengths with black fishnet stockings. At the top of each limb, there are children's toys, sweets and embroidered vulvas. The drilled and shackled legs are juxtaposed by resins inlaid with male sex toys. Two leather straps connect the back pair of the legs as the chairback. The cushion is in pink and made by machine and hand embroidered silk with beading and wire from the middle. Several black steel rods reinforce the chair at the bottom by connecting four ankles of the legs.

Step 2: Composition

The qualisigns in the above section all help manifest ideas about the body and integrity in sinsigns. The sinsign is a sign which consists of a reaction or resistance, an actual singular thing, an actual occurrence or fact. The sinsign is iconic in denoting some of its assembled objects such as the reclaimed prosthetic limbs, the lace-up cushion, and the embroidered vulvas, all of which function as a metaphor for a woman's identity and body. These also present, to a great extent, in the objects with other indexical properties, for instance, the fishnet stockings, childhood objects and male sex toys. The childhood objects at the tops of the legs are metonymic to innocence; the fishnet stockings and male sex toys are metonymic to sexuality and probably indicate a (forced) BDSM[19] relationship (or offer a synecdoche to pornographic and fetishistic sex scenes). If we connect all the parallel components together, the work could be considered as a narrative concerning women being trapped, hurt or forced in bondage to submit.

Step 3: Interpretation

Compared with the previous steps, the interpretation contains some more implicit messages. The title of the work: *Fushë Kosovë Sex Café Chair* is made up of two parts. First, 'Fushë Kosovë' is a region of the Balkans known for importing trafficked girls from Moldova before the girls are then forcibly trafficked to the UK and other European countries; second, the 'Café Chair' form itself belongs in the everyday, public environment on a mass scale, it is supposed to be comfortable and casual, for example as seen in Starbucks. But imagine sitting in Gorrill's chair, it does not necessarily make people feel pleasant or relaxed. In addition, when the word "Sex" is added on to the title, it instantly forms a connection with pornographic or sexually explicit activities, which are not legal and may be forced or brutal and without consent.

Contrary to this unusual and fetishistic object, a chair is such a common, everyday object in the modern world. The chair a person sits in often reveals his or her social status and comes to represent a social role.[20] Chairs have many meanings related to personal and lived experience because of their intimate relationship with our bodies and the strong anthropomorphic aspect to their structure, with legs, back, arms and seat that can represent the absence of their designer or owner.[21] Like any cultural construction,

19. BDSM is a variety of erotic practices or role-playing involving bondage, discipline, dominance and submission, sadomasochism, and other related interpersonal dynamics.

20. Anne Massey, *Chair* (London: Reaktion Books, 2011), p. 50.

21. Galen Cranz, *The Chair: Rethinking Culture, Body, and Design* (New York: W.W. Norton, 1998).

22. Ibid. See also Hung Wu, *Space in Art History* (Shanghai, 2018).

23. Massey, *Chair*, p. 50.

24. Online reference at: www.celesteprize.com/artwork/ido:52448/.

25. Email interview with Helen Gorrill, 13 March 2018.

chairs have a complex history and set of meanings. Chairs first became a vital sign of power relations between the rulers who sat and the ruled who knelt or stood beneath them in ancient Egypt, and, in many cultures, different types of chairs remain embedded in power relations that are differentiated by age, class, and gender.[22]

The development of electric chairs for execution is one example that represents an 'ultimate symbol of control and discipline' and entered the cultural landscape when Andy Warhol worked with the haunting image of an empty chair on his screen-printing pieces from 1963—the last execution by electric chair in New York state taking place the same year.[23] Other contemporary artists, such as Joseph Kosuth, Ai Weiwei, Joseph Beuys, and Edward and Nancy Reddin Kienholz, have explored different indexes, symbols and representations of the chair in their work; often indicating the presence or absence of human relations in terms of power, repression and objectification.

Gorrill encourages the viewer to sit in the chair and engage with its drilled and shackled legs juxtaposed by resins inlaid with male sex toys and childhood objects. Some viewers have commented online that the *Fushë Kosovë Sex Café Chair* makes them feel unsettled and is provocative as it represents the authority of the person (trafficker) controlling the sitter (trafficked girls).[24] Gorrill told me she was inspired by Allen Jones' work in the 1960s and Hans Bellmer's disjointed limbed dolls in the 1930s. However, as a previous victim of domestic violence, most of her work has revolved around gender issues, for example, taking a critical view of how women are seen in society and repressed through religion.[25] In *Fushë Kosovë Sex Café Chair*, Gorrill conveys her sympathy for the trafficked girls, and investigates the enforcement and reactions to patriarchal society.

My point of comparison for Helen Gorill is Chinese artist Jingjing Lin's work *Dress* (2006–2009). If we apply the same analysis to this work, we find that Lin also poses a question about where women are placed in society in terms of gender identity, even though the object here is a wedding dress.

The white wedding dress is a highly symbolic part of the complex set of interlocking relationships concerning marriage and marriage rituals that ties women in the West

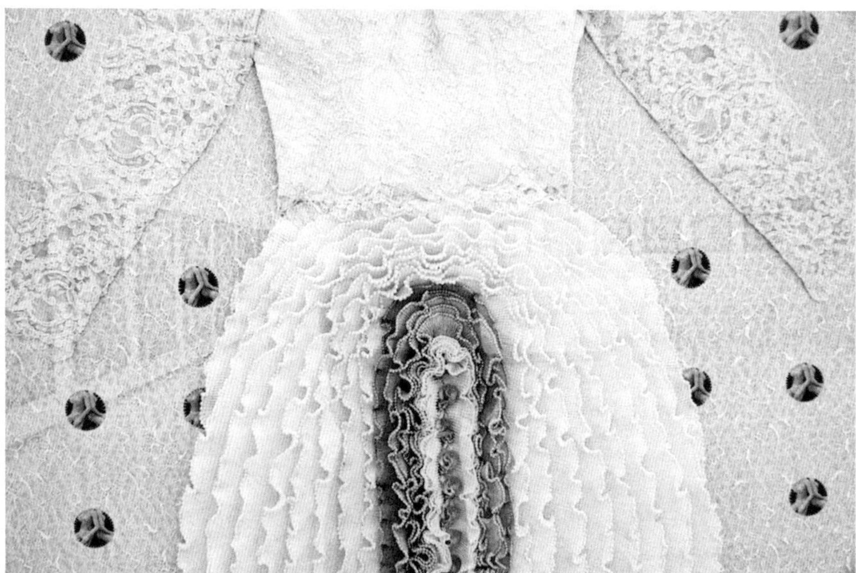

Jingjing Lin, *Dress*, 2006–2009, installation view

as much as Asia closely to changing cultural traditions in a larger sense.[26] Lin uses this dress to explore femininity itself with the materials and installation and how this form of femininity—white, lacy, detailed, pure, and yet still drawing attention to sex and women's sexual vulva—reflects on the contradictions and complexities of marriage for women.

Looking at Gorrill's *Fushë Kosovë Sex Café Chair* and Lin's *Dress* simultaneously, we find a touchpoint between two works in making gender power relations visible by means of the fragmented and imperfect female body. This can be read in at least three ways. First, both the limbs and the genitals (body parts) in Gorrill and Lin's installations present the existence of aspects of femininity indicated by objects closely associated with female bodies, but the body itself is absent. This absent presence of a woman's actual body could perhaps be considered as an indexical sign and the objects function as metonymy and synecdoche. The body understood through fragments encourages the viewer to complete their reading by assembling the fragments.

Second, both works have fetishistic and de-fetishistic elements. I found that Linda Nochlin's *The Body in Pieces*[27] aids this reading as she focuses on how cut-off elements in

26. Helen Bradley Foster and Donald Clay Johnson, *Wedding Dress across Cultures* (Oxford: Berg Publishers, 2003); Maria McBride-Mellinger, *The Wedding Dress* (New York: Random House, 1993).

27. Linda Nochlin, *The Body in Pieces: The Fragment as a Metaphor of Modernity* (London: Thames & Hudson, 1994).

28. Ibid., p. 38.

29. Sally O'Reilly, *The Body in Contemporary Art* (London: Thames & Hudson, 2009).

30. Galili Shahar, 'Fragments and Wounded Bodies: Kafka after Kleist', *The German Quarterly* 80, no. 4 (2007), pp. 449–467.

modernist paintings function, especially the women's legs and feet in Édouard Manet and Eugène Disdéri's work. Nochlin suggests the fragmentation of women's legs and feet can be seen as fetish in these male artists' work. In this reading, gender difference is the major factor in constituting the meaning of the body parts: male artists representing women's bodies.[28] In both Gorrill and Lin's work, there is no reversal of gender roles: i.e. women artists representing men's bodies, instead the use of women's legs and sex organs de-fetishizes the attached assumptions or fantasies by male (artists) to women, challenges the male gaze and indicates the imbalance and repression of women's role and social position under power relations.

Third, the female body does not always appear as an idealization of beauty. This is different to the dominant approach of traditional painting by male artists that took female body as "dreamy goodness".[29] Both Gorrill and Lin's work shows the imperfection of women. According to Shahar, the 'fragments, like wounds, have the texture of a cut'; they are broken or unfinished texts that embody 'allegories of crisis and loss in history and present moments of absence'.[30] Like the wounded body, the fragment bears the form of a rupture and stands as evidence of deficiency and imperfection. These fragmented female bodies represented by combinations of objects in sculpture and installation allude to absence and suffering in women's lives.

I want to indicate that these methods might provide new possibilities for reading and interpreting contemporary artworks in a transnational way from a feminist standpoint. The touchpoints form a structure to grasp the meaning of their work that could enable greater understanding of cultural differences and at the same time the uniqueness of different kinds of women's art production.

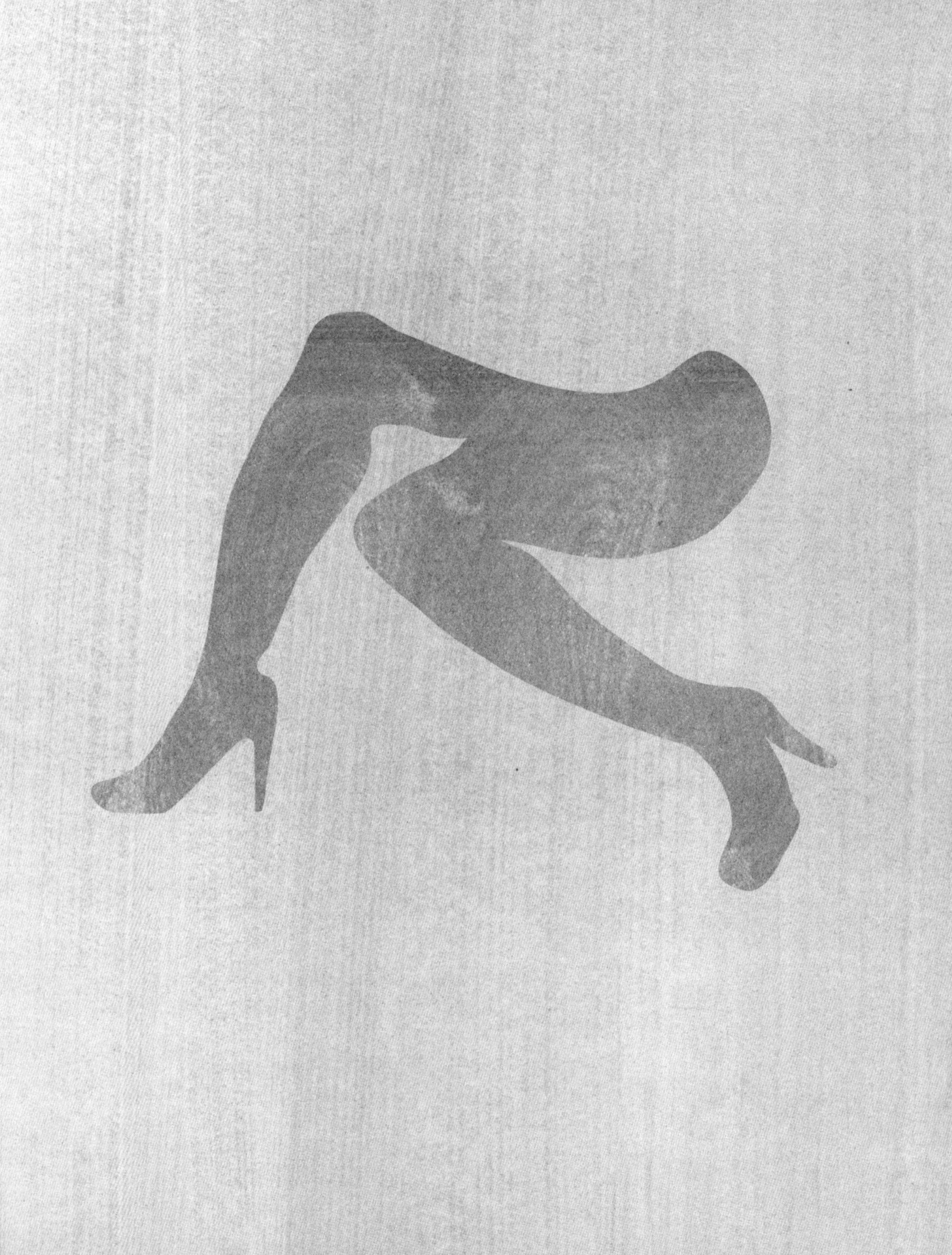

VISUAL ACTIVISM AND MARGINALIZED COMMUNITIES IN ONLINE SPACES

Camille Waring

1. Aneurin Bosley, 'Escort Agency: A Personal Touch Services: Selling Sex in Cyberspace', *The Internet Business Journal* (January 1995), p. 4.

2. Stewart Cunningham et al., 'Behind the screen: Commercial Sex, Digital Spaces and Working Online: Technology in Society', *Technology in Society* (May 2018), pp. 47–54, https://doi.org/10.1016/j.techsoc.2017.11.004.

3. Jean Burgess, 'Remediating Vernacular Creativity: Photography and Cultural Citizenship in the Flickr Photo-Sharing Network', *Spaces of Vernacular Creativity*, eds. Tim Edensor et al., (London: Routledge, 2009), pp. 130–140.

The internet has been a platform used by sex workers to sell sex since the mid-1990s and provided new means for sex workers and customers to find each other through web-based sex work sites, the first of which began online in September 1994.[1] The internet has been widely heralded for allowing independent sex workers, most notably, female sellers of sex to flourish, but it has also allowed for a proliferation of online spaces such as social media platforms that facilitated the formation of sex worker communities. As a communication tool, the internet has created spaces for visual and verbal exchanges across society, but it is also a place where the circulation of images and personas around sex work predominantly use anonymized or masked forms of identity. In the 1990s, the creation of "sex working identities" to sell commercial sex or to create "stigma-coping strategies" in manufactured identities, enabled and empowered many female sex workers to protect themselves and avoid association with whore stigma, moral condemnation and nefarious stereotypes, but it has also led to developments today where women are now experimenting with their own photographic self-representations and online identities differently.[2] Coupled with the digital democratization of photography online, through technical advancements in digital photo and web-based technologies as well as the proliferation of image-sharing platforms,[3] female sex workers have started to author their own visual content in these online spaces.

However, this new emergent area of photography in (female) sex worker self-authored photographs and in manufacturing new kinds of sex-working-identity online has been overlooked by academia despite considerable scholarly attention to how and why digital sex work is performed online[4] and studies of selfie culture that have overlooked why sex workers post selfies online. These female sellers of sex are no longer the 'passive female image subjects in an industry of active male image-makers'.[5] As contemporary sex workers, they have moved on from the standard academic finding that men control the images of sex work and they are only passive victims, exposed, visible and vulnerable or workers doing nothing more than enthusiastically performing patriarchal stereotypes of sexual servility. These assumptions about female sex workers are set into a fixed and well-recognized visual narrative that they cannot escape from, and this is replayed daily in the media and cinemascapes.[6] It is this situation that has created a voyeuristic gaze structured by a binary narrative of voyeurs looking either at the unrepentant harlot upholding the structures of patriarchy or a hapless and deviant pitiful victim of circumstance. This narrow visual portrayal of men's oppression of women reproduces "a politics of pity" and has resulted in a hegemonic visual representation that encourages the idea that the only way of interpreting images of sex workers is to see the women themselves as ripe for "rescue".[7]

In the digital revolution, and with the mass sharing of photography online, photographs now play a vital role in the sale of sex and in pornography as a multi-million-dollar industry. Words still matter and have their allure, but digital photographs are now fundamental to the transaction of sex for money. Independent (female) sex workers, however, are now major imagemakers in the sex industry, a role facilitated by the massive changes the internet has brought to the sex industry, embodying a technology-led disruption that has changed the fundamental economics of sex work. To civilians, situated outside of the institutions where sex work operates, the posting of visual content by sex workers on social media platforms may appear to be simply the posting of pornographic content in order to attract male buyers of sex. The danger in categorizing all the photographs of sex workers posted online as nothing more than sexually explicit

4. Elena Adriana Jeffreys, 'Sex Worker Organisations and Political Autonomy from Funders: Case studies of Scarlet Alliance Australian Sex Workers Association and Empower Foundation (Thailand)', PhD Thesis, School of Political Science and International Studies, The University of Queensland, 2018; Angela Jones, 'Sex Work in a Digital Era', *Sociology Compass* 9, no. 7 (2015), pp. 558–570.

5. Donna M. Hughes, 'Prostitution Online', *Journal of Trauma Practice* 2, no. 3–4 (2004), pp. 115–131.

6. Danielle Hipkins, and Kate Taylor-Jones, eds., *Prostitution and Sex Work in Global Cinema: New Takes on Fallen Women* (New York: Springer, 2017).

7. Camille Waring, 'Whoretography: Sex Workers as Image-Makers' PhD thesis, University of Westminster, 2019. This is a fate that seems to escape the white heterosexual male seller of sex, who in the mediascape and cinemascapes is often depicted as empowered, pensive and offering a much-needed community sexual service to women through a series of photographs that see them in acts of spreading sexual good vibes across the internet, far from the heterosexual man of colour who is depicted as a nefarious character tricking white women into paying them for their sexual services and very far from the fate of the female sex worker in the mediascape who appears in media photographs as infantilized and victimized.

8. Teela Sanders, '"It's Just Acting": Sex Workers' Strategies for Capitalizing on Sexuality', *Gender, Work & Organization* 12, no. 4 (2005), pp. 319–342.

9. Samantha Cole, 'Trump Just Signed SESTA/FOSTA, a Law Sex Workers Say Will Literally Kill Them', *Vice* 11 April 2018, www.vice.com/en_us/article/qvxeyq/trump-signed-fosta-sesta-into-law-sex-work.

marketing content is that it leads to a misunderstanding of more complex intentions as to why full-service sex workers post self-portraits and portraits online. A consequence of this monolithic attitude renders sex workers vulnerable to online censorship and persecution by those who seek to deny sex workers the right to participate in online visual platforms in order to block "pornographic" content completely or restrict its use to post-18 "adult" sites. The visual stereotyping of women through art, media and cinema acts as a blindfold that enables people to forget that sex workers are individual human beings like everyone else. This limited thinking must be challenged.

The definition of being a full-service individual sex worker is someone who engages in sexual intercourse or sexual acts in exchange for money, and this involves varying degrees of physical contact with clients,[8] should be conducted without physical or circumstantial coercion, and without being employed by a third party such as brothel, escort agency, online escort agency or pimp. The easy availability of information on the internet has revolutionized sex workers' marketing techniques and the verbal and visual vocabulary of sex work but who controls the circulation of images on the net is still a battleground. Whilst the internet has opened up spaces for sexual and gender emancipation of previously marginalized groups such as non-binary and trans individuals, BDSM and women sex worker communities, these groups and those identified with many transgressive sex sub-cultures are now disappearing at an alarming rate, a disappearance spearheaded by government legislation that seeks to remove sex workers' sites and platforms from sharing any images deemed "pornographic" and punish them for having the audacity to occupy visible space online.[9] There is, however, a photographic rebellion taking place amongst the most highly marginalized of oppressed and stigmatized communities online, namely, those out as female sex workers who actively identify as a full-service individual sex worker online. This is a bold and courageous move where their online presence is often met by real-life consequences: including horrible acts of misogynistic violence, being fired from civilian employment, the loss of children through family courts, being excluded from banking services, and ceremonially removed from social media platforms. These

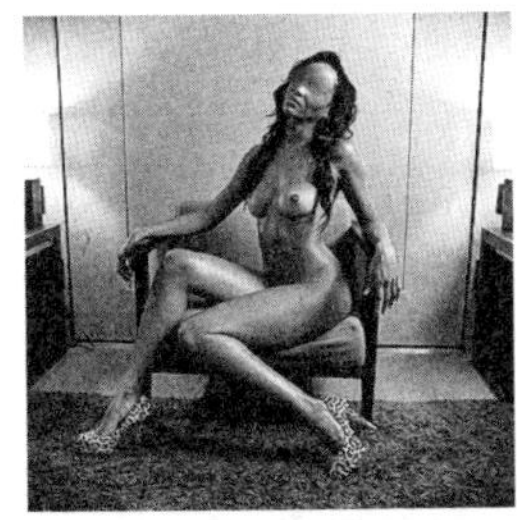

Canadian sex worker, *Untitled*, c. 2015, orphan photograph

Camille Waring

are the direct consequences of highly organized trolling by people (companies and governments) who want to block pornography on the internet and who target female sex worker social media accounts in particular and by the social media companies themselves who engage in shadow banning and search banning that results in sex workers being de-platformed, ghettoized, hidden, sporadically banned or suspended.[10]

In the face of government-sanctioned oppression and censorship through the implementation of legislative regimes of SESTA/FOSTA the newly implemented Porn Ban[11] and the EU Article 13 Copyright Directive,[12] and the rise of the surveillance technologies[13], women and trans women sex workers face an incredibly unwelcoming environment that seeks to push them back offline. It's possible to view legislative crackdowns that seek to push sex workers from public (and private) online spaces as forms of state-sanctioned social, class and ethnic cleansing of the internet, a moral gentrification of sorts to force sex workers out of public online spaces and into the "dark web". The crackdown is not a new phenomenon in terms of the social engineering around attempts to control sex work and is part of an ongoing weaponization against the circulation of certain types of photography that has been happening for over twenty-six years since the first sex work website appeared online.[14]

In this context, the self-portrait of the independent female sex-worker has become a powerful means of self-expression for sex workers, and there is now a political urgency at the heart of some sex worker portraits. However, are they a radical act of political empowerment? Do they offer creative resistance in terms of an aesthetic form of resistance to oppression? And are they a tool of women's sexual self-expression that can occupy and challenge often hostile and unwelcoming online spaces?

Visual activism can be defined as the use of, in this case, digital photographs shared in online social media platforms by oppressed others which is recognized as a form of activism and protest.[15] Sex worker visual activism is a way for the often ignored and wilfully misinterpreted voices of sex workers to effect social and political change using networked digital photographs. The possibility that visual activism

10. Anonymous, 'Bβ Liaraslist', *Liaraslist*, 2019, https://liaraslist. org/#h.ysjvuvkw0jd3.

11. Andrew Griffin, 'K-Porn-Ban-Blocks-When-Date-Get-Around-How-To-Pornography-Internet-Adult-Websites', *The Independent*, 17 April 2019, www.independent.co.uk/life-style/gadgets-and-tech/news/uk-porn-ban-blocks-when-date-get-around-how-to-pornography-internet-adult-websites-a8874761. html.

12. Anonymous, 2019; 'Article 13 Copyright Directive', https://www. article13.org/.

13. Rivkah Brown, 'How Facial Recognition Is Being Used To Target Sex Workers', Newstatesman.com, May 2019, www.newstatesman.com/science-tech/privacy/2019/05/how-facial-recognition-being-used-target-sex-workers?amp&__twitter_impression=true.

14. Waring, 'Whoretography'.

15. T.J. Demos, 'Between Rebel Creativity and Reification: For and Against Visual Activism', *Journal of Visual Culture* 15, no. 1 (2016), pp. 85–102.

 Feminist Art Activisms and Artivisms

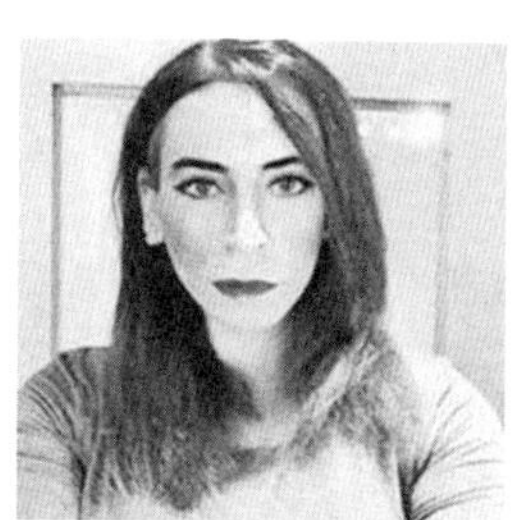

Cloe Amelia Lapper, transgendered sex worker, *Untitled* (self portrait), c. 2013

16. Teela Sanders et al., 'The Point of Counting: Mapping the Internet Based Sex Industry', *Social Sciences* 7, no. 5 (2018), pp. 233–241.

in this form can reshape, re-imagine, and redefine visual landscapes and through this reshape political and social landscapes remains. In this sense, the circulation of these photographs produced by independent women sex workers can become activism and protest. The protest would lie in the photograph's making, circulation and viewing. The aim of these sex workers who post photographic content online would be to create forms of solidarity between sex workers in online communities, in addition to generating paying audiences and sex buying clients, enabling sex workers to showcase themselves as real human beings and allow people with various opinions and vested interests in sex work to be able to interact more directly with the women featured in the photographs. Only through such platforms on the internet do sex workers, like other citizens, have access to an unfettered form of communication that allows them to challenge social constructs that influence their lives.[16]

Through my doctoral research, I have learnt of many many ways in which sex workers are engaging in visual activism, and I am conflicted about writing about such methods if it means causing harm to individual workers. However, we must document this visual fight back as sex workers themselves are reshaping visual landscapes in order to reshape political social landscapes.

Maya, an undocumented sex worker who lives and works in New York City was smuggled into the United States when she was five years old by her parents seeking a better life. Maya epitomizes the new millennial politicized sex worker who has harnessed the power of social media and the "face-out" selfie where her face is revealed. Maya is already doubly criminalized, as a sex worker in a state where it is a criminal offence to advertise sex for sale and as an undocumented illegal immigrant. Through the posting of self-portraits online, Maya challenges notions about her existence as a sex worker who does not fit into the dominant binary narrative described earlier nor is she a trafficked migrant sex worker, working for others. Maya's posting of face-out photographs is a remarkable, bold act of unrepentant visual activism. When asked about why she posts face-out photographs in public online spaces, her responses are both shocking and heart-breaking:

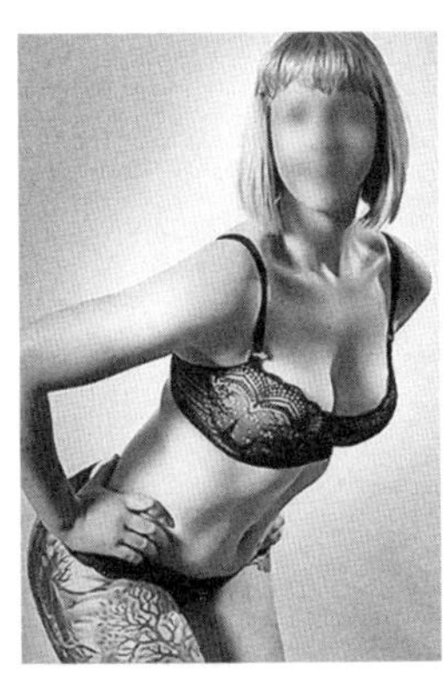

Unknown Australian sex worker, c. 2014, orphan photograph

Camille Waring

Selfies show my evolution of how I'm going as
a person, how I'm feeling that day. It's a way of
expressing my body, things I can't really express
anywhere else. There are several photos I took
recently of me attending protests, just hanging out,
a few sexy selfies and I tagged it with 'I am just
doing my part to contribute to white genocide'.
People think "white genocide" is real. I think the
tide is shifting… more people were talking about
migrant sex workers and I feel like you can't separate
sex workers from immigration because it's tied to
racial fears, the white panic around sex workers.
They (anti sex work prohibitionists and government
agencies) are trying to use facial recognition
software to find people like me, they are trying to
make us come out from underground, they don't
understand why we are hiding from them, they just
want to save us when we don't want to be saved, they
are trying to find us, trying to understand our visual
language to hunt us out, they don't really view the
selfies we post online as activism, art or as critical
thought.

Maya has weaponized and politicized her self-portrait as
a sex-worker and is wielding it against the state which seeks
to punish her for her very existence. For Maya, this form of
visual activism is a liberating performance of gender and
sexuality, and an opportunity to challenge notions about
race, sex working women of colour and not a form of
female self-objectification.

When speaking with sex workers it is difficult not
to imagine that the backlash against sex workers occupying
online spaces is happening because they (the sex workers)
became too comfortable on the internet and forgot who
was looking at them: not just clients and stalkers, but states
and the big tech bros of Silicon Valley. State agencies, like
U.S. Department of Homeland Security Immigration and
Customs Enforcement (ICE), are motivated by the same
prurient fascination with sex workers, searching for them
online in order to remove their images from the internet
and the undocumented or illegal immigrants from their
state. When I asked Maya about what the consequences

   Feminist Art Activisms and Artivisms

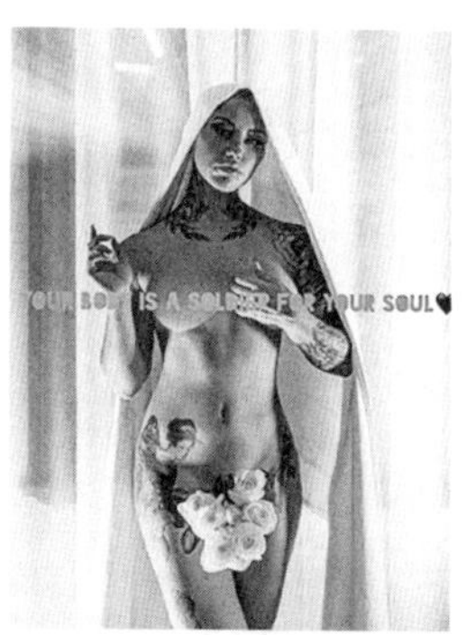

Marcella Romain, Australian sex
worker and visual artist, *Faith and
Fury* (self portrait), 2019

for her are of showing her face, Maya points to how to use surveillance culture to her advantage.

> I don't know why they (ICE) have not gone after me yet I think it's because, I'm hoping it's because me posting my photographs online keeps me kind of safe maybe, that my celebrity status as a sex worker and outspoken activist keeps me from being arrested and people would notice if I disappeared. When they try to go after the sex industry they don't go after the people who profit at the top of the industry, they don't go after the owner of Porn Hub because he's in tech, so he has not been impacted by any policy and that's how the anti-sex-work-feminists work, they are not targeting the men in the Tech industry that are profiting from the sex industry, they are just targeting us.

The most controversial form of visual activism is to show your face as a sex worker online as Maya did. "Face Out" refers to the phenomenon when sex workers publish photographs on websites and social media platforms without hiding the face by pixilation, blurring or other artistic intervention. The women may not be out as a sex worker by name, or out in their real-life communities and to their families, but they are out through the publication of images without any attempt to conceal their identities. The motivations for doing so are complex but typically, where posted by independent female sex workers, the reason for doing this is generally an act of defiance against shame and stigma. Using photography in this way is not only a political tool for activism, but also a trust-building marketing tactic, because their clients can see them also. This decision to post a "face-out" is not the same as when sex workers are outed by others or by clients on sex buyers' forums or just by those with whorephobic attitudes trying to incite real-life violence against them. A "face out" photograph makes a blatant statement about a woman who refuses to be ashamed of her choice of employment, makes visible the person behind the visual stereotype and is a way for sex workers to reclaim their visual representation in online spaces. Being "face out" as a sex worker can only be seen as a defiant politicized radical

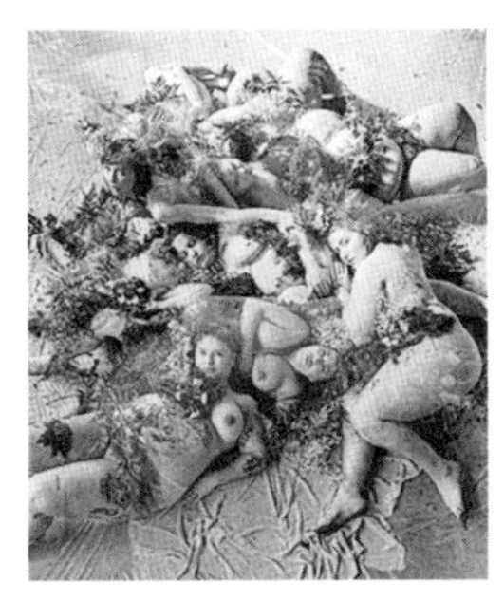

Heather Hunter, Australian sex worker, *Flesh and Flowers*, 2019. Photo: Logan Cherry Photography

Camille Waring

act in the face of stigma and shame that mandates that sex workers transgress notions of respectability.

Sex workers are also posting their photographs without sex worker specific hashtags and hijacking civilian work hashtags to avoid Instagram's algorithms that target accounts for removal. Sex workers are changing the visual style of the photographs they post to avoid detection by Instagram when the content of photographs are scanned, for example, bringing BDSM out of the dungeons and photographing BDSM practitioners in brightly lit hotel rooms so the photographs blend in with the brightly coloured imagery of most mainstream Instagram influencers.

The relationship between sex workers posting visual content online and the gendered aspect of online visual culture cannot be ignored—particularly as it relates to patriarchy and attitudes that surround sex work and the debate that surrounds female-generated photographs.[17] Sex workers and non sex working women who photographically self-document online face a shared criticism, that renders self-portraits to a visual expression of female vanity and narcissism facilitated by the rise of digital technologies. Such theories shape our understanding of self-representation online. Posting self-authored photographs in feminist terms is often seen in black and white terms, as either a progressive or regressive act.

Gabby, a chronically ill sex worker, uses photography to make sense of her "multiple online personas". She talks about how the photographs that she posts online explore her relationship with her image, both intentionally constructed and inadvertently presented. Gabby's visual activism stems from her awareness of sex worker visual marketing and the inevitable blurring of boundaries that comes from maintaining multiple online personas.

> In an image-saturated culture, where our self-worth (and for many sex workers: our livelihood) is determined by likes, shares and retweets, the curation of a digital persona becomes increasingly important. In the interconnected world, reality and lived experience often become less important than our social network and our social reach. My truth and current state are reflected in the image that I am creating.

17. Lian Duan, 'Textual Body in City Space: A Psychoanalytic Study of the Representation of Female Body in Contemporary Photography and Its Social Meaning', *Comparative Literature: East & West* 15, no. 1 (2011), pp. 116–140.

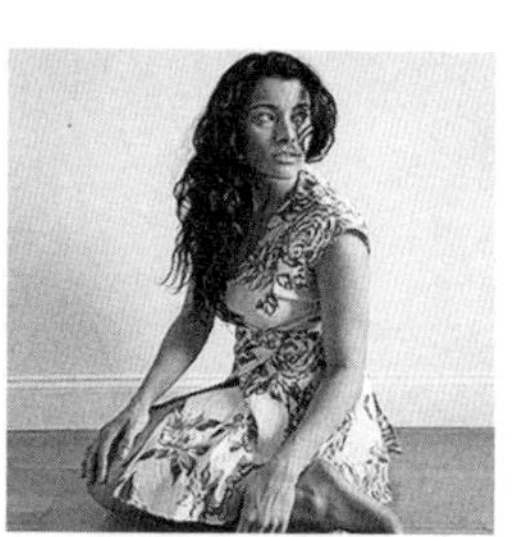

Maya Morena, sex worker, *Untitled* (self portrait), 2019

   Feminist Art Activisms and Artivisms

18. Waring, 'Whoretography'.

19. Duan, 'Textual Body in City Space'.

90% of my work is behind a computer, setting up appointments, marketing and taking calls. There is the assumption that I am always dressed, made up and ready to go. In these images, I incorporate my current state into pre-constructed images of my fetishized self as a lingering reminder of the less constructed components of reality. These images question how we present ourselves and construct our identities through social media and examine the process in which we curate truth.

Like Gabby, Lindsay uses photographs in ways that have her thinking about how her body, as a trans disabled woman sex worker, is disseminated through a variety of digital lenses imposed by the audiences and consumers of her visual content.

It becomes an almost Frankenstein-like assemblage comprised of the ideas that my viewers have about it. Particularly as a trans and disabled person, I was thinking about how much of the materiality of my body, being subject to so much state surveillance, changes as I navigate the sex work floor.

The politically motivated sex worker has morphed from the early twenty-first century when many photographs were highly constructed marketing images, to the rise of the first wave of celebrity sex workers circa 2012 who harnessed the power of Twitter and Instagram to create a visual persona for themselves into this new breed of politically inspired, motivated and no longer silenced sex worker who boldly uses the photograph as a weapon against censorship.[18]
There is now a quiet and unnoticed and previously undefined digitally networked rebellion taking place. Sub-versive, and determined, the contemporary political online sex worker has turned the photograph into a protest. Sharing these images online is a protest against another form of premediated and brutal online oppression imposing a social and racial cleansing of the internet in which sex workers are bearing the brunt of a moral gentrification that would see them thrust back to a pre-digital networked world where sex work was tolerated only because it remained unseen.[19]

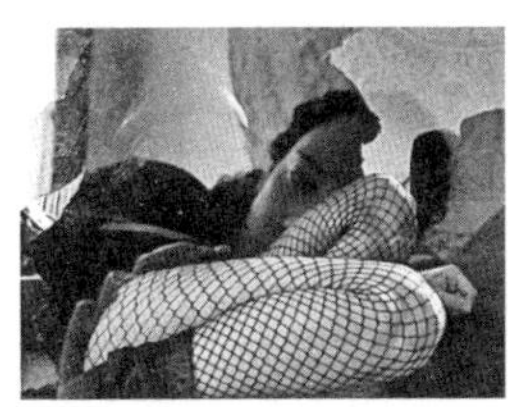

Gabriella Stein, sex worker, *Untitled* (self portrait), 2019

Individual female sellers of sex and small collectives of sex workers, in seemingly unconnected and certainly not organized ways, have turned the photograph into a tool of political protest, and a statement about the right to exist in online and offline spaces.

Sex workers have unwittingly, and perhaps unknowingly, become visual activists in the face of an unrelenting internet crackdown that is seeing them evicted from online spaces *en masse* and shoved back into the unsafe and unnoticed back alleys. Female sex workers have begun using visual elements creatively in their visual practices to expand their political engagements, create a politicking aesthetic, and redefine our understanding of pornography, as the pornographic image becomes a statement about exclusion and inclusion from online platforms. Through sex worker-led visual activism, female sex workers are forcing an evolution in the photographic ecology and the visual culture of online sex work. Sex workers are using photography and online social spaces as platforms for activisms and of course, historical offline sex work activism is intertwined with photographs of protesting sex workers.[20] The censorship of online sex culture and the eviction of sex workers from the open internet necessitate the use of user-generated visual data created by sex workers as a form of visual activism and necessitate sex workers adding new meaning to their photographs that are too often dismissed as pornography or just marketing material to entice male buyers of sex.

It is one thing for the walls of suburbia to be adorned with replica paintings of historical socially acceptable courtesans painted by French artists and purchased from Ikea, it is another thing entirely to expect to have to share online spaces with real sex workers who are now accessible and visible in suburbia from the couches and desks positioned to face those faux pieces of Ikea art. With the advent of digital photography, pornography as a mass industry of visual images, and the internet as the world's largest image database, photographs of sex workers have left the art world and are now readily accessible in people's homes. The figure of the female sex worker features heavily in cinema and media. Sex workers who ply their trade online, (and rightly so) are visible in online spaces, the expansion of photography to the internet has had a significant effect

20. Lilian Mathieu, 'An Unlikely Mobilization: The Occupation of Saint-Nizier Church by the Prostitutes of Lyon', *Revue française de sociologie* 42, no. 1 (2001), pp. 107–131.

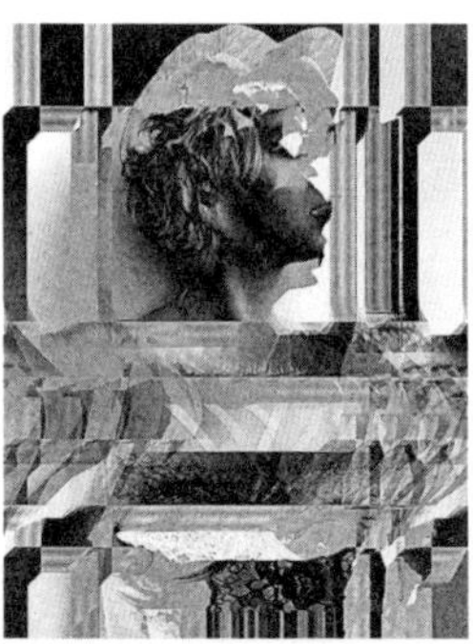

Lindsey Weiss, sex worker, *Untitled* (self portrait), 2019

   Feminist Art Activisms and Artivisms

21. Daniel Rubinstein and Katrina Sluis, 'A Life More Photographic: Mapping the Networked Image', *Photographies* 1, no. 1 (2008), pp. 9–28.

SEX WORK IS WORK

on society, online digital photographs have caused shifts in the way sex working bodies are seen.[21] This audacity of the sex worker to take up visible space online has been met with a harsh government crackdown whose aim is to push them back into spaces deemed acceptable for sex workers to be, the street corner where they can be easily policed or framed in art. Sex work depicted in art has been censored for a variety of reasons, but changing cultural attitudes towards sex work have also changed how sex work is depicted in different art forms, styles and artistic mediums. These visual portrayals have typically been created by non sex working individuals and this situation has created and largely maintains the standard voyeuristic gaze that depicts sex workers either as hapless victims or as complicit harlots upholding the social structures that underpin patriarchy.

This is why independent sex workers should be considered as at the forefront of visual activism, in an image-saturated internet, fighting for the right to exist in off and online spaces. Regardless of one's political or moral views regarding sex work or the terminology used to describe the practice of selling sex, sex workers have a fundamental basic right to exist visually in online spaces free from hate, stigma, and violence. Through sex worker-led visual activism, female sex workers are disrupting the hegemonic views that shape the general understanding of sex work by providing an alternative visual discourse and challenging the response to sex workers as only ripe for "rescue". Whilst these examples may seem random and unconnected, when you look at online sex work on a larger scale you see beautiful rhythmic connected patterns of resilience and resistance, previously undefined in academia. In these spaces, the sex worker's photographic revolution has the power to shift visual landscapes about identity, challenge visual cultural reference points in the media and cinemascapes and ultimately force a shift in how we consider the social and political landscape of sex work in terms of who makes images of sex.

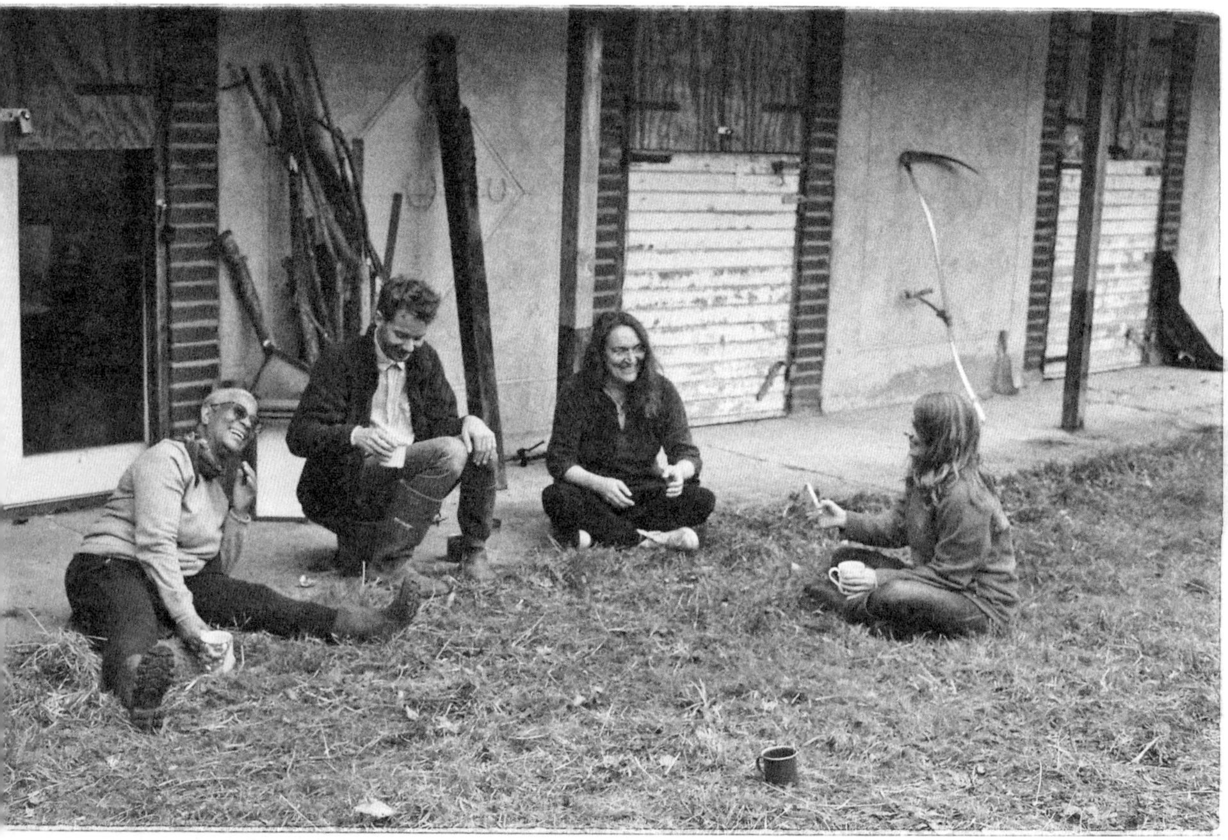

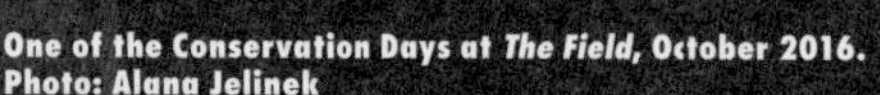

One of the Conservation Days at *The Field*, October 2016.
Photo: Alana Jelinek

FEMINIST ARTIVISMS
Examples of an Art History

Alana Jelinek

1. Alana Jelinek, 'The Field: An Art Experiment in Levinasian Ethics', in *Living Beings: Perspectives on Interspecies Engagements* (London: Bloomsbury, 2013); Alana Jelinek 'A Response to the Issues Raised in the Special Ethics Edition', *Ethnos: Journal of Anthropology* 87, no. 1 (2017), pp. 105–112; 'Cherry Laurel (Prunus laurocerasus): Prunus laurocerasus and Other Species', in *Botanical Drift: Protagonists of the Invasive Herbarium*, ed. Khadija von Zinnenburg-Carroll (Berlin: Sternberg Press, 2018), pp. 209–220.

Second-wave feminism taught us the personal is political, that our politics comes from a position, from a specific standpoint. So, I will introduce myself for those who haven't met me before. I am an artist. I have been an artist for my entire adult life, which is now middle-aged. I have exhibited nationally and internationally, sometimes in prestigious venues with artists of renown, more often in small venues outside the established art world. Usually I work with, and have as my audience, a small coterie of friends, and friends of friends, as well as strangers who often become friends. My model for being an artist is an old-fashioned one. I don't use social media. I have no followers. Instead, small groups of people come together in physical locations as participants in socially engaged work, or as more traditional audiences. My audiences are mostly comprised of fellow artists and I, in turn, am part of their audiences. This is how it used to be in the art worlds of the 1960s, 1970s and 1980s, a period I know about from historical record, not necessarily from personal experience. Occasionally I write about my art. Most often I write about the role and value of art—all art—in society, e.g. *This is Not Art: Activism and Other 'Not-Art'* (IB Tauris, 2013) and *Between Discipline and a Hard Place: The Value of Contemporary Art* (Bloomsbury, 2020–2021).

For this essay, I will describe—if briefly—one of my own art works, which I have written about before,[1] and two art works by women artists, namely Numbi (by Kinsi Abdulleh) and Idle Women (by Rachel Anderson and Cis O'Boyle), in order to elaborate an "ecological" way of thinking about art in the round. I offer an ecological approach to art history inspired by the feminist philosophies of Karen Barad and Donna Haraway because, despite the fact that the idea of the white male artist leading culture from the front is actively derided throughout the contemporary art world, it nevertheless continues to inform art world decision-makers and gate-keepers. What keeps the avant-gardist genius paradigm going, despite decades of critique, is the myth of progress, which is dependent on a hierarchy of achievement. Exceptional actors are sought to perpetuate the idea of genius.

However, when these exceptional actors are women, their achievements tend to remain obscure. For example, the Swedish artist Hilma af Klint (1862–1944) is now considered the originator of Modernist abstraction, yet she remains generally unknown. The position of originating genius is most often given to men and old ideas of genius maintain disproportionate market prices for white men, disproportionate biennial and gallery exhibition opportunities for men, alongside the everyday gross sexism that #MeToo and #NotSurprised made public.[2] Janet Sobel, for example, may be the progenitor of Jackson Pollock's drip paintings but she remains eclipsed, a fact encouraged by those invested in policing what genius could and should look like. 'Greenberg was always careful to state that there were precedents for individual aspects of Pollock's achievement. Tobey being one example of an acknowledged forebear, [with] Krasner

2. Nadja Sayej, 'See Change: The Battle against Sexual Harassment in the Art World', *The Guardian*, 20 February 2018; Arina Aristarkhova, 'MeToo in the Art World: Genius Should Not Excuse Sexual Harassment', *Salon* 7 (May 2018); Matthew Blackman, 'Zipped Mouths over Alleged "Racial Slurs and Sexual Innuendo" at Zeitz Mocaa', *news24*, 10 June 2018.

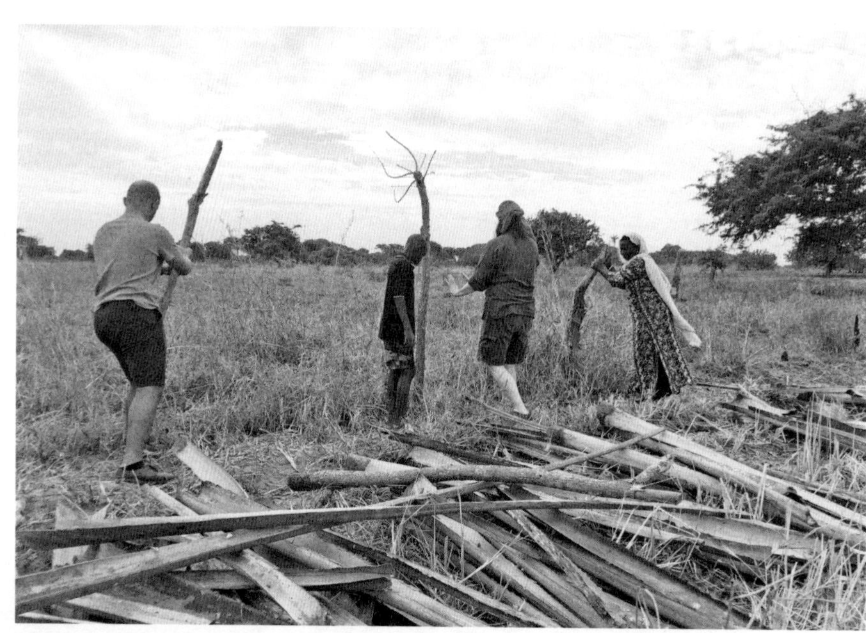

The Gambia Numbi Retreat, January 2019. Photo: Kinsi Abdulleh

3. Caroline A. Jones, *Eyesight Alone: Clement Greenberg's Modernism and the Bureaucratization of the Senses*, (Chicago: University of Chicago, 2008), pp. 220–222.

and Sobel'.[3] That Greenberg and Pollock together went to see Sobel's drip paintings in 1946 remains little known.

Because the achievements of women and anyone from outside the paradigm of Greatness are periodically erased, swept under carpets of white male achievement, there are good reasons for feminist art historians and post-colonialists to sift through history and geography in order to find alternative canons of artists —geniuses—who were once renowned but are now overlooked and marginalized. However, simply adding examples to a catalogue of Greats, scouting unknown territory in the pursuit of the novel and the as-yet-unknown, just as the plant hunters of the nineteenth century did, simply maintains an inherently problematic model. Lying at the foundation of progressivist notions of culture and politics is the idea of a special, exceptional few leading a bovine, recalcitrant mass towards Enlightenment. We are so wedded to this type of narrative that the scheme does not alter even when we choose to canonize variants on the theme of genius, those once

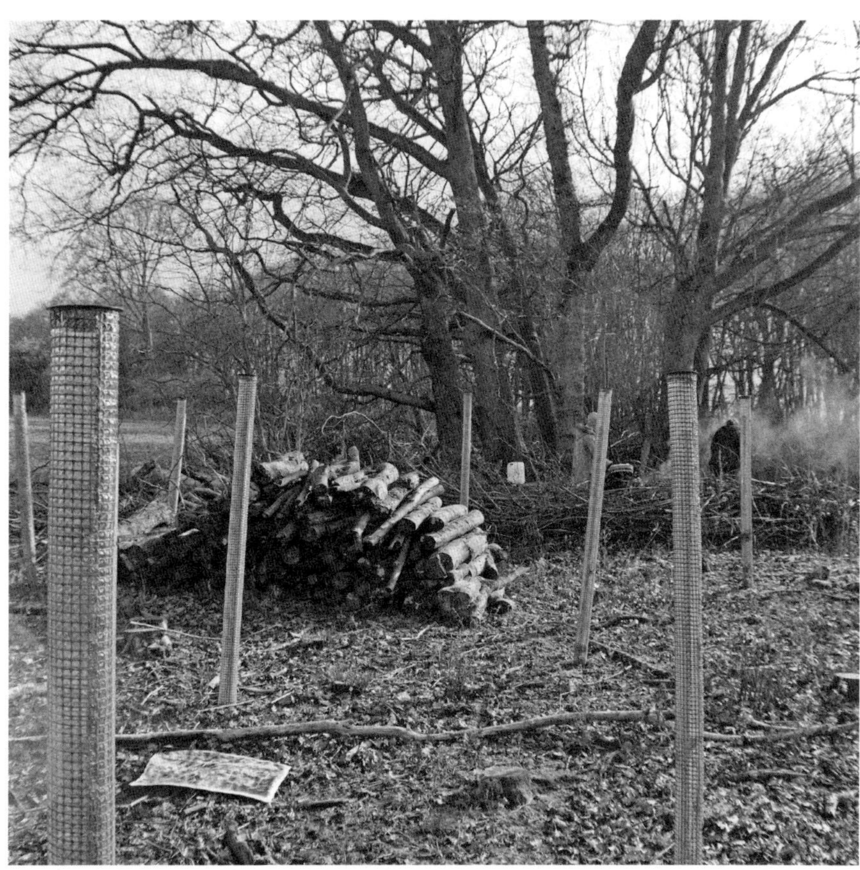

One of the monthly Conservation Days at *The Field*, May 2017. Photo: Martin Pankhurst

excluded by virtue of birth or belief, as if this is enough.
Instead, we should question the problematic in the model.
If we are to leave the masculinist, white supremacist model
behind once and for all, a completely different way of understanding art and how art-making is related to everything else
is required.

The science of ecology provides metaphors that help
visualize the potential for this. Ecology is the study of interrelationships between species: between individuals within
species in relation to other proximate species in a given and
specific context. By contrast, much traditional art history
focuses on the individual, the singular organism—to employ
the ecological term—and the individual is understood as
exemplar, as extraordinary. In traditional art histories, the
individual organism is generally not considered in relation
to her wider context, to the rest of her "species" (be it to
artists or to fellow human beings) living and working in a
specific location. Exceptions to this model sometimes occurs
when art history is written as the succession of art historical
movements in which particular individual artists become
exemplary of the movement. The artist in this model remains
either fruit fly or Koko the gorilla.

Fruit flies are one of the most intensively studied
organisms in molecular and cell biology. Individuals and
whole generations are investigated as "model organisms",
considered primarily in terms of mutation, in order to
understand particular biological phenomena. This approach
to biology parallels progressivist art history, in that developments in art and culture are understood as occurring
through a series of mutations. Further, by analogy, each
artist understood as model organism provides insights for
the wider population and the expectation is that discoveries
made in the "model organism" will provide insight into the
workings of other organisms. In addition to the artist as
model organism, some exceptional individuals, such as Koko
the gorilla, are studied for their embodiment of progress and
human achievement. It was considered a human achievement
that the gorilla had mastered language well enough to convey
relatively complex ideas and feelings. Traditionally art historians investigate the artist as an organism in isolation, and
narrate the purpose of art as a story of progress and human
achievement, like Koko.

A rarer form of traditional art history describes a community, in the ecological sense, enumerating those factors that sustain or deplete a given population of artists. If one describes a population in the ecological definition, looking beyond an individual organism, one arrives at a "culture" or "eco-system", here defined as many individuals of the same or different "species" living together in a given location. The ecological community includes predators and prey and, in this metaphor, it might include funders, dealers, patrons and wider material conditions, such as the presence of affordable studios to rent and the socio-political climate.

While these types of histories—the community, population and model organism perspectives—may be valuable for their accounts of art, they nevertheless fail to consider the wider web of relations and pressures that enable—or disable—artistic practice. By default, they tend to retain the myth of artist as genius leading society from the front as well as the myth of meritocracy, as if an individual organism somehow deserves its position in a community because it is judged as successful as a predator or used as prey. What is missed is the impact of the various intellectual, physical,

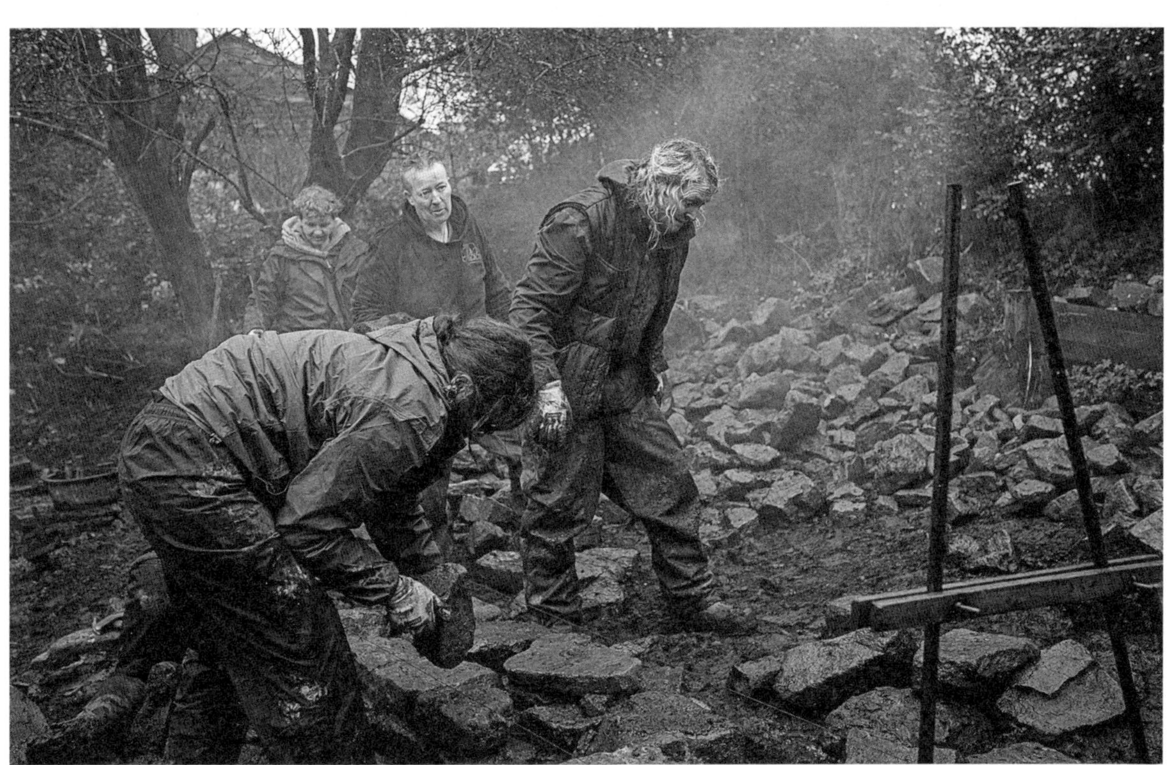

Idle Women, *Physic Garden Dry Stone Walling*. Photo: Jessie Leong

economic, technological, geographical, social, and normative
factors that enable or disable art and particular individual
artists. Art-making occurs as a consequence of numerous
social relations and the impact of social, physical and other
resources. At any given period in any given location, there
are always artists who did not form part of a given art movement—either as a community or population—who remain
unobserved by historians writing after the fact.

Employing ecological metaphors for understanding
art in society helps us to see that changes happen over time
through a complex web of relations. Evolution (so to speak)
occurs because of the relationship of artist populations to
their environment, of individuals in relation to each other
and also to wider conditions. The art an artist makes is an
emergent property of specific conditions and not the singular
act of a superlative organism. Institutions, both physical and
discursive, are part of the ecological environment, the biome,
so to speak. The result of institutional choices to support
or deny resources, to include and exclude conceptually and
sometimes literally, creates conditions that determine or
inform the art of any time in any location. In an ecological
view, art is the emergent property of a wide variety of
factors. None is deterministic.

The art works of terra incognita, Numbi Arts and
Idle Women, can be described in this way, just as any art
can be. Each art project is the product of individual artistic
vision and ambition, in dialogue with others, and also a
navigation of constrained resources, changing opportunities
and the ability and luck to forge new paths when none were
immediately apparent. Each group produces art works
that reflect aspects of contemporary artistic discourse and
preoccupations, while also embodying personal responses to
prevailing conditions and navigating personal commitments
to ethics and to art.

My own work with terra incognita arts organization
(1997–2017) culminated in a 9-year project called *The Field*
(2008–2017), in which London-based community groups
and artists were invited to a 13-acre ancient woodland
and grassland 1 mile north of Stansted Airport runway
in Essex. It is easy to describe *The Field* conforming to
the typical teleological art historical model in which one
artwork begets another, citing artistic precedents, such

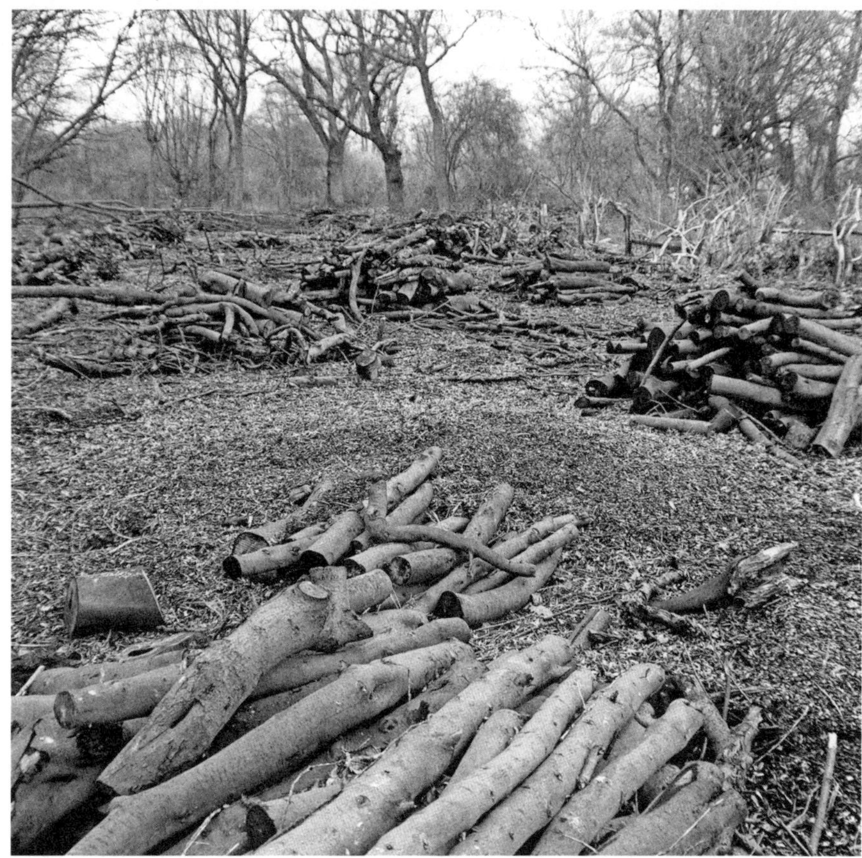

Felled the Cherry Laurel at *The Field*, 2016. Photo: Martin Pankhurst

4. www.thelandfoundation.org/about.

5. Brett Christophers, *The New Enclosure: The Appropriation of Public Land in Neoliberal Britain* (London: Verso, 2018).

as Land Art and Rirkrit Tiravanija's *The Land* project in Thailand (1998 ongoing).[4] This is true. *The Field*, as art, could only occur within a historical context in which artistic practice can include interventions large and small in the "natural" context, and working with precedents such as Agnes Denes, *Wheatfield—A Confrontation: Battery Park Landfill, Downtown Manhattan*, 1982. What is also true is that by 2008, artists' studios had been closed or rents had risen to extortionate levels, squatting was no longer an option, and public land had been largely privatized: the "new enclosures" of public land had occurred and they too have been critiqued.[5] London's art world seemed to have been eviscerated by commerce and a hungry generation of artists who knew nothing other than an inflated art market and globalized biennial circuit. These conditions informed

Alana Jelinek

The Field. There was also the long twelve years working as an artist only for it to get harder to make a living and to make art, living on the penultimate floor of a tower block with no access to the ground. Much of this also forms context and reasons behind the inception of Numbi in 2009 and Idle Women in 2015.

Kinsi Abdulleh of Numbi and Rachel Anderson of Idle Women had been active participants of *The Field*, helping to form its unique contribution to art, as regular and important contributors to the project, particularly through the annual Moot Point event (2009–2016). Moot Point was an opportunity to *moot*, or interrogate, an idea using both discursive and art-practice techniques over a weekend of camping at *The Field*. Each year a different mooter suggested the moot and invited guests as participants in a collective interrogation of ideas such as revolution, hospitality and failure.

However we need also to understand the other factors vital to the genesis of any art, beyond a narrative of influence and progress, if we are to understand art "ecologically" in a different way. In a public talk by Kinsi Abdulleh about her art practice, it was striking how many people she cited compared with most artist's talks, including those who are similarly "socially engaged".[6] She speaks about her art within a network of practices, at the junction of various artistic and community concerns, subsequent of turns of fortune and responding to the vagaries of life. As a black British artist, as an African woman, as a Somali refugee and a migrant to Britain, Abdulleh was drawn to specific people as mentors, colleagues, teachers and friends. She is conscious of these choices, but we all make them. Consequently her choices combined with the opportunities different decades afforded her: some doors were open to her, while others remained shut. She describes the formative influence of Sudanese British ceramicist Mo Abbaro (a name largely forgotten, swept under that carpet of white male achievement) and black British artist Rita Keegan, who introduced her to 'feminism and art marking and women making art'. She described how, in the 1990s, Oxford House in London's Bethnal Green worked with the Somali community so Abdulleh ended up

6. Artists' talk: Socially-engaged art practice in Tower Hamlets with Kinsi Abdulleh and Saif Osmani. Transcript from recording (18 April 2019) at Tower Hamlets Local History and Archives, 277 Bancroft Road, London E1 4DD.

AN ECOLOGICAL WAY OF THINKING ABOUT ART

volunteering because that was the only way I could get a studio. You volunteered for two days doing workshops with schools and community groups … and then you had a studio. I had a whole studio to myself. I had a whole print room to myself. They did a lot of work with Somalis. That's where I got into politics.

Aware of the networks that enable her art and those who influence how she thinks and makes art, Abdulleh honours the rhizome, as a means to explain the interrelationships between herself and others, remembering and naming the nodes. She is aware of the ecosystem that sustained, and continues to sustain, her practice. This is not a posture of inclusion, or lip service to Deleuze, but the habit of a lifetime and a way of seeing she terms "African", by which she means an awareness of mutuality and interdependence.

The Numbi project I discuss here is *Retreat* because it has direct links to *The Field*, however it exists on land negotiated with the traditional Gambian owners of Kartong village, obtained African style. Money could have changed hands so that ownership is sealed in perpetuity, in the way that western culture privileges, but it hasn't. Instead Abdulleh made an agreement to do something productive on a piece of land bestowed through traditional ownership mechanisms. The *Retreat* will revert to the community along with the new buildings, growing areas, tools, books and equipment for the use of the people, once Numbi is done. By contrast, once land on which *The Field* project had taken place was sold, after 9 years as a terra incognita project in receipt of conservation funding for the reintroduction of native tree species, the social, ecological and conservation benefits were more or less immediately reversed.

Like *The Field*, Numbi's *Retreat* may appear to be something other, more like ecology and conservation, perhaps even development, instead of art. There is no specific outcome. It is process-led and responsive to the needs and vision of participants. It is negotiated. We know it is art because it builds on and is in dialogue with artistic precedents, including *The Field,* but also a wider array of African art practice brought to London's attention via Numbi's ambitious residency programme with Rich Mix,

Shoreditch, London (2013–2018) and recorded in the various editions of Numbi's *Scarf* journal.

Idle Women was similarly a response, in part, to the crushingly market-preoccupied London art world of the second decade of the millennium and the conditions that asphyxiated life as a London-based artist at that time. Originally the Idle Women project was imagined in three distinct phases, beginning with a residential scheme for women artists on narrow boats on the canals of Lancashire, called *On the water*, and enabled through an Arts Council England grant. Idle Women was to work with Heart of Glass on all the manifestations of their project, which is a relatively new arts organization based in St Helens, Lancashire. There was also to be a land-based project, a long-term durational art project inspired by, and in response to, *The Field*. However, plans altered in response to changing conditions so Idle Women initiated *Physic Garden* (2018 ongoing) instead.

Whereas *The Field* was privately owned, *Physic Garden* was crowd-funded, and Idle Women work in part-nership with a women's refuge, Humraaz, and a commercial sponsor, Weleda, in part to make up the shortfall in

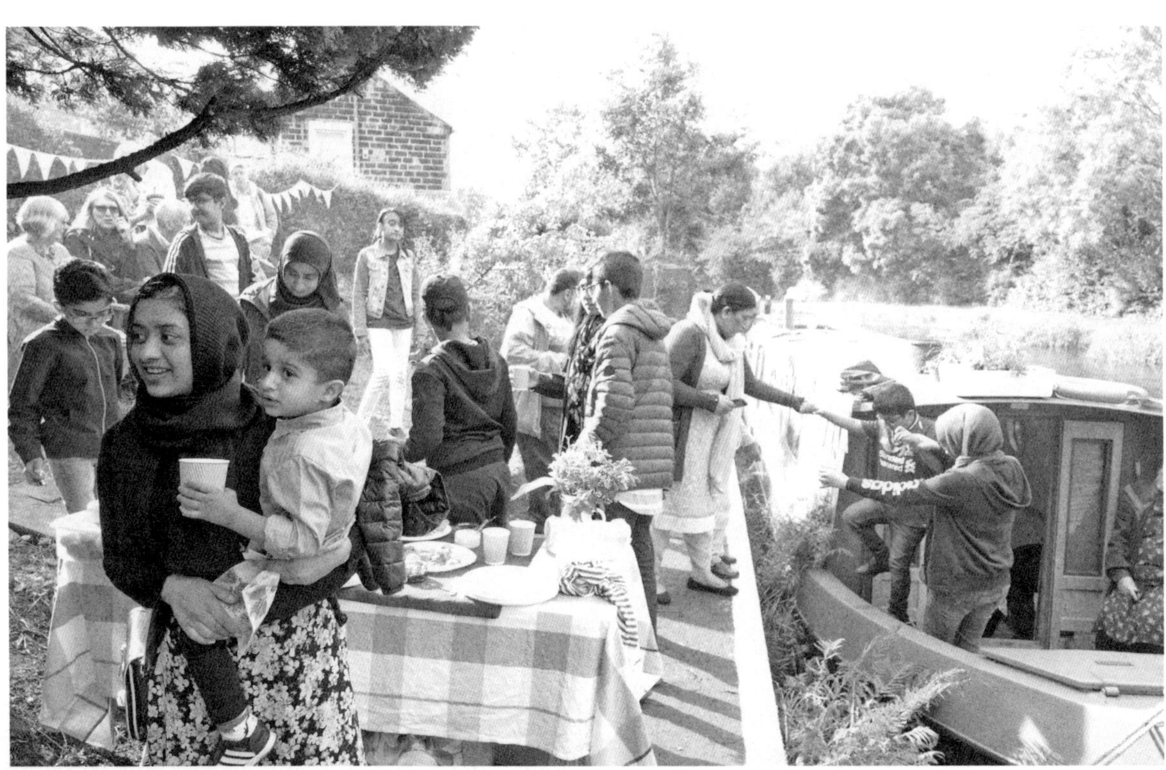

Idle Women, *Physic Garden Community Celebration*, 2019. Photo: Rachel Anderson

achieving the purchase price. There are many artistic differ-ences between terra incognita's *The Field* and Idle Women's *Physic Garden*, details of which lie beyond the scope of this essay, however the often-overlooked impact of location and funding regimes, as well as ownership models, also determine some of the differences between the two. I wish to highlight the impact of these ordinarily overlooked aspects here, attempting to account—to some extent—for the art in ecological terms.

What all the projects have in common, in addition to being durational, participatory and land-based is that none are strictly collaborative. Instead each is guided by the lead artists' intentions for their respective projects. There are physical and material differences between each of the projects, as well as differences in how they are constituted, their locations, how they are run and their reception by the art world. An ecological view of art takes account of all the processes and pressures involved, the material conditions, prevailing economics and legitimating discourse, locations, and participants, in addition to the vision of the individuals involved, in order to create and enable art to exist.

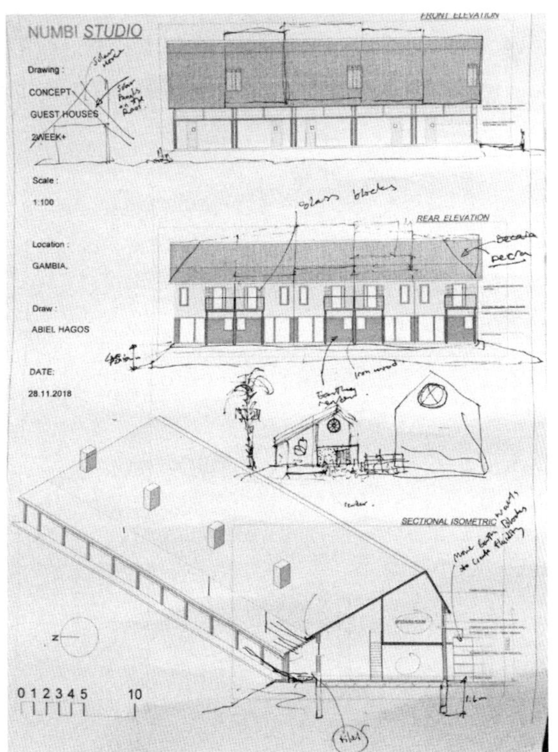

Numbi Studio, eco village drawing, architect: Abiel Hagos

3D render of site plan for Numbi

ART ACTIVISMS
AND ARTIVISMS

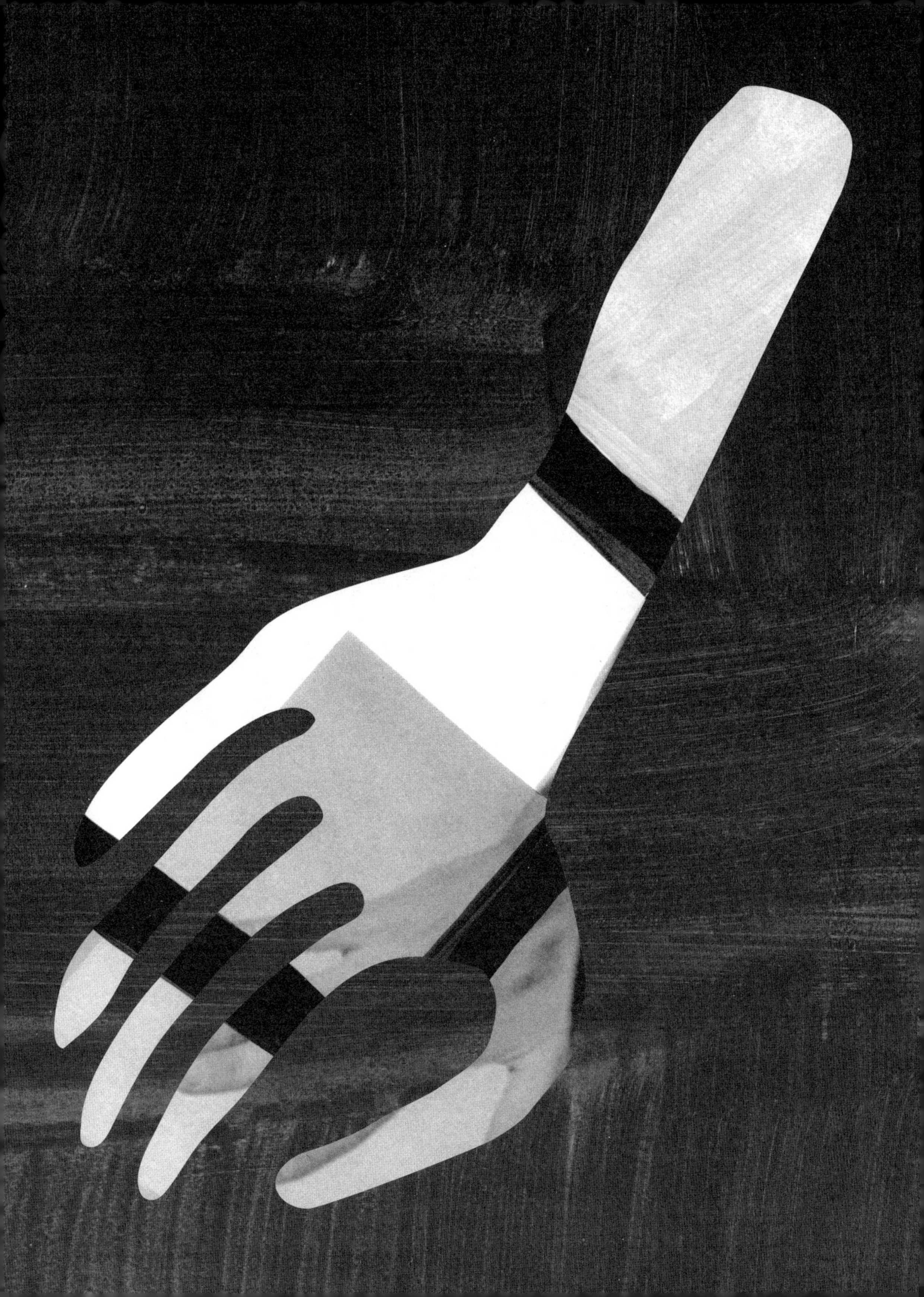

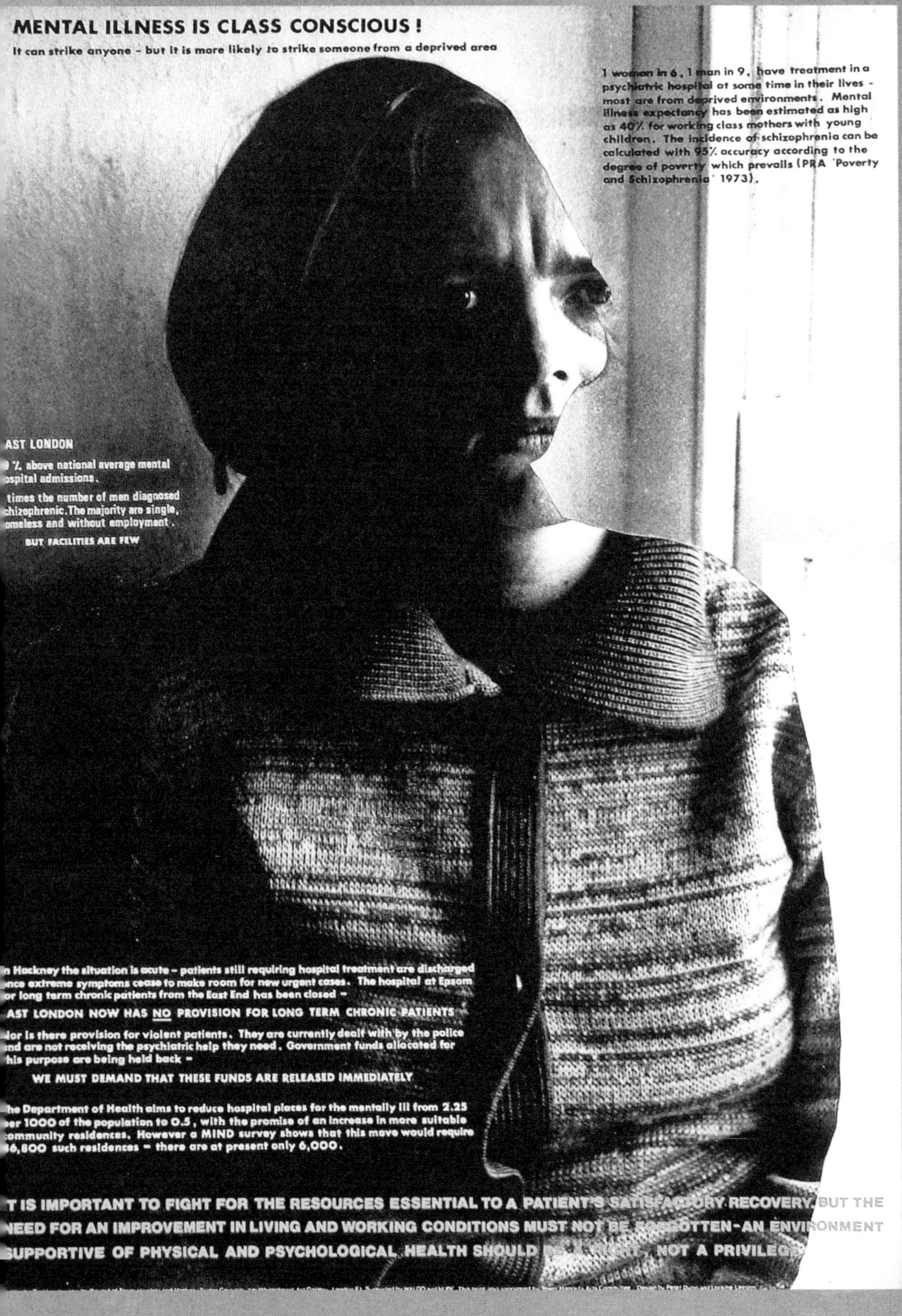

Loraine Leeson, East London Health Project © Dunn and Leeson, 'Mental Illness is Class Conscious', 1979, A2 poster, offset litho. Produced and distributed in conjunction with East London Trades Councils, health workers' unions and the Women's Health Information Collective.

THE THINGS THAT MAKE YOU SICK

Loraine Leeson

In the light of the current resurgence in feminist thought, I have found myself reflecting on the extent to which social engagement and activism in my art practice has been guided by the tenets of feminism. It certainly commenced at the height of feminist activism in the late 1970s, and many of those values and approaches have underpinned the work then and since. These encompassed a focus on social and civil rights, redistribution of wealth, economic and political equality, and recognition of the value of difference, issues that were addressed through processes of making visible, facilitating voice, valuing experience, exploring narratives other than the dominant, and addressing identities from the inside out, with consideration of representation playing a central role. This may not seem surprising, except that the subject of the work has addressed wider social issues and

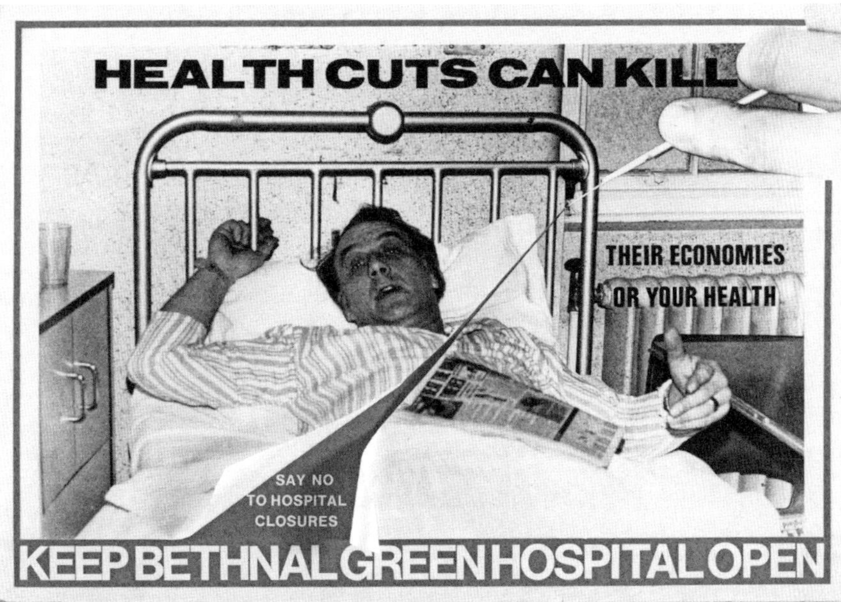

Peter Dunn and Loraine Leeson, Bethnal Green Hospital Campaign, 'Health cuts can kill', 1978, A2 poster, offset litho

only rarely focused on those specific to women. The Left at that time was nevertheless in many ways closely, though imperfectly, aligned with the women's movement, each with their multiple factions. *Beyond the Fragments*,[1] published in 1979, proved a useful point of reference for those of us straddling the productive, if shifting, positions of each.

Much of my confidence as a young artist was indeed fostered through involvement in women's groups and initiatives such as Tower Hamlets Women's Art Forum, and the various events and published articles generated through Camerawork, including the First Festival of Women Photographers,[2] though all still very much outside the mainstream. The work itself however was developed in collaboration with my long-term partner Peter Dunn. We had both studied at Reading University, where our art history tutor Caroline Tisdall, a close colleague of Joseph Beuys, introduced us to his works and concepts, and we subsequently became members of his Free International University. This provided a foundation for our ongoing creative practice and supported our growing interest in interdisciplinarity plus a belief that working outside of art institutions was where, as artists, we were most likely to contribute to social change. Following early attempts at exhibiting work on social issues in public, we were seeking situations where art might take on a more meaningful role. One such opportunity presented itself in 1978 while on a fellowship running community film and video workshops in Bethnal Green, East London. At around the same time, the local hospital went into occupation as a protest against threat of closure.

1. Sheila Rowbotham et al., *Beyond the Fragments: Feminism and the Making of Socialism* (London: Merlin Press, 1979).

2. The First Festival of Women Photographers was organized and curated by Shirley Read at Camerawork, circa 1982.

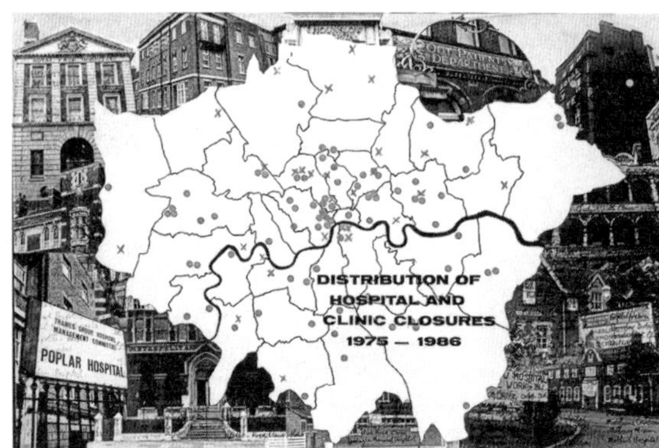

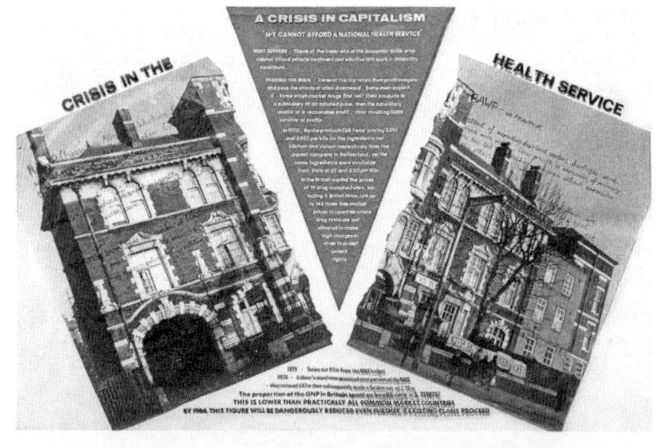

all images
Peter Dunn and Loraine Leeson, exhibition for Bethnal Green Hospital Campaign, 1979, A1 photomontage on card. Exhibition panels created for the foyer of Bethnal Green Hospital to inform visitors of the wider social and political context that lay behind the campaign. Also used in other hospitals under threat.

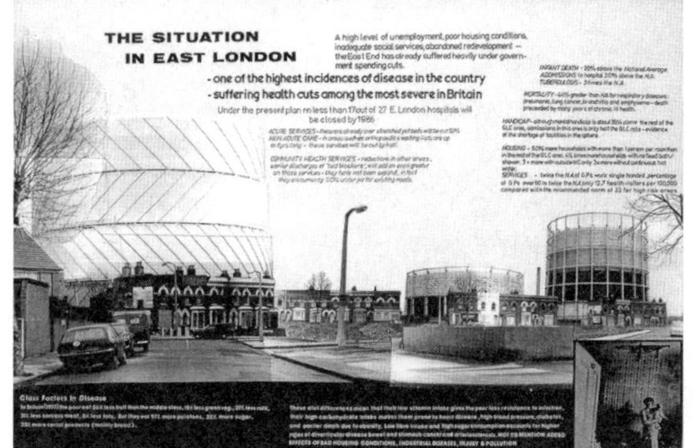

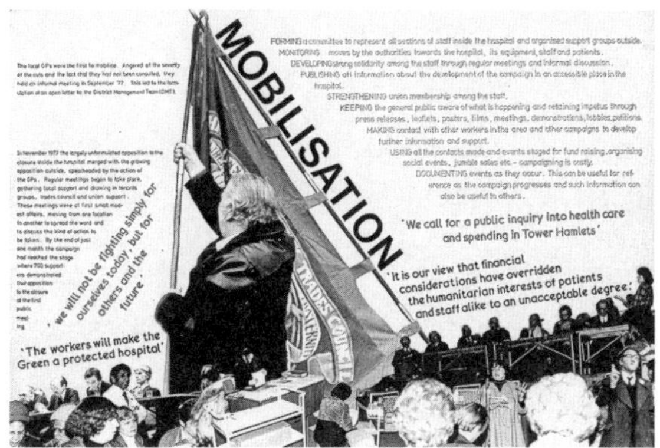

3. This and the following paragraphs are derived from a text produced by Peter Dunn and Loraine Leeson for the exhibition 'The Things That Make you Sick', London, ICA, 2017.

Bethnal Green's small community hospital was under threat as part of the first wave of cutbacks in the National Health Service, through which many small hospitals were closed. It was nevertheless highly valued for its continuity of care and accessibility to local residents, and continued to work to capacity. Once its facilities were withdrawn, patients would have nowhere to go except to extend already over-long waiting lists in other hospitals. In 1977, following orders for closure, its staff decided to "occupy" the hospital while a campaign was mounted to safeguard its future. The only people to move out of the hospital were therefore the administrators. Doctors, nurses and other staff continued to perform their duties, GPs continued to refer patients, people continued to attend the casualty department and ambulance drivers continued to respond to emergency calls. While patients remained at the hospital, the health authority had a duty to pay staff salaries—and so the occupation took effect.[3]

Peter and I were initially approached for a video to support the campaign. This led to a series of posters, followed by an exhibition for the hospital foyer to inform users of the hospital of the wider social and political context that lay behind the campaign. Background knowledge of the history of art had already informed us of art's ability to confer power, consolidate knowledge and celebrate achievement, and through the work for this campaign we sought to draw on these attributes to support a cause we felt worth fighting for. The experience offered fruitful lessons in the effectiveness of collaboration as an artistic strategy

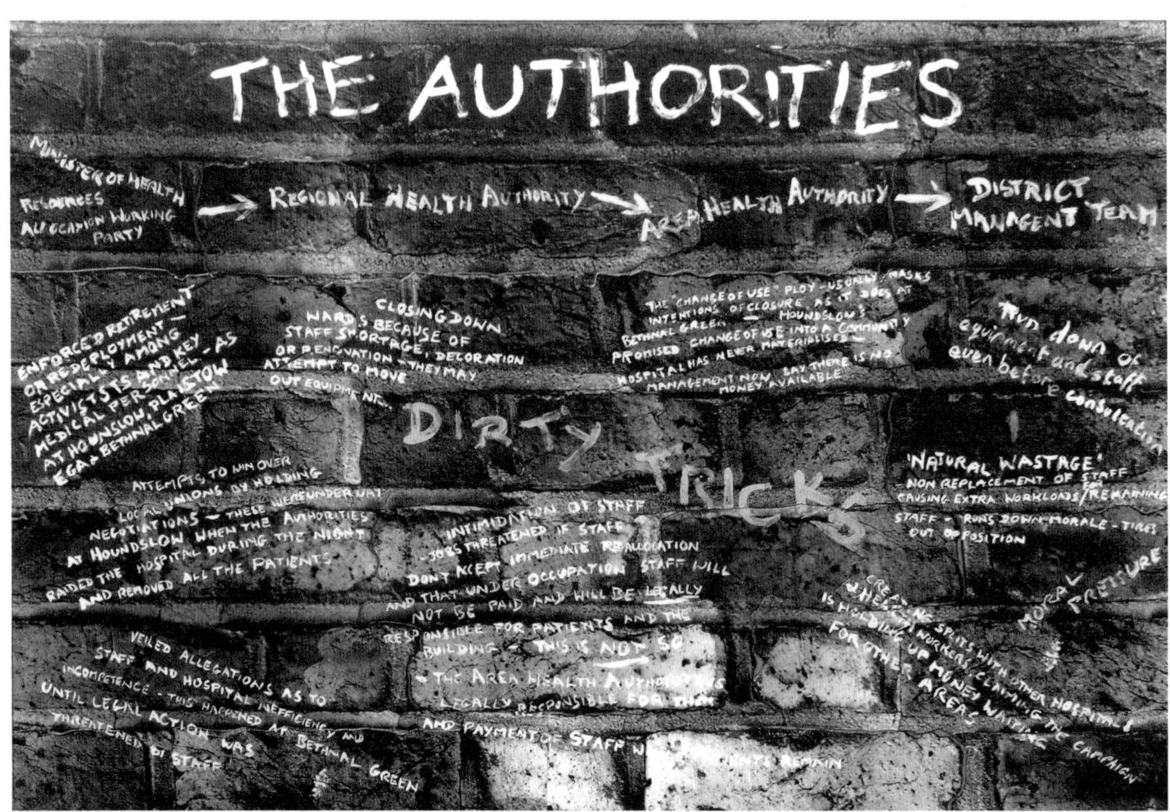

pp. 232, 233
Peter Dunn and Loraine Leeson, exhibition for Bethnal Green Hospital Campaign, 1979, A1 photomontage on card.
Exhibition panel created for the foyer of Bethnal Green Hospital to inform visitors of the wider social and political context that lay behind the campaign. Also used in other hospitals under threat.

together with the opportunity to explore the construction of
narratives beyond the mainstream from the perspective of
those directly involved.

Following the success of the campaign, the East
London trades councils planned to use leftover campaign
funds to disseminate information about health issues to the
local population in light of further NHS cuts. They recognized the potential role of art in this as offering a new, visual
approach for the broader campaigning. A steering committee
was established that included members of local trades
councils and health workers' unions. Peter and I worked
with this group to determine a visual form most suited to
its potential audience, and arrived at the idea of the "visual
pamphlet"—essentially a poster containing information that
could be used in health venues such as doctors' surgeries
and hospital waiting rooms. The collaborative processes
employed in devising and realizing this work, learned from
the union activists, thereafter continued to inform our art
practices.

Eight different posters were produced over the
two years of the project and widely distributed within
the health sector. Through these we developed our use of
photomontage, experimenting with "cut and paste" methods,
while Peter also introduced photographic "sets". One of
the steering group's priorities was on women's health, which
led to a series of posters that I produced with the Women's
Health Information Collective.

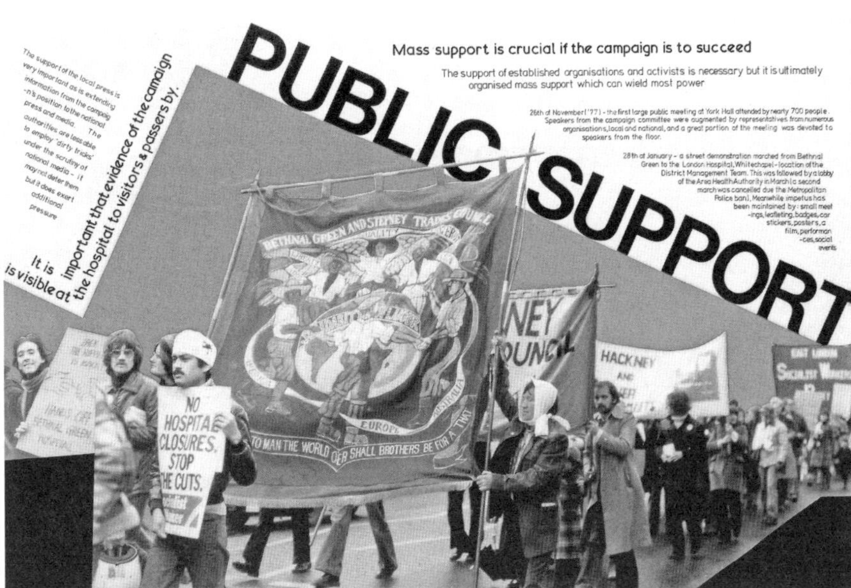

Although this work was created for locations outside of art institutions, wider interest in socially orientated art was growing, leading to inclusion of the Bethnal Green hospital campaign work in 'Art for Whom', curated by Richard Cork at the Serpentine Gallery in 1978 and the East London Health Project posters in 'Issue—Social Strategies by Women Artists', curated by Lucy Lippard for the ICA in 1980. All this work then returned to the ICA in 2017 as 'The Things That Make You Sick', curated by Juliette Desorgues.

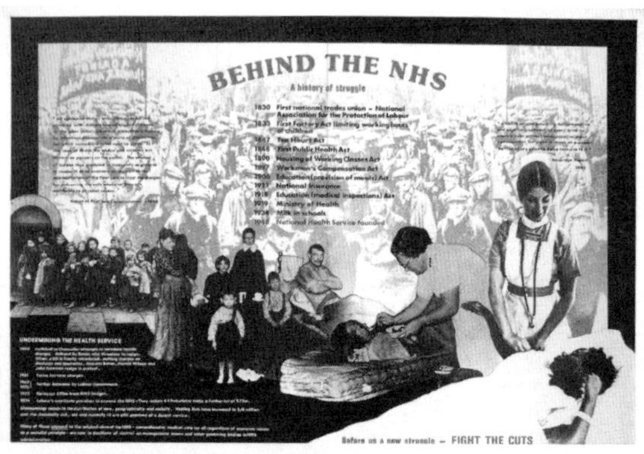

Loraine Leeson, East London Health Project © Dunn and Leeson, 'Behind the NHS', 1979, A2 poster, offset litho. Produced and distributed in conjunction with East London Trades Councils, health workers' unions and the Women's Health Information Collective.

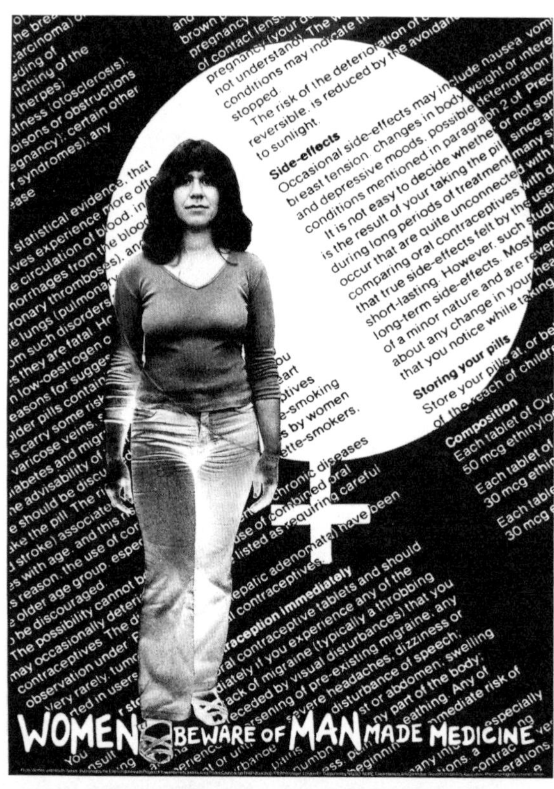

Loraine Leeson, East London Health Project © Dunn and Leeson, 'Women beware of man made medicine', 1980, A2 poster, offset litho. Produced and distributed in conjunction with East London Trades Councils, health workers' unions and the Women's Health Information Collective.

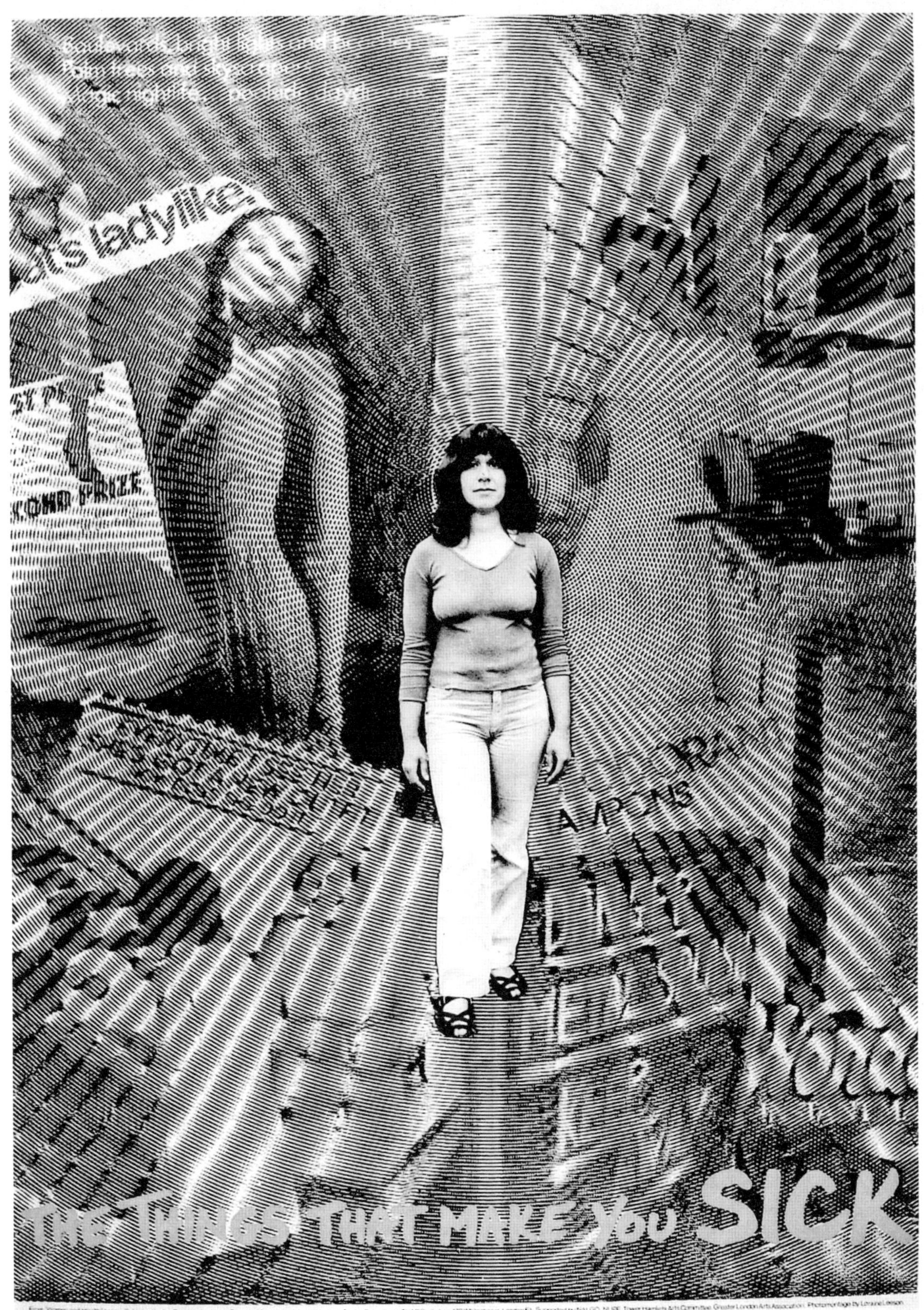

Loraine Leeson, East London Health Project © Dunn and Leeson, 'The Things that Make You Sick', 1980, A2 poster, offset litho. Produced and distributed in conjunction with East London Trades Councils, health workers' unions and the Women's Health Information Collective.

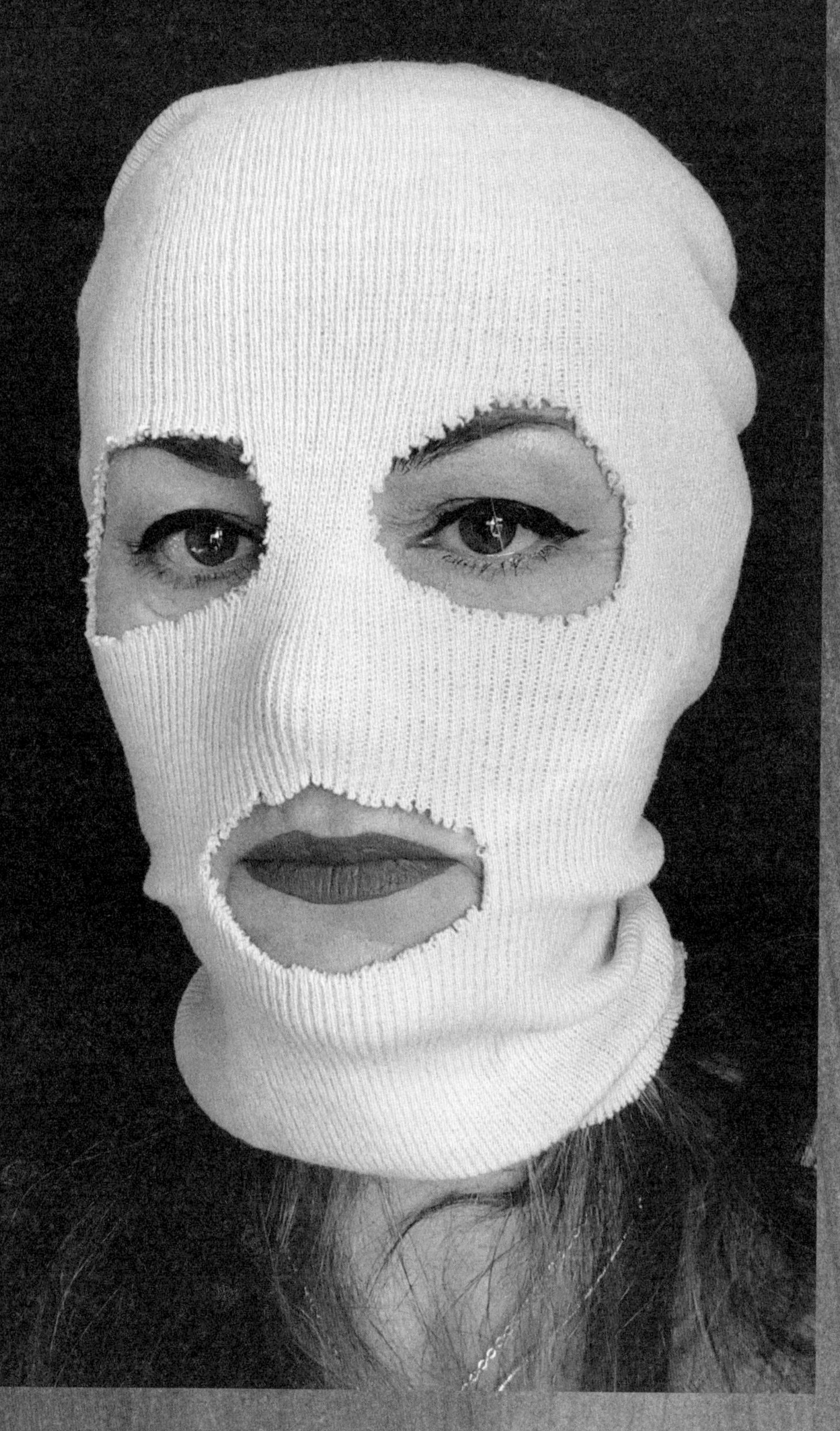

Paula Chambers, *Self Portrait: We Are All Pussy Riot*, 2019.
Courtesy of Paula Chambers

MATERIALIZING DISSENT
Pussy Riot's Balaclavas, Material Culture and Feminist Agency

Paula Chambers

1. Alison Bartlett and Margaret Henderson, 'What is a Feminist Object? Feminist Material Culture and the Making of the Activist Object', *Journal of Australian Studies* 40, no. 2 (2016), p. 2.

On 21 February 2012, the Russian feminist performance group Pussy Riot were arrested for staging a direct action in the Cathedral of Christ the Saviour in Moscow. The media attention this arrest and subsequent trial brought created worldwide notoriety, helped in no small part by the striking visuals of the homemade brightly coloured balaclavas worn by the group. The wearing of these "feminized" balaclavas created a visually recognizable sign for their symbolic act of political resistance, and became an activist symbol adopted by people all over the world to demonstrate their support for Pussy Riot's protest for gender equality and women's civil rights in Russia.

What were the specific material qualities of Pussy Riot's balaclavas? How did these objects come to embody both material and feminist agency? In 'What is a Feminist Object? Feminist Material Culture and the Making of the Activist Object' (2016), Alison Bartlett and Margaret Henderson, following Baudrillard's *The System of Objects* (1968), identify four major categories of feminist objects: corporeal things, world-making things, knowledge and communicative things, and protest things.[1] They propose a feminist system of objects within which the material culture of feminist activism is defined by the primacy of an object's political agency. Pussy Riot's homemade balaclavas sit within this material frame of reference as an example of feminist material culture of dissent, activism and political agency. In this, they are linked to a considerable history of textiles and symbolic objects embedded in other forms of material feminist protests undertaken by women—from the banners and flags of the suffragettes to the white headscarves worn by the mothers of the disappeared at the Plaza de Mayo in Buenos Aires, Argentina or the weaving of clothing and objects into chain link fences at women's anti-war protest camps, like Greenham Common.[2]

2. Alexandra M. Kokoli, 'Pre-Emptive Mourning Against the Bomb: Exploded Domesticities in Art Informed by Feminism and Anti-Nuclear Activism', *Oxford Art Journal* 40, no. 1 (March 2017), pp. 153–168.

Pussy Riot first came together in 2010 as a performance group operating as a feminist punk band of young Russian women. Their intention was to highlight, through direct action performances, the social injustices and corruption of the Russian government system, with a particular focus on Vladimir Putin as an oppressive patriarchal figurehead. The group operated with an open collaborative structure and remained open to all women who shared the Pussy Riot ethos and this characteristic of the organization produced an ever-changing line-up of women who remained anonymous behind their homemade balaclavas.

In February 2012, Maria Alyokhina (Masha), Nadezhda Tolokonnikova (Nadya) and Yekaterina Samutsevich (Katya), three of the five women performing in the Cathedral of Christ the Saviour in Moscow that day, were arrested whilst giving a noisy, impromptu and disruptive (albeit very brief) rendition of their punk prayer *Mother of God, Chase Putin Away*. Only these three members of the group were tried and convicted in the very public trial that followed. They were charged with hooliganism and blasphemy ostensibly because the action took place on the soleas, the raised platform in front of the altar in Russian Orthodox Cathedrals reserved for the preaching of male priests. The media attention given to the trial and the injustice of the harsh sentence meant that Pussy Riot's case attained world-wide attention and the group became icons of feminism for a generation of young women across the globe. The most striking visual aspect of the women who performed as Pussy Riot—and this could be as many as twelve at some performances—was the wearing of brightly coloured balaclavas. In journalist Masha Gessen's informative account of the rise and subsequent arrest and trial of Pussy Riot, *Words Will Break Cement: The Passion of Pussy Riot* (2014), she explains the decision of the group members to adopt the balaclava as a strategy of anonymity to avoid

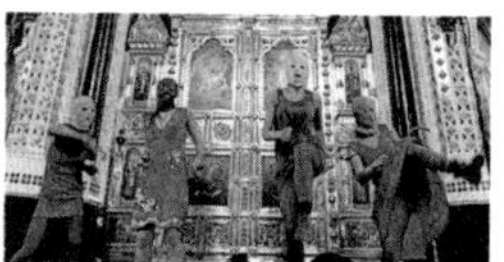

Pussy Riot, performance at Cathedral of Christ the Saviour, Moscow, 2012, publicity photograph

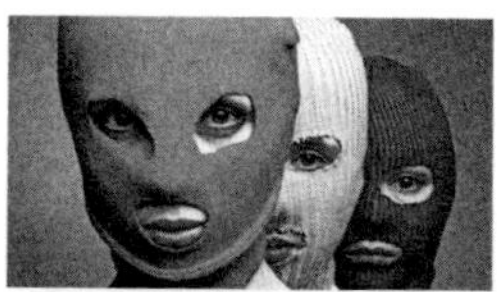

Pussy Riot's Balaclavas, 2012, publicity photograph

3. Masha Gessen, *Words Will Break Cement: The Passion of Pussy Riot* (London: Granta Publishing, 2014), p. 69.

4. Nadya Tolokonnikova, *Read and Riot: A Pussy Riot Guide to Activism* (London: Coronet, 2019), p. 35.

arrest and because it allowed for an ever-changing line-up of members where individual identification was discouraged:

> As they rehearsed, it became clear that they needed staging and visuals and costumes. 'Because if we got up there and started screaming, everyone would think we were stupid' … 'Stupid chicks just standing there screaming'. First they came up with wearing balaclavas, which would make them anonymous—but not like the Russian special forces, who kept their identities hidden behind black knit face masks with slits for the eyes and mouth, but like the opposite of that: their balaclavas would be neon-coloured. Then they would need dresses and multi-coloured stockings, to show that whole getup was intentional. Bright, exaggerated makeup showed surprisingly well through the slits in the balaclavas.[3]

Co-founder and one of the most public representatives of Pussy Riot, Nadya Tolokonnikova, recently published *Read and Riot: A Pussy Riot Guide to Activism* (2019). In this manual, Tolokonnikova discusses the DIY ethos of Pussy Riot's performances, and of the liberation and sense of empowerment wearing the balaclava gave her and the other women performing.

> Early on, I discovered that when I'm wearing a mask I feel a little bit like a superhero and maybe feel more power. I feel really brave, I believe I can do anything and everything, and I believe that I can change the situation. We played at being superheroes, Batwoman or Spider-women, who arrive to save our country from the villain, but we were choking on laughter looking at ourselves: a fur hat pissed on by a cat with narrow slits for eyes, a nonworking guitar, and for the audio system a homemade battery that leaks acid.[4]

There was a joyful sense of liberation experienced by Tolokonnikova and the others, manifest in the choice of brightly coloured clothing and the balaclavas worn by the group, as Tolokonnikova explains,

But why the bright colours? It was really a dumb reason: we just didn't want to be taken for terrorists in black balaclavas. We didn't want to scare people; we wanted to bring some fun, so we decided to look like clowns.[5]

Masha Alyokhina, in her opening courtroom statement in 2012, also makes the point that the Pussy Riot balaclava as mask was not intended as a disguise, but as an intentional feminist strategy of resistance.

> Tights and dresses are a part of the Pussy Riot image, and the balaclavas, identified in the indictment as "masks", are not a disguise, but a conceptual element of our image. Pussy Riot does not want to the focus of attention on girls' appearances, but creates characters who express ideas.[6]

In this context, Pussy Riot's balaclavas as objects that were perceived as both threatening and frivolous can be seen to be examples of tactical frivolity. The 'characters who express ideas' echoes Tolokonnikova's statement that Pussy Riot's intention was to have some fun and to look like clowns. As masks, Pussy Riot's balaclavas also signify collective identity and forms of political solidarity between the women who wear them. Pussy Riot's balaclavas were specifically conceived and produced with the intention to make feminist things happen.

The use of brightly coloured outfits for the purpose of feminist protest is a material strategy adopted by other activisms also, the wearing of pink Pussy Hats at the Women's March on Washington in January 2017 being one example of what has become known as "tactical frivolity".[7] Tactical frivolity involves the wearing of pink and sparkly costumes at protests and demonstrations, a material embodiment that brings to mind carnivalesque connotations of dressing up and mask wearing, where bodily participation in acts of political subversion is both transformative and liberating. This exaggerated sense of femininity, Pollyanna Ruiz argues, evokes the fragility often associated with femininity and as such places responsibility of the protestor's safety in the hands of the authorities.[8] Masking as a strategy,

5. Ibid.

6. Pussy Riot, *Pussy Riot! A Punk Prayer for Freedom* (New York City: The Feminist Press, 2012), p. 39.

7. A.T. Kingsmith, 'Why So Serious? Framing Comedies of Recognition and Repertoires of Tactical Frivolity Within Social Movements', *Interface: A Journal for and About Social Movements* 8, no. 2 (2016), p. 295.

8. Pollyanna Ruiz, 'Revealing Power: Masked Protest and the Blank Figure', *Cultural Politics.* 9, no. 3 (2013), p. 273.

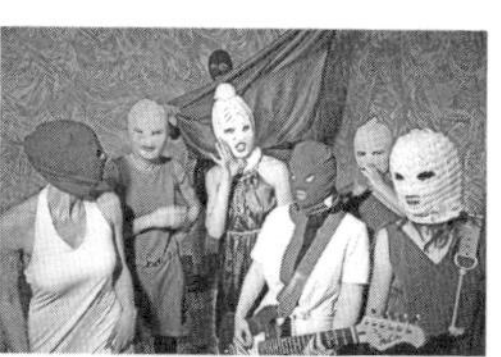

Pussy Riot, 2012, publicity photograph

   Feminist Art Activisms and Artivisms

9. Ibid.

10. Ibid., p. 277.

11. Bartlett and Henderson, 'What is a Feminist Object?', p. 159.

Ruiz states, is one that has cohesive qualities, as a material strategy of political protest it 'has utilised both the threatening and the frivolous … to create an enormously effective and imaginative organizational tool'.[9] The mask, Ruiz goes on to explain, is not a disguise but a strategy to draw attention, it downplays the role of the individual and foregrounds collective political endeavours, the wearing of masks as a form of political protest signifies collective identity. The use of masks as a politicized material strategy deliberately blurs the boundaries between us-and-them. '… the mask does not negate identity; instead it signifies the possibility of a multiplicity of identities'.[10]

Bartlett and Henderson's proposal is that a feminist system of objects is defined by the primacy of the object's political agency. They state that, 'feminist objects are intrinsically activist objects, that is, the women's movement remade and invented objects to make feminist things happen'.[11] Studying the pictures of various members of Pussy Riot in their neon-coloured balaclavas it becomes apparent that these objects have been hastily made from woolly hats, the type known as "beanie" hats that can be rolled down, the eye and mouth holes have been cut roughly, often too large to actually obscure much of the wearer's face. Nevertheless, the effect is striking, and the DIY process of making the balaclavas allow for this strategy to be easily copied by any and all who choose to identify with the Pussy Riot ethos of women's right and social justice. The balaclava becomes not only a powerful visual symbol of group identity but always an effective tool for masking individuality. Wearing the balaclava indicated an identification with "the cause", "the group's protest" for as long or short a time as the women involved felt necessary. Slavoj Žižek, in *Comradely Greetings: The Prison Letters of Nadya and Slavoj* (2014), argues the adoption of the balaclava was a conceptual political strategy that undermines the notion of the individual,

> They (Pussy Riot) are conceptual artists in the noblest sense of the word: artists who embody an idea. This is why they wear balaclavas: masks of de-individualisation, of liberating autonomy. The message of their balaclavas is that it doesn't matter which of them got arrested—they're not individuals,

they're an idea. And this is why they are such a
threat: it is easy to imprison individuals, but try to
imprison an idea![12]

The fact that people all over the world (men as well as
women), linked by social media and global communications,
took up the Pussy Riot balaclava as a visual material display
of solidarity with the ideas of the group, has a kind of
uncanny multiplicity, as if the group was infinitely reproduc-
ible; one is cut down (or imprisoned) and another magically
springs up in her place.

I imagine the women sitting at home of an evening
with a pile of beanie hats, bought, stolen, borrowed or
found. And sorting through for a suitably coloured hat that
might clash pleasingly with their bright tights and dresses,
while happily cutting away until the required eye holes and
mouth holes were achieved. This may have taken more than
one attempt as this type of woolly hat is stretchy and it
would be easy to cut the holes too low or too high, something that would only be discovered once the "balaclava"
was tried on in front of a mirror. I imagine laughter and
joy at the simplistic brilliancy discovered in this strategy
of material subversion, perhaps several women together
laughing convivially at each other, perhaps wearing their new
balaclavas all evening to drink wine, beer or vodka together.
Perhaps I will make one myself. I agree with Tolokonnikova,
why should there not be joy and laughter in revolution and
resistance.

Bartlett and Henderson's four categories of feminist
objects usefully define: i) "corporeal things" for the body
or of the body; ii) "world-making things", that bring
into being a feminist world in creative and cultural terms;
iii) "knowledge and communicative things" that can be
described as communicating a feminist message or way of
being in the world; and iv) "protest things" that are crucial
for the production and dissemination of feminist political
discourse via material culture. This is an egalitarian model
where no category is more valuable than another and most
feminist objects sit in more than one or sometimes all of
these categories.

Pussy Riot's balaclavas are "corporeal things" in
that they are worn as headgear, and are made from items of

12. Nadezhda Tolokonnikova
and Slavoj Žižek, *Comradely
Greetings: The Prison Letters of
Nadya and Slavoj* (London: Verso,
2014), p. 12.

pre-existing clothing, woolly hats. They are things for the body. That the materiality of this particular form of political protest became its defining feature is interesting here for a couple of reasons; firstly, the hasty process of "hacking" the hats to perform a function other than that intended by its manufacturer has resonances with Bartlett and Henderson's identification of the activist object as frequently having been produced through collaboration but an object that cannot be attributed to a single creator. Also, in relation to the domestic and feminized nature of the materiality itself (brightly coloured woolly hats are most often worn by women and girls), of the imagined process undertaken to transform these objects of femininity into objects of political resistance. Bartlett and Henderson give another example of the feminist identified clothing as the dungaree, a unisex item of clothing that refuses and rejects sexual objectification. The power suit is another example because it mimics the costume of men in the workplace and has become a form of dress that Bartlett and Henderson term "feminist camou-flage". Pussy Riot's balaclavas too were originally worn as a sort of feminist camouflage, they ensured a certain level of anonymity and allowed for a changing line-up within the group. They also disguised the identity of group members and enabled them to avoid detection and arrest, at least until February 2012.

Pussy Riot's balaclavas are "world-making things" in that they bring into being a feminist world in creative and cultural terms. As a performance group with a specifically feminist agenda, Pussy Riot set out to subvert the traditional distinctions between art and politics through the imaginative transformation of feminine material culture as a symbolic gesture of activist political resistance. The adoption of the brightly coloured handmade balaclavas by fans and supporters across the world made Pussy Riot into a global phenomenon and brought to light the inequalities and injustices experienced by women in Putin's Russia. In this sense,

feminist culture is generative: we observe the creation of a material culture that accompanies production of feminist ideology and knowledge. And feminist culture is performative: it makes possible a feminist way of being in the world, and a feminist

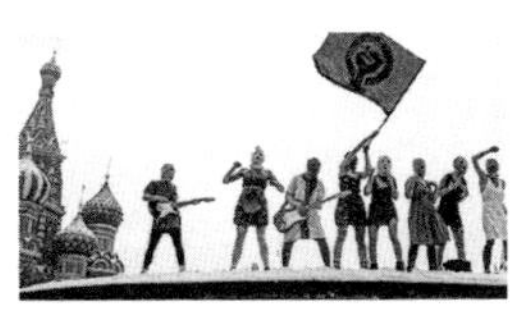

Pussy Riot, performance in Red Square, Moscow, 2012, publicity photograph

way of imagining the world—a specifically feminist counterculture.[13]

13. Bartlett and Henderson, 'What is a Feminist Object?', pp. 164–165.

Some examples given by Bartlett and Henderson of "world-making things" are Patti Smith's seminal album *Horses* (1975), and craft-based feminist art-making that utilizes the skills and materials of traditional women's craft processes such as knitting, crochet and embroidery.

Pussy Riot's balaclavas are "knowledge and communicative things" in that they communicate a feminist message or way of being in the world. As objects that are intrinsic to the performative spectacle of the group, the brightly coloured balaclavas can be seen as materiality that critiques existing patriarchal and phallocentric knowledge systems, and constructs an alternative feminist viewpoint. Pussy Riot were, and still are, very active online. They upload videos of performances and respond to comments and questions via various social media platforms. Pussy Riot's political intention was always to be world facing. In addition to their original intent as objects of symbolic defiance to Russia's oppressive political system, the balaclavas have, through online dissemination, come to embrace a wider frame of reference, an activist feminist politics of and for the twenty-first century. Bartlett and Henderson cite feminist publications such as *Spare Rib* (1972–1993) as examples of knowledge and communicative things.

Pussy Riot's balaclavas are "protest things" in that they are the material culture crucial to the production and dissemination of feminist political discourse. It would be fair to say, I think, that Pussy Riot may not have captured the public imagination in quite the way they have if it were not for the material strategy of wearing the brightly coloured balaclavas. These objects, in part at least, made political protest occur. As objects that are primarily used for political protest, Pussy Riot's balaclavas can be seen as crucial for the production and dissemination of feminist political discourse via material culture. The handmade protest banners of women's marches such as 'Reclaim the Night' against violence against women are examples given by Bartlett and Henderson of protest things.

The ambivalence and ambiguity of craft as art practice has proved an ideal medium for subversive political

14. Kokoli, 'Pre-Emptive Mourning Against the Bomb', p. 154.

15. Ele Carpenter, 'Activist Tendencies in Craft', 2010, https://research.gold.ac.uk/3109/1/Activist_Tendencies_in_Craft_EC.pdf (accessed 2 June 2018).

16. Carpenter, 'Activist Tendencies in Craft'.

17. Ibid.

activities due not least to its ability to expose 'patriarchal domesticity as contradictory, fragile and frayed at the edges'.[14] A study of feminine material culture in this context offers an invaluable perspective on the women's movement when it is understood as a materialization of social forms and relations. If, as I believe, we live out social relations through materiality, then feminist reconfigurations and reinvention of craft objects are also part of the transformation of the structures of knowledge.

Pussy Riot's adoption of brightly coloured balaclavas as a performative material strategy with feminist political intention and a craft-centred material engagement can be analyzed alongside other potentially subversive activities such as craftivism and yarn bombing, activities often presented in the media in a derogatory manner. The making and wearing by many of the Pussy Riot balaclava, as a materialization of feminist activism is an exercise in community action organized for and by women. The fact that it draws on many craft-based community projects centered around women's traditional craft skills; sewing and quilting bees, knitting groups, and yarn bombing, was their means of creating an action in which a large number of people could organize. This is an indication of a collaborative process identified by Bartlett and Henderson as one that marks the feminist activist object.

However, as Ele Carpenter warns, the dismissal of craftivism as "woolly activism", is symptomatic of an underlying sexism due to the connotations of white middle class, middle aged women who are perceived to undertake these activities.[15] Pussy Riot's craftivism, in contrast, was presented in the media as inflammatory and dangerous, the women themselves as victims of an unjust system or conversely as hysterical political anarchists. However, Carpenter makes the case for DIY craft processes as effective and legitimate political agency. Radical crafting, she proposes, is 'a social process of collective empowerment, action, expression and negotiation'.[16] Art activist craft practice is performative and interventionist, integrating gesture and agency, 'Here the simplest action is carefully planned to take or reveal responsibility for a socio-political convention, explored through collective creativity and individual volition. It is active resistance and transformation.'[17] The practice of craftivism defined in these terms enables art-activist objects produced to be placed within Bartlett and Henderson's system of feminist objects. The materials chosen all have the aesthetic and technology of craft, the "hacking" of the woolly hats, objects that when cut into are in serious danger of unraveling, are materially disruptive. The reinvention of brightly coloured woolly hats as balaclavas, objects more usually associated with undercover crime and violence, disrupts the symbolism of these objects and repurposes them for feminist use. As "corporeal things", craftivism produces things for the body or of the body. As "world-making things", it brings into being a feminist world in creative and cultural terms. As "knowledge and communicative things" it communicates a feminist message or way of being in the world. And as "protest things" it is crucial for the production and dissemination of feminist political discourse via material culture and in open-access digital platforms as the manifestation of feminist social relations.

Despite media representation (or maybe because of it), Pussy Riot have become feminist icons, and their hastily made woolly balaclavas symbols of feminist protest. Pussy Riot's balaclavas remake and reinvent the material culture of feminism, as evidenced through their global success as feminist activist material objects. The feminine materiality of Pussy Riot's balaclavas manifests itself as a feminist object with value as a symbol of political agency, an object of feminist material culture whereby the mechanics by which these activist objects are brought into being (physical making and online dissemination) becomes one in which, 'The scale of production and the distribution and circulation of feminist objects exemplify the activist object's repurposing of artefacts, and signify the political ideology of the women's movement.'[18] The balaclavas were objects that bring into being the possibility of a feminist material culture, and as such contribute to the visibility of feminist political protest. As corporeal things the balaclavas identify the body as a key signifier of feminist identity and allegiance. As world-making things they are part of feminist cultural activities. As knowledge and communicative things they produce, record, and distribute feminist thought and knowledge, hence legitimizing this work. And as protest things they are the material culture that makes political protest occur. Pussy

18. Bartlett and Henderson, 'What is a Feminist Object?', p. 168.

   Feminist Art Activisms and Artivisms

Riot's brightly coloured balaclavas are objects with feminist material agency, they are activist objects that materialize radical strategies of feminist dissent.

A quick and easy DIY guide to making your own Pussy Riot balaclava

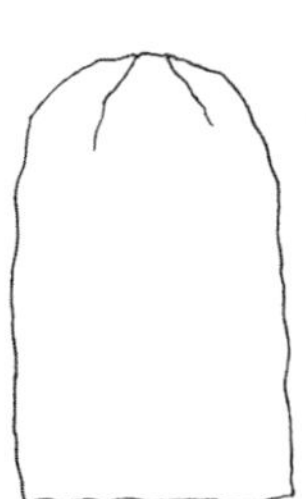

Step 1 - Take one 'beanie' hat in as bright a colour as you can find. The cheap acrylic types work best. For a true DIY ethos, borrow, find or steal a hat. Roll down to its full length.

Step 2 - Mark out the positions for eye and mouth holes. Eye holes at approx. 20cms from the top, mouth hole at approx. 30cms from the top.

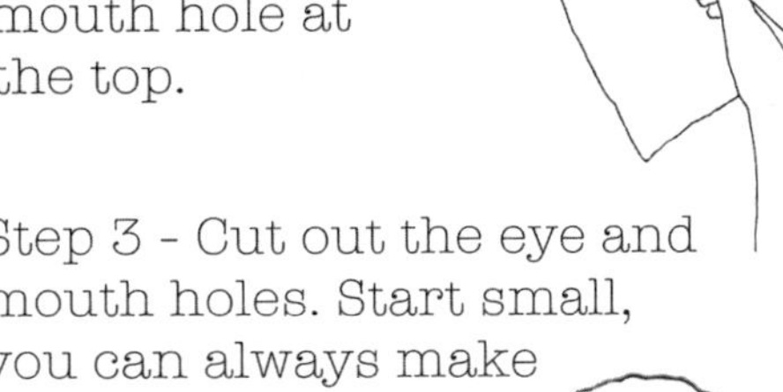

Step 3 - Cut out the eye and mouth holes. Start small, you can always make the holes bigger. For the proper Pussy Riot look, cut carelessly.

Step 4 - Wear your Pussy Riot balaclava to protests, sit-ins, and activist demonstrations of all kinds. Enjoy!

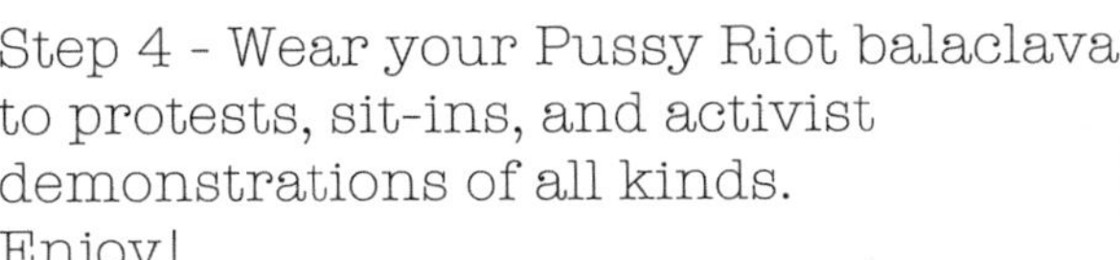

Copyright, Paula Chambers 2019

Paula Chambers, *A quick and easy DIY guide to making your own Pussy Riot balaclava*, 2019, instructional diagram. Courtesy of Paula Chambers

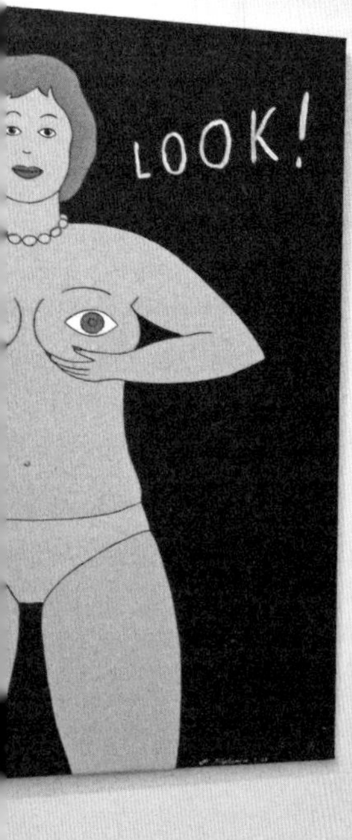

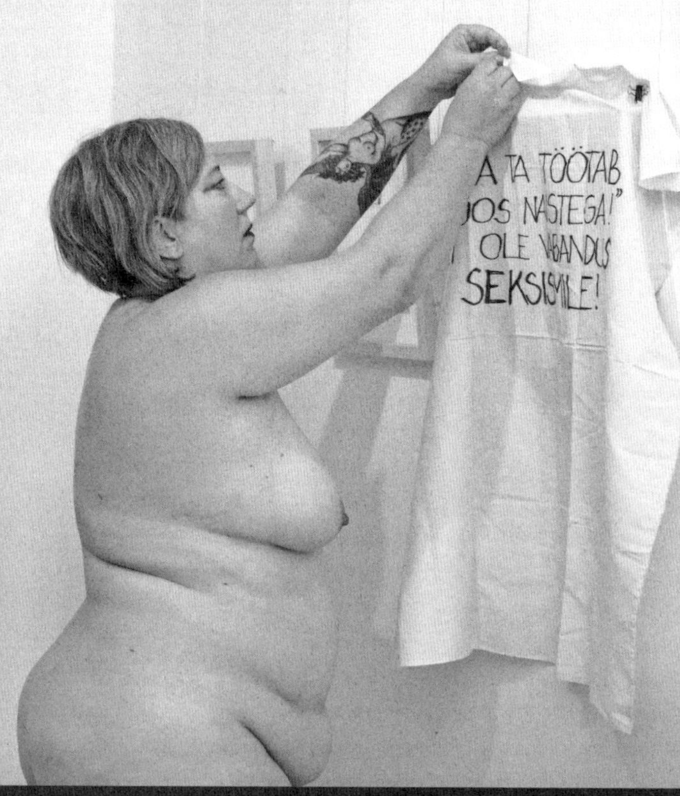

Mare Tralla, *No 'But' Can Be Used as an Excuse for Sexism!*, 2019, performance.
Photo: Alar Raudoja

NO, BUT…

Mare Tralla

1. See documentation on http://www.tralla.net/. Among these activities, I co-curated with Eha Komissarov, Reet Varblane, the first Estonian feminist exhibition 'Est. Fem' (1995); a touring Estonian-British feminist exhibition 'Private Views' (1998–1999), accompanied by a book *Private Views: Spaces and Gender in Contemporary Art from Britain and Estonia* (eds. Angela Dimitrakaki et al., 2000). Since 1994, I have also regularly contributed to Estonian newspapers.

Thursday, 27 June 2019

I am travelling from Tallinn to Pärnu. Curators Maarian Kivila and Jan Leo Grau have invited me to take part in an exhibition 'Woman & Woman' at Pärnu City Gallery. About an hour into my journey, I receive a message from Maarian: 'We are just unpacking Marko Mäetamm's works. What do you think?' An image of one of his works is attached: a caricature-like painting of a nude woman standing with a cat pushed into her vagina. What do I think? I am sad and angry. My first thought is to turn back and refuse to exhibit next to these kinds of sexist works. After all, I had a conversation with the curator a few months earlier, when she told me that she had invited him to the show and that he is doing somewhat "feminist" works. I had my doubts!

My second thought is to take a spray-can and simply cover up his images. Honestly, I am fuming, and I don't like this feeling at all. I had just been writing a text for this book and was almost finished with it. Now I can't concentrate and feel the urge to do something. Since the mid-1990s I have been an outspoken feminist in Estonia.[1] I question if the curator is deliberately trying to provoke me. She explains to me that it's just his humour and he really doesn't mean it in an offensive way and that he is a nice guy. Honestly, when will women stop excusing men's sexist behaviour? When can we talk about this in Estonia, when can we, women, be heard?

I arrive in Pärnu and see the rest of his works. I feel sick in my stomach. In the 1990s, I would have written something about his works, now with the background of direct-action activism in London I have a different urge.

He has been made aware of my feelings and is quick to respond by making the gallery sign a contract of responsibility. Marko is one of the most successful male artists in Estonia; he has represented the country twice at Venice Biennale, he has received The Order of the White Star from the president and he is a recipient of an annual artists' salary, which is only given to handful of artists in the country.

In the middle of the night, I receive a message from Marko. He is worried that I will do something to his works. He tries to explain to me how his works are not sexist and how the curator has taken them out of context and how for years he has made works about domestic violence, but has no such experience himself, and how he can't stand how Estonian men treat women and how he is different, after all he is a nice guy. He also tells me that none of his friends find his works sexist.

I try to explain patiently what sexism is, how he is not aware of his privilege and his position in society, about gender and patriarchy, about power and misogyny. He tells me that he is not successful and has no privileges, also that I am mistaken reading his works as sexist and that he will firmly stand by them. It is his right, of course!

I realize, talking to him about patriarchy, power and privilege, that I talk as a feminist activist, who has had to think and assess her own privilege at different times and in various social settings. Before the trip to Estonia, I made a drawing about my privilege living in London in 2019 to illustrate the text I was then writing to this volume. I was preoccupied with assessing my own privilege and thought that it is something every person would do at some point in their life, especially when faced with the need to do so. In the activist and feminist art circles we talk about privilege just as much as we talk about power and how to change the balance of it. I had not realized that the Estonian cultural elite doesn't even know what this word means and that the successful white middle-class heterosexual Estonian man sees himself as the most deprived creature on planet Earth.

Saturday, 29 June 2019
Opening of the exhibition. The gallery is full of people. I don't see who they are, I am concentrating only on what I will be doing shortly. The curator talks about the show, the artists and their

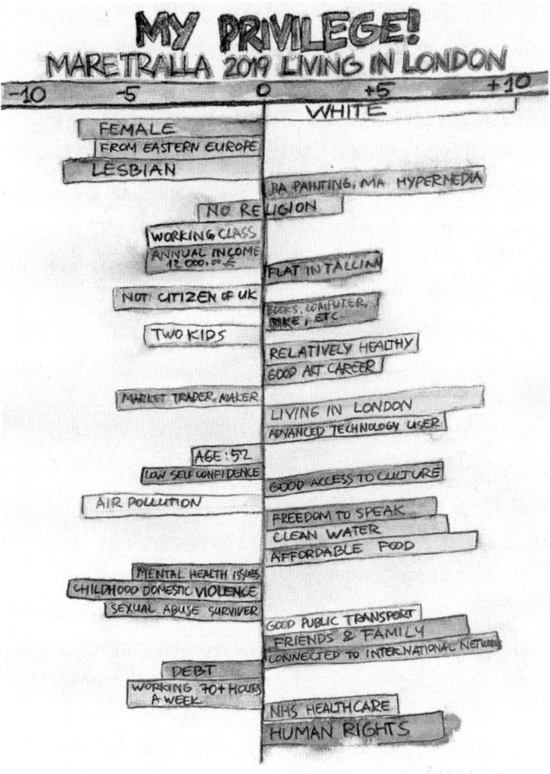

Mare Tralla, *My Privilege 2019*, 2019, watercolour, 60 x 42 cm

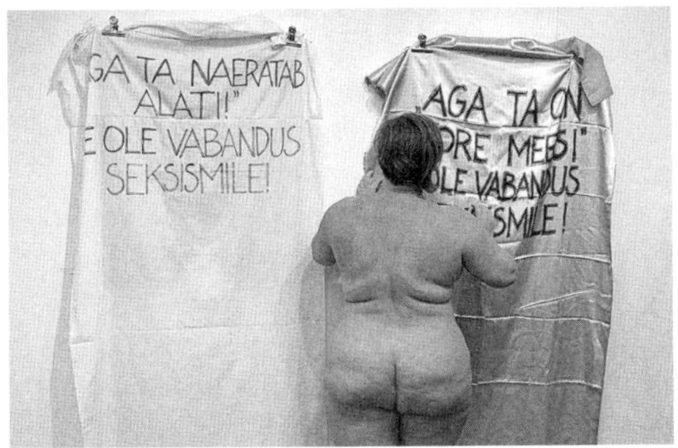

Mare Tralla, *No 'But' Can Be Used as an Excuse for Sexism!*, 2019, performance. Photo: Alar Raudoja

works. I think she is finished, there is an applause. It's my cue. I have been thinking a lot about what to do and have made up banners with slogans to cover his works.

I undress. Some people notice. I move to the room in the gallery where his works are on display. I feel strong being naked. I decided to make the action naked because his works depict sexist nude imagery of women: 'a cat forced into a woman's vagina'; a woman holding her breasts with eyes for areolas and a text "LOOK" next to it; a caricature of a woman with the text: 'An incredibly ugly girl with her hands in her underpants'; a woman peeing with one leg up in the air with the text: 'One night I met a woman with a strange behaviour so strange I did not know what to think' and so on.

Some people follow me, but most remain in the main gallery. I began in silence to cover his works with my banners:

'But He Works with Women!' Can Not Be Used as an Excuse for Sexism! 'But He Smiles Always!' Can Not Be Used as an Excuse for Sexism! 'But He Did Not Mean It This Way!' Can Not Be Used as an Excuse for Sexism! 'But He Is a Nice Guy!' Can Not Be Used as an Excuse for Sexism! 'But He Talks with

**Soft Voice!'
Can Not Be Used as an
Excuse for Sexism!
'But He Loves His Wife!'
Can Not Be Used as an
Excuse for Sexism!
'But This Is His Humour!'
Can Not Be Used as an
Excuse for Sexism!**

Throughout the action, Marko stands very close to me, less than a metre away and points his camera to document if I cause any damage at all to his works. Furthermore, he tries to instruct me on how to cover his works. Experiences from protesting and keeping cool, while the police try to engage with you come in handy: I stay calm and carry on. All the works covered, I lead the people out of his room. I take a piece of white fabric and staple it across the doorway, blocking the entrance. I write on to it 'No "But" Can Be Used as an Excuse for Sexism!' and walk away. The men in the room applaud Marko and loudly congratulate him on his strong works. The women remained silent.

I stay away for a while, waiting for people to leave. I feel still sad and angry, even deflated.

When I enter the gallery again, the women quietly tell me: 'Great! Well Done!'

There are a few journalists, who have been waiting to talk to me. I tell them about patriarchy, power, gender and sexism, why I did the action, and that it was not only about one male artist's works, but about the overwhelming sexism and violence against women in Estonian society, especially now with the new ultra-right-nationalist-homophobic government. I feel a bit better, thinking they understood why I had to do this action. I also assume that no-one really cares as I made the action in a small gallery in Pärnu. Afterwards, I drink too much.

Sunday, 30 June 2019

Massive hangover. I hear that sometime during the evening, Marko made his counter-action. I wonder what it was. The gallery is closed today, but we have arranged to meet up with the curators to see how to show the documentation of my action. Marko has taken my banners off his works and left them on the floor. Apparently, he had explained during his action the meaning behind his works. I hear it and find it even more sexist then the works.

Sometime in the afternoon, I learn that the local paper has published in their online version three different stories about the exhibition and my action: a general conversation with the curators, then one based on my interview, but somewhat weirdly cut short and not using my words, not talking about sexism, and it doesn't make any connections to wider issues in society, which I had tried to explain to the journalist. And the third, longest piece, is where Marko explains everything from his point of view and the author tries to give him all her sympathy. It is evident that the journalist was somewhat taken in by it all.

2. Video of performance *No "But" Can Be Used as an Excuse for Sexism!*, https://vimeo.com/345313337.

We sort out everything in the gallery, I upload the video of my action to Vimeo,[2] make some social media posts and then go to the Ladies Beach with some friends, where you are allowed to sunbathe naked. I have never been there before. On higher ground, above the Ladies Beach a few men stand naked and look down at the women. It feels like the men are birds of prey, observing and hunting. So much for a safe space for women only!

I get a message from the other journalist, from one of the main newspapers. He missed the opportunity to publish the first story about my action and is not happy. I see a lot of interest on social media and I am beginning to realize that my little action may cause some larger trouble.

In the evening I travel back to

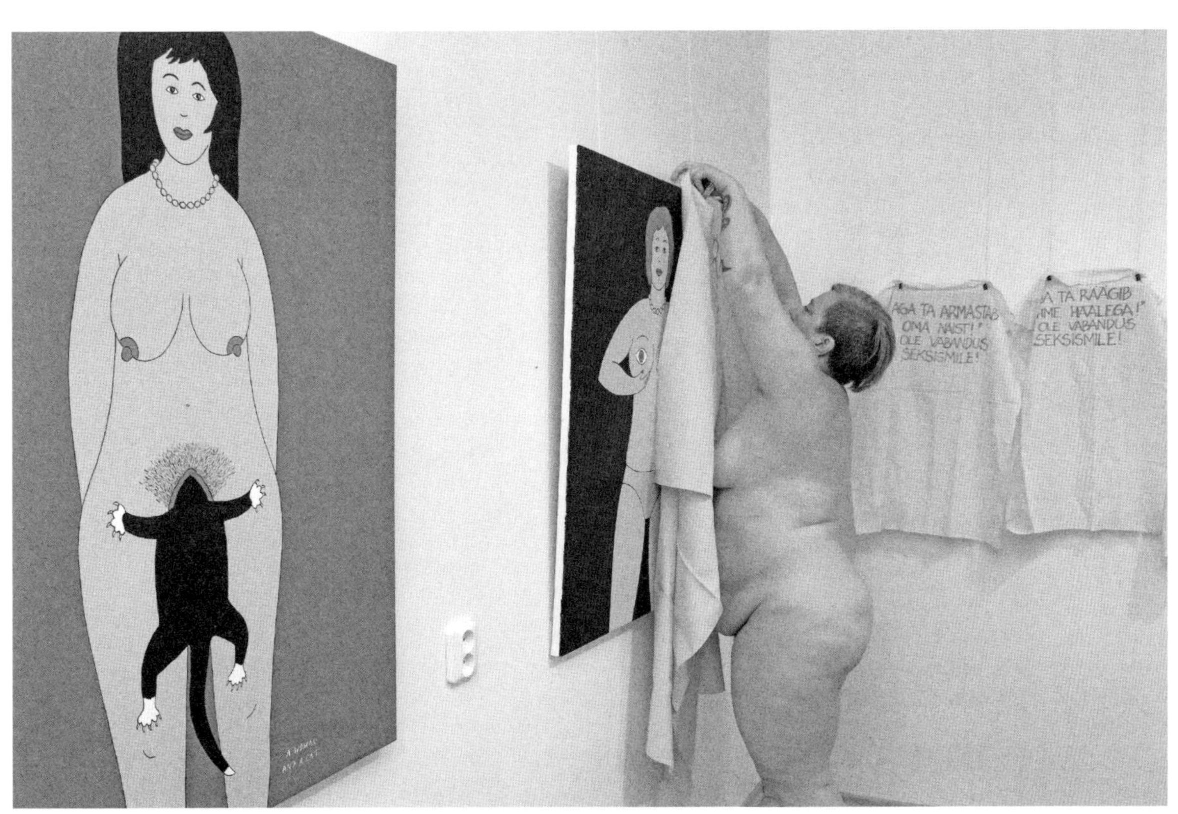

Mare Tralla, *No 'But' Can Be Used as an Excuse for Sexism!*, 2019, performance. Photo: Alar Raudoja

Tallinn with my friend Mari, who is trying to explain to me that calling someone out and telling them that they are privileged is also a violent act and by labelling them this way I am being sexist. I've known Mari since we were teenagers at art school. We have been through a lot together. However, when it comes to issues of gender and feminism, our understandings are very different. We agree to disagree.

Monday, 1 July 2019

I am in Tallinn, just for two more days. I have far too many non-art related things to sort out before I leave. Mainly, I need to paint the windows of my flat or otherwise they will rot away. It's a big job. There are many comments on social media and a few thousand views of my video. A second article is published in *Eesti Päevaleht*, one of the main daily newspapers. It's mainly descriptive and the author doesn't take sides. Good.

The weekly *Eesti Ekspress* contacts me. They've decided to make a personal story about me, because of the action and the buzz it's creating. I have had issues with their journalist Krister Kivi in past, so I am apprehensive. I agree that he comes to my place. He is late. At first, he acknowledges the history we had. It's a good start. I talk really fast and probably too much as I am far too emotional and there is too little time. Somehow, we end up talking about very personal issues: the experiences of domestic violence and sexual abuse

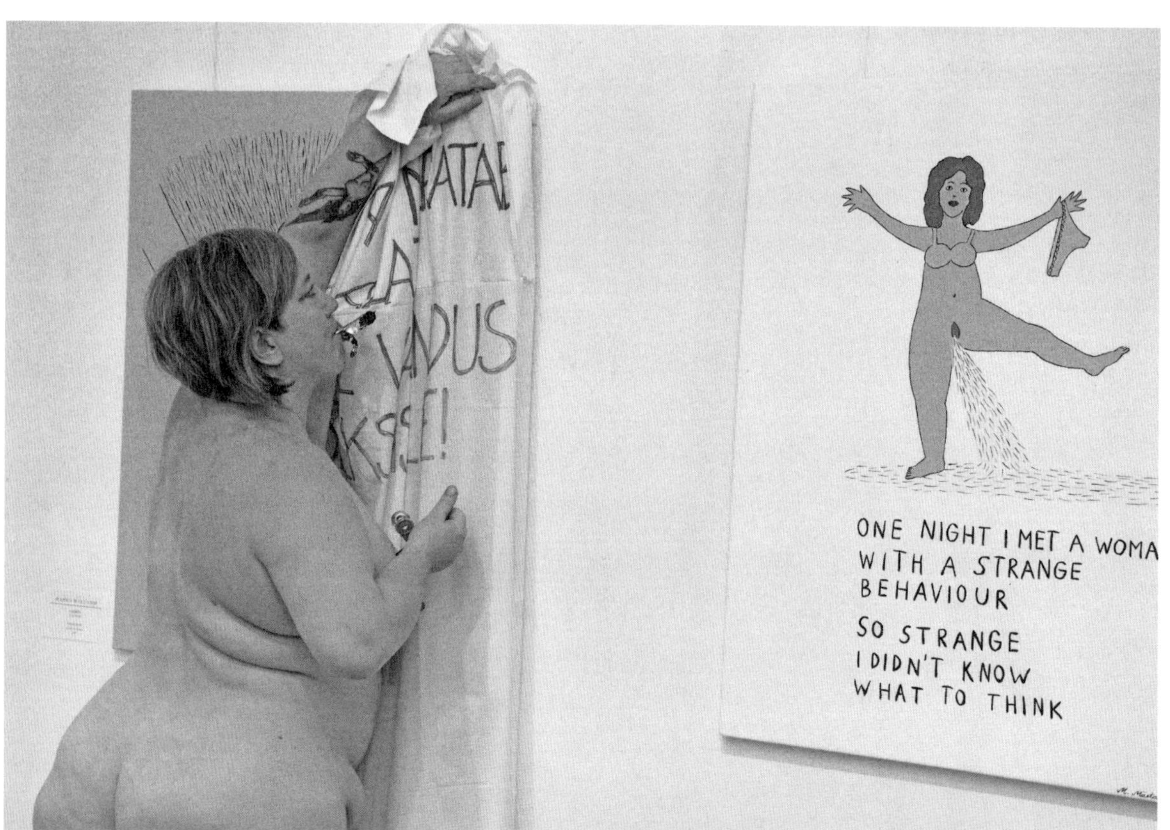

Mare Tralla, *No 'But' Can Be Used as an Excuse for Sexism!*, 2019, performance. Photo: Alar Raudoja

in my childhood. I think I have just ripped the skin off my body. He is surprisingly respectful and asks if I am sure that it should go in. I decide it needs to go in. My only worry is how my family will take it.

Tuesday, 2 July 2019
Over 20,000 people have viewed my video. A few men have tried to post threats and nasty comments to my timeline on Facebook. There seems to be an overwhelming public defence of Marko's freedom of speech and right of expression. In private, I receive tens of messages from women telling me how they admire my bravery and how it was time to talk about sexism. Some post supportive messages to social media, too. I keep calling artist Kadi Estland in London to talk about it all. She has been a great support. So has my girlfriend Donna.

I take some time out and have a long walk. There are several missed calls from a number I don't know. I call back. It's the TV. They want me to come to the studio and be filmed for a daily programme, *Ringvaade*. I tell them that I am already leaving Estonia in a few hours.

They convince me that there is enough time and that they will make sure I will not miss my flight.

Meanwhile, I receive a proof copy of the article from Krister Kivi. I think it's actually quite good. He has included a little overview of the types of online commentaries my action has received. They are overwhelmingly nasty: from suggestions to imprison me indefinitely on the grounds of insanity to wishing to kill me. Krister advises me to not read any.

I dash to the ETV studio. I sit there with presenter Anna Pihl and wait for Marko Mäetamm, who is late. I am told artists are not usually invited to *Ringvaade* (what artists do is not considered important enough for a daily affairs programme). A man from the crew comes and sits next to me: 'So, you are playing it together and doing a PR campaign for yourself and Marko!' I try to explain that it's not a PR campaign and that the issues of sexism are real and need to be taken seriously and that as a woman I was genuinely offended by these works. Then he turns towards the presenter and tells her: 'In Estonia we don't have problem with sexism! You agree with me, we don't.' She looks a bit taken aback. He continues: 'But I do remember that guy was a bit disrespectful and sexist towards you during the election debate. But he is an idiot. And you handled it very well!' She smiles and says nothing. I am speechless. Marko arrives, he seems nervous. I am tired and worried about missing my plane. At some point during the interview Marko explains that his works are about women's superior power over men. The presenter keeps nodding in agreement with him. It seems futile, I try to explain how men have the power in society and how any man needs to be aware of his position and privilege. We are from different worlds and seem to speak different languages. As a feminist activist I think of accountability and challenging patriarchy, as an ignorant man he is afraid of me taking everything away from him.

It's a quick ride to the airport. On reflection, I wish I would have done better a job for the TV. I think of so many things I should have challenged him on.

Wednesday, 3 July 2019

Back in London. More articles in the Estonian press, my video has almost 30, 000 views. I hear that the new ultra-right nationalist government in Estonia is planning to set up a department, which will deal with the country's most burning issue: how to stop fertile women leaving Estonia and especially the countryside.[3] I watch catch-up of the TV series of Margaret Atwood's novel *The Handmaid's Tale*. Reality and fiction have blurry borders.

For a while I have been trying to find a way to consolidate my personal life, my art practice and my activism. Often, they blend together. Yet, I have a strong ethical need to separate my art practice from activism. In recent years, activist practices have been commodified by art institutions and far too often artists and activists flirt with the attention of the artworld. From personal experience, including the latest action in Pärnu, I know how politically driven practices get sensationalized by the media and the art-world, how the issues raised by this work are overlooked or totally ignored. Furthermore, we are living at times of political anger, where empathy seems to have become extinct.

3. The proposed department is to deal with population and family issues under the Minister of Population.

4. Catwalk4Power project supporting and empowering women living with HIV. It was initiated and supported by Positively UK and Act Up London Women in 2017, www.facebook.com/Catwalk4Power/ and https://actuplondon.wordpress.com.

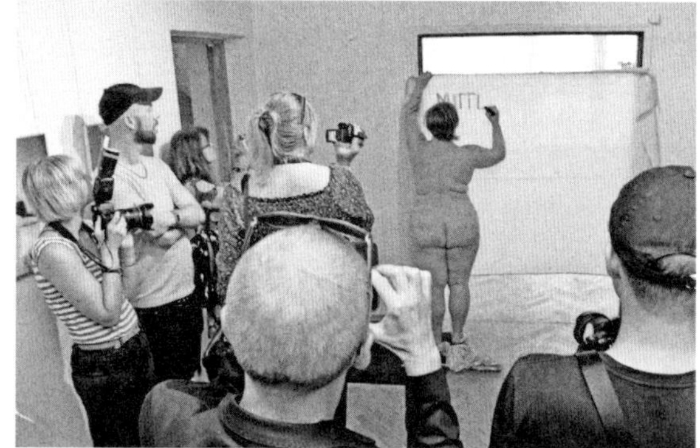

Mare Tralla, *No 'But' Can Be Used as an Excuse for Sexism!*, 2019, performance. Photo: Alar Raudoja

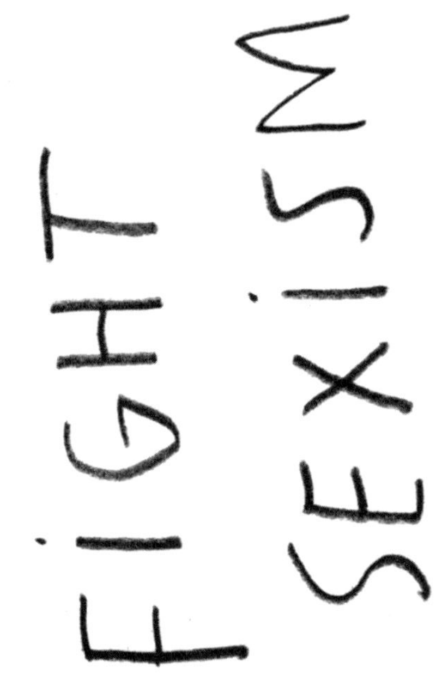

Feminist Art Activisms and Artivisms

As activists and artists, we react to this anger with our own anger, often without time to reflect, without time to think, we are permanently in a state of political emergency. We are continually reproducing anger and by reproducing anger we also reproduce power and injustice. Personally, I have a need to break out of this Moebius strip of anger. This is why I have recently been involved in the kind of unpaid activism connected to communities of women, particularly women living with HIV.[4] I am an ally in this work, my role varies from someone who shares her creative skills to the one who cooks or organizes food for the meetings and anything in between. I feel very passionate about giving some of my energy, time and privilege to help women speak their stories, to take their space and be proud. And it is really important that the women are safe and able to decide for themselves which space they want to claim.

I myself claim back my London bubble, and hope that for a few days I don't have to explain what the words privilege, patriarchy and power mean.

My London bubble didn't work this time, but the power of the naked female body did; since 3 July, Estonian ultra-nationalist neo-Nazis linked with USA hate groups have been leading local and international online hate campaigns against me. They initiated criminal and civil liability investigations to punish me, which ultimately found no breach of law by me and, six month later, articles related to the performance are still appearing in Estonian media.

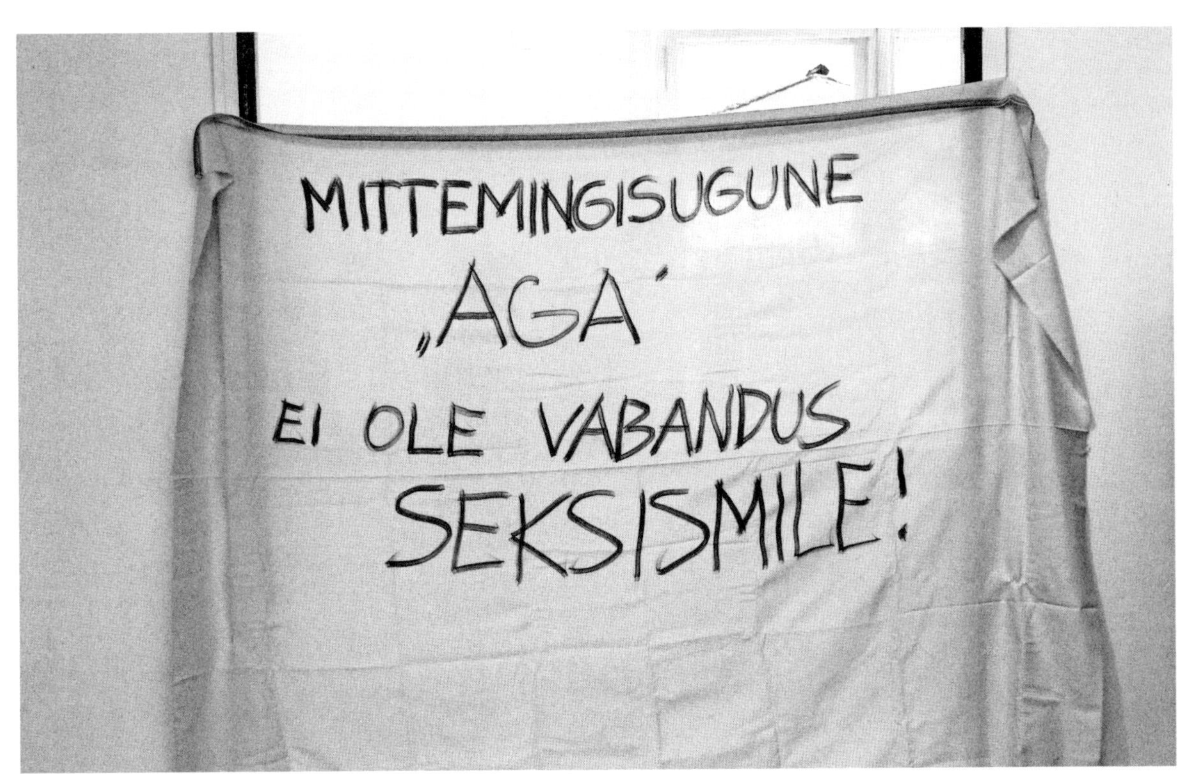

Mare Tralla, No 'But' Can Be Used as an Excuse for Sexism!, 2019, performance. Photo: Alar Raudoja

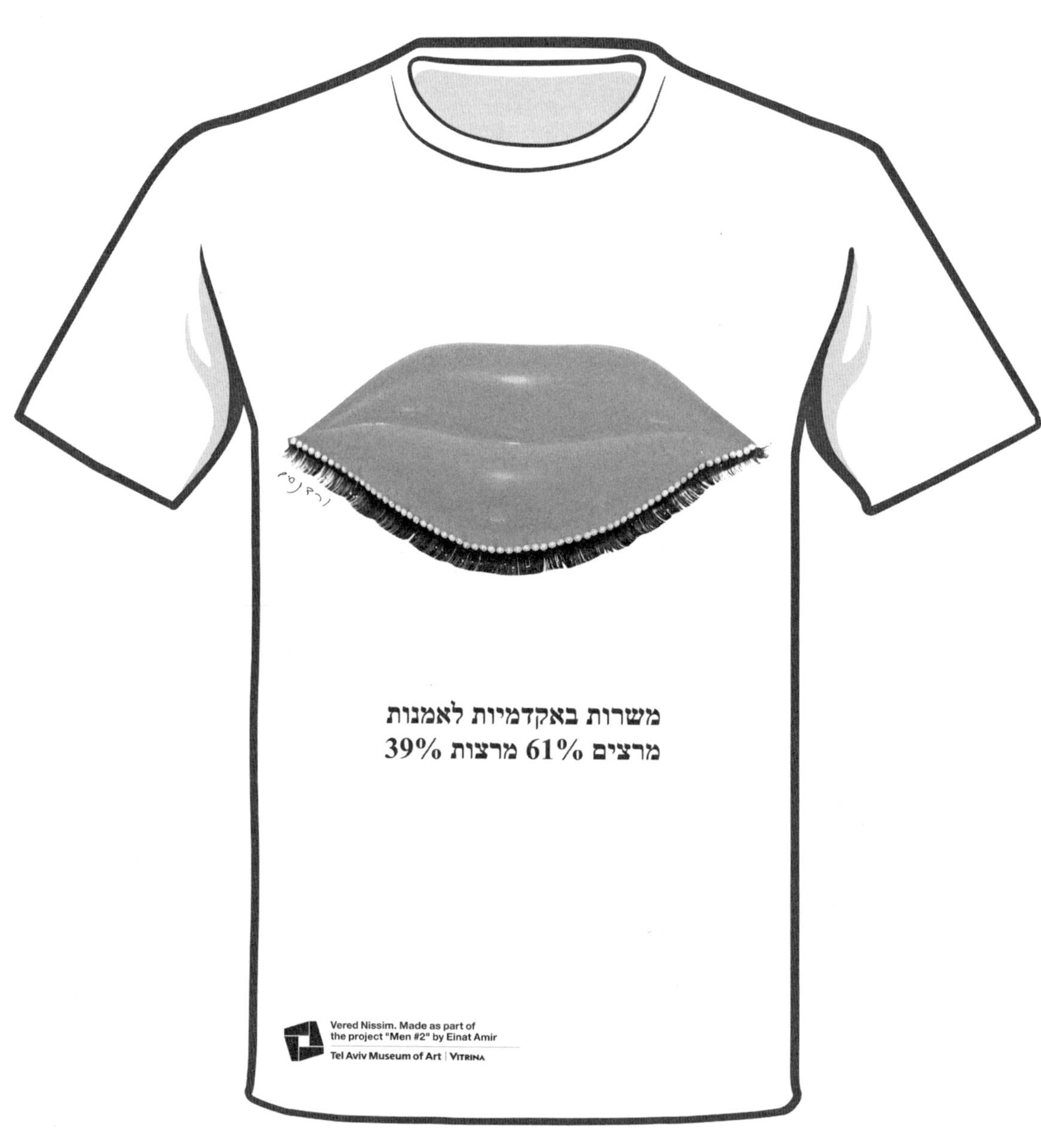

Einat Amir, *Men #2*, 2016, T-shirt designed by Vered Nissim, produced by Vitrina, Tel Aviv Museum.
(Text on t-shirt: Tenure positions in the art academies—61% male 39% female)

FEMINIST ART ACTIVISM IN ISRAEL
Subversive Strategies in Public Spaces

Tal Dekel and Lior Elefant

1. Norma Broude and Mary D. Garrard, eds., *The Power of Feminist Art: The American Movement of the 1970s, History and Impact* (New York: Abrams, 1994); Mary Jo Aagerstoun and Elissa Auther, 'Considering Feminist Activist Art', *NWSA Journal* 19, no. 1 (Spring 2007), pp. vii–xiv; Tatiana Volkova, 'The Chronicles of Russian Art', in *Global Activism: Art and Conflict in the 21st Century*, Peter Weibel, ed., (Cambridge, MA: MIT Press, 2013), pp. 515–530; Lucy Lippard, 'Trojan Horses: Activist Art and Power' (1984), *Feminism, Art, Theory: An Anthology 1968–2014*, Hilary Robinson, ed., (Chicester: Wiley Blackwell, 2015), pp. 69–79; Maura Reilly, *Curatorial Activism: Towards an Ethics of Curating* (London: Thames & Hudson, 2018).

2. bell hooks, *Feminism is for Everybody: Passionate Politics* (London: Pluto Press, 2000); Estelle Freedman, *No Turning Back: The History of Feminism and the Future of Women* (New York: Ballantine Books, 2007).

3. Lippard, 'Trojan Horses'.

4. G. Trajtenberg, 'Between Modernism and Gender in Israeli Art [in Hebrew]', *Israeli Modernism or Modernism in Israel*, Oded Heilbronner and Michael Levin, eds., (Tel Aviv: Resling, 2010), pp. 99–156.

5. For an in-depth examination of the reasons, see Tal Dekel, 'From First-Wave to Third-Wave Feminist Art in Israel: A Quantum Leap', *Israel Studies* 16, no. 1 (2011), pp. 149–178. A comparative analysis and historical review of feminist art in other countries are beyond the scope of this paper, but can be found, for example, in: Claire Johnston, 'Women's Cinema as Counter-Cinema' (1973), in *Feminism and Film*, ed. E. Ann Kaplan (Oxford: Oxford University Press, 2000), pp. 22-33; Harry

Many scholars have examined the various correlations between feminism, art, and activism.[1] Since the early 1960s, art has played a significant role in the social processes that propelled forward the social-political movement of feminism around the world.[2] Many women found in art a medium for expressing protest and resistance, articulating a feminist stance that challenged the traditional social order, seeking outlets even beyond the realm of museums and galleries. Feminist art is one form of activist art, asserts Lucy Lippard,[3] and is a critical social practice designed to address the real world, challenge the social, political, and economic hierarchies, and integrate research and theory, artistic activity, and social critique both in and outside the gallery. Unlike the Kantian approach, in which art is viewed as a meta-entity not subordinated to or affected by social, political, or cultural developments,[4] theoreticians of feminist art prioritize exploring the contexts of art within a given social reality, i.e., they critically examine the power relations, structures and dynamics that connect the artwork itself with the artists, the representatives and structures of the art establishment, the network of art criticism, and the audience at large.

For a variety of reasons, only in the 1990s did Israeli women artists begin to systematically and rigorously create art in public places from a critical, feminist perspective, two decades or more after such feminist art had proliferated globally.[5] Mapping and writing this nascent history in Israel is in itself a feminist act. Moreover, locating and articulating such activist art within the field of scholarly endeavour will help link scholarship with activism in the arts in Israel and push for social change. Here, through several case studies, we examine feminist art activism in public space, as feminist interventions, that have been created in Israel over the last decade. We discuss their strategies, audiences, socio-cultural contexts, and artistic characteristics through an examination of the complex and multi-layered relations between images and the projects themselves as acts of protest or resistance. The artists, as we shall see, merge activist strategies for radical change in Israeli society with art that challenges the social reality and exposes the power relations within it. Our approach combines Bourdieu's field theory,[6] artistic analysis of their ethnographic "specificity" and reception theory as we aim to understand not only the work of art itself, but the field of art—its institutions, organizations and power relations—in which it is embedded.

Examining the gender-art nexus and the power balance between them is not new, and many feminist scholars have explored the subject in depth.[7] Some, however, have challenged the feminist analysis of writers and activists who placed gender at the centre of their analysis, turning it into the main—indeed the sole—analytical lens through which they view power relations in the contemporary world. They argue that using a single focal point, gender, does not suffice for a complex, nuanced analysis or factoring in one rubric the many differences between women, in intersectional terms, or across and combined with nation-bound, ethnic and racial differences.[8] In light of this critique, and from a perspective that advocates taking diversity into account in order to deepen our understanding of feminist-activist visual art in public spaces in various permutations, the women artists discussed here are diverse not just ethnically, but also in terms of class, age, religion and stage in their artistic careers.

In selecting these artworks, from among many in metropolitan Tel Aviv and its boulevards, well-respected museums, major theaters or the internet, we chose pieces that received broad public exposure and had high visibility and impact beyond the purview only of art aficionados: art that entered the mainstream through social institutions or popular public spaces. The works discussed below all had

Justin Elam, 'Editorial Comment: Theatre and Activism', *Theatre Journal* 55, no. 4 (2003), pp. vii–xii; Wilma De Jong, Martin Shaw and Neil Stammers, *Global Activism, Global Media* (London: Pluto Press, 2005); Carolyn M. Byerly and Karen Ross, *Women and Media: A Critical Introduction* (Malden, MA: John Wiley & Sons, 2006); many articles in the journal, *n. paradoxa International Feminist Art Journal* (1998–2017); Amy E. Hughes, *Spectacles of Reform: Theater and Activism in Nineteenth-Century America* (Ann Arbor, MI: University of Michigan Press, 2012); Skadi Loist and Ger Zielinski, 'On the Development of Queer Film Festivals and Their Media Activism', *Film Festival Yearbook 4* (2012), pp. 49–62; Danica Minić, 'Feminist Publicist Strategies: Women's NGOs' Media Activism and Television Journalism in Serbia and Croatia', *Media, Culture & Society* 36, no. 2 (2014), pp. 133–149; Emma Cox, *Performing Noncitizenship: Asylum Seekers in Australian Theatre, Film and Activism* (London: Anthem Press, 2015); Leshu Torchin, 'Conditions of Activism: Feminist Film Activism and the Legacy of the Second Wave', in *Diversity, Difference, and Multiplicity in Contemporary Film Cultures*, eds. L. Mulvey and A.B. Rogers (Amsterdam: Amsterdam University Press, 2015), pp. 141–148.

6. Pierre Bourdieu, *Sociology in Question* (Thousand Oaks, CA: Sage, 1993).

7. Broude and Garrard, *The Power of Feminist Art*; Linda Nochlin, 'Why Have There Been No Great Women Artists?' (1971), in *The Feminism and Visual Culture Reader*, ed. Amelia Jones (London: Routledge, 2003), pp. 229–233; Whitney Chadwick and Tirza True Latimer, 'Becoming Modern: Gender and Sexual Identity after World War I', *The Modern Woman Revisited: Paris between the Wars*, eds. Whitney Chadwick and Tirza True Latimer (New Brunswick, NJ: Rutgers University Press, 2003), pp. 3–20; Angela Dimitrakaki, *Gender, artWork and the Global Imperative: A Materialist Feminist Critique* (Manchester: Manchester University Press, 2014).

8. Kimberlé Williams Crenshaw, 'Mapping the Margins: Intersectionality, Identity Politics, and Violence against Women', *Stanford Law Review* 43, no. 6 (1991), pp. 1241–1299; Maria Lugones, 'Purity, Impurity, and Separation', *Signs: Journal of Women in Culture and Society* 19, no. 2 (1994), pp. 458–479; G. Clement, *Care, Autonomy, and Justice: Feminism and the Ethic of Care* (Boulder, CO: Westview, 1996); Patricia Hill Collins, *Black Feminist Thought: Knowledge, Consciousness, and the Politics of Empowerment* (London: Routledge, 2000); Nira Yuval-Davis, 'Intersectionality and Feminist

 Feminist Art Activisms and Artivisms

Politics', *The European Journal of Women's Studies* 13, no. 3 (2006), pp. 193–209; Aristea Fotopoulou, 'Intersectionality Queer Studies and Hybridity: Methodological Frameworks for Social Research', *Journal of International Women's Studies* 13, no. 2 (2012), pp. 19-32; Evelien Geerts and Iris van der Tuin, 'From Intersectionality to Interference: Feminist Onto-Epistemological Reflections on the Politics of Representation', *Women's Studies International Forum* 41, no. 3 (November 2013), pp. 171–178.

9. Although these groups certainly have vivid activist feminist art created in Israel, and we acknowledge the importance of this work, unfortunately it has not yet had widespread exposure or been recognized in the mainstream media. See Tal Dekel, 'Subversive Uses of Perception: The Case of Palestinian Artist Anisa Ashkar', *Signs: Journal of Women in Culture and Society* 40, no. 2 (2015b), pp. 300–308; Tal Dekel, 'Welcome Home? Israeli-Ethiopian Women Artists and Questions of Citizenship and Belonging', *Third Text: Critical Perspectives on Contemporary Art and Culture* 29, no. 4–5 (2016), pp. 310–325; A. Nasrallah, 'Art, Abject, and Feminism: The Work of Hannan Abu Hussain [in Hebrew]', *Migdar: An Interdisciplinary Journal for Gender Studies* 5 (2018); E. Yerdai, 'To Be Black and Beautiful in Israel [in Hebrew]', *Migdar: An Interdisciplinary Journal for Gender Studies* 5 (2018).

10. Benjamin H.D. Buchloh, 'Conceptual Art 1962–1969: From the Aesthetic of Administration to the Critique of Institutions', *October* 55 (Winter 1990), pp. 105–143; Andrea Fraser, 'From the Critique of Institution to an Institution of Critique', *Artforum* 44, no. 1 (2005), pp. 100–106.

11. Danica Minić, 'Feminist Publicist Strategies: Women's NGOs' Media Activism and Television Journalism in Serbia and Croatia', *Media, Culture & Society* 36, no. 2 (2014), pp. 133–149.

public exposure beyond neighbourhood galleries or small venues. As a result, this paper does not discuss the activist art of Israeli women who are, for example, Palestinian or Ethiopian-born.[9]

The first part of our argument deals with one of the most common practices in feminist activism—raising awareness in public spaces about gender inequality in the artworld through counting and presenting statistics; part two examines the struggle for visibility and public representation of women's lives through performance; and part three considers collective feminist activism in public spaces, aiming to manifest daily incidents and struggles of women.

Some of the artworks discussed here have not been examined from a scholarly perspective before, and we view their citation and inclusion in the field of the discourse about feminist-activist art as contributing to activism in and of itself. We want to locate their activity within the fields of art and feminism and position them as part of a complex artistic dynasty with roots and history. Too often, artworks and their creators in Israel are read without context, as historically disconnected from broader trajectories of art, which further excludes and erases many women artists from memory and the artistic canon, or assigns these works an inferior status in the general field.

Feminist Institutional Critique — The Israeli Take

Institutional critique, which took root in the west in the mid-twentieth century, aimed its critical arrows at the art institutions in the world and those who headed them, while exposing the covert power relations in this field.[10] Nonetheless, this critique was not limited to writings by art theoreticians and critics; artists also began to express their protest and criticism of shortcomings within the art world in their own work.

Danica Minić indicates that feminist art activists began working for change in the 1960s and 1970s through methods that included monitoring ("head counting") and consciousness raising.[11] Examples are evident in the activities of many women artists in the 1970s and later from the 1980s, even though it is the US activist artists' groups such as the

Guerrilla Girls and WAC, and more recently Micol Hebron's *Gallery Tally* project which have become well-known.[12] Activists would count the number of female artists whose works appeared in museums or the number of images of women in museums, and would publish their findings as percentages of the total or in absolute numbers.[13]

In 2016, Israeli artist Einat Amir collected data on gender inequality in the Israeli art world. In the activist spirit of the Guerrilla Girls, Amir invited five women artists to design T-shirts that displayed these findings, which would be sold to the public at large (as merchandise). One of the T-shirts, for example, noted the discouraging statistic: 'Solo shows in the Israel Museum and the Tel Aviv Museum: 70% men, 30% women'. Another said: 'Artists in galleries: 61% men, 39% women'. As part of the ongoing art work, Amir asked her male teachers in the Midrasha Faculty of Arts in Beit Berl College—one of the most respected art academies in Israel—to wear the shirts with the incriminating data and thereby exhibit the inequalities for which they themselves, as prominent and influential teachers, were largely responsible. The teachers agreed to wear the shirts with their indictments in public space, whether in the spirit of co-operation or in ironic, postmodern self-awareness.

Another part of that project by Amir, called *Men #2*, was a live art installation in the Tel Aviv Museum of Art where Amir's male teachers, who were her mentors during her Midrasha studies, read out loud to the audience Rebecca Solnit's article 'Men Explain Things to Me' (2015). This performance took place while they were wearing the shirts with the harsh statistics, noting the unequal ratio of male to female teachers in the art colleges and the number of female students and lower-ranked female teachers in those colleges.

Lippard notes that one salient characteristic of feminist art activism is that it extends over time and engages both within and outside the mainstream art world.[14] In the spirit of Lippard's point, Amir's project was a long-term one—from the initial data collection in archives and libraries, through linking up and working with other Israeli women artists who collaborated in designing the T-shirts, and through the performative actions of art teachers wearing the shirts on the campus and in city streets, and culminating the project as a live event in a major, mainstream institution—the Tel Aviv Museum of Art.[15]

12. Whitney Chadwick, *Women, Art and Society* (London: Thames & Hudson, 1990), p. 347; Hilary Robinson, 'Activism and Institutions', in *Feminism, Art, Theory: An Anthology 1968–2014*, ed. Hilary Robinson (Oxford: John Wiley & Sons, 2015), p. 44; Catherine G. Wagley, 'With "Gallery Tally Project" Micol Hebron Examines Gender Inequality in the Art Market', *ArtNews*, 25 May 2016, www.artnews.com/2016/05/26/with-gallery-tally-project-micol-hebron-examines-gender-inequality-in-the-art-market/ (accessed 25 June 2019).

13. Josephine Withers, 'The Guerrilla Girls', *Feminist Studies* 14, no. 2 (1998), pp. 284–300; Anne Teresa Demo, 'The Guerrilla Girls' Comic Politics of Subversion', *Women's Studies in Communication* 23, no. 2 (2000), pp. 133–156.

14. Lippard, 'Trojan Horses'.

15. The project website: www.einatamir.com/men2.

16. Shulamid Lev-Aladgem, 'Ethnicity, Class and Gender in the Israeli Community Theatre', *Theatre Research International* 28, no. 2 (2003a), pp. 181–192; Shulamid Lev-Aladgem, 'From Object to Subject: Israeli Theatres of the Battered Women', *New Theatre Quarterly* XIX, no. 2 (2003b), pp. 139–149; Shulamid Lev-Aladgem and Anat First, 'The Israeli Community Theatre as a Site for Performing Gender and Identity', *Feminist Media Studies* 4, no. 1 (2004), pp. 37–50.

17. Hagar Tzameret-Kertcher et al., eds., *The Gender Index: Gender Inequality in Israel* (Jerusalem: The Van Leer Jerusalem Institute, 2016).

Visibility in Local Terms — Performing and Occupying Space

Amir, like the Guerrilla Girls in the United States, and other art groups in Europe, Africa, Asia, and Central and South America, works in plastic and graphic art as well as installations and performance: all of which have a proven track record of activism. But this is not the case for the performing arts and theatre in Israel.[16] Only in 2016 were the performing arts added as a category to the "Gender Index", an annual feminist research project that measures gender inequality in Israel, and within it "actors" was the only rubric tested. The findings were that men exceeded the numbers of women by 55% to 45%.[17]

A seminal event in this artistic field took place in May 2017, when an evening dedicated to original performance works of women was held in the theatre school of the Kibbutzim College of Education, Technology and the Arts. Entitled *Yotzrot Shinuy* (*Women Creating Change*),

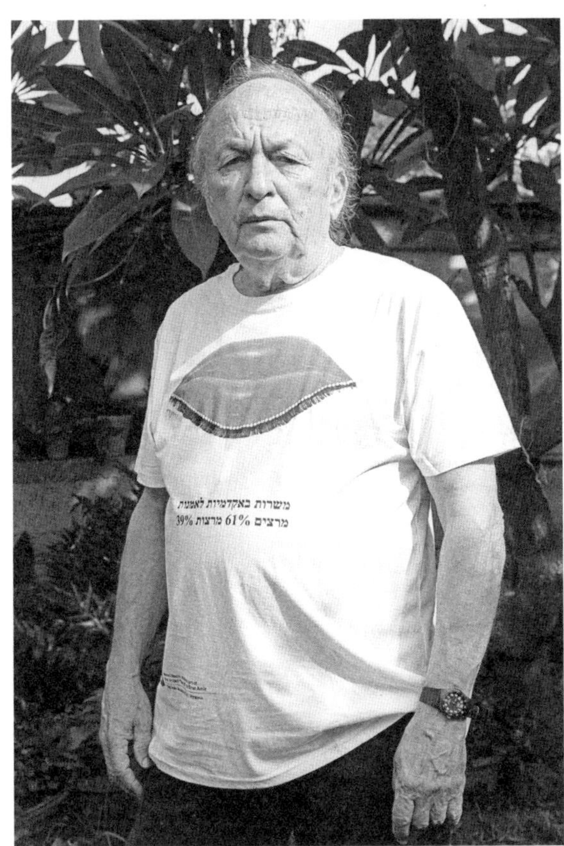

Einat Amir, *Men #2*, 2016, Yair Garbuz wearing T-shirt designed by Vered Nissim (produced by 'Vitrina', Tel Aviv Museum of Art). Photo: Einat Amir

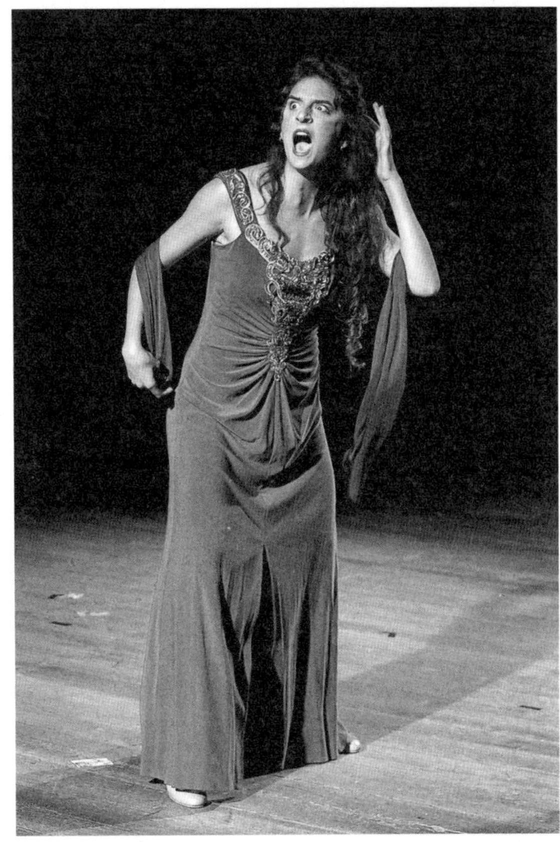

Maayan Preedan and Tamar Amit-Joseph, *Women Creating Change*, 2017, performance by artist Yarden Nikfahama. Photo: Amir Liberman

the one-hour event was a collection of monologues, dialogues, and scenes written, directed and performed by women, reflecting on the world from their perspectives. The production was the brainchild of two women, Maayan Preedan and Tamar Amit-Joseph, students in the college, supervised by Moran Arbiv-Gans, one of their teachers. Preedan and Amit-Joseph had realized during their studies how few performance works were created by women in Israel, so they decided to invite female students to submit proposals for the project, by putting up posters throughout the college campus, adding to the call some data from the major performance and theatre organizations in Israel showing that only a small percentage of the works are by women.[18] Preedan and Amit-Joseph did not believe that findings about inequality in the performing arts and the importance of correcting it would be controversial, and were surprised to encounter considerable opposition to the project mainly among male but also among some female students. Claims were made that the data were distorted, and that 'feminists are trying to take over the place'. Nonetheless, in contrast with the widespread opposition, several female students were delighted and enthusiastic about having the opportunity to submit a proposal for the project.[19] Itzik Weingarten, head of the Theatre Department at the Kibbutzim College of Arts, gave immediate support to the project, and encouraged the artists. He even allocated funding, including hall rental, lighting, and institutional support, all of which are necessary for an independent student projection.

This feminist activity, a first of its kind in the field, was manifested not only by the insistence that all the works be by women, but also that the content would be about women. Under the guidance of Arbiv-Gans, thirteen submissions were selected on a variety of subjects (rape, harassment, masturbation, prostitution, obsessiveness, love, body hair, sexual orientation, ageism, etc.) all of which were influenced by cardinal issues in the Israeli society, such as militarism, ethnic power relations between Mizrahi and Ashkenazi women, and the effect of religion on local women.

The diverse perspectives of the performances exposed the audience to a wide range of experiences, opinions, and outlooks of Israeli women, and gave public

18. Only 13% of the works performed in major theatres were directed by women in 2015, and only 18% in 2016. M. Asheri, 'A Forum for Supporting and Promoting Women in Theatre was Formed at the Initiation of the Directors' and Actors' Guild [in Hebrew]', Ha'aretz, 2 May 2018, www.haaretz.co.il/1.6052244 (accessed 19 June 2019).

19. The quotes are taken from the comments on the Facebook pages of these women.

20. O. Lubin, 'The Space and the Gaze [in Hebrew]', *Where Am I Situated? Gender Perspective on Space*, ed. R. Halpern (Hertzliya: Friedrich Ebert Foundation, 2013), pp. 17–76.

21. The scope of this article prevents us from elaborating on these key issues in Israeli society. For further reading on Israeli militarism and gender power relations see: Hanna Herzog, 'Homefront and Battlefront: the Status of Jewish and Palestinian Women in Israel', *Israel Studies* 3, no. 1 (Spring 1998), pp. 61–84; Dalia Sachs, Amalia Sa'ar and Sarai Aharoni, '"How Can I Feel for others when I myself am Beaten?': The Impact of the Armed Conflict on Women in Israel', *Sex Roles* 57, no. 7 (2007), pp. 593–606. About ethnic power relations in Israel see: Henriette Dahan-Kalev, 'Tensions in Israeli Feminism: the Mizrahi Ashkenazi Rift', *Women Studies International Forum* 24, no. 6 (November 2001), pp. 669–684; Tal Dekel, 'Breaking the Pattern, Creating New Paths: Feminist Mizrahi Artists in Israel', *Revista de História da Arte* 12 (2015a), pp. 93–105.

exposure to subjects considered "personal". In Israel, much like in other countries around the world, patriarchal society constructs a hierarchy between "personal" space (private, intimate, and emotional, all considered female) and "public" space in which social and "political" life evolves (based on science, facts, and objectivity) are all considered male.[20] However, by introducing original pieces dealing with women's experiences in the IDF (Israeli Defense Force) and the rising militarism and chauvinism in the country, and two short performances about the experiences of Mizrahi women in Israel which reveal the ethnic tension between Jewish women of Europe origin and of North African origin living in Israel, the performances exposed the audience to points of view which are unique to the Israeli context.[21] By presenting the perspectives of women on a public stage, *Women Creating Change* challenged the view that the personal/female is inferior to the public/male and indeed that there is a dichotomy between them.

Women Creating Change honed a diverse range of feminist practices in various fields: women acting students also wrote, directed, produced, and danced; women training as directors acted, wrote, sang, and performed music; and male acting students appeared in scenes written by women. In addition, by virtue of Preedan and Amit-Joseph's call for women to bring their writing to the stage, the duo promoted other women, not just themselves, encouraging them, working closely with the performers and writers—sometimes from the early writing stages—up to the performance itself. In so doing, Preedan and Amit-Joseph crafted an activity whose main goal was to advance other women, although interestingly it was solely Preedan and Amit-Joseph who were exposed to the angry reactions, opposition, and latent violence directed at the production. The production was open to view by the general public and not just to students, and despite the strident criticism, it succeeded beyond expectations, adding more shows to the original schedule of performances.

PUBLIC SPACES

Collective Work — Religion, Class and Gender

In Jerusalem, a group of feminist religious Jewish women belonging to the art collective Studio Mi'Shelach (A Studio of Her Own), organized an outdoor exhibition entitled 'In Her Image' to mark International Women's Day in 2017.[22] This exhibition emerged from a workshop run by Jerusalem's Yad Sarah Family Center, which taught photography using smartphones to religious and ultra-Orthodox women who had survived domestic violence and have low-incomes. Images for the exhibition were created by all involved— the instructors, the staff (including social workers and the Family Center director), and the women themselves who had experienced the violence. All were committed to the artistic process and contributed images, as equals.

Two urban venues in mid-town Jerusalem—the Shatz pedestrian mall and Bezalel street—were selected as the public space for the exhibition. These are trendy gathering places, locations of artistic activity, and in close proximity to well-known art institutions—the Jerusalem Artists' House gallery and the old Bezalel Academy of Arts and Design. The venues were chosen to give the women who experienced violence not only a sense that their artistic capabilities deserve a "real" exhibition, but also to give public exposure to them and their painful life stories, in contrast with the years of concealment of their oppression in their abusive

22. A. Lev, 'In Her Own Image: Photography Exhibition in the Public Space in Jerusalem [in Hebrew]', *Artists: Israeli Art*, 19 May 2017, www.amanim.com/michalsa241/ (accessed 19 June 2019).

Studio of Your Own collective, *In Her Image*, 2017, installation view. Photo: Tzipi Mizrahi

23. For more about feminist art in religious Jewish context see: David Sperber, *Jewish Feminist Art in the US and Israel, 1990–2017*, Ph.D. dissertation (Ramat Gan: Bar Ilan University, 2017).

24. Reilly, *Curatorial Activism*, p. 21.

25. A. Zorea, 'Bezalel Street: A Unique Street Exhibition of Women's Photographs [in Hebrew]', *Kol Ha'Ir*, 12 March 2017, www.kolhair.co.il/jerusalem-news/2870/ (accessed 19 June 2019).

family setting, which in the Israeli context has a special social characteristic, as they all come from Ultra-Orthodox communities, who tend to be much less cooperative with police and any kind of authorities when domestic violence occurs, and cover up domestic violence in marriage because of their extreme conservative community norms.[23] The photos by the women were hung on the street-light poles and this was an intrusion into mainstream urban space.

Thus, one could see passing pedestrians, women and men, secular and religious, lifting their eyes to the streetlights to look at the artwork overhead. Striking among the photos was the image of wet laundry hanging out to dry, alluding to the cover-up and concealment of the violence the women experienced in their homes. Another photo captures a window display of a store no longer in business—two armless and legless mannequins, one upright and the other prone on the floor, indicate the neglect and violence clearly evident in the entire scene.

Curatorial Activism and 'Becoming Minor'

Maura Reilly has coined the term "curatorial activism" to refer to the organizing of art exhibitions of sensitivity and urgency that champion social change by:

> Attempting to ensure that the under- or un-repre-sented, the silenced, and the "doubly colonized"—those subjected by both empire and patriarchy, for example—are no longer ignored … a driving force as a curator is therefore wholly activist; the aim is to be consistently counter-hegemonic.[24]

Reilly notes the need to curate exhibitions of women artists and feminist art, in particular, as well as art by Others, as curatorial corrective action whose purpose is to end the exclusion of women artists from the narratives of contemporary art and art history in general. "Curatorial activism" describes precisely the collective project A Studio of Her Own and the perspective of its curators—Noga Greenberg and Yael Horen-Danino.[25]

However, it also goes beyond this because this project highlights the strong sense of being a stranger in one's own town which is characteristic of women in public space. This sense of foreignness is better described as a realization of the politics indicating how to overturn the politics of "becoming-minor" that holds a real possibility of resistance. The political function of the concept 'becoming-minor' is derived from the writings of the philosophers Gilles Deleuze and Félix Guattari and articulated by Ohad Zehavi: 'Minoracy is political action aimed at undermining the forces of oppression, resisting the powers of authority, escaping the inevitability of violence.'[26] Identification with a group that is 'becoming-minor' is an ongoing process that continues to challenge the values of the majority order and can coexist with the experience of foreignness: 'Minoracy urges us to make ourselves strangers in our own world so that the strangers in our world might enjoy a place of their own, in our vicinity.'[27] Although foreignness is ostensibly threatening to the mainstream majority—and results in feelings of separation and non-belonging for the minority—for those who choose the political stance of resistance, and identify with, support and encourage the alternative visions of different parts of society as "becoming-minor", it is the only strategy that can make the articulation of different feminist perspectives possible.

The life experiences of being a woman in the patriarchal culture of Israel, which is particularly chauvinist in its ethno-nationalism, allows for extremes of foreignness and alienation to meet with intimacy and solidarity and co-exist, despite the seemingly inherent contradiction between these conflictual feelings. Their co-existence enables the creation of something different, something new, only if mutual tolerance is permitted, and when they are allowed to blend and merge with a sense of local belonging and community. The artistic activism of women who identify themselves as feminist artists often gives presence to gendered body experiences of women in a patriarchal space that is hostile to them. Dissolving the boundaries between the private and public spheres is a known feminist strategy; in-depth analysis of this transgression and its reflexive deconstruction are critical to an understanding of feminist art activism in Israel.

26. Ohad Zehavi, 'Minoracy', Mafte'akh: A Lexical Review of Political Thought 1 (2010), p. 37.

27. Ibid., p. 44.

   Feminist Art Activisms and Artivisms

28. Robinson, 'Activism and Institutions', p. 44.

These examples of Israeli activist feminist art are linked to the notion of "becoming-minor" in the very essence of the oppositional and radical politics it entails. Moreover, it is art created to foster and promote discourse about a wide variety of gender, class, ethnic, national, and religious issues and dialogue between diverse women from different social groups. Some works do this through humour or irony, others use controlled rage or overt anger and protest, yet others use critical-performative re-creation. The feminist artists and organizers discussed here, creating as cultural activists, formalize in artistic visual terms a range of subjects that require exposure and transformation, and their work becomes a tool to connect with and build audiences for reflexive thinking about local burning social issues.

There are many common denominators between Israeli artists involved in feminist activism and artists doing similar work in other countries: internet activism, protest in public space, monitoring and head-counting, and the forming of artist collectives are some examples. However, the local framework of the artists based in Israel makes them distinct in many ways that influence their strategies and the content of their work on ageism and youthism in light of local demographics, chauvinism and the Israeli-Palestinian conflict, ethnic minorities and immigration, conflicting religious background, and civil rights in the State of Israel. This local framework does not overlook issues that are global concerns, shared by countless women, such as motherhood, sexuality, or the labor market. These activist feminist artworks created in Israel in recent years offer fresh perspectives on subjects that have not been spoken about before in Israel through visual means, and their content unfolds elements that are disruptive and subversive, with the potential for a change of public consciousness.[28] They seek to challenge conventional strategies in the field of art, whether in the performing arts or in the graphic and plastic arts, contemporary activist feminist artists working in public spaces in Israel today offer a daring, radical vision of a more just and equitable society.

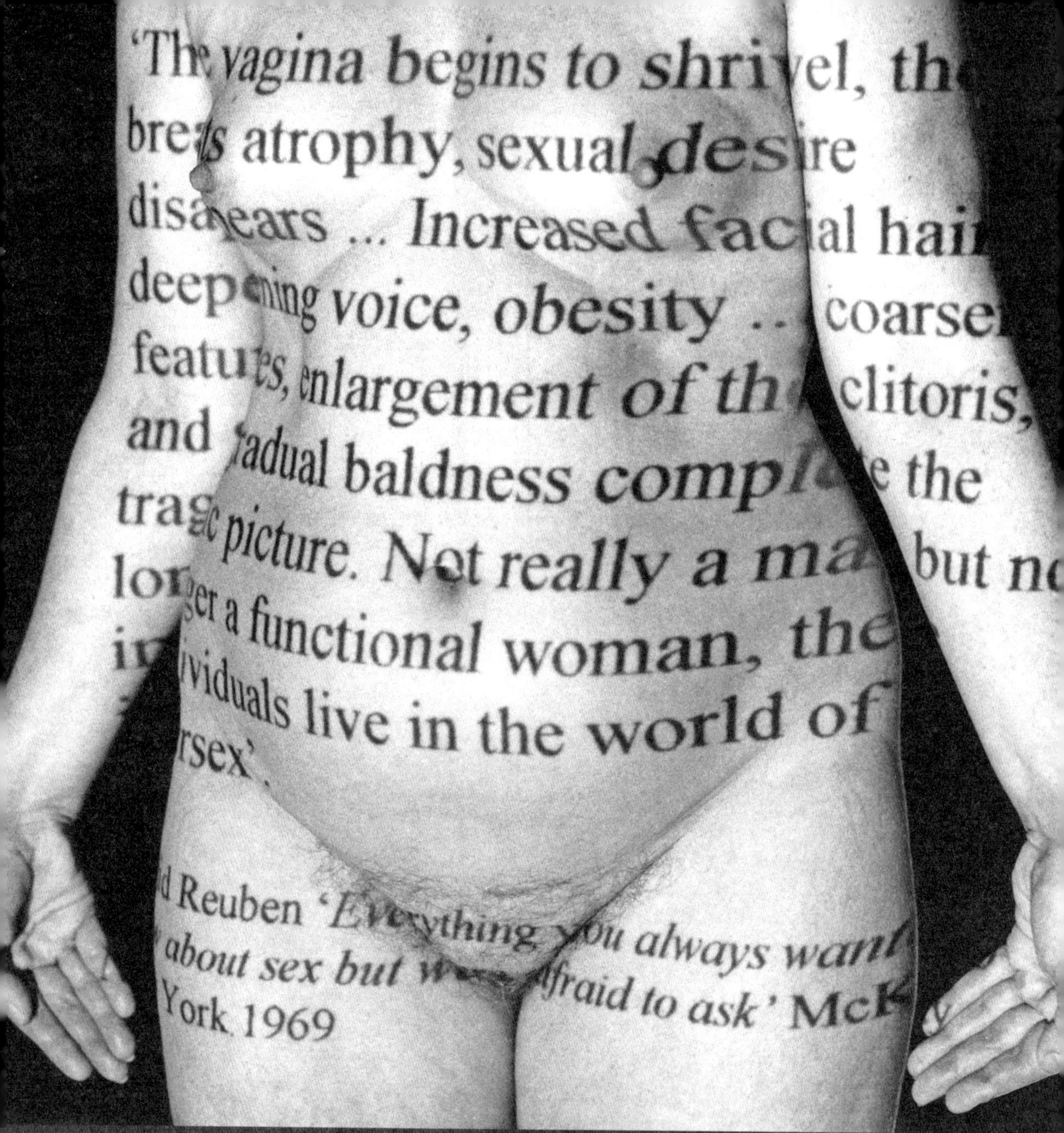

Rosy Martin and Kay Goodridge, *When the vagina begins to shrivel...*, from *Outrageous Agers*, 2000, photographic black and white print , 49.2 × 38.7 cm

OUTRAGEOUS AGEING AS ACTIVISM

Rosy Martin

1. This essay draws upon and develops arguments addressed in: Rosy Martin, 'Challenging Invisibility: Outrageous Agers', *Gender Issues in Art Therapy*, Susan Hogan, ed., (London: Jessica Kingsley Publishers, 2003); Rosy Martin, 'Outrageous Agers: Performativity and Transgressions', *Ageing Femininities: Troubling Representations*, eds. Josephine Dolan and Estella Tincknell, (Cambridge, MA: Cambridge Scholars Press, 2012). For more images of the works, see the website: www.outrageousagers. co.uk. A video of the performance 'I feel like chicken tonight', https:// vimeo.com/192169316. For recent work see www.gravitygravitas. com, www.rosymartin.info, www.rosymartin.co.uk.

The one position within the diversity debate that we will all embody, if we are lucky, is (old) age. While the proportion of older people within the population is growing, ageing itself is too often presented only as a crisis or problem. For many, ageing in Western societies is now seen only in terms of a loss of power particularly after retirement from waged work, even if, historically, that may not always have been the case and "age limits" to ending paid employment are constantly being extended. The apparent value of listening to one's elders is shifting, even in Asia, as today internet searches replace wisdom gleaned from older people and younger people claim their own autonomy. It really is about time that society globally took the issues surrounding ageism seriously and actively challenged current attitudes and policies towards its older people. Changing attitudes to ageing should become a vital issue for all with a renewed focus on how best to enjoy good and fulfilling lives and how to provide care and support to those who need it.

I first took this issue of ageism as a focus for my photographic art and research practice when I turned fifty.[1] I have always chosen to address issues of social and cultural formation in my work, most often through examining my personal experiences as a route to making the too often overlooked or invisible palpable. Looking back now, as a woman in my early seventies, this could seem to have been a little premature. But the lived reality for women is once the peri-menopause starts and the physical and psychological changes begin to become manifest, the brutal awareness kicks in of how mainstream media and the language of advertising misrepresents, or even worse, just ignores older women.

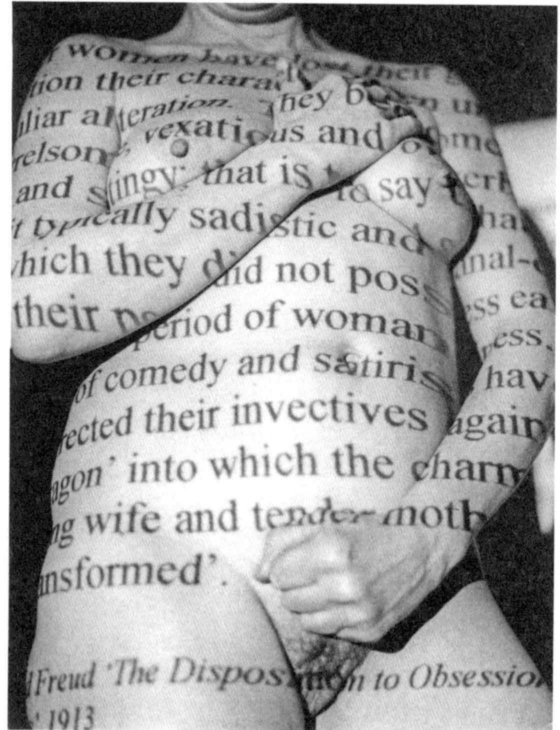

Rosy Martin and Kay Goodridge, *After women have lost their genital function…*, from *Outrageous Agers*, 2000, photographic black and white print, 49.2 × 38.7 cm

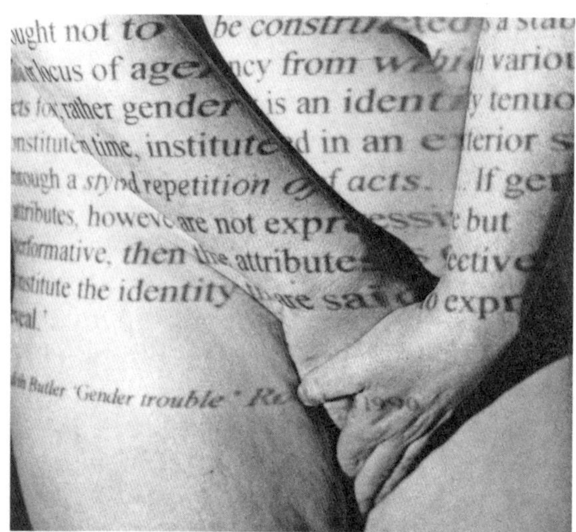

Rosy Martin and Kay Goodridge, *Gender ought not to be constructed as a stable identity or locus of agency…*, from *Outrageous Agers*, 2000, photographic black and white print, 38.7 × 38.7 cm

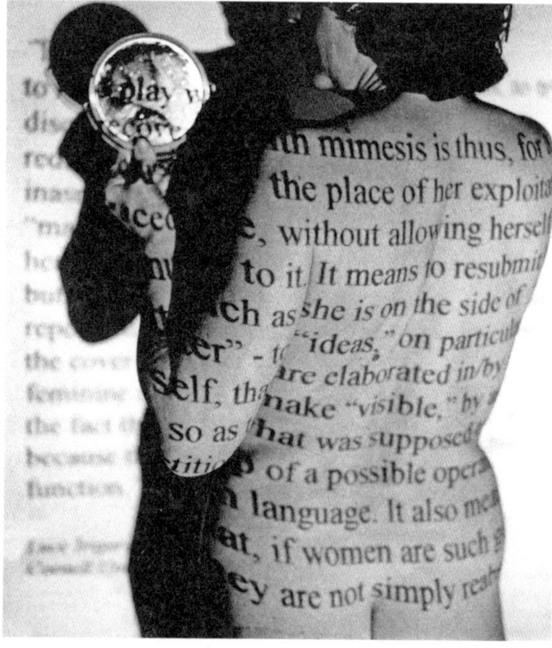

Rosy Martin and Kay Goodridge, *To play with mimesis* from *Outrageous Agers*, 2000, photographic black and white print, 49.2 × 38.7 cm

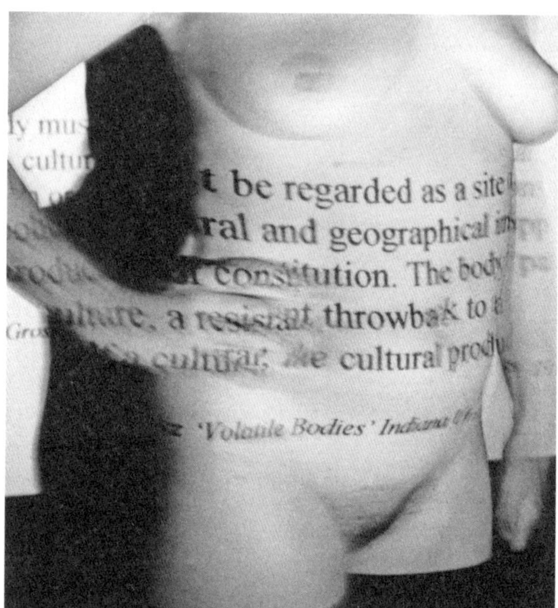

Rosy Martin and Kay Goodridge, *The body must be regarded as a site of social, political, cultural and geographical inscriptions, production or constitution…*, from *Outrageous Agers*, 2000, photographic black and white print, 38.7 × 38.7 cm

2. Fiona Sturges, 'Madonna's Age Isn't Relevant: Her Music Is', *The Guardian*, 5 June 2019.

Caught in that too familiar dilemma between disavowal and acceptance, many women are habitually denying or defying their chronological age for nearly half their life. Why is it considered a compliment to be told 'you don't look your age'? What does any particular age past-fifty look like anyway? In the West, we now live in a culture of amplified discontent and for women especially, this is channelled and intensified by advertising and reality TV makeover shows, focused upon the idealized appearance of the youthful body.

Where does one look for images of middle-aged and older women not embedded in the culture of re-touched and botoxed youthfulness? The cosmetics industry seems to endorse a fear of ageing—all those "anti-ageing" products sold to everyone over twenty or so—but despite their luxurious claims to hold back time, revitalize, and renew through recourse to the discourses of science, plastic surgery, war or even magic, time will tell as our skin is damaged by exposure to sunburn and pollution. Cosmetics' names like 'Instant illusions airbrush away primer' interestingly appropriate the language of Photoshop and digital interventions. It's not enough to disguise those giveaway signs of ageing, now the customer has to be "instagram ready" too.

In our currently celebrity-obsessed popular culture there was always shape-shifting Madonna, with her continuing re-invention and the re-articulation of iconic Hollywood images of women. But now she has turned sixty, the popular and music press is obsessed with her age, an approach not pursued for Mick Jagger or Paul McCartney.

> In fighting to do her job at sixty, Madonna is, as ever, blazing a trail … In the minds of her most vicious detractors she would be better off binning the fishnets, putting on a nice cardie and waiting for death. Even the more moderate language used in relation to her is revealing. "Dignity" crops up a lot, as does "appropriate" and "growing old gracefully". When men talk about women ageing gracefully, they are not acting out of concern. They're telling them to know their station, to sit down and shut up. Madonna told Vogue recently 'People have always been trying to silence me for one reason or another … Now I'm being punished for turning sixty.'[2]

The media obsession with the youthful older body produces a heroine/victim dichotomy of extremes in which older women are either properly maintained or "letting themselves go", are either super-fit marathon runners or couch potatoes, are either mature polished consumers or abject pensioners shivering in the loneliness of poverty. There are too few visible examples in contemporary media culture of "lived in" female bodies that signify a rich, complex lifetime of experience.

Medical discourses on the menopause underline the rhetoric of lack and loss. The World Health Organization defines menopause as an estrogen deficiency disease. The vivid imagery of atrophy, withering, and decline used to describe "senile ovaries"[3] reiterates Dr. Reuben (1969) who considered the menopause to be a time of sexual degeneration, which he [sic] characterizes as "tragic", once the reproductive function is lost:

> The vagina begins to shrivel, the breasts atrophy, sexual desire disappears ... Increased facial hair, deepening voice, obesity ... coarsened features, enlargement of the clitoris, and gradual baldness complete the tragic picture. Not really a man but no longer a functional woman, these individuals live in the world of intersex.[4]

Similarly, for Freud, a woman of fifty was "elderly", dysfunctional in sexual reproductive terms and therefore sexually redundant and invisible.

> After women have lost their genital function their character often undergoes a peculiar alteration. They become quarrelsome, vexatious and overbearing, petty and stingy; that is to say that they exhibit typically sadistic and anal-erotic traits which they did not possess earlier, during their period of womanliness. Writers of comedy and satirists have in all ages directed their invectives against the "old dragon" into which the charming girl, the loving wife and tender mother have been transformed.[5]

3. Emily Martin, *The Woman in the Body: A Cultural Analysis of Reproduction* (Boston: Beacon Press, 1992), p 39.

4. David R. Reuben, *Everything You Always Wanted to Know about Sex but Were Afraid to Ask* (New York: McKay, 1969), p. 242.

5. Sigmund Freud, *The Disposition to Obsessional Neurosis* (1913), Section 12, pp. 323–324.

6. Judith Butler, *Gender Trouble* (London and New York: Routledge, 1990).

7. Margaret Morganroth Gullette, 'The Other End of the Fashion Cycle: Practicing Loss, Learning Decline', *Figuring Age: Women, Bodies, Generations*, ed. Kathleen Woodward (Bloomington, IN: Indiana University Press, 1999), pp. 34–55.

Freud here slides between medical and popular cultural discourse with an ease that suggests the play of stereotypes in his "scientific" thinking, or even a personal prejudice. The "old dragon" of Freud's construction of ageing femininity can be traced through a range of popular cultural forms of his time: pantomime, music hall, legitimate theatre and the comic seaside postcard.

Stereotypes of older women circulating in contemporary popular culture and medical discourse constitute ageing femininity in terms of decline and redundancy. However, such "common sense" beliefs hide the potential fluidity of identities.

> Gender ought not to be constructed as a stable identity or locus of agency from which various acts follow; rather gender is an identity tenuously constituted in time, instituted in an exterior space through a stylised repetition of acts. ... If gender attributes, however, are not expressive but performative, then these attributes effectively constitute the identity they are said to express or reveal.[6]

Butler's position in *Gender Trouble* provides a basis for potential subversions that expand the notions of what a post-menopausal woman might be or become: it suggests ways in which transgression offers a route to oppositional ways of representing ageing.

The demand for constant change which fuels the fashion cycle itself holds implicit messages of redundancy and obsolescence, through which we are taught to despise and cast off the styles of previous years. Whilst the internet is full of "advice" and "influencers", it seems rather to be the recurrent story of keep on shopping and yet a variety of styles that would provide for the full range of differences amongst women, including ageing, is not available. Consumer culture and the "life cycle" of clothes, in which 'dissatisfaction is our most important product',[7] presents all of us with an arena in which we are taught to discard once-loved garments with which we identified and by so doing, old fashions and old age are worryingly elided.

For the photographic series *Outrageous Agers*, I worked collaboratively with Kay Goodridge. We spent many

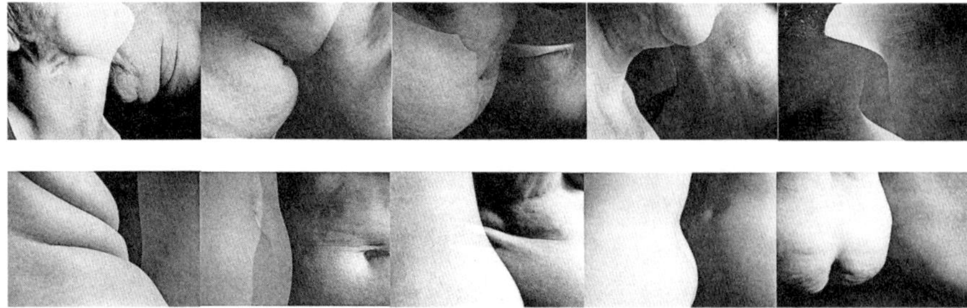

Rosy Martin and Kay Goodridge, *Bodyscapes*, from *Outrageous Agers*, 2000, C-type colour photographic prints, 61 × 91.5 cm (each)

hours together, using our therapeutic skills to uncover and own our fears and prejudices about our own ageing. This deep connection enabled us to create a safe space to work, using many of the phototherapeutic techniques[8] I had developed previously in my work with Jo Spence. We aimed to use photography in dialogue, firstly between ourselves and then with our audience to intervene in dominant cultural constructions of ageing female identities that attempt to fix and define, rather than allow space for fluidity, mobility and non-fixity. We transgressed these dominant stereotypes in a bid to transform them, through parody, ridicule, and embracing the carnivalesque, using our own bodies performatively.

> The body must be regarded as a site of social, political, cultural and geographical inscriptions, production or constitution. The body is not opposed to culture, a resistant throwback to a natural past; it is itself a cultural, the cultural product.[9]

Through our conversations we identified those body parts that were sites of on-going anxieties which could be characterized as our "ugly bits", e.g. triple chins, bellies, cellulite-pitted buttocks and thighs, and love handles. We experimented with double exposures (in camera) by overlapping the images, for example when photographing our flabby bellies firstly breathing out whilst relaxing muscles and then breathing in whilst tensing the muscles. We also cropped in very close, to allow the images to transgress the boundaries of the frame in the same way that our bodies were transgressing the framing of a stereotype. When we eventually

8. Rosy Martin, 'The Performative Body: Phototherapy and Re-Enactment', *Afterimage*, November–December 2001, and Rosy Martin, 'Inhabiting the Image: Photography, Therapy and Re-Enactment Phototherapy', *European Journal of Psychotherapy and Counselling* 11, no. 1 (March 2009), pp. 35–49, both reproduced in *Phototherapy and Therapeutic Photography in a Digital Age*, ed. Del Loewenthal (London and New York: Routledge, 2015), pp. 69–81.

9. Elizabeth Grosz, *Volatile Bodies: Toward a Corporeal Feminism* (Indiana, IN: Indiana University Press 1994), p. 23.

 Feminist Art Activisms and Artivisms

10. Rachel Gear, 'The Old Hags Are Laughing: A Response to Outrageous Agers', *Make 87* (March–May 2000), p. 29.

made selections from the resulting photographs, we discovered that by placing images together as a continuous frieze of colour photographic prints, one image merged with the next. Our preconceptions shifted, these had become aesthetically gorgeous bodyscapes that countered the discourses of abjection that dominate contemporary attitudes towards the ageing female body. As one reviewer observed:

> The act of looking at the undulating folds and contours of the skin becomes pleasurable and manifold, as though the artists are playfully interrogating our assumptions of how the ageing body should appear... By engaging with the dynamics of representing the old(er) female nude, the absence of the older woman in visual art is challenged. Within a patriarchal frame, only the smooth, healthy body is considered an appropriate body type for art: anything other than this is out of bounds/ monstrous.'[10]

We also used multiple exposures, in camera, to examine the sense of having an unstable body, foregrounded by our own experiences, for example that of feeling fit and healthy one day, the next crippled by rheumatism and strained knee joints. By overlapping images of movement to represent instability with images frozen by flashlight, we made visible this sense of occupying an unstable body, which contained echoes of its history, and projections towards its future, within itself. We used a similar technique to make portraits of each other combining movement and stasis to make visible ideas of change and instability. We created traces of both the past and the future within the images, for example in one image of Rosy, the movement gave back the bright auburn-red colour to the hair, in another the loose movement of the jaw offered up an image of a premonition of extreme old age.

Ignoring the implicit notice 'no woman over 30 need enter' we re-visited the fashion chain Top Shop on Oxford Street, London to play with and perform the stereotype of "mutton dressed as lamb" by choosing and trying on a range of trendy club-wear, lycra-stretched sequins, leopard-skin prints and PVC, clearly not marketed to us.

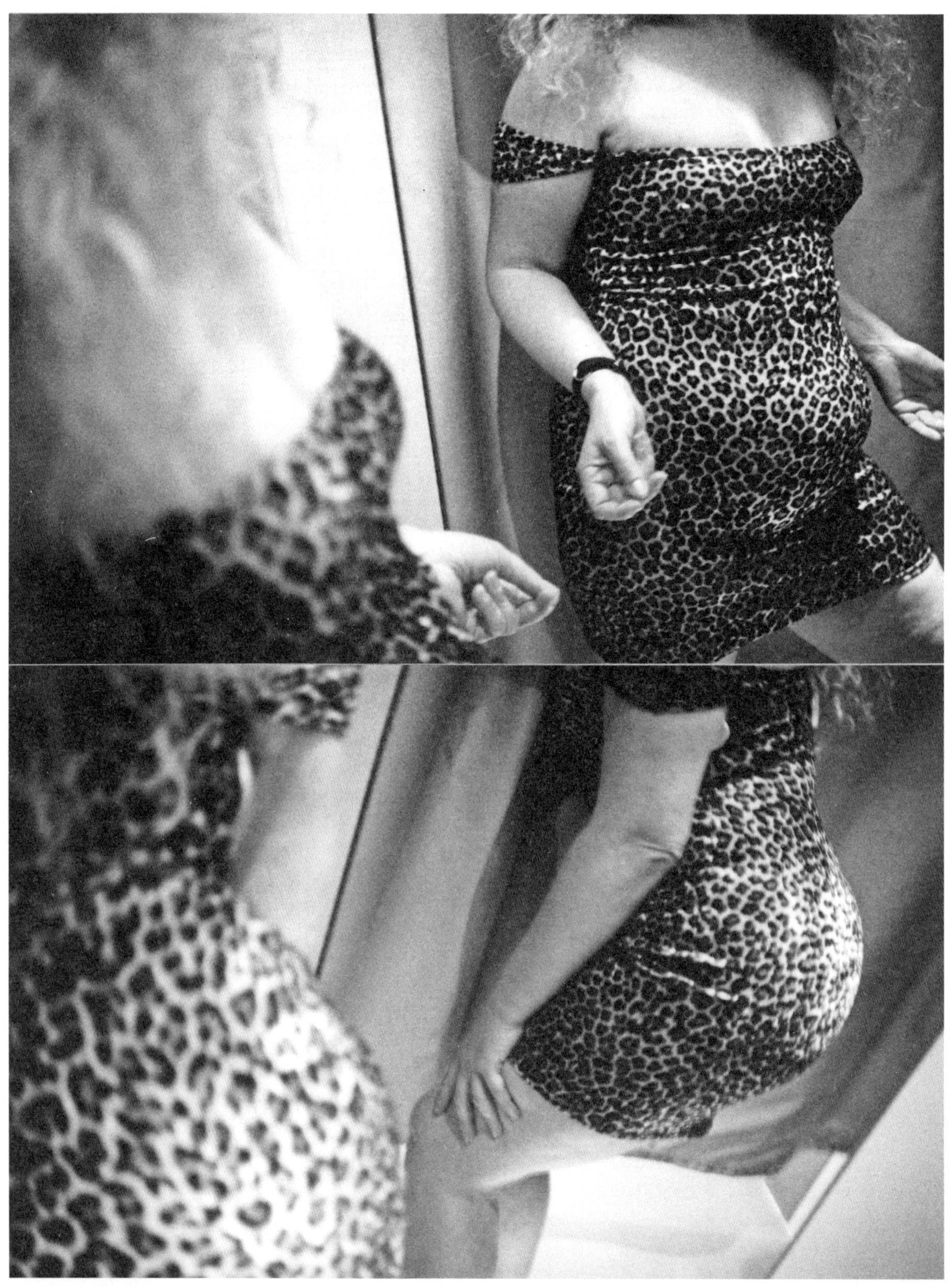

Rosy Martin and Kay Goodridge, *Trying it on—Leopard skin dress*, from *Outrageous Agers*, 2000,
colour duratrans lightbox, 76.2 × 101.5 cm

11. Chris Arnot, 'Cellulite for Sore Eyes', *The Guardian*, 3 February 2000, p. 12.

12. Ibid.

13. Mikhail Bakhtin, *Rabelais and His World* (1965), trans. Helene Iswolsky (Cambridge, MA and London: MIT Press, 1968).

Squeezed into the frame, our bodies mirror the desire and discontent of the loss of the anyway already impossible "perfect" body. Trying on youth in a tiny changing room, the flesh of the body reasserts itself through the stretched fabric, it cannot be contained or forced to fit within fashion's parameters. But alongside this unease, we were celebrating the carnivalesque fun and ambiguity of the images, as tendrils of hair fall upon plunging necklines and bums most definitely do look big in this. The mirrors of the changing room reflected back the performative aspects of the work and reinforced the act of looking, both of the viewer as voyeur inside the changing room and us as both fashion model and photographer. When we exhibited this work, we made large (60" x 40") light-boxes, montaging together series of images, to cite, challenge, subvert, and create a parody of fashion and advertising photography. Chris Arnot reviewing the exhibition in 2000 had a mixed response to these images:

> A large bottom stretches tight leopard-skin to comic postcard parody. A big, bare thigh, pitted with cellulite, protrudes from a short skirt below a bare bulging midriff. The unsightly lumps are juxtaposed with lovely feminine shoulders and hints of cleavage.[11]

He misses the subversive intent of the images, responding with disgust when viewing an un-retouched photograph of ageing flesh, whilst also acknowledging our work as 'challenging assumptions with wit and a defiant, if rather desperate, air of celebration'.[12]

Given that we had focused upon our bodies and the subversion of popular cultural practices we decided our next move should be to play with the striptease. However, we would have to make it outrageous. Our performative approach was intentionally carnivalesque and transgressive, drawing its inspiration from engagement with Bakhtin's (1965) work on Rabelais and his notions of "grotesque realism".[13] The grotesque body he addresses is the open, protruding, extended, secreting body, the body of becoming, process and change, which may be seen as in opposition to the Classical body, characterized as monumental, static, closed and sleek, the idealized body that haunts the psyche

of desire, the always impossible to physically embody ideal.
  Allowing ourselves to inhabit the "monstrous feminine" was immediately liberating. We used Kay's studio, an
all-white room that looked like an empty gallery space and
we dressed in many layers of sensible smart black clothes,

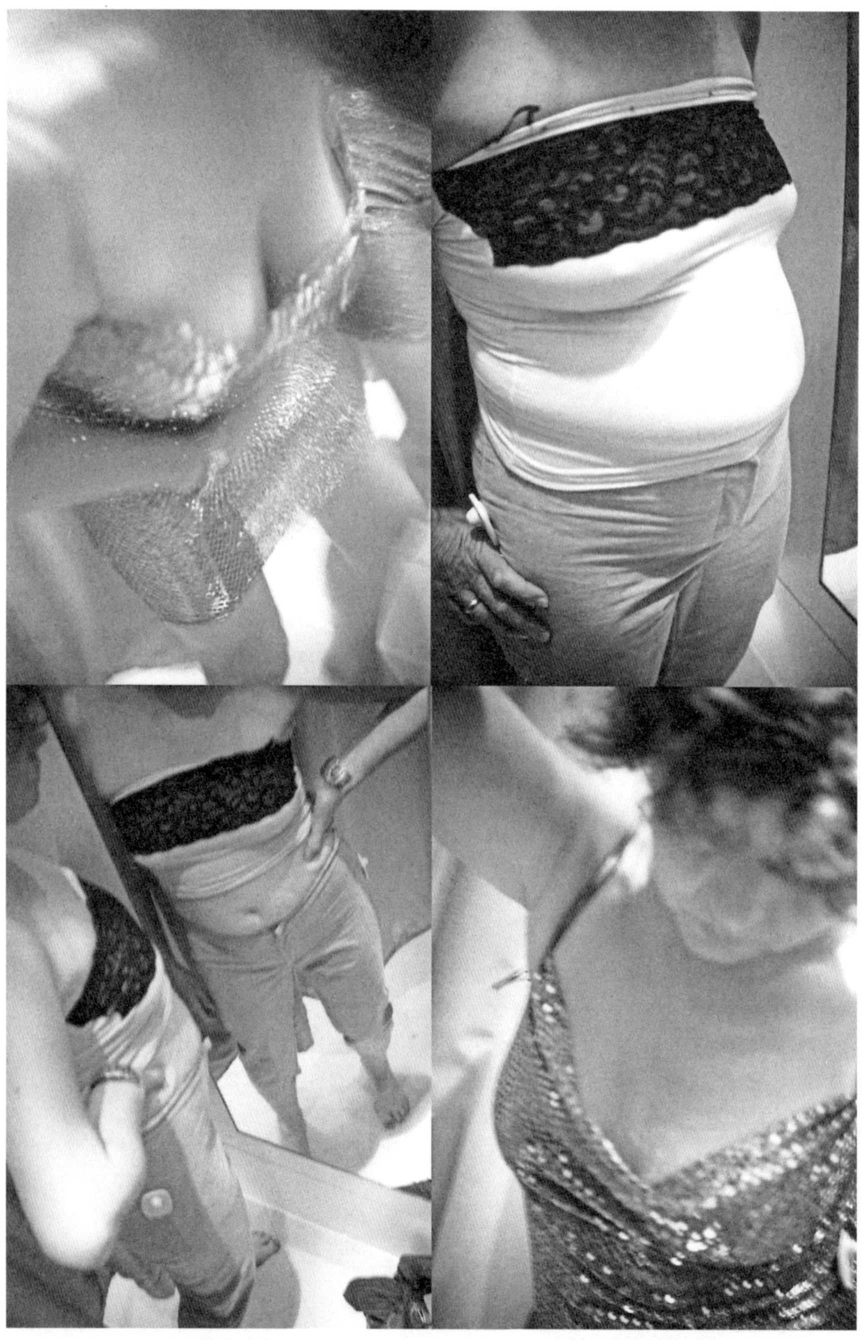

Rosy Martin and Kay Goodridge, *Trying it on—desire and discontent*, from *Outrageous Agers*, 2000,
colour duratrans lightbox, 101.5 × 152.5 cm

14. Gear, 'The Old Hags Are Laughing', p. 29.

15. Barbara W. Walker, *The Women's Encyclopaedia of Myths and Secrets* (San Francisco: Harper & Row, 1983).

16. Luce Irigaray, *The Sex Which is Not One*, trans. Catherine Porter (Ithaca, NY: Cornell University Press, 1985).

as if attending a private view. We videoed the proceedings, as we slowly and playfully removed layer upon layer, underneath which lay another visual twist, inspired by my experience of a sprained ankle; tubi-grip covered our arms and legs. Although this is usually connected to the damaged, elderly body, we used it as a second skin Tubigrip as the new lycra. As we peeled it off it also made a visual reference to Victorian silk stockings, whilst its seductive undertones were undercut by our laughter. Reviewers had little difficulty grasping the point of our striptease parody.

> Several key words spring immediately to mind: riotous, positive, powerful and, of course, outrageous. ... Martin hums and sings 'The Stripper' throughout, bawdy at first and then slowing down to a rhythmic gasp which evokes an excited heartbeat... . What is most appealing is that they look and sound as if they are enjoying themselves, as though they are revelling in peeling off the stigma of old age.[14]

In a series of ten scripto-visual works, theoretical texts by Reuben, Freud, Bakhtin, Plath, Irigaray, Gullette, Butler, Grosz, Macdonald, and Walker which I chose as exemplars of defining or defiant texts, were projected onto our fragmented naked ageing bodies to challenge, subvert and make visible the inscriptions of medical, psychoanalytic and cultural discourses upon the body. (Some of these are included within this chapter). The aim was to shift from the position taken by Reuben to that of Walker,[15] through the theoretical strategies of Bakhtin (which were ambivalent) to Irigaray (the chosen quote 'to play with mimesis is thus, for a woman, to try to recover the place of her exploitation by discourse, without allowing herself simply to be reduced to it ...'[16] sets out the questions to be addressed), and on to Grosz and Butler (who offer differing routes through positioning by discourse). The intention was to stress the multiplicity of texts and images that circulate around this shifting ground, the destabilized body, and effect a re-reading through how we interacted with the texts, as they became inscribed onto our flesh, through projection. The authority of the normative and clinical prescriptions of Reuben (1969) and Freud

(1913) is undermined by the exuberance and presence of the vitality of the living, breathing body. Not all of the text is easily visible, and is distorted by the disruptive and excessive body upon which it is projected. It is the very surface of the skin that is written upon by the projected words. The photographic process, which "writes with light", materializes this. Flesh overpowers word. The body thus animated, answers back.

The poses were carefully chosen with reference to key art historical sources and to comment upon the texts projected upon them. For example, in the image using the quote from Butler (1990) on the performativity of gender, the pose is that of the *Venus pudica*,[17] covering the pubis with the hands, performing the Classical pose of femininity, with the excessive, transgressive body of middle age. The *Venus pudica* pose is challenged in the image using the quote from Freud (1913). The image is taken from a low angle, which gives a sense of power to the figure, defying the quote. The hand does not cover, but rather, in the form of a fist, resists and contests any "loss of genital function".[18] We chose to use black and white prints for this series to formally echo the idea of the authority of the printed word, which we subverted.

I have returned recently to this question of ageing, working with Verity Welstead, who although twenty years younger than me, is also feeling and confronting the impacts of what it means to be viewed as ageing now. We shared our stories and our feelings about how it was to be seen as older women in supportive and empathetic exchanges, in which we could each gain understanding of each other's specific circumstances. The age gap between us and our diverse life circumstances produced insightful similarities and differences. We brainstormed ideas as to how to make these experiences visible and ways of confronting any fears or trepidation. Fundamentally, the support we gave one another was key to being willing to explore and play with the projections of others. Trips to department stores (Selfridges and Debenhams) on Oxford Street to be "made up" and "styled" provoked some dissonance. Whilst the women who assisted us were polite enough, though they were clearly a bit phased, as indeed were we by their interpretations of what would "suit you". We also searched the internet for advice for 'how

17. Nanette Salomon, 'Uncovering Art History's "Hidden Agendas and Pedigrees"', *Generations and Geographies in the Visual Arts*, ed. Griselda Pollock (London and New York: Routledge 1996), pp. 69–88.

18. Freud, *The Disposition to Obsessional Neurosis*, pp. 323–324.

19. Viktor Shklovsky and Alexandra Berlina, ed., *Viktor Shklovsky: A Reader*, trans. by Alexandra Berlina (London and New York: Bloomsbury, 2017).

to dress as older women' and riffed on the recommendations.

Verity and I decided to search for beige or taupe clothes, that all too ubiquitous supposedly safe older women's colour choice, ironically cited as 'this year's colour' by the fashion press. I knew full well already that beige drains any colour from my face. I have the fair complexion and freckles that go with having had red hair. If my aim was to look ill or tired, a camel coat always sufficed. Trips to charity shops, hunts through our wardrobes and short-term purchases provided us both with an array of beige clothes. Having admired each other's finds when we met for our photography session, we also took the time to connect and face our fears about making ourselves intentionally ugly and unappealing, whatever that might mean, and as a means to accept how we are. We took it in turns in front of the camera and bounced ideas from one another. Wrinkled tights, awkward stances, hiding within and behind beige, curling up on the floor and struggling to get up, or even allowing myself to look as if I was out for the day from a care home, we were playing with appearances and allowing ourselves to make the worst of it. My mother's woollen vest, in soft beige offered us a unifying image pairing, an honesty which we both embraced for *Studies in beige*.

We then chose to examine our bodies for those infamous "signs of ageing" that advertisers and the media focus upon: wrinkles on our hands and faces, widening waistlines and sagging bellies. Using a macro lens and video, we made these strange through extreme close-up, cropping, and active performances, for example using our bellies as drums. How mysteriously could we show our bodies so that the viewer would be uncertain as to what they were looking at? These acts of defamiliarization, or "making strange" link to the work of the Russian formalists:

> The purpose of art is to impart the sensation of things as they are perceived and not as they are known. The technique of art is to make objects "unfamiliar", to make forms difficult to increase the difficulty and length of perception because the process of perception is an aesthetic end in itself and must be prolonged.[19]

This is a very useful strategy, especially when dealing with subjects that can be too often simplified or rendered as "cliched", and indeed for women surveying their bodies too often loaded with feelings of disgust and disaffection learnt from dominant media or the internet's replication of idealized (unobtainable) perfection and advertising. Defamiliarization offered a way for us to move, albeit slowly and with some apprehension towards playing with our representations of ourselves. Interestingly when we reviewed the images and videos we had made some weeks later, we could not immediately identify exactly where on our bodies some of the images were from, or whose body was whose. Whilst initially we did want these images to be strange, even repellent and shocking, the more important aspect was to show just how ordinary, commonplace and ubiquitous real lived-in flesh is.

We also played with instructions from the internet on 'how to make a good selfie'. We applied "face time" software to our portraits, which is used by celebrities to "enhance" their looks, distorting and adding emphasis for a supposedly desired effect, such as enlarging the eyes or filling the lips. The result is bizarre and on an older face ends up making visible just how grotesque such enhancements are. We used the tricks of analogue portrait photographers, Vaseline on the lens, and various diffusing and masking techniques to dissolve our portrait images to a ghostly absent presence. We printed these photographs in pairs on silk, as a comment upon the invisibility of older women. What if we valued wrinkles? What if we searched each morning for new wrinkles as a sign of beauty? A goal reached? A wondrous thing? As opposed to turning away in disgust, horror, disbelief, even despair? Can our images begin to reveal this shift to acceptance?

Looking back now on all the work I had done on ageing, either with collaborators, primarily Kay Goodridge, Seija Ulkuniemi and Verity Welstead or in running workshops with older women on these issues,[20] I find that my attitudes have changed somewhat. The need to speak out and be seen as older women and to command respect is still vital. I am more accepting of who I am, the age I now occupy and those hard acts of letting go. If gravity wins, as indeed it must, when will older women be honoured for

20. Rosy Martin, 'Look at Me! Representing Self: Representing Ageing: Older Women Represent Their Own Narratives of Ageing, Using Re-enactment Phototherapeutic Techniques', *Gender Issues in International Arts Therapies Research*, ed. Susan Hogan (London and New York: Routledge, 2019).

their gravitas? Must we all wait till we are dead, or in our eighties or nineties to be recognized for our contributions to art practices? A sudden flurry of exhibitions by very old or dead women artists hardly suffices to compensate for generations of neglect. Is it always better late than never?

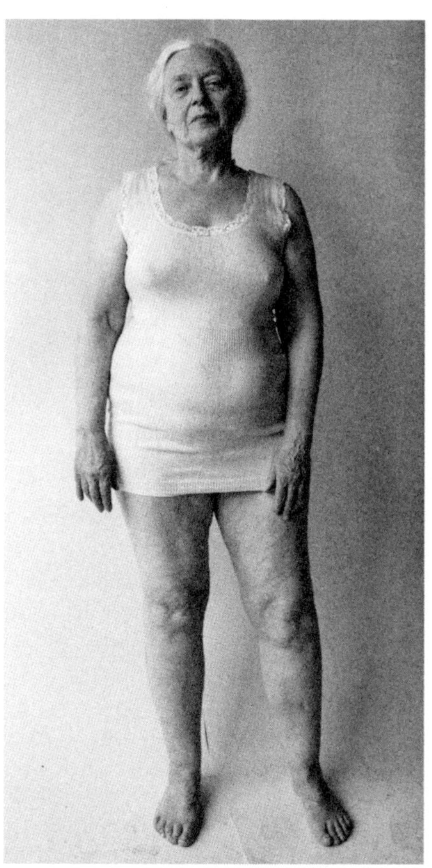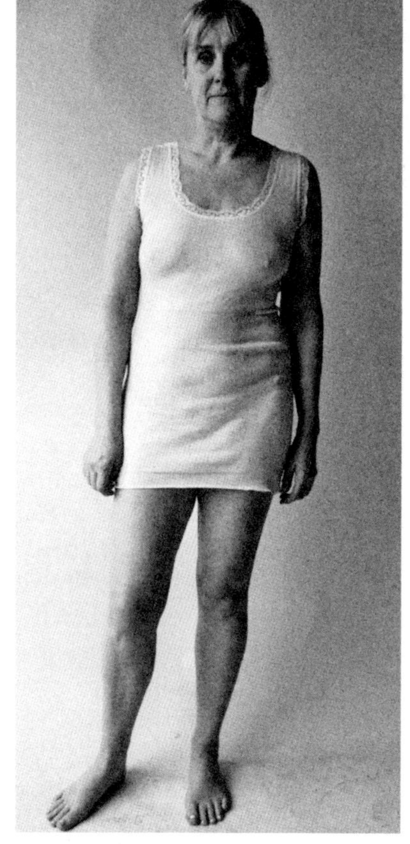

Rosy Martin and Verity Welstead, *Studies in beige*, 2018, colour C-type print, 100 x 100 cm

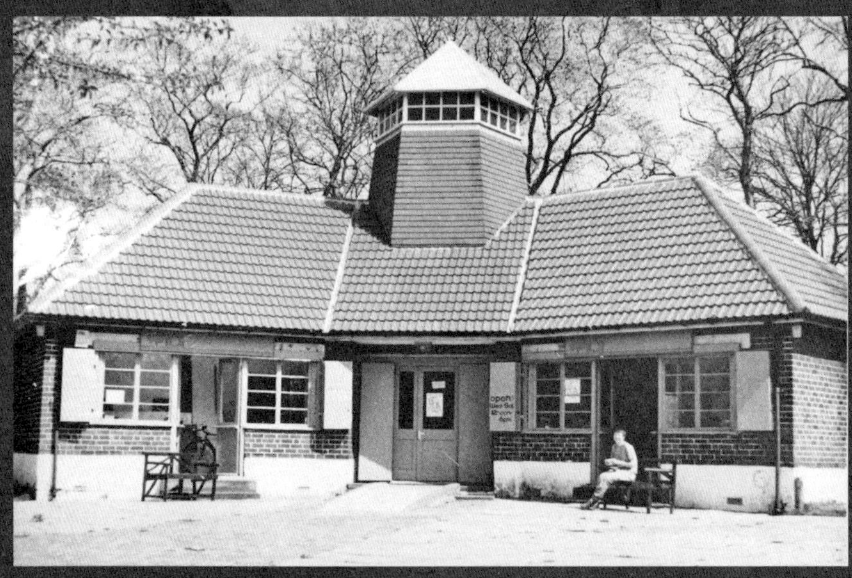

The Pavilion Women's Photography Centre, Leeds, date unknown.
Courtesy of Pavilion/Feminist Archive North

FEMINIST*ING* PHOTOGRAPHY The Pavilion Women's Photography Centre— Looking Back to Act Forwards

Gill Park

1. Andrea Fisher, *Let Us Now Praise Famous Women: Women Photographers for the US Government 1935 to 1944* (London: Pandora, 1987), p. 3.

2. Griselda Pollock, 'Action, Activism and Art and/as Thought: A Dialogue with the Artworking of Sonia Khurana and Sutapa Biswas and the Political Theory of Hannah Arendt', *e-flux* 92 (June 2018), www.e-flux. com/journal/92/204726/ action-activism-and-art-and-as- thought-a-dialogue-with-the- artworking-of-sonia-khurana- and-sutapa-biswas-and-the- political-theory-of-hannah-arendt/ (accessed 1 May 2019).

'Her history is, then, no longer the disclosure of a lost and distant past; it is a relation, a writing and thus, a production of our present.'[1] Andrea Fisher's words about how history produces a relation to the present can productively be juxtaposed with Griselda Pollock's thoughts on activism and art in 2018 where she discusses how we should consider the very different politics facing artists in the 1970s who were active within feminism:

> In the 1970s, art did not expect feminism. At the very same time, the emerging Women's Liberation Movement, as we knew ourselves at that moment of intense social and political activism, did not place art high on its list of priorities. At best artists might be useful for making posters and other agit-prop materials. At worst, art was a bourgeois distraction irrelevant to the struggles in which women were involved for equal pay, personal safety, sexual self-determination, and control over their own fertility and bodies in conditions of neo-colonial and intensifying class conflict and aggravated racism.[2]

Pollock argues that while art and feminism have been mutually transformative, we are still confined to conventional art historical categories and methods. For instance, she asks, how often is "feminist" used as an adjective to describe a style, an iconography, an authorial intention, missing the transformation demanded of such art-historical concepts by the force of feminism as intervention and effect?[3] Likewise, in the recent BBC documentary *Rebel Women: The Great Art Fightback* (2018), artist Mary Kelly notes that there has been a tendency to create a divide between feminist theory on the one hand and feminist politics on the other. Mary Kelly's own artwork is indeed an example of the way in which feminist theory, art practice and politics has converged. Her famous scripto-visual work *Post-Partum Document* (1973) was informed by Kelly's direct observations of the psychic dimension of women's labour through collaborations with women factory workers and nightcleaners, her work for the Artist's Union, and her own experiences of motherhood, as much as her deep investigations into language, representation and conceptual art strategies.

My recent research has focused on the history of one feminist space that was part of the feminist transformation in art during the so-called "second wave" of the Women's Liberation Movement, through which theoretical work on representation, art-making and feminist politics converged. This space is The Pavilion Women's Photography Centre (The Pavilion), which opened in Leeds as a feminist photography project (1983–1993), and continues under the name "Pavilion" as a contemporary arts commissioning organization. My role as director of Pavilion (2012–2017) was the motivation for my academic research into The Pavilion's little-known feminist history. In reconstructing this under-recognized political-aesthetic experiment, I have sought to understand the way in which the disruption of the photographic image was one manifestation of feminist politics in the 1980s. Furthermore, in looking back at this one small, precarious project in Leeds, I am seeking to "act forward", locating strategies of political exhibition-making in the present-day. In doing so I am drawing on Mieke Bal's concept of a "preposterous history", in which she argues that, 'an engagement of contemporary culture with the past

3. Ibid.

4. Mieke Bal, *Quoting Carravagio: Contemporary Art, Preposterous History* (London and Chicago: University of Chicago Press, 1999), p. 1.

5. Walter Benjamin, 'Theses on the Philosophy of History', in *Illuminations*, ed. Hannah Arendt (London: Fontana/Collins, 1977), p. 254.

… has important implications for the ways we conceive of both history and culture in the present'.[4] Bal's articulation of the past as being actively reworked for the present in turn draws on the writings of Walter Benjamin who conceptualized *Jetztzeit* ('a past charged by the time of the now') by which he floated the idea that the past only becomes intelligible later when it produced a present that can belatedly recognize the significance of the past.[5]

The Pavilion was founded in May 1983 by three graduates from the Department of Fine Art at the University of Leeds—Dinah Clark, Shirley Moreno and Caroline Taylor. It emerged against the backdrop of the UK miners' strike, deindustrialization, race riots, Thatcher's dismantling of the welfare state and the violent murders of women in Leeds by Peter Sutcliffe, the "Yorkshire Ripper". Established in a renovated park pavilion in the Woodhouse Moor area of the city, close to the University of Leeds, its founders sought to make an intervention into the social and political sphere and the lived experiences of women in its immediate

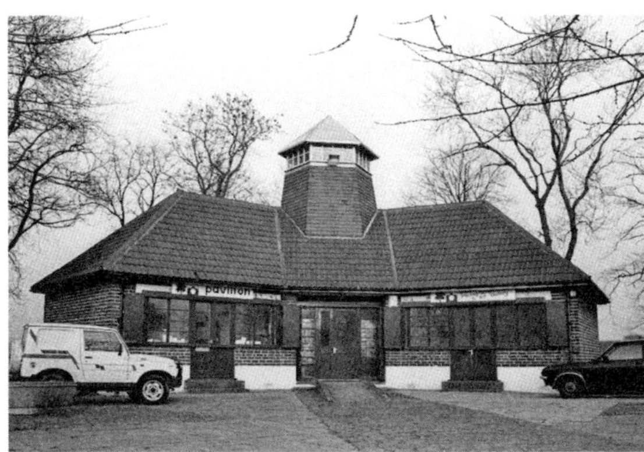

Exterior view of The Pavilion, date unknown.
Courtesy of Pavilion/Feminist Archive North

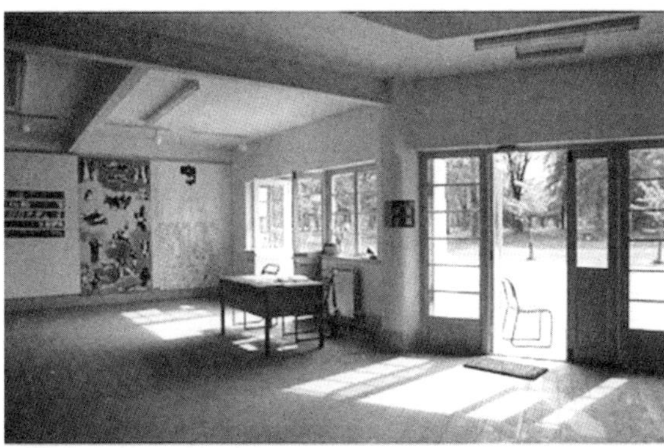

Interior view of The Pavilion, date unknown.
Courtesy of Pavilion/Feminist Archive North

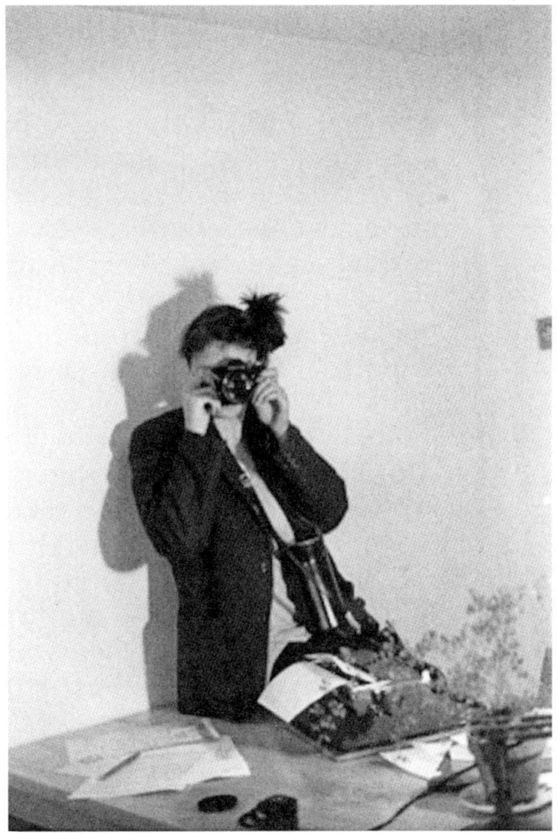

Caroline Taylor (Pavilion founder), date unknown.
Courtesy of Pavilion/Feminist Archive North

local community. The outcome was a decade-long radical programme of photographic exhibitions that centred on women's experiences while investigating urgent theoretical questions about art and our social relations. The organization taught working women to make photographs when the technology and resources for making images was mostly unavailable to them. It also exhibited work by leading figures in the critical debates about the image and 'the politics of representation' in an era dominated by media imagery of women. It sought to examine both the photographic image and technology in relation to areas of women's lives ignored in the media image world. Finally, it engaged with issues of race and class as they intersected with gender. In her chapter 'The light writing on the wall: the Leeds Pavilion Project', published in 1986, one of The Pavilion's founders Shirley Moreno described the relationship between art and activism as it was conceptualized at The Pavilion:

> Leeds is historically an area of women's activities; the female labor force has been of major significance to local industry and has therefore played a crucial role in the development of the city. This has assisted the growth of a strong local women's movement. The Peter Sutcliffe murders and the resultant militant action against sexist imagery has encouraged debate and concern about the effect pictures have on women's lives. There is a large women's arts movement, with nowhere to exhibit and also almost nothing significant to see, as the facilities for the visual arts in Leeds are appalling. All these factors made Leeds the perfect place for the [Pavilion Women's Photography] Centre.[6]

The Pavilion's initial project lasted ten years, but the name survived through various forms from its original function as exhibition centre and darkroom to its role as contemporary arts commissioning agency. I argue that The Pavilion became a significant space during its operating years because it made visible photographic practices that were equally concerned with artistic experimentalism, theory and activism, bringing these different poles of activity into relation with one another. I name this convergence of art and politics

6. Shirley Moreno, 'The Light Writing on the Wall: The Leeds Pavilion Project', in *Photographic Practices: Towards a Different Image*, eds. Stevie Bezencenet and Philip Corrigan (London: Comedia, 1986), p. 115.

during the 1980s: "feminist*ing* photography". "Feministing photography" is a means to describe a particular artistic focus on a critical analysis of, and activism within, the realm of representation. Charged with the politics of the women's movement, artists showing at The Pavilion did not use photography simply as a fine art medium but as a site of critical inquiry, in order to address complex questions of sexual difference and the entanglements of gender, class and race. Artists such as Maud Sulter, Marie Yates, Ingrid Pollard, Brenda Agard, Chila Kumari Burman, Sirkka-Liisa Konttinnen, Jo Spence and Rosy Martin who all showed at The Pavilion during its founding decade were asking deep questions about the relay between social experiences and the image. They addressed women as image, while seeking to re-image women in a wider range of lived experiences, identities and conditions. This was informed by feminist theory, notably theories of ideology, and psychoanalytical theories of the unconscious, subjectivity and sexual difference. Of equal importance was The Pavilion's desire

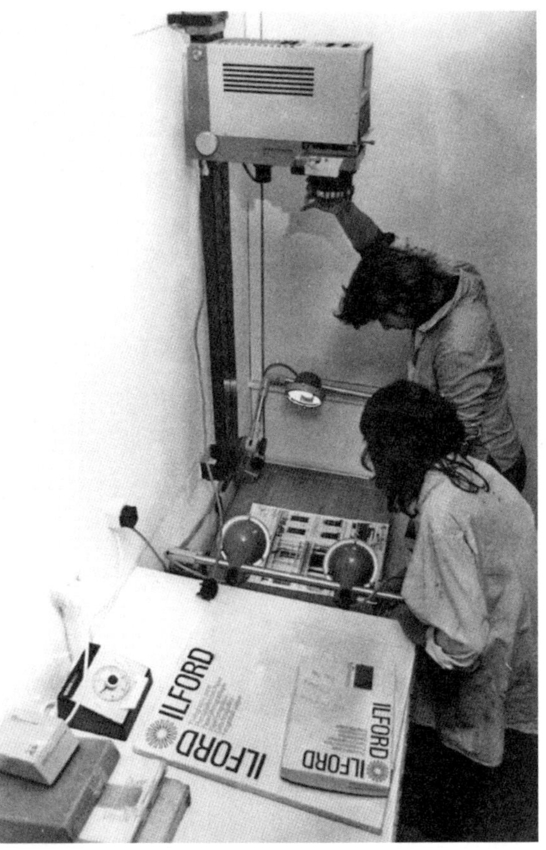

The Pavilion darkroom, date unknown.
Courtesy of Pavilion/Feminist Archive North

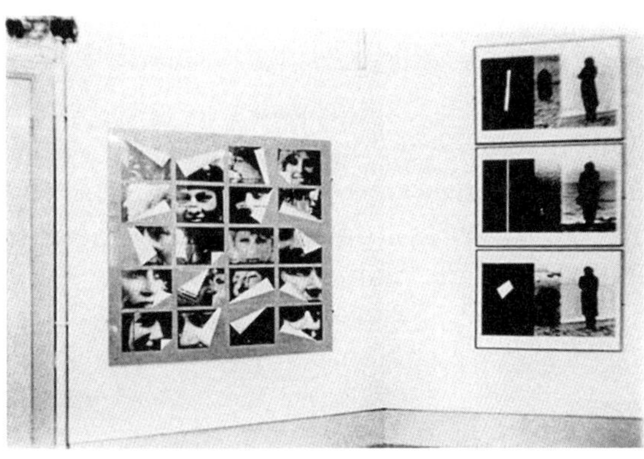

Marie Yates and Yve Lomax, *The Image in Trouble*, 1984, installation view.
Courtesy of Marie Yates

to enable opportunities for local women who were neither artists nor academics, but for whom accessing the means of photographic production became an important tool in their self-determination. Thus, a darkroom was as important to its work as the exhibition space.

The work of The Pavilion is one example of a feminist art project that saw the convergence of debates about feminism, representation and photography, which were in turn informed by a generation of politicized artists who came together in the late 1970s and early 1980s. The relationship between art and activism during this moment is not, however, self-evident. Much of the recent discourse on feminist histories has focused on the way in which different generations of feminists superseded—or else regressed from—the 1970s as feminism's foundation. In her analysis of feminist journal articles, Clare Hemmings has identified three narratives in feminist discourses: "progress", "loss" or "return".[7] In her reading of progress, the 1970s are presented as a period of feminist activism while the 1980s are seen as a decade of theoreticism and "identity politics", both of which are often seen to have been "overcome" in the 1990s. For some the shift into more theoretically rich feminist discussions represents a loss of activism, for others it signals progress from naïve activism to deeper analysis of structures. The 1990s narrative of return to the 1970s or a mourning of its lost condition then involves an attempt to reconcile what has been presented as opposing modes of feminism.

In part, these narratives have been conditioned by the introduction of "feminist theory" into academia as a distinct intellectual discourse. The tendency has thus been for feminist histories to be misread as fitting into either "theoretical" or "activist" feminism. The Pavilion by contrast represents one instance in which such oppositions were not enacted, but rather negotiated differently through a specific framework at the intersection of art education, feminism and exhibition practice, and mediated by cultural practices on photography. The Pavilion is a significant case study precisely because it defies such over-simplified generational narratives, because it was a project that was committed, during the 1980s, to both an intense engagement with certain theoretical resources—informed by its relationship to the educational space at the University of Leeds, where Griselda Pollock was

7. Clare Hemmings, *Why Stories Matter? The Political Grammar of Feminist Theory* (Durham and London: Duke University Press, 2011).

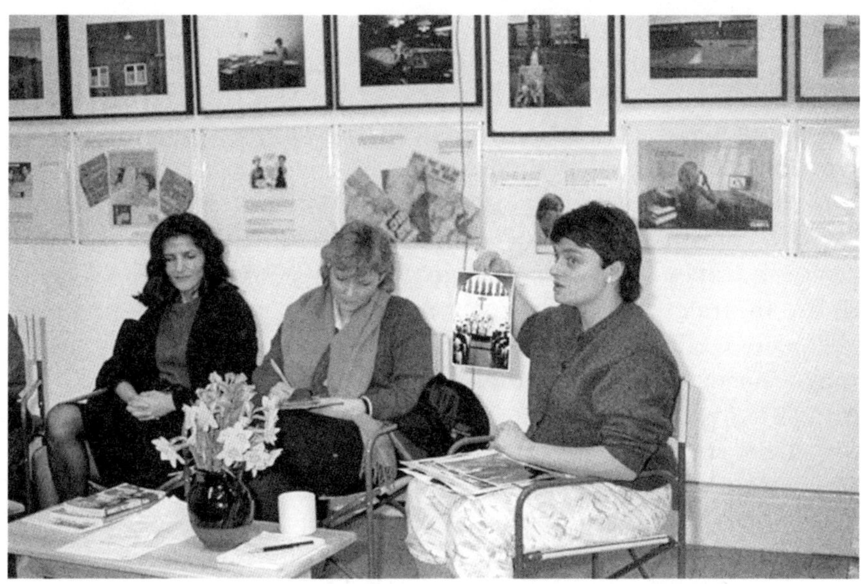

Public talk at The Pavilion, from left to right: Mitra Tabrizian, Griselda Pollock and Joanne O'Brien, date unknown. Courtesy of Pavilion/Feminist Archive North

8. Sarah James, 'The Truth About Photography', *Art Monthly* 292 (December 2005–January 2006), www.artmonthly.co.uk/magazine/site/article/the-truth-about-photography-by-sarah-james-dec-jan-2005-06 (accessed 2 May 2019).

making her feminist interventions into art and history— and to activating social change among the women from the immediate communities around its site, who both used The Pavilion's open darkroom and visited its exhibitions. For the women involved in The Pavilion, photography was not simply a fine art form but was both a process to which women needed access to represent themselves and a key site of feminist interrogation of ideology, representation, subjectivity and sexual difference. As Sarah James has argued, in a 2019 article for *Art Monthly*, following Steve Edwards' critique, the dominance of postmodern photographic theories today have 'allowed for no reading of it outside of representation, and therefore allowed for no reality or meaning' to question its construction institutionally or in the art market.[8] Instead, as a counter-strategy, we need to continue to consider the way in which representations have real effects, while also considering the creative strategies to make visible unseen, unspeakable experiences, emphasizing agency, meaning-making and history.

I want to emphasize here that my historical investigations of The Pavilion's early activity have been propelled by my experiences of working within the contemporary art field. Throughout my research I have asked: What could I discover about the nature of feminist struggle and strategies of resistance both past and present from looking closely at a specific artistic, political intervention in the 1980s? The current-day *Pavilion* is a very different organization from the one that was founded in 1983. In the 1990s, it retracted its explicit feminist focus and it moved out of the original park pavilion. Over the years its priorities have adapted to shifts in the financial and political landscape. Its modes of practice are necessarily different to what they once were. The art market now dominates the possibilities for artists to make and show work and most of the artists Pavilion works with are circulating in a highly marketized international circuit of biennials and blockbuster exhibitions. Photography has been absorbed into the mainstream categories of art in Britain and art, since the 1990s, has taken a multiplicity of forms that had yet to be imagined in the 1980s. The means of production and of distribution have shifted enormously, not least through the development of digital technology. Indeed, Pavilion's main programme now focuses on the commissioning of artist video and audio work, which has emerged as arguably the primary medium of artwork of a critical, political nature. The gap between then and now must be acknowledged. The world has changed and art has changed with it. Yet while there are differences there are also continuities and the current artistic moment is marked by a desire by contemporary curators to produce conversations with feminist art of the 1970s and 1980s.

One continuity between then and now has centred on the struggle for the financing of political-aesthetic experiments. My experience of programming contemporary art has given me direct experience of the struggle to negotiate with public funding bodies particularly in the English regions. In this struggle there is nothing new. In March 1984, less than a year after The Pavilion had opened its doors, the Yorkshire Arts Association—then the regional branch of the Arts Council of Great Britain—withdrew its offer of regular funding to the organization. In April 1984, Arts Council officer Simon Roodhouse wrote a report on a visit to The Pavilion. The report stated that this was:

9. Barry Lane, unpublished internal memo, 'YAA regional visits', 11–13 April 1984, ACGB/33/1.

A rather dispiriting visit. Yorkshire Arts Association had withdrawn program support because of a number of issues—shortage of funds, ineffective management, lack of local authority support and growing exclusiveness of events (women only). Both the gallery and darkroom are now functioning and run by voluntary effort, but both seem to lack direction and energy.[9]

Between 1983 and 1984, various reports make repeated reference to the Pavilion's so-called "exclusiveness", its lack of professionalism, or its lack of direction and vision. Conversely, however I have identified The Pavilion as an organization that was radically breaking down the boundaries between artist and audience and acting as a platform for exciting aesthetic innovations, both driven by a desire for social change. Yet its *inclusivity*, its commitment to social change and its presentation of groundbreaking visual practices were illegible to the major public funding bodies during the 1980s. In 2011, this historic hostility found its parallel when the current-day Pavilion programmed two screenings of work by Hito Steyerl, whose extraordinary films—which address the distribution of images as part of global capitalism—have gained international attention in many biennials and been described as 'an art for our times'. An Arts Council England [ACE] assessor attended the screenings at Pavilion and in her report, complained that Steyerl's work was "too long" and "esoteric". That same year, Pavilion was removed from ACE's portfolio of regular funding. The staff team felt strongly that this was a censorship of critical, experimental yet socially engaged work itself linked to an increasing condescension by the funders towards arts audiences and art spaces in the English regions. How could the current-day Pavilion continue to pursue the relationship between politics and aesthetics in relation to its current constituencies? How can art escape from the confines of an art-world that continually reduces it to commodity or spectacle?

Potentially making space for close and careful research into historic projects that have been constantly demeaned or have disappeared is in itself a form of feminist activism, where this can provide the evidence that feminist

spaces point to new relationships between art and politics.
The mutual transformations of politics and aesthetics
that must be credited to feminism have yet to be fully
acknowledged in the institutions that are now, belatedly,
collecting and exhibiting that work. My own investigations
into feminism and photography add to the growing demand
to recognize the politics of feminist works, which does not
reduce artwork to an aesthetic style nor make "feminist" a
signifier of politics or politics as extraneous to art, but rather
shows that "feministing" was a complex operation producing
meaning and as much about the media, the technology and
the political message.

One formative moment in my own current thinking
about the relationship of art to feminism in the current
moment—and in tracing parallels between then and
now—was when I encountered the group Voice of Domestic
Workers (formerly known as Justice for Domestic Workers)
(see chapter by Marissa Begonia and Amy Charlesworth).
This group of women migrant domestic workers have
regularly collaborated with arts organizations because of the
particular pertinence of the image to their struggle, which
has to do with their demand to make visible their work as
work, in a society that both undervalues and yet relies upon
this kind of socially reproductive labour.

In 2014, my own contribution to their work was
to raise a small amount of funding in order to commission

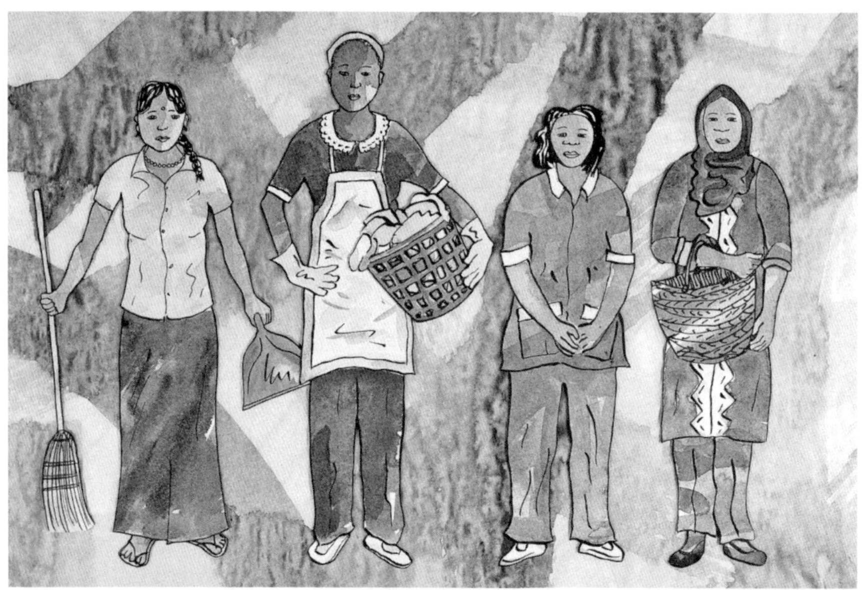

Leeds Animation Workshop & Justice for Domestic Workers Leeds, *They Call Us Maids: The Domestic Workers' Story,*
2015, video still. Courtesy of Leeds Animation Workshop/Pavilion

the feminist film collective Leeds Animation Workshop to produce a short animation film made in collaboration with domestic workers in Leeds, that would tell the story of the journey taken by thousands of women from the Philippines to the Arab Gulf States, and then to Britain to work in private homes. The final short film, scripted by Terry Wragg from the accounts of domestic workers, used animations, hand-painted by artist Jo Dunn, to narrate the experiences of women who had been neglected, sexually abused, enslaved and subjected to violence at the hands of their employers. The film became a tool to support the campaigns of the wider Domestic Workers group, who wanted to counter the isolation and invisibility they faced working alone in private homes, while also making the political demand that their "work" is work. This example of artistic activism develops important socialist feminist questions about the nature of women's oppression. I reflected, for example, on the work of Jo Spence and the Hackney Flashers (both of whom had shown at The Pavilion) and whose work made visible the contributions women make to the relations of production and reproduction. I also reflected on the way in which the Black Women's Movement has revealed that, within the Anglo-American world, the labour of working-class women of colour has been integral to the on-going reproduction of Western capitalism. I began to see how the feminist questions raised in the 1980s—if recognized for the way in which they meaningfully addressed the entanglements of gender, class and race—are not confined to the past but absolutely pertinent to the ongoing feminist global struggle in the era of so-called multiculturalism.

At the same time, my research into The Pavilion also made me think more deeply about the nature of the image. I was interested in what the position of this specific group of women workers from the Global South had to do with the images of economic migrants, asylum seekers and refugees within the British media, and particularly since 2011 and the start of the Syrian Civil War. How could the present-day Pavilion, as a contemporary cultural practice, reflect on the nature of our relations under global capitalism through its public visual arts program? Meeting members of the Voice of Domestic Workers thus catalysed for Pavilion a new curatorial project, which looked at the question of representation in relation to the attitudes, perceptions and realities of migrant workers in the present-day, within Pavilion's local Leeds community. In 2016, in my capacity at Pavilion, I applied for funding from the Heritage Lottery Fund (HLF) to undertake a project that would 'make visible the contributions of the migrant workforce to industry in Leeds' whilst considering how Britain's economic dependence on migrant labour was accompanied by a lack of public representation of migrant subjects. I named this project *Interwoven Histories*.

A desire to discover the story of migrant workers in Leeds and why it was invisible, led me to identify traces of a history that was not self-evident within the public, institutional memory of industry in the city. It forced me to confront the problematic of the archive–so familiar to all of us seeking to "do" feminist history, aware that certain histories do not have archives waiting to be discovered, as Gayatri Spivak's work so brilliantly addresses.[10] The gap between archival representation and the historical socio-economic reality of Leeds was perfectly illustrated when I spoke to curators from the Leeds Industrial Museum based at the former Armley Mills. The museum's own collection of historical material, derived from its history as a textiles mill, contains documentary evidence of a white working-class labour force, but no material relating to migrant labour even while newspaper evidence shows that Leeds actively sought migrant workers in the post-war years.

How then, did feminist knowledge, drawn from my own research into The Pavilion's history, inform my approach to this historical curatorial project? One way was in understanding the value of lived experiences, or to draw on Stuart Hall's term, "the Living Archive". As part of this contemporary curatorial project, we (Pavilion's team) spoke with first-generation migrants about their experiences of arriving in Leeds from Jamaica, St Kitts & Nevis, India and Pakistan. By listening to first-hand experiences, we began to build up a picture of a post-war Leeds that was dependent on its migrant workforce but that was also entangled with a deep-rooted racism. For example, one retired woman recounted that, having arrived in Leeds from the Caribbean, and having made a job application by telephone, she was invited to interview. On arriving at the office, however, her

10. Gayatri Chakravorty Spivak, 'The Rani of Sirmur: An Essay in Reading Archives', *History and Theory* 24 (1985), pp. 247–272.

POLITICS OF REPRESENTATION

 Feminist Art Activisms and Artivisms

11. Derrick Boothroyd, 'Many Colored Workers Are Over-Sensitive', *The Yorkshire Post and Leeds Mercury*, 10 December 1955, p. 5.

12. Stuart Hall, 'Assembling the 1980s: The Deluge—and After', *Shades of Black: Assembling Black Arts in 1980s Britain*, eds., David A. Bailey, Ian Baucom and Sonia Boyce (Durham: Duke University Press, 2005), p. 17.

prospective employer, surprised by the colour of her skin, subsequently informed her that a job was no longer available. This experience was corroborated by representations from the time. For example, we found a newspaper article, published in 1955 in *The Yorkshire Post and Leeds Mercury*, which ran the headline 'Many coloured workers are over-sensitive'.[11] This headline was symptomatic of this particular newspaper's transformation of migrant labour into a "social problem". Thus, the project uncovered racism in testimonies of lived experience, but also at the level of representation in the media. We were aware that we were not simply going to "discover" a documentary archive offering evidence of migrant workers *at work*, but we could see that the complex picture of migration was being produced in the *convergence* of different historical resources: documentary photography, archival film footage, works of art, creative writing, workers' magazines, lived experiences, mainstream news reports and alternative community publications. In planning for the installation, and as we assembled the material on the walls of Pavilion's office, we could see that putting together different types of representations side by side allowed the contradictions of the 'migrant story in Leeds' to emerge without the need for lengthy wall-texts. This was interesting to me because of the currency of "montage" as a feminist practice. During the 1920s and 30s, "photo-montage" was deployed in Weimar Germany by artists such as Hannah Höch in order to make visible a critique of the rising fascist ideology. Feminist artists such as Jo Spence in the 1970s and Maud Sulter in the 1980s then remobilized this strategy in order to denaturalize the racist, sexist representations that idealized women as wives/mothers or sexual objects. As Stuart Hall argues in his paper 'Assembling the 1980s', moving away from the documentary photograph to photo-montage 'better approximates the complexity of real relations it seeks to explore and contest'.[12]

The final exhibition produced as the culmination of the *Interwoven Histories* project (for which Pavilion's Will Rose and Kerstin Doble must be credited) was a configuration of panels that brought together the divergent material gathered through the research project in an installation at the Leeds Industrial Museum. For example, the aforementioned article from *The Yorkshire Post & Leeds*

Mercury was positioned in conjunction with a reproduction of a *Chapeltown News* article that named the institutional racism of the Leeds police force. Added to the documentary evidence of racism and resistance were pieces of poetry, reproductions of artworks, and documentation of the Leeds carnival, which together evidenced the creative, aesthetic contributions brought to the city by its migrant populations. While few of the selected images within the exhibition documented a migrant worker at work, the exhibition overcame this "problem" of invisibility of their contribution to the culture of the city. It presented positive images of migration, while also denaturalizing the discourse that presents the figure of the migrant as either victim or problem. In staging this recent project, a theoretical understanding of the archive's opacity, and of the way in which the invisibility of migrant representations serves the interests of the political *status quo*, produced a curatorial aesthetic strategy that reveals the ongoing productive potential of the politics-aesthetics relation that ultimately draws on the politico-aesthetic innovations of the feminist art movement in the 1980s.

In a recent essay entitled 'Insights from Italy: Pleasure, Plurality and Shaping the Present', Jo Anna Isaak notes that 'there has been a radical rejection of the theoretical 1980s. Work done at that time by avowedly feminist artists—work drawing upon theoretical writings—is now often rejected as didactic, illustrative, intellectually elitist or arcane'.[13] In returning to The Pavilion, however, I did not find an organization that was 'intellectually elitist or arcane'. While theory has continued to develop new concepts, the legacy of my research into The Pavilion is a continued desire to disavow the division between politics and aesthetics that persists in the contemporary art-world. Instead, re-engagement with The Pavilion's feminist priorities has offered me a model for creative resistance in the present day. My research into The Pavilion motivated me to develop new work on the lived experiences of migrant women living in Leeds. It was resourced by understanding photography as a language that is productive of meaning, which necessitates political analysis. Finally, it remobilized specific visual strategies, informed by an archive of "feministing photography" that found creative ways to articulate the complexity of our social relations today.

13. Jo Anna Isaak, 'Insights from Italy: Pleasure, Plurality and Shaping the Present', *Politics in a Glass Case: Feminism, Exhibitions Cultures and Curatorial Transgressions*, eds. Angela Dimitrakaki and Lara Perry (Liverpool: Liverpool University Press, 2014), p. 40. See also Jo Anna Isaak *Feminism and Contemporary Art* (London: Routledge, 1996).

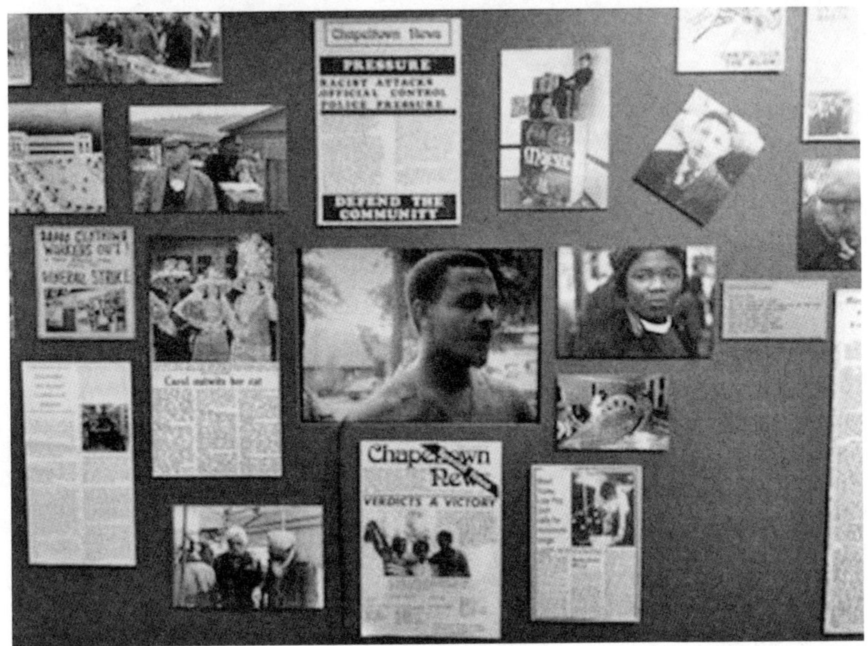

Interwoven Histories, 2017, exhibition view. Courtesy of Pavilion

The concept—"feministing photography"—has significance for the writing of feminist art and curatorial histories. Artistic practices were, and continue to be, addressed by The Pavilion through attention to the high-level critical debates about the image, through experimental artistic practices and through a commitment to social and political change. The concept of "feministing photography" underpins the significance of The Pavilion Women's Photography Centre as a radical cultural practice that must be read as part of the wider history of a politicized artistic culture in Britain that has yet to be fully assessed. It has revealed photography as a primary instrument of critical art practice at a particular historical and political moment. It has also expanded on an understanding of the relation of feminist theory and politics to the history of contemporary art practice. In this example of the contemporary application of "feministing photography"—it became a route to show the necessary relationship between theoretical work, art practice and political struggle in the past in relation to the challenges facing cultural practices in the present.

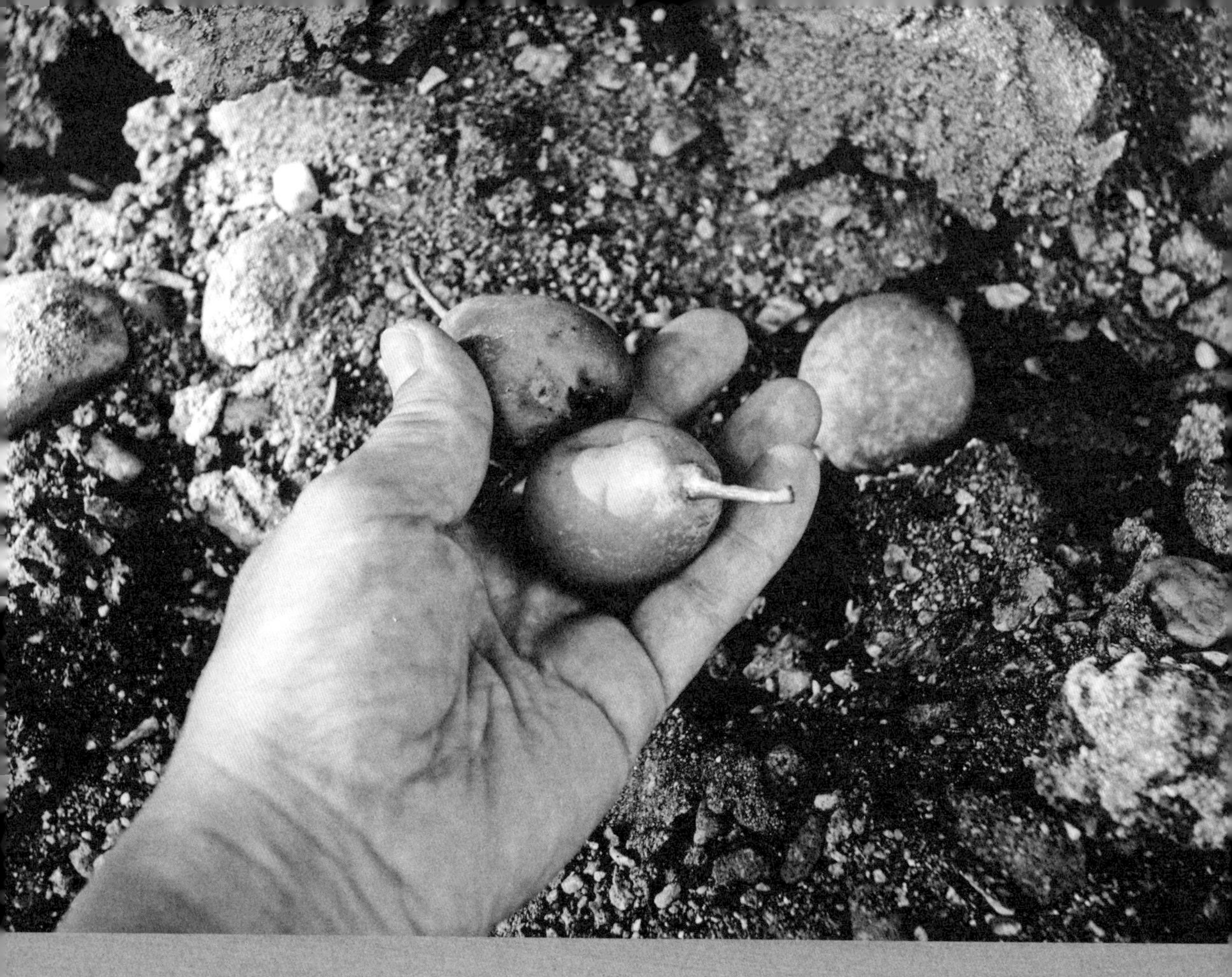

Zdena Kolečková, *Made in Ghetto*, 2012, photography, part of the installation

STRANGE BODIES, STRANGE NATURE
Corporeal and Environmental Artivisms of Lenka Klodová and Zdena Kolečková

Martina Pachmanová

Just a few months before the 1989 Velvet Revolution in former Czechoslovakia, a group of women who later called themselves Prague Mothers strolled through the capital city with their children of various ages, some of them still in prams, with banners asking the communist apparatchiks to share the information about the worsening environmental situation and the growing air pollution that affected not only the capital city but also—and most importantly—regions with mining and chemistry industry in the north of the country. Another purpose of this happening was to collect signatures of random passers-by on a petition and to deliver it to the participants of the international meeting of ministers of the environment that was organized in Prague at that time. In the same year, another group of women—this time from the dissident circles—manifested on the central square in Prague their frustration about the lack of sanitary napkins available to purchase with a public exposure of basic women's hygienic needs related to the menstruating body. This symbolism about the failure of the supply chain and the needs of women unmasked the hypocrisy of the collapsing regime more than many other political protests, as this was the first time during the communist era when solely women had demonstrated against the regime and on topics that were largely irrelevant to their male contemporaries.

Recollecting how these two often-marginalized events in 1989 nevertheless contributed to the demolition of the totalitarian system, I would like to discuss the work of Lenka Klodová and Zdena Kolečková who both freely follow this legacy of late-Socialist women's engagement in body politics and environmental issues. Both artists were born in 1969, the first year of the twenty-year-long Soviet occupation of Czechoslovakia, and they grew up during the so called "normalization",[1] the period characteristic of paralysis of the public space and persecution of any politically oriented civic activities. They both entered the Czech art scene after the collapse of communism in East Europe and in their work, they have been confronting patriarchal attitudes and traditional gender-based hierarchy of dualisms (culture/nature, mind/body etc.), while investigating nature and re-conceptualizing biology. Although not explicitly activist, their projects treat nature, body and motherhood not in terms of naturalism or fixed essence but as a site of social and political inscription and—most importantly—production.

Lenka Klodová records the beginnings of her art career in the following way:

> I have had a family of three children since the beginning of my studies at art school; this was determining for my life and work. This existential situation, the eternal stress of time and the persistent need to do many things at one, forced me—when looking for inspiration—to exploit myself alone and my own feelings and experiences. When everyone somehow fell asleep in the evening and I had free time for creating, I couldn't just turn all that inwards and engage with something such as abstract painting. I could only turn and move among ideas grounded in the life of a woman, a mother.[2]

Although motherhood has always been regarded as more of a barrier to creativity than its motor, and although linking art with motherhood might throw us into the trap of the alleged biological essence of our identities, Klodová has taken child care and maternity as a source of her art and

1. The term "normalization" refers to the period of Czechoslovak history that began with the firm seizure of power by politicians loyal to the Soviet Union and followed the invasion by Warsaw Pact troops in 1968. It lasted until 1989.

2. Lucie Jandová, 'O ženách, pornu a hornících: Rozhovor s Lenkou Klodovou' ['On Women, Pornography and Miners: Interview with Lenka Klodová'], Nový prostor, no. 116 (2002), p. 28.

3. Martina Pachmanová, 'Všednodenností za uměleckou metafyziku: Rozhovor s Lenkou Klodovou' ['Reaching Art Metaphysics through the Everyday: Interview with Lenka Klodová'], *Někdy v sukni: Umění 90. let* [*In Skirt, Sometimes: Art of the 1990s*], ed. Pavlína Morganová, exh. cat. Brno/Prague 2013, p. 102.

4. For the figure of the 'playful (laughing) mother' see Susan Rubin Suleiman, *Subversive Intent: Gender, Politics and the Avant-Garde* (Cambridge, MA: Harvard University Press, 1990).

intellectual rebellion that started already during her studies at the Academy of Arts, Architecture and Design in Prague. In 1996, she made her end of semester project as a living sculpture. *Golden Kids*, or *Goldies* (the Czech equivalent for addressing somebody we love as "Darling", "Ducky", or "Sugar") consisted of an installation in which her children were dressed in gold and strolled around, played, drunk, ate, drew during the performance… 'It was not only my despair and lack of time but also—and mainly—the need to cross over the traditional genres, forms and disciplines which in this case ended by a living action.'[3] Although Klodová did not pass the exam [and had to retake the semester or leave!] (significantly all the members of the jury were men), it was an important impulse for her further projects, often performances and public-art-based, that have confronted the stereotypical notions about female body, womanhood, maternity, sexuality, pornography and, as we shall see, also ecology.

Lenka Klodová employed the concept of a rebelling and playful mother[4] in many other projects in the late 1990s and 2000s. In her *Travestishow* (2001), she glued a tiny moustache on her face and dressed in a leather jacket, pink shirt, dandyish hat and Doc Martens, to challenge not only fashion gender codes but also the prevailing norms of nuclear family. In this public performance, s/he breastfed her newly born son in a shopping centre car park, exposing the tension between the extreme phallic posture of hard and

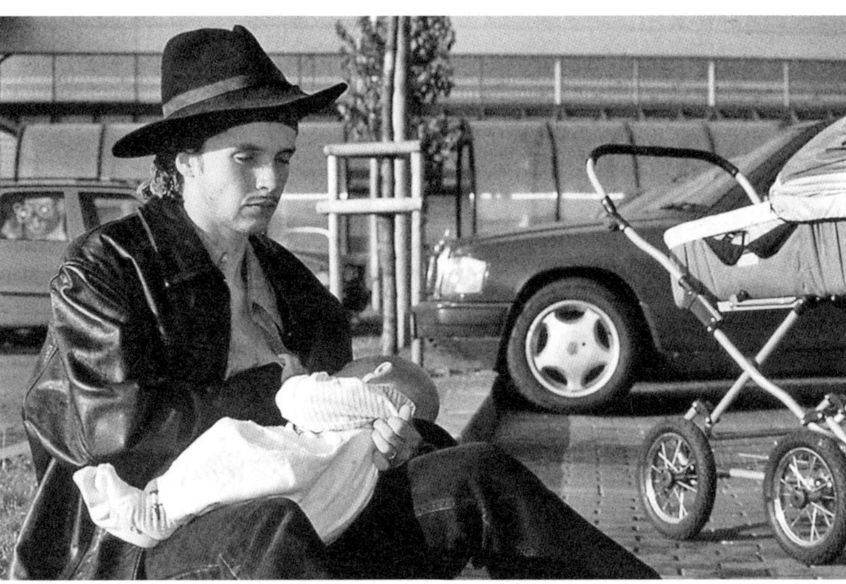

Lenka Klodová, *Travestishow*, 2001, performance

un-compromising masculinity with love, care, and tenderness toward the baby. Although she revealed the "true" manhood as a fiction, a garb, a disguise, as something that can be put on and off, she also opened the way to the radical concept of motherhood as a game with a subversive activist potential. Klodová approached the female body not only as a place of reproduction (procreating and childbearing) but also as a place of production (creativity and self-transformation). If the traditional psychoanalytical model of gender difference presupposes woman's masochism and passivity, and if it understands motherhood as the fulfilment of the internal natural woman's need to give birth and satisfy the needs of others, Klodová has upturned it. She has shown that the maternal body can become a source of playing for the woman/mother herself but mainly the motor of her social rebellion.

In 2003, she organized a performance *Are You Afraid of Maternity?* in which a woman, this time her friend, repeatedly exposed her pregnant belly on a forest roadside to the occasional tourists and cyclists, mocking the routine reality of men's public exposure of their genitals. Reactions were varied: surprise, fright, laughter, disgust, misunderstanding… Confronting the public with a physical (not photographed) evidence of pregnancy and playing the maternal version of male exhibitionism, Klodová—with a touch of humour—broke a taboo. The 'naked, protruding belly brings about a complete transformation of life in which thousands of worries accompany a life-long commitment' she wrote in her monograph published in 2006 and titled, symptomatically, *Pregnant Songs*.[5] Pregnancy is usually not talked about in public (our mothers used to wear wide dresses to hide their swelling bellies) no matter how praised

5. Lenka Klodová, *Pregnant Songs*, exh. cat. Prague: Divus, 2006.

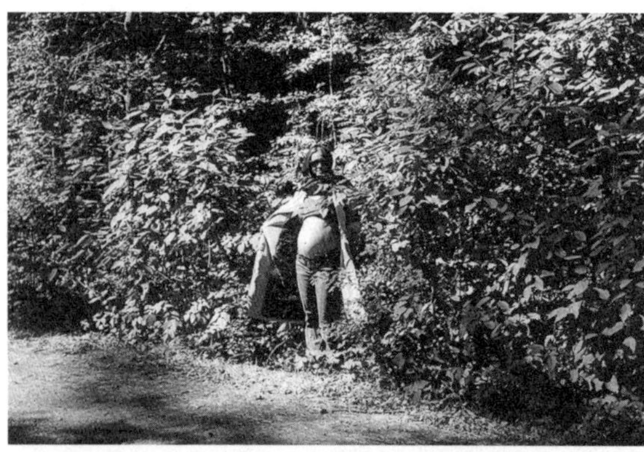

Lenka Klodová, *Are You Afraid of Maternity?*, 2003, performance.
Courtesy of artist

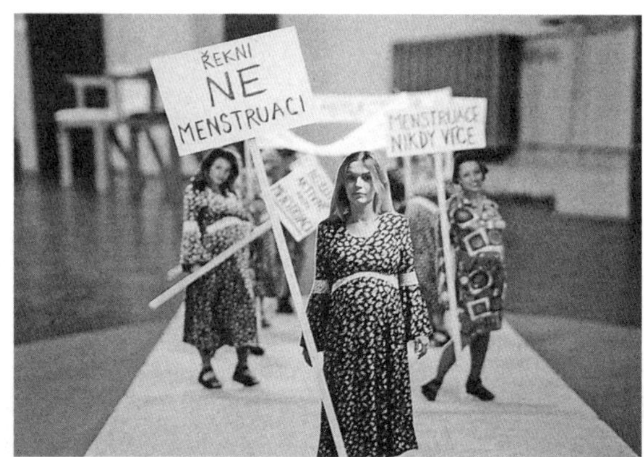

Lenka Klodová, *Demonstration*, 2004, installation

the state of motherhood is in most Western societies. The pregnant woman stands in Western culture as a non-erotic polarity of the fetishized female body of ideal proportions, but she also stands as an antithesis of reason and intellect. She is adored for the miracle of giving new life but still she is regarded in this state as "not herself". Pregnancy, as Klodová also wrote in her monograph, is probably the most crucial break in woman's life but one that is most associated with the risk of schizophrenia and of a romanticized dissolution of the "self" into or with the "other".

That the maternal is also political for Klodová is also manifested in her photo-installation *Demonstration* (2004) which is—in its formal and activist aspects—also closest to the above-mentioned demonstrations of Prague Mothers. Here, she transformed the theme of the monthly cycle and presented a group of pregnant women, including herself, who demonstrated for a higher birth rate. If pregnancy is usually conceived as a time of peace, rest, and inactivity, Klodová showed its emancipatory, even activist, potential. The slogans 'Say NO to menstruation', 'Fight actively against menstruation', 'No more menstruation', 'For life without menstruation', 'Menstruation—a desolation of mankind' and other purposefully simplistic proclamations on banners carry, obviously, an ambivalent message. The demonstrating female crowd does not protest against the menstrual bleeding as an injustice that "nature" committed on women; vice versa: it demonstrates for a utopia of a permanent pregnancy, for the omnipresent and excessive maternity which is a threat—not a support—of patriarchal society. Klodová—of course, quite hazardously—appropriates the strategies of natality politics, which was—especially in the twentieth century—a highly popular and frequently misused weapon for many regimes to preserve their national or racial identity, and takes them to the extreme. In a humorous, yet subversive, way she transformed women as reproductive machines and foot soldiers of the political propaganda into an autonomous mighty force that, at least symbolically, undermines the 'catastrophe of (maternal) identity' as women's only identity (Julia Kristeva). As we can see from Klodová's other projects—including *Belly-Backpack* (2006) in which she designed a special backpack in the shape of a pregnant belly to be used to claim the mountains, or *Female Winners* (2006), a series of large-scale outdoor prints depicting pregnant women as Olympic champions[6]—she always thinks about motherhood as a state of playful, humorous, and rebellious existence.

In her recently published book *Naked Situations*, Lenka Klodová points out that the exposure of the pregnant body is still seen as something inappropriate, offensive. To give an example of how much anger the pregnancy can arouse when it is not celebrated as some sacred state but when is related to activism and is, moreover, sexualized, she quotes the words of the current president of the Czech Republic, Miloš Zeman. In 2014, he gave an interview that was publicly broadcast, in which he presented the activities of Pussy Riot as being that of:

> a pornographic group that is minimally guilty for criminal act of rowdiness in the Orthodox Church, not even taking into consideration that one of its members participated in the public sex in the advanced state of pregnancy—simply a normal hooliganism that is related to pornography. … This is a really perfect example of a political prisoner.[7]

In the same book, Klodová systematically examines various aspects of human nakedness from the perspective of art, anthropology, medicine, biology or pornography, and also surveys her own work with the medium of the body (mostly her own body). It is here where her artivism perhaps most clearly meets women's environmental protests from the late Socialist era. Her twenty-something years long explorations of the crossovers between women's bodies (her body), maternity and art have their political, emancipatory and also

6. They were exhibited as a public art project at Artwall, outdoor exhibition site in the centre of Prague, just under the former 1950s giant monument of J.V. Stalin. For more see: http://cca.fcca.cz/en/galleries/artwall/2005/lenka-klodova-vitezky/.

7. Miloš Zeman quoted in Lenka Klodová, *Nahé situace* [Naked Situations] (Brno: HOST, 2016).

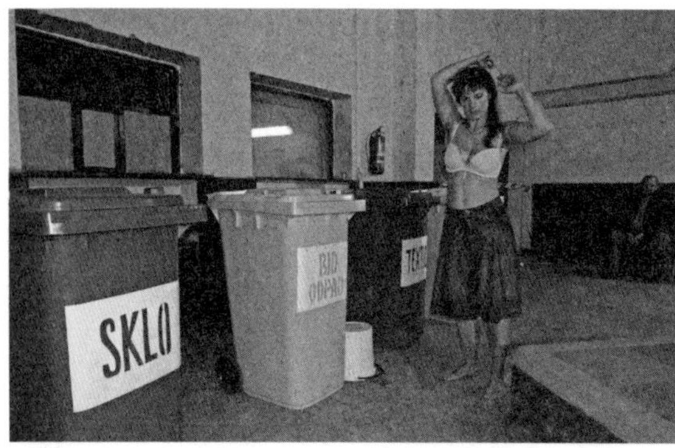

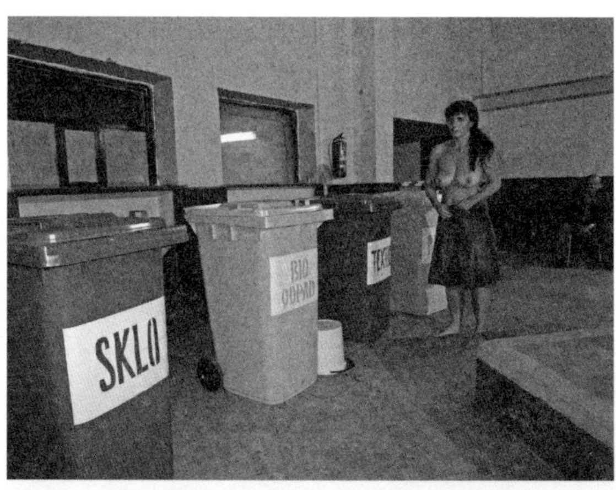

all images
Lenka Klodová, *Recycling*, Performance Festival Malamut, Ostrava, Czech Republic, 2006. Courtesy of artist

8. Ibid.

ecological motivations. In her performance *Recycling* (2006), she describes how:

> I am taking off parts of my cloth, shoes and jewellery, in a common, non-exhibitionist way, just like I do every evening. I am sorting them from the perspective of materials and throwing them to relevant containers. In the end, already naked, I am peeing into the container signposted bio.[8]

The naked body is for her both the battleground but also the medium of resistance. She approaches the body as both a symptom of culture and the product of nature (that's why its secretions primarily belong to the bio-containers and not to museums), it is individualized yet it is just one part of many other bodies that form the living environment. As she writes,

> an interesting feature of human nakedness is that when it is manifested it can in many cases arouse many, often contradictory responses at the same time. This ambivalence is typical for accepting human nakedness—it is also given by a fact that there are two totally different types of naked bodies—my body and the body of someone else … Nakedness can be closed in privacy and experienced as a highly intimate state. But it can also go out and let the cultural habits, stereotypes, rules and historical "givens" pouring on its skin. Consciously and even unconsciously nakedness is approached by social sciences, politics as well as art as a testing "stone" for exploring freedom and manipulation. It is a strongly political issue in the sense of both

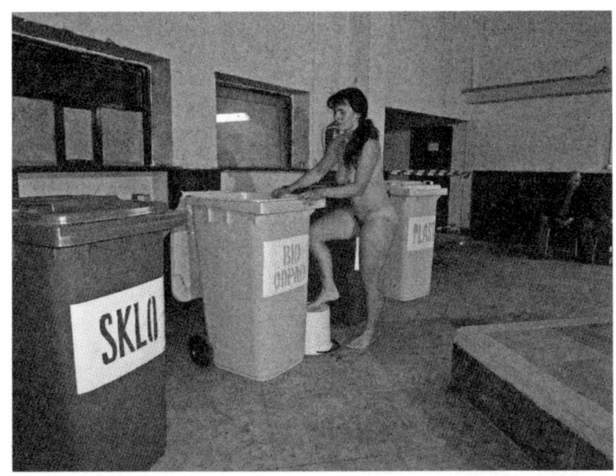

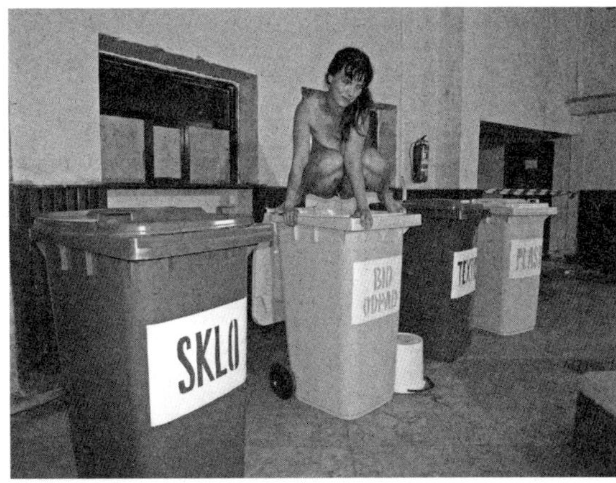

"high" (state) and "low" (personal) politics.[9]

Zdena Kolečková grew up and still lives in one of the most ecologically devastated regions of communist Czechoslovakia and the site of many historical traumas, including the massacre of Sudeten Germans in July 1945, part of the *wilde Vertreibung* (fierce expulsion) of ethnic Germans after World War II (1945), the North Bohemian city of Ústí nad Labem. The degradation of the natural environment (so much criticized by Prague Mothers in 1989) that went in hand with social degradation of these "second-rate" citizens (including her own German grandmother) have been the major sources for her multimedia work in which she connects artistic processes with deep scientific research.

Although the environmental situation has been slowly improving in the Czech Republic, Ústí nad Labem still suffers from heavy water and air pollution. Ecological catastrophe in this region has created many levels of discrimination in the politics here, against ethnic Germans and local Roma. There is collective guilt in the plundering of natural resources, and the degradation of the environment due to industry, even though many people have only one or two generations of connection with the land because of this history.[10]

Jiří Černický, another important artist related to this region, recently claimed:

> My family lives in a pre-fab house [built during communism] where, when you go out to the balcony in the morning and the local gasworks lets the gas to the air you are likely to vomit. I also remember climbing the chemical dump with other kids during my childhood where the acid pools easily ate away your boots.[11]

Exploring and thematizing consequences of crude materialism and rampant consumerism, colonization, pillage and displacement form the core of most of Kolečková's recent projects.

In 2012, she started to experiment with cooking and preserving. Her project *Made in Ghetto* was related to the peripheral district of Předlice in Ústí nad Labem. Under the

9. Ibid., p. 48.

10. Although much has been done to build the dialogue with the wrongly expelled families of ethnic Germans who did not collaborate with the Nazis, not only many local people but even many Czech politicians are Germanophobic and, even today, spread paranoia of German hoards taking over the country.

11. Jiří Černický, 'Environmentální víla' ['Environmental Fairy'] *Zdena Kolečková, Podivná botanika a jiné příběhy* [*Strange Botany and Other Stories*], exh. cat. Prague 2018, p. 4.

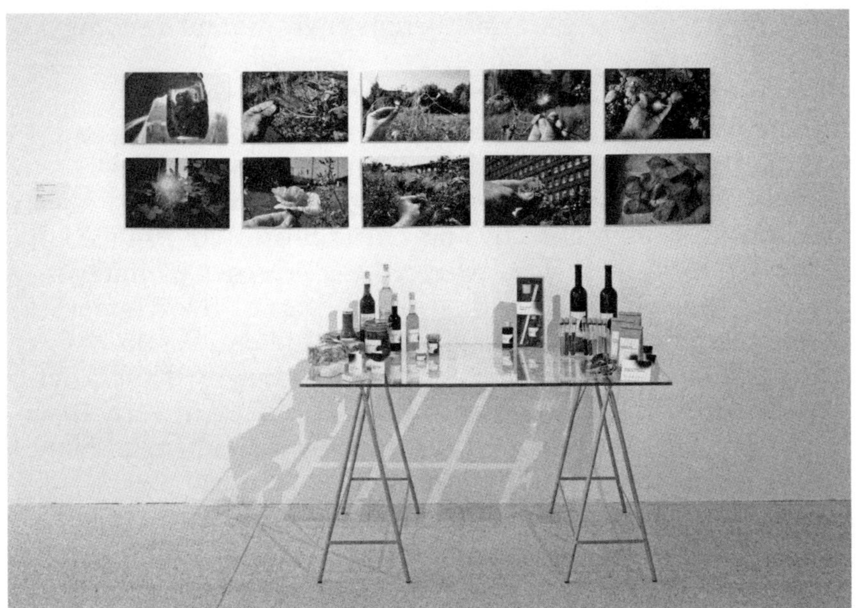

Zdena Kolečková, *Made in Ghetto*, 2012, installation. Photo: Martin Polák

communist regime, the once prosperous pre-war industrial and residential locality was destined for extinction because it was a major brown coal mine, and today this area is fatally threatened by processes of economic decline and social exclusion, and country-wide has become known as a Roma Ghetto. For the whole year, the artist picked, gleaned and harvested various widely growing plants, herbs and fruits and produced from them jams, honey, wine, juices, creams and detergents from original local—Czech as well as German—recipes. She then sent her home-made products for tests in a laboratory. Most of her products did not meet basic hygiene requirements, due to the environmental exploitation of the place. Not only did Kolečková turn attention towards the domestic, mostly women's work, in making these items, but she also drew attention to the environmental issues affecting them and rendering them unsafe to eat. The final products combined with the test results reveal the visible social aspects of the given locality. In her recipes, she nevertheless showed that even in the place which most white people avoid as a ghetto of "unadaptable ones" (as Roma are sometimes called in local media) there remains an unexpected richness of colours and tastes that should be cared for, as well as that the current environment's ecology has poisoned this possibility.

One of the most complex and compelling of Kolečková's projects related to environmental issues was realized in her processual installation *Chemistry Tea & Mercury Coffee/Perpetuum racionalis* (2017–2018), part of her exhibition 'Strange Botany and Other Stories' in Prague City Gallery.[12] Here, she again analyzed the presence of undesirable substances affecting the surroundings of Spolchemie, the largest industrial plant in Ústí nad Labem. While transforming the gallery space into a laboratory, Kolečková grew plants from seeds watered by water taken directly from the river of Bílina that flows just next to the industrial plant. This time her final products are tea and "coffee" blends whose packaging looks again just like the usual labels from health food stores. The set of products and the architectonic model of Spolchemie accompanies a video featuring the artist drawing water, collecting it and using it for watering herbs and vegetables. Through these means —and with the help of experts—she attempts to trace the extent of their contamination by dangerous heavy metals, including mercury, and hydrocarbons.

Combining scientific methods of "hard" science (that is traditionally ascribed to men) with soft skills and processes like gardening and domestic gastronomic experiments (ascribed to women), Kolečková examines, classifies, analyzes and categorizes the samples. In this approach, she has developed a strategy that is highly critical and politically charged but, on first sight, appears to an audience as a beautiful, lyrical and poetic display. Her experiments with plants link these organisms directly to the fate of the inhabitants of the city with whom they share an identical environment. 'Just behind the wall of Spolchemie there are two dorms for

12. Prague City Gallery, 14 March–17 June 2016.

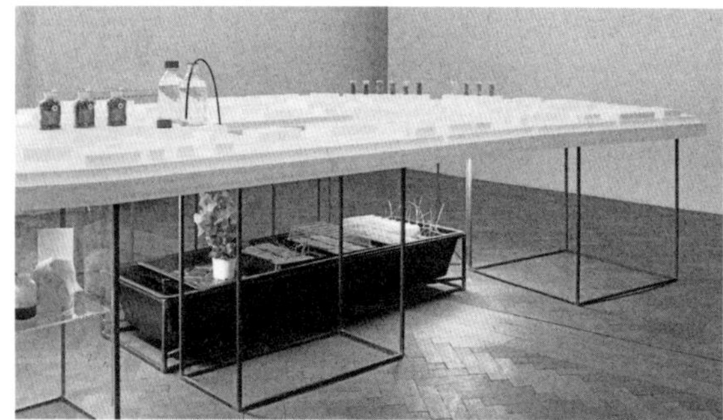

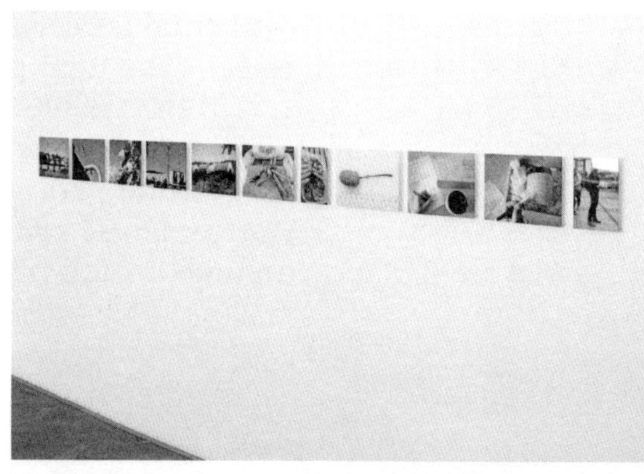

all images
Zdena Kolečková, *Chemistry Tea & Mercury Coffee Perpetuum racionalis*, 2018, installation. Photo: Martin Polák

socially weak groups which is a typical example of business with poverty. Just two hundred metres further, people grow vegetables and consume them as well', comments the artist. But just as herbs are beautiful, their appearance hides danger (as found in the evidence of poisonous molecules presented by their chemical analyses). The piece contains another message, perceived locally, in that local plants, just like people, are often stigmatized since their appearance and behaviour is different from the (white) majority. Thus Kolečková's project should not be related only to ecology but also to the no less burdensome issues of social and economic (in)equality and (in)justice in this region of the Czech Republic.

This project also marked the moment when Kolečková eradicated the boundary between art and research, on the periphery of which she had been operating for many years. Fully mindful of the unsustainability of social engineering and humankind's indifference to the environment, she passed through the hallowed portals of the intellect in order to draw attention to tangible signs of environmental devastation and force the art world to adopt a more responsible attitude, above all to stop treating nature as simply an external model for representation, manipulation and material appropriation. At the same time, she wanted to show that a collaboration between art and science—as well as a symbiosis between nature and culture—could be a win-win situation: art would acquire the tools necessary to meet the challenge posed by environmental degradation, while science was able to advance into an environment that could lend a new emotional dimension to its pragmatic, objectivizing character. In addition, the routine repetition of the same activity, a feature more symptomatic of the scientific method (the incessant rationalism and utility intrinsic

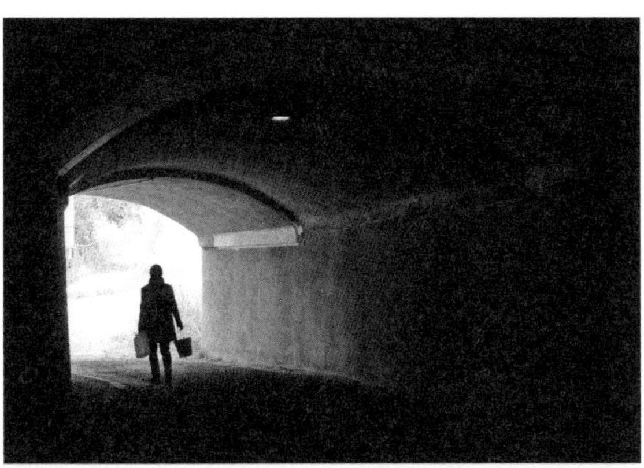

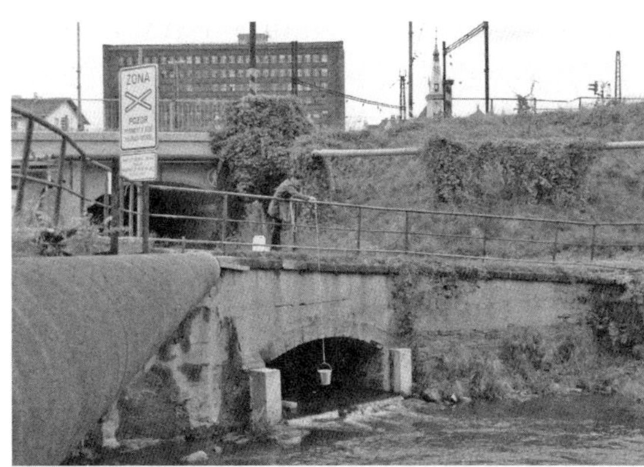

to the Latin *perpetuum racionalis*) than free artistic creativity,
here becomes the prerequisite for a declared responsibility.
On the art scene, a commitment to the surrounding world,
be this the human or biotic community, demands discipline
(though not disciplinarianism), and yet must not ignore the
experience of its own mental and physical existence. Finally,
through monotonous rituals (collecting the water, feeding
the plants, taking measurements, etc.), Kolečková got closer
to a cyclical awareness of time and thus interrogated the
imperative of linear progress that modern science is based on
and to whose ambitions even nature is now falling victim.

In 1989, the Prague Mothers asked the communist regime,
just before its collapse, to report openly on the ecological
catastrophe that was slowly but surely hitting many countries
in former East Europe, including Czechoslovakia, and
that had terrible consequences on the health of all, but
mainly children. Now, thirty years later, we know that
the catastrophe is far from over and that it is not only the
problem of the former East but affects the entire planet.
Kolečková does not move with the current environmentalist
flow that recently started to attract many artists who
sometimes superficially and calculatingly appropriate issues
of climate change and sustainability as either a "lift" to
visibility or as means for formal and aesthetic innovation
rather than ecological revolution. She has been stubbornly
addressing issues that challenge the apparent economic,
cultural and mental comfort we live in for more than two
decades now.

    In the 1990s, the German philosopher and feminist
Ulla Zöhrer-Ernst wrote that contemporary philosophical
considerations were characterized by 'a loss of concern
for human life, a failure to participate in human suffering,
and a lack of interest in the destruction of planet Earth by
advanced technology', and that such considerations were
as distant as they could be from that which is concrete and
tangible. The dominant approach of contemporary thinking
about life, she believed, was

> mediated by the findings of individual sciences,
> attempting in abstract principles, numbers, measure-
> ments and comparisons to pin down the object of

13. Ulla Zöhrer-Ernst, 'Die Philosophin als feministisch interessierte Intellektuelle', *Die Philosophin* no. 4 (1994), pp. 51–52.

investigation in pure form devoid of all feelings, as though the head were cut off from the body and all considerations abstracted from everyday questions.[13]

The radical revision of mechanistic understanding of nature is a core not only of current environmentally oriented discussions, but also an appeal to revise the traditional Western understanding of body, corporeality and sexuality as the opposites of mind and culture. Overcoming such dualism that is one of the foundations of Western philosophy lies also at the centre of Klodová and Kolečková's work. Their practice takes a non-instrumental but also non-essentialist and non-moralizing approach to bodies, bodily functions, natural processes as well as subaltern sites and subjects, making them important forces in making ethics of care part of artistic creativity without resigning to social and political agency. Just like the Prague Mothers in May 1989, who courageously exposed their bodies and offsprings to communist police that tried to scatter their demonstration in order to confront the political establishment and undermine its foundational paternalism, the two artists stubbornly confront the society with discomforting images but both have also sought to present data, artworks and publications, to ask the questions which will destabilize the practical-technical, rationalist and profit-oriented essence of contemporary neo-liberal society.

We need to ask: whose economic and political interests are served by the continuous withholding of information about the environment we live in? Do we really know what is contained in those gorgeously and professionally packed products we consume? How can we understand better the life of those who live in poverty, who are culturally and even ethnically different from us who write and publish, and who don't even bother to think about ecology when their first priority is merely to survive? Can we define our identity only by our ignorance about or removal of "others'" cultures, both past and present? How can we build our wealth and success on a basis other than simply financial profit and dominance and exploitation of nature? Do we want our children to live in a world full of superficial beauty and smart technologies or screen cultures, but one without nature or even real care for their environment?

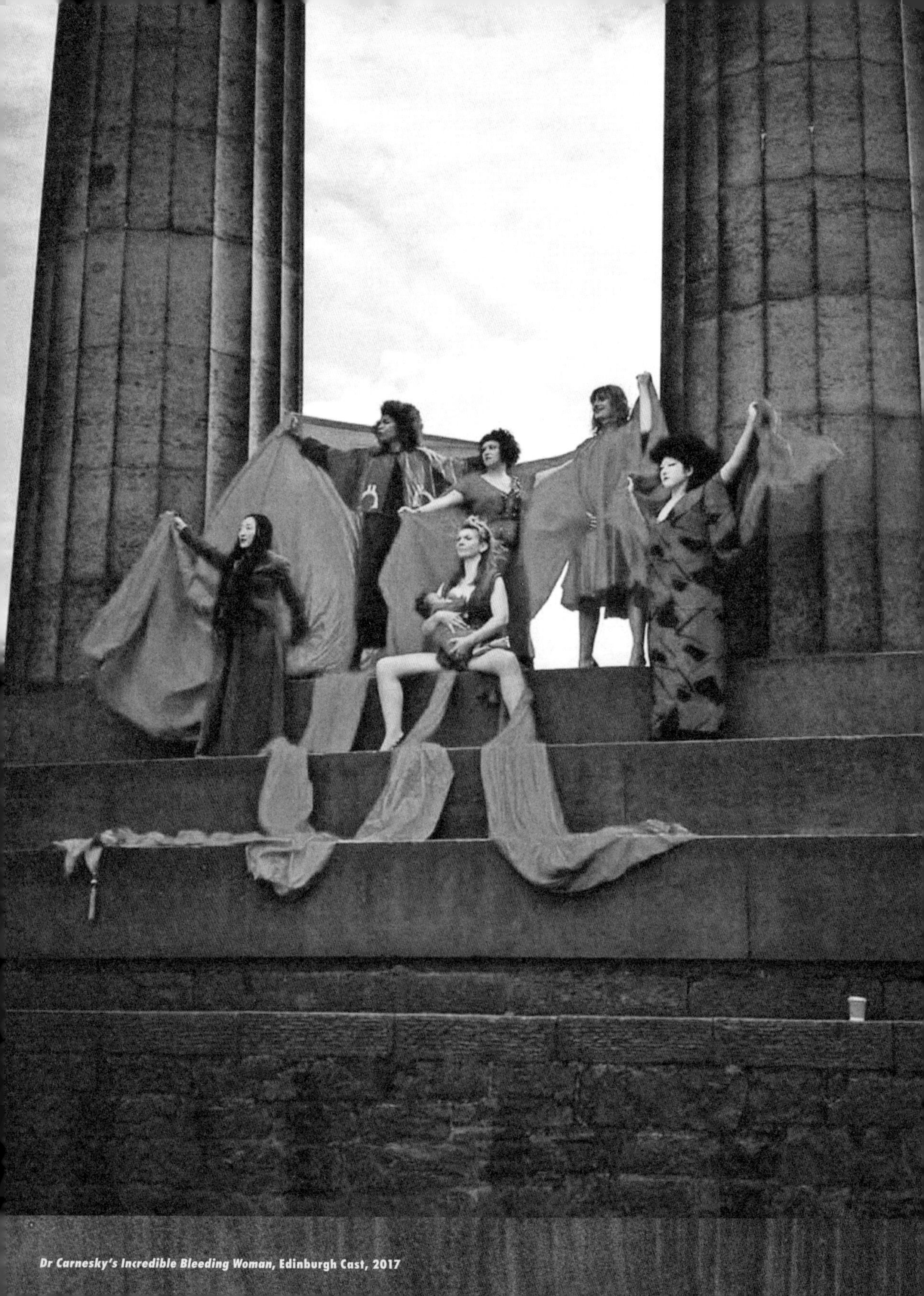

Dr Carnesky's Incredible Bleeding Woman, Edinburgh Cast, 2017

MENSTRONAUTS A GO GO

Marisa Carnesky

1. http://carnesky.com/project/
dr-carneskys-incredible-bleeding-
woman/.

Firstly, as many good cabarets begin, let me introduce myself to you: I am Marisa Carnesky, a UK-based performance maker and performer who fuses a variety of traditions and cultural politics into a live art practice that includes solo and group shows. These performances happen in all sorts of places including theatre stages, nightclubs, old factories and forests, on ghost trains made from pieces of old showman's rides, and in the streets with activist groups like Extinction Rebellion and the Menstronauts.

In 2015, I first premiered *Dr Carnesky's Incredible Bleeding Woman*,[1] a live art/new cabaret show, touring from 2016–2018, that examined existing religious and cultural menstrual rituals with the intention of reinventing new alternative feminist performative ones. The project created these rituals using theories that ranged from anthropological studies of synchronicity in traditional human cultures to the autoethnographic testimonies from the performers involved. A unique group of intersectional cabaret and live

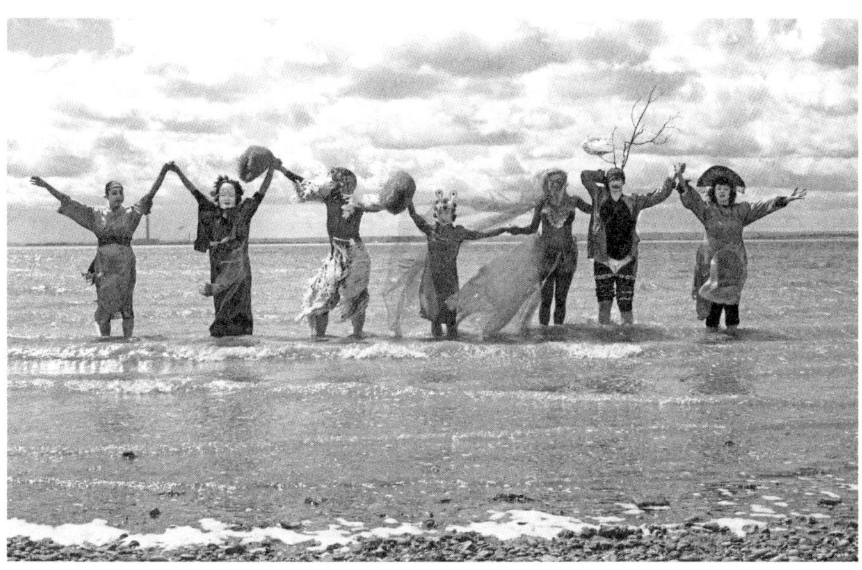

The original cast of *Dr Carnesky's Incredible Bleeding Woman*, 2016, from left to right: Amy Ridler, Nao Nagai, Rhyannon Styles, Fancy Chance, Missa Blue, Helen Plewis, Marisa Carnesky, publicity image, taken in Southend. Courtesy of photographer Sarah Ainslie

artists joined me in this cabaret, bringing a range of skills, cultural interests and backgrounds from hair hanging, stage magic and sword swallowing to live art practice and queer journalism. Aesthetically, the performance work drew on traditional entertainment tropes of bleeding women in popular culture and media, from classic horror film imagery of women possessing paranormal powers when menstruating, to women bleeding in stage magic performance and parodies of sanitary product advertisements. A reflexivity in the research enabled ideas for revisioning and reinventing rituals associated with menstruation into contemporary feminist performance and activist practices. This approach to the creation of the original performance rituals emerged from a highly structured practice-as-research PhD[2] in which the diverse group of performers became participants. The overarching desire of the work was to raise awareness and expand notions of the cultural identity of menstruation, exposing hidden mythologies, reframing popular representations and exposing ingrained social taboos in mainstream Western consciousness.

The show began with a performative lecture, led by me as "Dr Carnesky", a camp character developed from aspects of my persona and aesthetic interests informed by historical and thematic research. "Dr Carnesky" presents her "Menstruants", my collaborating team of performers, as if she were an anthropologist exhibiting her subjects, a flamboyant circus showwoman, a *magicienne* with sleight of hand tricks, and a carnival sideshow con artist posing as a doctor. This eccentric academic lecturer, using slides and films, both upholds and defiles the institution of instruction about the body, as she plays with the tradition of ethnographic shows in Victorian popular entertainments, the politics of cultural appropriation and perceptions of traditional anthropology, to explore the magic of menstruation. She asks the audience through her evidence to question the very origins of magic: 'What if I told you the origins of all magic, of all ritual, since the beginning of time was menstrual, would you believe me?' The cabaret then offers a unique performance experiment in synchronicity where the "Menstruant" participants each perform their own individually devised rituals live. The performance swings between the fictional, the factual and the autoethnographic, working with abject images, horror and

2. Marisa Carnesky, 'Dr Carnesky's Incredible Bleeding Woman: Reinventing Menstrual Rituals Through New Performance Practices', PhD, Middlesex University, 2019.

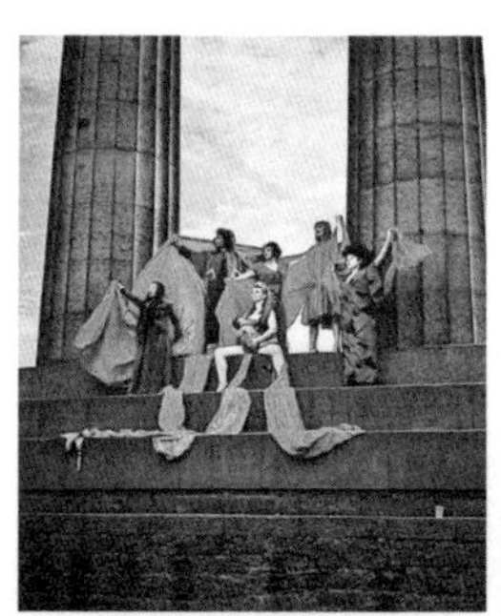

Dr Carnesky's Incredible Bleeding Woman, Edinburgh Cast, 2017

   Feminist Art Activisms and Artivisms

3. Quote from script of performance, *Dr. Carnesky's Incredible Bleeding Woman.*

4. Julia Kristeva, *Powers of Horror* (New York: Columbia University Press, 1982). See also Donna J. Haraway, *Staying with the Trouble: Making Kin in the Chthulucene* (Durham and London: Duke University Press, 2016).

variety stage tropes for added drama and timing. Questions are then posed to the audience.

The character of "Dr Carnesky" is a punk-cabaret *détournement* of the archetypal Aunt Flo in menstrual advertising—the popular euphemism for getting your period—and a formal Mistress of Ceremonies, crossing into moments of hysteria and horror. At moments, she is authoritative like a supposed medical instructor, at others, an illegitimate entertainer dealing in shock, taboo and spectacle, or a female parody of the "showman" in the tradition of variety theatre who linked the acts and spoke directly to the audience. If a showman denotes a certain flair for spectacle and bravado, or exploitation of the extraordinary, exemplified by P.T. Barnum or Derren Brown, what could a showwoman be? A showwoman is a rarely used term often employed to describe female proprietors of fairground rides. "Dr Carnesky" was a female counterpoint to the term showman. This showwoman does not exploit or control her subjects, but collaborates with them, perhaps because she shares their visceral experiences in words and actions. In this show, the façade of the camp in the showwoman character fades to reveal more intimate personal testimonies. The showwoman and her exhibits become a group, a coven, a community of women bound by shared experiences of loss, shame, abjection and subsequently activist reclamation of their bodily cycles.

Dr Carnesky's Incredible Bleeding Woman experimented with and re-worked magical illusions when "tinctures and ointments" were distributed to the audience. The ideas of merging the setting of the institute with a carnivalesque sideshow enabled Dr Carnesky to present her "snake oil" extracted from 'Medusa's own cave as the elixir that causes the audience's glasses to become rose tinted with menstrual blood'.[3] The metaphor of the historical travelling carnival sideshow as a place of ritual disorder and transience, where borders collapse and the forbidden is permitted, and where human bodily taboos are broken was the backdrop in these early performances of the project for the exploration and exhibition of the menstruating woman and the secrets she traditionally holds.

This cabaret explored abjection,[4] radical anthropological perspectives on witchcraft, the origin of the commune and the revelation of hidden menstrual mythological figures.

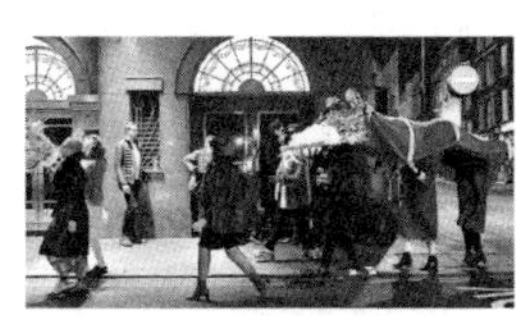

Menstronauts, Red Riding Hood March, 2016. Photo: Claire Lawrie

Marisa Carnesky

It further unpacked and addressed the parallels between trans-activism and menstruation as metaphors for rebirth, proposed feminist reclamations of death-defying nineteenth-century carnival sideshow skills and new theories of understanding misogyny in stage magic. It was a menstrual activist call to arms, combining personal testimonies which were both serious and emotive with the researched material in a manner that was both rigorous and a spoof of research modes themselves. Drawing together aspects of autoethnography, memoir and imagined fictions, the work combines and intersperses aspects of lived experience into a performative landscape that draws from the proposed real and the fictional.

The rituals of menstruation known from traditional human cultures and devised for this cabaret sound not unlike rituals of queer and experimental cabaret artists in London. Transgression of gender norms, transformation through costume and makeup into a ritualized persona, enactments of rebirth, destruction and reconstruction of identity, breaking sexual taboos, all these themes are regularly played out by cabaret artists in popular cutting-edge London cabaret clubs like Duckie in The Royal Vauxhall Tavern. The first work-in-progress performances of *Dr Carnesky's Incredible Bleeding Woman* took place at the Radical Anthropology Group and Duckie, placing the reinvention of menstrual rituals in front of audiences in the heart of subversive London.

Menstrual Activists and Spiritualists Unite

Menstrual activism is at the forefront of current feminist debate, uniting in its cultural diversity a worldwide struggle for the ritually unclean, the disempowered, duly sanitized and highly tabooed bleeding women to decipher how to gain more respect for menstruation without giving up any of the freedoms women worked so hard to earn. Menstruation represents a hotbed of issues in how we live and work and about how we understand bodily diversity and difference and its social and cultural recognition. Menstruation as a subject is going through a cultural revolution in 2018–2020, with the loudest voices and most focus on the subject since

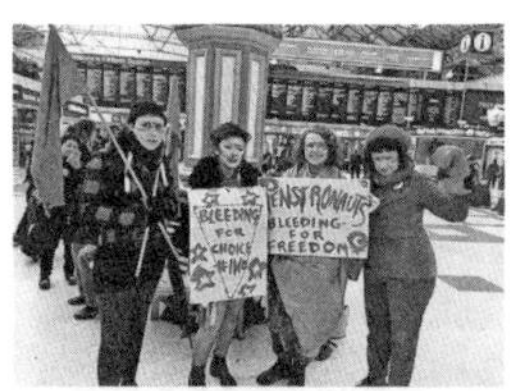

Menstronauts at Victoria Station, London

5. Germaine Greer, *The Female Eunuch* (London: Paladin, 1971).

6. Anita Diament, *The Red Tent* (London: St Martins Press, 1997).

7. Chris Bobel, *New Blood: Third-Wave Feminism and the Politics of Menstruation* (New Jersey: Rutgers University Press, 2010), p. 168. For other references on menstruation, see Chris Knight, *Blood Relations Menstruation and the Origins of Culture* (London and New Haven: Yale University Press, 1991); Penelope Shuttle, and Peter Redgrove, *The Wise Wound: Myths, Realities, and Meanings of Menstruation* (London: Marion Boyars Publishers, 1999) and the Menstruation Research Network website, https://menstruationresearchnetwork.co.uk/.

the feminist debates of the 1970s were typified by Germaine Greer's famous quote 'If you think you are emancipated, you might consider the idea of tasting your own menstrual blood—if it makes you sick, you've got a long way to go, baby.'[5]

Anita Diamant's 1997 bestselling novel *The Red Tent*[6] has proved inspirational to a growing trend of menstrual spiritualists in the US who became known as the Red Tent Movement. They combine a feminist spiritualist approach to celebrating menstruation as a sacred rite of passage to be ritualized and shared between mothers and daughters on a girl's first cycle and continued then throughout the rest of women's menstrual lives. The aim is to offer a new supportive collective menstrual environment where women can share stories and experiences as a fundamental step towards recognizing the importance of the female bodily cycle and addressing how it is both commonly devalued and medicalized. Bringing together a community of women in temporary spaces defined by interior red draping, Red Tent feminists reclaim menstruation as a central experience of womanhood, but in doing so they also risk reinforcing reductive stereotypes of femininity solely defined by reproductive function. Women who, for a variety of reasons, do not menstruate and do not see their reproduction as central to their identity have felt excluded from the Red Tent Movement. As Chris Bobel identifies, in redefining menstruation, feminists must address a contemporary state of womanhood, rather than an essentialist notion of nature and the biological:

> Is it possible to simultaneously acknowledge real social, political and cultural forces that continue to shape the menstrual experience in destructive and oppressive ways without falling into the treacherous essentialist trap that locates identity in the biological body?[7]

As gender roles become less fixed, the idea of the womb as a site of reproduction and the experience of the menstrual cycle as defining notions of femininity has becomes obsolete for many. Third-wave feminists who call for a blurring of gender roles and identities reject the idea of an exclusive safe space focussed on women's reproductive potential. If the

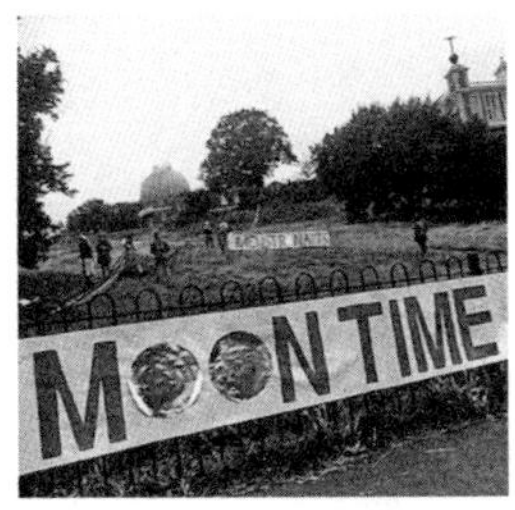

Menstronauts, Greenwich Meridian Action, 2016

Marisa Carnesky

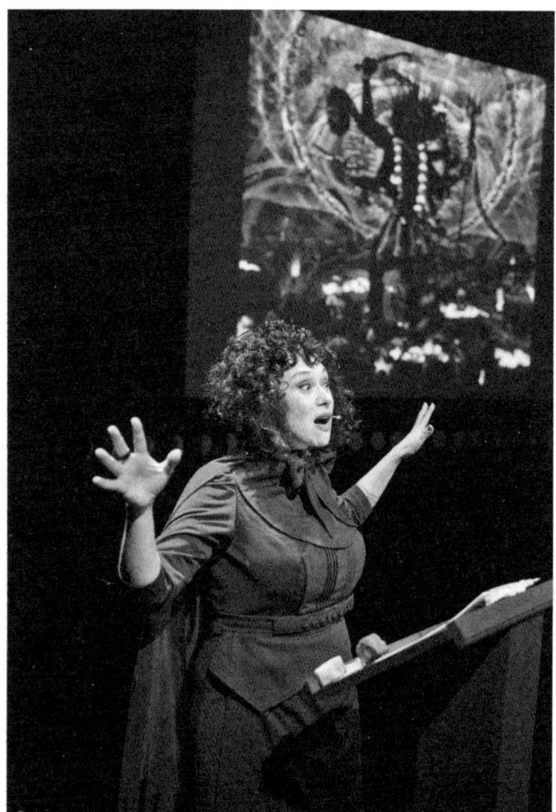

Marisa Carnesky in *Dr Carnesky's Incredible Bleeding Woman*, 2019, live theatre show, 55', Soho Theatre, London. Courtesy of photographer Claire Lawrie

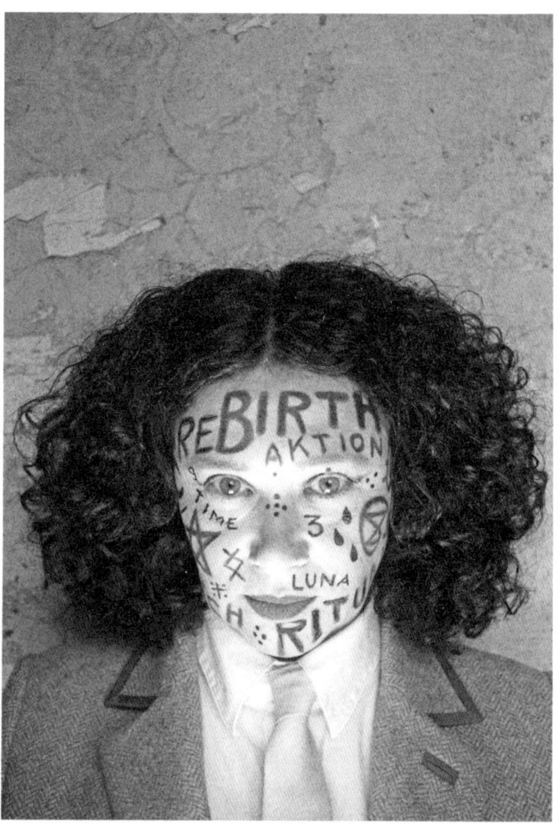

Marisa Carnesky, *Showwoman. Ritual. Action*, 2019, publicity photo at the British Library. Courtesy of photographer Ruth Bayer

Red Tent Movement is to address the diversity of all people who identify as feminists, it is necessary to engage with other current feminist debates and broaden its message to 'transgender, androgyne, inter-gender, bigender, bio, third gender, neuter/neutrois/agender, genderqueer and gender fluid, and more, say third wavers'.[8]

Bobel offers a valid critique of the Red Tent subculture by arguing that queer notions of gender are needed but as yet no comparable popular queer version of the Red Tent Movement that explores a mindful approach to the experience and concept of human cyclical renewal has surfaced. The Menstronauts proposed to create such an alternative, fusing the spaces between menstrual activism, queer identity, menstrual art and menstrual spiritualism.

8. Bobel, *New Blood*, p. 164.

9. http://
radicalanthropologygroup.org/.

The Menstronauts

The performance activist vein of the project grew as the project developed from its first workshops into the group's engagement with performing the rituals outdoors in the landscape in public outdoor spaces and, within the show, a call-to-arms to its audiences. It was at the last work-in-progress preview that was staged for International Women's Day at the Archaeology Lecture Hall as a special event for the Radical Anthropology Group[9] that a question and answer session after the performance opened up the idea of an activist group: the Menstronauts.

Questions from the audience asked what next, how could people get involved, how could we utilize the energy in the room to reach more people? Questions were also posed as to what happened to the participants as a result of performing the rituals, and whether anything changed for them as a result of the experiment? As the question was asked, the immediate answers proved crucial for how the project would develop. The panel, which was made up of myself (Dr Carnesky), the cast and Dr Camilla Power from Radical Anthropology Group, agreed that we were going to open out the themes of the work and start an activist group that any woman could join. The initial idea was that, like the performers in the show, the group would meet on every dark new moon to create and perform ritual actions outdoors on the landscape. Anthropologist Ingrid Lewis offered her house in Brixton as the meeting location. A small group started to meet made up mainly of women created from participants of Carnesky's Finishing School, the *Bleeding Woman* cast, audience members from the show and members of the Radical Anthropology Group (RAG). The Menstronauts started to take shape in April 2016. At the first meeting we had a round table discussion to consider what this activist group might look like and do.

One of the processes that the group had to go through over the coming months was to understand and differentiate the relationship of the group to both the *Dr Carnesky's Incredible Bleeding Woman* and to the Radical Anthropology Group. One of the central discussions in the group was the way to approach creating menstrually themed performative actions and identifying what we hoped to achieve.

Menstronauts feel that a disregard for the cycles of the human body echoes a disregard for the cycles of the planet and for each other. We seek to reclaim time through respect for the bodily cycles we evolved as humans, and for the original cultural means of counting time—the waxing and waning of the moon.[10]

10. Unpublished text, posted initially on Facebook, 2018.

11. http://lunarchy.weebly.com/.

Radical Anthropology Group member and founder Power had been involved in the 'Government of the Dead' activist performance group. The style of their performative protest is exemplified by their performance tableaux during marches, including the 2009 G20 demonstration. She brought her unique knowledge and style of activism forward to the group and particularly proposed an agenda that was inspired by these actions under the name of *Lunarchy*, which is a banner title and website resource under which the various activist projects of the radical anthropology group were brought together.

> We need to stop. Turn the world upside-down! Once a month, each time the moon dies, let's act to quench the fires. It means pulling out capitalism's plug. It means going on strike. It means switching off and staying out on strike until full moon. It means dying to this world as the moon does, emerging refreshed and renewed. Death followed by new life.[11]

Discussions about how the Menstronauts' actions would differ from the Government of the Dead and *Lunarchy* made for an interesting debate about the different political agendas and modes of activist approaches. Should the Menstronauts continue in the tradition of the actions of these groups, using bold agitprop, and shocking Grand Guignol style imagery? How could the Menstronauts be fluid, creating actions that could be viewed from a wider feminist perspective and encompass contemporary issues arising from menstrual topics? How could the Menstronauts develop new performative activist languages that firstly addressed the taboo just of menstruation itself and link it successfully to wider issues as part of a growing feminist activist movement and part of global resistance to patriarchal injustices?

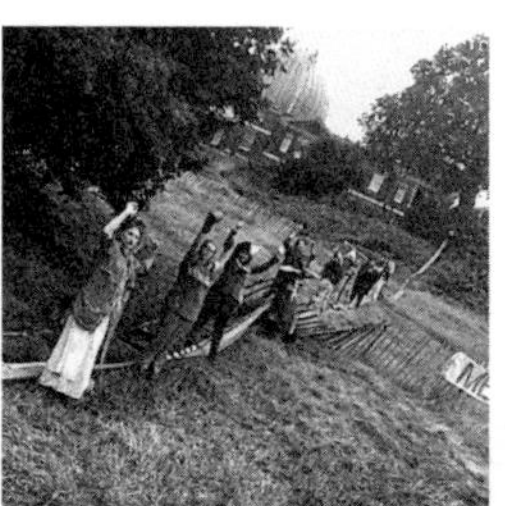

Menstronauts, Greenwich Meridian Action, 2016

    Feminist Art Activisms and Artivisms

MENSTRUAL REVOLUTIONS

The Menstronauts took the rituals beyond the realm of the personal and created collective menstrually themed activist rituals, tackling issues around women's reproductive rights and eco-feminism through shared public performance experiences, joining protests including Irish and Polish Women campaigning for abortion rights in 2016 and 2018 and creating performance events in Greenwich, Soho and East London from 2016–2018.

The Menstronauts were made up of intersectional, gender fluid, queer feminist, activist and artist attendees. One of the key differences which emerged between the different generations of feminists and activists in the group when it came to talking about menstrual activism in 2016–2017 was the introduction to many of what a queer menstrual agenda could look like. Moreover, a significant discussion began on whom the movement would be open to and how a manifesto or rather a "moonifesto of the Menstronauts" would be worded. We needed to decide if we were a "woman only" group and if so what did that mean and who did it exclude? Were we open to trans women who had never menstruated, to trans men who had menstruated? Was menstruation to be something that had to be a physical literal experience or could it be a metaphor for cyclicity, renewal and rebirth for all genders inclusive of a non-binary narrative? It became clear from the attendees that the Menstronauts must be as fluid, as gender queer and as open as the people who came to be part of the actions.

Another challenge for the Menstronauts was keeping a consistent group going that would meet monthly. We started our actions with an idea led by Camilla Power to meet in Greenwich Park by the Observatory on the meridian line and create a large red "snake" of fabric to mark Midsummer's night which then happened to fall that year on the new dark moon. We had about five metres of red cloth and the idea was to drape it down the hill, as a serpentine shape, to create a representation of a red snake or river of blood cutting through the Greenwich meridian, thus reclaiming moon time. We then put up a banner that said "moon time" and read and discussed our possible *Moonifesto*. This was interrupted by a visit from the police who were driving around the park patrolling: they agreed we could finish our meeting and then move on. There were eleven of us present.

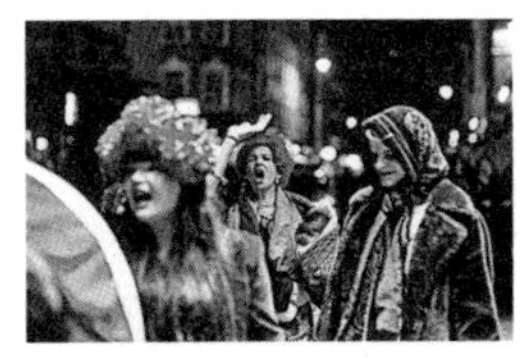

Menstronauts action with London Fourth Wave Feminists, 2017

Marisa Carnesky

We met every month for a year at The Cock Tavern in Euston in May 2016 with a workshop where Menstronauts was agreed as the name of the group. The Greenwich *Moontime* June 2016 gathering was the first outdoor performance action. We had a meeting at Hyde Park Corner and joined a demonstration in support of Polish feminists against oppressive abortion laws. We performed a parade around the streets of Soho with a giant wolf puppet during the Halloween season, which we named 'The Menstronauts Red Riding and the Wolf March' in Autumn 2016. We met on 26 February 2017 to commemorate the Match Girls strike, which we entitled 'Women, Blood and the Red Flag'. The last meeting was at Downing Street on International Women's Day, 8 March 2017, to take part in an action with London Fourth Wave Feminists.

The Menstronauts continued to meet working towards potential actions. In 2019, a meeting was held to see how we could contribute to the Extinction Rebellion. On 15 April 2019, Extinction Rebellion (XR) occupied a series of major London sites in protest for ten days. In collaboration with fellow 'Clown Witch Priestess' Lucy Hopkins, I created the 'Regeneration Game' especially for XR, which was formed over a month in the run-up to 15 April, each Thursday at 6pm, through our "performance activist" training offerings in the belly of the XR headquarters in Euston. Some weeks, fifty people showed up ready to think about performing in the streets and creative ways to protest. Lucy introduced the idea of playing an improvization clown theatre game inspired by one of her teachers John Wright. Its rules are simple, yet its outcomes are myriad: the performers play like children creating temporary worlds with improvised characters and scenarios known as "flocking". Sometimes on the ground, sometimes screaming, crying or laughing, the game was not so much a follow-my-leader as a co-operative effort to create interweaved, interlaced mass performative actions of the absurd.

The following week I led a workshop on creating a regenerative performance identity, piecing together images, themes and issues inspired by the practice of the Menstronauts. We ended up with some deeply innovative concepts flying around the room and green witches against fracking with anti-pollution wands were coming into being.

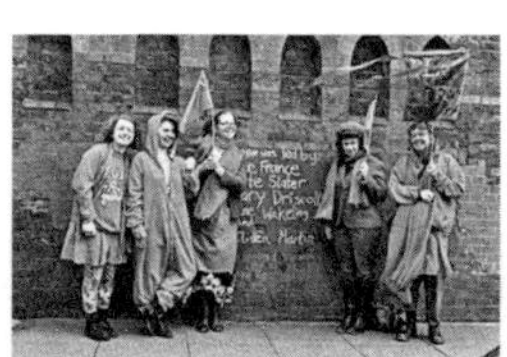

Menstronauts Match Girl Action, 2017. Photo: Ruth Bayer

   Feminist Art Activisms and Artivisms

12. *Marisa Carnesky: Showwoman. Ritual. Action* was performed at the British Library, London on 12 July 2019, 19:00–20:30.

The aim for the activist participants was to turn up and play the game in a newly formed performance persona. On 15 April, we all assembled in Parliament Square. I was dressed in red as a Menstronaut, proposing the connection the themes of the cycle of the body to the cycle of the planet.

My performance activism with firstly the Menstronauts and then with XR and the Regeneration Game, has its roots in experimental cabaret performance and autoethnographic research and continues to unfold in cyclical waves of actions and ideas. It is a central and guiding part of my practice leading to new performative languages and collaborations. Post the XR rebellion I began a new show and performance activist strategy, combining all I have learnt. *Showwoman. Ritual. Action* premiered at the British Library as part of their writing season in July 2019.[12] For me, activism and artivism combine the following: practice, practice, practice, research, research, research: collaborate, collectivize, commune, act.

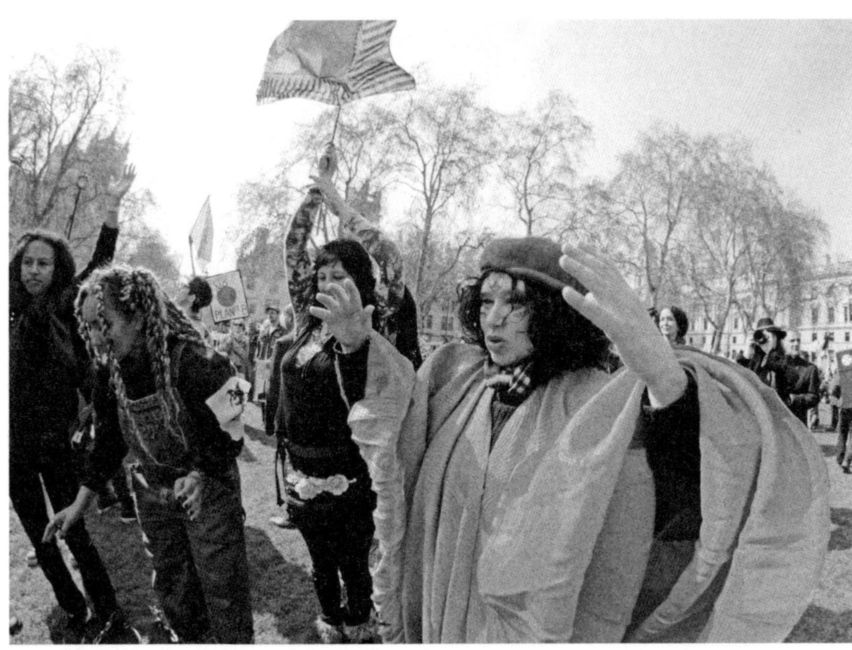

Marisa Carnesky, playing the Regeneration Game at Extinction Rebellion action, Parliament Square, London, 2019. Courtesy of photographer Ruth Bayer

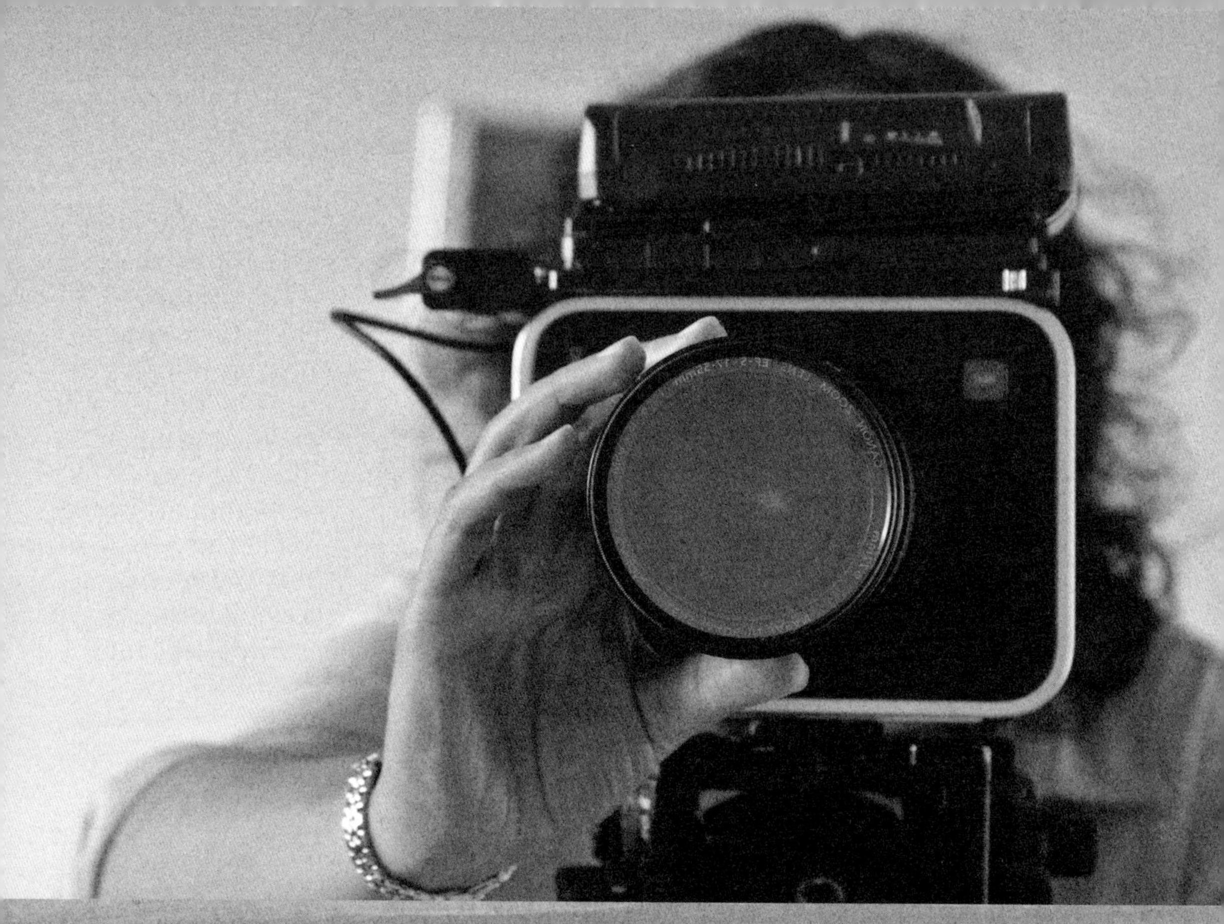

Myself behind the camera, reflected in the mirror

WOMEN, AGENCY, DOCUMENTARY
First Cut of *Shahla*

Pune Parsafar

My film *Shahla* (18 min.) is part of a longer documentary, made up of six discrete episodes, narrating the lives and struggles of six Iranian women activists. This documentary film aims to challenge the dominant portrayals of Iranian women, primarily in Iran's official cinema. It aims to reinforce female agency by presenting narratives about these

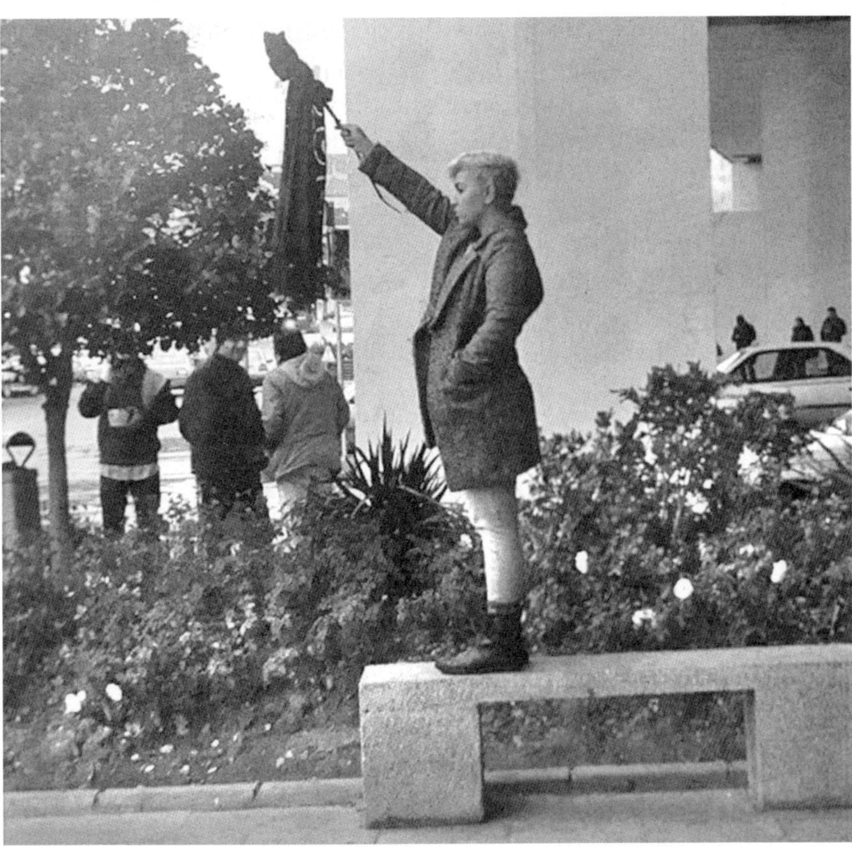

A girl of the Revolution Street in Tehran publicly protesting against compulsory veiling by holding her hijab on a stick, 2018

women as agents of change. These narratives provide an
active platform to explore questions of representation, experimenting with cinematic forms and styles, and searching
for and developing new, more progressive approaches. The
work challenges the current misogynistic representations
of Iranian women that dominate Iran's official cinema, and
the postmodernist representations prevalent in much of
mainstream films in the West. *Shahla* is an application of
this critical perspective, which I will discuss below to demonstrate some of the choices I made in its making, for example,
in the adoption of the documentary form, in the choice of
participants, in the narrative design and in the particular use
of colour and personal objects.

The idea for my research and film started very
naturally from observation and then critical thinking both as
a consumer of films and my own professional experience as
a documentarist with many years of experience in documentary video making and broadcasting. I began by considering
how the portrayal of Iranian women in cinema had
presented me with images I was uncomfortable with, to say
the least, and which I found at odds with my own experience
as a woman from Iran and with the reality of the lives of the
women in that society as I know them from personal experience. I therefore set out to challenge these representations,
critically examine them and explore the ideological meanings
that underpin them. Based on this critical evaluation, my aim
was to contribute, through my documentary film, to novel
ways of representing women, gender and sexuality in cinema,
within a modern, emancipatory and feminist perspective.

Broadly speaking, three perspectives on the
representation of Iranian women in cinema (with their
inevitable overlaps) could be said to make up the cinematic
landscape of representation, both in Iran and the West,
that I was confronted with and which formed my starting
point. These are 1) Orientalist, 2) conservative, religious
and misogynistic, and 3) modern and emancipatory feminist
perspectives.

The Orientalist and cultural-relativist view of
Iranian woman has been prevalent in cinema in the West.
Even in films with modern settings, Iranian women have
been portrayed in a variety of roles, but overwhelmingly as
helpless victims, submissive wives, concubines, traditional

homemakers, devout Muslims, belly dancers, etc. At times, they have figured as mere shadows in the background, as extras, or chador-clad[1] and tucked away in homes; or have been conspicuous by their total absence in public, in plots centred around men's lives and experiences. Even modern films reproduce these images (or lack of an image) of the women from ancient Persia or Arabia (akin to the women of the Arabian tales or harems, portrayed in Orientalist paintings, for example). A modern variant of the Orientalist perspective is the cultural-relativist view, which offers a similarly conservative, backdated and distorted image of the present-day Iranian woman. These images have increasingly come to be seen as grotesque, stereotypical and out of place as information about the Iranian society and the reality of the lives of Iranian women has increased. Dynamics such as demographic movements and interactions (migration), the global information and communication revolution and, crucially, the social protests and revolutions of recent years, since 2009, in Iran, North Africa and the Middle East, have helped to bring the contrast between these images and the real lives and struggles of women in Iran to full view.

Immediately after the Islamic state came to power in Iran in March 1979, woman in cinema, TV and print was effectively erased, and when she came back, her body was veiled, in stipulated black and dark colours, following the imposition of compulsory hijab in public. The conservative, religious, and misogynistic perspectives manifest themselves in the representation of Iranian woman in Iran's official cinema at two broad levels: first, there is an extreme form which is the result of the oppressive, regressive and extremely conservative legal and political context of the Iranian society and the current political and religious-led system in place. The typical image of the woman here mirrors the perspective and ideal of the religious and political establishment. She is conservative, a home-maker, dependent on the man, meek, god-fearing, chaste, and a sinner, if she pursues her own goals at their expense; at best, she can be a victim, saved and forgiven at last by the mercy and compassion of a man; at worst, the cause of man's temptation and downfall. The second, less extreme form, is a result of a dominant perspective within Iranian cinema, which also portrays a meek and conservative image of the Iranian woman, out of step with the actual lives and outlook on life of the modern, defiant and unwieldy Iranian woman, when she refuses to accept her unequal social position as dictated by the law, and challenges them by fighting to survive within and despite the rules she has no control over. There is overlap here, of course, with the Orientalist and cultural-relativist perspectives within Western cinema.

> Within the broad context of responses to the global phenomenon of migratory movements, it remains a poignant fact that political as well as media discourses consistently deny or minimise female protagonism … reducing the panoply of migrant women's roles to contributions to domesticity and depicting them as dependent, economically passive subjects, often contextualised solely in terms of family reunification, domestic service, and sexual work.[2]

Though Isolina Ballesteros is writing here in the context of migrant women, the same can be said about the way Iranian women have been depicted in the political and media discourses in the West, and more brashly, of course, in Iran. Challenging this through film was one of my motivations in embarking on this research and making this documentary.

There are some modern, emancipatory, feminist perspectives evident in the portrayal of the Iranian woman, in both documentary and fiction, but particularly

2. Isolina Ballesteros, 'Female Transnational Migrations and Diasporas in European "Immigration Cinema"', *Exile through a Gendered Lens: Women's Displacement in Recent European History, Literature, and Cinema*, eds. Gesa Zinn and Maureen Tobin Stanley (New York: Palgrave Macmillan, 2012), pp. 143–168.

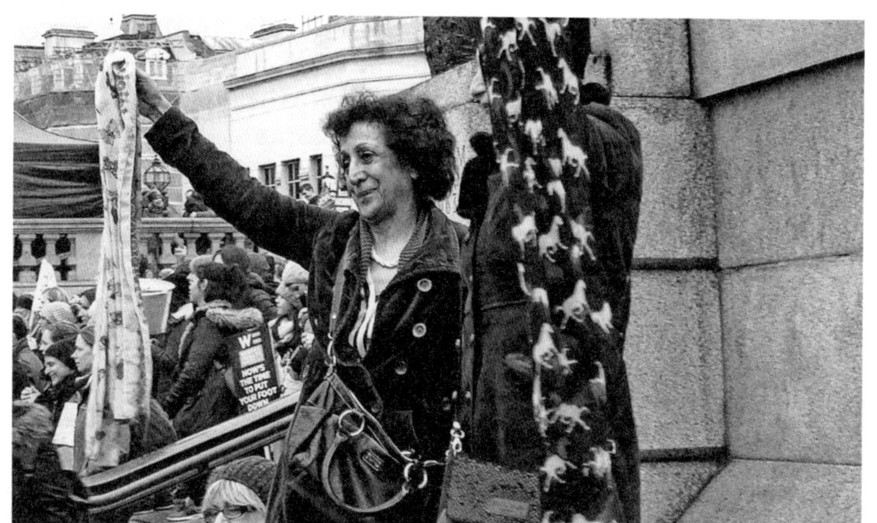

Shahla Daneshfar, the protagonist of *Shahla*, a workers' rights and political campaigner, symbolically removing the hijab in solidarity with Iran's Girls of Revolution Street, International Women's Day 2018, Trafalgar Square, London

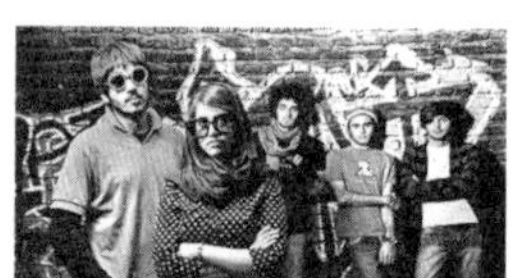

The cast of *No One Knows About Persian Cats* (Bahman Ghobadi, 2009)

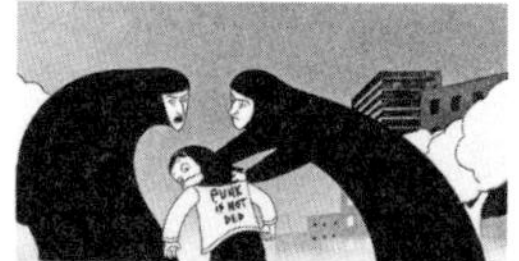

From a scene of *Persepolis* (Marjane Satrapi, 2007)

3. Claire Johnston, 'Women's Cinema as Counter-Cinema', *Notes on Women's Cinema*, ed. Claire Johnston (London: Society for Education in Film and Television, 1973), pp. 24–31.

documentary, within the Iranian underground film scene and Iranian diaspora. This milieu has produced, and is producing, interesting films, with clear departures from the traditional perspectives that have dominated Iranian cinema, specifically in dealing with the portrayal of women and issues of religion, gender and sexuality. Nevertheless, this is still in development, and is hampered by lack of funding and resources, and is rarely promoted to larger audiences. There is a greater correspondence here with the lives, preoccupations and concerns of present-day Iranian women and the key issues that make up the real discourse of Iranian society and population today; issues such as compulsory veiling, women's sexuality, marriage, age of marriage, child abuse, right to divorce, custody of children, equal access to employment, inheritance, the penal code, legal redress, etc. Those involved in this fervent film scene are often young filmmakers (predominantly in the underground film space inside Iran) and a mix of young and exiled veteran filmmakers and visual artists outside Iran, in the Iranian diaspora. The backdrop to this development is both the political, legal and social constraints of the past few decades in Iran, as well as the lack of a credible and more authentic representation of Iranian life and society, specifically produced by Iranian woman, in the mainstream cinema in the West. My own film and research, which I shall write more on below, sits within this emergent critical movement in art and cinema in Iran, and which I hope will give a clearer voice to it.

Claire Johnston in her seminal essay 'Women's Cinema as Counter-Cinema' (1973), emphasized how mainstream cinema is 'an expression of the dominant ideology and cannot be neutral'.[3] Johnston proposed that women's cinema should disrupt 'the fabric of the male bourgeois cinema within the text of the film' and build an avant-garde, counter-cinema to challenge the male-dominated language of cinema. Historically, feminist film theorists have recognized the influence of a range of radical film (and theatre) theories and practices on feminist film, which are considered avant-garde and oppositional to the dominant system of meaning-making. The most commonly cited examples of this method are Sergei Eisenstein's montage innovation and Bertolt Brecht's *Verfremdungseffekt* (alienation, de-familiarization), which interrupts the identification of the viewer with the characters and the narrative, and Jean-Luc Godard's Marxist choice of cinematic forms and styles.

Elin Diamond in 'Brechtian Theory/Feminist Theory: Toward a Gestic Feminist Criticism' (1988) proposes an intertextual reading of Brechtian theory and feminist theory, claiming 'a recovery of the radical potential of the Brechtian critique and a discovery for feminist theory'.[4] Similarly, Iris Smith suggests that we adopt, and adapt, Brechtian ideas, especially the idea of "Gestus", in gender studies, noting that 'Brecht probably sensed … that dilemmas facing women, as estranged and disenfranchised members of society, could articulate his own views. It remains for feminists to capitalize on their potential for gender studies'.[5] My documentary sits within a similar intertextual reading of Brechtian theory and feminist theory, in which I wanted the protests of a group of "disenfranchised" women to be the voice of a society rejecting an intensely misogynistic and repressive establishment.

In 'The Revolutionary Film: Problem of Form' (1934), Samuel Brody considers documentary form as the 'medium of revolutionary film production' under the capitalist system. Distinguishing different genres of documentary at the time—newsreel, "synthetic documentary" and the educational short—Brody calls documentary the filmic "weapon" for the working class.[6] Talking in the context of slum dwellers, Bill Nichols in his book *Introduction to Documentary* (2017) states that documentary traditionally has given the opportunity to the subjects to 'speak for themselves'.[7] My documentary aims towards a filmic representation of a group of activist women, their thoughts and actions, or, as Nichols puts it, to offer 'aural and visual representations of some part of the historical world'.[8] There is a long tradition of showing women as activists, who are protesting against oppression and discrimination. *Nightcleaners* (Berwick Street Collective, 1975) and *The Willmar 8* (Grant, 1981) are examples of many documentaries, which show campaigns by women workers in the 1970s over unequal pay based on sexual discrimination. These films have played an important role both in giving a voice to feminist campaigns and eternalizing their hard work in the history of women's rights, as well as experimenting with filmic forms and styles, which push the boundaries.

4. Elin Diamond, 'Brechtian Theory/Feminist Theory: Toward a Gestic Feminist Criticism', *TDR* 32, no. 1 (Spring 1988), pp. 82–94.

5. Iris Smith, 'Brecht and the Mothers of Epic Theater', *Theatre Journal* 43, no. 4 (December 1991), pp. 491–505.

6. Samuel Brody, 'The Revolutionary Film: Problem of Form', *The Documentary Film Reader: History, Theory, Criticism*, ed. Jonathan Kahana (Oxford: Oxford University Press, 2016), pp. 247–248.

7. Bill Nichols, *Introduction to Documentary* (Bloomington: Indiana University Press, 2017), 3rd. ed., p. 159.

8. Ibid., p. 31.

9. 'Statement by women documentary makers: "We are angry and upset about the violent treatment of women who are protesting against compulsory hijab"' (original Farsi title), RFI, https://bit.ly/321w9fP (accessed 1 July 2019).

10. 'Academy calls for release of Iranian film-makers', BBC, https://bit.ly/2XjAZqe (accessed 1 July 2019).

11. 'Iran arrests two journalists as crackdown gathers pace', Reuters, https://reut.rs/2XhE7Tu (accessed 1 July 2019).

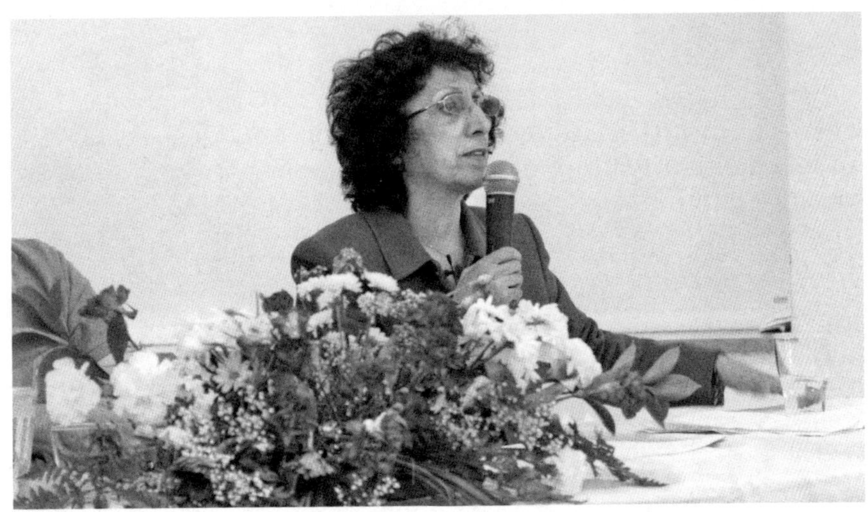

Shahla Daneshfar speaking at a Conference of the Worker-communist Party of Iran, May 2016

In Iran, documentary has historically proved to be an ideal filmic tool, especially for women, as a voice to get across their demands and use it as a platform for social protest. In 2018, 68 Iranian women documentary filmmakers in a petition to the government and members of the National Assembly, criticized the violence against women who protest against compulsory hijab in streets. They stated that due to being documentary filmmakers, they experience a great deal of restrictions and obstacles in the areas related to women, and so have constantly tried to express those problems.[9] In return, the Islamic Republic has been suspicious of documentary makers, watching them closely and applying harsh restrictions. In September 2011, the government arrested and imprisoned six independent Iranian documentary makers for alleged activities damaging to the regime.[10] In 2016, the filmmaker Keywan Karimi was arrested for making the documentary *Writing on the City* (2015), which was an account of the history of graffiti in Tehran. He was sentenced to six years in prison and 223 lashes. His charges were "propaganda against the regime" and "insulting the sacred".[11] This is in addition to many filmmakers, who have had to leave the country as a consequence of their work, such as Lila Ghobadi and Moslem Mansouri, makers of underground documentaries, such as *Epitaph* (1998) about women prostitutes in Iran.

Pune Parsafar

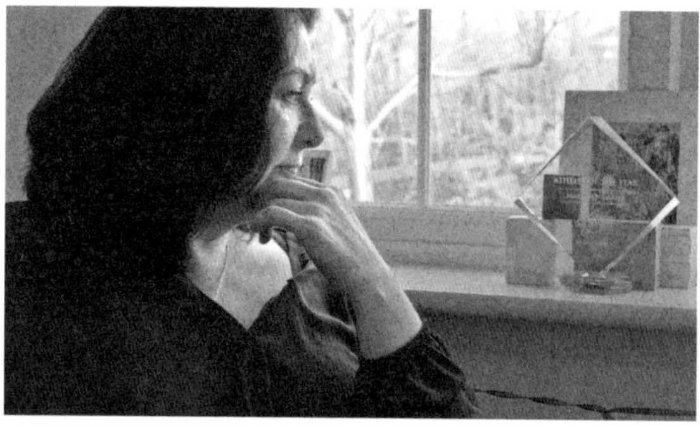

Maryam Namazie, a participant in my film, a rights campaigner and critic of political Islam, beside her Atheist of the Year Award, Kazimierz Łyszczyński Foundation, Warsaw, 2014

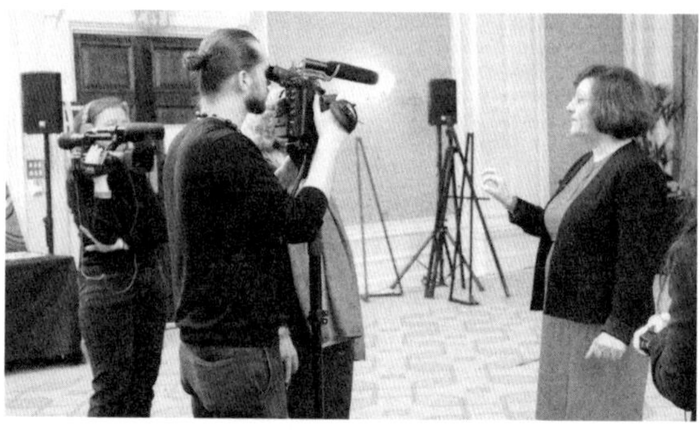

Mina Ahadi, a participant in my film, a women's rights and political activist, on the fringe of the 1st International Atheist Day Event, London, March 2019

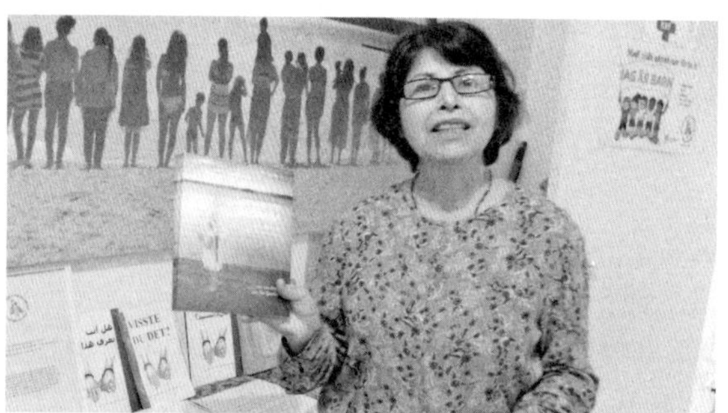

Farideh Arman, a participant in my film, introducing *Summer's Sheerest Light*, 2014, by Lars Åberg and Åsa Sjöström on Farideh's Women's Rights Association, Malmö, Sweden

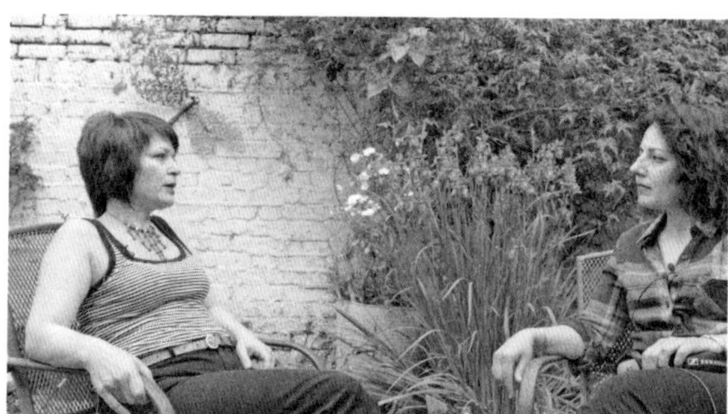

Shiva Mahbobi (left), a participant in my film, a rights campaigner and former political prisoner at the age of 16, in conversation with me in her garden in London, 2017

I wanted to present women in this documentary as the agents of change, as subjects who contribute to the creation of networks of sociality and solidarity for women and for social justice and human rights. In a society living under a systematic state misogyny enshrined in its laws and built into its ideology, women have become important agents for change in opposing this regime, not just for themselves but for society as a whole. In a society whose political and religious establishment rests on the disenfranchisement of women, which ideologically justifies its rationale for exist-ence by denying human status to women, women can become powerful agents for change. While it is not a simple question of substituting the Marxist notion of the proletariat with female agency as the agent of change for social transforma-tion in a capitalist society, women's agency and mobilization is nevertheless an important adjunct to (and an ally of) the working class. Marx says of the working class that it cannot

12. Karl Marx, 'A Contribution to the Critique of Hegel's Philosophy of Right. Introduction', *Karl Marx: Early Writings* (London: Penguin Classics, 1992), pp. 453–479.

liberate itself without at the same time liberating the entire enslaved humanity.[12] The women under this aggressive misogynistic system cannot achieve change in their situation without at the same time upending the system as a whole. Hijab (the obligatory Islamic headscarf) is a case in point. The abolition of compulsory hijab questions the ideology of the state and its whole justification for existence.

As an Iranian woman who was forced to wear the hijab as a child right after the Islamic regime came to power in 1979, I have first-hand experience of systematic misogyny and state gender segregation on many levels. I could not make sense of why we had to wear heavy and cumbersome clothes in order to go to school. I could not understand why I was being forced to cover myself, although I was not any less than my male cousins, who did not have to. Since leaving Iran, it has been a long struggle to overcome the emotions of constant intimidation and humiliation, of being reminded to live by the Islamic rules and act according to behaviour considered appropriate for a *good* woman. In my film, I decided to portray myself and my women participants released from their enforced mobile cages—the hijab—and as the modern, secular protagonists that they are. I wanted to reflect and amplify their voices, a voice that goes beyond the stereotypical picture of a woman from the "Islamic East", and show how they are influential participants in the major political and social discourses and activisms of the day. During filming, as we were sitting in different gardens and living rooms, I asked about my participants' public presence, whether as a partisan in Sanandaj, a political prisoner in a women's prison in Kermanshah (both cities in the west of Iran), or a speaker at a protest rally in Tehran or a secularist conference in London. In the film-making, I

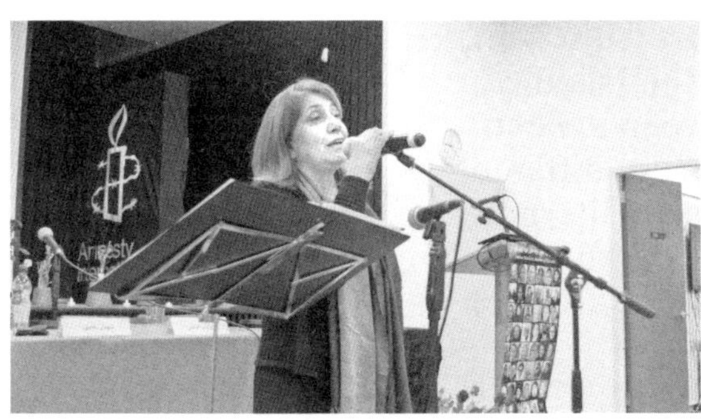

Mersedeh Ghaedi, a participant in my film, former political prisoner and a justice campaigner, speaking at an event in London, honouring the 'Mothers of Khavaran', who have been campaigning for redress for their loved ones executed during the 1980s political genocide in Iran, and buried in the unmarked mass graves of Khavaran, in the outskirts of Tehran.

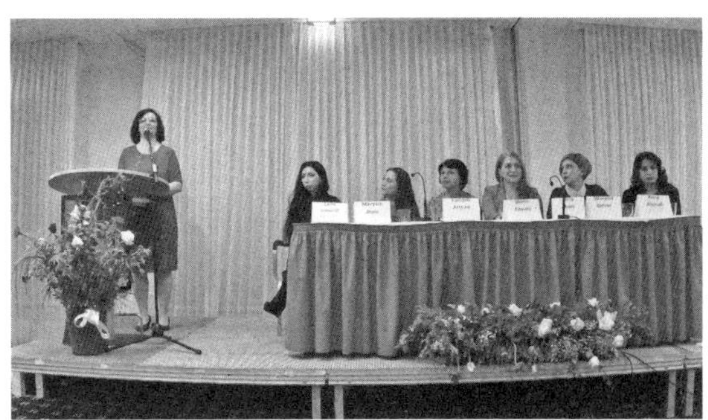

A scene from a session of the 'Rebellious Women Seminar', held in Cologne in 2017, debating the struggles of women from Iran and the Middle East for freedom and equality against Islamic laws and governments.

was looking for stylistic and substantive means to construct an image of Iranian women that is modern, rebellious and taboo-breaking, precisely to counter the existing stereotypes of Iranian official cinema.

Choosing women *activists* as participants in my film was a decision to construct an image of Iranian women which challenges the stereotypical representations (often as "good submissive housewives") both in numerous films of the Iranian official cinema and in Western fiction, such as in *Not Without My Daughter* (Gilbert, 1991) and *House of Sand and Fog* (Perelman, 2003). Asghar Farhadi's films are good examples of how women, whether central as in *About Elly* (2009) or in supporting roles, as in *A Separation* (2011), are subordinated to male power intellectually and physically. Farhadi is not afraid to show violence against women in his films and blame it on the woman's emotional and irrational behaviour and decisions. In *About Elly*, the reasons behind the actions by women are momentary pleasure or completely unknown as in the final death. In *A Separation*, the wife is inconsiderate to the illness of her father-in-law and would only like to pursue her own will, which results in her leaving her teenage daughter behind. In *The Past* (2013) the (Iranian) ex-husband is calm, caring and logical, and we are never wholly convinced why the (French) woman, who is trapped in another troubled relationship and failing her parental responsibilities, divorced him. Even the supporting female roles in his films are not spared this view. Although likable in the first instance, they appear ungrateful to the men's generosity. They are cunning creatures, who stop at nothing to gain what they desire. My choice of activist women, and the associated characteristics that come along with it, is to create, in complete contrast to this type of representation, a feminist iconography, which challenges the characterizations and portrayals mentioned above.

My film has an exclusively female cast from Iran, who have proven track records of opposing the Islamic regime in Iran. As a result of this, they all live in exile in Europe as political refugees. These women, from different backgrounds and with different ages, discuss an alternative take on women's lives in Iran in recent history. The six women in my film, together, represent important areas of social protest in the current Iranian society.

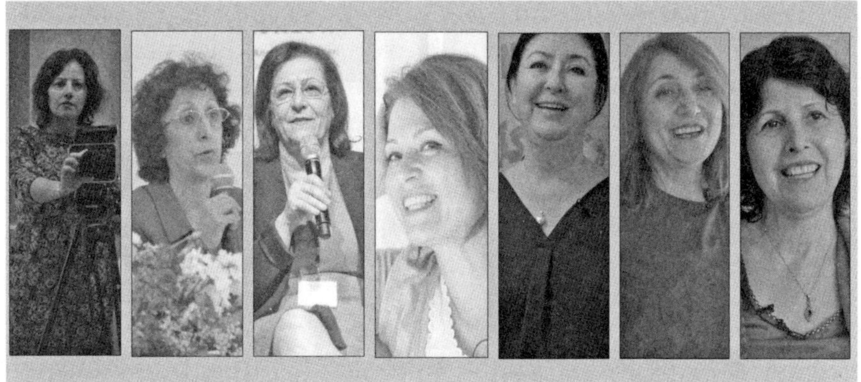

The participants in my documentary, from left to right: Pune Parsafar, Shahla Daneshfar, Mina Ahadi, Shiva Mahbobi, Maryam Namazie, Mersedeh Ghaedi and Farideh Arman

13. A movement of public protests by women in Iran against compulsory hijab that started in December 2017, inspired by Vida Movahed who stood on a utility box in Tehran's Revolution Street, removing her hijab and hoisting it on a stick.

14. Sharon Smith, 'The Image of Women in Film: Some Suggestions for Future Research', *Feminist Film Theory: A Reader*, ed. Sue Thornham, (Edinburgh: Edinburgh University Press, 1999), pp. 14–19.

Along with this key political motivation behind my film, I have been contemplating an iconography appropriate to my genre, producing a feminist film, an alternative avant-garde documentary that is critical of the dominant image of women in Iran. Therefore, my camera focuses on events led by women, such as meetings, rallies, conferences and organizations, whose agendas revolve around women's rights and human rights. For instance, I have filmed them at specific events where many of my women are present in groups and protest collectively, expressing clearly their campaign mottos including workers' rights, freedom of expression, against compulsory hijab and for release of jailed political activists. In my film, I include footage of one woman, Shahla, as a workers' rights activist in constant contact with Iran and with worker activists on the ground, as well as on International Women's Day rally in 2018 in Trafalgar Square in London holding out a headscarf as a sign of protest against compulsory veiling in solidarity with the Girls of Revolution Street[13] and their protest against compulsory veiling.

In my film, women are not just seen participating in protests about national and international human rights issues, but they also discuss, propose and advocate solutions. They appear in settings, which challenge gendered conceptualizations of the workplace. My film acts on Sharon Smith's analysis of feminist documentary (1999),[14] which suggests showing women in a wider range of roles, positioned as active and not passive and freed from the typical conventions of subservient roles to men. My women are the founders, heads and/or speakers of their organizations and have worked hard to make real changes in people's lives and a major impact in society. During my interviews, I made sure to illustrate these achievements. By showing Iranian women in empowering roles in international public forums as agents of change, I aim to substitute the negative images for positive ones, subverting the gender-based conventions of both fiction and documentary.

Having six participants helped me to approach my narrative as a collection of personal narratives, and this forms the structure of my documentary. My film therefore adopts the approach of ensemble films which are made up of many key actors who are given roughly equal weight during the story and which 'stress a sense of collectivity and community', in contrast to the popular sole "protagonism" in Hollywood cinema.[15] While they share a commonality in what they do, the specific domain each covers is the focus of separate narratives, which I let freely develop in my interviews. Each of these domains/protagonists complements the others, and they all link up as a patchwork to build the bigger narrative for the documentary.

In contrast to the depiction of women in Iranian cinema, I have employed the colour red, seen in red lipstick and red clothing of the women filmed. Sometimes, it was already a choice by my participant, and at other times, my suggestion, and agreed by my participant. The use of

15. Ernest Mathijs, 'Referential Acting and the Ensemble Cast', *Screen* 52, no. 1 (Spring 2011), pp. 89–96.

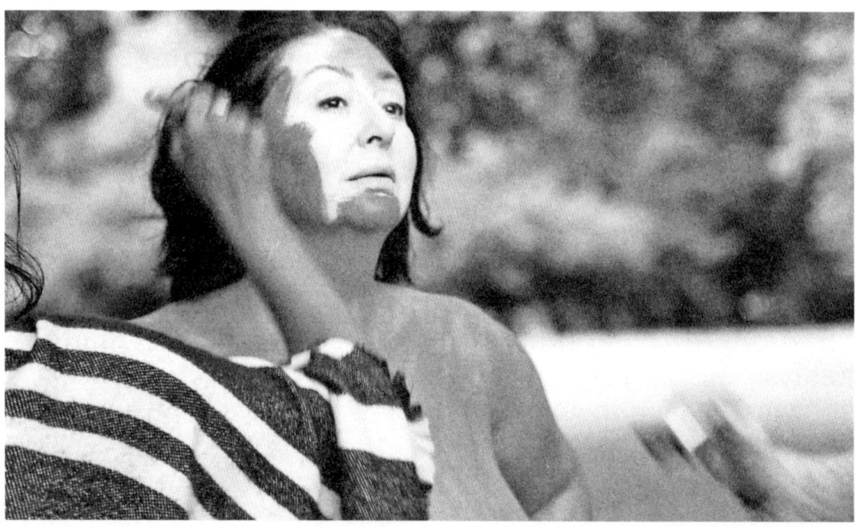

Maryam Namazie receiving a body paint during a bodypainting event in solidarity with Ex-Muslims, in a north London park, September 2017

the colour red is in opposition to dark colours, especially black, as the symbolic colour of Islamic modesty, eternal mourning for the dead and the Islamic Republic as a whole. I have also included scenes in which the women in the film put on makeup. In this way, I am showing details of their private lives which Iranian women have been prevented from expressing freely, but also depicting a normal, everyday life of these women.

In addition to colour, I have made use of personal objects, such as photos, letters, memorabilia, wherever I could, in order to depict the private lives of my participants, alongside their political lives. As well as enriching their stories, these personal items and photos act as tropes for their modern-day and progressive character, which challenge the traditional, stereotypical images of Iranian women prevalent in the official cinema in Iran and in much of the mainstream films in the West.

In my film, I appear in the narrative of the film, not just as the interviewer who asks questions but also as the camera-woman, sound-recordist and producer-researcher for the film. The decision to include myself in the frame was a deliberate choice to position myself alongside my other protagonists, as someone who has lived through a similar experience and who, with her film and camera, is engaged in the same battle.

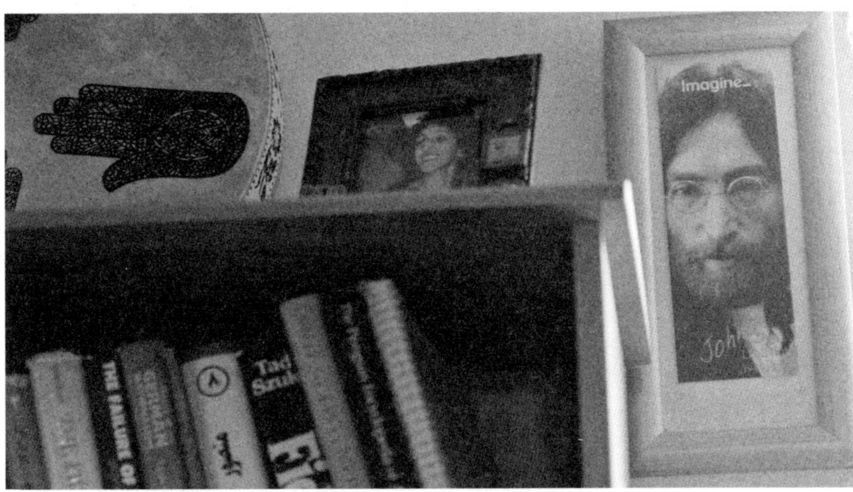

Use of personal items and photos as tropes which challenge the traditional, stereotypical images of Iranian women prevalent in the official cinema in Iran and in much of the mainstream films in the West.

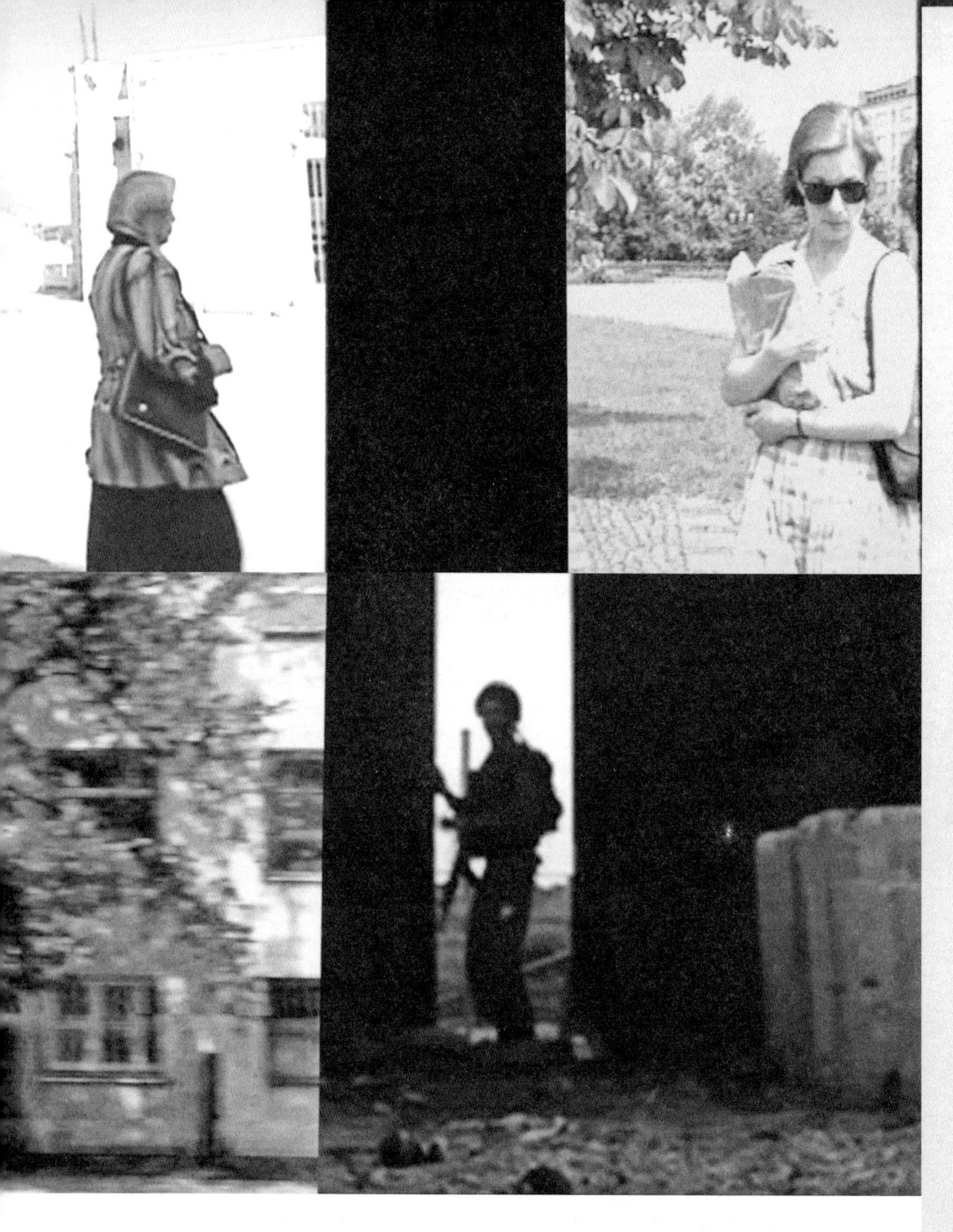

'WE REFUSE TO BE SCAPEGOATS' An Essay on the Painful Journey Towards un Censored a New Art Work

Pam Skelton

un Censored is the name of a work in progress, a video installation I am making that explores an archaeological and multidirectional approach to the politics of memory shaped by the conflicted and contested histories of Israel, Palestine and Poland.

There are two strands to my contribution. The first maps the trajectory of my journey through this project across the disputed pasts and uncertain futures which bridge histories, spaces, places and times spanning the Holocaust to different moments in the long-standing Israeli-Palestinian conflict. The second strand is adapted and re-invented for this book, as images and text, in the form of transnational and transgenerational multi-voice dialogues constructed as encounters between figures who live or have lived through occupation or as either activists or witnesses. These are the ones who give testament and hold to account the power mongers, and invaders who hold limitless power and create intolerance and hatred at the expense of peace.

un Censored is a work of solidarity born of the desire for a gathering of activists, academics, artists, citizens and refugees who have lived through different struggles and who have experienced the realities of oppression and life under occupation. Like all reflective work on conflict in

Israel-Palestine, it is transgressive because it touches sensitive subjects that will disturb some or might cause offence to others because we have learnt that certain histories must be kept apart. Isolating histories makes it easier to deny human rights abuses and common ground with others. It is a convenient strategy for policy makers who choose to erase or marginalize politically inconvenient histories of populations living through conflict and put the blame on the people who they are oppressing. There are a growing number of voices in opposition, they cannot be stopped: they speak out against the creation of camps and walls and checkpoints, expulsions and racisms, they refuse to be censored and they refuse to be scapegoats.

Palestine   Israel

Denial, sociologist Eva Illouz suggests, is the mind's capacity to block out, forget, push aside and minimize information that is uncomfortable or painful to the self and she goes on to say that this is precisely what Israel has done in exhibiting three stages of denial in its treatment of the Palestinians since the formation of the state of Israel in 1948, and these denials allow it to stay blind to its status as an occupying power. The three forms of denial that Illouz identifies are 1) the erasure of memories, 2) the denial of knowledge of the conflict and ignoring the consequences of their actions from themselves and others and 3) a form of denial that is the gaze that sees but does not register.[1]

Avraham Shapira's book *The Seventh Day: Soldiers' Talk About the Six Day War* (the Arab Israeli War of 1967) is made up of candid dialogues between two generations of Israeli soldiers and poets who talk about what James Young has identified as their 'extremely complicated relationship between collective Holocaust memory, their sense of patriotism and their reasons for fighting in the war'.[2] In 1948, half of the population of Israel was made up of Holocaust survivors, many of whom could identify with the fate of the Palestinians with sentiments of sympathy and remorse: 'it is these visions of the Holocaust that compel us to fight… but at the same time we do not want to lose that sense of identity

1. Eva Illouz, 'Israel is in National Denial regarding the oppression of Palestinians', *Haaretz*, 11 November 2015, www.haaretz.com /israel-is-in-national-denial-regarding-its-oppression-of-palestinians-1.5420257. As an example of this in reading art, see Juli Carson's essay 'Art of the Impossible: The Jewish Renaissance Movement in Poland', which points to a psychoanalytical reading of denial, http://yaelbartana.com/text/deflections-anti-mirrors-2.

2. James E. Young, 'When Soldier-Poets Remember the Holocaust: Antiwar Poetry in Israel', *Writing and Re-writing the Holocaust: Narrative and the Consequences of Interpretation* (Indiana University Press, 1988).

3. Avraham Shapira (ed.), *The Seventh Day: Soldiers' Talk About the Six-Day War* (London: Penguin, 1971), p. 217.

4. Ibid., pp. 38–39.

5. Ibid.

6. Anat Livne and David Netzer, 'Holocaust, Democratic Values and Jewish-Arab Dialogue: The Work of the Center for Humanistic Education at the Ghetto Fighters' House Museum', in *Holocaust Education in a Global Context*, eds. Karel Fracapane and Matthias Haß (Paris: UNESCO/ Topography of Terror Foundation, 2014), pp. 216–217.

with the victim'.[3] In the 1960s, the state of Israel came to identify and articulate militarization and victimhood with the Holocaust as a necessary pre-condition to the nation's survival and defence against what they perceived as the permanent threat of annihilation to the Jewish state.

> Menachem: I felt uneasy about being a victorious army, a strong army. If I had any clear awareness of the World War years and the fate of European Jewry it was once when I was going up the Jericho road and the (Palestinian) refugees were going down it. I identified directly with them. When I saw parents dragging their children along by the hand, I actually almost saw myself being dragged along by my own father.[4]

Moving and important as this book is for insight into soldiers' attitudes at the time, women do not have much of a voice in *The Seventh Day*, their role in Israel is in their support for their families. Palestinian women are simply identified as part of refugee families with their children:

> Berala: I found a satchel belonging to a child who must have been in the first grade. It didn't make me too happy. Although when I flipped through the pages of a textbook I saw a picture of a rifle with a bayonet pointing towards Israel. All the same it's not just the guilty who suffered… We saw refugees. People going along with their donkeys carrying all sorts of bits and pieces. We thought more generally in terms of the whole of humanity. Wars are bad. Even when you win them.[5]

In a comparative study of school history textbooks published in Israel in the years from 1948 to 2006, Anat Livner and David Netzer show how they serve 'the educational establishment as a tool to provide a selective structuring of events, to categorize and shape the content, and also to hide and erase parts of history' and especially to 'mobilize the memory of the Holocaust as a cornerstone of Israeli youth'.[6] This process serves the creation of a hegemonic narrative that describes the history of a nation and

the territory it claims 'as well as cultivating the nations
norms by which it abides'.[7]

In 2002, the militaristic construction of the Israeli
Separation Barrier saw fit to carve up the land to keep
Israelis "safe" behind an eight-metre high concrete barrier,
barbed wire and checkpoints in a country where every
Palestinian is considered a potential terrorist. Instability
and war are motivated by economic incentives described by
Naomi Klein as "Disaster Capitalism",[8] an industry where
the financial incentives are huge. As we know, Israel is not
alone in its ambition to turn 'itself into a fortified gated
community, surrounded by locked-out people living in
permanently excluded red zones'.[9] Nevertheless, the creation
of the Israeli Separation barrier

> allows Israel not to see itself as aggressive, violent,
> cruel, possessive, a violator of human rights, by
> projecting all these traits onto the Palestinians
> beyond the wall. The wall is not perceived by
> the Zionists as an aggressive act; it is perceived
> as a protective act, an act of self defense… thus
> preserving its basic assumption that is the "good"
> "just" victim.[10]

Lithuania   Israel

The collapse of the Soviet Union in 1989 and the fall of the
Berlin Wall revealed a parallel world, which previously had
only been imagined and now could be visited. It brought
into focus a Lithuania that had been off limits and was a
place of particular significance by virtue of my family having
emigrated from there to Britain. During my research trip
to Poland, Lithuania and Ukraine in the summer of 1993,
I focused on searching for and recording the remnants of
Jewish life before the war and the genocidal legacy of the
aftermath. It was an experience that shaped my research
interests and my art practice. I could now acknowledge
my generational relationship to the Jewish genocide and at
the same time the inability or impossibility to imagine the
catastrophe that befell the many millions of people who were

7. Noga Kadman, *Erased from Space and Consciousness: Israel and the Depopulated Palestinian Villages of 1948* (Bloomington, IN: Indiana University Press, 2015), p. 34.

8. See Naomi Klein, *Shock Doctrine: The Rise of Disaster Capitalism* (London: Penguin Books, 2007) or Antony Loewenstein, *Disaster Capitalism: Making a Killing Out of Catastrophe* (London: Verso, 2017).

9. Naomi Klein, 'Losing the Peace Incentive: Israel as Warning', in *Shock Doctrine*, pp. 423-442.

10. Wendy Brown, Walled States, Waning Sovereignty (New York: Zone Books, 2014), p. 123.

    Feminist Art Activisms and Artivisms

11. From this encounter with Itzak Dogim, Pam Skelton's *Dangerous Places—Ponar* (1994–1995) emerged, a seven-channel video installation, opened Ferens Art Gallery, 4 December 1994. See also Griselda Pollock, 'Dangerous Places—Ponar: An Installation by Pam Skelton', *Third Text* 10, no. 36 (Autumn 1996), pp. 45–53. Itzak Dogim was one of 40 slave labourers who, for four months, dug up from the pits 60,000 corpses and burnt them and was among the eleven who survived after they excavated a tunnel to escape from the pit where they lived. See Vasily Grossman and Ilya Ehrenburg, *The Complete Black Book of Russian Jewry* (New York: Routledge, 2017).

also victims of fascism.

Vilnius, Lithuania was the birthplace of the Leeds branch of my family, the Hurwitzes. Twenty kilometres from Vilnius is the Panerai forest known as Ponar by the Vilnius Jews who, before the war, frequented it as a favourite picnic spot. It was there that I met Itzak Dogim. Itzak was part of a Jewish delegation from Israel, of Holocaust survivors on a commemorative trip to their countries of origin. My chance encounter with Itzak Dogim on this 1993 field trip was completely unexpected and made a profoundly deep impression. Itzak narrated his story to my camera of his incarceration and escape from Ponar, on which I based the video installation *Dangerous Places—Ponar* (1995–1996).[11] In December 1994, I visited Itzak at his home in Rishon LeZion in Israel. This was my first and only trip to Israel and it was during that visit that I started to understand on a day-to-day level the increasingly difficult situation experienced by Palestinians and tasted the militaristic aggression underlying everyday life.

Polish   Polish Jewish

In summer 1996, I met Magdalena Nowacka Jaccotta in Poland who shared with me her childhood memories of life in the Arian side of Nazi-occupied Warsaw. Her memories of life in Warsaw inspired me and led me to consider more about how the traumatic past returned to haunt her and other Polish people. I returned to Warsaw that October with the intention of researching Polish memory of the Warsaw ghetto. I began this project with the help of a curator at Ujazdowski Castle Centre for Contemporary Art, Warsaw and the Polish Jewish Historical Institute, Żydowski Instytut Historyczry Polsce, who turned their backs on me as soon as they understood the focus of the project. I had naively opened a Pandora's box revealing long-standing antagonisms and deeply held views of a conflicted history that spans Polish-Israeli politics up until today. I completed as much work as I could and shelved the project until in 2013 its presence emerged to take a prominent place in my current research.

I started to realize the terms of a bitter debate and undervaluing of Polish suffering in which the memory narratives of Jews and Poles are enacted 'in a kind of perpetual competition creating two divergent memorial perspectives, a Jewish and a Polish one'.[12]

Six million Poles died during World War II (1939–1945), three million of them were Polish Jews alongside millions of others who died as a result of Nazi Germany's aggressive policies in Germany and in occupied countries: Jews, Roma, political dissidents, resistance fighters, homosexuals, the disabled were all targeted. Poland having appeared to have absorbed German guilt is blamed for the Nazi death camps in Poland.

Israeli Professor, Daniel Blatman, has been appointed chief historian of a new commemorative project in Warsaw, the Warsaw Ghetto Museum, scheduled to open in 2023. The project is controversial because it takes a more inclusive approach to Jewish and Polish memory, acknowledging that Poland's history during Nazi occupation 'is formed out of two narratives not one' and that 'the wall that separated Jews and Poles during the Holocaust, was created neither by Jews nor Poles; it was created by the Germans'. Daniel Blatman has nevertheless been widely condemned for the direction that the museum will take. His argument remains:

> Is it really such a great sin to look at the wider picture? To take a more inclusive approach to the study of Nazi-occupied Poland? Is it really so terrible to tell the history of the Warsaw Ghetto from the perspective of the entire occupied, tormented and devastated city where the ghetto existed?[13]

Yael Bartana's *Europe Will Be Stunned* (2007–2011) proposes the return of 3.3 million Polish Jews to Poland in an epic film trilogy and fictional Congress of the 'Jewish Renaissance Movement in Poland'. The project is an interplay of art and politics, drama, history, documentary and parody transgressing the complicated realities and contested memory politics of Polish, Israeli and Palestinian realities. The return of the Jews to Poland with a subtext of the

12. Konstanty Gebert, 'Conflicting Memories: Polish and Jewish perceptions of the Shoah', *Holocaust Education in a Global Context*, eds. Karel Fracapane and Matthias Haß (Paris: UNESCO/ Topography of Terror Foundation, 2014), pp. 28–39.

13. Daniel Blatman, 'Warsaw Ghetto Museum Historian: A Tale of History, Force and Narrow Horizons', *Haaretz*, 4 January 2019, http://1943.pl/en/professor-daniel-blatman-in-the-warsaw-getto-museum/.

IMPLICATED SUBJECTS

 Feminist Art Activisms and Artivisms

14. See https://culture.pl/en/event/the-power-of-imagination-1st-international-congress-of-the-jewish-renaissance-movement and Yael Bartana and Erika Balsom, 'Embrace Weakness! A Conversation, in *Yael Bartana: Trembling Times*, exh. cat. Lausanne (Musée cantonal des Beaux-Arts, 2017).

15. Rebecca Lewin, 'Yael Bartana Review', *This is Tomorrow: Contemporary Art Magazine* (2011), http://thisistomorrow.info/articles/venice-biennale-2011-yael-bartana.

16. Yifat Gutman coined the term memory activism. Affiliated with the globally circulating paradigm of historical justice, memory activist groups assume that a new understanding of the past could lead to a new perception of present problems and project alternative solutions for the future in Yifat Gutman, *Memory Activism, Reimagining the Past for the Future in Israel-Palestine* (Nashville, TN: Vanderbilt University Press, 2017).

return of the Palestinians to their homelands. The trilogy begins with Sławomir Sierakowski, a leftist leader of the Jewish Renaissance Movement in Poland, who delivers an impassioned plea for the return of the Jews to Poland to an almost empty stadium. In the second film, the returned Jews construct their settlement in a park in Warsaw city centre using the watch tower and stockade design used to build kibbutzim in Palestine in the 1930s. They are eerily reminiscent of concentration camps. The final film depicts Sławomir's funeral after his assassination.[14] Bartana's project engages the aesthetics of revolutionary Soviet cinema together with the legacy of European anti-Semitism, colonialism, socialism and Zionism to present art as a controversial political tool to provoke discussion. It is an important artwork and 'a powerful indictment of the conflicted memory of Poland and Israel and the present policies being enacted as a result of that history'.[15] With the erosion of freedom of speech, I doubt that it would find favour in the current political climate.

Witch hunts are currently taking place in Britain, Europe and the USA against anyone who criticizes Israeli policy on the treatment of Palestinians. This silencing has been normalized and enforced through the so-called International Holocaust Remembrance Alliance (IHRA) definition of antisemitism, whose examples falsely equate criticism of Israel with antisemitism.

We must speak out against censorship, for if today there can be no debate, no discussion, no voice, no criticism, there is no representation. Then, how can we act against the historical consciousness that buttresses contemporary far-right politics? Memory activism may offer an opposition to it.[16] If free speech is illegal then what is the fate of dissenting voices? If academics or artists who speak out are driven out from our universities, or are pushed to the margins; if artists only serve the art industry; if there are no counter narratives who will represent the unrepresented, not the press in their suppressing or disguising of facts on the ground.

Palestinian artist Larissa Sansour's two-channel monumental film, *Heirloom* (2019), filmed in black and white presents a post-apocalyptic dystopia future in an underground bunker in Bethlehem and acts as a warning.

Its flashes of grainy archive film clips of old Jerusalem that existed before 1967 are testimony to the lost inheritance shared by these two women in an intergenerational narrative of connectivity and loss. Bethlehem is Sansour's family home onto which she projects a stark, melancholic vision inhabited by two women whose 'individual narratives and personal experience' meet and 'where memory and forgetting compete'.[17] But what is the value of 'belonging and heritage' in a world where everything has been destroyed? Can anything be recovered and if not, what will the future hold? To take the narrative further, we must take the future into our own hands.

The contents of *un Censored* are sourced from websites created by peace activists and human rights groups and my own collection of Warsaw ghetto interviews. I am not an activist, I seldom put myself on the front line and feel more at ease avoiding crowds. I have approached this work from the only position I am capable of, which is through strength of feeling towards the subject and through trial and error applied in the spirit of explorative experimental practice-based visual art strategies of trial and error, which are shared in the excerpts which follow.

Two sections of the script from *un Censored*

An encounter with Ahed Tamimi: a Palestinian youth activist from the village of Nabi Saleh in the West Bank[18] and Gil Hillel: an Israeli peace activist who served at Sahlav Military Police Patrol in Hebron in the West Bank and broke the silence.[19]

Ahed Tamimi: I cannot think far into the future because the occupation prevents it.

Gil Hillel: I decided to break the silence because as a country, as a society I want us to examine the reality that we live in.

17. See Nat Muller, *Larissa Sansour, Heirloom*, exh. cat. Venice (58th Venice Biennale, Danish Pavilion), 2019.

18. Source: *Living Resistance Tour* FOSNA, www.youtube.com/watch?v=cMWuk_mi5kw.

19. Source: *Breaking the Silence*, Courtesy of Breaking the Silence, 2019, www.breakingthesilence.org.il/testimonies/videos/93551.

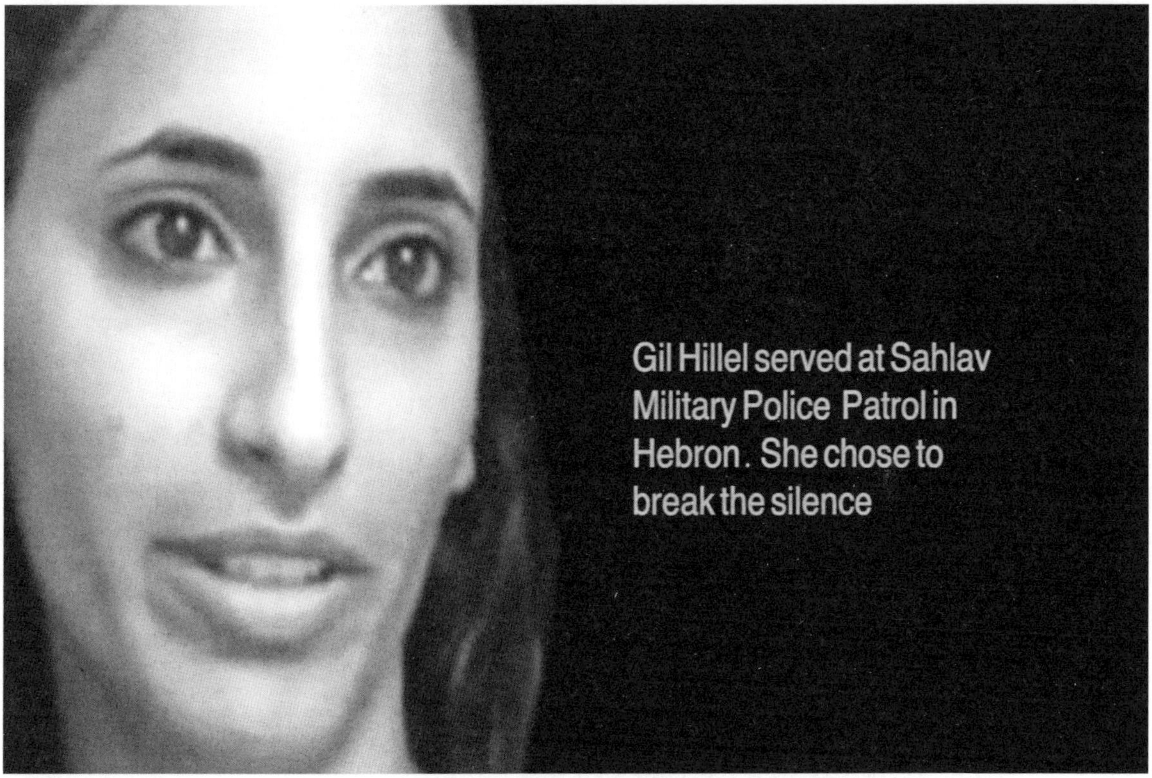

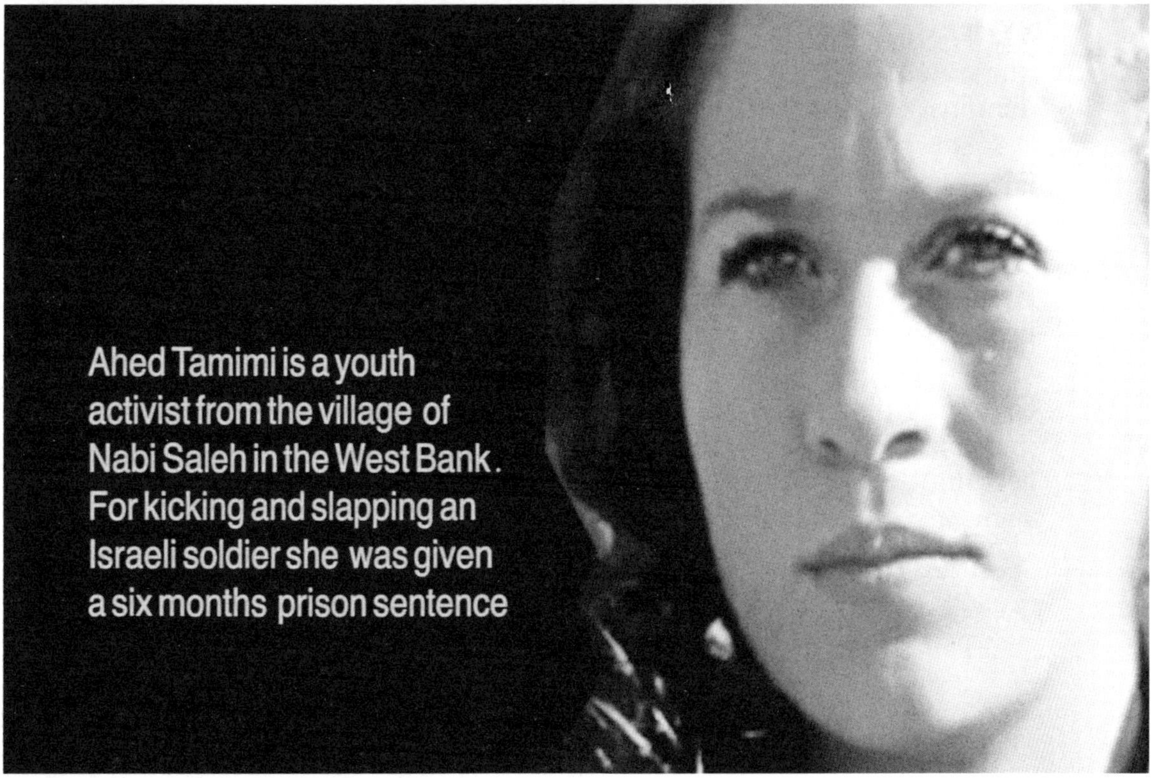

Pam Skelton, *un Censored*, 2019, video stills/artwork in progress

AT: You know we can see the ocean, but we cannot go there because of the occupation. It's only 30 minutes away, but its forbidden for us to go there unless we get Israeli permission.

GH: I want to look it in the eye and say okay, we are a conquering nation.

AT: I cannot think far into the future… every village in this area has a settlement around it or a military base or some physical presence of occupation.

GH: When I enlisted I said to myself okay? I'll have to do this. I'll go to the most combat focused unit there is, and I'll give it my touches of humanity.

AT: When I used to go to play in the street the army would enter the village and start shooting.

GH: And I turned into a monster and I can't look myself in the eye and for that I'm not alone.

AT: There are settlers down below trying to take our water spring, so we decided to lead a peaceful demonstration.

GH: There is no way out of becoming that violent aggressive person which I have become.

AT: In one day of protesting 1,000 gas canisters can be shot at us—in just one day!

GH: I ask that anyone who sees my testimony to just think about it. It's the reality of anyone who gets limitless power. It's what we turn into. It's our society.

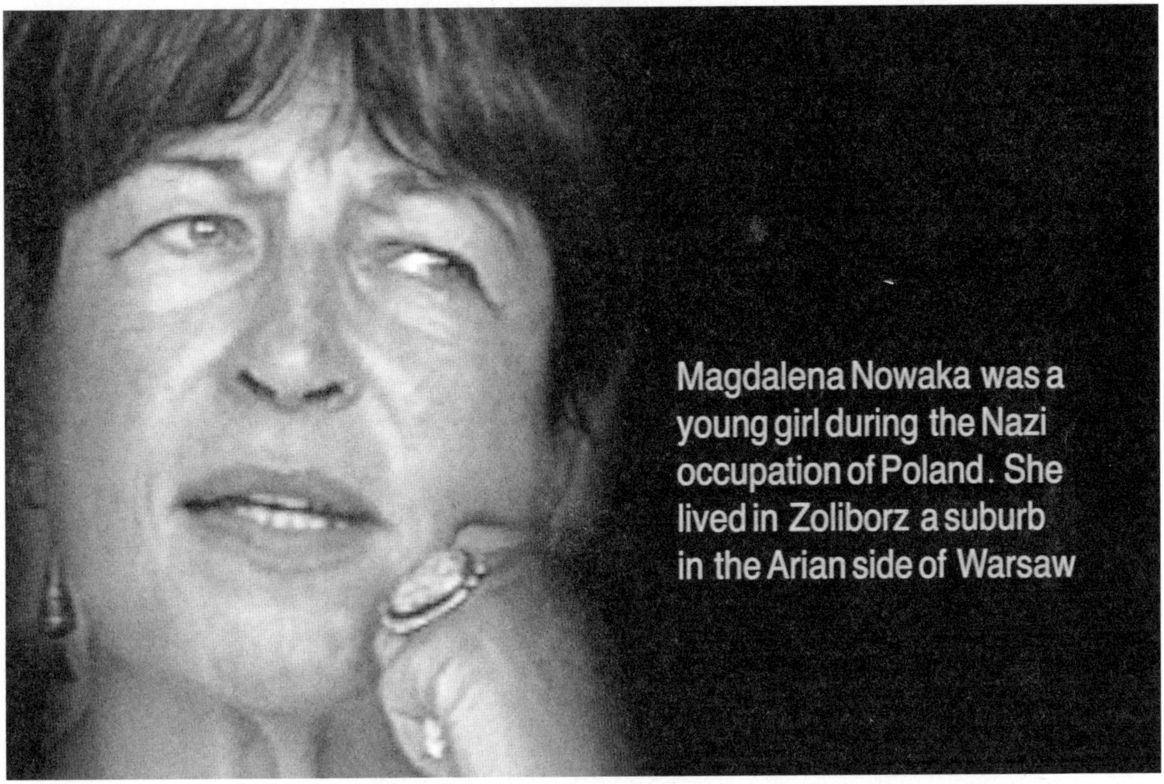

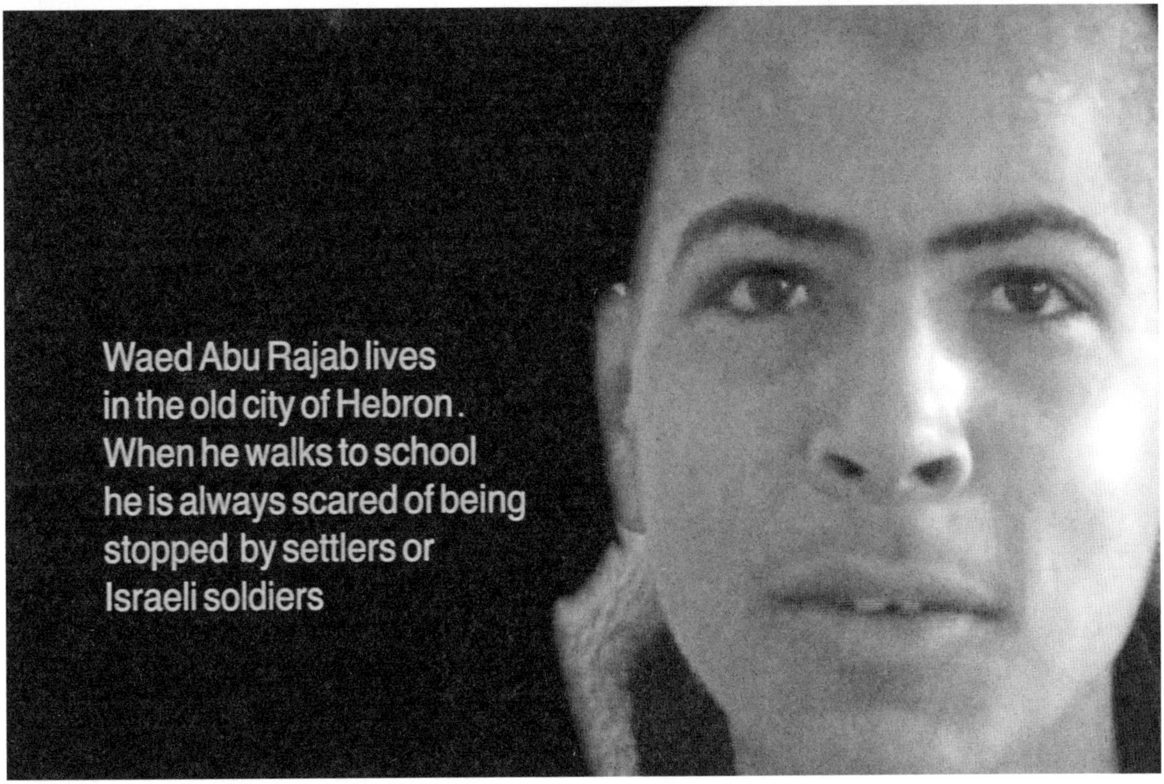

Pam Skelton, *un Censored*, 2019, video stills/artwork in progress

An encounter with Magdalena Nowacka: a schoolgirl in an Arian district of occupied Warsaw[20] and Waed Abu-Rajab: a schoolboy in Hebron in the occupied West Bank.[21]

20. Source: Pam Skelton's video collection recorded in 1996. Courtesy of Magdalena Nowacka, 2019.

21. Source: Walking to School with Waed in Hebron, 2016 UNRWA (United Nations Relief Agency for Palestinian Refugees in the Near East), www.unrwa.org/newsroom/videos/walking-school-waed-hebron.

Magdalena Nowacka: Well there were no schools, so I would go with five other girls to some private home to learn say mathematics. I had to go over two streets and two alleys. I'll never forget when I wanted to cross the alley where the big truck with the Germans with their helmets on, well they were sitting, and they were driving out, so I backed off letting them go because they were ruling the place.

Waed Abu-Rajab: This is my home, over there is my school. I have to go through checkpoints without problems it would take 10 mins to walk to school. When the soldiers check the people, it takes more than half an hour. If the soldiers don't stop us the settlers will. Every day is different, every day they make new rules. When I go through the first checkpoint they check me. When I go through checkpoint 106 they check me again.

MN: And I'll never forget, I'll never forget when I wanted to cross the alley where the big truck with the Germans was when I backed off they stopped. And then I wanted to go forward again, because I was late already, and the moment I started they would start the engine again and it was such a nasty game. I'll never forget that. I was terrified they would run me over. That's what I thought. Then finally at the last moment I just ran across fast, and well I won for the moment, but I was always scared.

WA-R: When I go through checkpoint 106 they check me again. The soldiers stare at us all the time. They always ask, where are you going, how old are you? You always have to keep your birth certificate in your pocket. Sometimes they take someone away. We see many terrible things. We are always scared.

The activist groups and individuals who have created,
maintained and contributed to these online platforms are a
vitally important resource, disseminating counter-narratives,
alternative futures and hope for the future. Their value is
indispensable, and their reach potentially vast, where they
foster understanding and peaceful resolutions to conflict. I
see the opportunity for artists as well as activists to consider
how these gateways enable the circulation of dissenting
voices to be heard more clearly and more effectively in our
society, such as encounters with Palestinian youth activist
Ahed Tamimi and Gil Hillel, an Israeli veteran who served
in the Israeli army and broke the silence, and Magdalena
Nowacka, once a schoolgirl in Warsaw and Waed-Abu
Ragab, a schoolboy in Hebron.

Bad expirienced
am not safe for my first
boss.

WHOSE HOUSEWORK, WHOSE ARTWORK? The Voice of Domestic Workers

Marissa Begonia and Amy Charlesworth

1. Martha Rosler, 'For an Art Against the Mythology of Everyday Life', *Decoys and Disruptions: Selected Writings 1975–2001* (Boston: MIT Press, 2004), p. 8.

In an early essay, Martha Rosler claimed:

> Cultural products can never bring about substantive changes in society, yet they are indispensable to any movement that is working to bring about such changes. The clarification of vision is a first step toward reasonably and humanely changing the world.[1]

For our purposes, the "movement" in question is a grassroots campaign and support group for migrant domestic workers in the UK, namely Justice for Domestic Workers (J4DW), who formed in London in 2009. Since their formation, the group has campaigned in public, regularly appeared in the press as a voice for domestic workers, lobbied UK Parliament, represented themselves at the United Nations and undertaken countless emergency rescue and support services for abused (and enslaved) peoples throughout the UK. In 2013, a further satellite group was constituted in Leeds as a result of protests around a domestic worker's court case in Yorkshire. In 2017, the group became a registered charity, at the same time, they renamed themselves as: Voice of Domestic Workers (VoDW). The arts are a mainstay of the group's broader education programme, which also includes ESOL and IT classes, legal advice sessions and access to healthcare support, all organized by the members of VoDW. Aesthetic literacy, for the group, has functioned as a core device for communicating difficult and diverse experiences enabling the formation of a common politics and a successful campaign: whether this be through painting and printing, filmmaking, theatre, song, dance or poetry. As a group they have collaborated extensively with artists, writers, programmers, and curators since their formation. For example, their longstanding work with curator Louise Shelley, who, until 2018, led the *Communal Knowledge* programme at The Showroom gallery in London, has continued beyond the walls of a singular institution and expanded the terms of the initial encounter (Shelley is now a Trustee and Treasurer for VoDW). Members have worked on projects nominated for the Turner Prize (with artist Ciara Phillips in 2014) and most recently alongside Hito Steyerl for her 2019 exhibition at the Serpentine Galleries.[2]

In the following exchange, Marissa Begonia (founder and co-ordinator

2. See www.theshowroom. org/exhibitions/ciara-phillips- workshop-2010-ongoing and here: www.youtube.com/ watch?v=NEhwb2M9ltI for a short clip on the project with Hito Steyerl.

3. From June 2019, the VoDW Leeds branch will serve as a base to increase the presence of the organization in the regions in order to support migrant domestic workers in households (or currently undocumented) outside of London.

4. At the time, Park was Director of Pavilion, she is now based at The University of Leeds and The University of Newcastle.

5. As part of Teresa May's (then home secretary) 'hostile environment' policies in 2012 the UK government changed the law so that migrant domestic workers (MDW) could only come to the UK under the non-renewable six-month tied visa system. Prior to this, migrant domestic workers, like Begonia, could renew their visa over a five-year period and apply for indefinite leave to remain (leading to British citizenship). See Anne Karpf, 'When Escaping an Abusive Employer is a Crime: The Trap Britain Sets for Filipino Domestic Workers', *The Guardian*, 15 January 2019, www.theguardian.com/ lifeandstyle/2019/jan/15/when- escaping-an-abusive-employer-is- a-the-trap-britain-sets-for-filipino- domestic-workers.

6. At the time of writing, the film has been screened at over forty film festivals and events, across the UK and internationally. In 2016, it won two awards, one for Best Short Screenplay award at the Philippine International Film Festival, Los Angeles and was shortlisted for the Arts and Humanities Research Award for Research in the Arts—Innovation Award. In 2017, it won the Film Ambassador Trophy, awarded by the Film Development Council of the Philippines, and was awarded The Best Film on Modern Slavery in the UK (awarded March 2018).

7. See 'Mindless Culture, Unskilled Labour', a conversation between Laura Guy and Rehana Zaman, 2015 for a thoughtful account of Zaman's film *Some Women, Other Women and all the Bittermen* (2014), which features many of the Leeds-based VoDW's group, www. academia.edu/27982523/Mindless_ Culture_Unskilled_Labour_An_ interview_with_Rehana_Zaman.

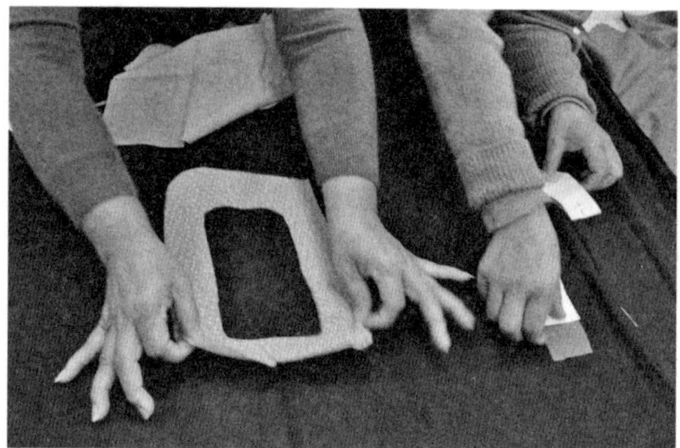

Voice of Domestic Workers Leeds, banner making workshop, 2013. Photo: Amy Charlesworth/Gill Park

of VoDW) and Amy Charlesworth (lecturer in Art History at The Open University) discuss the work that was accomplished and the aspects that were left unsaid (or undone) during the initial formation of the regional group, which took place over a two-year period, 2013–2015.[3] We hope the interview framework instigates greater parity between our two voices and works to cut loose the too often polarizing positions of interviewer (having authorial direction) and interviewee (assigned a vulnerability): a dynamic which is all too often adopted unthinkingly. Central to the building of the Leeds VoDW group was the production of two artists' films. *They Call Us Maids: The Domestic Workers' Story* (2013) is a short film made by longstanding feminist co-op, Leeds Animation Workshop, commissioned by Gill Park (Director of Pavilion, Leeds, UK, see chapter: Gill Park) and Amy Charlesworth.[4] The film, scripted and edited by Terry Wragg and animated by Jo Dunn, examines, through the lens of one story, the violence and exploitation faced by migrant domestic workers in the UK on the Overseas Domestic Worker Visa which ties (mostly) women to their employer.[5] The film was made in 2015 after a two-year period of getting to know one another through conversations, watching films, campaigning, workshops and sharing meals together.[6] This period was simultaneously shaped by the involvement and close working partnership (and friendship) the emergent group had with artist Rehana Zaman, who was working on her film *Some Women, Other Women and all the Bittermen* (2014).[7]

Marissa Begonia: I remember that it was a very exciting journey on the way to Leeds, J4DW (now VoDW) were in two coaches, for the first time, with a total of seventy-six passengers who were members. We stopped in Manchester to join the Union rally of 50,000 people against austerity and cuts in the NHS at the Conservative Party's annual conference while they were still in a coalition government with the Liberal Democrats. We couldn't move forward because there were so many coaches, so we got off the coaches and joined the rally for a short time. We heard the welcome speeches but we had to return to our coaches as agreed with the comrades watching and maintaining the flow of the rally. We headed off to Leeds, full of excitement. For us it was a new adventure to explore what we could offer to the domestic workers in the northern city of Leeds but also how our presence could influence the employers and community there. How we would begin to organize when everything was blank? I was not truly aware how much Amy and Gill who we went to meet would understand us nor whether they realized how complex the condition of domestic workers is, with work, visas etc. It was also a big question mark how many migrant domestic workers worked in Leeds, who are they, what work do they do? I wondered, could we rely on our members who migrated to Leeds to help us reach-out to other domestic workers? We did have fifty migrant domestic workers who I knew were mostly undocumented and I knew this was one reason why it was difficult to engage them. How could we gain their trust and help them overcome their fear the way we had done in London? Should we adopt a different approach? How would local people in Leeds (and its local council) respond to precarious work such as ours? Was (and is) this type of work simply not visible and the workforce too unknown and isolated?

We did talk initially about providing English classes and possibly doing an art class every month, a Sunday session. I know we struggled because of lack of funding that even VoDWs couldn't produce funding for an outreach programme to keep the Leeds community going. I'm imagining what we could have done differently so we could get more support?

Amy Charlesworth: At the time we met I was doing a PhD and working, both as a teaching assistant and also within the regional arts infrastructure. I worked at The Henry Moore Institute too and had booked the use of the conference room for us; the many voices and languages reverberating throughout the usually still space of the galleries as I welcomed you all up the stairs to the offices was memorable. At the time I'd been reading a lot about the labour of care and domestic work, the debates from the 1970s within feminism in the West around "wages for housework" and the relation between waged and un-waged labour. I was focussed on

how these politics intersected with (mostly) art made by women at the time. I'd also been reading many social policy reports on gendered migration and considering the arguments around the greater inclusion of women in waged work in the West from the 1970s onwards relied heavily on the outsourcing of domestic and care work to (mostly) women of colour, and/or women trapped in economic hardship. At the time, there seemed to me, to be many overlaps and synergies between the VoDW campaigns (and work with artists), this longer history in the UK and its interactions with global politics and the experiences of women of colour. During the course of our meetings it became clear that my assumptions, while striving for commonalities were in no way sufficiently attentive to the unique specificities of people's experiences and individual circumstances. As we got to know each other as a group, we sought representatives from Unite the Union and local Filipino community organizers in Leeds to attend our meetings (important to this were the individual energies of everyone now involved). Despite these efforts it became obvious that we needed to embed and network VoDW within the fabric of "third sector" and other organizations and charities involved in political organizing in Leeds and Yorkshire. With time and money consistently on a shoestring, efforts got funnelled—not unsurprisingly, given mine and Gill's own backgrounds—through the arts. One event which worked very well was

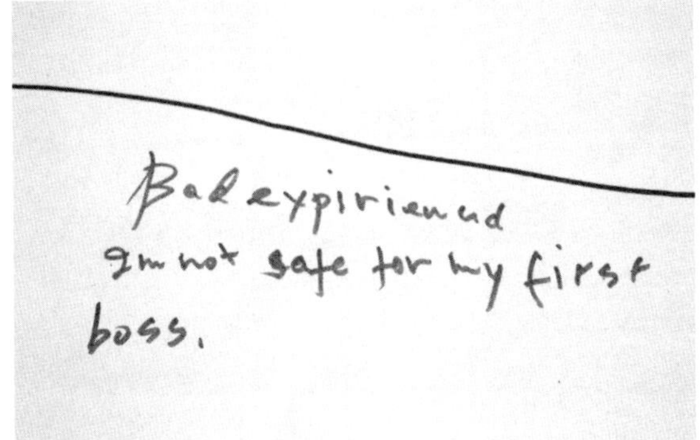

Voice of Domestic Workers Leeds, workshop, 2013.
Photo: Amy Charlesworth/Gill Park

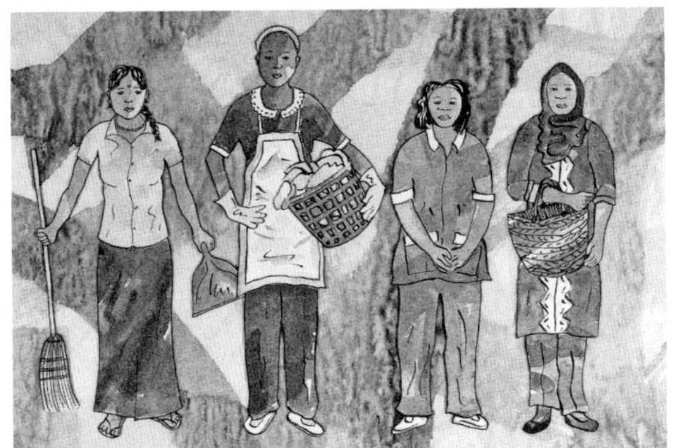

Leeds Animation Workshop, *They Call Us Maids: The Domestic Workers' Story*, 2015, film still, 7'. Courtesy of Leeds Animation Workshop

the public screening we did together at the independent cinema Hyde Park Picture House, in Leeds. We showed Colin Welland's BBC *Play for Today Leeds United!* with an introduction by us all.[8] It felt really important to position VoDW in proximity to past worker struggles, many of whom were first generation migrants to the city.[9] You recently reminded me, Marissa, that this resulted in VoDW doing a documentary for *Inside Out* BBC Yorkshire and Lincolnshire in 2016.

Artworks *about* political issues or artworks *made* politically are often categorized as distinct from one another, with the latter understood as more radical in approach and function. Animation, as a form, cannot be so easily categorized. The decision to commission LAW made sense for a number of reasons, not least the long history they have as a collective committed to feminist principles and social justice. We hoped, given their engagement with teaching animation, this would translate into a skills sharing experience too. How do you see *They Call Us Maids* operating? Do you think it'll have purpose beyond its immediate use given it was our intention it functioned as a campaign film of sorts for VoDW? And if it doesn't, does that matter to you, and the organization more widely?

Marissa Begonia: This was our first and only animated film, we have used it to host panel events and raised public awareness about the condition of migrant domestic workers during the year after it was produced. It was also shown in some independent cinemas with a wider audience and was nominated for and won some awards. We were also invited by some academics to show the film and talk more about the domestic worker's plight, we took that opportunity to gather their support and we did receive positive actions; some of them would ask how they could help and offer to talk or write to their MPs or help us campaign and others offered donations.

There was some criticism, like it wasn't real because it's animated but actually it was real stories of members of the VoDWs. People asked why we used cartoons when we have real people? But I loved the process which ensured the domestic workers themselves were directly involved in the making of the film. We learned and watched how Leeds Animation did the film. It was also good to see the Leeds Animation studio and their other work.[10] We also felt very privileged to have done most of the Sunday workshops in Leeds City Art Gallery. Amy and Gill did their very best to accommodate us during this period. It wasn't difficult to convince domestic workers (from both London and Leeds) to share their stories because— due to the form the film would take—it wouldn't show their faces, the animation protected their identity, all we needed was for them to share their stories. I did remember Terry saying that she found it difficult to understand the complexity of our stories so we did talk to her many times until she wrote the final script. The film works

10. Leeds Animation Workshop (LAW) was founded in 1978 to make and distribute films on social issues. It is an independent, not-for-profit women-run co-op and remains committed to feminist and collectivist principles.

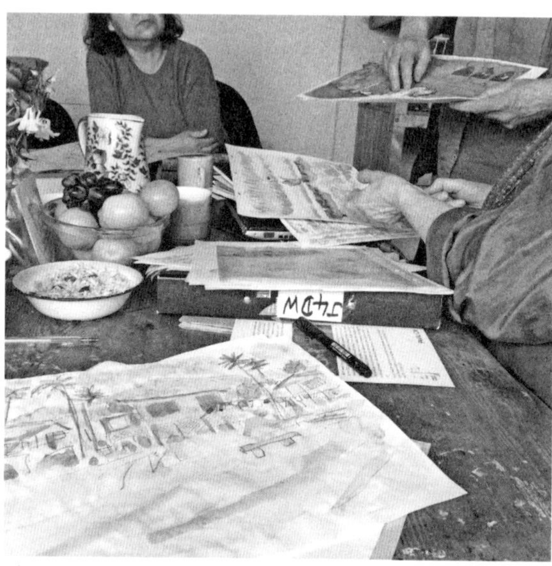

Voice of Domestic Workers Leeds, animation workshop, 2014.
Photo: Amy Charlesworth

Feminist Art Activisms and Artivisms

well for raising awareness because it is short and the animation makes it feel accessible for different audiences

You and Gill planned to show the film in schools as a way to help educate a younger audience. I thought it was brilliant idea but wasn't not sure if teachers would actually welcome this? I did experience being asked by the child I was caring for (in my place of work) to help raise awareness in her school, however, it didn't happen in the end because the school changed what they wanted to do on that day. At a different level, VoDW is very open to students who are doing their research on migrant domestic workers but what frustrates me sometimes is their lack of interest in talking directly to domestic workers. I often think how can they even complete their work without this? There's so much ignorance because of their inability to talk and discuss things directly to domestic workers. It is no good only speaking to me because I am not experiencing what the workers are experiencing now.

AC: Gill and I never secured the funds to implement the school idea you mention. The film was shown to community groups through a screening at The Open University in Milton Keynes, which did include a younger audience. An important element to screening films is the conversations that happen afterwards. Gill and I screened *They Call Us Maids* as part of a longer film programme, *Images and Journeys*, devised with, and for, newly arrived asylum seekers in Leeds. These screenings were initially for a closed workshop, attendees then, in turn selected a programme of films for a public audience. As mentioned before, it felt important to try and find ways to place the campaign on VoDW within the regional context, within histories past and present. The film also won an award from the Film Development Council of the Philippines in 2017. Of course, the politics of distribution are just as important as the politics of production. Despite the many long-standing connections that Leeds Animation Workshop have, given their place within independent film networks in the UK and further afield, I know distribution takes consistent effort and remains an issue long after the film is made. There are two elements that are important to this, not only who gets to screen the film, but how it is screened. I recall you telling me, Marissa, how you felt ensuring a member of VoDW being present results in greater ownership over the representation. Gill and I secured funds for the production however the importance of funds for distribution, given we would need to ensure travel and time, where possible, could be covered if a member of VoDW were to attend future screenings is just as necessary. Your second point, to my mind, raises, more broadly the issue of time, and lack thereof. All the while, as a group, you are managing a range of requests and the need to raise awareness but this leaves you open to careless engagement which all too often feeds little back into the growth and sustainability of the organization, repeating the mistake of rendering you objects of study and diminishing the acute need to understand and make visible your role as workers and contributors to the economy of the UK.

Our meetings in Leeds were often difficult, not to organize, but in terms of growing members in the regions. There was a great deal of inconsistency in terms of numbers, sometimes we would have large groups, other times we would struggle to get more than one or two domestic workers to come along. On occasion, we had potential members attend with their employer's young children, for others the minimal time off from their almost 24/7 jobs meant spare time was extremely stretched. Often Gill and I would use funds secured from small council or arts grants to ensure both yourself and another member from London could attend. The presence of you (and members, such as Georgina) was invaluable, indeed, a necessity for ensuring domestic workers attended our meetings, mostly held on Sundays. In many ways the Leeds regional group began from within the infrastructure of contemporary art (Gill and I as supporters, facilitators, administrators and fundraisers) and it quickly became apparent how ill-equipped we were (structurally, institutionally and also, to a certain extent, personally) to deal with the complex needs of domestic workers. I wondered if you could say something about the regional context? Perhaps you could talk a little about the specific case of Cristy and what, as a group, we were able to do through the *They Call Us Maids* film.

MB: Cristy was in the UK under the old Overseas Domestic Worker Visa. The only problem with the old Overseas Domestic Worker Visa was how much power was still in the hands of the employer. The domestic worker needed the support of their employer (proof of funds, a contract and letter of support) every year in order to renew their visa. For Cristy, this support fell through meaning she was not able to renew her visa and also needed to find domestic work elsewhere. Once she found a new employer, she experienced abuse and they also withheld wages. When Cristy reported this abuse to the authorities they immediately locked her up because they believed the employer, who had reported Cristy for stealing. The judgment on her case was also unjust and this left Cristy so devastated, hopeless and traumatized. There was little we could do to help her. The old visa system was not perfect and there was plenty of room for improvement but it did allow domestic workers to exercise their rights as workers, they could fight their case in the Tribunal Courts and claim unpaid wages. It worked for many domestic workers like me and I am now a British citizen. But instead of improving the old Overseas Domestic Worker Visa, the UK government removed all the rights of domestic workers. So, since 2012, VoDW have struggled to help domestic workers under the new visa system. What we can do is provide emergency accommodation for them after we have rescued them from an abusive employer but we can do little to help them in terms of their visa because once their six-months visa has ended, they automatically become undocumented. The more unprotected the domestic workers are, the more they will be subject to abuse and exploitation as "illegal" workers.

While there is National Referral Mechanism of Trafficking Law the need to prove that one has been abused is hard for domestic workers as there are no witnesses and rarely any evidence as they often work in isolating conditions within the private space of the home. The National Referral Mechanism (NRM) effectively changes the status of these women from workers to victims. Domestic workers are victims of slavery and trafficking but also they are workers whose worker rights (and contribution to the economy) have been denied entirely by the UK Government and communicating this particular issue remains the big challenge for our organization and our campaigns. We continue to organize, educate and mobilize domestic workers and art has been our tool to show these injustices and be more visible to society. The film and Cristy's involvement in it helped awaken Leeds to these issues and we got a lot of support for her particular case. It is not always just about raising public awareness but also awakening the politicization of the domestic workers themselves. Art, for us, is a powerful tool.

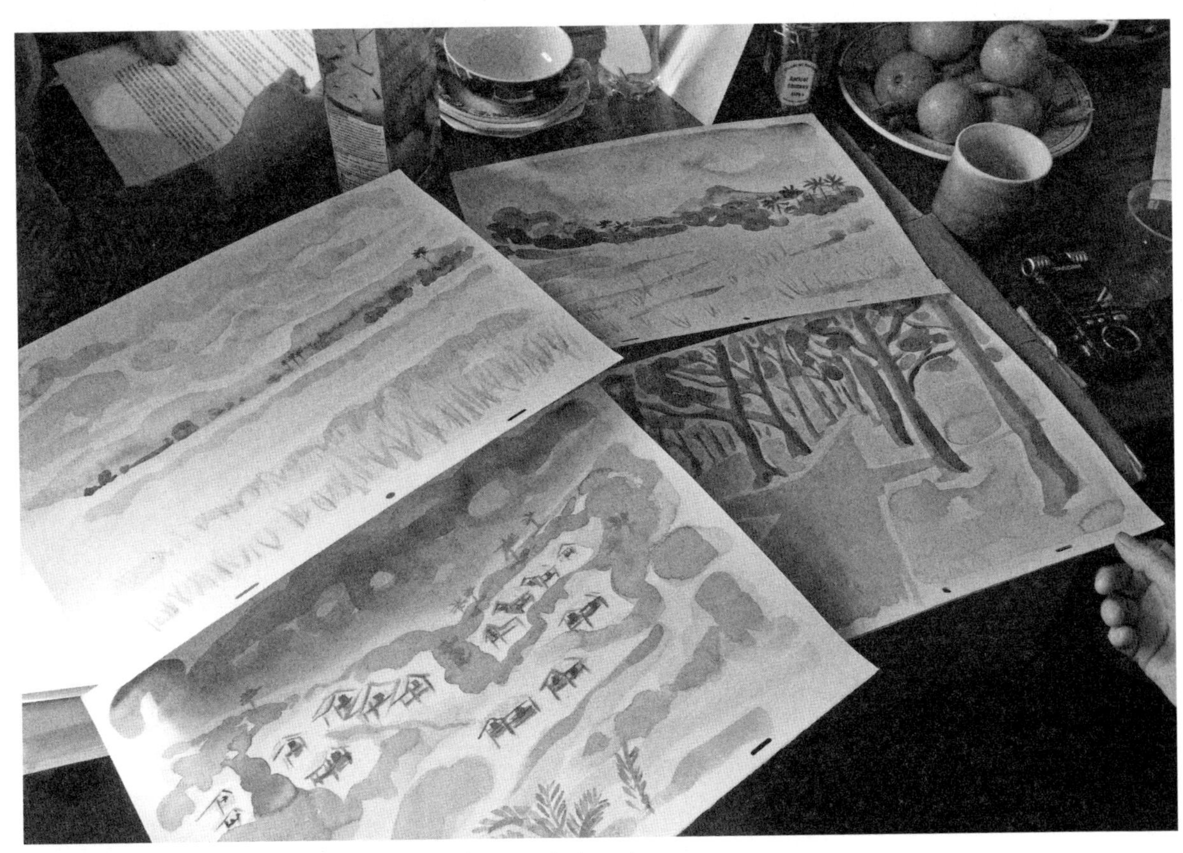

Voice of Domestic Workers Leeds, animation workshop, 2014. Photo: Amy Charlesworth

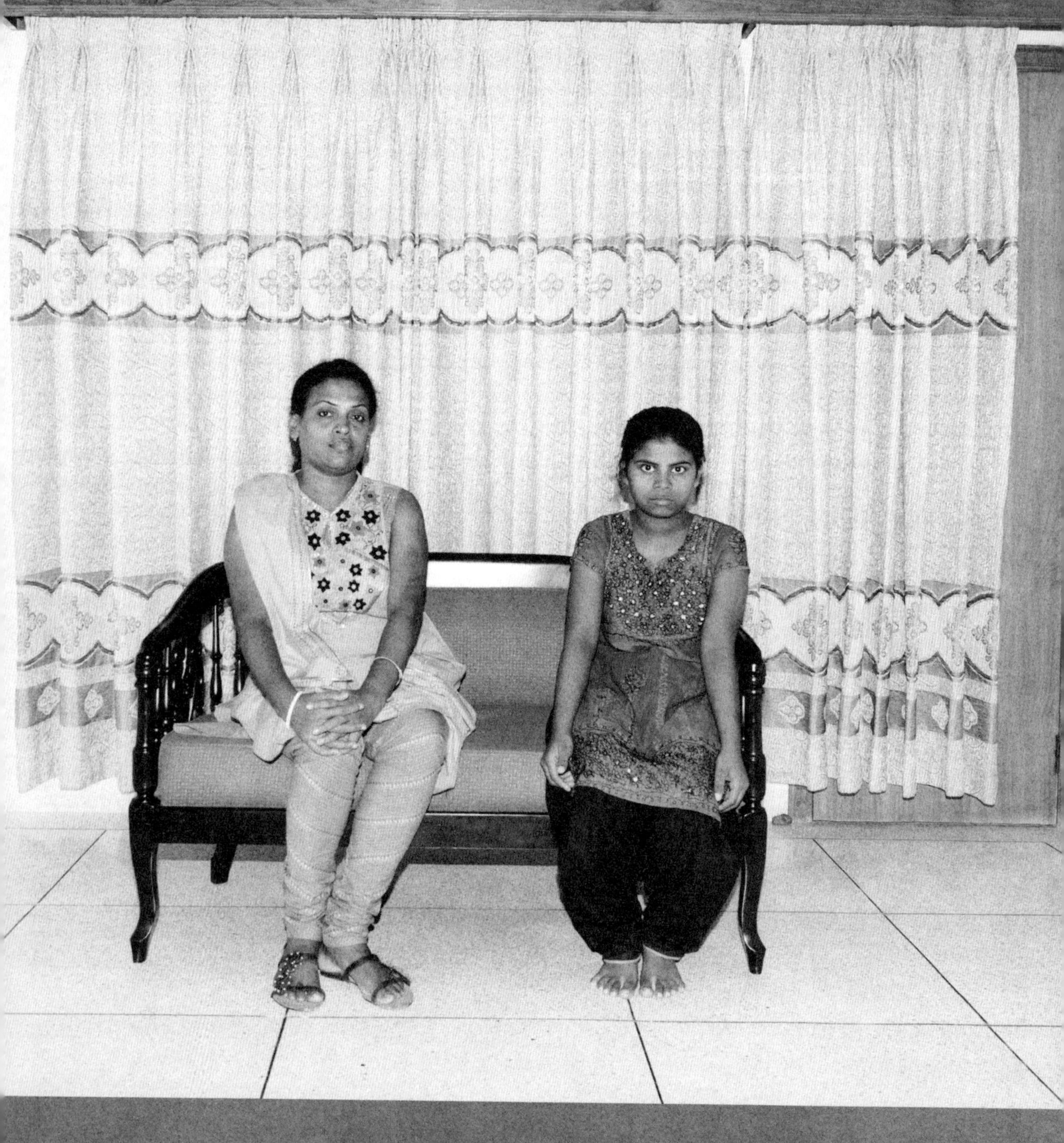

Jannatul Mawa, *Close Distance*, 2011–2014
Anu Shaha (left), aged 39, is a middle class housewife, living in Lalmatia, Dhaka. Puspa Das (right), aged 13, is a housemaid who is staying in this city for the last four years to feed her family. Keeping a home servant is a common scenario among both middle and upper classes in Dhaka.
Photo: https://mawaspace.wordpress.com/projects-2/close-distance/

LIVING PORTRAITS
Expanding the Archive of Representations for Indian Domestic Workers

Sreyashi Tinni Bhattacharyya

1. Benjamin Weiser and Vivian Yee, 'After Being Indicted, Diplomat Is Allowed to Leave the Country', *The New York Times*, 9 January 2014.

2. Ibid.

On 12 December 2013, Devyani Khobragade, India's Deputy Consul General in New York, was arrested by the Federal District Court in Manhattan and charged with 'visa fraud and making false statements in connection with her treatment of a domestic worker, Sangeeta Richard'.[1] Represented by the victim service agency Safe Horizon, Ms. Richard had accused her employer of illegally underpaying, overworking, and exploiting her. The indictment stated that even when Ms. Richard expressed her dissatisfaction with the working conditions and requested to return to her family in India, Ms. Khobragade denied the request and actively withheld her employee's passport to restrict her mobility. The case quickly inspired anger in India, as Ms. Khobragade's attorneys attested that the charges were "false and baseless" and that the arrest was a breach of international protocol as she was entitled to diplomatic immunity. The outraged response predominantly sympathized with the employer. Some local South Asian shopkeepers even argued that Ms. Richard was "fortunate" and should "be thankful" as '[she was] doing well compared to how [others were] doing in their home country'.[2] A few anti-human trafficking advocates cited several similar criminal cases to validate the experiences of isolation, exploitation, and victimization of migrant domestic workers. In the midst of these polarized perspectives, Preet Bharara, one of the prosecuting United States attorneys in Manhattan, presents a pertinent dilemma: 'One wonders why there is so much outrage about the alleged treatment of the Indian national accused of perpetrating these acts, but precious little outrage about the alleged treatment of the Indian victim.'[3] Bharara poignantly presents an asymmetrical paradigm in which two female, Indian-national migrants have been given unequal social concessions and political privileges. The historic and gendered root of this curious, but unfortunately unsurprising, asymmetry will be the topic of this chapter.

In a petition to the Delhi High Commission, Sangeeta Richard's husband Philip goes as far as to state: 'The treatment of Sangeeta by Devyani Khobragade is tantamount to keeping a person in slavery-like conditions.'[4] The history of slavery is in fact incredibly pertinent to the history of labour in colonial and post-colonial India. After the British Empire declared its abolition of the Atlantic Slave Trade in 1807, they instituted a new form of East Indian "indentured servitude" in the Caribbean.[5] Indentured servitude provided a new euphemism under which the colonial regime could continue to control bodies for economic self-interest. Historian Markus Vink argues that recovering the phrase "Indian slavery"—enacted by calling a slave a slave—erases the economic, contractual relationship depicted by the term "indentureship".[6] The simplistic conflation of these different forms of oppression erases the meticulously repulsive procedures by which people in power constructed new guises to install similar, if not the same, oppressive regimes in disparate communities. I would argue that modern, systemized domestic servitude in India emerged from a re-articulation of ideas and practices derived from British colonial slaving ideologies.

Despite a few civil society movements supporting Sangeeta Richard, the Khobragade-Richard case has been primarily remembered as an international diplomatic row between the United States and India. Khobragade was ultimately given diplomatic immunity and impunity; she has continued her career as an Indian Foreign Service Officer. Meanwhile, after multiple reported threats towards her and her family, Richard has disappeared from the public purview—her fate remains unknown. When trying to imagine Sangeeta Richard's life today, the only image my mind produces is one of abundant absence—I can create multiple narratives of her fate but cannot concretely situate

3. Ibid.

4. Debarshi Dasgupta, 'The Other Side of the Story', *Outlook India*, 30 December 2013.

5. Ron Ramdin, *Arising from Bondage: A History of the Indo-Caribbean People* (New York: New York University Press, 2000), p. 5.

6. Andrea Major, *Slavery, Abolitionism and Empire in India, 1772–1843* (Liverpool: Liverpool University Press, 2012), p. 19.

ASYMMETRICAL PARADIGMS

   Feminist Art Activisms and Artivisms

7. Saidiya Hartman, 'Venus in Two Acts', *Small Axe 26* (2008), p. 2.

8. Ibid.

9. Tina M. Campt, *Listening to Images* (Durham and London: Duke University Press, 2017), p. 5.

her in a fully embodied reality. The lives of domestic workers within India have been meagerly sketched out in recent literature. However, the lives of transnational migrant domestic workers have been lost in the international expanse. The sea of Black Atlantic theory could provide a framework to recover the lives of transnational migrant domestic workers. Saidiya Hartman's foundational text, 'Venus in Two Acts' asks and answers:

> Who is Venus?... There are hundreds of thousands of other girls who share her circumstances and these circumstances have generated few stories. And the stories that exist are not about them, but rather about the violence, excess, mendacity, and reason that seized hold of their lives, transformed them into commodities and corpses, and identified them with names tossed-off as insults and crass jokes.[7]

Hartman coined the term "critical fabulation" in an attempt to interweave the experiential, the fantastical, and the archival to recover and heal the historic ruptures and erasures of the lives of disenfranchised, exploited women.[8] Additionally, Tina Campt offers "listening to images" as a

> method that opens up the radical interpretive possibilities of images and state archives we are most often inclined to overlook, by engaging the paradoxical capacity of identity photos to rupture the sovereign gaze of the regimes that created them by refusing the very terms of photographic subjection they were engineered to produce.[9]

Given the dearth of material on modern transnational Indian migrant domestic workers, I turn to these two Black feminist scholars as their work destabilizes the static archive to privilege the construction of an embodied archive. By forming bridges between historic and contemporary methodological approaches to women workers, I choose to generate an archive of living portraiture of Indian domestic workers and their encounters with power and their enactments of protest. Informed by artworks, news archives, and ethnographies, this archive of portraiture exposes how domestic space and work in India has been historically ordered and gendered. In untangling the 'processes by which hierarchies are established, reproduced and challenged', an intersectional analysis of "gendering" acknowledges how a complex matrix of hierarchical, social and cultural constructions of identity inform a gendered experience of domestic work.[10] The multiple living portraits of women domestic workers create an imagined space within which I hope to recover and reconcile the fate of Sangeeta Richard.

When addressing the feminization of labour with regard to domestic workers and carers, many contemporary scholars frame 'the classic gendered divide between *public* and *private* spheres and their attribution to *productive* and *non-productive* labor' as an explanation to a gendered asymmetry in migrant labour markets.[11] Indrani Chatterjee traces the feminization of domestic labour to the nineteenth century, when serving the indigenous elite and colonial officers in city centre, was viewed as "unproductive" labour, as it did not participate in the extraction of commoditized materials, such as: cotton, sugar, or coffee.[12] Characterized by a "conceptual apartheid", Chatterjee discusses how the segregation of the domains of female and male labour made the exploitation within domestic labour invisible.[13] South Asian artist and social activist, Jannatul Mawa's series *Close Distance* invites viewers into a private sphere by making a public representation of it. Her portraits document a mundane, yet unusual scene: two women, an employer and her employee, sit passively, side-by-side, sharing their domestic space. The photographs are accompanied with thorough captions, in which Mawa names both women and defines them by their ties to the setting, as a *house*wife and a *house*maid. The linguistic act of naming not only binds both women to their domestic space, but also distinguishes them by indicating their differing assigned roles in the house, as employer and employee. The simplified setting heightens the viewer's attention to the individuals and the characteristics that define each of them. Face forward, straight shoulders, hands on lap, no expression. The housemaids all sit in strict, uniform, linear postures. The housewives sit as they like. Some place their arms on their arm rest, some tilt their head, some lean back into the comfort of their couch, and some show a hint of a smile. These small permutations of

10. Nadje Al-Ali, 'Diasporas and Gender', in *Diasporas: Concepts, Intersections, Identities*, eds. Kim Knott and Sean McLoughlin (London and New York: Zed Books, 2010), p. 119.

11. Helma Lutz, 'Gender in the Migratory Process', *Journal of Ethnic and Migration Studies* 36, no. 10 (2010), p. 1652.

12. Indrani Chatterjee, *Gender, Slavery, and Law in Colonial India* (New Delhi and New York: Oxford University Press, 1999), p. 3.

13. Ibid.

14. Lutz, 'Gender in the Migratory
Process', p. 1650.

a seated pose indicate the housewives' dominance and agency over their body and their space, in comparison to restricted "modest" movements of their housemaids. Despite their physical proximity, their social roles delineate an imagined barrier.

Each of the portraits in Mawa's archive utilizes a repetitive format and structure—a housewife and a housemaid sitting together in a shared private space. While the standardized setting clearly codifies the reign women claim over the private sphere, the variable gestures also illustrate that simplified, discrete distinctions between "public" and "private" spheres cannot wholly explicate the power dynamics formed within Indian domestic work. From the mid-1990s, research on migrant women workers (in intra-national as well as inter-national situations) shifted its perspective from one of Women's Studies to that of Gender Studies.[14] By addressing gender as a 'socially acquired and

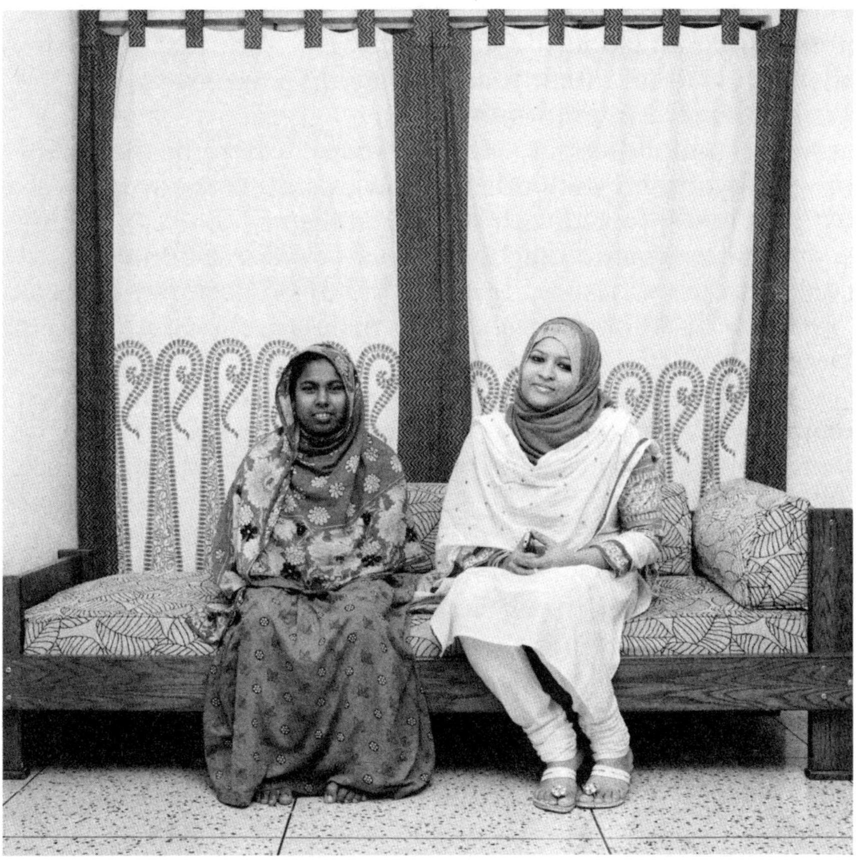

Jannatul Mawa, *Close Distance*, 2011–2014.
Farhana Munir (right), aged 38, is a housewife living in the Kalyanpur area, Dhaka. Rupali (left), aged 27,
her home servant for the last year, is staying in to feed her and family. Keeping a home servant is common scenario
among both middle and upper classes in Dhaka. Photo: https://mawaspace.wordpress.com/projects-2/close-distance/

performed identity', this new perspective strived to 'move away from monolithic and universalistic notions of the "female" and "male" by studying gender relations as expressions of asymmetry, inequality, domination and power not only between the genders but also within one gender category'.[15] Fixations solely on the feminization of labour are often criticized for producing reductive narratives that erase the complex means by which domestic workers are exploited *within* a feminized domain. While Mawa doesn't directly discuss such asymmetrical power dynamics, by placing Mawa's portraits in conversation with different ethnographic studies on Indian domestic workers, her images begin to elucidate the underlying matrix of class- and caste-based asymmetries that create the silent, but visible barrier we see between each pair of women in these representations.

Geeta Menon's ethnographic study of the Karnataka Domestic Workers' Union (KDWU) in Bangalore elaborates on the feudal roots of modern conceptions of domestic work. In the previously dominant agrarian economy, employees were hired by landowners to conduct agricultural and household labour.[16] Often they were compensated with shelter and food, rather than being paid a money wage.[17] With greater in-migration of women agrarian workers into service-based industries, Menon argues: 'often the mentality of employers and state officials towards domestic work and workers is still tinged with semi-feudalism'.[18] The continuing economic transaction of bonded slavery and serfdom is evident in the widespread perception of domestic workers as "servants", and of domestic work as relatively valueless and "undignified".[19]

Indrani Chatterjee argues that the social dynamics of Indian slavery was conceptualized as 'a dialectic between alienation and intimacy, not as a static problem of "unfreedom", coerced labor, "commodity" or property'.[20] Political networks of the kin/clan group demarcated obligations and responsibilities, which make it difficult to categorically 'delineate slavery from other forms of servitude because almost all forms of labor were influenced by extra-economic compulsions to some degree and few were ever entirely "free"'.[21] Nupur Chaudhuri addresses the colonial regimes by which these forms of "unfree" labour were concretized by British social customs.

15. Ibid., pp. 1650–1651.

16. Geeta Menon, 'The Challenge of Organizing Domestic Workers in Bangalore: Caste, Gender and Employer-Employee Relations in the Informal Economy', *Organizing Women Workers in the Informal Economy: Beyond the Weapons of the Weak*, eds. Naila Kabeer, Ratna Sudarshan, and Kirsty Milward (London: Zed Books, 2013), p. 182.

17. Ibid., p. 182.

18. Ibid.

19. Ibid.

20. Major, *Slavery, Abolitionism and Empire in India, 1772–1843*, p. 21.

21. Ibid. pp. 20–21.

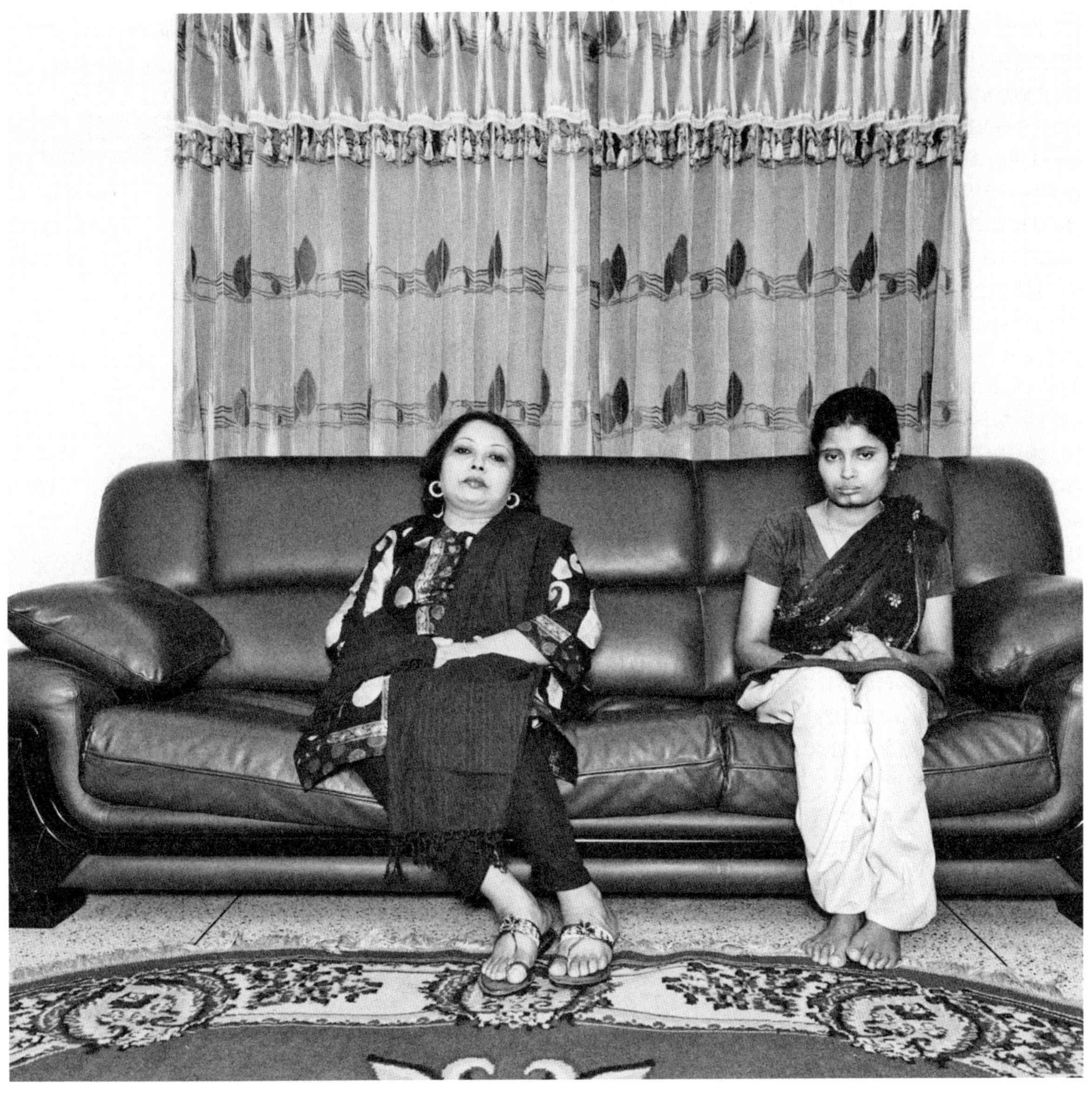

Jannatul Mawa, *Close Distance*, 2011–2014.
Shela Ali Nera (left), aged 42, is a housewife living in a middle-class neighbourhood at Green Road, Dhaka. Yeasmin (right), aged 19, her home servant for the last five years, is staying in to feed her and her family. Keeping a home servant is a common scenario among both middle and upper classes in Dhaka. Photo: https://mawaspace.wordpress.com/projects-2/close-distance/

From the beginning of British rule in India, British *memsa-hibs*—the British wives of officials, military officers, mission-aries, and merchants—published letters, advice manuals, and autobiographies that encompassed their relationship with local domestic workers.[22] Memsahibs were encouraged to dismiss 'the annoying acts of servants' as childlike anomalies and absurdities.[23] These "annoying acts" included their reli-gious practices, their spoken languages, their eating habits; any practice that deviated from a British social norm was regarded as primitive, defunct, and infantile.[24] Naming them the 'Great Unwashed', memsahibs emphasized the domestic workers' "dirty" bodies as markers of their immorality and inferiority.[25] All these constructions imagined local domestic workers as naturally subservient creatures. In turn, Raka Ray and Seemin Qayum argue: '[Indians became] subjects as well as objects of modernization, [desperate] to get a grip on the modern world and make themselves a home in it through particular conceptions and constructions of domestic spatiality and sociality.'[26] The British colonial domination of Bengali society manifested in the fostering of a new domestic ideal for Bengali housewives.[27] Didactic literature instructed Bengali housewives how to become sophisticated *bhadramahila* (gentlewoman).[28] This literature enforced codes of conduct for "mistress-servant" relationships, that placed both parties under supervision and surveillance—women domestic workers were doubly watched as their movements were scrutinized by both the male and female gaze of their masters and mistresses.[29]

While these historical analyses illuminate the crys-tallization of domestic work within the realm of "feminized domains", they do not fully expose the underlying, founda-tional logic of the stigmatization and scrutiny of domestic workers. Sara Dickey's ethnographic study on domestic work in India's urban spaces discusses how class-based power dynamics create the ideological distinction between the 'safe, pure, ordered space of the inside and the dangerous, contaminated, disordered space of the outside', and they inform the role of middle- and upper-class women to protect the sanctity and stability of the latter space.[30] She argues:

> Employers feel that this mixing [of outside and
> inside spaces] threatens the security of their homes

22. Nupur Chaudhuri, 'Memsahibs and their Servants in Nineteenth-Century India', *Women's History Review* 3, no. 4 (2006), p. 549.

23. Ibid., p. 555.

24. Ibid., p. 552.

25. Ibid., p. 554.

26. Raka Ray and Seemin Qayum, *Cultures of Servitude: Modernity, Domesticity, and Class in India* (Stanford, CA: Stanford University Press, 2009), p. 32.

27. Ibid., pp. 48–49.

28. Ibid., p. 50.

29. Ibid., p. 194.

30. Sara Dickey, 'Permeable Homes: Domestic Service, Household Space, and the Vulnerability of Class Boundaries in Urban India', *American Ethnologist* 27, no. 2 (2000), p. 470.

31. Ibid., pp. 462–463.

32. Ibid., p. 464.

and class standing. Yet, because the presence of servants is a necessary marker of class, employers attempt to contain the threat by buttressing the symbolic boundaries of the household, controlling domestic workers' movements through space, and manipulating workers' closeness to and distance from employers… Unraveling the construction of this threat reveals critical aspects of… how the domestic, even when ideologically separated from other aspects of human life, is inextricably bound to and mutually constitutive of broader political and economic structures.[31]

Dickey notes how class is one of the 'most potent idioms of identity' in contemporary India, coded by income, occupation, education, fashion, eating habits, modes of speaking, etc.[32] Employers (middle- and upper-class matriarchs) hire

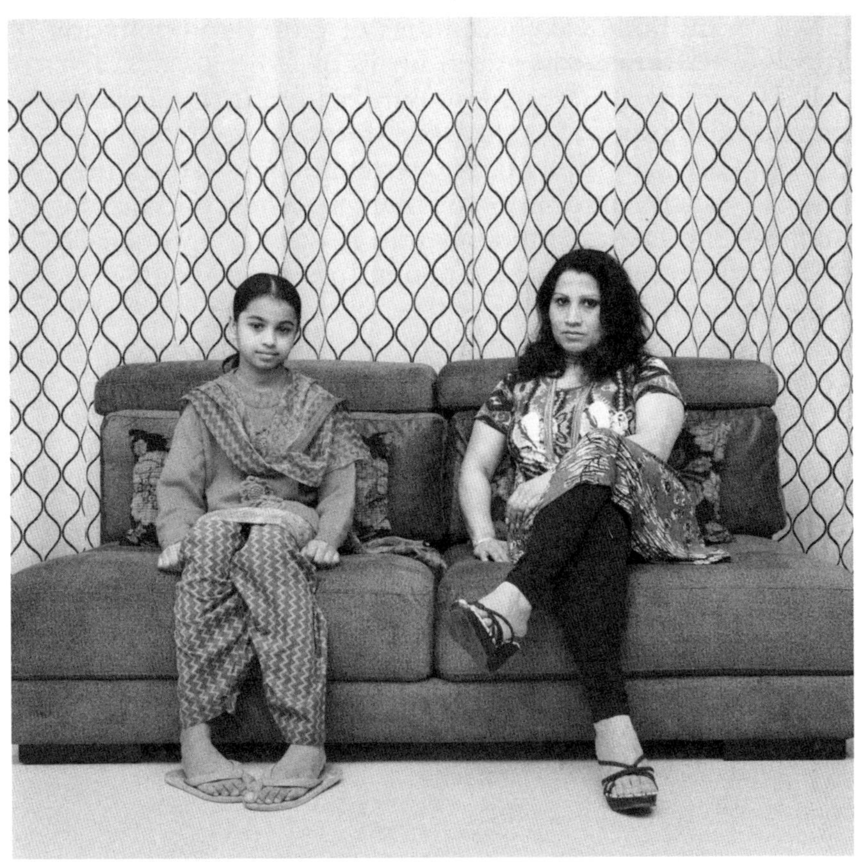

Jannatul Mawa, *Close Distance*, 2011–2014.
Sharmina Hossain (right), aged 45, is a housewife living in the Dhanmondi area, Dhaka. Kulsum (left), aged 11, her home servant for the last two years, is staying in to feed her and family. Keeping a home servant is common scenario among both middle and upper classes in Dhaka.
Photo: https://mawaspace.wordpress.com/projects-2/close-distance/

domestic workers (lower-class women) selectively based on codes of sameness and deference.[33] The employees are expected to conform to the employer's codes of cleanliness and hygiene, language, taste and manners, and loyalty to uphold the employer's prestige and image.[34] However, in regards to fashion, domestic workers are expected to dress neatly, but must not wear clothing that closely resembles those of their employers.[35] Furthermore, as employers often donate old but serviceable clothing to domestic workers—often regarded as a representation of an employer's kindness—Dickey argues that this also functions to reduce the import of objectionable, lower-class culture such as "dirtiness" and "shabbiness".[36]

Kathinka Frøystad further untangles this class-centred argument, by stating that the characterization of lower-class culture as objectionable and threatening to ordered, pure society is rooted in caste-based ideologies.[37] The relegation of tasks that comprise domestic work (i.e. cleaning toilets, washing floors, dishwashing, washing clothes, etc.) is based on Brahminical conceptions of purity and pollution. Substances correlated to these forms of work are characterized as *tamogun* (tainted, impure materials that include human waste, spoiled and leftover food, alcohol, beef, etc.) and are avoided by upper-caste families.[38] Given the historic societal association of these materials and tasks with Shudras and Dalit (commonly referred to as "untouchable") castes, upper-caste families appoint lower- or middle-caste domestic workers to perform these tasks.[39] These examples exhibit that employers construct a gendered space to produce and protect the social hierarchies that separate and privilege

33. Ibid., p. 479.

34. Ibid., pp. 474–477.

35. Ibid., p. 479.

36. Ibid., p. 478.

37. Kathinka Frøystad, 'Master-Servant Relations and the Domestic Reproduction of Caste in Northern India', *Ethnos* 68, no. 1 (2003), p. 90.

38. Ibid., p. 80.

39. Ibid., p. 81.

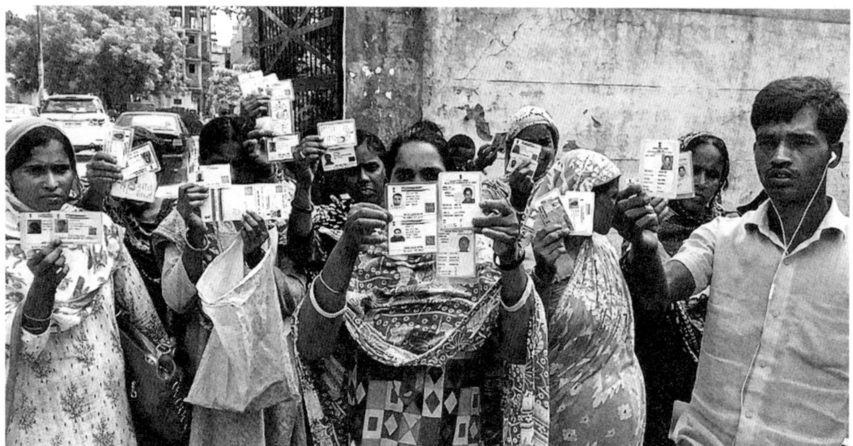

Abhishek Dey, 'Branded as Bangladeshis: In Noida, anger turns to fear for domestic workers after police raid', 14 July 2017. Photo: *Scroll:in*

40. Abhishek Dey, 'Branded as Bangladeshis: In Noida, anger turns to fear for domestic workers after police raid', *Scroll:in*, 14 July 2017.

employers over their domestic workers.

When re-examined through these narratives, Jannatul Mawa's women start telling multiple stories. We begin to notice Farhana Munir's coordinated *salwar kameez* (traditional South Asian tunic and pants) and *hijab* against Rupali's mismatched patterned shroud. Sharmina Houssain's elegantly crossed legs against Kulsum's timid, inverted feet. Still bright white sandals against peeping bare feet. Shela Ali Nera's *zari* (woven gold) covered kameez against Yeasmin's simply sequined stole. The modern fit of her tunic and leggings against her traditionally worn, somewhat oversized *salwar kameez*. Purposefully placed hands against clenched fidgeting hands. Each minute difference tells tales of these specific class- and class-coded conventions.

Jannatul Mawa's collection of private, semi-staged portraits can be interwoven with many news images that have been quickly captured for news reports. Often, we find graphic images of domestic workers lying on the floor after having been beaten, or images of a crowd of workers gathering in public spaces during a protest. The most striking news image I have come across was taken by Abhishek Dey and published alongside a news story in *Scroll India*, a progressive online media platform. The image captures a group of women and men directly addressing the camera.[40] Each individual is only partially visible, parts of their faces or their bodies are obstructed by hand-held documents: Aadaar biometric identity cards, Electoral Photo Identity cards, driver's licences, and Permanent account number (PAN) cards. It is unclear who staged the photograph, if the format was decided upon communally or instructed by the photographer. Regardless, the image has a sense of intention. Unlike other news images, it seems to cross into the realm of reportage photography by capturing a decisive, narrative moment. I propose this image as a portrait akin to Mawa's photographs. Foregrounded by various state-issued identity documents, the specific name, age, clothes, and postures of each individual is diminished and given secondary priority. The primary priority is a public declaration of their citizenship. This novel format was published on 14 July 2017, two days after a large protest instigated by domestic workers in Noida, Uttar Pradesh.

In the morning of 12 July 2017, an unprecedented dispute between a domestic worker and her employer surged into "a full-blown riot" at the Mahagun Moderne, a luxury gated community.[41] A crowd of protesters jumped over the balcony of the employer's ground-floor apartment, shattered the dividing glass-door, and ransacked the apartment while the employer and her family hid in their locked bathroom.[42] The clash was between Johra Bibi, a domestic worker, and her employer, Harshu Sethi, a schoolteacher. In light of multiple conflicting narratives regarding the dispute, the central accusations are as follows: Ms. Sethi had accused Ms. Bibi of stealing 17,000 rupees from a safe in the apartment; Ms. Bibi had accused Ms. Sethi of withholding two months' salary, falsely accusing her of theft, physically assaulting her, and holding her captive in the apartment.[43] Ashok Yadav, the community's Head of Security, reflects on the incident:

> The fact is that it is a symbiotic relationship between the madam and the maid. Right now, the residents are very angry and shocked at the violent way the mob attacked the society. But before long, they will have to find new maids. How will life go on otherwise?[44]

Yadav holds onto a romanticized idea of natural co-dependency and proximity in a domestic work employer-employee relationship. Given the predominance of such responses and sentiments, it is integral to understand the centrality of ideations of proximity and distance in conceptualizing, challenging, and re-constructing a gendered space.

Prior to these trends in urban development, most employers owned bungalows within which they offered shacks or "servants quarters" in their compound for full-time domestic workers that restricted these same workers to their employer's home.[45] Ray and Qayum present historic, cultural codes of civility and shame that clearly delineated between the perceived civility of the home and the promiscuity of the street. Low-caste women, who were obliged to work outside their homes as domestic workers, gained protection from a public, stigmatizing gaze by remaining bounded to the employer's home. Tripti Lahiri, author of *Maid in India: Stories of Inequality and Opportunity Inside Our Homes*, says

41. Suhasini Raj and Ellen Barry, 'At a Luxury Complex in India, the Maids and the Madams Go to War', *The New York Times*, 15 July 2017, www.nytimes.com/2017/07/15/world/asia/at-a-luxury-complex-in-india-the-maids-and-the-madams-go-to-war.html.

42. Ibid.

43. Sohil Sehran, 'Mayhem in Noida's Mahagun Moderne Society After Maid is Beaten Up', *Hindustan Times*, 19 July 2017, www.hindustantimes.com/noida/noida-society-mahagun-moderne-attacked-by-mob-after-maid-beaten-up-by-resident/story-ae8SgUzC36eXKcpV2O4aYK.html.

44. Raj and Barry, 'At a Luxury Complex in India, the Maids and the Madams Go to War'.

45. Frøystad, 'Master-Servant Relations and the Domestic Reproduction of Caste in Northern India', p. 81.

46. Ibid.

47. Menon, 'The Challenge of Organizing Domestic Workers in Bangalore', p. 185.

48. Ibid.

49. Raj and Barry, 'At a Luxury Complex in India, the Maids and the Madams Go to War'.

50. Frøystad, 'Master-Servant Relations and the Domestic Reproduction of Caste in Northern India', p. 81.

51. Ibid.

52. Menon, 'The Challenge of Organizing Domestic Workers in Bangalore', p. 181.

that the dominant culture of live-in employees '[gives] them little opportunity to build networks and compare notes' that may inspire collective actions or unionization.[46] Menon concurs that for the KDWU it was extremely difficult to protect live-in domestic workers given the spatial boundaries of this kind of employer's home. While

> of all domestic workers, [Menon] found [live-in domestic workers] the most likely to be in bonded labor situations… and vulnerable to sexual abuse… It was difficult to make contact with these workers, or for them to get the time to leave the household to attend meetings

states Menon.[47] The rigid construction of inside and outside in relation to the employer's home reinforces the control of employers over live-in domestic workers and hinders domestic workers from seeking opportunities to protest mistreatment.

However, the urbanization and "apartmentization" of cityscapes has drastically changed the spatial experience of domestic workers and their opportunities to collectivize. The current proliferation of luxury household developments on the peripheries of large Indian cities has been mirrored by a significant rise of adjacent slum neighbourhoods.[48] Lahiri characterizes this polarization as 'a perfect setup for an us vs. them clash'.[49] This setup occurs in two ways. Firstly, the experienced isolation of live-in domestic workers in bungalow settings changes due to the growth of population living in apartments. Given the increased proximity of physical and social household spaces within apartment complexes, live-in domestic workers are more likely to come into contact, run errands, and form community with others in a similar situation. Secondly, "apartmentization" often causes employers to reduce the number of live-in domestic workers, alongside the decrease in physical living space available.[50] Many employers have shifted to hiring visiting, part-time domestic workers.[51] According to Menon, slums that often neighbour these apartment complexes become 'labor colonies: places from where various employers sourced their workers'.[52] As the slum becomes increasingly constituted as both the home and the market of domestic workers,

EMBODIED ARCHIVES

it emerges as a potential site for organizing collectively. Ultimately, the spatial boundaries of employers' home have become more permeable to the escape and transmission of information, creating an arena in which both live-in and visiting domestic workers may collectivize not only within the apartment complexes and within the slums, but also across the two spaces. A handful of domestic workers' unions have been formed to organize skill-based trainings, respond to accusations of theft, formalize wage and bonus payment systems, address caste- and religion-based divisions between workers, and provide resources for organizations handling sexual harassment cases.[53] We find that within modern contexts, domestic workers are renegotiating and reconstituting these dominant power structures enforced by their employers. While class, caste, and gender were once used to segregate and control domestic workers, current civil society movements challenge this logic by enacting their freedom both inside and outside the employer's home.

However, these civil society protests have been repeatedly suppressed. The residents of Mahagun Moderne responded to the protests by deciding to ban "Bangladeshi" domestic workers (who constitute the majority in this case) from working in their apartment complex.[54] They also filed complaints to the police with false accusations of their employees being illegal, Muslim immigrants from Bangladesh started a small Twitter campaign, #MaldaInNoida, and requested the Uttar Pradesh government to evict the workers from the adjacent slum.[55,56] The selective reference to an earlier, unrelated January 2016 protest in Malda and the violence between Hindus and Muslims it recalls is significant. Mahagun Moderne residents, who are predominantly Hindu, chose to threaten the rights of their employees by stigmatizing their religion and ethnicity, and questioning the legality of their citizenship. The employer's attempts to control women domestic workers continue through incorporating other hierarchical social and cultural conventions—i.e. religion, ethnicity, and citizenship—into the already gendered matrix of their employment and lives.

Samita Sen reflects on Karl Marx's statement regarding 'homeworking' as the '"invisible threads" of capitalism, the "outside departments" of factories', when

53. Ibid.

54. Sehran, 'Mayhem in Noida's Mahagun Moderne Society After Maid is Beaten Up'.

55. Raj and Barry, 'At a Luxury Complex in India, the Maids and the Madams Go to War'.

56. Bidisha Mahapatra, '#MaldaInNoida: Twitter Reacts Against "Bangladeshi" Immigrants over Mahagun Mob Violence', Hindustan Times, 13 July 2017, www.hindustantimes.com/noida/maldainnoida-twitter-reacts-against-bangladeshi-immigrants-over-mahagun-mob-violence/story-CgXFG0zUMtkovJiCLtVcNM.html.

57. Samita Sen, 'Women, Work and Household in Industrialising Asia', *Women Workers in Industrialising Asia: Costed, Not Valued*, ed. Amarjit Kaur (Houndmills, Basingstoke: Palgrave Macmillan, 2003), pp. 82–84.

58. Praveena Kodoth, 'Structural Violence Against Emigrant Domestic Workers and Survival in the Middle East', *Journal of Interdisciplinary Economics* 28, no. 1 (2016), p. 85.

59. Ibid., p. 83.

60. Ibid., p. 85.

61. Ibid., p. 87.

62. Ibid., p. 88.

63. Praveena Kodoth and V.J. Varghese, 'Protecting Women or Endangering the Emigration Process: Emigrant Women Domestic Workers, Gender and State Policy', *Economic and Political Weekly* XLVI, no. 43 (2012), 62.

asserting that the feminization of labour in India pushed women to the peripheries and forced them into informal, casual employment—participating in the growth, but not privileged by mobility, of global capitalism.[57] The living portraits presented above clarify the historic and gendered power dynamics of Indian domestic work and how they have been repeatedly and methodically imagined, enacted, and reconfigured to assert one woman's right over the other.

These extant dynamics are reiterated in the international sphere of migrant domestic workers. In response to the moral panic generated due to reports of abuse and exploitation of women migrant domestic workers, the Indian government enacted the Emigration Act of 1983 to protect Indian women. Unfortunately, these policies reproduced analogous practices of selective surveillance and ambivalence within these policies asymmetrically privileges and regulates the mobility of women migrants based on their class, caste, and trade. Praveena Kodoth critiques the Indian government's imposed restriction on specifically women migrant domestic workers (WMDW), challenging the government's defence of its 'conservative position… as being in the interests of women'.[58] Given that the emigrating domestic workers to the Middle East were predominantly from socially and economically disadvantaged communities in Kerala and Andhra Pradesh, Kodoth asserts that these forms of restriction are in actuality underpinned by a 'gendered, caste- and class-based nationalism that view women domestic workers as degrading'.[59] Furthermore, she argues that these protectionist restrictions have the opposite effect on women migrants by: 1) creating structural conditions for the abuse and exploitation of migrant domestic workers, and 2) undermining the social and economic mobility pursued by migrant domestic workers.[60] Kodoth compares how restrictions on terms of employment by supportive and liberal emigration policies of major proactive Asian sending countries, such as the Philippines, Sri Lanka, and Indonesia.[61] Most significantly, emigration policies institute and encourage embassies to stand on the front line to protect domestic workers.[62] Kodoth and Varghese, however, note the attitude of Indian embassies towards [women domestic migrant workers] is described as "negative", "passive" or "reluctant".[63] India's protectionist policies re-iterate an oppressive gendered space on a transnational scale. These paternalistic policies undermine the economic logic of lower-class and -caste women migrants, and characterize their actions as deviant to a nationalist project of socialized, gendered morality.[64] The paralleling practices of selective surveillance and ambivalence within these policies asymmetrically privileges and regulates the mobility of women migrants based on their class, caste, and trade.

Entangled in such emigration policies, we find Sangeeta Richard. Richard's entry in the United States was contingent on having signed a contract of employment that promised the payment of fair wages, aligning with Fair Labor Standards. When the stipulated wages and working conditions were not fulfilled, both Indian and American national labour policies and international human rights failed to provide adequate protection to Richard. Leah Briones' Capable Agency Approach provides a framework that addresses unequal development (that which privileges certain migrants over others) and how it is a 'problem rooted, but also structured transnationally, by [migrant worker's] lives in the host country as well as back in their homeland'.[65] She critiques the efficacy and feasibility of agency- and rights-based policies produced to protect migrant domestic workers. She decisively states: 'agency itself is insufficient... examining agency and resistance in Foucaultian terms does not escape the hold of dominant powers'.[66] Briones challenges the romanticization of worker's resistance movements as the social security and economic

64. Kodoth, 'Structural Violence Against Emigrant Domestic Workers and Survival in the Middle East', p. 88.

65. Leah Briones, 'Capability and International Labor Migration for Domestic Work', in *Empowering Migrant Women: Why Agency and Rights Are Not Enough* (Burlington: Ashgate Publishing Limited, 2009), p. 15.

66. Ibid., pp. 4, 10.

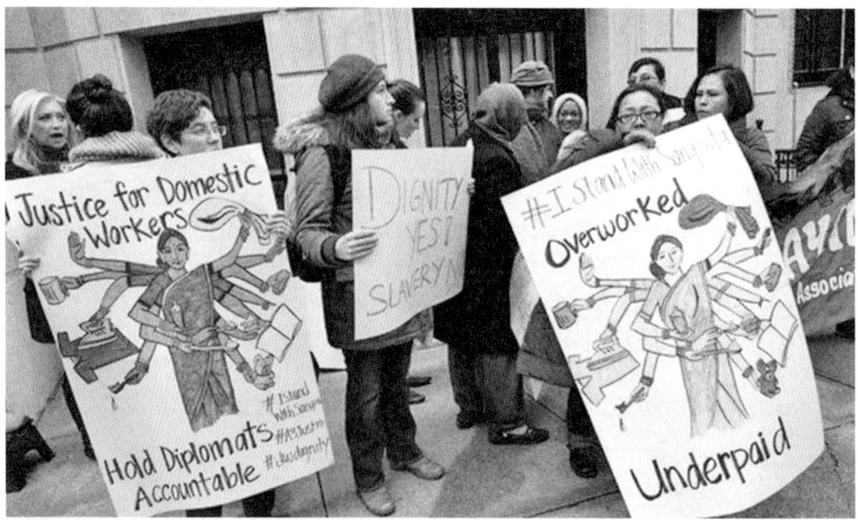

The BBC's Nada Tawfik reports, 'Devyani Khobragade: New York maids protest at Indian consulate', 13 December 2013. Photo: James Cooke

67. Ibid., p. 9.

68. Ibid., p. 15.

69. 'Khobragade Affair: Protests for Sangeeta Richard in New York: Against US in Chennai', *The Hindustan Times*, 21 December 2013.

mobility of women is compromised based on the multiplicity of their identity.[67] While many laws exist to supposedly protect women on paper, social conventions prevent them from being enacted and practised successfully by disenfranchised women. Briones demands a paradigmatic shift that centralizes migrant empowerment by reconstituting their access to power: protect livelihoods to increase migrants' capability for securing their rights.[68]

In a demonstration outside the Indian Consulate in New York supporting Sangeeta Richard, protestors chanted: 'They say diplomatic immunity, we say accountability', and 'they say protect the traffickers, we say protect the workers'.[69] They carried hand-drawn posters featuring a woman with multiple arms; each hand was either serving a cup of tea, ironing a shirt, dusting furniture, spooning out food, or playing with a child. The posters read: 'Overworked, Underpaid', and 'Dignity YES! Slavery No!' Iconographically referencing maternal Hindu deities, the woman illustrated could be viewed as an Indian reincarnation of Saidiya Hartman's mythological Venus. Multiple facets of Richard's character are captured within one portrait; she is simultaneously a deity, a care-taker, a cook, a housekeeper, a nurse, a maid, a nanny... somewhat revered but ultimately exploited. As a living portrait, the image celebrates the sanctity of the domestic space while also exposing the violent burden of performing domestic work. Disturbingly so, the remanence of this bold, assertive, and divine figure starkly contrasts the fleeting, irrecoverable image of Sangeeta Richard (and of Johra Bibi). While theirs and others' images have faded over time, the political enactments of Indian women domestic workers have inspired a plethora of visual culture, ethnographies, and new articles. While artists, like Jannatul Mawa, might attempt to document the complexities of Indian domestic work, these images are ultimately hollow without the embodied practices of women workers themselves. It is only through the process of weaving enactments of protest and self-representation into the archive of domestic work that we can begin to imagine the intricacies of the lives of Indian migrant domestic workers.

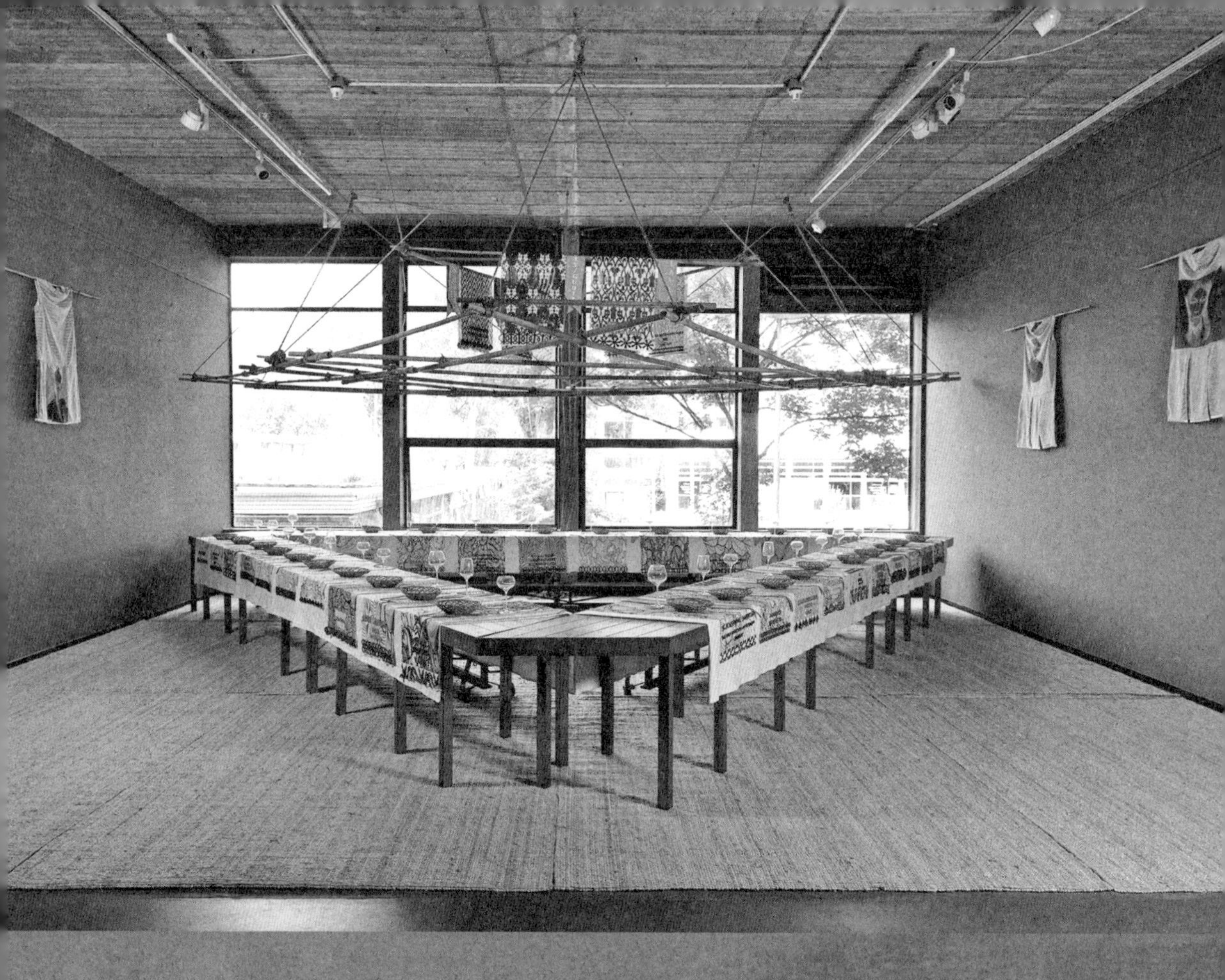

Patricia Kaersenhout, *Guess Who's Coming to Dinner Too?*, installation view, WOW Amsterdam, 2017.
Photo: Aatjan Renders

MONUMENTAL ACTIVISM
Judy Chicago's *Dinner Party* in Feminist Art Making

Elke Krasny

1. Gail Lavin, *Becoming Judy Chicago: A Biography of the Artist* (Oakland: University of California Press), p. 251.

2. I want to thank Tanja Ostojić for drawing my attention to Patricia Kaersenhout's work at the symposium 'Feminist Art Activisms and Artivisms' (Middlesex University, London, 2 July 2018), organized by Katy Deepwell, which made possible such fruitful learning and generous exchange.

Feminist artists of the 1970s concerned with developing a radical critique of patriarchy used dinner parties as fertile territory for artistic experimentation. *The Dinner Party* by artist Judy Chicago is perhaps the best-known example harnessing the representational and symbolic power of a dinner party. In a 1978 interview, the artist stated, 'women have never had a Last Supper, but they have had dinner parties where they facilitated conversation and nourished people'.[1] Chicago created a feminist monument honouring women's cultural, spiritual, and historical importance in Western Civilization. Having sparked public controversy and critical debates within feminism, this iconic sculpture with its celebration of central core imagery, was permanently installed at Elizabeth A. Sackler Center for Feminist Art at the Brooklyn Museum in New York City in 2002. Here, I examine two artistic responses to *The Dinner Party*: Suzanne Lacy's 1979 *The International Dinner Party* and Patricia Kaersenhout's *Guess Who's Coming to Dinner Too?*, the first rendering of which was shown in 2017.[2] These three artworks exemplify the interconnectedness of art making, feminist activism, and monument activism. The latter is a specific kind of activism and includes actions against monuments that represent values of patriarchy, colonialism, white supremacy, imperialism, or fascism, but also actions for new monuments remembering histories of the forgotten, the marginalized, and the oppressed. The two responses to Judy Chicago's work, recognized even at the moment of

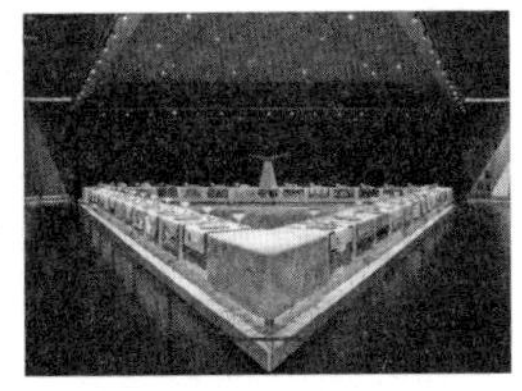

Judy Chicago, *The Dinner Party* (1974–1979), installed at the Elizabeth A. Sackler Center for Feminist Art, New York, since 2007

385

its first exhibition as a monument within feminist art, are connected by their artistic expansion beyond the framework of Judy Chicago's Western-centric and White-centric feminism. Nevertheless, taken together, these three dinner parties present an exemplary constellation of feminist art works in which the artistic critique remains appreciative, yet radically expands the notion of feminism into feminism(s). I will examine the different strategies adopted in Suzanne Lacy's and Patricia Kaersenhout's works as social and political feminist activism(s) and connect them to larger trends in feminist struggles and critiques.

The International Dinner Party
Living Monument Created by Women of All Cultures

> **Dear Sisters,**
> **We would like to ask you to participate with us in a worldwide celebration of ourselves! We are asking women in many countries to host dinner parties honoring women important to their own culture. These dinner parties held simultaneously in March 1979, will create a network of women-acknowledging-wome which will extend around the world.**[3]

Celebrating the momentum feminism had gained in the US throughout the 1970s, the above invitation was sent out by mail or fax in early 1979 by a group of eight California-based artists, 'Suzanne Lacy, Thea Litsios, Linda Preuss, Audrey Wallace, Susan Brenner, Shannon Hogan, Adrienne Weiss, and Sharon Kagan'.[4] The invitation was extended to women's groups, women's organizations, feminist activists, and feminist artists. Eventually, the collective effort became known as *The International Dinner Party* by artist Suzanne Lacy, who links its scale to the political experiences of her generation.

> Protests were important in general for my generation, starting with the Civil Rights, through Vietnam, farm workers organizing, feminist protests like Take Back the Night marches. ... Scale is an important lesson from that era too, that numbers of bodies make a difference.[5]

3. 'An International Dinner Party to Celebrate Women's Culture', invitation, 1979 (Suzanne Lacy's International Dinner Party Archive).

4. Ibid.

5. Catherine Wood, 'Art as Life, Art as Politics, Art as Political Action: An Interview with Suzanne Lacy', in *Politics in a Glass Case: Feminism, Exhibition Cultures and Curatorial Transgressions*, eds. Angela Dimitrakaki and Lara Perry (Liverpool: Liverpool University Press, 2013), p. 122.

6. Nicole Van de Ven and Diana E.H. Russell, *Crimes Against Women: International Tribunal Proceedings* (Berkeley: Russell Publications, 1990), p. 7.

7. Ibid.

8. 'An International Dinner Party to Celebrate Women's Culture', invitation, 1979 (Suzanne Lacy's International Dinner Party Archive).

9. Ibid.

10. Jocelyn Olcott, *International Women's Year: The Greatest Consciousness: Raising Event in History* (New York: Oxford University Press, 2017), p. 5.

11. Ibid., p. 8.

The decade of the 1970s had not only witnessed large numbers of bodies taking to the streets, but also other forms of large-scale gatherings and worldwide exchanges between women. Lacy mentions the International Tribunal on Crimes against Women as a source of inspiration. In 1976, this self-organized people's tribunal brought together 2000 women from 40 different countries whose goal was to jointly create testimonies on the specificity of crimes committed against women. 'Sisterhood is powerful! International sister-hood is more powerful!'[6] was the tribunal's slogan. Feminist internationalism was at its core. 'Our struggle must not only be conducted within nations, but across national bound-aries.'[7] Large-scale participation, international feminist networks beyond national boundaries, and the gathering of collective evidence from many different parts of the world, are the lessons learned from the making of *The International Dinner Party*.

The invitation to *The International Dinner Party* describes Chicago's *The Dinner Party* as follows:

> For 4½ years, artist and writer Judy Chicago, aided by over 250 artists and designers, historians and craftspeople, has been creating this work which pays homage to 39 women who have been major contributors to Western Civilization, and lists 999 others who have left their mark.[8]

The activist motivation was to expand such a dinner party to 'living women of all cultures'.[9] The 1970s were marked by an international turn in feminism. This is maybe best under-stood through the large-scale gathering of women during the first UN Women's Conference in Mexico City with 2000 official delegates and 6000 women participating in the NGO tribune. 'The gatherings in Mexico City … had been designed precisely to encourage First World participants to listen to Third World participants.'[10] This dimension of First World Women looking at the history and achievements of Third World women was blatantly absent from Judy Chicago's Dinner Party. Nevertheless, this international turn in feminism motivated *The International Dinner Party*. The NGO tribune in Mexico City 'honored lived experience as a form of expertise'.[11] Worldwide feminist activism with its

Elke Krasny

foundation in "lived experience" connects to the feminism practised in a "living artwork". 'We see this as a "living art work", in which all of us will be performers in a gathering together and honouring of women from around the world.'[12]

The invitation emphasized the collective spirit and the international turn in feminism.

> We would like to create with you an 'International Dinner Party Event', in which women from many cities and countries host their own dinner party, paying homage to women in their area who have contributed to our lives. The size, format or style of your dinner party is up to you, as well as the women you will honor and how you choose to do so.[13]

The International Dinner Party presents an example of international feminist activist social practice. The conceptual strategy driving this social art practice artwork is characterized by autonomy and independence when it comes to the different dinner parties, yet strategically planned and choreographed when it comes to the timing of the large-scale event. 'If each of our dinner parties occurs on the same evening, we will form a continuous 24 hour celebration around the world (because of time differences.)'[14]

The follow-up Instructions sent to women interested in contributing, signed by Suzanne Lacy and Linda Preuss, assigned women the task to send a 'telegram...—telling us who you are and who you are celebrating'.[15] The telegram messages are evidence to the diversity in women's culture and the wide range of women honoured. 'We are all Stars. Four in Paris Honour the Nameless Women', reads one of the telegram messages sent from Paris. German artist Ulrike Rosenbach and her Schule für kreativen Feminismus (School for Creative Feminism) sent this postcard message from Cologne: 'In Dedication to more than 6000 women, who were persecuted and burnt as witches in Germany and other parts of Europe, we will have a 24-hours symbolic hungerstrike on March 14th as a contribution to your "Dinner-Party".' The New-York based artists Ana Mendieta and Mary Beth Edelson gave a 'Party to Honor Louise Bourgeois'. Avoiding a tribute to Chicago, they chose to honour instead Louise Bourgeois. 'The invited guests were

12. Suzanne Lacy and Linda Preuss, 'Instructions', 1979 (Suzanne Lacy's International Dinner Party Archive).

13. 'An International Dinner Party to Celebrate Women's Culture', invitation, 1979 (Suzanne Lacy's International Dinner Party Archive).

14. Ibid.

15. Suzanne Lacy and Linda Preuss, 'Instructions', 1979 (Suzanne Lacy's International Dinner Party Archive).

asked—if they were in the mood—to come dressed as a famous herstorical or contemporary women artist.' Out of the twenty women who had accepted the invitation, seventeen attended the party. 'Louise Bourgeois came as herself, Ana Mendieta came as Freda Kahla (sic!), Mary Beth Edelson came as Leanor Fini (in Leanor's ritual moon Goddess costume), … Hannah Wilke came as herself ….' Ajuda, Anette, Dorine, Leila, Ligia, Malu, Marhel, Maris, and Zezé signed with their first names only and self-identified as 'a group of Brazilian feminists living in Rio de Janeiro'. The group describes plans for a three-day public seminar on women's reproductive rights, family planning, contraception, abortion, and on women's rights over their bodies. '… this will be the first time that this whole complex of problems is discussed from a feminist point of view. It is really about time too!' A feminist group in Edinburgh, UK, and a Women's Group in Christchurch, New Zealand, expressed their solidarity with women in Iran. Only a few days before *The International Dinner Party*, Iranian women had taken to the streets of Teheran to protest against what is today known as the Iranian Revolution or the 1979 Revolution. Iranian women sought to protect their hard-won civil and personal liberties.

For the opening of *The Dinner Party* at the San Francisco Museum of Modern Art on 14 March 1979, Lacy had a map of the world printed and hung at the wall. The text-panel displayed next to the map of the world explains

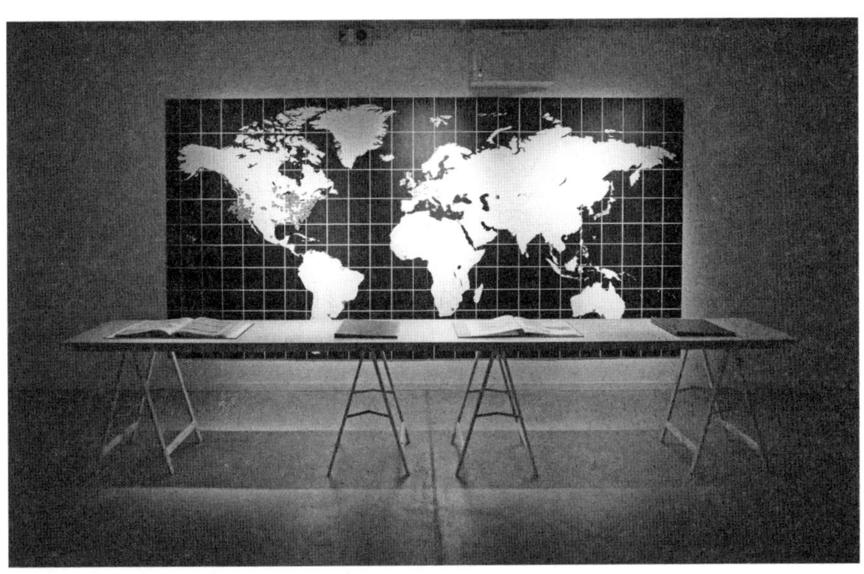

Suzanne Lacy's *International Dinner Party* in feminist curatorial thought installation view, Zurich University of the Arts, 2015. Photo: Alexander Schuh

about *The International Dinner Party Event* and states that all the women 'shared their events with us through telegrams and we in turn placed emblems on the map to give visual representation to their participation'.[16] This text, signed by Lacy, makes the collective women-led event an art work "dedicated to" Judy Chicago, Lacy's teacher and mentor.[17] 'I wanted to acknowledge Judy and the people who worked on it, to pay tribute to their work with my own.' In a several-hours long performance, the arrival of the telegrams was marked by Lacy on the map aiming to produce a powerful image of the worldwide territory of women staging international dinner parties all giving testimony for the importance of women's culture.[18] The map and the collected documents of the telegrams, letters, and photographs pull together the large-scale and globally dispersed dinner parties into a manageable picture and coherent display of documents. While the invitation is an expression of the international turn in feminism, the map betrays its failure. 'Pass this information on to women in other cities and countries so our network can continue to expand. We particularly need to know of women in the Middle and Far East, Africa and South America.'[19] The map with barely any red triangles in the regions mentioned in the invitation, and also very few triangles in both Western and Eastern Europe shows the limits of the networking efforts.[20] Constrained by lack of contacts and lack of other languages, the project is conceptually dedicated to honour and celebrate "living women of all cultures", yet fails to succeed in overcoming the limits to First World, White and Anglo-centric feminism. The large-scale NGO tribune at the United Nation's world conference of women with its emphasis on lived experience compares to the intent of the living art work of *The International Dinner Party*. While the tribune resulted in achieving "disunity", precisely because First World women finally did listen closely to Third World Women, the same does not hold true for *The International Dinner Party*.[21]

16. *The International Dinner Party*, wall text, 1979 (Suzanne Lacy's International Dinner Party Archive).

17. Ibid.

18. I have written elsewhere on the ambivalence of the map, a tool of imperial-colonial power, and of Western-centric distorted representation. See Elke Krasny, 'Putting on the Map: Suzanne Lacy's International Dinner Party', in *Participation in Art and Architecture: Spaces of Interaction and Occupation*, eds. Martino Stirli and Mechtild Widrich (London and New York: I.B. Tauris, 2015), pp. 89–106.

19. Suzanne Lacy and Linda Preuss, 'Instructions', 1979 (Suzanne Lacy's International Dinner Party Archive).

20. Extending this work into Northern Europe, the post-Yugoslav and the post-Soviet territory was my own response in the exhibition curated by Elke Krasny with Aktion Arkiv, Queering Yerevan, and Red Min(e)d on radical practices of collective care 'Suzanne Lacy's International Dinner Party in feminist curatorial thought' (Toni-Areal Galerie, Zurich, 21 March–13 April 2015). See Elke Krasny, *Suzanne Lacy's International Dinner Party in Feminist Curatorial Thought* (Vienna: OnCuratingPress, 2019) provides a detailed analysis of Lacy's work in the context of contemporary feminist and queer feminist collectives and their activist archives.

21. Elke Krasny, 'Suzanne Lacy's International Dinner Party in Feminist Curatorial Thought: A Curator's Talk', *Architecture and Culture* 5, no. 3 (2017), pp. 435–453.

22. Patricia Kaersenhout, 'For a performance …', https://twitter.com/pkaersenhout/status/874290157452767232.

23. Ibid.

24. Tori Egherman, 'All Art is Political: A conversation with Patricia Kaersenhout', *Global Voices*, 26 October 2018, https://globalvoices.org/2018/10/26/all-art-is-political-a-conversation-with-patricia-kaersenhout/.

Guess, Who's Coming for Dinner, Too?
Social Monument dedicated to Warriors of Resistance

'For a performance I am looking for 36 men who dare to dance a HAKA for women. Training done by a Maori. Fee €75 pp and a signed artwork.'[22] Celebrating and honouring the memory of warriors of resistance, the visual artist, womanist and cultural activist Patricia Kaersenhout put forward this call for participation on twitter at 8:39 on 12 June 2017.[23] She was searching for 36 men to dance for the 36 'female warriors who fought for justice and equality' to whom she dedicated her large-scale artistic appropriation of Judy Chicago's *Dinner Party*. Living and working in the context of Europe, where white privilege, the re-emergence of ethnonationalism, and normalized racism are still politically, socially, and culturally dominant, Kaersenhout turns *The Dinner Party* into a monument to Black Women and non-Western women.

Recent publications on race as well as on Black and immigrant feminist movements in Europe all indicate how race is a red-hot topic within feminism and society at large. Recent publications expressing resistant consciousness and working toward decolonization include Noah Sow's *Deutschland Schwarz Weiss. Der alltägliche Rassismus*, Gloria Wekker's *White Innocence: Paradoxes of Colonialism and Race* in 2016 and Grada Kilomba's *Plantation Memories: Episodes of Everyday Racism* of the same year, Reni Eddo-Lodge's 2017 book *Why I'm No Longer Talking to White People about Race* and *Relating Worlds of Racism: Dehumanisation, Belonging, and the Normativity of European Whiteness*, co-edited by Philomena Essed, Karen Farquharson, Kathryn Pillay, and Elisa Joy White and Françoise Vergès' *Un féminism décolonial*, both published in 2019. The formation of resistant Black European consciousness, diasporic knowledge production and what Walter Mignolo has referred to as "decolonial aesthetics", are salient points for Kaersenhout, who is literally and figuratively bringing 'Black women to the table'.[24]

The Netherlands, one of Europe's largest and most aggressive colonial empires with its brutal plantation system, has impacted traumatically on millions of people from Indonesia to Surinam(e). Yet, the Dutch colonial trauma, the history of enslavement, and the historical dimension of the plantation system have been conspicuously absent from Dutch historiography and contemporary critical discourse. In a 2018 interview, Kaersenhout stated:

> The Dutch don't do race. But now there is a black voice, a voice of color, that speaks back. Black people and people of color are no longer in a state of confusion about race. We know we are experiencing racism.[25]

Kaersenhout makes use of the art-activist strategy of appropriation. Harnessing the representative power of the iconic status of Chicago's monumental dinner party, she dedicates her dinner exclusively to Black women.

Judy Chicago's ceremonial banquet with its massive triangular table devotes the three wings of the triangle to Prehistory to Classical Rome, Christianity to Reformation, and American Revolution to the Women's Revolution. The first wing includes goddesses and female deities beyond European geographies such as Ishtar from ancient Mesopotomia, Kali from East India or Hatshepsut from Ancient Egypt.[26] While many of the goddesses and deities represented are non-Western, their inclusion is premised on the idea of ancient high cultures as predecessors of modern Western civilizations as developed in the discipline of history writing in the nineteenth century. Other women honoured by Chicago include, amongst others: Sappho, Hypatia, Christine de Pisan, Isabella d'Este, Susan B. Anthony, and Natalie Barney. The only plate that does not use elaborate vulva iconography but a mask to represent "the agony of enslavement" is dedicated to African-American abolitionist Sojourner Truth. This has sparked critical debate on tokenism—'Not just a token at the *Dinner Party*, Truth was also used as a token by the predominantly white Suffrage movement.'[27] It has equally been discussed as denying black women their sexuality—'This refusal to ascribe a vulva design to Sojourner Truth has been read as a racist denial of, or discomfort with, the African American woman's sexuality.'[28]

Kaersenhout appropriates the three-winged structure and counteracts the version of women's herstory

25. Ibid.

26. See Judy Chicago, *The Dinner Party: Place Settings*, www.brooklynmuseum.org/eascfa/dinner_party/place_settings.

27. Carolyn Gage, 'Guess Who's Not Coming to Dinner: A Feminist Reconsideration of "The Dinner Party"', *Rain and Thunder: A Radical Feminist Journal of Discussion and Activism* 2 (Spring 1999), p. 2.

28. Ibid.

29. Patricia Kaersenhout, 'Community Art Project: Guess Who's Coming to Dinner Too?', http://agalab.nl/opening-guess-whos-coming-to-dinner-too-by-patricia-kaersenhout/?lang=en.

through her version of Black women's herstory. The artist divides her table as follows: 'Warrior Queens and Divine Spirits', 'Slavery and Colonialism', and 'Colonialism and Contemporary Revolutionaries'. In 2017, the artist created her dinner party for 36 non-Western women, among them Queen Zenobia, Queen Gudit, Queen Nanny of the Maroons, Carlota Lukumi, revolt leader in Cuba, Sanité Bélair, the Haitian freedom fighter, Janey Begum Tetary, the Slave rebel of Suriname, Carmen Pereira, fighting in the War of Independence of Guinnea-Bissau and Cape Verde, N'Nonmiton, the Dahomey Amon, the female military regiment of the Kingdom of Dahomey, Lilian Masediba Ngoyi, leader in the anti-apartheid protest, and Amina Tyler, feminist activist in Tunisia. Kaersenhout's choices set forth a very different notion of understanding history. Her place settings reveal not only the invisibility of these women in mainstream history, but also represent resistance to the racialized power system and its contours of epistemic knowledge production in a White-centric nationalist history.

On the occasion of the opening of *Guess Who's Coming to Dinner Too* at WOW Amsterdam on 25 June 2017, 36 men danced a haka in honour of the 36 "heroines of resistance". The haka is a ceremonial Maori war dance performed for men going to war, but also for individuals who are honoured for their achievements. Here, the haka honours women warriors who wage war against slavery and colonialism and resisted the oppression through colonialist patriarchy with its white supremacy. The 36 men wore specially designed robes so each of the men was connected to one of the 36 women. The robes had 'images and texts about the heroines, all from non-western cultures'.[29] The men are literally and figuratively dressed in women's histories.

In terms of the actual making and producing of her installation, Kaersenhout embedded her project in Amsterdam West. This can be considered a novel type of community art work, not only consciously cultivating community culture, but equally collaborating with neighbourhood businesses. Kaersenhout worked with local women-run businesses, such as AGA LAB, GildeLab, and the fashion label BYBROWN. GildeLab is a production studio specializing in high-quality craft and producing small quantities. The fashion label BYBROWN designed the tunics worn by the men doing the haka dance and the trainee seamstresses at GildeLab sewed them. The table runners and the napkins were printed by the women at AGA LAB and embroidered and beaded by women in Africa and in Amsterdam West.[30] Stressing the interconnectedness and interdependence of local histories and diasporic relations just as much as forging and nourishing economic, social, and cultural ties between non-Western women, AGA LAB emphasized how 'the project has come about thanks to working closely with mainly non-Western women from WOW's immediate surroundings. Kaersenhout spoke with them and heard stories about their heroines and role models'.[31]

Referred to as "a social monument", the next edition of *Guess Who's Coming To Dinner Too?*, guest-curated by Vivian Ziherl, was shown at De Appel (October to December 2019). In commemoration of the Stonewall Riots, Kaersenhout has added two trans women to the table: Marsha P. Johnson and Sylvia. This growing social monument includes many forms of collaborative makings. Via Facebook, De Appel extended an invitation to a "community embroidery workshop" held at De Appel on 12 June 2019, imagined as a "Stitch-In", it was advertised as

> the opportunity to gather around the stories of the women being honoured, and in the company of guest of honour Emory Douglas, former Minister for Culture of the Black Panther Party. The event will be a social occasion of coming together, story-telling, and consciousness-raising. Embroidery skills are not compulsory. Please be sure to RSVP as spaces are limited![32]

While more than fifty people embroidered the table runners together, 'Emory spoke about care and intimacy within the Black Panthers'.[33] Table runners were also embroidered collaboratively with the migrant women organization Vrouw en Vaart. On Instagram, where Kaersenhout, in 2019, refers to herself as 'visual artist, pleasure activist, organic intellectual', she uses the hashtag #teamworkmakesthedreamwork and shares an image of the collaborative situation accompanied by the following caption: 'Embroidering the table

30. See Patricia Kaersenhout, 'Community Art Project: Guess Who's Coming to Dinner Too?', https://bybrown.nl/pages/guess-who-is-coming-to-dinner-too.

31. http://agalab.nl/opening-guess-whos-coming-to-dinner-too-by-patricia-kaersenhout/?lang=en.

32. De Appel, exhibition: 'Guess Who's Coming To Dinner Too?', artist: Patricia Kaersenhout, curator: Vivian Ziherl, press release (Amsterdam, 11 June 2019), www.facebook.com/events/de-appel/stitch-in-with-patricia-kaersenhout-and-emory-douglas/437993470322539/.

33. Patricia Kaersenhout, email to the author, 17 June 2019.

34. Patricia Kaersenhout, https://deskgram.net/p/ 20651416009606165508_ 6422361143.

35. Patricia Kaersenhout, email to the author, 17 June 2019.

36. Aby Warburg, *Der Bilderatlas Mnemosyne*, eds. Martin Warnke and Claudia Brink (Berlin: De Gruyter Akademie Forschung, 2012) and Maurice Halbwachs, *On Collective Memory*, ed. and trans. Lewis A. Coser (Chicago: University of Chicago Press, 1992).

37. Aleida Assmann, 'Transformations Between History and Memory', *Social Research: An International Quarterly* 75, no. 1 (2008), pp. 49–72.

38. Press release, Ibid.

runners for *Guess who's coming to dinner too?* With migrant women at the women's centre Vrouw en Vaart. We had wonderful conversations and lots of laughter.'[34] Over the summer of 2019, Kaersenhout worked on the glassware for her dinner table. While Chicago had individual plates and chalices for her 39 guests of honour, Kaersenhout conceived of a 'communal glass sculpture which symbolizes dining with the dead'.[35] Having researched Pre-Christian Peruvian and Colombian ceramics in the depot of the National Museum of World Cultures in Leiden, the artist developed the idea for vessels that symbolize eating and drinking as a communal, rather than an individualized activity. The glass work is being made in collaboration with the Glaslab in Leerdam. Following the emphasis on craft expressed in Judy Chicago's *Dinner Party*, Kaersenhout takes this up and translates this into contemporary strategies of community art making and local economies of production.

The idea of a "social monument" used to describe Kaersenhout's approach is of interest as it connects memory and history. Independently of each other, both art historian Aby Warburg and sociologist Maurice Halbwachs developed notions of social memory and collective memory at the beginning of the twentieth century.[36] Following memory scholar Aleida Assmann, the definition of social memory is 'embodied, grounded in lived experience that vanish with their carriers'.[37] A social monument then shares both the lived experience of those who are the memories' carriers and the "more durable carriers" of a monument that takes on a physical representation.

The exhibition at De Appel will be the occasion to stage meetings between truly exceptional women of colour who have made deeply significant social and artistic contributions, and yet who may not have had the opportunity to meet or engage in conversation… For example, a truly historic meeting will be staged between Dutch-American scholar and author of *Everyday Racism* Philomena Essed, and renowned Political Scientist and Chairperson of the National Committee for the Memory and History of Slavery of France, Francoise Vergès.[38]

While the social dimension of the monument is being
foregrounded, Kaersenhout's activism equally reaches for
a permanent installation of *Guess Who's Coming to Dinner
Too?* 'Kaersenhout's ultimate goal is to have the installation
travel around the globe and find its final resting place at
the Brooklyn Museum of Art in New York, where Judy
Chicago's work is also on show.'[39]

In Lieu of a Conclusion —
Opening Questions for Future Feminisms

Taken together, the three different dinner parties, Judy
Chicago's *The Dinner Party*, Suzanne Lacy's *The International
Dinner Party*, and Patricia Kaersenhout's *Guess Who's
Coming To Dinner Too?*, present different strategies of
monumental activism in feminist art making as they
shape form and, at the same time, embed their work in the
collective energy of women's communities. Chicago set up a
volunteer-based studio of a community of women contributing to the making of her artwork. She used the dinner as
an aesthetic form for a monument celebrating a religious
feminism 'offering a mythical past freed of patriarchy, where
goddesses ruled' and promoting an accomplished feminism
based in 'a liberal tradition of achievement, not a radical
vision of feminist sisterhood'.[40] For Suzanne Lacy, the dinner
was an activist form based in feminist networks of grassroots
activism in order to create a large-scale living monument
honouring the lived experience of meals to 'strengthen bonds
among women in both the women's labor movement of the
early twentieth century and the feminist community of the
1970s'.[41] *The International Dinner Party* is rooted in activism
and in art. The chosen materials and the formal features,
the map of the world and the collected telegrams document
the activism that resulted in a large-scale event with all
the contributing women understood to be performers. The
installation is the durable carrier for this living monument
that happened in 1979. Kaersenhout appropriates the
aesthetic strategies of Chicago's monument to feminism and
joins it to localized community-based art practices focusing
on the diasporic experience of non-Western women in the
European metropole. The questions these dinner parties

39. 'WOW presents Guess Who's
Coming To Dinner Too? Patricia
Kaersenhout', press release
(Amsterdam, 7 June 2017), www.
wow-amsterdam.nl/wp-content/
uploads/2017/02/Engels1.pdf.

40. Jane F. Gerhard, *The Dinner
Party: Judy Chicago and the
Power of Popular Feminism,
1970–2007* (Athens and London:
The University of Georgia Press,
2013), p. 142 and p. 132.

41. Suzanne Lacy, 'Interview'
*Feast. Radical Hospitality in
Contemporary Art*, ed. Stephanie
Smith, exh cat. Chicago (Smart
Museum of Art); The University of
Chicago, 2013, p. 76.

  Feminist Art Activisms and Artivisms

42. "Travelling" in the sense of 'through the discourse of intentionalism and a practice of narrativity' and the process of 'critical intimacy' described in Mieke Bal, *Travelling Concepts in the Humanities: A Rough Guide* (Toronto: University of Toronto Press, 2002), p. 283.

43. See Amelia Jones, ed., *Sexual Politics: Judy Chicago's Dinner Party in Feminist Art History* (Berkeley: University of California Press, 1996).

44. Suzanne Lacy, 'International Dinner Party (1979–2012)', www.suzannelacy.com/feast-radical-hospitality-in-contemporary-art.

45. Ibid.

46. On the potential of Lacy re-staging her own performative work following a curatorial invitation, see: Harriet Curtis, 'Restaging Feminism in Los Angeles: *Three Weeks in January* (2012): *Three Weeks in May* (1977)', *n.paradoxa* 34 (2014), pp. 77–85.

raise are different according to their historical specificity and context, yet they are also "travelling"[42] dinner parties extending their invitation to open up further questions and to understand how feminist consciousness is durational and has been expanding questions about, within and to feminisms.

Not only has Chicago's *The Dinner Party* provoked seminal feminist artistic responses by the two artists Lacy and Kaersenhout, but both Chicago's monumental installation and Lacy's large-scale performance have led to important curatorial interpretations offering re-interpretations, re-installations, re-stagings, re-performing, and re-citation. In 1996, Amelia Jones revisited *The Dinner Party*, which at the time was controversially critiqued for its essentialism, and critically re-contextualized the piece through her exhibition 'Sexual Politics: Judy Chicago's Dinner Party in Feminist Art History' (Armand Hammer Museum of Art and Cultural Center). This 1996 exhibition placed *The Dinner Party* in the sexual struggles that were part of Second Wave Feminism and central to finding liberated and liberating images beyond hetero-patriarchy and opened up the piece to a present-day re-investigation from an art historical perspective.[43] In 2013, curator Stephanie Smith placed Lacy's *The International Dinner Party* in the context of artistic practices dedicated to sharing meals and celebrating food in the exhibition, 'Feast'. This occasioned an outreach initiative in which 'Lacy invited participants throughout Chicago to host a dinner party in their home honoring a woman from their particular area'[44] and added a new collection of stories and images through a Facebook page and an archive organized by the Smart Museum of Art.[45] In 2015, I curated 'Suzanne Lacy's International Dinner Party in Feminist Curatorial Thought' at the Zurich University of the Arts and showed the 1979 piece in the context of emergent activist archives assembled and composed by feminist and queer feminist collectives in Northern Europe, the Post-Yugoslav and the Post-Soviet context in the twenty-first century. Emphasizing different aspects of the work, including the live dinner party in Chicago and the archival dimension in Zurich, allowed for re-interpretations and re-citations that extend, expand, transform, and update the work's meaning over time.[46] The potential of *The International Dinner Party* has not been exhausted and younger feminists continue to take up the baton.[47]

Judy Chicago sought to counteract the erasure of women from history under patriarchy, yet erased and rendered invisible non-Western women, while privileging notions of high cultural achievement and Western traditions of genealogy and historiography. In Kaersenhout's artistic critique, these aspects of *The Dinner Party* are rendered legible as a white hegemonic herstory. Kaersenhout chooses the strategy of strategic separatism to counteract Black women's, BRM Black Refugee Migrant women's, and non-Western women's invisibility in history and in herstory. She connects the idea of a social monument to dining with the dead. *Guess Who's Coming To Dinner Too?* is also equal parts rooted in activism and in art. Appropriating the distinct elements of *The Dinner Party*, these are translated into a sculpture incorporating non-Western traditions of art and craft.

Both Lacy's and Kaesenhout's artistic responses to *The Dinner Party* can be understood as artistic critiques, activist appropriations, and critical expansions. They provide evidence that disunity and conflict in feminisms leads to novel art historical forms of monumental activism through which feminist artists respond to each other's work. Lacy's large-scale living monument to international feminism could be performed again; extending its invitation in many different languages might produce a truly worldwide feminist moment today.[48] While the activist measure of creating multiple, simultaneous international dinner parties round the globe is inspiring, its promise remains to be fulfilled. Kaersenhout's social monument could include future live moments, even if it were to be permanently installed at its desired destination next to Judy Chicago's sculpture. As a new anti-capitalist and anti-racist feminism is taking shape, future art and activism will very much be needed to perform the labour of decolonizing feminism. While the activist measure of substituting black heroines of resistance for white heroines is powerful, the question of what a less iconic and less symbolically driven monumental feminist activism might look like remains wide open.

In September 1979, the year of *The Dinner Party's* first showing, Audre Lorde gave the paper 'The Master's

  Feminist Art Activisms and Artivisms

47. See also 'After Suzanne Lacy: Another International Dinner Party, 40 years after: An Event Hosted by Carlota Mir with Sam Hultin & School in Common', Stockholm, March 2019.

48. Krasny, 'Suzanne Lacy's International Dinner Party in Feminist Curatorial Thought'.

49. Audre Lorde, 'The Master's Tools Will Never Dismantle the Master's House', in *Your Silence Will Not Protect You* (London: Silver Press, 2017), pp. 92, 93. These were her comments at 'The Personal and the Political Panel' at the Second Sex Conference in New York.

Tools Will Never Dismantle the Master's House'. Lorde writes:

> But as Adrienne Rich pointed out in a recent talk, white feminists have educated themselves about such an enormous amount over the past ten years, how come you haven't also educated yourselves about Black women and the differences between us —white and Black—when its key to our survival as a movement?[49]

Forty years later, in 2019, when this essay is being written, this sharp observation resonates strongly with today's historico-political conjuncture as its classed, racialized, and sexualized power system that continues to redeploy feminist legacies newly entangled with critiques of patriarchal modernity, colonial capitalism, and its hegemonic patterns of history writing. Putting feminisms in question, the dinner party is an artistic format open to future feminist appropriation, re-citation, critique, and expansion and this indicates the enduring value of its aesthetic strategies and the lasting activism in the idea. The largest question and most difficult challenge remains the monumental deficit regarding a more complex study of her*stories rooted in disunity, nuanced difference, and creative conflicts between transnationally entangled, interconnected, and interdependent movements in and for feminisms.

WHERE WE'RE AT!

OTHER VOICES ON GENDER

SilvanaEditoriale

BOZAR BOOKS

WHERE WE'RE AT! Other Voices on Gender, Bozar, Brussels, 2014.
Catalogue edited by Christine Eyene

CURATING FROM A BLACK FEMALE PERSPECTIVE
A Testimony on Adversity and Resilience

Christine Eyene

1. Matthew Blackman, 'Inquiry launched into professional conduct of Zeitz MOCAA Director', *Artthrob*, 16 May 2018, https://artthrob.co.za/2018/05/16/inquiry-launched-into-professional-conduct-of-zeitz-mocaa-director (accessed 24 July 2019).

2. Matthew Blackman, 'An Open Letter to Jochen Zeitz and Mark Coetzee', *Artthrob*, 9 March 2015, https://artthrob.co.za/2015/03/09/an-open-letter-to-jochen-zeitz-and-mark-coetzee/ (accessed 24 July 2019).

3. Sean O'Toole, 'Zeitz MoCAA Cape Town: A Change in Leadership', *Contemporary And*, 18 May 2018, www.contemporaryand.com/fr/magazines/a-change-in-leadership (accessed 24 July 2019).

In May 2018, Matthew Blackman, a South African writer and former editor of *Artthrob*, one of South Africa's most important online art news platforms, published an article announcing that an inquiry was being launched into the professional conduct of the former executive director and chief curator of a now well-established museum of contemporary African art in Cape Town. The article spoke of "unconfirmed rumours" of "abuses of power" of an unknown nature and that 'although several people at the museum … ha[d] been asked for comment none ha[d] been forthcoming'. It also mentioned that the museum had received very little criticism, despite 'questionable institutional and curatorial practices'.[1]

From what I saw at the time, Blackman was one of the rare South African observers who had clearly and publicly voiced his concerns about the museum's governance. He did so in an open letter in 2015,[2] more than two years before the museum opened its doors. The letter was also mentioned by South African art critic Sean O'Toole in an article published in the online African art platform *Contemporary And (C&)* in which he commented that no one had ever responded to the points raised by Blackman.[3]

When the open letter was published in 2015, the comment section included remarks by a user named "Karl Max" who suggested Blackman interviewed Raphael Chikukwa, now deputy director of the National Gallery of Zimbabwe, and myself, since we were both collaborators of the concerned individual between 2009 and 2010. I was never approached by Blackman but had I been at the time, I would probably have refused to comment on the matter. Just like I had declined several press requests to share my views on the museum as it opened to great international acclaim in 2017. I always felt that the criticism should come from within the South African art scene, not from me.

Seeing how artists, galleries and curators had then been dazzled by the museum, its power as a financially backed project, the influence of the people behind it, the visibility to be gained in being associated with it, and how they advocated it without even questioning the professional history and character of the person at its helm, was interesting to observe. It also led me to distance myself from the South African art scene, a scene that I was passionate about, to which I owe my introduction to art and to black forms of cultural resistance.

While in my mind Blackman's open letter kept all of its relevance, by the time the museum had opened, it seemed to me that there was no point engaging with those issues anymore. I assumed it had been a situation accepted not only by the South African but also the global art world.

Who would have believed me ten years ago if I had talked about my experience working with the now suspended museum director? At the time, I felt that if I spoke, the African art scene would cast me away as someone bitter for having been robbed of a project I helped develop. Furthermore, in raising a certain number of issues, I did not want to be accused of 'playing the race card'. Then, in 2015–2017, it might have been seen as an act of attention-seeking from a killjoy ruining the greatest African artistic celebration of all time. So, I kept silent until May 2018, when questions about this character arose.

My decision to speak out, in the form of writing, came after reading Sean O'Toole's article, 'A Change in Leadership'. It got me thinking about invisibility. More particularly, women's invisibility. And whitewashing, which is very frequent in the art world. We see it in the power dynamics at play in the decision-making processes, in the act of further marginalizing under-represented voices, in the writing (out) of art history and even in the way that museum polemic was reported. Which is what prompted me to express

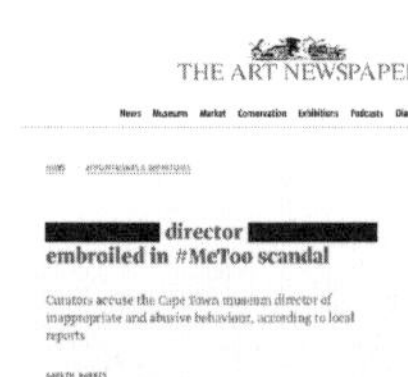

Heading of *The Art Newspaper*, online article by Gareth Harris, edited by Christine Eyene

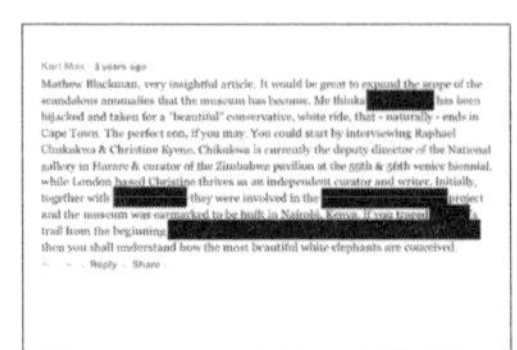

Comment by user named Karl Max in Matthew Blackman's *Artthrob* article, edited by Christine Eyene

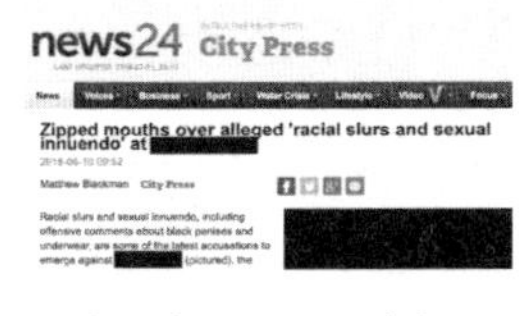

Heading of *News 24* article by Matthew Blackman, edited by Christine Eyene

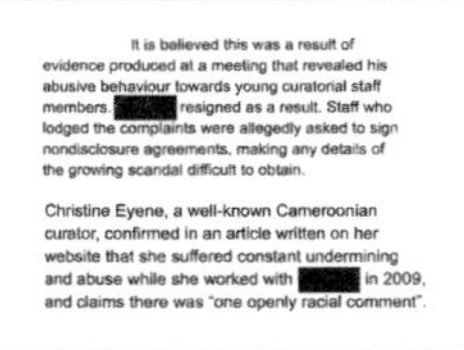

Excerpt of Matthew Blackman's article in *News 24*, edited by Christine Eyene

myself. I was interested in how the context and mechanism that led to my erasure predicted all the signs of a situation, the magnitude of which was now amplified because of the museum's high visibility.

It also has to be said that another reason for me to have remained silent was that I did not want my name to be associated with any project bearing that person's name. This collaboration, which I can honestly say was my worst experience in the arts ever, is not part of my résumé. I have tried to forget about it and I am lucky enough to have worked on more fulfilling projects before and after.

I am writing because I believe the discourses we make as curators should not be limited to curatorial statements or within exhibitions spaces. There are times when one needs to just paint a picture of our art scene as it is and say things as they are. I am fortunate to work at the University of Central Lancashire with the artist Lubaina Himid, CBE, on an interdisciplinary research project called Making Histories Visible, through which we address, and hopefully redress, issues of the marginalization and silencing of certain voices within art institutions. We do so as black female art professionals who are aware of how gender, race and class, to name but those three, impact on the functioning and vision of art institutions.[4] I owe it to the younger generation of curators in Africa and beyond to make this story known.

In May 2008, I was approached by the Dutch museum director of a now defunct museum to discuss the possibility to be involved in the artistic component of a global company's social responsibility programme. I did not immediately jump at the offer. Rather I considered it carefully because the effects of mixing corporate and art worlds are common knowledge. Eventually I accepted to join the project because of the culturally diverse team assembled by the curator leading the project. I was also very keen to collaborate with curators practising beyond the field of contemporary African art.

The lead curator, a white French woman, fostered a very collegial bond between our team, where we all contributed ideas and our expertise as co-curators of the project. She always valued our opinions, knowledge, skills and abilities. She is an avid sharer of art information and art news and allowed us space for research, including attending international art events when possible. Unfortunately, she left the project at the end of 2008 for reasons that I never got to properly pin down but I know they were linked to a professional disagreement. Before leaving, she ensured that some of the plans I had recommended were validated. As much as our team were disappointed that she left, we were equally happy to welcome the project's new lead, a white man hailing from a country with a past history of racial discrimination known as apartheid. This was a short-lived enthusiasm. For me, it turned out to be a year or so of moral abuse "in the workplace".[5]

First of all, we were all demoted, in what felt like a power-crazed move, from co-curators to advisors. Then, in one of our first email exchanges, a non-offensive yet direct response from me about the projects we had lined up for the year that he had planned to cancel was met with a 'Christine, I don't like your tone' and 'if you're not happy, you know what to do'. In other words, I was threatened with losing my job from the very moment he joined our team. From then on, I knew it was not going to be an easy ride, but I was determined to see the project I had planned through to realization.

What then ensued were countless acts of undermining, against which I was ill-equipped at the time because I had never encountered anything like that before, not even from more respected curators with whom I had worked in France, Morocco or England. Progressively, the decision-making process shifted from a collegial one to a one-man voice. Transparency became opacity, while the artistic orientations we had developed for months dissolved into a marketing spectacle that instrumentalized our African art scene. We were never consulted before a new member joined our team.[6] One by one I saw my colleagues being let go. I decided I would ensure I remained, until the collaboration I had initiated was delivered. After that, I knew my contract would be terminated and I had no intention of continuing working in such a hostile environment.

June to December 2009 marked my most difficult time being part of this project. I was the only member of the initial team, the only black person, and I was working (if one may call it so) with two white individuals who excluded me from all the important aspects of the project. I was denied

5. I am using quotes because the workplace was both a physical (office) and non-physical (multi-location events, emails) place.

6. The initial team of this African art project was replaced by two consecutive white persons that I prefer to leave out this testimony.

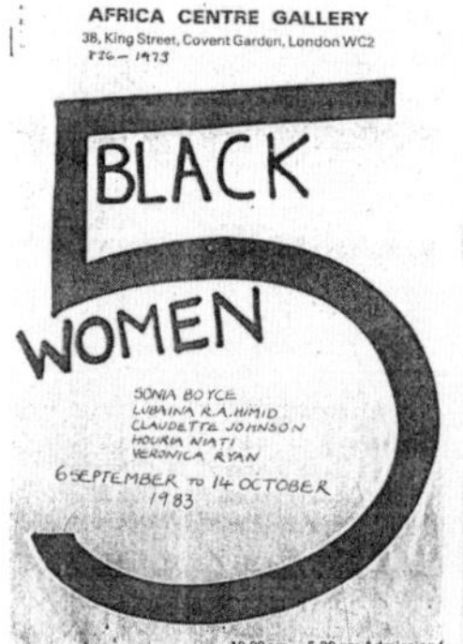

Brochure of exhibition 'Five Black Women' curated by Lubaina Himid at the Africa Centre, London, 1983. Courtesy Lubaina Himid and Making Histories Visible

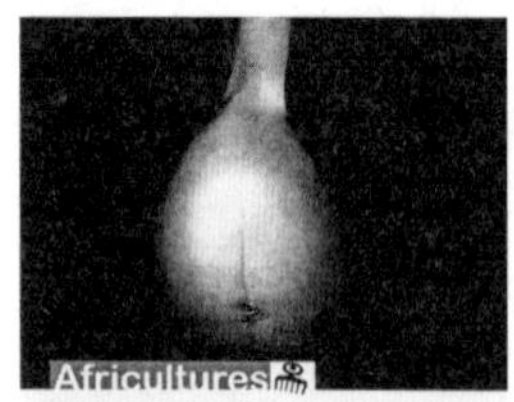

Cover of *Africultures*, no. 75 (February 2009), edited by Christine Eyene

7. For instance, in 2014, *eye.on.art* was the only art platform taking a clear position (from a French perspective) with regard to *Exhibit B*, the installation/performance by South African artist Brett Bailey consisting of re-enacting the human zoos by placing shackled black actors in cages. See Christine Eyene, 'Exhibit B: de quel racisme parle-t-on?', *eye.on.art*, 2 December 2014, https://eyonart.org/exhibit-b-de-quel-racisme-parle-t-on (accessed 24 July 2019).

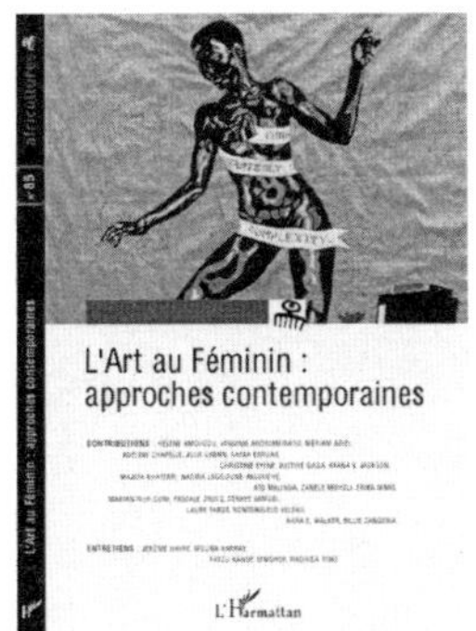

Cover of *Africultures*, no. 85 (June 2011), edited by Christine Eyene

the opportunity to attend international art exhibitions like the Venice Biennale, which is the most important event in the arts calendar. I found out this two-person team were to go to Venice as part of the project but that I was not included in that trip. I still went to Venice invited by another museum.

The way I was treated worsened from one collaborative project to the other and the disrespect was topped by an openly racial comment. At that point, I had been side-lined from almost everything including from the discussions on our partnerships with art biennales. When I was approached by one of the Manifesta 8 curators to collaborate with a project, I was told that it was great, but if I did it, there would not be any budget for it. As an advisor, none of my advice was ever taken on board, none of my ideas were ever valued, nor was my knowledge of the African art scene. When, in 2018, the art press spoke of an 'inquiry into professional conduct' and 'abuses of power', it revived the experience I had encountered ten years earlier. I also knew that the curators who complained about the individual in question probably experienced worse than I did.

I turned this adverse situation into a resilience geared towards plans for an independent curatorial and writing practice. From it was born my art news website *eye.on.art* as a way to control my information, express critical views[7] and, most importantly, share opportunities with the African and global art community. In June 2010, I curated 'FOCUS 10: Contemporary Art Africa' in Basel, an exhibition addressing Africa's under-representation at major Western art fairs. I had not anticipated this would mark the beginning of my career as an international curator. Other important collaborations were born out of this negative experience as I kept close ties with some members of our initial team. We came together and supported Raphael Chikukwa realize the first ever Zimbabwe Pavilion at the 54th Venice Biennale in 2011. This was a turning point not only for the Zimbabwean art scene but also in terms of representation of national African pavilions in Venice. I continued working as a curator, developing projects ranging from small-scale curatorial experiments to major international exhibitions.

My encounter with the legendary Lubaina Himid in 2012 led me to working with her on Making Histories

Visible, where I am still in position today. But even before ever having met her in person, Lubaina had had a major impact on my thinking through the exhibitions of black women artists she had curated from the early 1980s.
A newcomer to London in 2002, I found out about her work as an artist and exhibition maker while digging in the Africa Centre's archive, where I worked at the time. She and her peers Sutapa Biswas, Sonia Boyce OBE, Claudette Johnson, Marlene Smith, to name but a few, are at the heart of my interest in black feminist art. Their work visually translated experiences with which I identified. They developed discourses that not only helped me articulate my own exist-ence, but also informed my writing and curatorial practice. My first feminist exhibition, 'Women Speak Out (La Parole aux Femmes)' at Galerie le Manège, Dakar (Senegal) in 2011, was the first step towards reclaiming my voice as a black African female curator, after one year of being silenced by a white male.

This feminist curatorial practice is not aligned with a trend, nor is it some sort of detached curatorial exercise. It is deeply inspired by my own experience, including the one I just described. It is the prism through which I am touched by the creative souls I work with. And it continues to be motivated by the urgency to address all forms of inequalities as I witness them in society and in the arts.

This testimony was first published on my website under the title: 'On Ethics and Good Practice: An Open Discussion to Be Had in Africa', *eye.on.art*, 21 May 2018, https://eyonart.org/on-ethics, accessed 24 July 2019. The present piece is an adaption from my keynote speech at the conference Feminist Art Activisms and Artivisms held in July 2018.

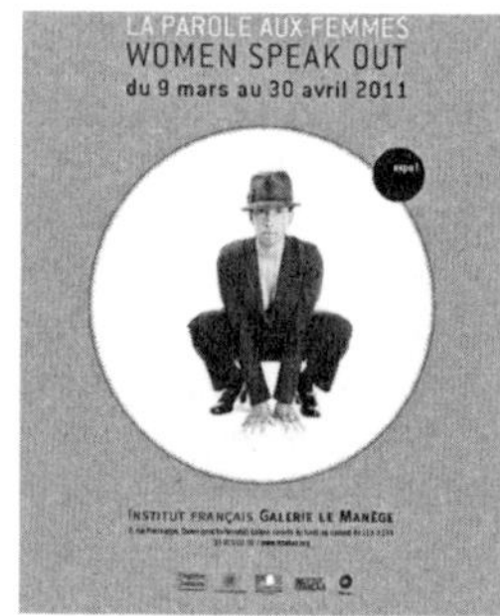

Poster of exhibition 'Women Speak Out', Le Manège, Dakar, 2011. Courtesy of Christine Eyene

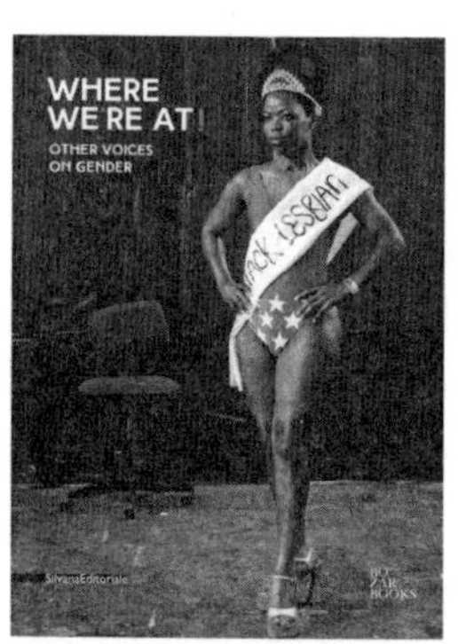

'WHERE WE'RE AT! Other Voices on Gender', Bozar, Brussels, 2014. Exhibition curated and catalogue edited by Christine Eyene.

    Feminist Art Activisms and Artivisms

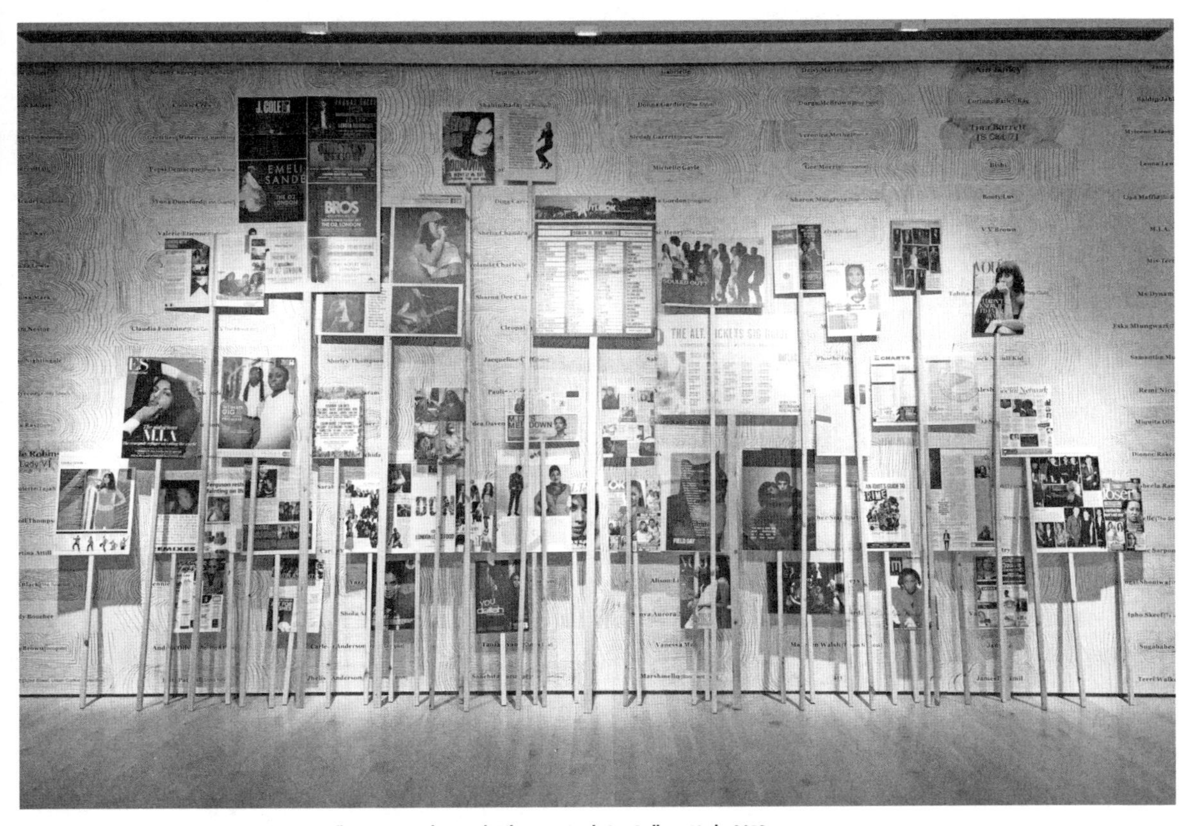

Sonia Boyce, Devotional, *1999–present*, installation view of 'Sounds Like Her', York Art Gallery, York, 2019,
a New Art Exchange exhibition curated by Christine Eyene. Photo: Chris Streek

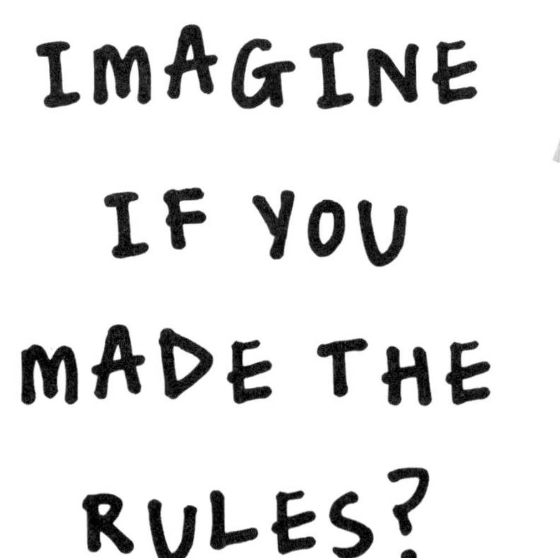

IMAGINE IF YOU MADE THE RULES?
YOUR RULE and WHY?
OPEN EARLY CLOSE LATE
SUPPORT YOUR LOCAL ARTISTS
what would you do differently at Tate Liverpool?

USING WORDS IN PRACTICE
Contemporary Art Collections as Agonistic Sites

Emma Curd

1. bell hooks, *Teaching to Transgress: Education as the Practice of Freedom* (New York: Routledge, 1994), pp. 167–175.

2. Michael Hardt and Antonio Negri, *Empire* (Cambridge, MA: Harvard University Press, 2000), p. 212.

bell hooks, in her essay 'On the Language of Power' (1994), theorizes language as an instrument to conduct counter-hegemonic action. For her, words have power to "challenge" and "assist", as much as "include" and "exclude", "dominate" or "emancipate".[1] As an artist-practitioner and action researcher working at the intersection between contemporary art and museums, I have spent my career exploring how words create communities, and, at the same time, those same words alienate and jettison others. My argument here focuses on examining the politics of discourse—words, language, and tone of voice—used by museum collections in their texts and labels about works of art and how these can be transformed by demands to democratize their role in the museum as one of the "Places of Power"[2] in our society.

Undertaken with the 'Community Collective', a group defined by their engagement with Tate Liverpool, I discuss two approaches which formed part of our work during a week-long residency on 'Art, Activism and Language: Feminist Issues in Museums and Galleries' (Tate Exchange, 2017). Part artwork, part action research project, these were designed to disrupt the dominant discourse in the 'DLA Piper Series: Constellations', Tate Liverpool and develop a new kind of agonistic democratic practice through dialogue. I was invited to write a proposal to suit the Tate's theme of "Production", which had been proposed by artist Clare Twomey for 2017 because of my doctoral research at Liverpool John Moores University,

one of the Associate institutions of Tate Exchange. In my
proposal I identified the words "co-production" and "co-cre-
ation" as subjects requiring analysis due to their aggregated
use by museum professionals in practice and in the field of
research. My ambition for the residency was to investigate
the ethics of co-labour, exchange and reciprocity between
Tate Liverpool and community producers when undertaking
processes to co-write interpretation for the collection.
Specifically, I was interested in creating a potential "toolkit"
to engender agonistic interventions in the future as well
as finding out how the institution ascribes authorship to
content producers and, at the same time, resists co-opting
community voices. When applying to Tate Exchange, I
extended their guidelines for "Associates" by making use of
my respective roles and connections to the artist collective
Quad Collective, and the artist-led studio organization The
Royal Standard, Liverpool. Significantly, these collective
groups are funded publicly via bodies such as Arts Council
England and Liverpool John Moores University and
privately, but it was due to this financial support that I was
able to undertake the research and involve them as participants. These are crucial aspects to consider when critiquing
the framework of educational spatial strategies such as Tate
Exchange. I believe that my intervention at Tate Exchange
was accepted because it was both financially self-sufficient
and offered a temporal "change-making" capacity only
without any long-lasting potential. In principle, although
the programme is designed to value input from "different
publics", its structural competence makes it difficult for
any of its collection interventions to be truly meaningful or

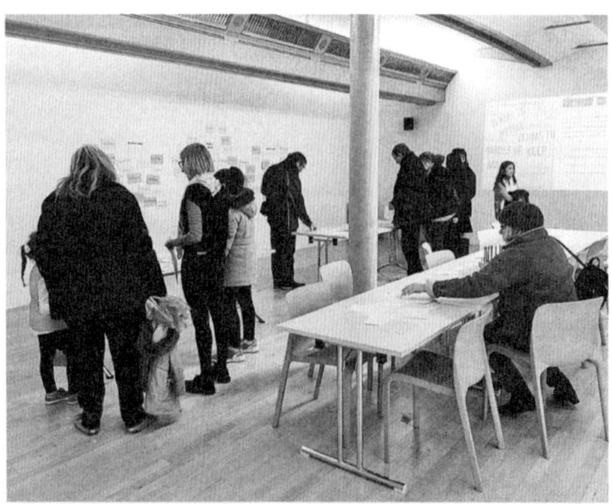

Quad Collective, *Shared Language*, 2017, documentation of workshop at
Tate Exchange, Liverpool. Photo: Jessica Fairclough

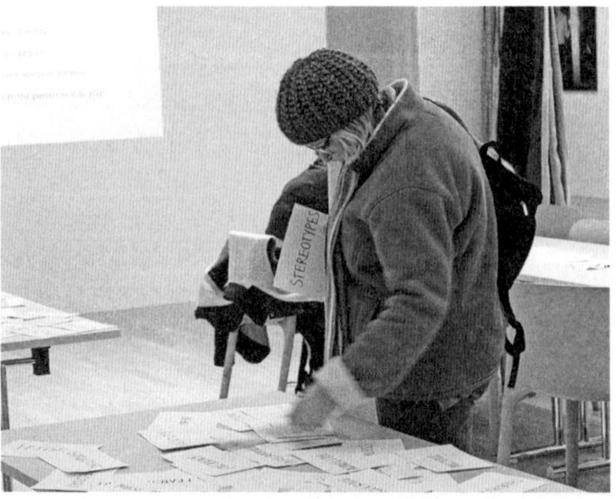

Quad Collective, *Shared Language*, 2017, documentation of workshop at
Tate Exchange, Liverpool. Photo: Emma Curd

3. Chantal Mouffe, 'Institutions as Sites for Agonistic Intervention', *Institutional Attitudes: Instituting Art in a Flat World*, ed. Pascal Gielen (Amsterdam: Valiz, 2013), p. 66.

4. Gilles Deleuze, *A Thousand Plateaus: Capitalism and Schizophrenia* (London: Athlone Press, 1980), p. 456, and Paolo Virno, *A Grammar of the Multitude: For an Analysis of Contemporary Forms of Life* (Los Angeles: Semiotext(e), 2004), pp. 66–70.

5. Kuba Szreder, 'Productive Withdrawals: Art Strikes, Art Worlds, and Art as a Practice of Freedom', *e-flux journal* 87 (December 2017), http://worker01.e-flux.com/pdf/article_168899.pdf.

6. Chantal Mouffe, *The Museum and Radical Democracy: European Museums in the 21st Century: Setting the Framework* (Milan: Politecnico di Milano Press, 2013), p. 18.

7. Chantal Mouffe, 'Institutions as Sites for Agonistic Intervention', *Institutional Attitudes: Instituting Art in a Flat World*, ed. Pascal Gielen (Amsterdam: Valiz, 2013), p. 66.

8. Susan Ashley, 'First Nations on View: Canadian Museums and Hybrid Representations of Culture', *eTopia* 13 (2005), pp. 31–40.

9. Chantal Mouffe, 'Art as an Agonistic Intervention in Public Space', in *Art as a Public Issue: How Art and Its Institutions Reinvent the Public Dimension*, ed. Jorinde Seijdel (Rotterdam: NAi Publishers, 2008).

10. Chantal Mouffe, 'Institutions as Sites for Agonistic Intervention', p. 66.

11. Chantal Mouffe, 'Deliberative Democracy or Agonistic Pluralism?', *Social Research* 66, no. 3 (1999), pp. 745–758.

transformative in the long term. In this essay I describe some of the practices that I designed to "hack" the system.

The contemporary art museum is an agonistic site in liberal democracy as a State-funded cultural institution and here I argue against the widespread notion that 'institutions of the art world have become complicit with capitalism and that they can no longer provide a site for critical art practices'.[3] Postcolonial critics have theorized routes to avoid collusion with institutions by fleeing, escaping, exiting, withdrawing or departing from the institutional, hegemonic landscape.[4] In discourses of contemporary art, recent waves 'of art strikes, boycotts, and occupations'[5] show that this theoretical approach may be the favoured tactic to avoid being complicit with any museums' empiricism and question their Imperialist and colonialist pasts. Despite the trend to blacklist museums as "Places of Power", I argue for their collections to be used as potential sites to confront hegemonic discourses and its resulting social stratification with the aim of including unheard, public voices in different narratives about the art objects they have acquired. This route is supported by Chantal Mouffe, who suggests that to disengage with museums would be 'to ignore the tensions that always exist within a given configuration of forces'.[6]

Frequently masked by their perceived neutrality,[7] art institutions are "Places of Power" where their competencies emulate colonial practices, as they collect, exhibit and educate and, because of their history, produce singular, authoritative and dominant narratives on art and culture.[8] As a political scientist, Mouffe positions contemporary art museums as possible sites for conflictual agonism to challenge hegemonic constructions of power and discourse[9] and to resist discursive occupation.[10] In her view, the development of democratic art practices requires "agonistic plurality" in which hegemonic practices must be countered to mobilize dissent and 'passions towards democratic design'.[11] Questioning hegemony is the key to creating counter discourses or minor narratives that disrupt the status quo. In my view, it is the practitioners most engaged with institutional critique, collaborative, useful or socially engaged art that can activate opportunities to represent and mediate agonistic plurality in museum spaces as sites for democratic discussion. The residency discussed is an example of how collections might develop agonistic and self-critical strategies and draws on Mouffe's theory to inform a critical art practice that takes discourse as its starting point.

Currently, it is expected that diverse categories of people take part in the public discourse associated with museums thus creating a "public sphere" in its audiences, and as viewers and spectators, by presenting many differing opinions and representations of thought and speech.[12] Institutions attempt to communicate with their publics via language; both in institutional text and in oral consultation.[13] In *Hegemony and Socialist Strategy*, Mouffe and Laclau conceive communication, or discourse theory, as an ideology that defines the world through discursive mediation. Their theorization—for our purposes—gives space to the central idea that text communicates hegemony through its author's hand. This is theorized as 'the drawing of political frontiers between "insiders" and "outsiders"'[14] to reduce the possibilities of surplus meanings. Consequently, in this view, all visible text in all public spheres prioritizes insider knowledge and therefore acts to exercise power. Hence, whilst museums have attempted to emancipate themselves and their visitors from the production of singular and dominant narratives via multi-mediation and the incorporation of multiple perspectives, there still remains a dichotomy between "them" and "us" as "insiders" and "outsiders" that continues to undermine their learning and participatory efforts.[15]

Attempting to combat the waves of criticism of elitist practices and limited audiences, museums have sought to redefine their visitors as "active citizens" and "interpreters" in efforts to increase inclusion, redefining their original purpose to educate the general public by solely presenting works of art.[16] Their outreach efforts to different communities in society are increasingly evident in the development of "invited spaces" for community consultation groups and attempts to involve specific categories of under-represented people—young, old, local and racially diverse[17] in an effort to represent practices of deliberative democracy. However, simply listening and respecting these community consultants is not enough to constitute a public sphere seeking to encompass agonistic plurality 'to exercise voice and influence'[18] over the reception of art because it does not address the selection of artists or exhibitions, and the display

12. Robin Boast, 'Neocolonial Collaboration: Museum as Contact Zone Revisited', *Museum Anthropology* 34, no. 1 (2011), p. 56.

13. Teun Adrianus van Dijk, *Discourse and Power* (New York and Basingstoke: Palgrave Macmillan, 2008), p. 54.

14. David J. Howarth, Aletta J. Norval and Yannis Stavrakakis, *Discourse Theory and Political Analysis: Identities, Hegemonies, and Social Change* (Manchester: Manchester University Press, 2000), p. 5.

15. Bernadette Lynch, 'Good for You, But I Don't Care!': Critical Museum Pedagogy in Educational and Curatorial Practice', *Art. School.Differences Symposium* (Zurich: ZHdK; University of the Arts, 2016); https://blog.zhdk.ch/artschooldifferences/en/forschungsvorhaben/.

16. Boast, 'Neocolonial Collaboration', p. 56.

17. Miranda Stearn, 'Contemporary Challenges: Artist Interventions in Museums and Galleries Dealing with Challenging Histories', in *Challenging History in the Museum: International Perspectives*, eds. Jenny Kidd et al. (Surrey: Ashgate Publishing, 2016), p. 111.

18. Andrea Cornwall, 'Unpacking "Participation": Models, Meanings and Practices', *Community Development Journal* 43, no. 3 (2008), p. 283.

19. Pablo Helguera, *Education for Socially Engaged Art: A Materials and Technique Handbook* (Taiwan: Jorge Pinto Books, 2013), p. 73.

20. Ibid.

21. Rolando R. Vázquez, 'Towards a Decolonial Critique of Modernity: Buen Vivir, Relationality and the Task of Listening', *Capital, Poverty, Development, Denktraditionen im Dialog: Studien zur Befreiung und Interkulturalität* 33 (2012), pp. 241–252.

and purchasing role of the collections. Arguably, in museums of contemporary art especially, deliberative democracy has yet to be represented in a meaningful way. As artist and educator Pablo Helguera observes about how museums organize: 'In contemporary art and in art history in general, the voice of the public is generally missing; it is the voice of the artists, the curators and the critics that appears to matter.'[19]

Emphasizing Helguera's proposition that the voice of the general public is still missing in conversations around contemporary art, it is my suggestion that collections of contemporary art have averted some of the more rigorous processes of implementing plurality due to their commitment to "contemporaneity". By exhibiting diverse collections of contemporary art, the museum offers "liberal" gestures towards "balance" and "representation", and attempt to claim that pluralism is constituent to what they do. This strategy effectively minimizes differences, assumes common held values and beliefs, and hides unarticulated embedded thought processes.[20] Furthermore, by the same logic, their textual mediation has not yet aligned itself to embrace the "vocabulary of relationality" or to challenge modernity's vocabulary of objectification, exploitation and autonomy.[21] As a result, it has not been a priority to decolonize their

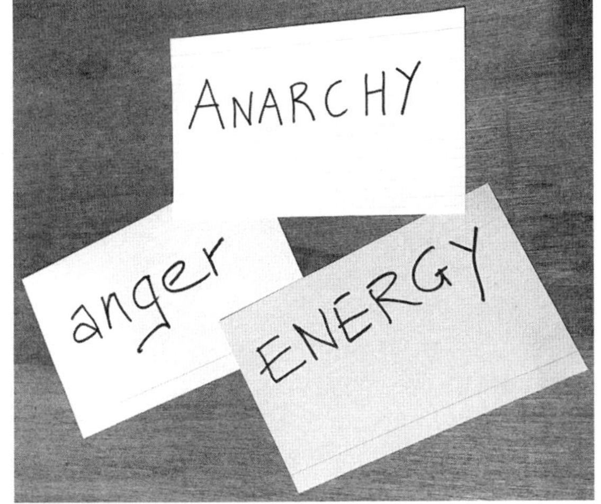

Publicly-produced additions to contribute to the 'word archive', *Shared Language*, documentation of workshop, 2017. Photo: Emma Curd

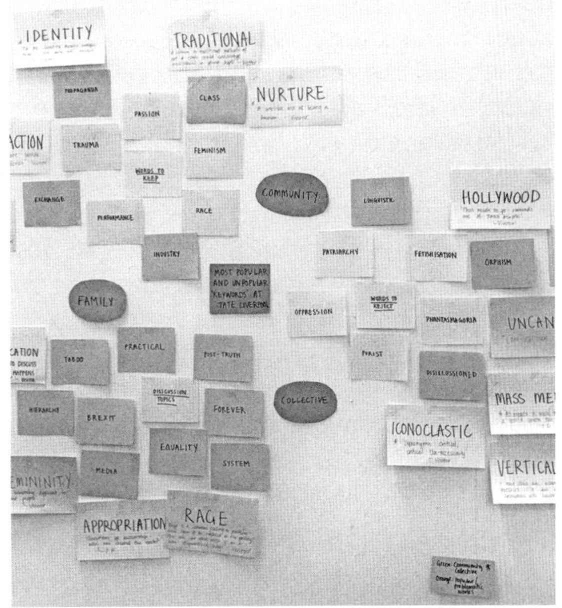

Publicly-produced additions to contribute to the 'word archive' and discourse analysis from *Shared Language* workshop, 2017. Photo: Emma Curd

narratives through analysing their own self-representation, even though many of their museological counterparts in historical and ethnographic museums have started this process because of the campaigns of indigenous groups.

Recently, several artists' groups have emerged, not just to protest numbers or visibility, but to argue for greater attention to the vocabulary museums use to describe their work. Feminist, decolonial artist collective Mujeres Creando from Bolivia, have positioned themselves critically towards the ways in which 'official art histories are inserted'[22] into museums and galleries. For them, one cannot separate colonial practices from patriarchal ones, and in their view, working decolonially can only be done through the creation of new vocabularies to rethink "every word" within 'the very field of language and poetics'.[23] For example, the common use of the words like "genius" and "pioneer" are synonyms for the word—colonist, colonizer, discoverer—and are central to the sexism as well as colonial vocabulary of Western, modernist discourse as it has constructed a progressive, linear view of art history. Other decolonial researchers have demanded the end of "contemporary" due to its implications within 'the negation of multiple pasts, of multiple histories and 'in the erasure of other worlds of meaning'.[24] In this way, decolonial research opposes the "single truth" of modernism that assumes itself as universal, pioneering and progressive, where post-colonial or feminist critics have sought inclusion. Instead, decolonial thought asks 'for what has been lost: what has been exploited, extracted, denied dignity, denied existence?'[25] Collections of contemporary art are asking themselves the same questions. For example, in 2017, the Van Abbemuseum hosted the symposium, 'Collections in Transition: Decolonising, Demodernising and Decentralising?', organized by L'Internationale, at which Rolando Vázquez posed the question: 'Can modern and contemporary art institutions…forego the privilege of controlling the locus of enunciation, overcome its epistemic enclosure and listen to the pluriversal?'[26]

Vázquez's question emphasizes how it is important to challenge how modernist discourses exclude and conceal the relationality of art history, objects and mediation. Unequivocally, in these discourses, decolonial feminism has proposed 'the reconstruction of museums' and sought to

22. María Galindo, 'Creativity Is an Instrument of Struggle and Social Change a Creative Act', *Afterall* 46 (Autumn/Winter 2018), p. 47. Mujeres Creando are a feminist art collective that formed in 1992 in La Paz, Bolivia.

23. Ibid.

24. Rolando R. Vázquez, 'Decolonial Thinking with Rolando Vázquez: The End of the Contemporary?, *Contemporary And*, 5 June 2017, www.contemporaryand.com/magazines/the-end-of-the-contemporary/.

25. Ibid.

26. Rolando R. Vázquez, 'The Museum, Decoloniality and the End of the Contemporary', paper presented at symposium 'Collections In Transition: Decolonising, Demodernising and Decentralising?', Van Abbemuseum, Eindhoven, 22 September 2017.

WORDS ARE TOOLS

27. Hilde S. Hein, 'Redressing the Museum in Feminist Theory', *Museum Management and Curatorship* 22, no. 1, pp. 29–42.

28. Sujit Chandrakumar, 'Guerrilla Girls: "The Art World Has Become an Instrument of the Rich and Powerful: We Are Fighting to Change That"', *Kochi News*, 11 December 2018, https://timesofindia.indiatimes. com/city/kochi/the-art-world-has-become-an-instrument-of-the-rich-and-powerful-we-are-fighting-to-change-that/ articleshow/67041158.cms.

29. Clare Ballinger, 'Navigating Multiple Research Identities: Reflexivity in Discourse Analytic Research', *Reflexivity: A Practical Guide for Researchers in Health and Social Sciences*, eds. Brendan Gough and Linda Finlay (Oxford: Blackwell Science, 2003), p. 67.

30. Silvio Ripamonti et al., 'Pushing Action Research Toward Reflexive Practice', *Journal of Management Inquiry* 25, no. 1 (2016), p. 55.

31. David Coghlan and Teresa Brannick, *Doing Action Research in Your Own Organization* (London: Sage, 2010), p. 17.

32. Nicholas Serota, in 'Tone of Voice Guidelines', ed. Rob Baker (London: Tate, 2016), guidelines/ internal document.

recognize its yet-unrealized potential for 'open-endedness and inherent pluralism'.[27] Some argue that the same feminist, pluralistic mechanisms have already been adopted in collections of contemporary art since the emergence of radical feminist interventions initiated by collectives such as the Guerrilla Girls, as the 'conscience of the art world', to undermine the canon. However, even if the numbers of women artists are increasing in the international contemporary art world, and we 'have seen a change of consciousness about the need for intersectional diversity in the arts… we haven't seen the system change very much' in many places, like India, where this quote originates.[28]

Two reflexive, interdisciplinary methods, discourse analysis[29] and Participatory Action Research, also conceived as 'reflexive dialogical action research',[30] were employed during the residency to help investigate how the discourse within the collection was directed at different "communities of practice".

Both methods have been useful in reflecting on the micro and macro implications of power and authority in the uses of language and new tools to develop usable (or accessible) knowledge.[31] The methods described below are just two in an action research "toolkit" that I have developed to challenge institutional discourse and the barriers that prevent a pluriversal discourse from emerging in museum collections.

FAX-BAKing: An Exercise in Discourse

In the first method, I took Tate's most recent 'Tone of Voice Guidelines' to understand how language is used to inform all written communications at Tate. In this document, former director, Nicholas Serota states that 'invitation and dialogue, rather than Olympian instruction, have become the necessary voice of the institution'.[32] Using this sentence as a foundation for my enquiry, I adopted a playful art-based model to conduct a critical discourse analysis of the document. My analysis was also based on the *FAX-BAK* project created by the artist collective known as BANK (who have since dispersed). In *FAX-BAK*, the group annotated gallery press releases, marked them out of ten—the marks were always

Emma Curd, *FAX-BAKing* at 'Art, Activism and Language: Feminist Issues in Museums and Galleries' at Tate Exchange, Liverpool, 2017, annotated and redacted Guidelines Document

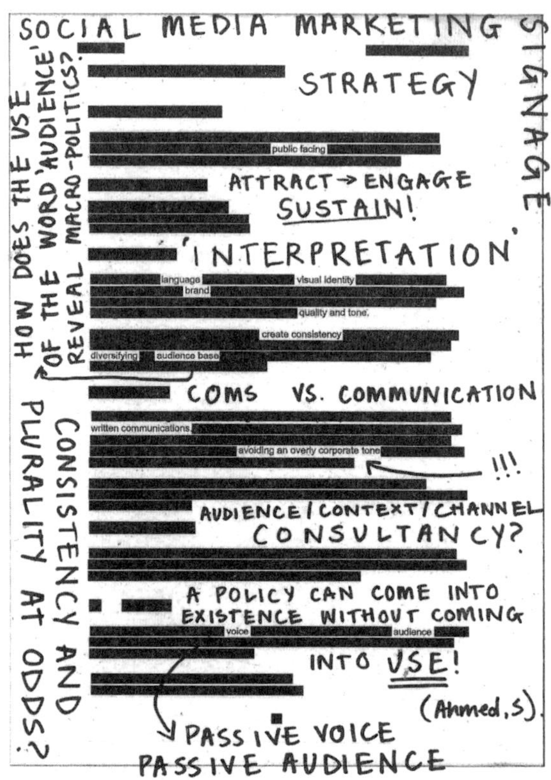

Emma Curd, *FAX-BAKing* at 'Art, Activism and Language: Feminist Issues in Museums and Galleries' at Tate Exchange, Liverpool, 2017, annotated and redacted Guidelines Document

painfully low—and faxed them back to the gallery they came from. BANK's motivation for this form of institutional critique was to challenge the increasingly corporate art industry and its usage of "developmentspeak"[33] that proliferated in the late 1990s and 2000s. My use of this technique was a form of "artivism"[34] due to the challenge it presents to "artspeak" which 'when used by the systems that support art, not only perpetuates certain power structures but also obfuscates or undermines the efficacy of critical discussion'.[35]

However, instead of focussing on "artspeak" as a language game of "insider" knowledge, I considered instead the areas where the inclusion of user-generated content could contribute. This was done individually to inform the residency and to guide an open discussion conducted with Community Collective where we were able to reflect on the

33. Andrea Cornwall and Deborah Eade, eds., *Deconstructing Development Discourse: Buzzwords and Fuzzwords* (London: Practical Action Publishing, 2010), p. xiii.

34. Chantal Mouffe, 'Institutions as Sites for Agonistic Intervention' (2013), p. 69.

35. Dan Fox, 'Poisoned Pen', *Frieze* 100 (June–August 2006), p. 31.

36. Chantal Mouffe, 'Deliberative Democracy or Agonistic Pluralism?', *Social Research* 66, no. 3 (1999), pp. 745–758.

37. Julia Kristeva, *Desire in Language: A Semiotic Approach to Literature and Art* (New York: Columbia University Press, 1980), p. 36.

38. Norman Fairclough, *Analysing Discourse: Textual Analysis for Social Research* (London: Psychology Press, 2003), p. 17.

four dominant tonal values that Tate aim for in their textual interpretation, which are; Approachable, Alert, Animated and Authoritative. As we have already discussed, the purpose of the residency's interventions was to challenge "authoritarian order"[36] and pursue practices invested in agonistic pluralism. Reviewing this document enabled those in the residency to consider how the term "voice" is only used in relation to Tate's, which remains a one-way broadcast about items in the collection. In this use of voice, there remains a lack of public "intertextuality"[37] and no texts that might 'draw upon, incorporate, recontextualize and dialogue with other texts'[38] where oppositional voices or perspectives were actually used. As a result, it became my ambition to create a project that focussed on the voices of individuals and collective identities to create greater intertextuality and to recognize difference. In practice, this method manifested itself as a process with users to create a collaborative word index from which the action research project manifested. Spreading across the walls of Tate Exchange, the word

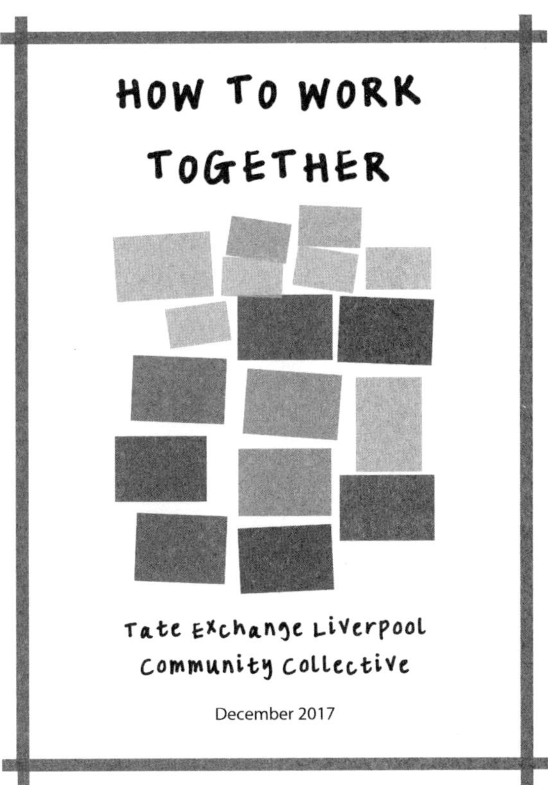

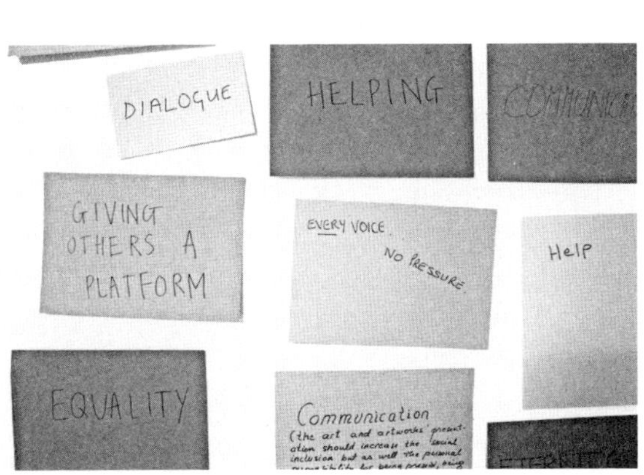

Collaborative outputs from How We Work Together workshop, 'Art, Activism and Language: Feminist Issues in Museums and Galleries' at Tate Exchange, Liverpool, 2017. Photo: Rene Matić

Emma Curd and Community Collective, front page from zine made as an outcome from How We Work Together workshop, 'Art, Activism and Language: Feminist Issues in Museums and Galleries' at Tate Exchange, Liverpool, 2017

index accumulated and multiplied as a visual representation of temporary vandalism 'to bring an end to what you are supposed to reproduce'.[39] Meanwhile, although the index was not a permanent fixture for Tate Exchange, producers were able to leave their mark in the hope they could centre themselves in minoritarian terms.

'How We Work Together' in Action

This workshop was organized with seven members of Community Collective who had expressed an interest in intervening in "artspeak" in the collection. Recruitment was done via email and social media due to our pre-existing collaboration, which had been cultivated over two years. The How We Work Together workshop was intended to explore how we might work in collaboration to produce a glossary of terms for Tate Liverpool's collection. Taking creative democracy as a starting point, we set out to produce a working set of rules to guide our collaborative work and enable everyone to have the same rights as more privileged individuals, like myself as "resident artist" who organized or initiated the group. This was a crucial foundation for the toolkit. Intended as a method toward a rediscovery of micro-politics, the creation of collective values also sought to encourage mutual creativity and co-production, and avoid feelings of exploitation. Values like "being present", "listening to others", "respect differences in opinion" and "taking responsibility"[40] were prominent amongst those raised by individuals. It could be argued that these responses echo practices of "deliberative democracy"—which prioritize consensus—and provided a "contact space"[41] to enable conflictual ideas, narratives and discourses to emerge later. For one collaborator, the words "safe" and "space" were suggested to discuss a place where publics might engage with collections in a low-pressure environment without fear of "getting it wrong" or having a conflictual perspective. Gallery educator Emily Pringle has theorized the creation of a "safe space" as a place where publics are able to build self-confidence through the validation of different learner's interpretation.[42] This was reflected in our workshop where we agreed that one way that this could be achieved is by the

39. Sara Ahmed, 'Institutional as Usual: Diversity Work as Data Collection', *Feminist Killjoys*, 24 October 2017, https://feministkilljoys.com/2017/10/24/institutional-as-usual/.

40. Seyla Benhabib, *The Claims of Culture: Equality and Diversity in the Global Era* (Oxford: Princeton University Press, 2002), pp. 19–20.

41. Kye Askins and Rachel Pain, 'Contact Zones: Participation, Materiality, and the Messiness of Interaction', *Environment and Planning: Society and Space* 29, no. 5 (2011), p. 803.

42. Emily Pringle and Jennifer Dewitt, 'Perceptions, Processes and Practices around Learning in an Art Gallery', *Tate Papers* 22 (Autumn 2014), www.tate.org.uk/research/publications/tate-papers/22/perceptions-processes-and-practices-around-learning-in-an-art-gallery.

43. Mouffe, 'Deliberative Democracy or Agonistic Pluralism?', p. 755.

44. Andrew Flinn, 'An Attack on Professionalism and Scholarship?: Democratising Archives and the Production of Knowledge', *Ariadne: Web Magazine for Information Professionals* no. 62 (2010), www.ariadne.ac.uk/issue62/flinn/.

creation of a system where all voices are valued similarly to "expert" voices, via the representation of counter narratives in the collection. Through these suggestions and others, we began a process of building a common language by articulating words with different meanings and stories. Additionally, by restricting rational agents (i.e. curators and experts) to the workshop, agonism remained at the core of the exercise due to the understanding that their presence might "eliminate passions" or 'relegate them to the private sphere'.[43] This was suggested as one way that we might cultivate confidence amongst collaborators who otherwise might be apprehensive to speak their mind; especially if their view conflicted with what was seen as empirical information. Consequentially, recording and representing voices that countered expertise was a vital way to enable collaborators to renegotiate their idea of legitimacy and feel comfortable to express their thoughts.

In the session, another person stated that we needed opportunities for new "narratives/storytelling". What emerged from this framing was for the need for Community Collective to flesh out their own identities and stories—both collectively and individually—in a way that communicated the voices of those involved in the act of interpreting collections. Over the last twenty years, projects outside of contemporary art, such as the *Human Library* (2000), have created opportunities for people to define themselves in their own words. Specifically, the objective of the *Human Library* is to challenge dominant discourse by redefining identity with people, words and voices. Still in collections of contemporary art, user-generated content infrequently enters the gallery due to fear that the addition of these voices attack 'standards, professionalism and scholarship'.[44] Hence, the question 'who gets to tell stories about art?' remains a pertinent question. In summary, this method provided a resource for the residents of the project to reflect on during our work together and this is an ongoing process. Moreover, the differences that were raised in this workshop have become part of an online re-interpretation project and resource titled *The People's Glossary* (www.thepeoplesglossary.co.uk). The aim of which seeks to represent agonistic, user-generated discourse to challenge Tate Liverpool's dominant model and is open to users for searching and adding to keywords,

EQUITABLE PLURALITY

meanings and interpretations as a process for building a common language.

Focusing on the use of language as a way to confront authoritarian forces, I have also shown one individual and one collective practice that sought to challenge the aesthetics and discourses of museum "voice". I have emphasized that these can only take place whilst rejecting the exodus theory and seeking engagement with these institutions. Processes informed by decolonial feminism proved useful in regard to working relationally through dialogue and understanding of difference.[45] Moreover, through this work it was emphasized that not only is the act of speaking inseparable from the act of listening, but recognition, representation and redistribution are all also required to challenge the canon of contemporaneity. Mouffe's idea of democracy as "agonistic pluralism" demands that conflictual differences must be recognized, represented and be 'seen as a fund of necessary polarities between which our creativity can spark like a dialectic'.[46] If we are to consider institutions of art as truly pluralistic or agonistic, then these contingencies must be regarded to inform all collections. Which in turn returns us to the question; why do 'those at the heart of museum representational practice (…) resist the dialogic turn?'[47]

45. Vázquez, 'Towards a Decolonial Critique of Modernity', p. 244.

46. Audre Lorde, 'The Master's Tools Will Never Dismantle the Master's House', *Feminist Postcolonial Theory: A Reader*, ed. Reina Lewis (New York: Routledge, 1999), p. 27.

47. Catherine Styles, 'Dialogic Learning in Museum Space', *Ethos* 19, no. 3 (2011), p. 12.

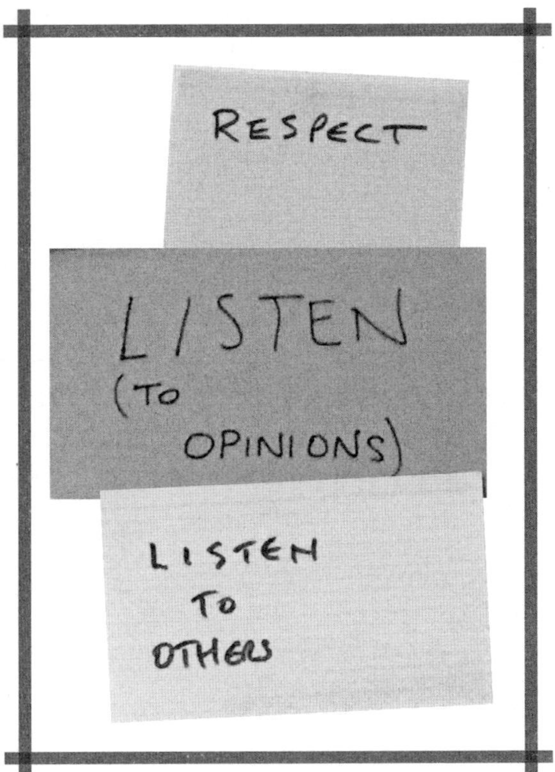

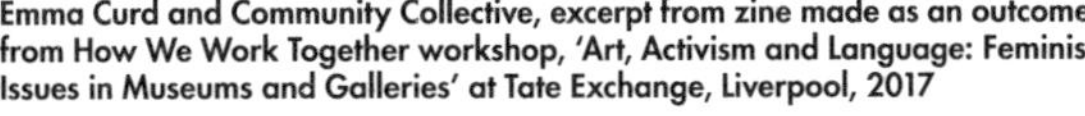

Emma Curd and Community Collective, excerpt from zine made as an outcome from How We Work Together workshop, 'Art, Activism and Language: Feminist Issues in Museums and Galleries' at Tate Exchange, Liverpool, 2017

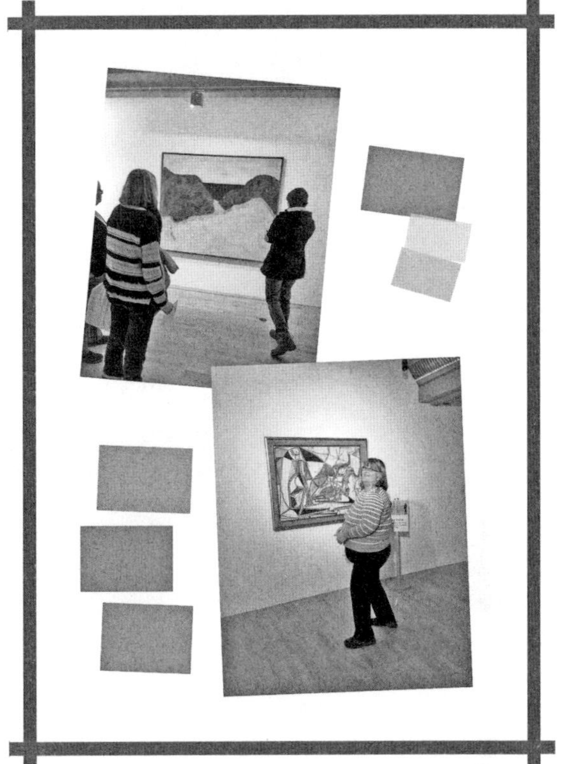

Emma Curd and Community Collective, excerpt from zine made as an outcome from How We Work Together workshop, 'Art, Activism and Language: Feminist Issues in Museums and Galleries' at Tate Exchange, Liverpool, 2017

ABOUT THE AUTHORS

Linda Aloysius is an artist and researcher who was awarded her PhD in Art by Goldsmiths College, University of London in January 2018. Aloysius is Senior Lecturer and Module Leader at University of East London and Associate Lecturer at Central Saint Martins, University of The Arts London. Her work explores 'Morphological Activism', which recognizes figurative sculpture as uniquely positioned to generate new structures to combat the marginalization of working-class women's creativity within the realms of art and cultural production, with particular emphasis on the longstanding inequalities experienced by working-class single mothers who want to live and work as artists. Recent selected Fieldworks include *New Model Army: Behind Tate Modern: Morphological Activism and Working-Class Single Mothers (2018–19)* and *New Model Army: Invisible Labour (2017–18)*. Selected publications include 'New Model Army, Invisible Labour (2017–18)', *Feminist Review* (2018) and 'Not Fallen but Felled', *Museological Review* (2016). She lives and works in London. – www.lindaaloysius.com

Marissa Begonia is an activist and domestic worker. Begonia is founder and co-ordinator of Voice of Domestic Workers. In addition to speaking at numerous public events and rallies, Begonia has written 'A Day Travel', in *Tongues*, ed. Rehana Zaman (PSS publishing, 2019) and 'We Build Families: The Aesthetics of Domestic Labour' with Louise Shelley and Jenny Richards, *Grand Domestic Revolution Handbook*, eds. Binna Choi and Maiko Tanaka (Valiz, 2014). Begonia was born in the Philippines and received her British Citizenship in 2014. She lives and works in London.

Sreyashi Tinni Bhattacharyya (born 1994) is a Bengali artist, researcher, and curator. She completed her BA in both Art History and Visual Arts from Oberlin College, USA. She has held positions at the Baltimore Museum of Art, the Peggy Guggenheim Collection, Venice, the Allen Memorial Art Museum, Oberlin, and the National Museum, New Delhi. In autumn 2016, she independently curated '(Anti)Corporeality: Reclaiming and Re-presenting the Black Body' at the Allen Memorial Art Museum. Her current research explores genealogies of Indian exploitative labour through the lens of womanhood, nationalism, and civil society movements. She is currently finishing an MA in Migration and Diaspora Studies at SOAS University of London, UK. – www.cargocollective.com/ sreyashibhattacharyya

Marisa Carnesky is an artist, showwoman and practitioner-researcher. She is interested in the use of spectacle; fairground rides, magic illusions and grand ritual as a means of creating highly accessible provocative work, rooted in popular culture that promotes cultural and political discourses. In 2004, she founded and is Creative Director of Carnesky Productions, a performance and theatre company responsible for original large and small-scale interactive performance works (including *Carnesky's Ghost Train*, 2004–2014, *Carnesky's Incredible Bleeding Woman*, 2015 Ongoing and alternative stage school Carnesky's Finishing School). She lives and works in London.
– www.carnesky.com

Paula Chambers (born 1966) is an artist, academic and arts educator. She is currently Subject Leader for Sculpture on BA (Hons) Fine Art at Leeds Arts University. Recent solo exhibitions include 'Home (dis)Comforts' at Dye House Gallery, Bradford, and 'Transcendental Housework' at Stockport Art Gallery. Recent group exhibitions include 'HOME STRIKE', l'étrangère Gallery, London with Su Richardson, Malgorzata Markiewicz and CANNAN. Recent publications include 'The Nightdress I Wore to Give Birth In: Performative Materialities and Maternal Intersubjectivities', *Performance Research: A Journal of the Performing Arts* (2017), special issue 'On the Maternal'. Chambers lives and works in West Yorkshire.
– www.paulachambers.co.uk

Amy Charlesworth is lecturer in Art History at The Open University. Most recently she has written 'Contemporary Art: Movement, Migration and Other Histories', *Art After Empire: From Colonialism to Globalisation* (Manchester University Press, 2018) and 'Absence and Saturation in Chantal Akerman's *De l'autre côté* (From the Other Side)', *The Oxford Art Journal* (2017). Charlesworth lives in Leeds and works in Milton Keynes, UK.

Emma Curd is an artist, action-researcher and education researcher. Having undertaken practice-based doctoral research at Liverpool John Moores University between 2015 and 2019, she continues her work in arts-based methods as Research Assistant and Associate Fellow in the Faculty of Arts, Professional and Social Studies. Curd's practice is dedicated to creating frameworks to facilitate discussion around language and its relationship to power whilst working with a broad range of communities. Recent residencies include 'Visible Voices', Bow Arts, London, 2018 and 'Art, Activism and Language: Feminist Issues in Museums and Galleries', Tate Exchange, Liverpool, 2017. Curd lives and works in Liverpool, UK.
– www.emmacurd.co.uk/about.html

Katy Deepwell (born 1962) is the founding editor of KT press, who published *n.paradoxa: international feminist art journal* (1998–2017) and *n.paradoxa's MOOC* (a mass open online course in 2017) (https://nparadoxa.com), as well as a series of ebooks. Since 2013, she has been Professor of Contemporary Art, Theory and Criticism at Middlesex University, London. Her books include: *All-Women Art Spaces in Europe in the Long 1970s* co-edited with Agata Jakubowska (Liverpool University Press, 2018); (ed.) *Feminist Art Manifestos: An Anthology* (KT press, 2014); *Women Artists between the Wars* (Manchester University Press, 2010); *Dialogues: Women Artists from Ireland* (IB Tauris, 2005); (ed.) *Women Artists and Modernism* (Manchester University Press, 1998); (ed.) *Art Criticism and Africa* (Saffron Books, 1997) and (ed.) *New Feminist Art Criticism: Critical Strategies* (Manchester University Press, 1995). She lives and works in London. – www.ktpress.co.uk

Tal Dekel (born 1968) is an art historian. She is head of the Visual Literacy Studies Program (M.Ed) and head of the Curatorial Track at the Kibbutzim College, Tel Aviv. She is Chair of the 'Association of Women's Art and Gender Research', and was formerly Chair of the Gender Studies Forum at Tel Aviv University. Dekel specializes in visual culture and focuses on the correlations between activism, feminism, migration and transnationalism.

Recent publications include: *Transnational Identities: Women, Art, and Migration in Israel* (Wayne State University Press, 2016); *Gendered: Art and Feminist Theory* (Cambridge Scholars Publishing, 2013), *Ageism and Gender in Israeli Art* (2019). Dekel lives and works in Israel. – www.taldekel.net

Emma Dick (born 1977) is a researcher and practitioner working in the areas of textiles, international development and gender. She studied Turkish with Islamic Art and Archaeology at Hertford College, University of Oxford, and a Masters in Design Practice in Textiles as Fashion at Glasgow School of Art. She is currently Senior Lecturer in Fashion Visual Cultures at Middlesex University, London and Director of Projects and Training for SPINNA Circle, a non-profit organization working to empower women in fashion and textiles globally. She recently published an article 'Performing Eurasia in the textiles and clothing businesses along the Silk Road' in the *Cambridge Journal of Eurasian Studies* (2018), alongside her ongoing collaborations with Kathleen Mullaniff noted in this volume. Dick lives and works in London.

Lior Elefant (born 1981) is a PhD candidate at the Sociology and Anthropology department at Ben Gurion University of the Negev, Israel. She is also Chair of the Israeli Women in Film and Television Forum, and the founder and editor of the Israeli feminist media magazine *Politically Corret*, and a feminist media activist. Elefant specializes in gender and feminist studies, LGBTQ and cultural activism, and focuses on creative industries—film, theatre and media. Elefant lives and works in Tel Aviv, Israel.

Christine Eyene is an art historian, critic, curator and research fellow in contemporary art at the University of Central Lancashire, where she works on Making Histories Visible, an interdisciplinary visual arts research project led by Lubaina Himid OBE, Professor of Contemporary Art. Her research and curatorial interests range from African and Diaspora arts, feminist art, to non-object-based practices like sound art. She is Artistic Director of the 5th Biennale Internationale de Casablanca 2020. Her recent projects include *Sounds Like Her*, UK touring, 2017–2020; 'RESIST! The 1960s Protests, Photography and Visual Legacy', BOZAR, Brussels, 2018; 'Murder Machine '(part of EVA International), Ormston House, Limerick, 2016; 'All Of Us Have A Sense Of Rhythm', David Roberts Art Foundation, London, 2015; 'WHERE WE'RE AT! Other Voices on Gender', BOZAR, Brussels, 2014; 10th Dak'Art: Biennale of Contemporary African Art, multiple venues, Dakar, 2012; 'Reflections on the Self: Five African Women Photographers', Southbank Centre, London, 2011.
– www.eyonart.org

Abbe Leigh Fletcher (born 1976) is a filmmaker. She studied at Camberwell College of Art, London College of Communication and the Royal College of Art and is Senior Lecturer in Filmmaking at Kingston School of Art. She has a background of documentary and experimental filmmaking, with particular focus on the impact of family life on creativity. Recent exhibitions include: 'Railwaywomen', Heritage Open Day, Ropley, 2018; 'Women on the Railway' event, Winchester, 2018; *My Mild-Mannered Mother-in-law from Mildmay* at 'Film maker in the Family', BFI, London, 2016; *Pulpo y pandereta*, 'The Beast and the Body' event, De Lane Lea, London, 2014; *The Road to Gibara*, MuFest Madrid, 2011; Cine Pobre Film Festival, Gibara, 2010; Film Directing 4 Women Film Festival, London, 2010; *Under Construction*, Cine Pobre Film Festival, Gibara, 2009; Reading Film Festival, 2009; Diversions Experimental Film Festival, Edinburgh, 2008. Recent publications include: *Small is Beautiful: Miniature Worlds and Microeconomics*; blog on E.F. Schumacher and Bluebird Toys (1981–1998) (2019). Fletcher lives and works in Hampshire.
– www.abbeleighfletcher.com

GraceGraceGrace includes Katharine Meynell, Teresa Albor and Lady Helena Vortex, all of whom identify as older. Collectively they perform gender and ageing. Recent performances include: *Pantomime Unicorn*, Cabaret Melancholique, London, 2018; 'The Small Publishers' Fair', Conway Hall, London, 2018; 'DAYLIGHTING', Wellcome Trust, London, 2018; *LOUISE*, Riga Performance Festival, Riga, 2018; *7 signs of aging*, Anarchist Feminist Party, London, 2018; GraceGraceGrace one month residency at Yinka Shonibare's Guest Projects (ACE funding), London, 2018; *Manifesto*, FiLiA's annual conference, Institute of Education, London, 2017; *Do you see me?*, INLAND, 198 Gallery, Brixton/London; SLAP performance/workshops, Jerwood & Yorkshire Dance, York; Venice Experimental Video and Performance Art Festival, Palazzo Ca' Zanardi, Venice; The Nunnery Gallery, Bow Arts, London;WORM at Humber Street Gallery, Hull, 2017. Recent publications include: *GraceGraceGrace explore gen-age** (*gender and ageing) (2019). All three live and work in the UK.
– www.gracegracegrace.moonfruit.com

Alana Jelinek (born 1968) is an artist who writes theory of art. Her practice investigates the terrain where ecological concerns meet a history of colonialism and she has worked on a number of multi- and inter-disciplinary projects with anthropologists since 2009. She uses a wide range of media to explore and research specific ideas and in this sense her work lies in the tradition of conceptual art. She has written novels, worked in live art and performance, made internet-specific art, worked on participatory projects and she continues to use oil paint when it's the right medium for the enquiry. She is the author of *This is Not Art: Activism and Other 'Not-Art'* (IB Tauris, 2013). Her current research is on 'Between Discipline and A Hard Place' (Bloomsbury, forthcoming), for a book in which she discusses ethics, inter-disciplinary working as artists, the politics and ecology of art, and how art is a knowledge-forming discipline. Jelinek lives in London and works at the University of Hertfordshire.
– www.alanajelinek.com

Sonja van Kerkhoff (born 1960) is an artist, curator, occasional guest lecturer and reviewer who has studied at The Dunedin School of Visual Art, Otago University, the Maastricht School of Visual Art and Leiden University. Recent curated exhibitions include: 'The Poetic Condition', NorthArt, Auckland, 2018. Recent art projects include: lectures and workshops for Creative Circles, Burnlaw, Northumberland, 2018; *The Colorfield Performance*, a land art project coordinated by Dirk Hakze, Sloten, Friesland, the Netherlands, 2018; Arte Italia Tautoko Māori Foundation residency, Irsina, Italy; *He Punawai Hohourongo: Peace, Water, Power*, SCANZ + InterCreate, Parihaka, Taranaki, Aotearoa/New Zealand, 2018. Since 2017, she has been writing for Art New Zealand. She has been based in Kawakawa, Aotearoa/New Zealand and The Hague, The Netherlands, since 2017. – www.sonjavank.com

Alexandra Kokoli is Senior Lecturer in Visual Culture at Middlesex University London and Research Associate at VIAD, University of Johannesburg. An art historian and theorist originally trained in comparative literature, Kokoli researches the aesthetic mobilization of discomfort to political ends, focusing on art practices informed by and committed to feminism, the fraught but fertile relationship between feminism and psychoanalysis, mourning and shame. She curated 'Burnt Breakfast' and other works by Su Richardson, Goldsmiths, London, 2012, and, with Basia Sliwinska, 'HOME STRIKE', l'étrangère, London, 2018. Her books include *The Feminist Uncanny in Theory and Art Practice* (2016); and (as editor) *Feminism Reframed: Reflections on Art and Difference* (Cambridge Scholars Publishing, 2008); and *The Provisional Texture of Reality: Selected Talks and Texts by Susan Hiller, 1977–2007* (Les presses du réel, 2008). Kokoli is the recipient of a Paul Mellon mid-career fellowship (2019) for her research into the legacies of the women's peace camp at Greenham Common, focusing on the aesthetics and politics of feminist anti-nuclear activism.

Elke Krasny (born 1965) is a Professor of Art and Education at the Academy of Fine Arts Vienna. She is a cultural theorist, urban researcher, educator, and curator. Her work focuses on critical practices in architecture, urbanism, and contemporary art addressing ecology, economy, labour, memory, and feminisms. Recent exhibitions include: 'Suzanne Lacy's International Dinner Party in Feminist Curatorial Thought', KTH Stockholm, 2017 and Zurich University of the Arts, 2016. Recent books: *Suzanne Lacy's International Dinner Party in Feminist Curatorial Thought* (OnCuratingPublishing, 2019); *Critical Care: Architecture and Urbanism for a Broken Planet*, co-edited with Angelika Fitz (MIT Press, 2019). Krasny lives and works in Vienna. – www.elkekrasny.at

Loraine Leeson (born 1951) is an artist who studied at St Martins College of Art, Reading University and the Hochschule der Künste, Berlin and is currently Senior Lecturer at Middlesex University. Leeson is particularly known for her socially engaged work with East London communities, mainly realized in the public domain. Recent exhibitions of her practice have included: 'The Things That Make You Sick', ICA, London, 2017 and 'Feminist and…', Mattress Factory, Pittsburgh, 2012, while her retrospective 'Arts for Change' toured NGBK, Berlin, SPACE, London, A-Space, Toronto, and City Library, Dublin, 2005–2008. Her monograph *Art:Process:Change: Inside a Socially*

Situated Practice was published in 2017 by Routledge. Leeson lives and works in London.

Laura Malacart (born 1968) is an artist and lecturer on photography, documentary and art theory and holds a PhD on voice agency and representation in fine art moving image ('MUVE: The Museum of Ventriloquial Objects', Slade School of Fine Art, UCL). Her practice is collaborative, interdisciplinary and conceived as a tool to address the asymmetries of a globalized society and their historical underpinnings. Recent solo exhibition include 'Speak Robert' at the Artists' Pavilion at the 57th Venice Biennale (2017) and 'The Little Book of Answers', a participatory performance, Turbine Hall at Tate Modern, London (2015). Group exhibitions include 'Drone Britannia', an interactive sound installation at the Oval Cricket Ground for 2018 ArtNight and *A Very British Pictionary Game*, a participatory performance at Turner Contemporary in Margate with 2017 Venice Agendas. Recent articles include 'The Rebirth of the East India Company: Buy Who You Want to Be', a conversation with sociologist Sara De Jong in *Open Democracy* (2017) and 'The Little Book of Answers Vol. 1' in *n.paradoxa* (2016). Malacart lives and works in London.
– www.lauramalacart.info

Rosy Martin (born 1946) is an artist-photographer, psychological-therapist, workshop leader, lecturer and writer. She explores the relationships between photography, memory, identities and unconscious processes using self-portraiture, still life photography, digital imaging and video. From 1983, with Jo Spence, she pioneered re-enactment phototherapy. She has exhibited internationally since 1985, including Tate Britain (2015–2016), Peltz Gallery London (2014), Durham Art Gallery (2010), Documenta 12, Kassel (2007), Focal Point Gallery, Southend-on-Sea (2001), Randolph Street Gallery, Chicago (1991 and 1994), Tokyo Metropolitan Museum of Photography (1991), and The Photographers' Gallery, London (1987). Recent publications include essays in *Gender Issues in International Arts Therapies Research* (Routledge, 2019); *Home/Land* (Liverpool University, 2016); *Phototherapy and Therapeutic Photography in a Digital Age* (Routledge, 2013); *The Photograph and the Album* (MuseumsEtc, 2013); *Ageing Femininities, Troubling Representations* (Cambridge Scholars Publishing, 2012). She lives and works in London.
– www.rosymartin.info

Alice Maude-Roxby is Fine Art Programme Leader at Middlesex University. She has produced films, books and exhibitions in response to the ways in which live art or ephemeral works are recorded and understood through documentation, how artists' practices inform teaching and workshops, and how artists collaborate. She published 'The Delicate Art of Documenting Performance', in *Art, Lies and Videotape: Exposing Performance*, ed. Adrian George (Tate Publications, 2003); *On Record: Advertising, Architecture and the Actions of Gina Pane*, with Françoise Masson (Artwords Press, 2004); *'Past-Present-Future' in Double Exposures: Performance as Photography, Photography as Performance*, eds. Manuel Vason and David Evans (Intellect with Live Art Development Agency, 2015); *Censored Realities: Changing New York*, co-authored with Stefanie Seibold (Camera Austria, 2018). For John Hansard Gallery she curated 'Live Art on Camera' (2007) and 'Anti-Academy' (2013), and co-curated with Stefanie Seibold, 'Resist: be modern (again)' (2019). She lives in London.

Kathleen Mullaniff (born 1957, County Longford, Ireland) studied Fine Art at Camberwell University of the Arts, and Goldsmiths College University of London. Kathleen has been a Senior Lecturer at Middlesex University BA Fine Art course since 1990 and was a founder member of Chisenhale Studios and Gallery (1981–2007). She was awarded an AHRC grant in 2002 to research the botanical drawings of Pierre-Joseph Redoute. In 2004 she co-founded The Patternlab and took part in the Touch, Textiles, Technology collaboration across Europe, Goldsmiths College. Her exhibitions include: 'Textile and Memory', The Dick Institute, Killmarnock, Scotland, 2019; 'Personal Relations', Pulchri Studio, The Hague, 2017; 'Vernissage', Vicenza, 2017; 'Garland', MYB Textiles, Killmarnock, Scotland, 2015; 'Paisley: Exploding the Teardrop', responding to Buta/Paisley shawls in The National Gallery of Scotland, Paisley Museum Gallery and House, 2007; 'Purl', The Museum of Domestic Design & Architecture, London, 2004; 'Painting as a 'Foreign as a Language', Cultura Inglesa, São Paulo, 2002; 'Fabric Reinterpreting the House', Abbot Hall Art Gallery, UK, 2002. Mullaniff is a member of the London Group and lives in St Leonards on Sea, UK.
– www.kathleenmullaniff.com

Louise O'Hare (born 1982) is a curator, writer and editor. She was an editor at *Afterall* from 2013–2016 and completed her PhD at University of Northumbria (2019). Her research is focused on the political potentials of memoir, gossip and anecdote, feminism, and an expanded vision of the caring economy. She co-curated 'Safe', HOME Manchester, 2015; and founded the London Bookshop Map in 2011 as a project to disseminate writing by artists. Recent publications include: 'Havana-London Diary: Art Publishing, Sustainability, Free Speech and Free Papers', in *Whose Book Is it Anyway?* (OpenBook Publishers, 2019). O'Hare lives and works in Tower Hamlets, London.

Tanja Ostojić (born 1972, Yugoslavia) is Berlin-based performance and interdisciplinary artist, researcher and educator. She performed and exhibited at: 'Feminism is Politics!', Pratt Manhattan Gallery, New York, 2016; Busan Biennale, South Korea, 2016; 'Call the Witness', Roma Pavilion, Venice Biennale, 2011; 'Global Feminisms', Brooklyn Museum, New York, 2006; 'Performa', New York, 2009; 'Plateau of Humankind', Venice Biennale, 2001; ICA, London, 1999, among others. Recent solo exhibitions include: 'Lexicon of Tanjas Ostojić', MoCA Belgrade Salon, 2017; 'Tanja Ostojić: Body, Politics', Agency, Škuc Gallery, Ljubljana, 2012; 'Integration Impossible? Politics of Migration in the Artwork of Tanja Ostojić 2000–07', Kunstpavillon Innsbruck, Austria, 2008. She has published several books, including: *Lexicon of Tanjas Ostojić* (LADA, 2018); Ostojić and M. Gržinić, eds., *Integration Impossible? The Politics of Migration in the Artwork of Tanja Ostojić* (argobooks, 2009); *Strategies of Success/Curators Series* (La Box & SKC, 2004).
– www.misplacedwomen.wordpress.com
– www.tanjaostojicshop.wordpress.com
– www.van.at/see/tanja

Martina Pachmanová is Associate Professor at the Department of Art History and Theory at the Academy of Arts, Architecture and Design in Prague. As a researcher, writer and curator she specializes in gender, sexual politics and feminism in modern, post-war and contemporary art and visual culture, including design. She is an editor or co-editor of numerous books and exhibition catalogues, and author of several books: *Mobile Fidelities: Conversations on Feminism, History, and Visuality* (2001; KT press: www.ktpress.co.uk/pdf/nparadoxaissue19.pdf); *Unknown Territories of Czech Modern Art: Through the Looking Glass of Gender* (Argo, 2004); *The Birth of a Woman Artist from the Lemonade Foam: Gender Contexts of Modern Czech Art Theory and Criticism* (2013), among others. Besides several monographs of contemporary Czech women artists, including Milena Dopitová, she also published three monographs of forgotten Czech female modernists related to their retrospective exhibitions.
– www.umprum.cz

Gill Park studied art history and Art Gallery and Museum Studies at the University of Leeds. She is currently Lecturer in Curating at the University of Newcastle and Lecturer in Art Gallery, Museum and Heritage Studies at the University of Leeds. Her work addresses feminist art and exhibition histories with a particular focus on photography and the moving image. Prior to entering academia, Park was Director of Pavilion, where she curated a series of commissioned contemporary art projects with artists, outside of the traditional gallery space. Her latest book (co-edited) is *Intersecting Practices: Contemporary Art in Heritage Spaces* (Routledge, 2019). Park lives and works in Leeds, UK.

Pune Parsafar (born 1970) is completing her practice-based PhD, at the Faculty of Arts and Creative Industries at Middlesex University, London. She is currently researching representation of Iranian women in cinema, including in documentary and experimental genres. She has many years' experience of teaching, research and collaboration within documentary film and TV production in both Iran and the UK. Parsafar lives and works in London, UK.

Roxane Permar is an artist and Reader in Fine Art at the University of the Highlands and Islands, where she is a Research Fellow and Programme Leader for the MA Art and Social Practice in the Centre for Rural Creativity, Shetland College. She works collaboratively with Susan Timmins in *Cold War Projects*, using social engagement to facilitate exchange across cultures and political boundaries. Recent projects include *Northern Exchange: Cold War Histories and Nuclear Futures* in Iceland and a new collaborative project, *Home & Belonging*, with care-experienced young people and colleagues Siún Carden (Centre for Rural Creativity) and Sian Wild (Who Cares? Scotland).
– www.roxanepermar.com

Anne Robinson works with film as an artist educator, currently teaching at Middlesex University. Her art practice is concerned with the perception and politics of temporality. Recent film works include: *Wakeful* (2018) and *Thrashing in the Static* (2014) and curatorial projects: 'Supernormal' Festival and 'Over Time'. She is engaged with social change and collective practice in art and was a member of the See-Red Women's Collective. Her work is documented in *See-Red Women's Workshop: Feminist Posters, 1974–1990* (Four Corners Books, 2016). She completed a practice-led PhD in 2012, entitled *The Elusive Digital Frame and the Elasticity of Time in Painting*.
– www.annerobinsonartwork.org

Stefanie Seibold (born 1967) is an artist and teaches at the Academy of Fine Arts in Vienna, currently as head of Sculpture and Space Strategies. She works with performances, installations, objects, archives, video and texts including curatorial projects. In her practice she is interested in rephrasing influential rituals, gestures and speech acts that are applied to form subjects. Recent exhibitions include 'Resist: Be modern again' at the John Hansard Gallery, Southampton, 2019. Recent publications include: *Censored Realities/Changing New York*, co-authored with Alice Maude-Roxby (Camera Austria, 2018). She lives and works in Vienna, Austria.
– www.clevergretel.com

Pam Skelton (born 1941) is an artist based in London and was Reader in Fine Art at Central Saint Martins, London until she retired from that post in 2013. Her work explores memory, history and trauma revisited in the aftermath of WWII and the Holocaust. *Un Censored* will be exhibited at P21 Gallery, London in September 2020. Recent exhibitions include 'Salon for a Speculative Future', Chisenhale Artspace Studios, London, 2019; 'Cartographies of Life & Death', LSHTM, London, 2013; 'Archive of Exile', Bank Street Gallery, Sheffield, 2011. Recent publications include: 'Histories of Eye in the Sky', *Fotograf Magazine* (2017); 'Conspiracy Dwellings', *n.paradoxa* (2014); *Conspiracy Dwellings: Surveillance in Contemporary Art*, co-edited with Outi Remes (Cambridge Scholars Publishing, 2010). Her works have been supported by Arts Council England, Arts and Humanities Research Council, British Council, KulturStiftung des Bundes and West Midlands Arts.
– www.pamskelton.org

Mare Tralla (born 1967) is a queer-feminist artist and activist. She studied at Estonian Academy of Arts and at the University of Westminster. Recent exhibitions: 'Woman&Woman', City Gallery, Pärnu, 2019; 'The X-Files' [Registry of the Nineties], Art Museum of Estonia KUMU, Tallinn, 2018–2019; 'Give Up the Ghost: Baltic Triennial 13', Kim? Contemporary Art Center, Riga, 2018; 'Bastard Voices, Baltic Triennial 13', evening of performances, South London Gallery, London, 2018; 'Amor', Oi Futuro, Rio de Janeiro, 2016. Recent text contributions in: *Watched! Surveillance, Art and Photography*, eds. Louise Wolthers, Dragana Vujanovic and Niclas Östlind (Walther König, 2016); *re.act.feminism a performing archive*, eds. Bettina Knaup and Beatrice Ellen Stammer (Verlag für moderne Kunst Nürnberg, 2014); *quite queer*, ed. Claudia Reiche (Quite Queer, 2014). Co-edited: *Private Views: Spaces and Gender in Contemporary Art from Britain and Estonia*, co-edited with Angela Dimitrakaki and Pam Skelton (WAL, 2000). Tralla lives and works in London and Tallinn.
– www.tralla.net

Christina Vasileiou (born 1978) is a performance artist and educator. She studied at Royal Central School of Speech and Drama (MA Applied Theatre) and is currently completing an interdisciplinary PhD at Guildhall School of Music and Drama. Christina's performance art and participatory performance work focuses on the embodied practices of teachers' caregiving as affective performance in order to develop more critical understandings of what it means to be a teacher-carer. Recent shows include: *PaperCare*, Guildhall School of Music & Drama, London, 2018; *Transfixed*, Platform 1 Gallery, London, 2018; *Crowning*, Leyden Gallery, London, 2018. Vasileiou lives and works in London.
– www.christinavasileiou.com

Camille Melissa Waring (born 1975) is a visual artist, creative director, and commercial photographer. She is currently a third-year PhD candidate at the Centre for Research and Education in Arts and Media, University of Westminster. Recent work involves exploring issues related to photographic self-representation, body politics, sexuality, violence, feminism, surveillance, and censorship. Recent exhibitions include: 'Hyphen: An Exposition Between Art and Research', Ambika P3, London, 2019. Recent publications include: 'Lens-based violence and the online sex worker', in *Navigating Contemporary Sex Work: Gender, Justice and Policy in the Twenty-First century*, eds. Emily Cooper and Paul Maginn (2020). Waring lives and works in Paris.

Michelle Williams Gamaker (born 1979) is an artist filmmaker and Senior Lecturer in the Department of Art at Goldsmiths College, University of London. Williams Gamaker's key focus is the development of 'fictional activism': the restoration of marginalized brown characters as central figures, who return in her works to challenge the fictional injustices to which they have been historically consigned. Recent exhibitions include: 'Distant Relative', Tintype, London, 2019; 'As Seen on Screen', Walker Art Gallery, Liverpool, 2019; 'All About You' (with Julia Kouneski), The Koppel Project Hive, London, 2019; 'Women Power Protest', Birmingham Museum and Art Gallery, 2019; 'Essex Road 5', Tintype, 2018; 'Solitary Pleasures', Freud Museum, London, 2018; 'Library Interventions: Moving Knowledge', Blenheim Walk Gallery, Leeds, 2018; 'Living Beyond Limits: Queeratorial Project and History Repeats Itself', MIMA, Middlesbrough, 2018; BFI 62nd London Film Festival 2018; 'Concrete Jungle', Annka Kultys Gallery, London, 2017; 'Emma and Edvard: Love in the Time of Loneliness' (with Mieke Bal), Munch Museum, Oslo, 2017; 'The World Made New', Pi Projects, London, 2017. She is also Chair of Trustees at the arts commissioning organization Pavilion in Leeds.
– www.michellewilliamsgamaker.com

Virginia Yiqing Yang (born 1992) is a PhD student at Coventry University. Her research interests are in the area of women's studies and contemporary art with a specific focus on visual semiotics. Exhibitions and Events: 'Self-portrait', Glass Box Gallery, Coventry, 2017; 'Rear Window', The ETA Salon, FarGo Village, Coventry, 2015; 'Dotttt', Winchester School of Art Degree Show, Winchester, 2014; 'INSITU', Graphic Arts Exhibition, Winchester, 2013. Yang lives and works in Coventry, UK.

INDEX

Trump, Donald 139
Truth, Sojourner 392
Tuin, Iris van der 261
Tumbas, Jasmina 27, 28
Turalba, Josephine 107
Twomey, Clare 409
Tyler, Amina 393
Tzameret-Kertcher, Hagar 263

U

Ulkuniemi, Seija 284

V

Van de Ven, Nicole 387
Varda, Agnès 84, 85, 89
Varghese, Vin Joe 381
Vasileiou, Christina 124, 127, 128,
130–132
Vasquez Ramírez, Claudia 83
Vázquez, Rolando R. 413, 414, 420
Verblane, Reet 249
Vergès, Françoise 391, 395
Videkanić, Bojana 37
Vink, Marcus 368
Virno, Paulo 411
Voice of Domestic Workers (VoDW)
296, 297, 356, 358, 361, 362, 365
Volkova, Tatiana 259
Vrouw en Vaart 394

W

WAC 262
Wagley, Catherine G. 262
Walker, Barbara W. 281
Wallace, Audrey 386
Warburg, Aby 143, 395
Warhol, Andy 199
Waring, Camille 204, 206, 211
Warner, Michael 146
Warnke, Martin 395
Weibel, Peter 259
Weinberg, Rob 102
Weingarten, Itzik 264
Weingartner, Charles 65
Weiser, Benjamin 367
Weiss, Adrienne 386
Weiss, Lindsey 212
Weiwei, Ai 199
Wekker, Gloria 391
Welland, Colin 361
Welstead, Verity 282–285
White, Elisa Joy 391
Whyte, Peter 66
Widrich, Mechtild 390
Wildtrax 113–115, 120

Wilke, Hannah 389
William, Prince 138
Williams, Raymond 114
Williams Crenshaw, Kimberlé 260
Williams Gamaker, Michelle 40, 42,
45, 46, 49, 52, 53
Winnicott, Donald Woods 84, 91
Withers, Josephine 262
Women for Life on Earth 137
Women's Health Information
Collective 228, 233–235
Wood, Catherine 386
Woodward, Kathleen 275
Woolf, Virginia 49, 91, 138, 139
Worley, Matthew 114
Wragg, Terry 297, 359
Wright, John 326
Wu, Hung 199
Wylie, Alison 172

Y

Yadav, Ashok 378
Yates, Marie 291
Yeasmin 373, 377
Yee, Vivian 367
Yerdai, Efrat 261
Yiwei, Jiang 106
Young, James E. 344
Your Own 266
Yuval-Davis, Nira 260

Z

Zaman, Rehana 358, 359
Zehavi, Ohad 268
Zeman, Miloš 308
Zenobia, Queen 393
Zhao, Yiheng 196
Zielinski, Ger 260
Ziherl, Vivian 394
Zinn, Gesa 332
Zinnenburg-Carroll, Khadija von 215
Žižek, Slavoj 241, 242
Zöhrer-Ernst, Ulla 314, 315
Zorea, Avraham 267

COLOPHON

ACKNOWLEGDEMENTS

This book arose from the conference 'Feminist Art Activisms and Artivisms', (Middlesex University, 2 July 2018), organized by Professor Katy Deepwell on behalf of the Create/Feminisms cluster with the assistance of staff and students.
The initial conference and this book was supported by the Research Fund of the ACI Faculty, which the editor and Valiz gratefully acknowledge.
The editor would like to thank the contributors for their help and assistance in compiling this anthology and for their contributions and research.
The publisher would like to thank Sarah van Binsbergen for co-developing the PLURAL series.

EDITOR
Katy Deepwell

CONTRIBUTORS
Linda Aloysius, Marissa Begonia, Sreyashi Tinni Bhattacharyya, Marisa Carnesky, Paula Chambers, Amy Charlesworth, Emma Curd, Katy Deepwell, Tal Dekel, Emma Dick, Lior Elefant, Christine Eyene, Abbe Leigh Fletcher, GraceGraceGrace, Alana Jelinek, Sonja van Kerkhoff, Alexandra Kokoli, Elke Krasny, Loraine Leeson, Laura Malacart, Rosy Martin, Alice Maude-Roxby, Kathleen Mullaniff, Louise O'Hare, Tanja Ostojić, Martina Pachmanová, Gill Park, Pune Parsafar, Roxane Permar, Anne Robinson, Stefanie Seibold, Pam Skelton, Mare Tralla, Christina Vasileiou, Camille Melissa Waring, Michelle Williams Gamaker, Virginia Yiqing Yang

COPY-EDITING
Alice Tetley-Paul

PROOFREADING
Els Brinkman

INDEX
Elke Stevens

DESIGN
Lotte Lara Schröder
(incl. cover, backgrounds at opening pages chapters, added graphics)

PUBLISHER
Valiz, Amsterdam
Astrid Vorstermans & Pia Pol

www.valiz.nl

TYPEFACES
Amelia Pro, **Futura Std,**
Times New Roman MT Std

PAPER
Munken Pure 240 gr
Munken Print White 15 100 gr

PRINTING AND BINDING
Bariet/Ten Brink, Meppel

This book has been produced on
FSC-certified paper.

DISTRIBUTION
NL/BE/LU: Centraal Boekhuis,
www.cb.nl
GB/IE: Anagram Books,
www.anagrambooks.com
Europe/Asia: Idea Books,
www.ideabooks.nl
USA/CA/Latin America: D.A.P.,
www.artbook.com
Australia: Perimeter,
www.perimeterdistribution.com
Individual orders: www.valiz.nl

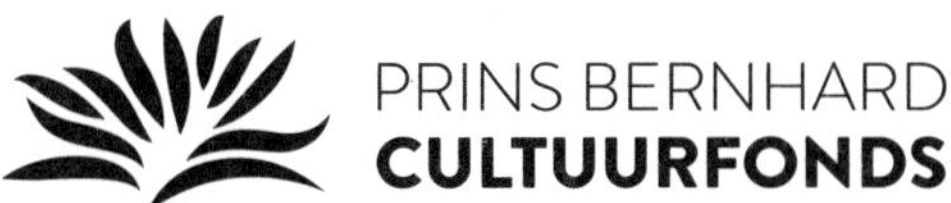

This publication received generous
support of the Prins Bernhard
Cultuurfonds.

This project has kindly been supported
by Middlesex University, London.

PLURAL

The PLURAL series focuses on
how the intersections between
identity, power, representation and
emancipation play out in the arts
and in cultural practices. The volumes
in this series aim to do justice to
the plurality of voices, experiences and
perspectives in society and in the arts
and to address the history, present and
future meaning of these positions and
their interrelations. PLURAL brings
together new and critical insights from
artists, arts professionals, activists,
cultural and social researchers,
journalists and theorists.
Series design by Lotte Lara Schröder

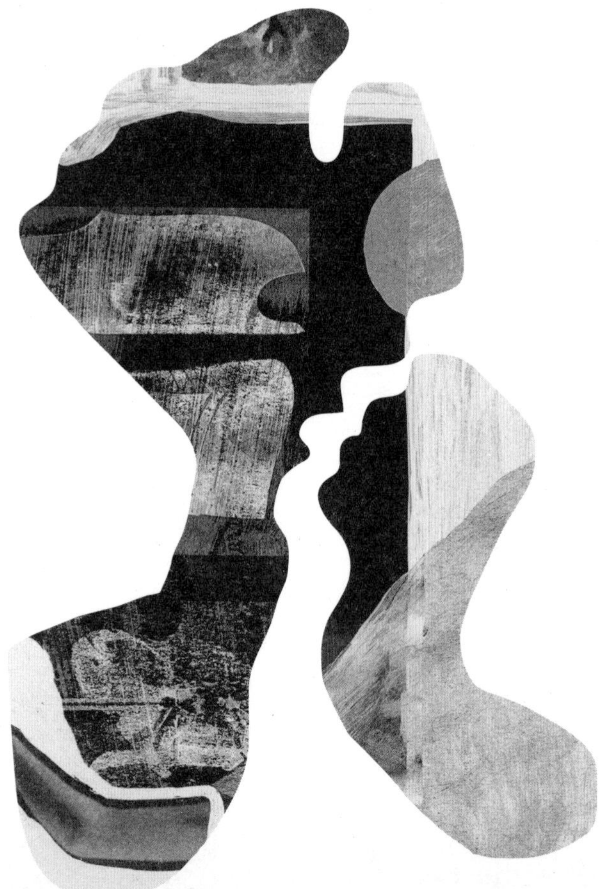

Feminist Art Activisms and Artivisms
is the first volume in the PLURAL series.

ISBN 978-94-92095-72-5
Printed and bound in the EU, 2020